ALSO BY **GRADY KLEIN** AND
YORAM BAUMAN, Ph.D.

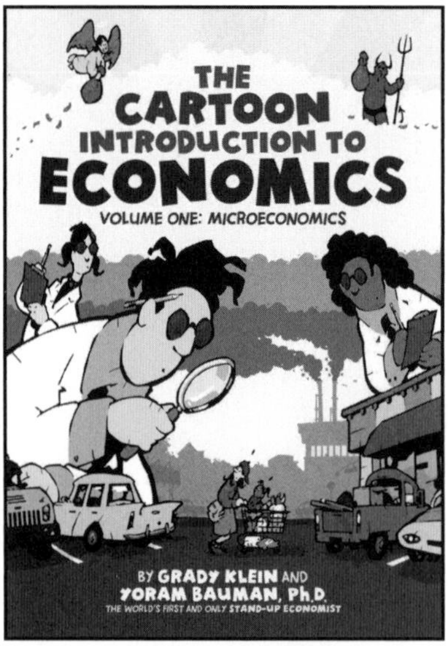
THE CARTOON INTRODUCTION TO ECONOMICS
VOLUME ONE: MICROECONOMICS
BY GRADY KLEIN AND
YORAM BAUMAN, Ph.D.
THE WORLD'S FIRST AND ONLY STAND-UP ECONOMIST

VOLUME ONE:
MICROECONOMICS

THE CARTOON INTRODUCTION TO ECONOMICS

VOLUME TWO: MACROECONOMICS

THE CARTOON INTRODUCTION TO ECONOMICS

VOLUME TWO: MACROECONOMICS

BY **GRADY KLEIN** AND
YORAM BAUMAN, Ph.D.
THE WORLD'S FIRST AND ONLY **STAND-UP ECONOMIST**

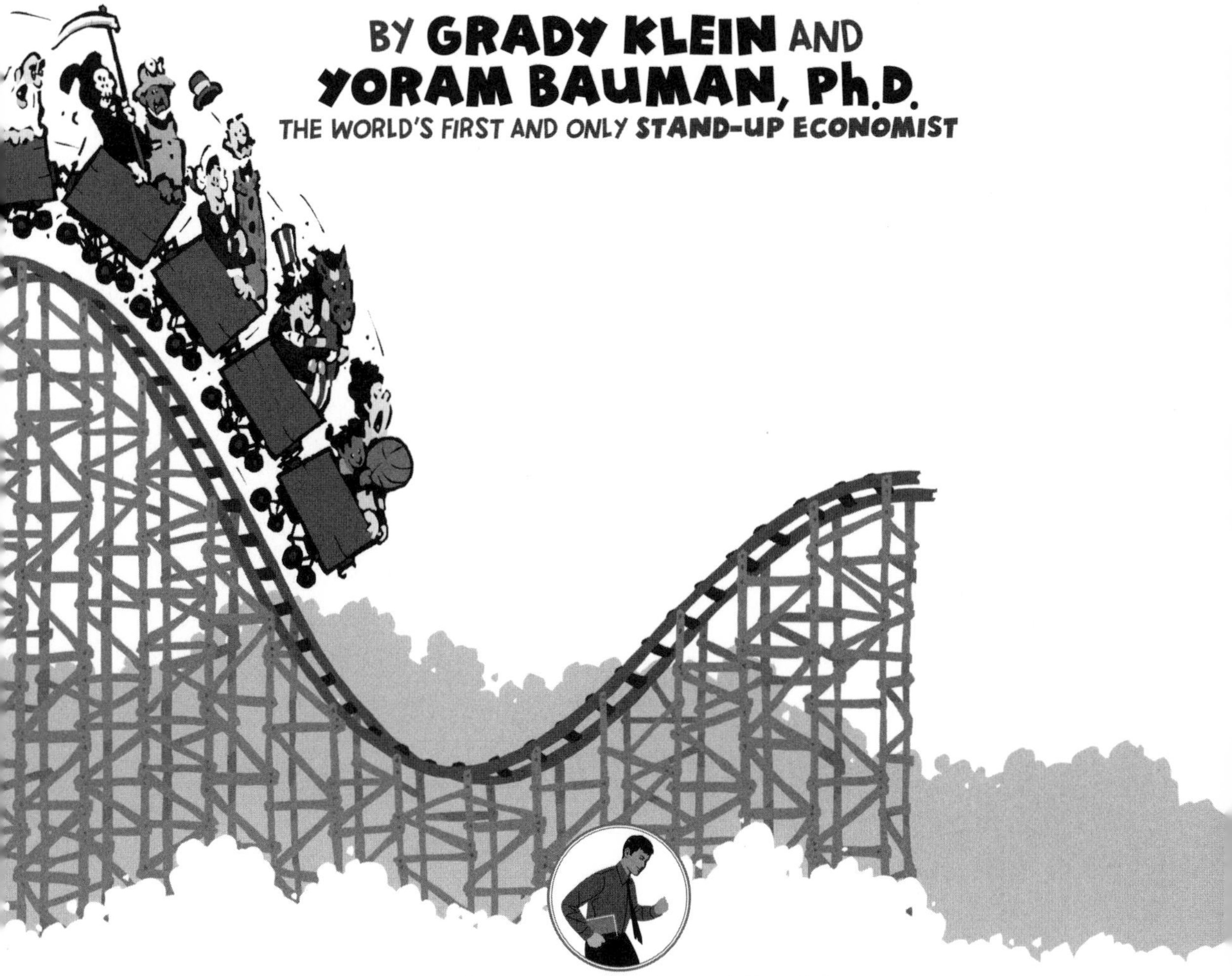

A NOVEL GRAPHIC FROM HILL AND WANG
A DIVISION OF FARRAR, STRAUS AND GIROUX
NEW YORK

HILL AND WANG
A DIVISION OF FARRAR, STRAUS AND GIROUX
18 WEST 18TH STREET, NEW YORK 10011

PRINTED IN CHINA
FIRST EDITION, 2012

LIBRARY OF CONGRESS CATALOGING-IN-PUBLICATION DATA

KLEIN, GRADY.
  THE CARTOON INTRODUCTION TO ECONOMICS / BY GRADY KLEIN AND
YORAM BAUMAN. — 1ST ED.
    V. ; CM.
  CONTENTS: VOL. 1. MICROECONOMICS.
  ISBN: 978-0-8090-9481-3 (PBK. : ALK. PAPER)
I. MICROECONOMICS. I. BAUMAN, YORAM. II. TITLE.
HB172. K67 2009
338.5—DC22

                                        2009015727

VOLUME TWO ISBN: 978-0-8090-3361-4

WWW.FSGBOOKS.COM

16 17 18 19

FOR ANNE AND LIAM AND BENJAMIN
—GK

FOR LAURA
—YB

CONTENTS

PART ONE:
A SINGLE MACROECONOMY

PART TWO:
INTERNATIONAL TRADE

PART THREE:
GLOBAL MACROECONOMICS

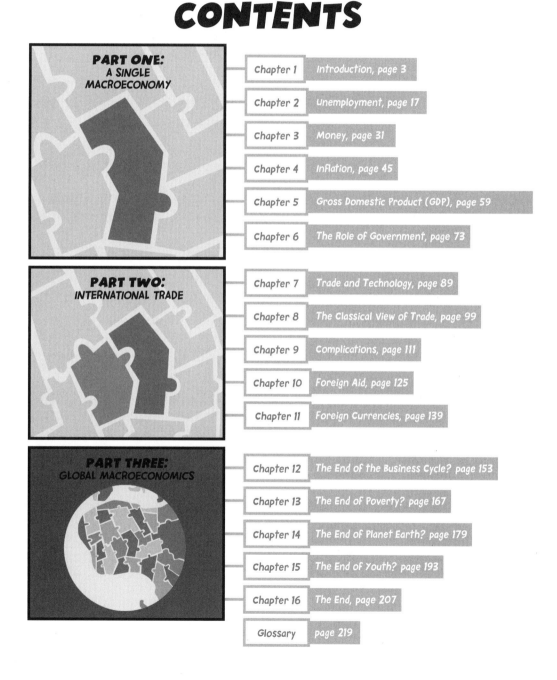

PART ONE
A SINGLE MACROECONOMY

CHAPTER 1
INTRODUCTION

ECONOMICS IS ABOUT **OPTIMIZING INDIVIDUALS!**

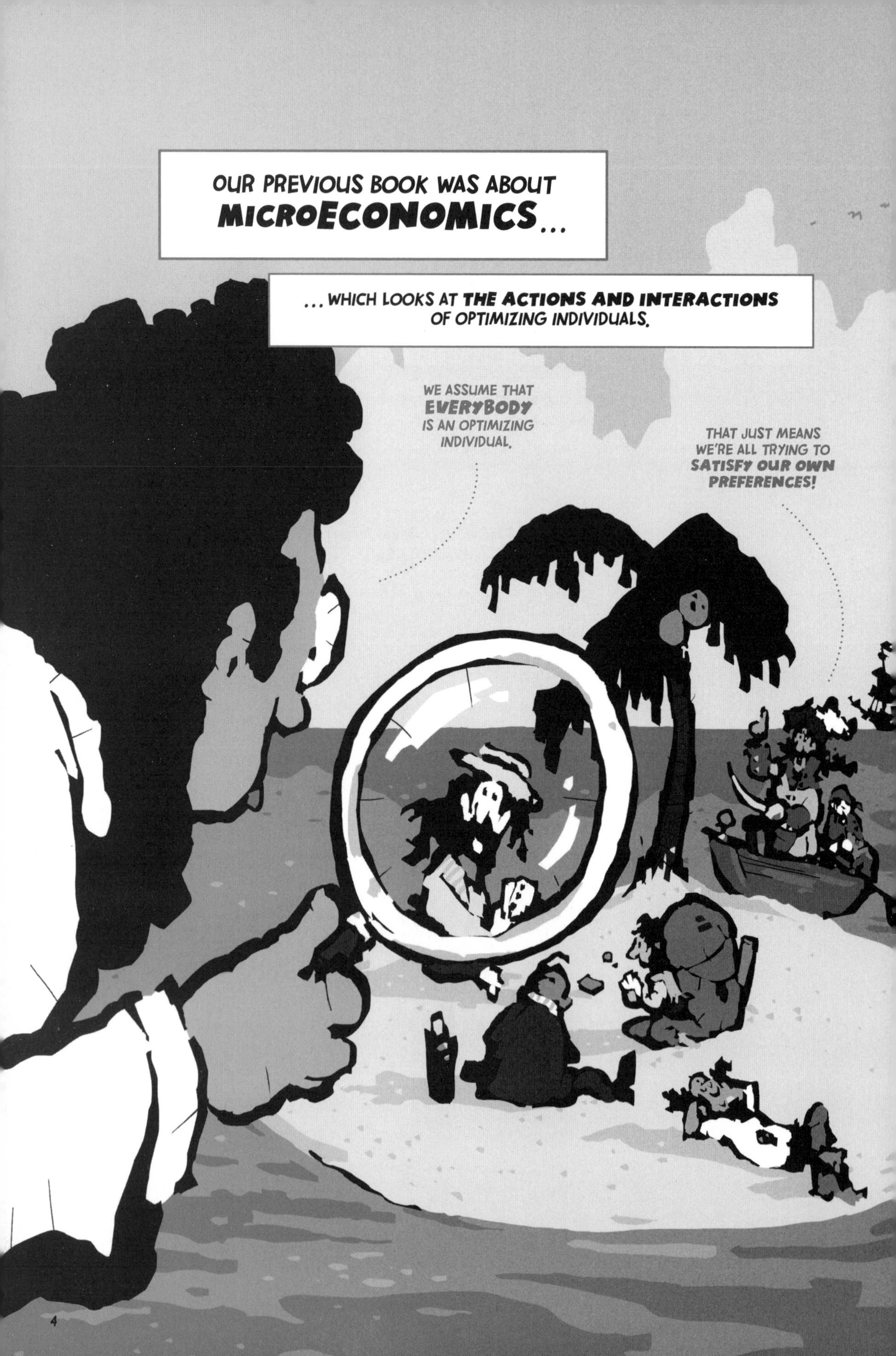
OUR PREVIOUS BOOK WAS ABOUT MICROECONOMICS...
...WHICH LOOKS AT THE ACTIONS AND INTERACTIONS OF OPTIMIZING INDIVIDUALS.
WE ASSUME THAT EVERYBODY IS AN OPTIMIZING INDIVIDUAL.
THAT JUST MEANS WE'RE ALL TRYING TO SATISFY OUR OWN PREFERENCES!

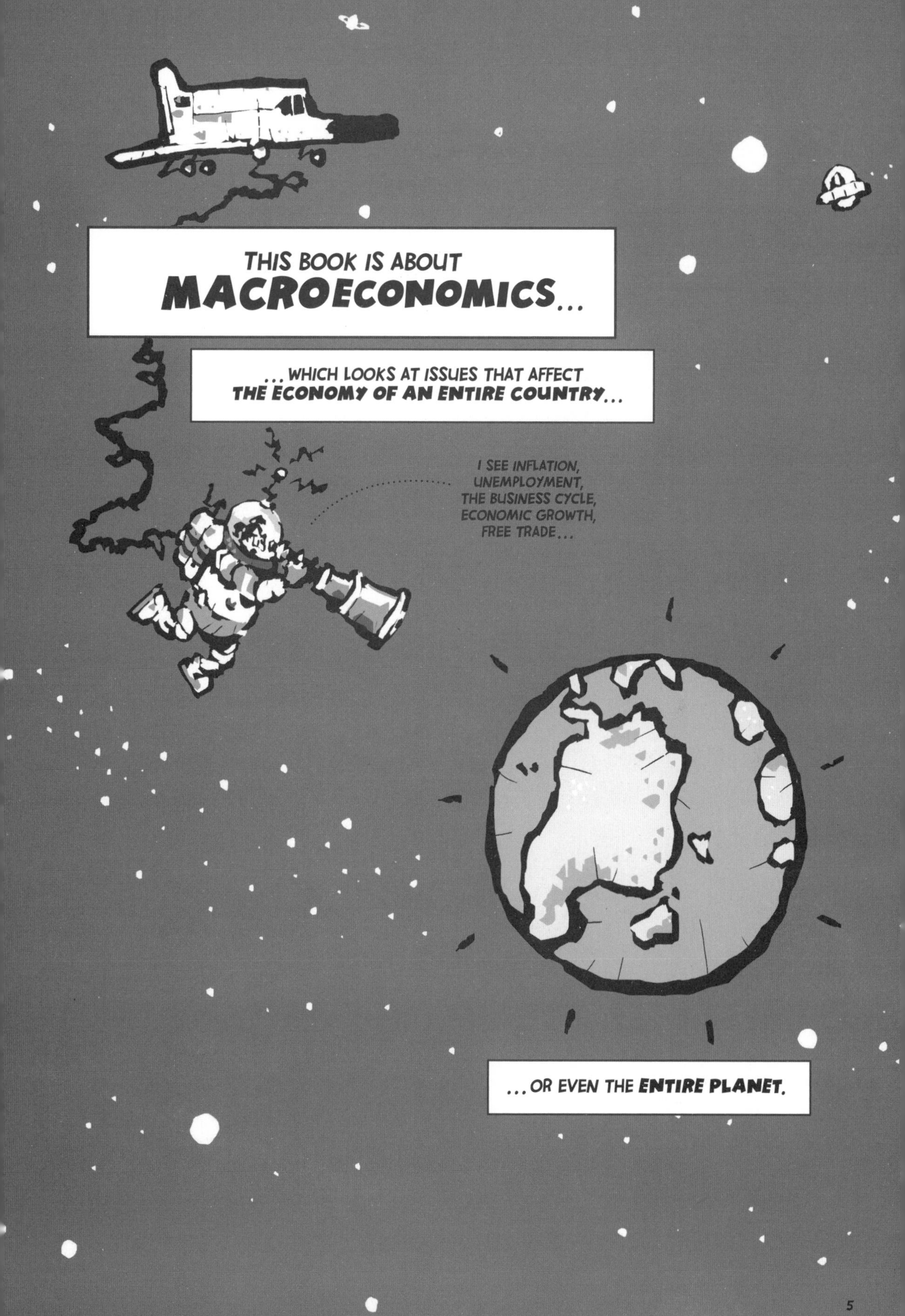

THIS BOOK IS ABOUT MACROECONOMICS...
...WHICH LOOKS AT ISSUES THAT AFFECT THE ECONOMY OF AN ENTIRE COUNTRY...
I SEE INFLATION, UNEMPLOYMENT, THE BUSINESS CYCLE, ECONOMIC GROWTH, FREE TRADE...
...OR EVEN THE ENTIRE PLANET.

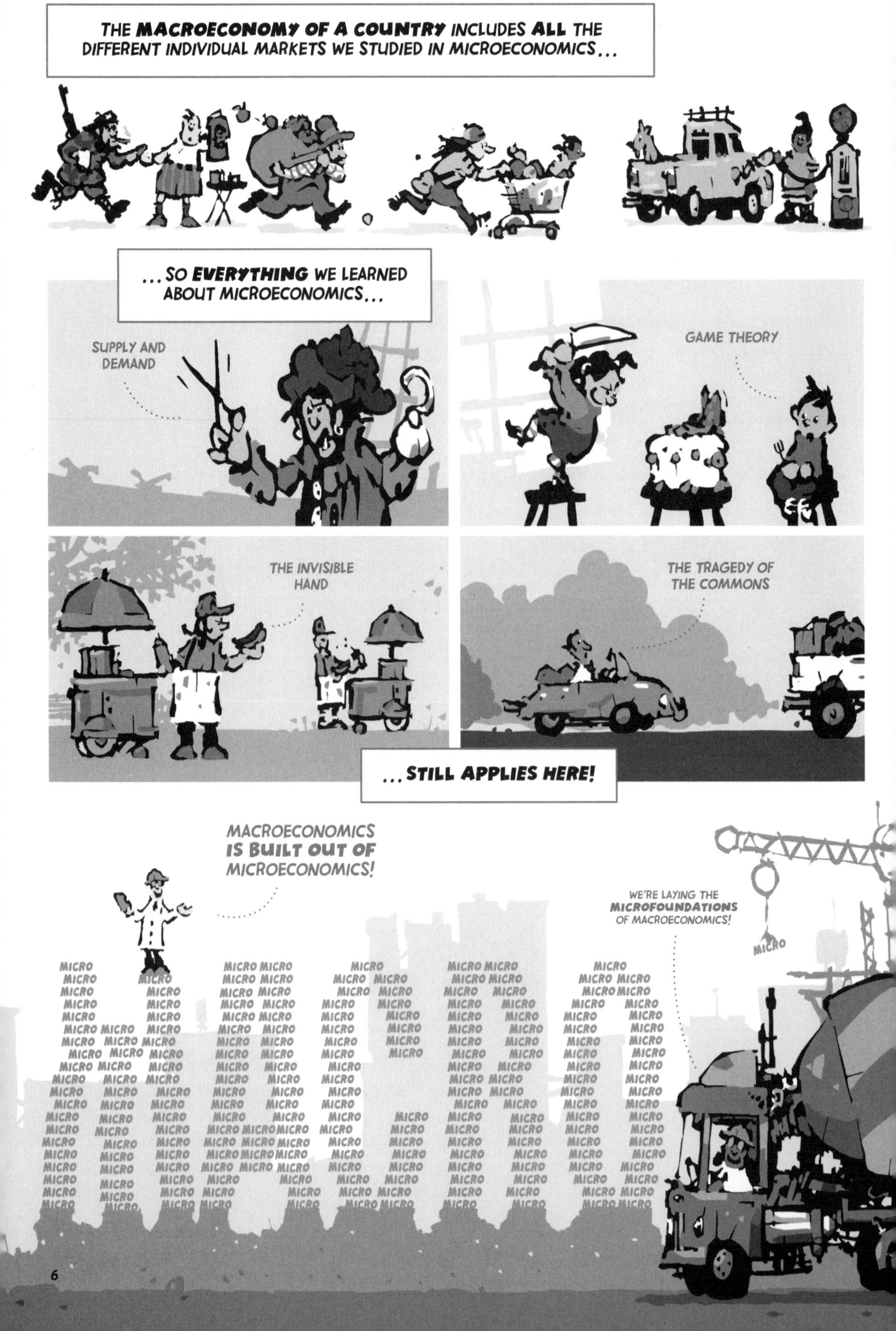

THE MACROECONOMY OF A COUNTRY INCLUDES ALL THE DIFFERENT INDIVIDUAL MARKETS WE STUDIED IN MICROECONOMICS...
...SO EVERYTHING WE LEARNED ABOUT MICROECONOMICS...
SUPPLY AND DEMAND
GAME THEORY
THE INVISIBLE HAND
THE TRAGEDY OF THE COMMONS
...STILL APPLIES HERE!
MACROECONOMICS IS BUILT OUT OF MICROECONOMICS!
WE'RE LAYING THE MICROFOUNDATIONS OF MACROECONOMICS!
MICRO

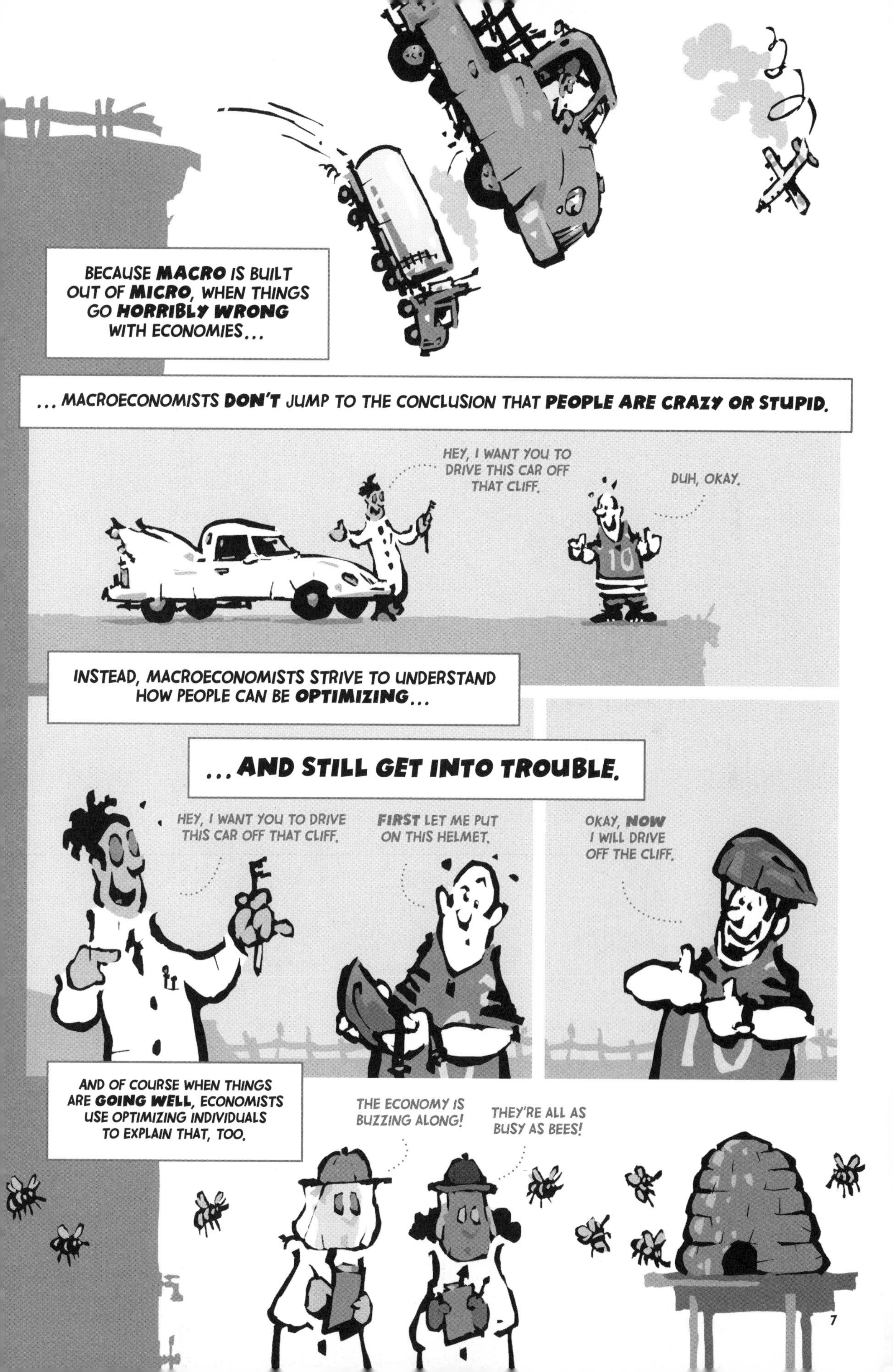

BECAUSE MACRO IS BUILT OUT OF MICRO, WHEN THINGS GO HORRIBLY WRONG WITH ECONOMIES...
... MACROECONOMISTS DON'T JUMP TO THE CONCLUSION THAT PEOPLE ARE CRAZY OR STUPID.
HEY, I WANT YOU TO DRIVE THIS CAR OFF THAT CLIFF.
DUH, OKAY.
INSTEAD, MACROECONOMISTS STRIVE TO UNDERSTAND HOW PEOPLE CAN BE OPTIMIZING...
... AND STILL GET INTO TROUBLE.
HEY, I WANT YOU TO DRIVE THIS CAR OFF THAT CLIFF.
FIRST LET ME PUT ON THIS HELMET.
OKAY, NOW I WILL DRIVE OFF THE CLIFF.
AND OF COURSE WHEN THINGS ARE GOING WELL, ECONOMISTS USE OPTIMIZING INDIVIDUALS TO EXPLAIN THAT, TOO.
THE ECONOMY IS BUZZING ALONG!
THEY'RE ALL AS BUSY AS BEES!

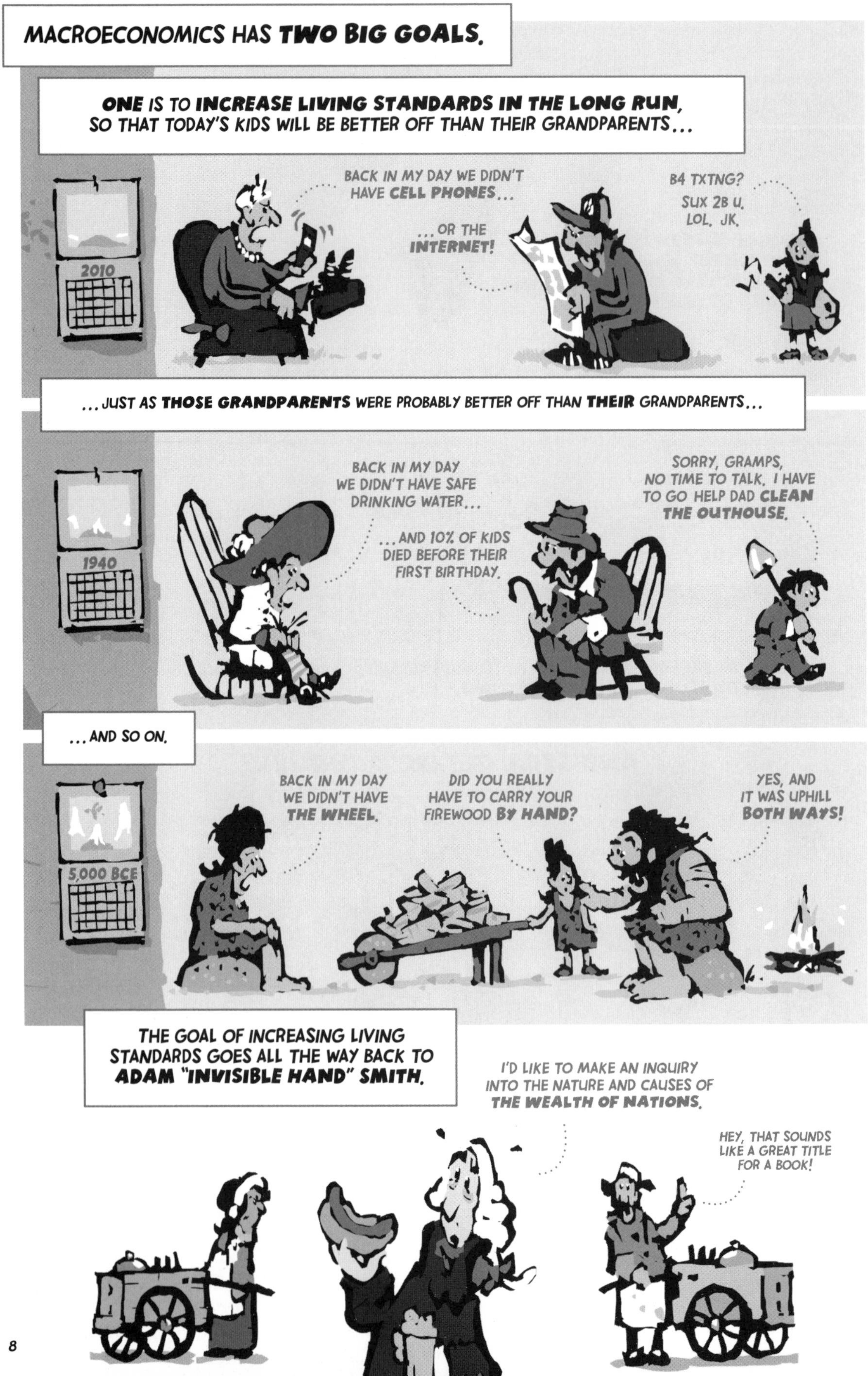
MACROECONOMICS HAS TWO BIG GOALS.
ONE IS TO INCREASE LIVING STANDARDS IN THE LONG RUN, SO THAT TODAY'S KIDS WILL BE BETTER OFF THAN THEIR GRANDPARENTS...
2010
BACK IN MY DAY WE DIDN'T HAVE CELL PHONES...
...OR THE INTERNET!
B4 TXTNG? SUX 2B U. LOL. JK.
...JUST AS THOSE GRANDPARENTS WERE PROBABLY BETTER OFF THAN THEIR GRANDPARENTS...
1940
BACK IN MY DAY WE DIDN'T HAVE SAFE DRINKING WATER...
...AND 10% OF KIDS DIED BEFORE THEIR FIRST BIRTHDAY.
SORRY, GRAMPS, NO TIME TO TALK. I HAVE TO GO HELP DAD CLEAN THE OUTHOUSE.
...AND SO ON.
5,000 BCE
BACK IN MY DAY WE DIDN'T HAVE THE WHEEL.
DID YOU REALLY HAVE TO CARRY YOUR FIREWOOD BY HAND?
YES, AND IT WAS UPHILL BOTH WAYS!
THE GOAL OF INCREASING LIVING STANDARDS GOES ALL THE WAY BACK TO ADAM "INVISIBLE HAND" SMITH.
I'D LIKE TO MAKE AN INQUIRY INTO THE NATURE AND CAUSES OF THE WEALTH OF NATIONS.
HEY, THAT SOUNDS LIKE A GREAT TITLE FOR A BOOK!

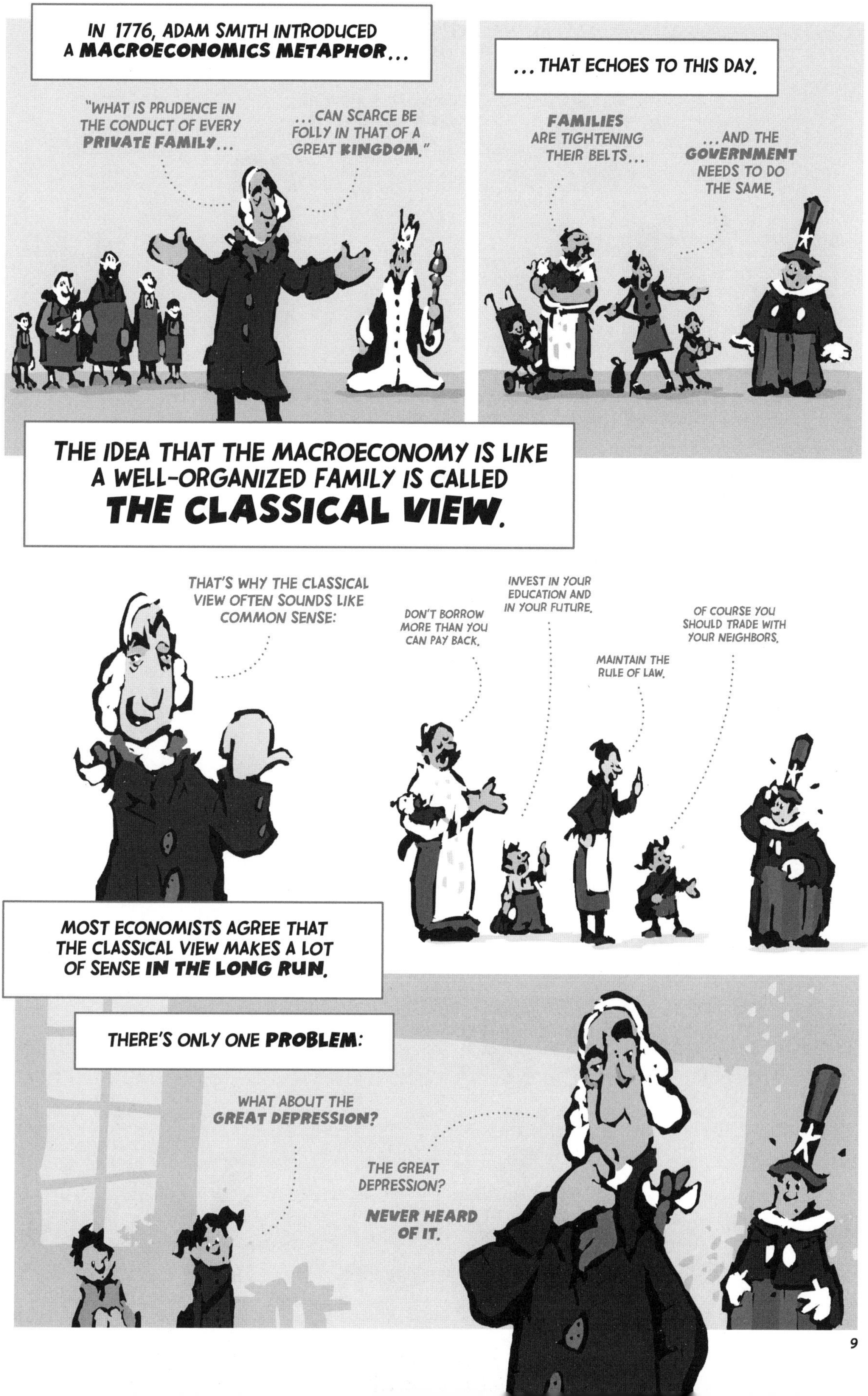

IN 1776, ADAM SMITH INTRODUCED A **MACROECONOMICS METAPHOR**...
"WHAT IS PRUDENCE IN THE CONDUCT OF EVERY **PRIVATE FAMILY**...
...CAN SCARCE BE FOLLY IN THAT OF A GREAT **KINGDOM**."
...THAT ECHOES TO THIS DAY.
FAMILIES ARE TIGHTENING THEIR BELTS...
...AND THE **GOVERNMENT** NEEDS TO DO THE SAME.
THE IDEA THAT THE MACROECONOMY IS LIKE A WELL-ORGANIZED FAMILY IS CALLED **THE CLASSICAL VIEW**.
THAT'S WHY THE CLASSICAL VIEW OFTEN SOUNDS LIKE COMMON SENSE:
DON'T BORROW MORE THAN YOU CAN PAY BACK.
INVEST IN YOUR EDUCATION AND IN YOUR FUTURE.
MAINTAIN THE RULE OF LAW.
OF COURSE YOU SHOULD TRADE WITH YOUR NEIGHBORS.
MOST ECONOMISTS AGREE THAT THE CLASSICAL VIEW MAKES A LOT OF SENSE **IN THE LONG RUN**.
THERE'S ONLY ONE **PROBLEM**:
WHAT ABOUT THE **GREAT DEPRESSION?**
THE GREAT DEPRESSION?
NEVER HEARD OF IT.

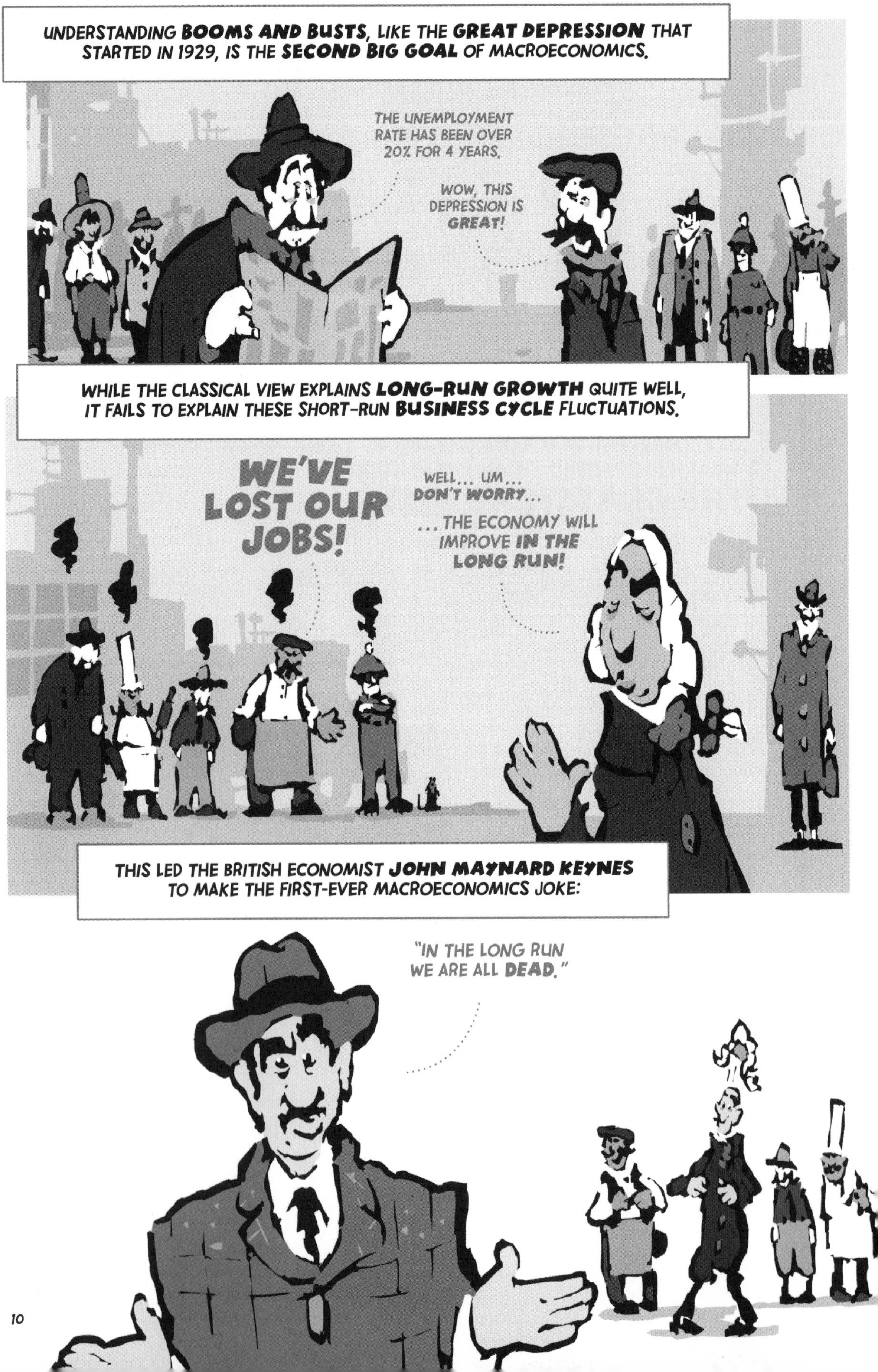
UNDERSTANDING BOOMS AND BUSTS, LIKE THE GREAT DEPRESSION THAT STARTED IN 1929, IS THE SECOND BIG GOAL OF MACROECONOMICS.
THE UNEMPLOYMENT RATE HAS BEEN OVER 20% FOR 4 YEARS.
WOW, THIS DEPRESSION IS GREAT!
WHILE THE CLASSICAL VIEW EXPLAINS LONG-RUN GROWTH QUITE WELL, IT FAILS TO EXPLAIN THESE SHORT-RUN BUSINESS CYCLE FLUCTUATIONS.
WE'VE LOST OUR JOBS!
WELL... UM... DON'T WORRY...
...THE ECONOMY WILL IMPROVE IN THE LONG RUN!
THIS LED THE BRITISH ECONOMIST JOHN MAYNARD KEYNES TO MAKE THE FIRST-EVER MACROECONOMICS JOKE:
"IN THE LONG RUN WE ARE ALL DEAD."

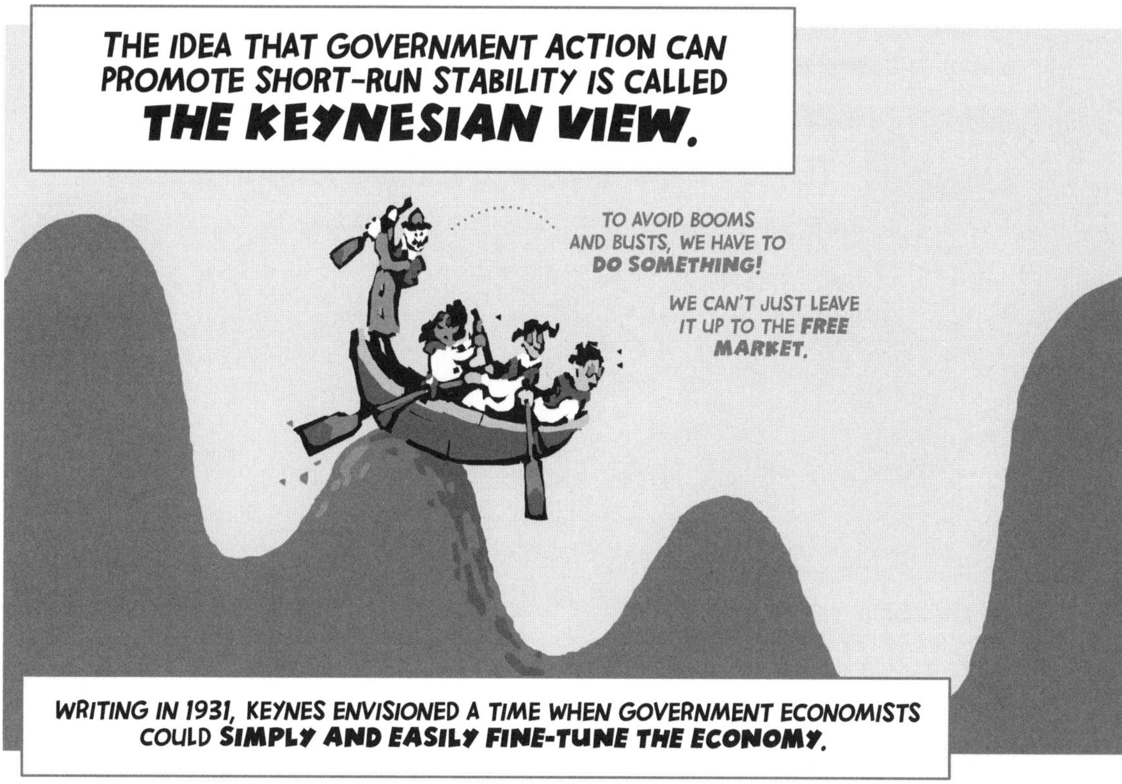
THE IDEA THAT GOVERNMENT ACTION CAN PROMOTE SHORT-RUN STABILITY IS CALLED **THE KEYNESIAN VIEW.**
TO AVOID BOOMS AND BUSTS, WE HAVE TO **DO SOMETHING!**
WE CAN'T JUST LEAVE IT UP TO THE **FREE MARKET.**
WRITING IN 1931, KEYNES ENVISIONED A TIME WHEN GOVERNMENT ECONOMISTS COULD **SIMPLY AND EASILY FINE-TUNE THE ECONOMY.**

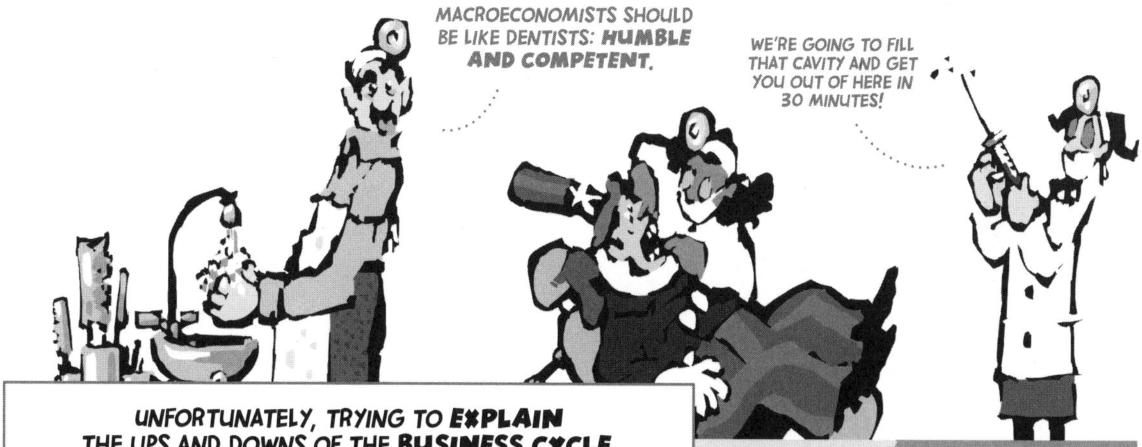
MACROECONOMISTS SHOULD BE LIKE DENTISTS: **HUMBLE AND COMPETENT.**
WE'RE GOING TO FILL THAT CAVITY AND GET YOU OUT OF HERE IN 30 MINUTES!

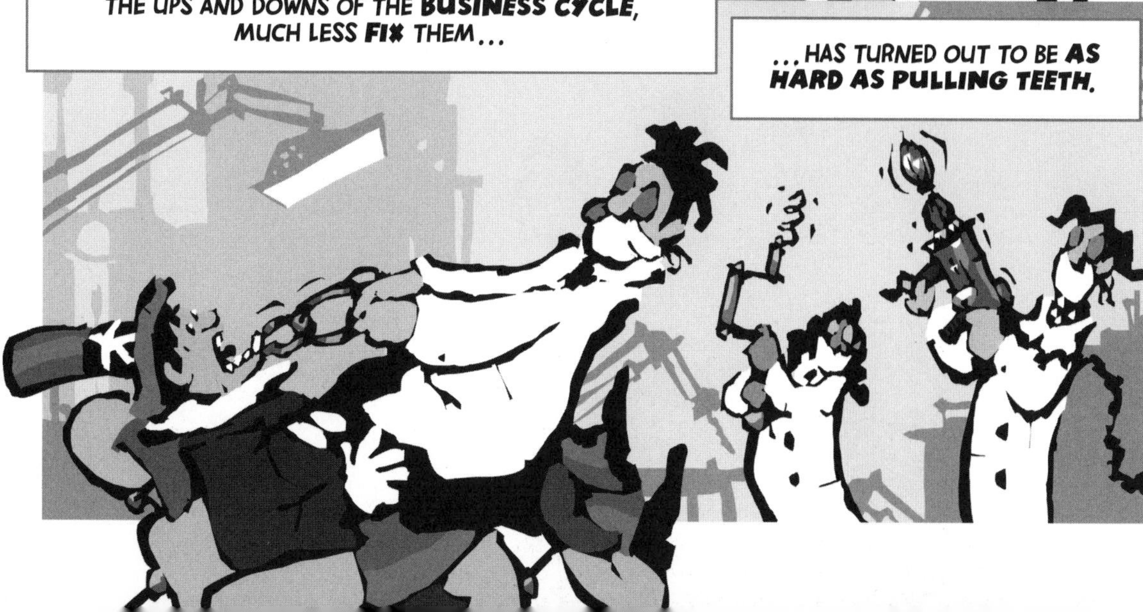
UNFORTUNATELY, TRYING TO **EXPLAIN** THE UPS AND DOWNS OF THE **BUSINESS CYCLE,** MUCH LESS **FIX** THEM...
...HAS TURNED OUT TO BE **AS HARD AS PULLING TEETH.**

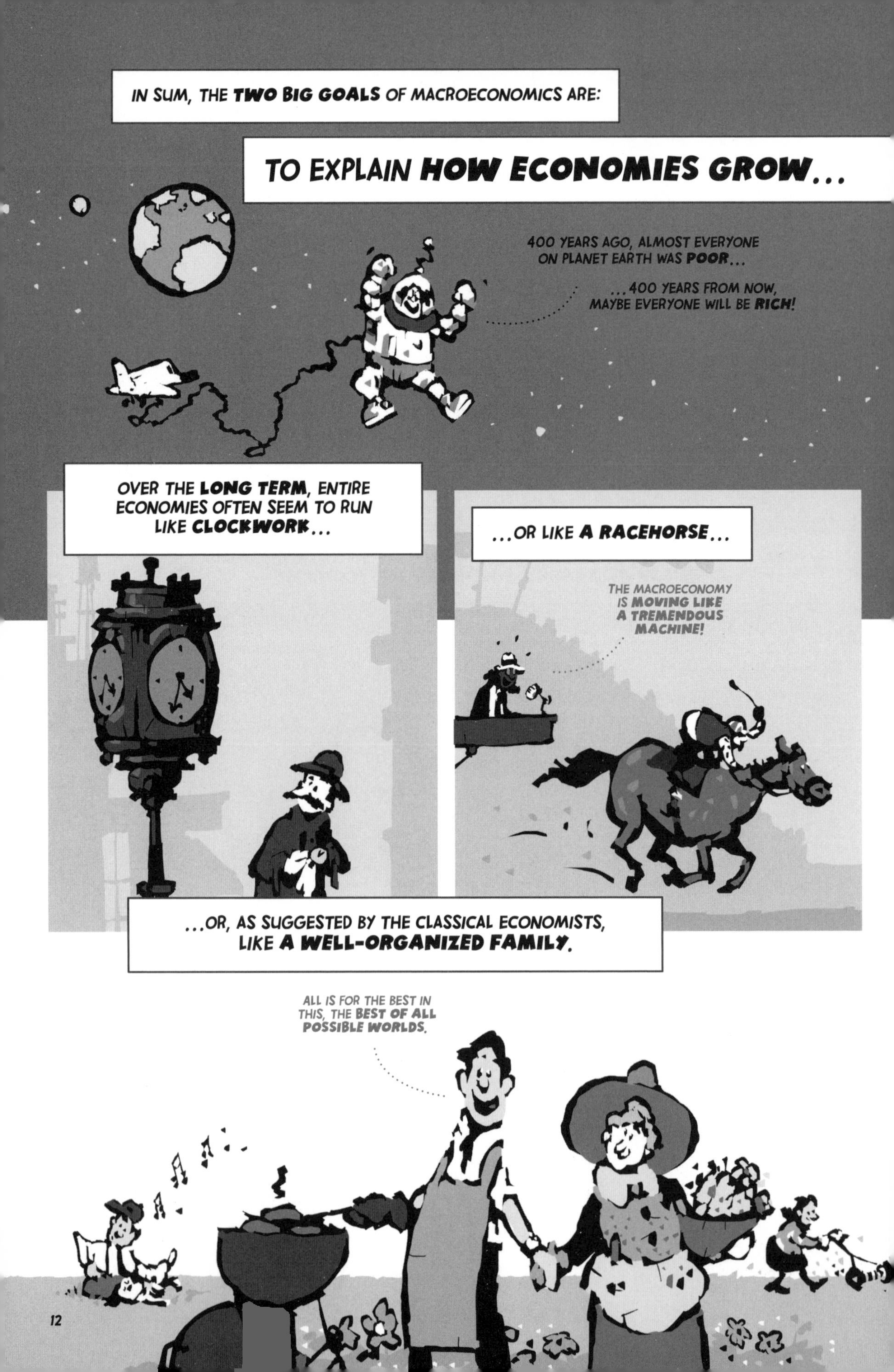
IN SUM, THE **TWO BIG GOALS** OF MACROECONOMICS ARE:
TO EXPLAIN **HOW ECONOMIES GROW**...
400 YEARS AGO, ALMOST EVERYONE ON PLANET EARTH WAS **POOR**...
...400 YEARS FROM NOW, MAYBE EVERYONE WILL BE **RICH**!
OVER THE **LONG TERM**, ENTIRE ECONOMIES OFTEN SEEM TO RUN LIKE **CLOCKWORK**...
...OR LIKE **A RACEHORSE**...
THE MACROECONOMY IS **MOVING LIKE A TREMENDOUS MACHINE!**
...OR, AS SUGGESTED BY THE CLASSICAL ECONOMISTS, LIKE **A WELL-ORGANIZED FAMILY**.
ALL IS FOR THE BEST IN THIS, THE **BEST OF ALL POSSIBLE WORLDS**.

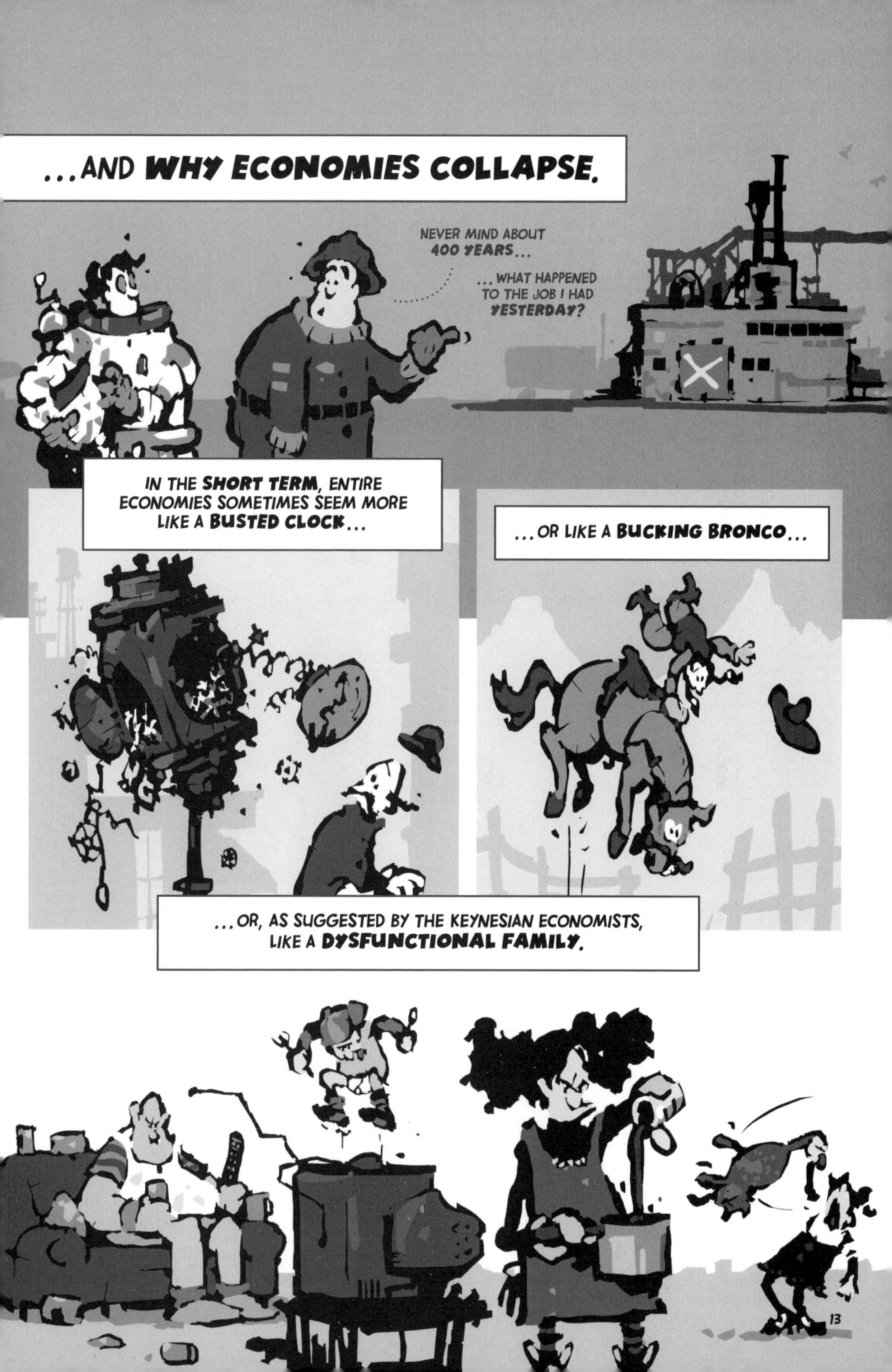
...AND WHY ECONOMIES COLLAPSE.
NEVER MIND ABOUT 400 YEARS...
...WHAT HAPPENED TO THE JOB I HAD YESTERDAY?
IN THE SHORT TERM, ENTIRE ECONOMIES SOMETIMES SEEM MORE LIKE A BUSTED CLOCK...
...OR LIKE A BUCKING BRONCO...
...OR, AS SUGGESTED BY THE KEYNESIAN ECONOMISTS, LIKE A DYSFUNCTIONAL FAMILY.

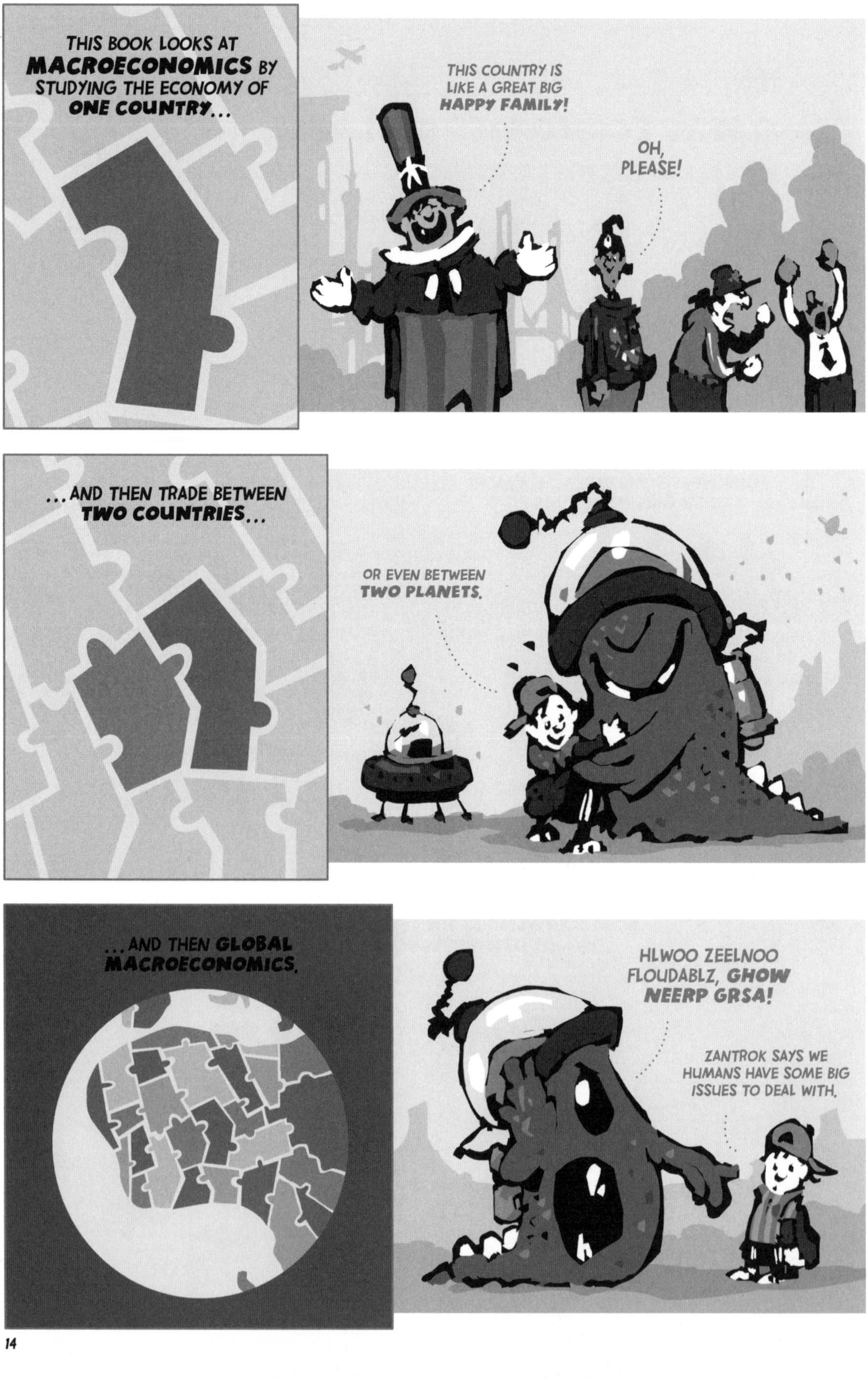
THIS BOOK LOOKS AT **MACROECONOMICS** BY STUDYING THE ECONOMY OF **ONE COUNTRY**...
THIS COUNTRY IS LIKE A GREAT BIG **HAPPY FAMILY!**
OH, PLEASE!
...AND THEN TRADE BETWEEN **TWO COUNTRIES**...
OR EVEN BETWEEN **TWO PLANETS.**
...AND THEN **GLOBAL MACROECONOMICS.**
HLWOO ZEELNOO FLOUDABLZ, **GHOW NEERP GRSA!**
ZANTROK SAYS WE HUMANS HAVE SOME BIG ISSUES TO DEAL WITH.

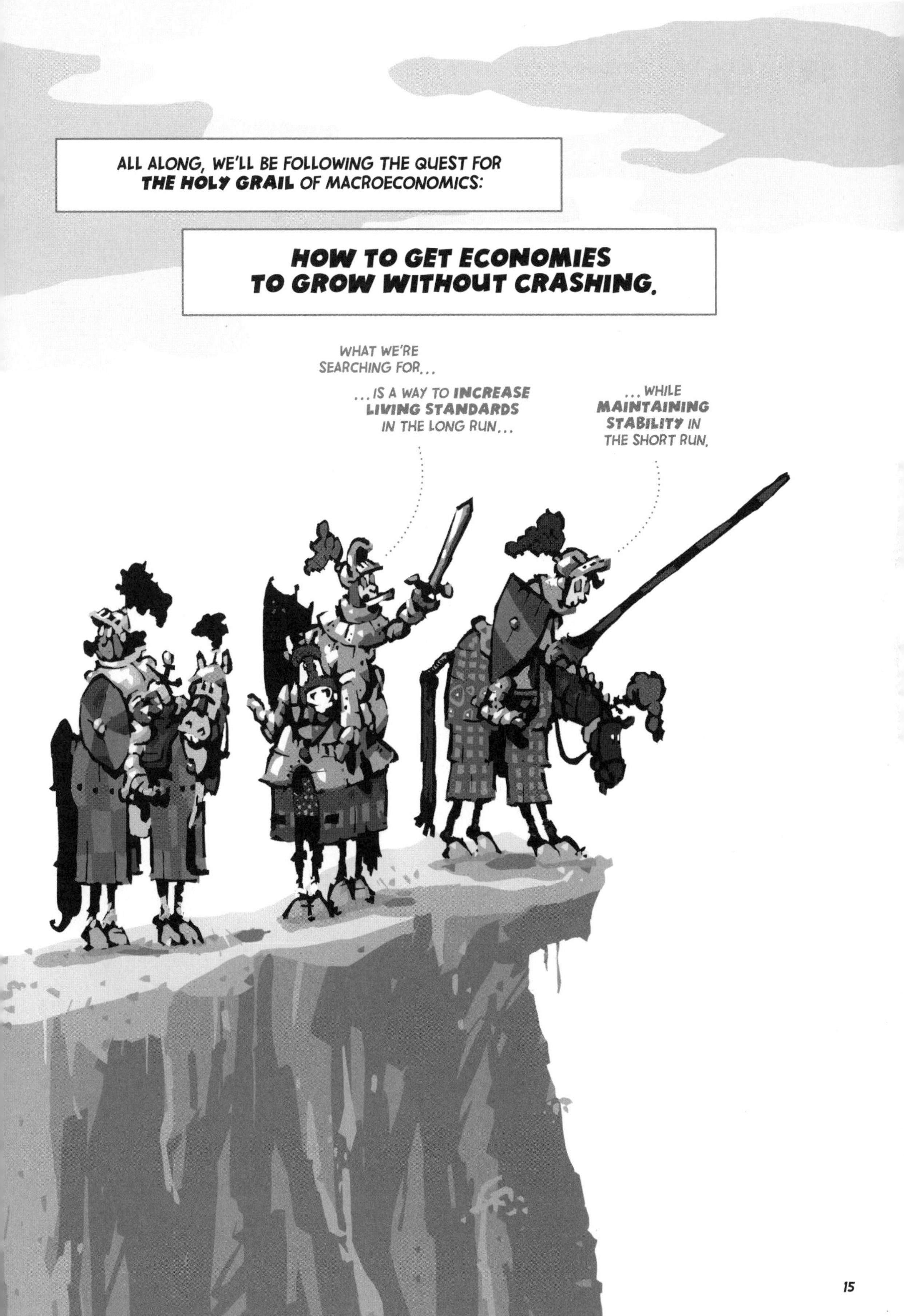
ALL ALONG, WE'LL BE FOLLOWING THE QUEST FOR **THE HOLY GRAIL** OF MACROECONOMICS:
HOW TO GET ECONOMIES TO GROW WITHOUT CRASHING.
WHAT WE'RE SEARCHING FOR...
...IS A WAY TO **INCREASE LIVING STANDARDS** IN THE LONG RUN...
...WHILE **MAINTAINING STABILITY** IN THE SHORT RUN.

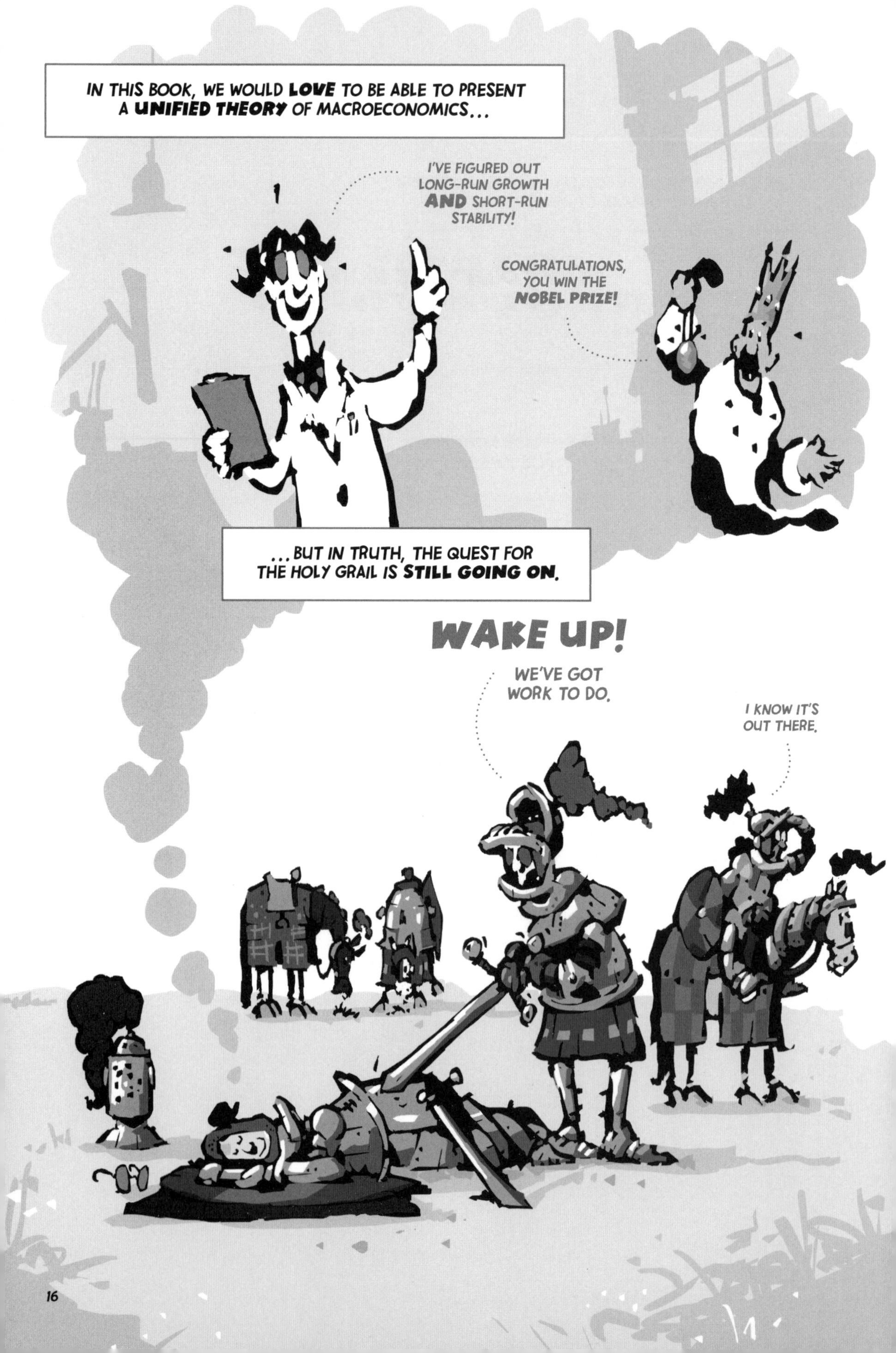
IN THIS BOOK, WE WOULD LOVE TO BE ABLE TO PRESENT A UNIFIED THEORY OF MACROECONOMICS...
I'VE FIGURED OUT LONG-RUN GROWTH AND SHORT-RUN STABILITY!
CONGRATULATIONS, YOU WIN THE NOBEL PRIZE!
...BUT IN TRUTH, THE QUEST FOR THE HOLY GRAIL IS STILL GOING ON.
WAKE UP!
WE'VE GOT WORK TO DO.
I KNOW IT'S OUT THERE.

CHAPTER 2
UNEMPLOYMENT

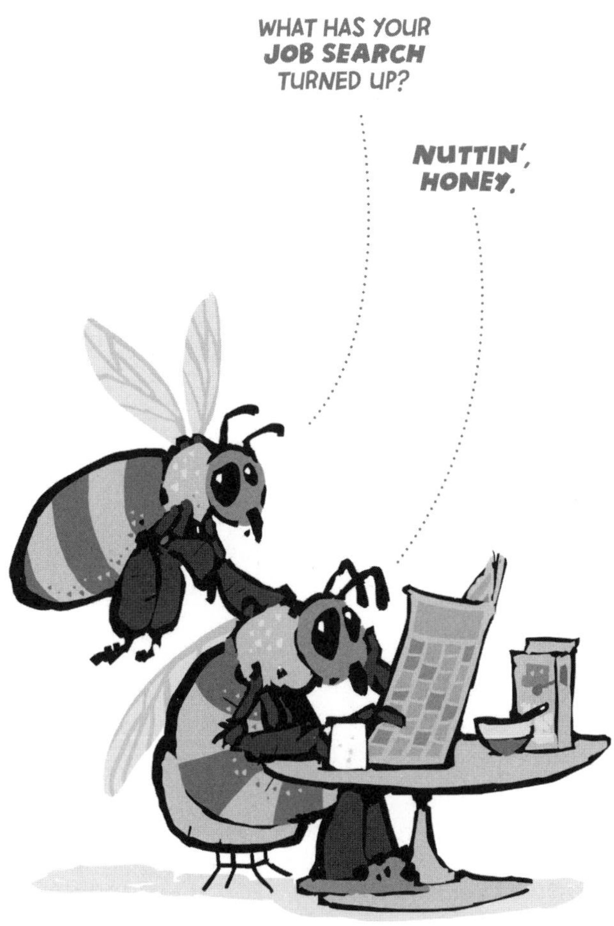
WHAT HAS YOUR JOB SEARCH TURNED UP?
NUTTIN', HONEY.

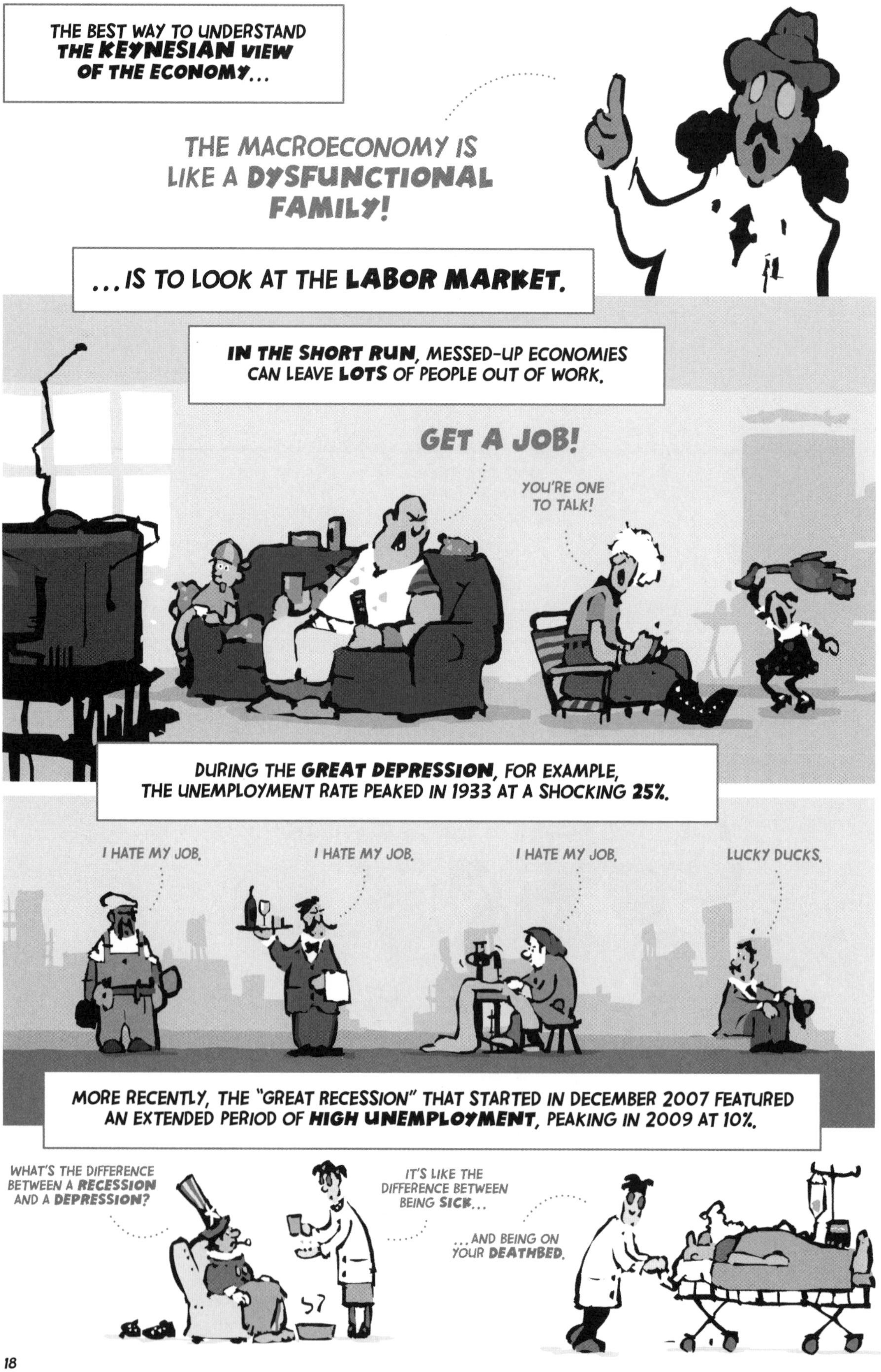
THE BEST WAY TO UNDERSTAND THE KEYNESIAN VIEW OF THE ECONOMY...
THE MACROECONOMY IS LIKE A DYSFUNCTIONAL FAMILY!
...IS TO LOOK AT THE LABOR MARKET.
IN THE SHORT RUN, MESSED-UP ECONOMIES CAN LEAVE LOTS OF PEOPLE OUT OF WORK.
GET A JOB!
YOU'RE ONE TO TALK!
DURING THE GREAT DEPRESSION, FOR EXAMPLE, THE UNEMPLOYMENT RATE PEAKED IN 1933 AT A SHOCKING 25%.
I HATE MY JOB.
I HATE MY JOB.
I HATE MY JOB.
LUCKY DUCKS.
MORE RECENTLY, THE "GREAT RECESSION" THAT STARTED IN DECEMBER 2007 FEATURED AN EXTENDED PERIOD OF HIGH UNEMPLOYMENT, PEAKING IN 2009 AT 10%.
WHAT'S THE DIFFERENCE BETWEEN A RECESSION AND A DEPRESSION?
IT'S LIKE THE DIFFERENCE BETWEEN BEING SICK...
...AND BEING ON YOUR DEATHBED.

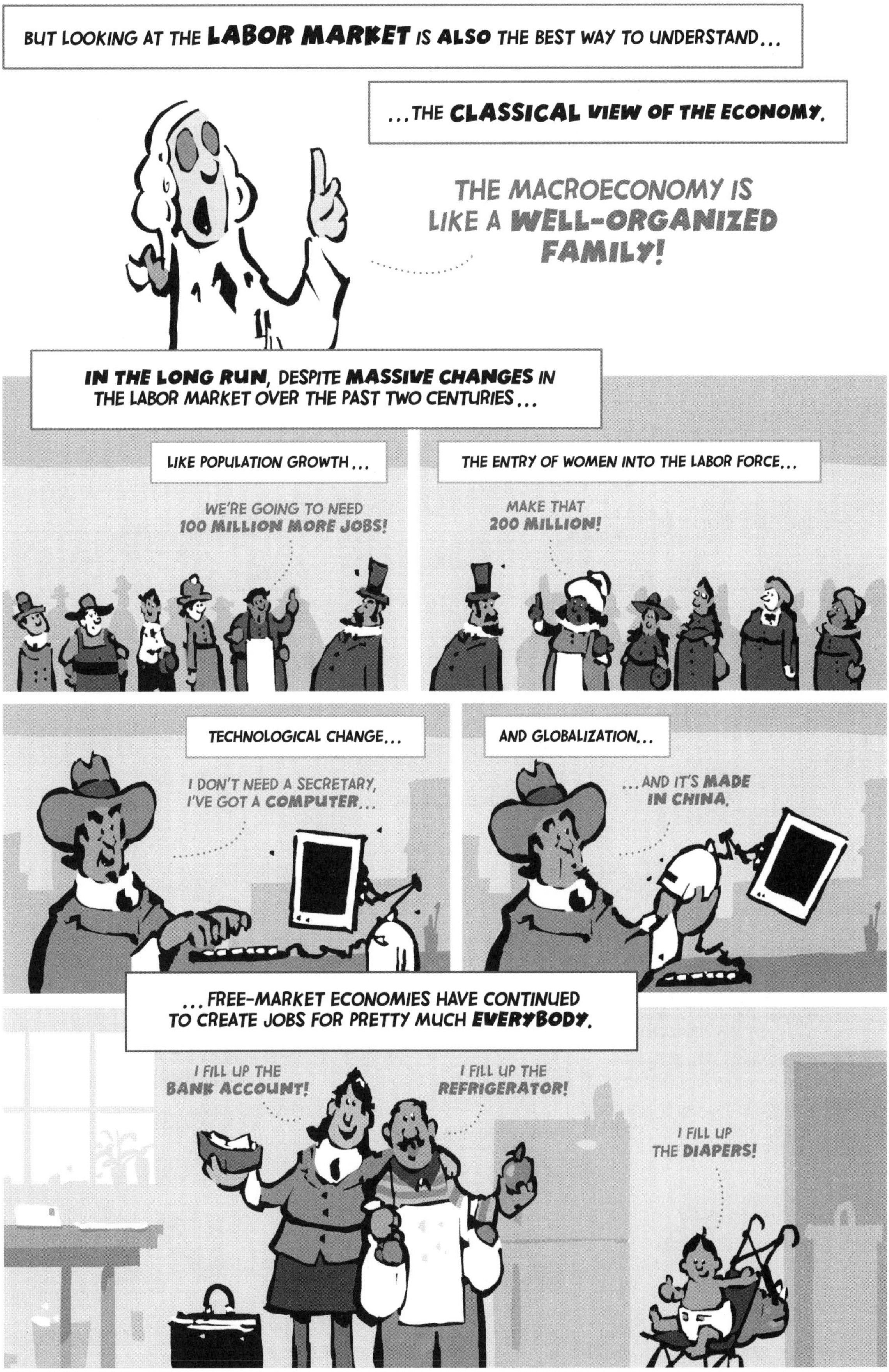
BUT LOOKING AT THE LABOR MARKET IS ALSO THE BEST WAY TO UNDERSTAND...
...THE CLASSICAL VIEW OF THE ECONOMY.
THE MACROECONOMY IS LIKE A WELL-ORGANIZED FAMILY!
IN THE LONG RUN, DESPITE MASSIVE CHANGES IN THE LABOR MARKET OVER THE PAST TWO CENTURIES...
LIKE POPULATION GROWTH...
WE'RE GOING TO NEED 100 MILLION MORE JOBS!
THE ENTRY OF WOMEN INTO THE LABOR FORCE...
MAKE THAT 200 MILLION!
TECHNOLOGICAL CHANGE...
I DON'T NEED A SECRETARY, I'VE GOT A COMPUTER...
AND GLOBALIZATION...
...AND IT'S MADE IN CHINA.
...FREE-MARKET ECONOMIES HAVE CONTINUED TO CREATE JOBS FOR PRETTY MUCH EVERYBODY.
I FILL UP THE BANK ACCOUNT!
I FILL UP THE REFRIGERATOR!
I FILL UP THE DIAPERS!

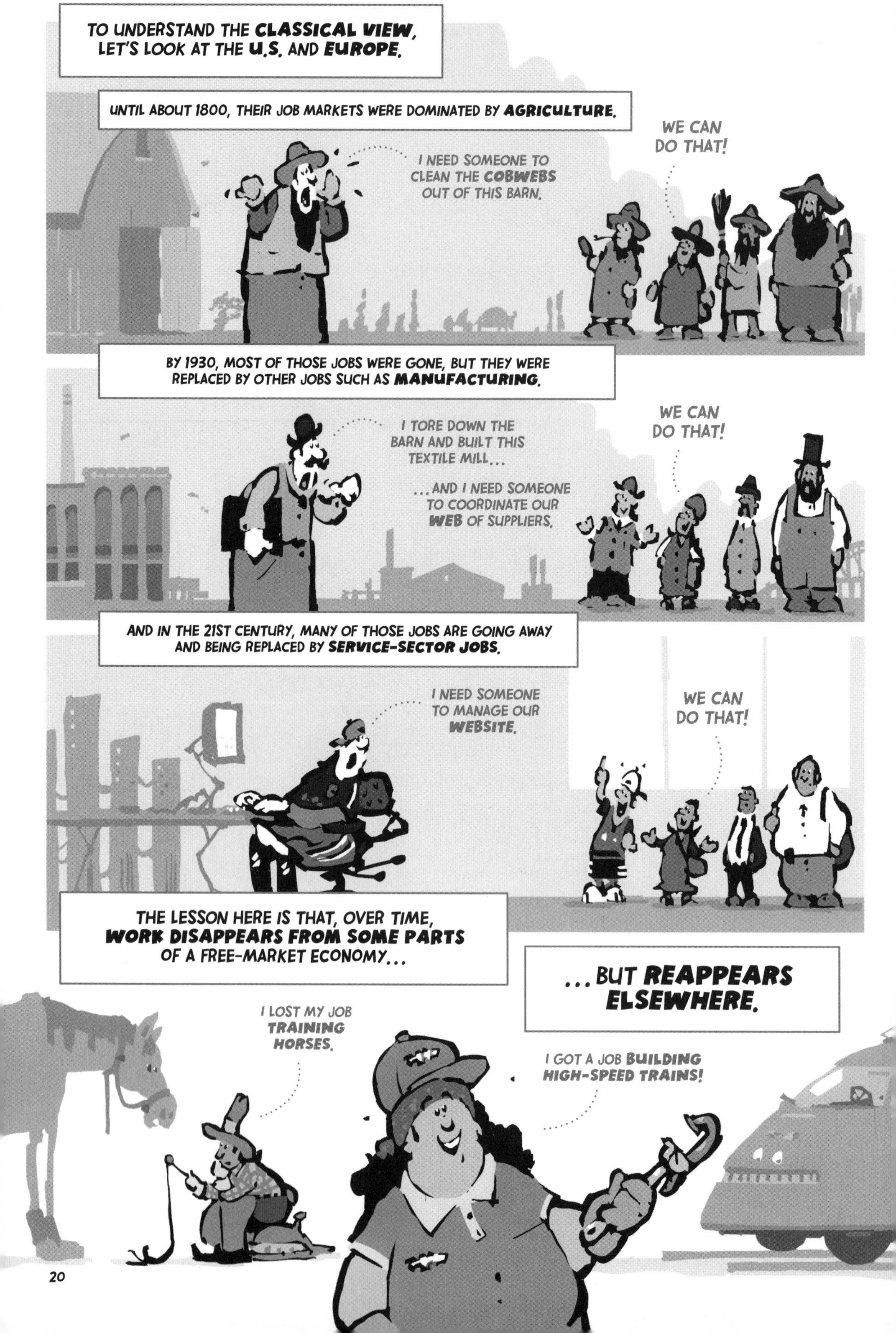
TO UNDERSTAND THE CLASSICAL VIEW, LET'S LOOK AT THE U.S. AND EUROPE.
UNTIL ABOUT 1800, THEIR JOB MARKETS WERE DOMINATED BY AGRICULTURE.
I NEED SOMEONE TO CLEAN THE COBWEBS OUT OF THIS BARN.
WE CAN DO THAT!
BY 1930, MOST OF THOSE JOBS WERE GONE, BUT THEY WERE REPLACED BY OTHER JOBS SUCH AS MANUFACTURING.
I TORE DOWN THE BARN AND BUILT THIS TEXTILE MILL...
...AND I NEED SOMEONE TO COORDINATE OUR WEB OF SUPPLIERS.
WE CAN DO THAT!
AND IN THE 21ST CENTURY, MANY OF THOSE JOBS ARE GOING AWAY AND BEING REPLACED BY SERVICE-SECTOR JOBS.
I NEED SOMEONE TO MANAGE OUR WEBSITE.
WE CAN DO THAT!
THE LESSON HERE IS THAT, OVER TIME, WORK DISAPPEARS FROM SOME PARTS OF A FREE-MARKET ECONOMY...
...BUT REAPPEARS ELSEWHERE.
I LOST MY JOB TRAINING HORSES.
I GOT A JOB BUILDING HIGH-SPEED TRAINS!

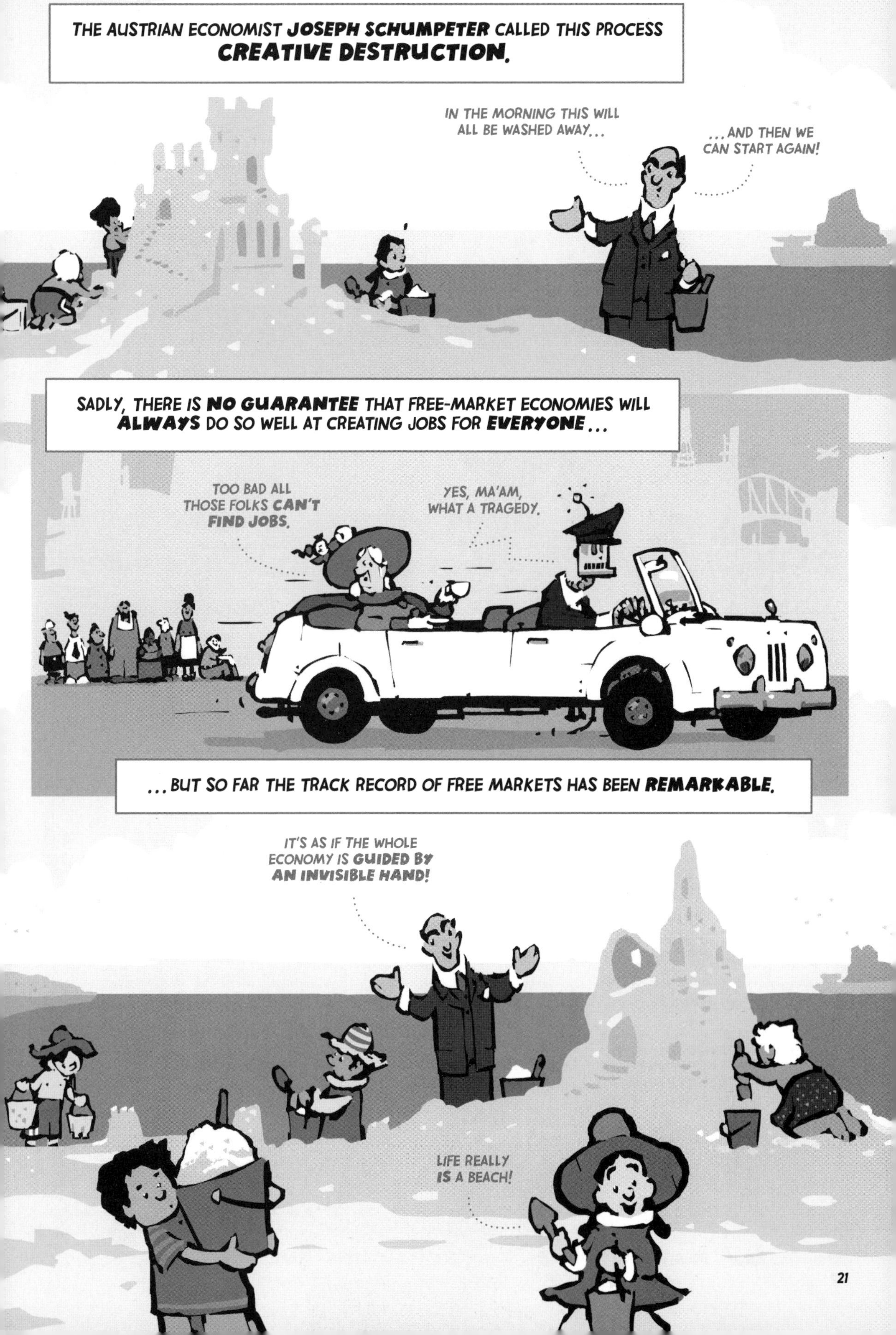
THE AUSTRIAN ECONOMIST **JOSEPH SCHUMPETER** CALLED THIS PROCESS **CREATIVE DESTRUCTION.**
IN THE MORNING THIS WILL ALL BE WASHED AWAY...
...AND THEN WE CAN START AGAIN!
SADLY, THERE IS **NO GUARANTEE** THAT FREE-MARKET ECONOMIES WILL **ALWAYS** DO SO WELL AT CREATING JOBS FOR **EVERYONE**...
TOO BAD ALL THOSE FOLKS **CAN'T FIND JOBS.**
YES, MA'AM, WHAT A TRAGEDY.
...BUT SO FAR THE TRACK RECORD OF FREE MARKETS HAS BEEN **REMARKABLE.**
IT'S AS IF THE WHOLE ECONOMY IS **GUIDED BY AN INVISIBLE HAND!**
LIFE REALLY **IS** A BEACH!

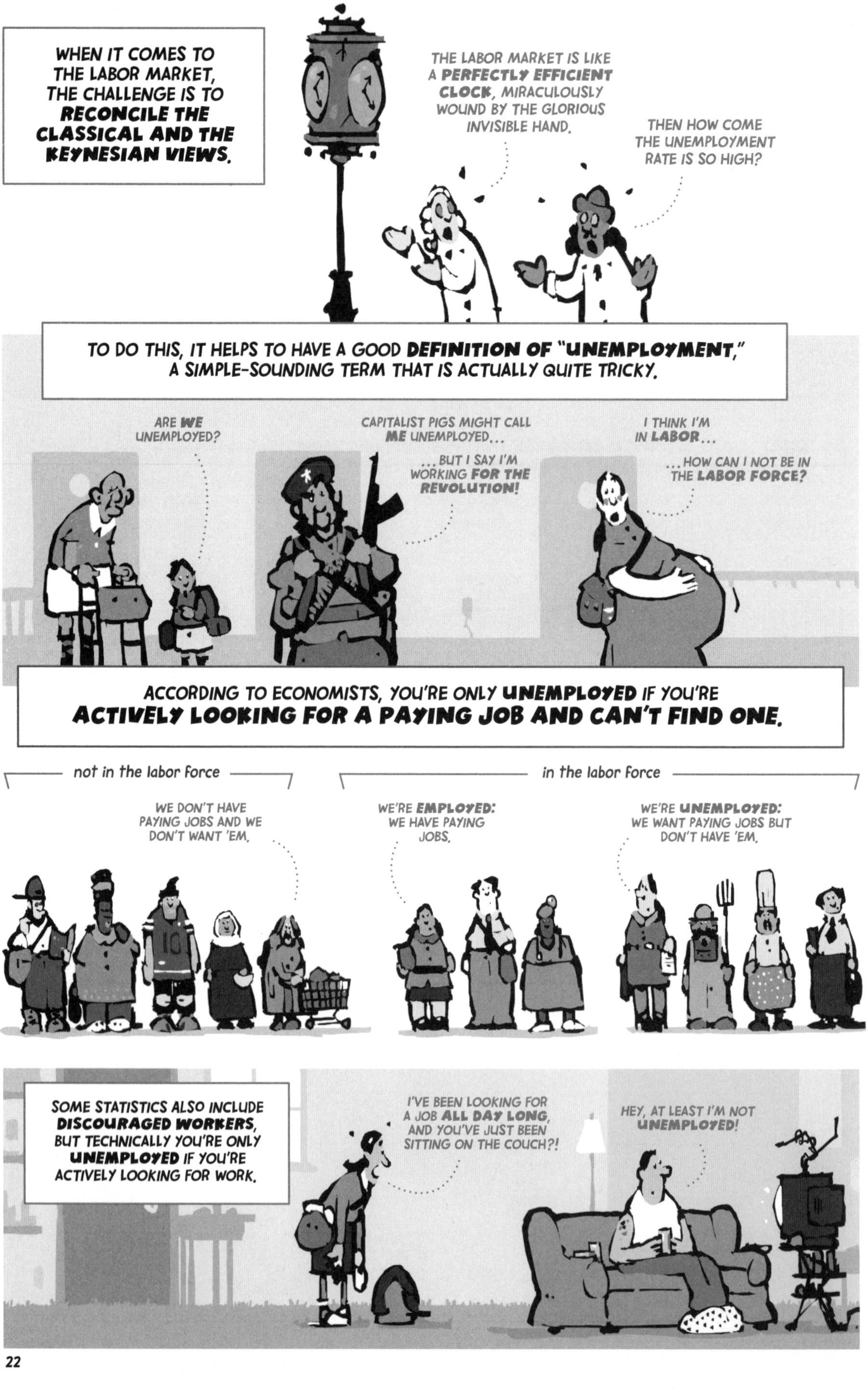
WHEN IT COMES TO THE LABOR MARKET, THE CHALLENGE IS TO RECONCILE THE CLASSICAL AND THE KEYNESIAN VIEWS.
THE LABOR MARKET IS LIKE A PERFECTLY EFFICIENT CLOCK, MIRACULOUSLY WOUND BY THE GLORIOUS INVISIBLE HAND.
THEN HOW COME THE UNEMPLOYMENT RATE IS SO HIGH?
TO DO THIS, IT HELPS TO HAVE A GOOD DEFINITION OF "UNEMPLOYMENT," A SIMPLE-SOUNDING TERM THAT IS ACTUALLY QUITE TRICKY.
ARE WE UNEMPLOYED?
CAPITALIST PIGS MIGHT CALL ME UNEMPLOYED...
...BUT I SAY I'M WORKING FOR THE REVOLUTION!
I THINK I'M IN LABOR...
...HOW CAN I NOT BE IN THE LABOR FORCE?
ACCORDING TO ECONOMISTS, YOU'RE ONLY UNEMPLOYED IF YOU'RE ACTIVELY LOOKING FOR A PAYING JOB AND CAN'T FIND ONE.
not in the labor force
in the labor force
WE DON'T HAVE PAYING JOBS AND WE DON'T WANT 'EM.
WE'RE EMPLOYED: WE HAVE PAYING JOBS.
WE'RE UNEMPLOYED: WE WANT PAYING JOBS BUT DON'T HAVE 'EM.
SOME STATISTICS ALSO INCLUDE DISCOURAGED WORKERS, BUT TECHNICALLY YOU'RE ONLY UNEMPLOYED IF YOU'RE ACTIVELY LOOKING FOR WORK.
I'VE BEEN LOOKING FOR A JOB ALL DAY LONG, AND YOU'VE JUST BEEN SITTING ON THE COUCH?!
HEY, AT LEAST I'M NOT UNEMPLOYED!

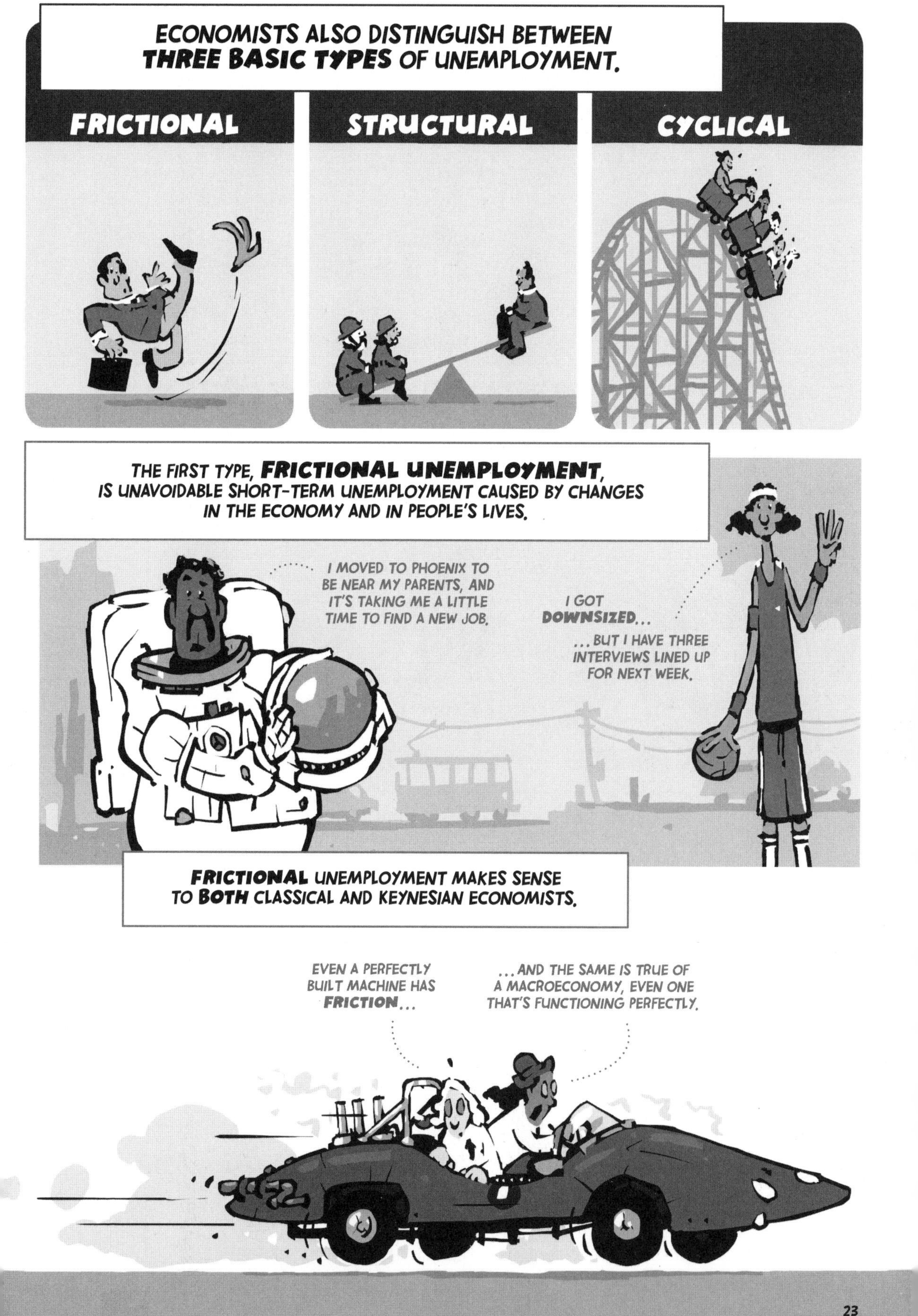
ECONOMISTS ALSO DISTINGUISH BETWEEN **THREE BASIC TYPES** OF UNEMPLOYMENT.
FRICTIONAL
STRUCTURAL
CYCLICAL
THE FIRST TYPE, **FRICTIONAL UNEMPLOYMENT**, IS UNAVOIDABLE SHORT-TERM UNEMPLOYMENT CAUSED BY CHANGES IN THE ECONOMY AND IN PEOPLE'S LIVES.
I MOVED TO PHOENIX TO BE NEAR MY PARENTS, AND IT'S TAKING ME A LITTLE TIME TO FIND A NEW JOB.
I GOT **DOWNSIZED**...
...BUT I HAVE THREE INTERVIEWS LINED UP FOR NEXT WEEK.
FRICTIONAL UNEMPLOYMENT MAKES SENSE TO **BOTH** CLASSICAL AND KEYNESIAN ECONOMISTS.
EVEN A PERFECTLY BUILT MACHINE HAS **FRICTION**...
...AND THE SAME IS TRUE OF A MACROECONOMY, EVEN ONE THAT'S FUNCTIONING PERFECTLY.

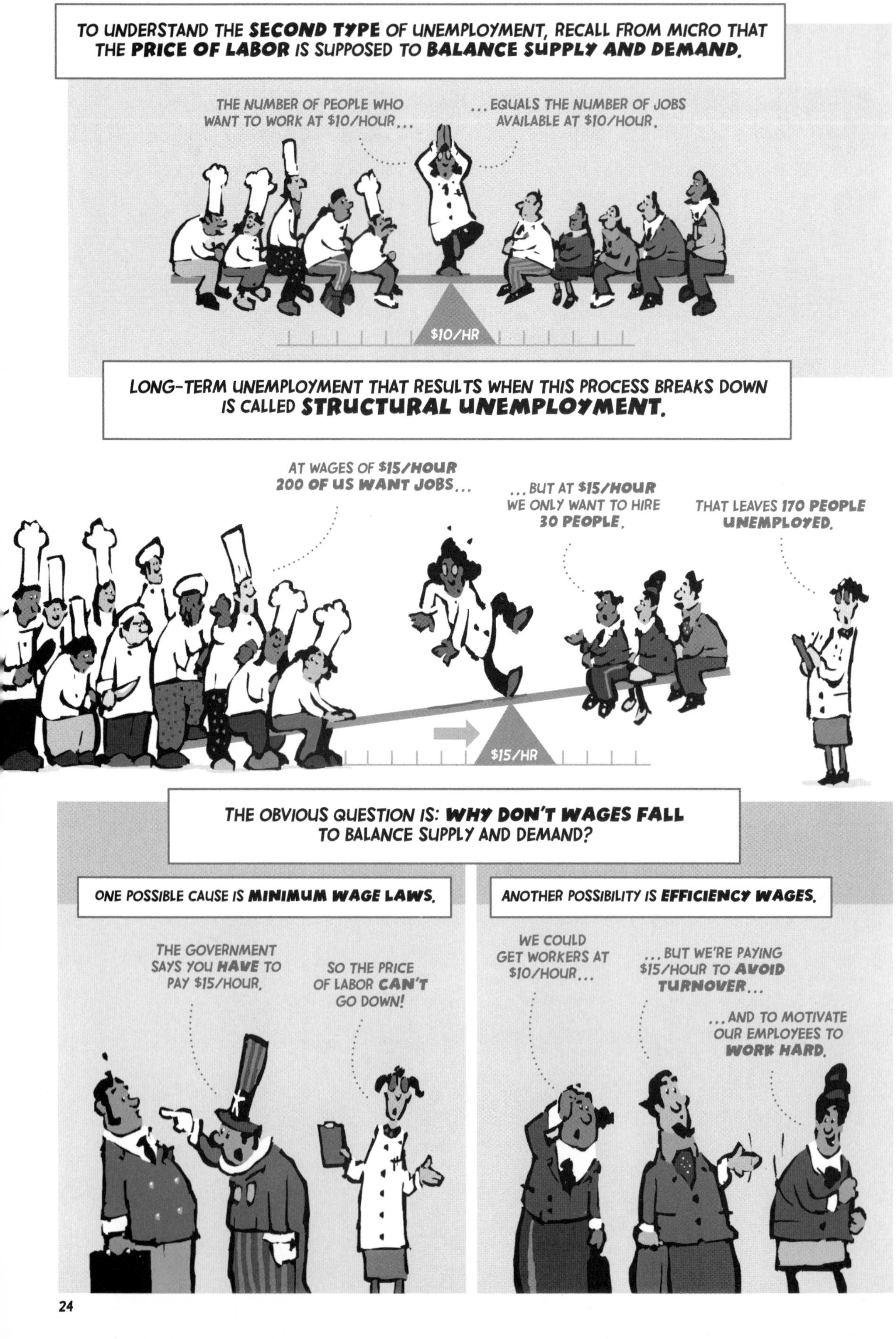
TO UNDERSTAND THE SECOND TYPE OF UNEMPLOYMENT, RECALL FROM MICRO THAT THE PRICE OF LABOR IS SUPPOSED TO BALANCE SUPPLY AND DEMAND.
THE NUMBER OF PEOPLE WHO WANT TO WORK AT $10/HOUR...
...EQUALS THE NUMBER OF JOBS AVAILABLE AT $10/HOUR.
$10/HR
LONG-TERM UNEMPLOYMENT THAT RESULTS WHEN THIS PROCESS BREAKS DOWN IS CALLED STRUCTURAL UNEMPLOYMENT.
AT WAGES OF $15/HOUR 200 OF US WANT JOBS...
...BUT AT $15/HOUR WE ONLY WANT TO HIRE 30 PEOPLE.
THAT LEAVES 170 PEOPLE UNEMPLOYED.
$15/HR
THE OBVIOUS QUESTION IS: WHY DON'T WAGES FALL TO BALANCE SUPPLY AND DEMAND?
ONE POSSIBLE CAUSE IS MINIMUM WAGE LAWS.
THE GOVERNMENT SAYS YOU HAVE TO PAY $15/HOUR.
SO THE PRICE OF LABOR CAN'T GO DOWN!
ANOTHER POSSIBILITY IS EFFICIENCY WAGES.
WE COULD GET WORKERS AT $10/HOUR...
...BUT WE'RE PAYING $15/HOUR TO AVOID TURNOVER...
...AND TO MOTIVATE OUR EMPLOYEES TO WORK HARD.

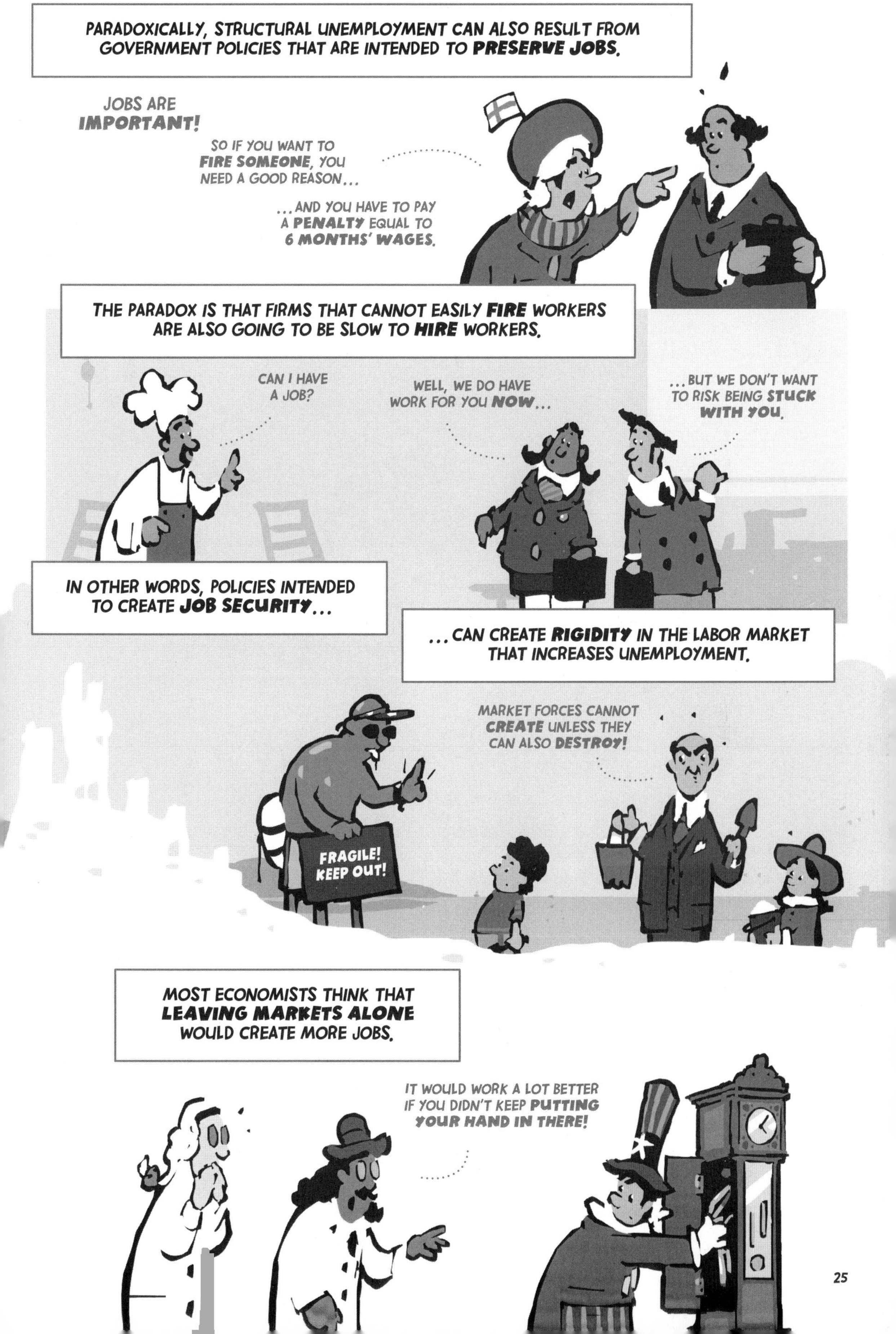
PARADOXICALLY, STRUCTURAL UNEMPLOYMENT CAN ALSO RESULT FROM GOVERNMENT POLICIES THAT ARE INTENDED TO PRESERVE JOBS.
JOBS ARE IMPORTANT!
SO IF YOU WANT TO FIRE SOMEONE, YOU NEED A GOOD REASON...
...AND YOU HAVE TO PAY A PENALTY EQUAL TO 6 MONTHS' WAGES.
THE PARADOX IS THAT FIRMS THAT CANNOT EASILY FIRE WORKERS ARE ALSO GOING TO BE SLOW TO HIRE WORKERS.
CAN I HAVE A JOB?
WELL, WE DO HAVE WORK FOR YOU NOW...
...BUT WE DON'T WANT TO RISK BEING STUCK WITH YOU.
IN OTHER WORDS, POLICIES INTENDED TO CREATE JOB SECURITY...
...CAN CREATE RIGIDITY IN THE LABOR MARKET THAT INCREASES UNEMPLOYMENT.
FRAGILE! KEEP OUT!
MARKET FORCES CANNOT CREATE UNLESS THEY CAN ALSO DESTROY!
MOST ECONOMISTS THINK THAT LEAVING MARKETS ALONE WOULD CREATE MORE JOBS.
IT WOULD WORK A LOT BETTER IF YOU DIDN'T KEEP PUTTING YOUR HAND IN THERE!

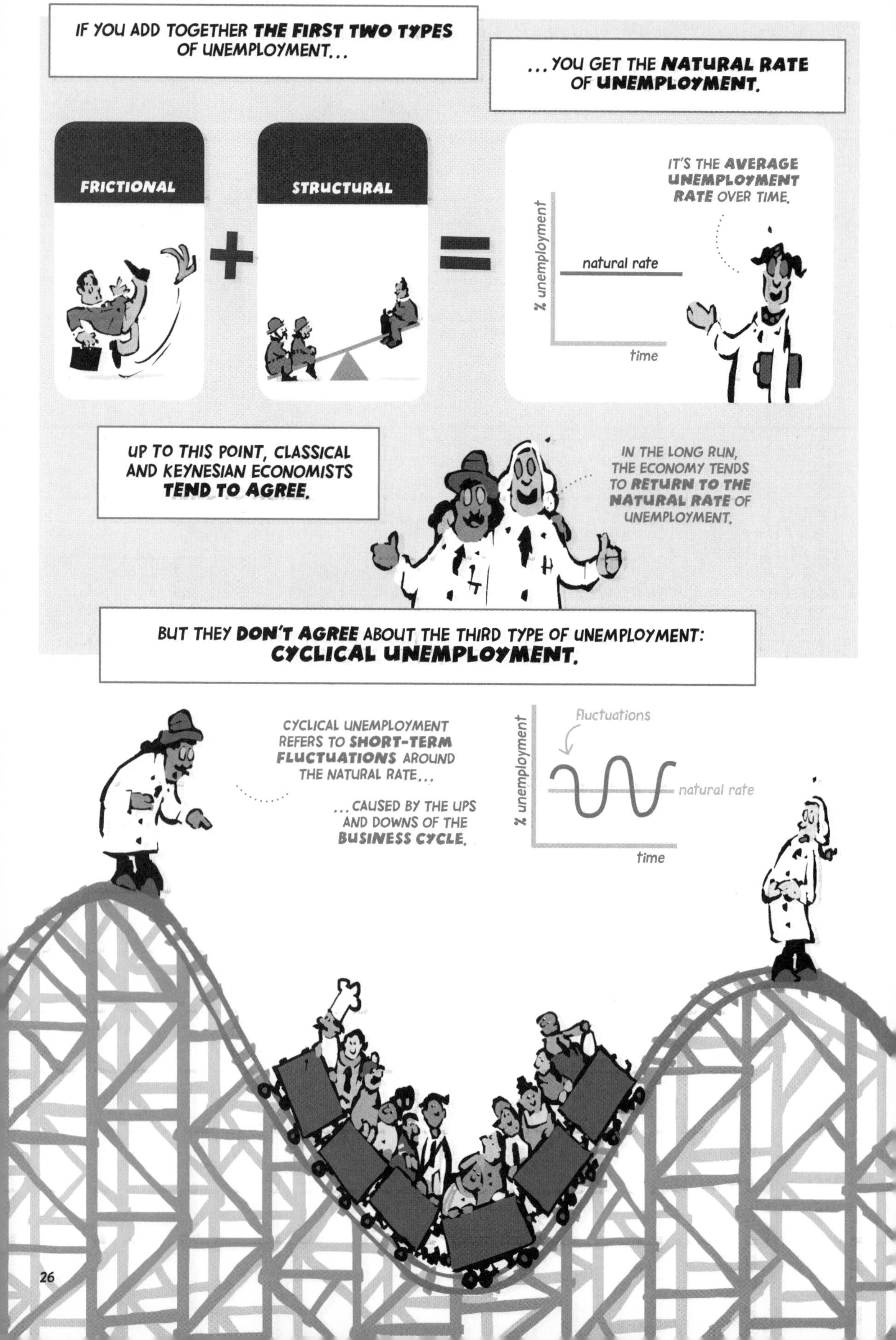
IF YOU ADD TOGETHER THE FIRST TWO TYPES OF UNEMPLOYMENT...
...YOU GET THE NATURAL RATE OF UNEMPLOYMENT.
FRICTIONAL
+
STRUCTURAL
=
% unemployment
natural rate
time
IT'S THE AVERAGE UNEMPLOYMENT RATE OVER TIME.
UP TO THIS POINT, CLASSICAL AND KEYNESIAN ECONOMISTS TEND TO AGREE.
IN THE LONG RUN, THE ECONOMY TENDS TO RETURN TO THE NATURAL RATE OF UNEMPLOYMENT.
BUT THEY DON'T AGREE ABOUT THE THIRD TYPE OF UNEMPLOYMENT: CYCLICAL UNEMPLOYMENT.
CYCLICAL UNEMPLOYMENT REFERS TO SHORT-TERM FLUCTUATIONS AROUND THE NATURAL RATE...
...CAUSED BY THE UPS AND DOWNS OF THE BUSINESS CYCLE.
Fluctuations
% unemployment
natural rate
time

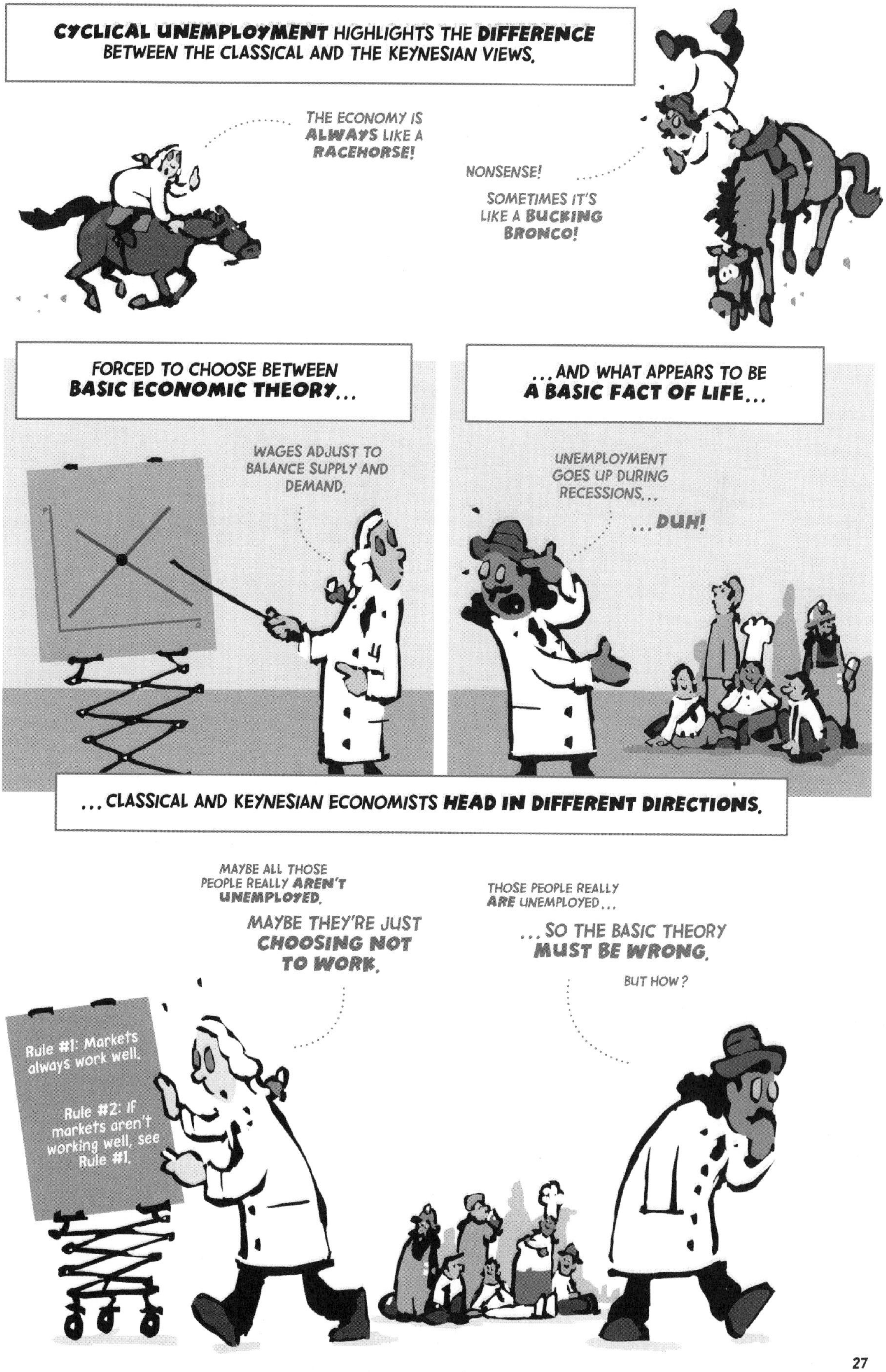
CYCLICAL UNEMPLOYMENT HIGHLIGHTS THE DIFFERENCE BETWEEN THE CLASSICAL AND THE KEYNESIAN VIEWS.
THE ECONOMY IS ALWAYS LIKE A RACEHORSE!
NONSENSE!
SOMETIMES IT'S LIKE A BUCKING BRONCO!
FORCED TO CHOOSE BETWEEN BASIC ECONOMIC THEORY...
WAGES ADJUST TO BALANCE SUPPLY AND DEMAND.
...AND WHAT APPEARS TO BE A BASIC FACT OF LIFE...
UNEMPLOYMENT GOES UP DURING RECESSIONS...
...DUH!
...CLASSICAL AND KEYNESIAN ECONOMISTS HEAD IN DIFFERENT DIRECTIONS.
MAYBE ALL THOSE PEOPLE REALLY AREN'T UNEMPLOYED.
MAYBE THEY'RE JUST CHOOSING NOT TO WORK.
Rule #1: Markets always work well.
Rule #2: IF markets aren't working well, see Rule #1.
THOSE PEOPLE REALLY ARE UNEMPLOYED...
...SO THE BASIC THEORY MUST BE WRONG.
BUT HOW?

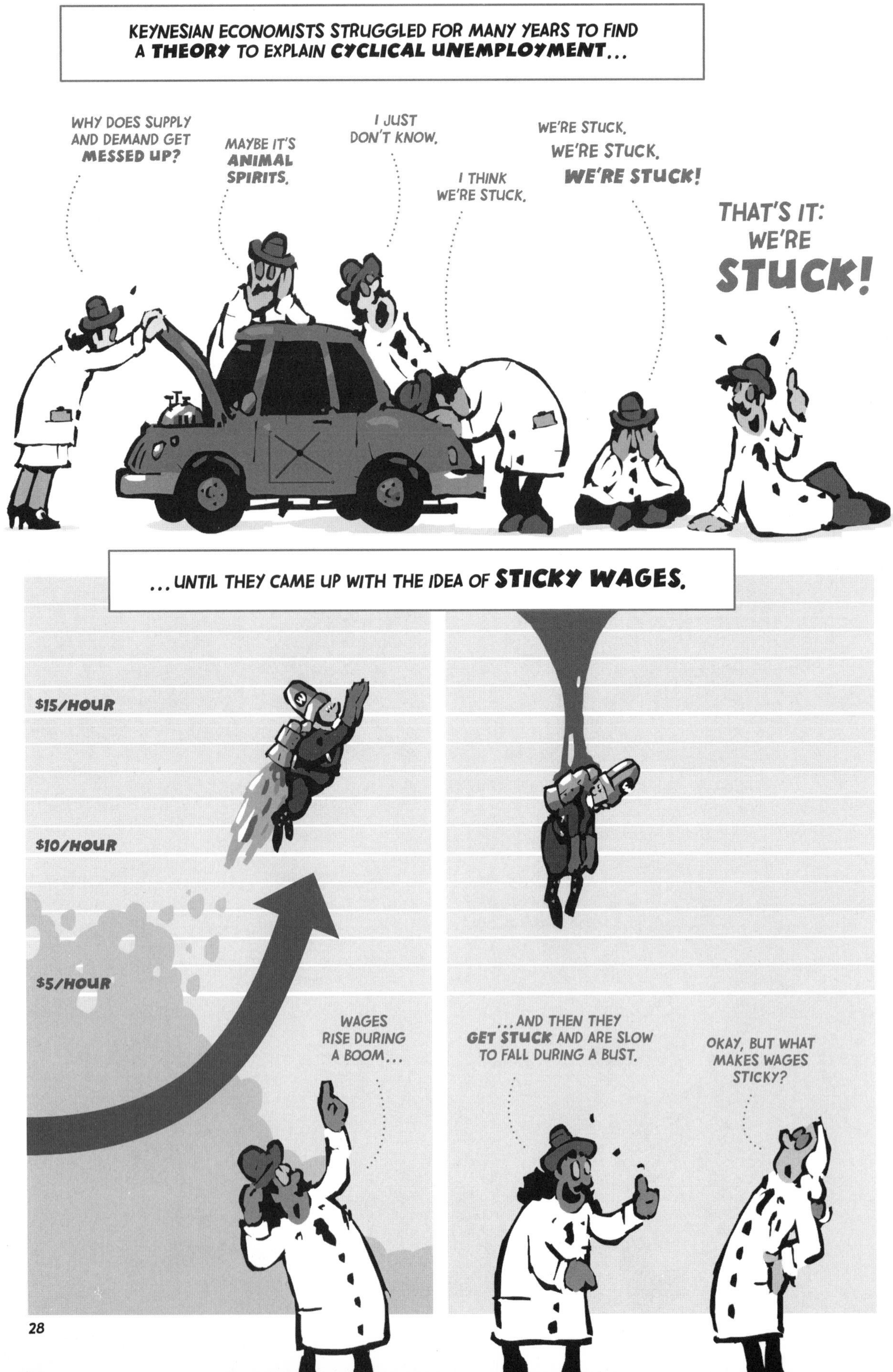
KEYNESIAN ECONOMISTS STRUGGLED FOR MANY YEARS TO FIND A **THEORY** TO EXPLAIN **CYCLICAL UNEMPLOYMENT**...
WHY DOES SUPPLY AND DEMAND GET **MESSED UP?**
MAYBE IT'S **ANIMAL SPIRITS.**
I JUST DON'T KNOW.
I THINK WE'RE STUCK.
WE'RE STUCK. WE'RE STUCK. **WE'RE STUCK!**
THAT'S IT: WE'RE **STUCK!**
...UNTIL THEY CAME UP WITH THE IDEA OF **STICKY WAGES.**
$15/HOUR
$10/HOUR
$5/HOUR
WAGES RISE DURING A BOOM...
...AND THEN THEY **GET STUCK** AND ARE SLOW TO FALL DURING A BUST.
OKAY, BUT WHAT MAKES WAGES STICKY?

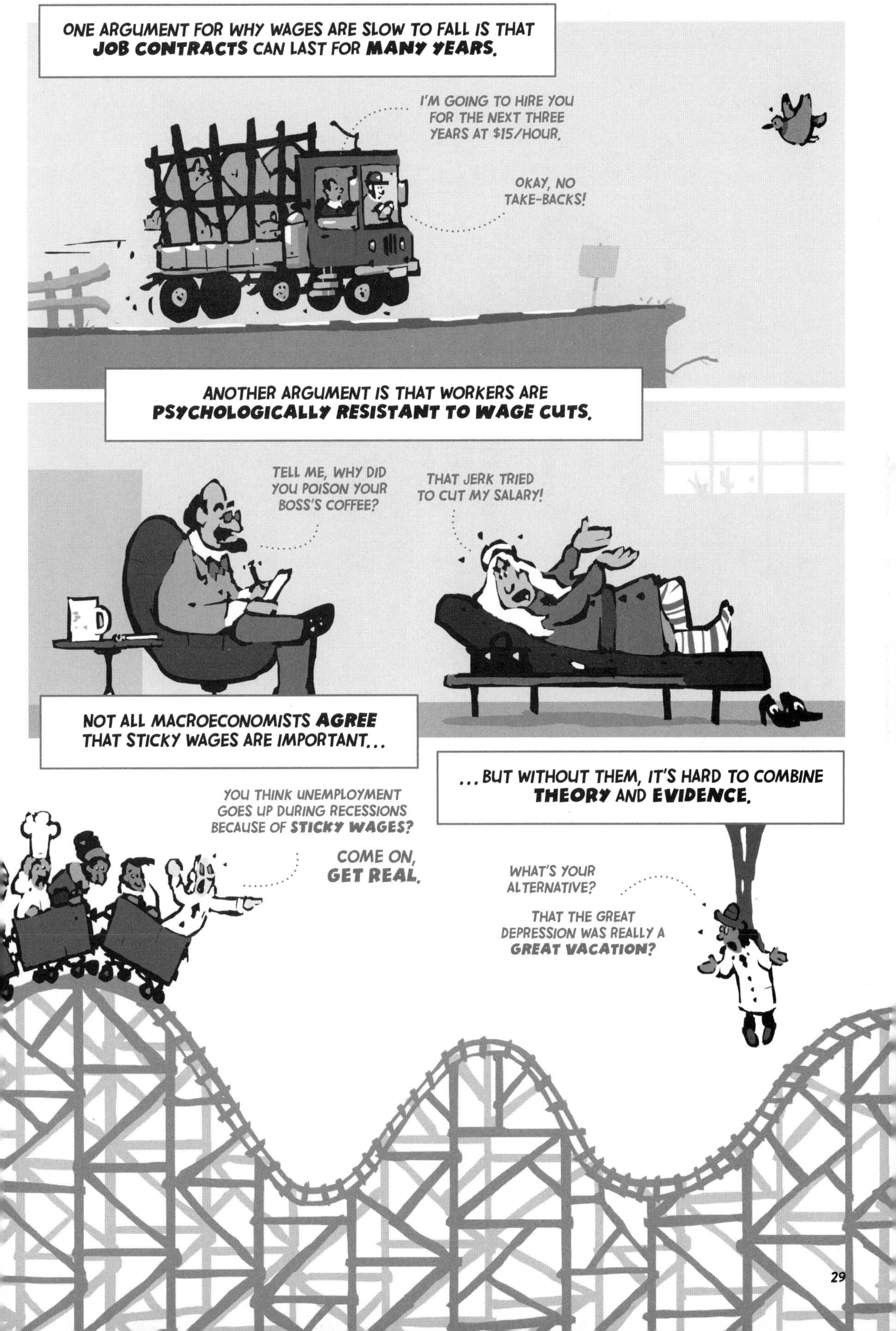
ONE ARGUMENT FOR WHY WAGES ARE SLOW TO FALL IS THAT JOB CONTRACTS CAN LAST FOR MANY YEARS.
I'M GOING TO HIRE YOU FOR THE NEXT THREE YEARS AT $15/HOUR.
OKAY, NO TAKE-BACKS!
ANOTHER ARGUMENT IS THAT WORKERS ARE PSYCHOLOGICALLY RESISTANT TO WAGE CUTS.
TELL ME, WHY DID YOU POISON YOUR BOSS'S COFFEE?
THAT JERK TRIED TO CUT MY SALARY!
NOT ALL MACROECONOMISTS AGREE THAT STICKY WAGES ARE IMPORTANT...
...BUT WITHOUT THEM, IT'S HARD TO COMBINE THEORY AND EVIDENCE.
YOU THINK UNEMPLOYMENT GOES UP DURING RECESSIONS BECAUSE OF STICKY WAGES?
COME ON, GET REAL.
WHAT'S YOUR ALTERNATIVE?
THAT THE GREAT DEPRESSION WAS REALLY A GREAT VACATION?

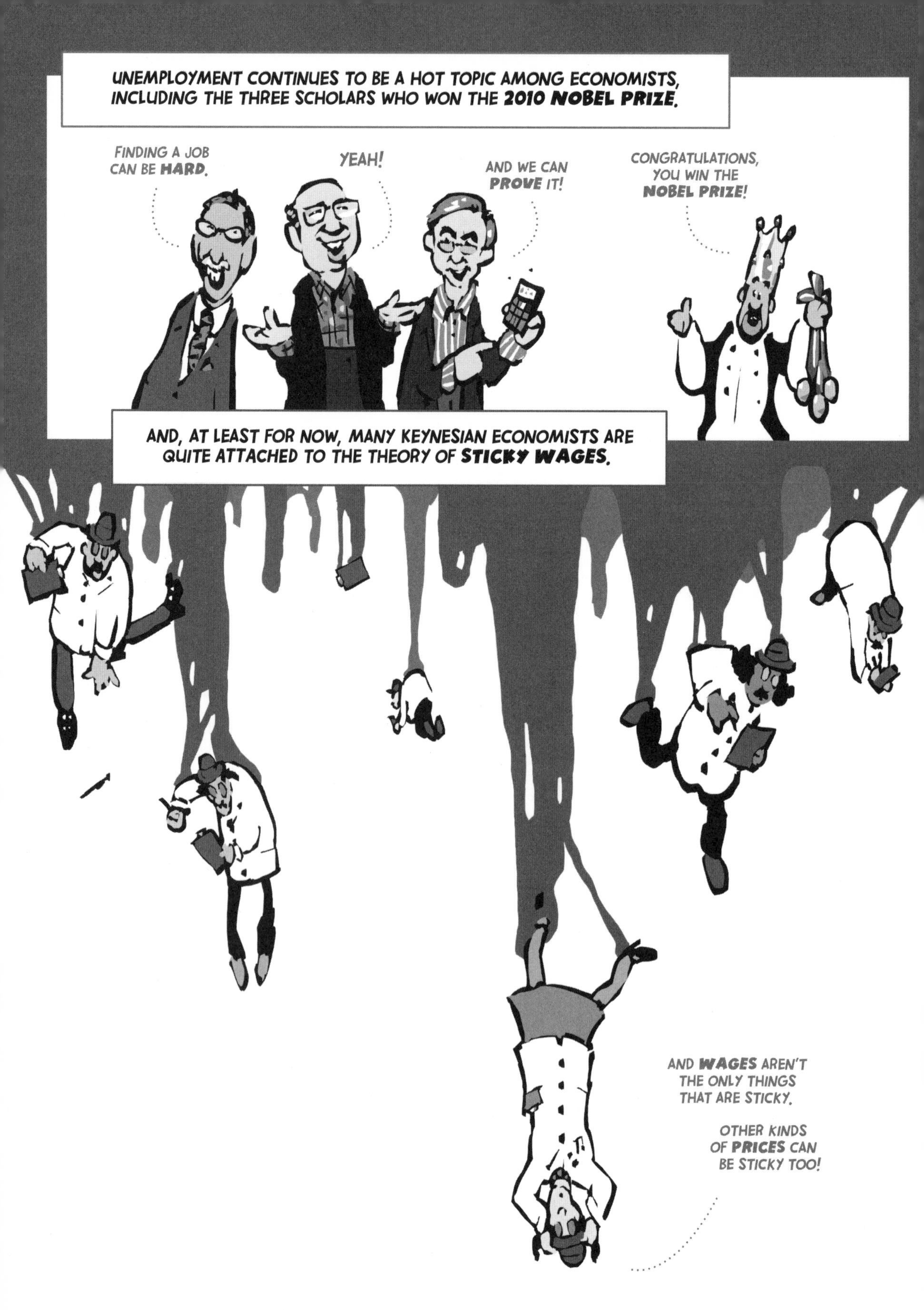

UNEMPLOYMENT CONTINUES TO BE A HOT TOPIC AMONG ECONOMISTS, INCLUDING THE THREE SCHOLARS WHO WON THE 2010 NOBEL PRIZE.
FINDING A JOB CAN BE HARD.
YEAH!
AND WE CAN PROVE IT!
CONGRATULATIONS, YOU WIN THE NOBEL PRIZE!
AND, AT LEAST FOR NOW, MANY KEYNESIAN ECONOMISTS ARE QUITE ATTACHED TO THE THEORY OF STICKY WAGES.
AND WAGES AREN'T THE ONLY THINGS THAT ARE STICKY.
OTHER KINDS OF PRICES CAN BE STICKY TOO!

CHAPTER 3
MONEY

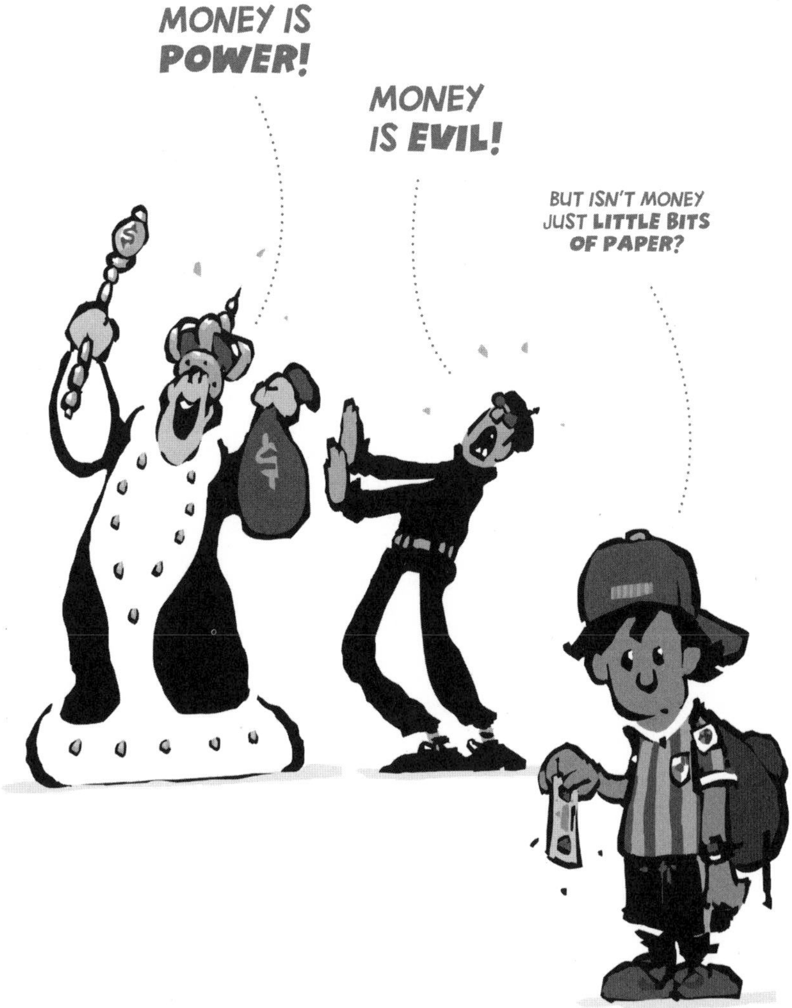
MONEY IS POWER!
MONEY IS EVIL!
BUT ISN'T MONEY JUST LITTLE BITS OF PAPER?

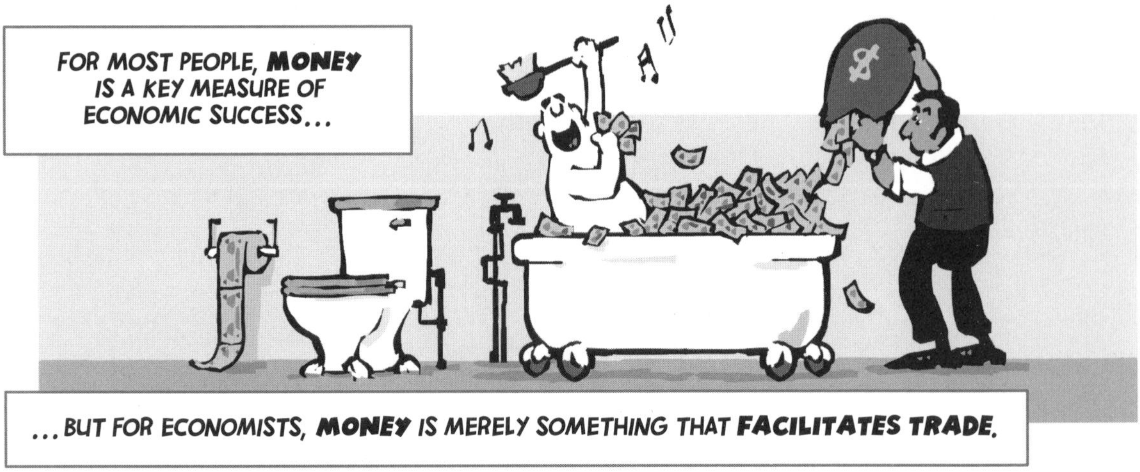
FOR MOST PEOPLE, MONEY IS A KEY MEASURE OF ECONOMIC SUCCESS...
...BUT FOR ECONOMISTS, MONEY IS MERELY SOMETHING THAT FACILITATES TRADE.

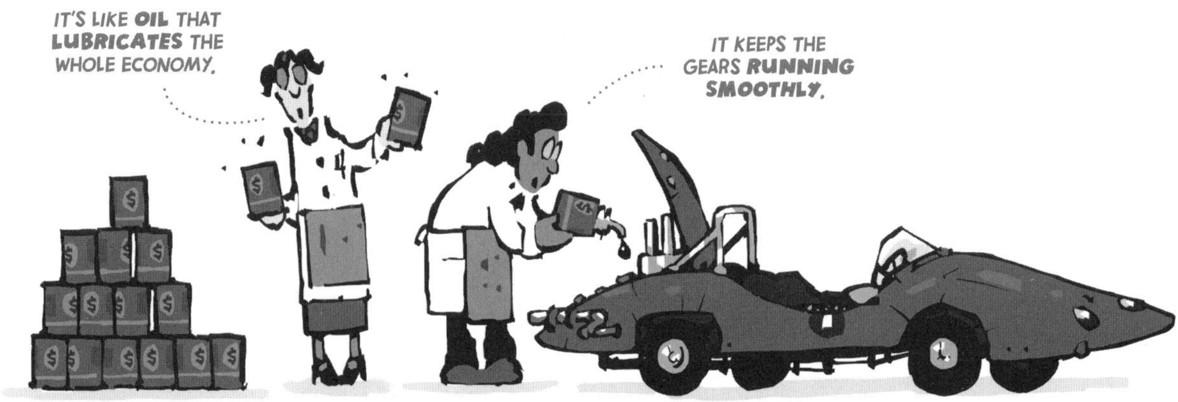
IT'S LIKE OIL THAT LUBRICATES THE WHOLE ECONOMY.
IT KEEPS THE GEARS RUNNING SMOOTHLY.

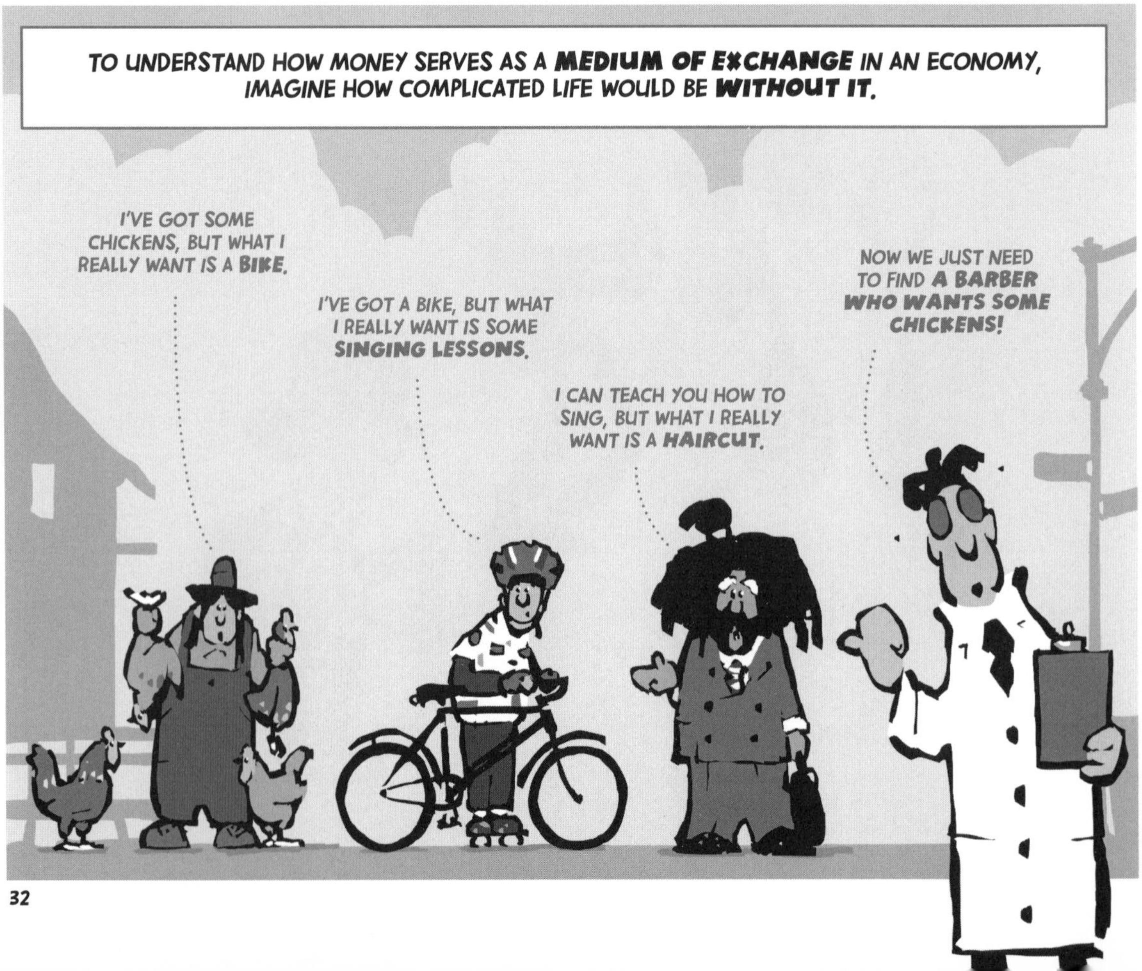
TO UNDERSTAND HOW MONEY SERVES AS A MEDIUM OF EXCHANGE IN AN ECONOMY, IMAGINE HOW COMPLICATED LIFE WOULD BE WITHOUT IT.
I'VE GOT SOME CHICKENS, BUT WHAT I REALLY WANT IS A BIKE.
I'VE GOT A BIKE, BUT WHAT I REALLY WANT IS SOME SINGING LESSONS.
I CAN TEACH YOU HOW TO SING, BUT WHAT I REALLY WANT IS A HAIRCUT.
NOW WE JUST NEED TO FIND A BARBER WHO WANTS SOME CHICKENS!

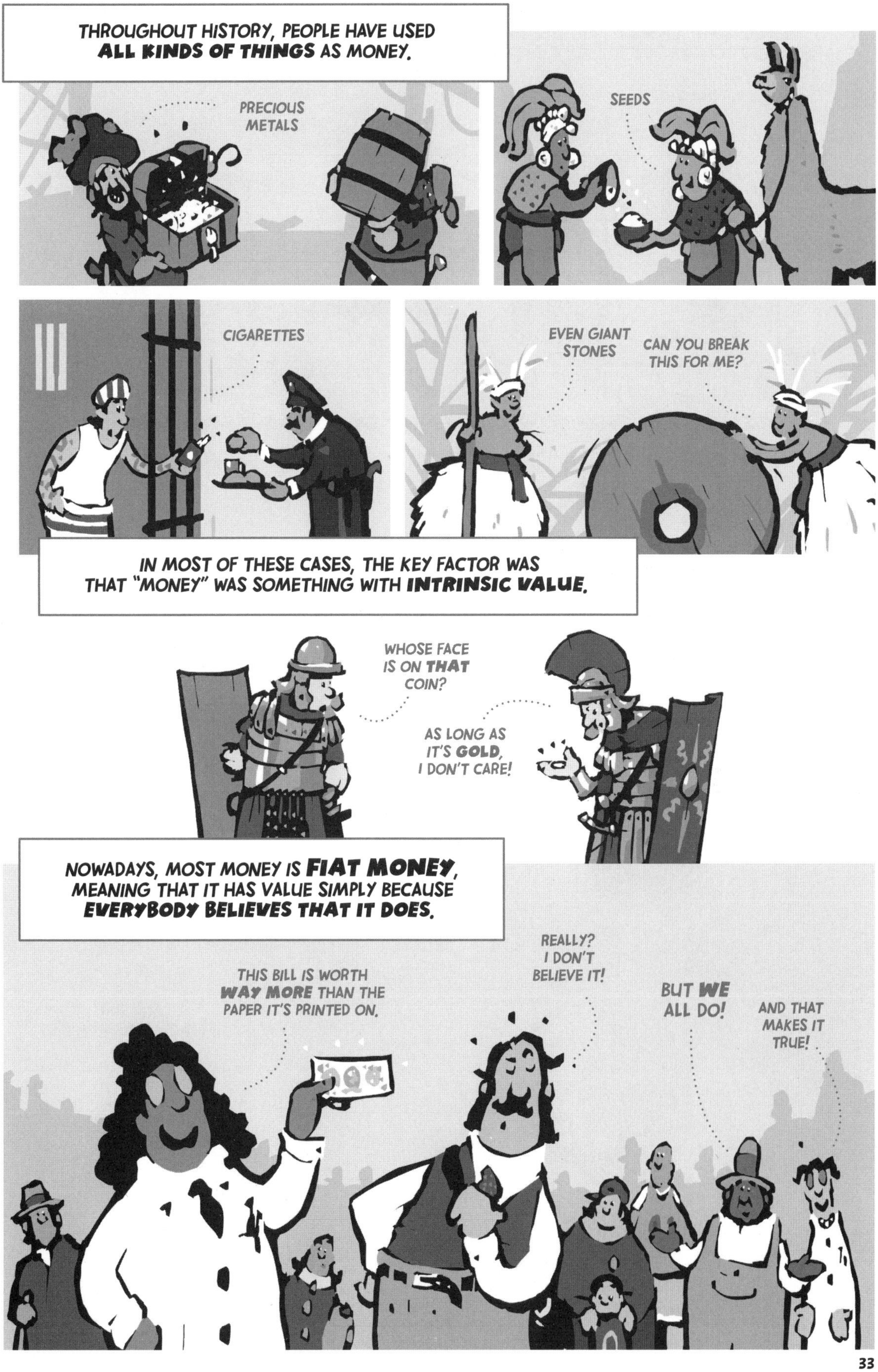
THROUGHOUT HISTORY, PEOPLE HAVE USED **ALL KINDS OF THINGS** AS MONEY.
PRECIOUS METALS
SEEDS
CIGARETTES
EVEN GIANT STONES
CAN YOU BREAK THIS FOR ME?
IN MOST OF THESE CASES, THE KEY FACTOR WAS THAT "MONEY" WAS SOMETHING WITH **INTRINSIC VALUE.**
WHOSE FACE IS ON **THAT** COIN?
AS LONG AS IT'S **GOLD**, I DON'T CARE!
NOWADAYS, MOST MONEY IS **FIAT MONEY**, MEANING THAT IT HAS VALUE SIMPLY BECAUSE **EVERYBODY BELIEVES THAT IT DOES.**
THIS BILL IS WORTH **WAY MORE** THAN THE PAPER IT'S PRINTED ON.
REALLY? I DON'T BELIEVE IT!
BUT **WE** ALL DO!
AND THAT MAKES IT TRUE!

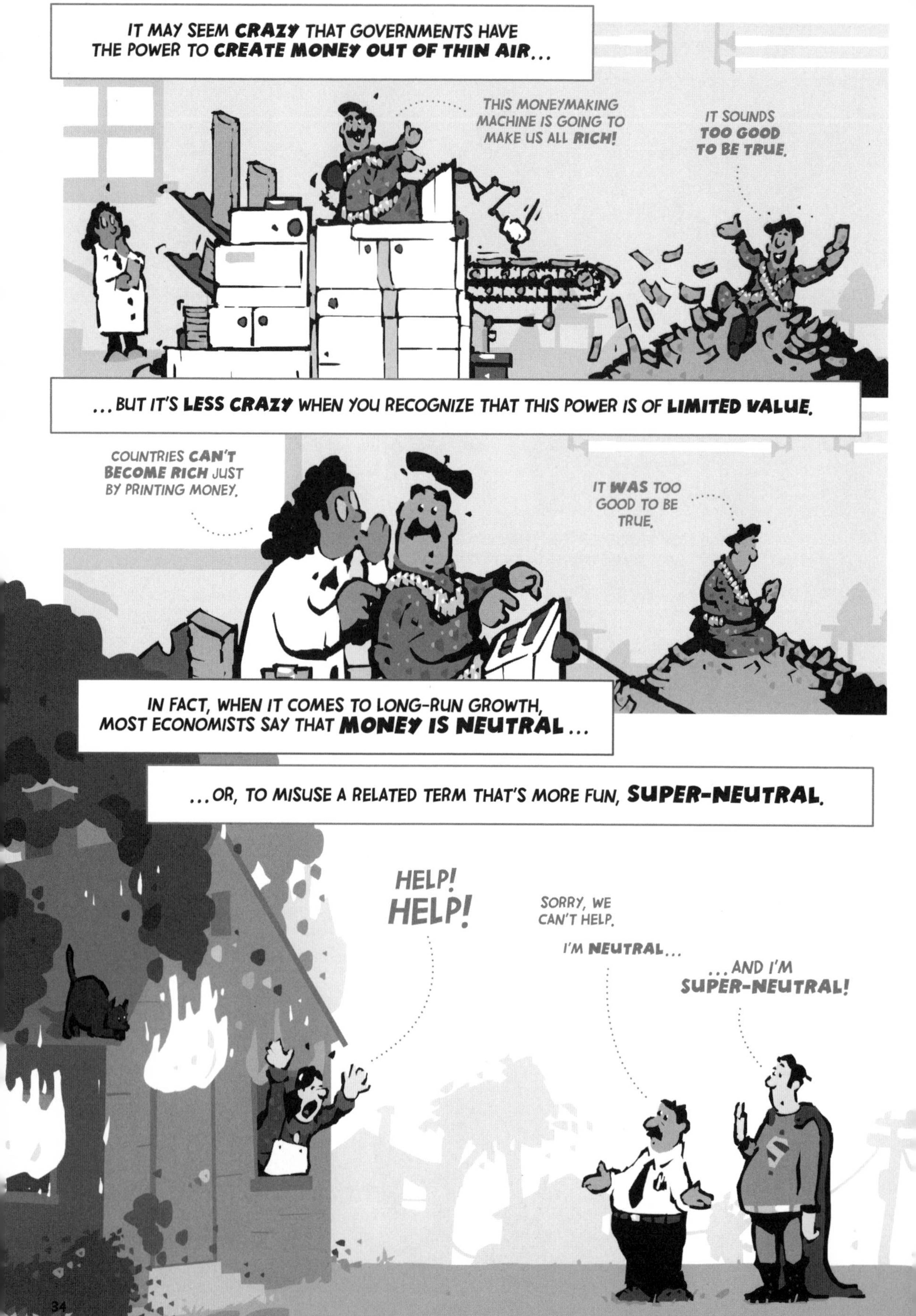

IT MAY SEEM CRAZY THAT GOVERNMENTS HAVE THE POWER TO CREATE MONEY OUT OF THIN AIR...
THIS MONEYMAKING MACHINE IS GOING TO MAKE US ALL RICH!
IT SOUNDS TOO GOOD TO BE TRUE.
...BUT IT'S LESS CRAZY WHEN YOU RECOGNIZE THAT THIS POWER IS OF LIMITED VALUE.
COUNTRIES CAN'T BECOME RICH JUST BY PRINTING MONEY.
IT WAS TOO GOOD TO BE TRUE.
IN FACT, WHEN IT COMES TO LONG-RUN GROWTH, MOST ECONOMISTS SAY THAT MONEY IS NEUTRAL...
...OR, TO MISUSE A RELATED TERM THAT'S MORE FUN, SUPER-NEUTRAL.
HELP! HELP!
SORRY, WE CAN'T HELP.
I'M NEUTRAL...
...AND I'M SUPER-NEUTRAL!

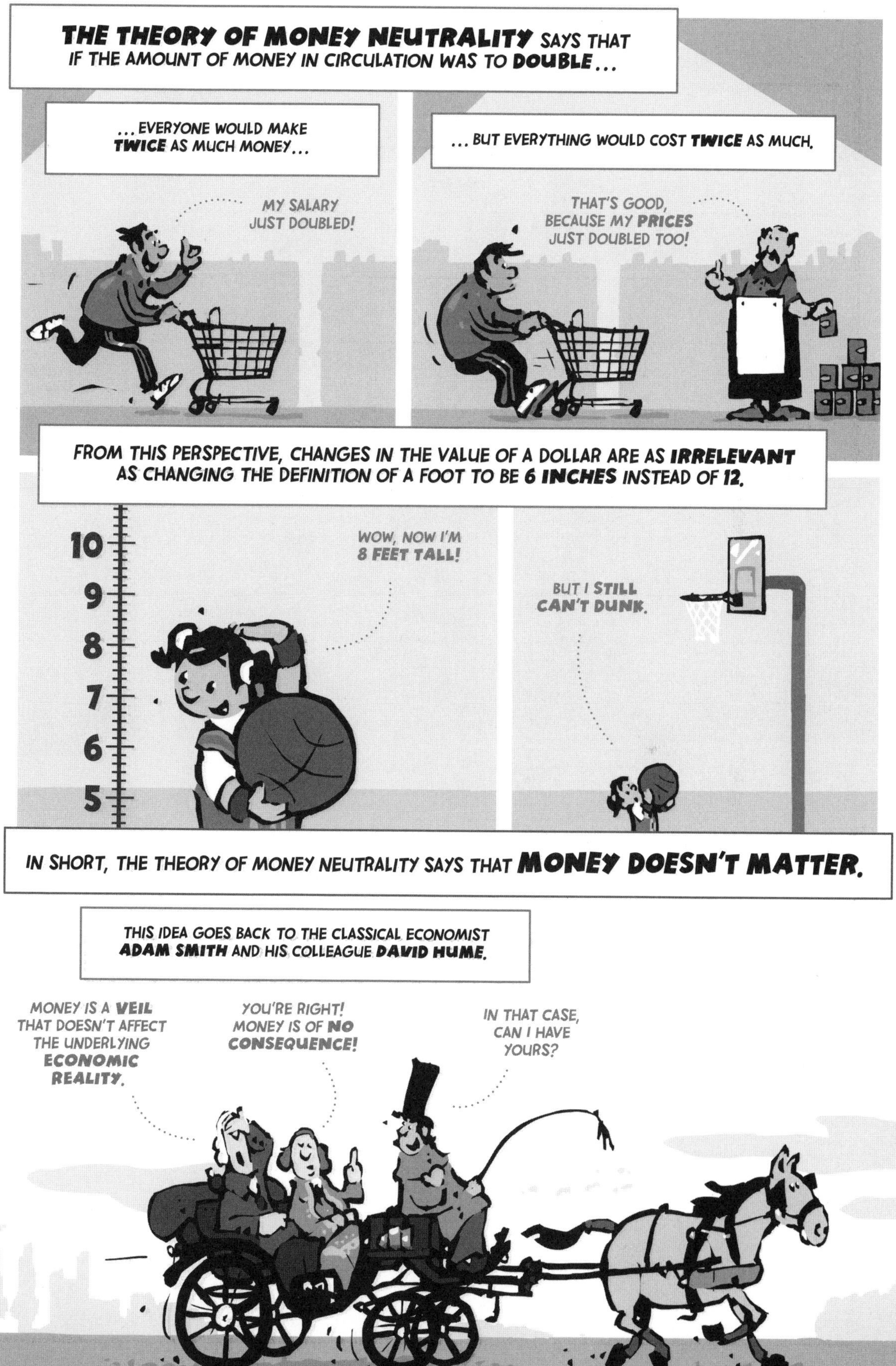
THE THEORY OF MONEY NEUTRALITY SAYS THAT IF THE AMOUNT OF MONEY IN CIRCULATION WAS TO DOUBLE...
...EVERYONE WOULD MAKE TWICE AS MUCH MONEY...
MY SALARY JUST DOUBLED!
...BUT EVERYTHING WOULD COST TWICE AS MUCH.
THAT'S GOOD, BECAUSE MY PRICES JUST DOUBLED TOO!
FROM THIS PERSPECTIVE, CHANGES IN THE VALUE OF A DOLLAR ARE AS IRRELEVANT AS CHANGING THE DEFINITION OF A FOOT TO BE 6 INCHES INSTEAD OF 12.
10
9
8
7
6
5
WOW, NOW I'M 8 FEET TALL!
BUT I STILL CAN'T DUNK.
IN SHORT, THE THEORY OF MONEY NEUTRALITY SAYS THAT MONEY DOESN'T MATTER.
THIS IDEA GOES BACK TO THE CLASSICAL ECONOMIST ADAM SMITH AND HIS COLLEAGUE DAVID HUME.
MONEY IS A VEIL THAT DOESN'T AFFECT THE UNDERLYING ECONOMIC REALITY.
YOU'RE RIGHT! MONEY IS OF NO CONSEQUENCE!
IN THAT CASE, CAN I HAVE YOURS?

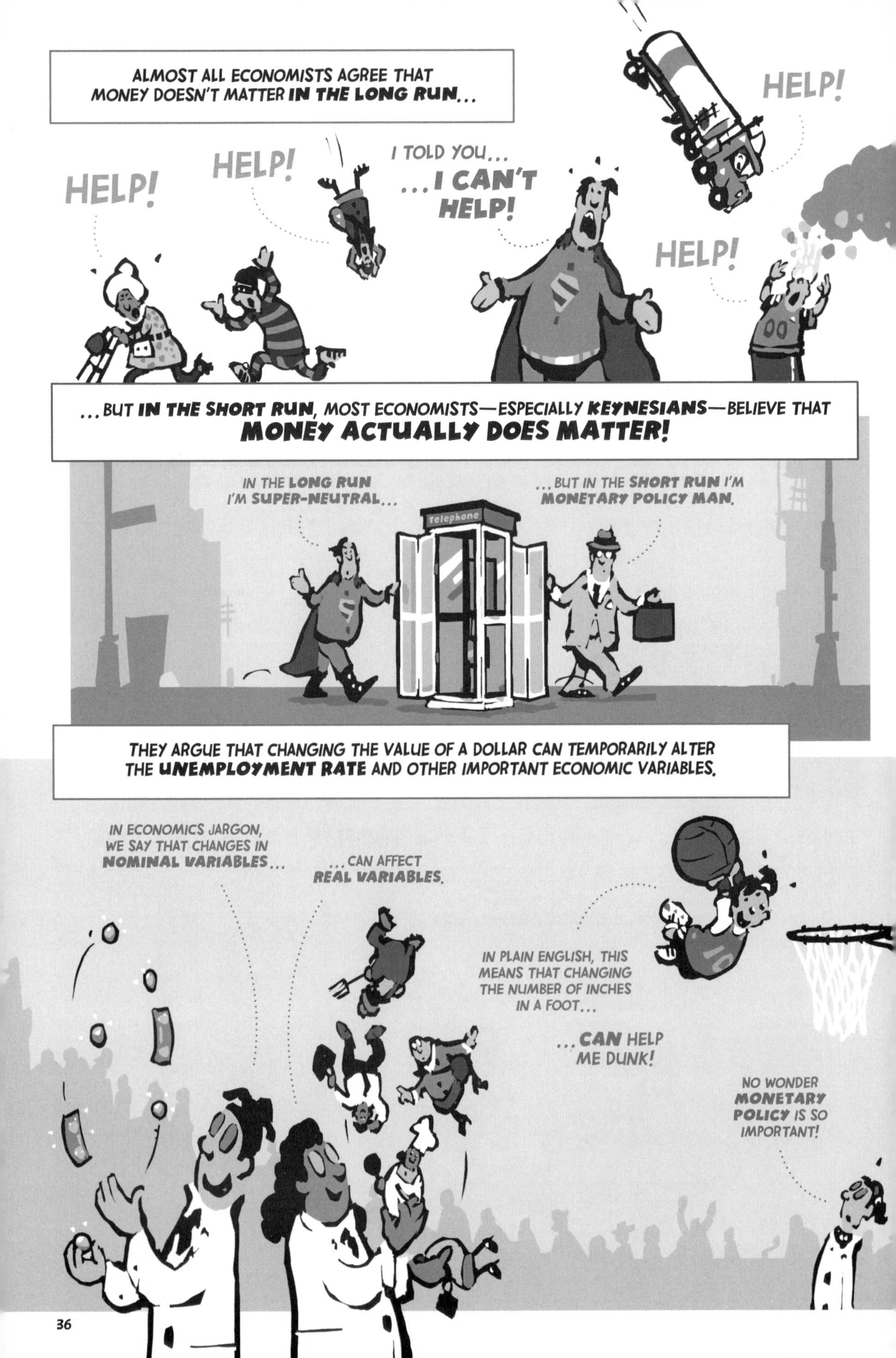
ALMOST ALL ECONOMISTS AGREE THAT MONEY DOESN'T MATTER **IN THE LONG RUN**...
HELP!
HELP!
I TOLD YOU...
...I CAN'T HELP!
HELP!
HELP!
...BUT **IN THE SHORT RUN**, MOST ECONOMISTS—ESPECIALLY **KEYNESIANS**—BELIEVE THAT
MONEY ACTUALLY DOES MATTER!
IN THE **LONG RUN** I'M **SUPER-NEUTRAL**...
Telephone
...BUT IN THE **SHORT RUN** I'M **MONETARY POLICY MAN**.
THEY ARGUE THAT CHANGING THE VALUE OF A DOLLAR CAN TEMPORARILY ALTER THE **UNEMPLOYMENT RATE** AND OTHER IMPORTANT ECONOMIC VARIABLES.
IN ECONOMICS JARGON, WE SAY THAT CHANGES IN **NOMINAL VARIABLES**...
...CAN AFFECT **REAL VARIABLES**.
IN PLAIN ENGLISH, THIS MEANS THAT CHANGING THE NUMBER OF INCHES IN A FOOT...
...**CAN** HELP ME DUNK!
NO WONDER **MONETARY POLICY** IS SO IMPORTANT!

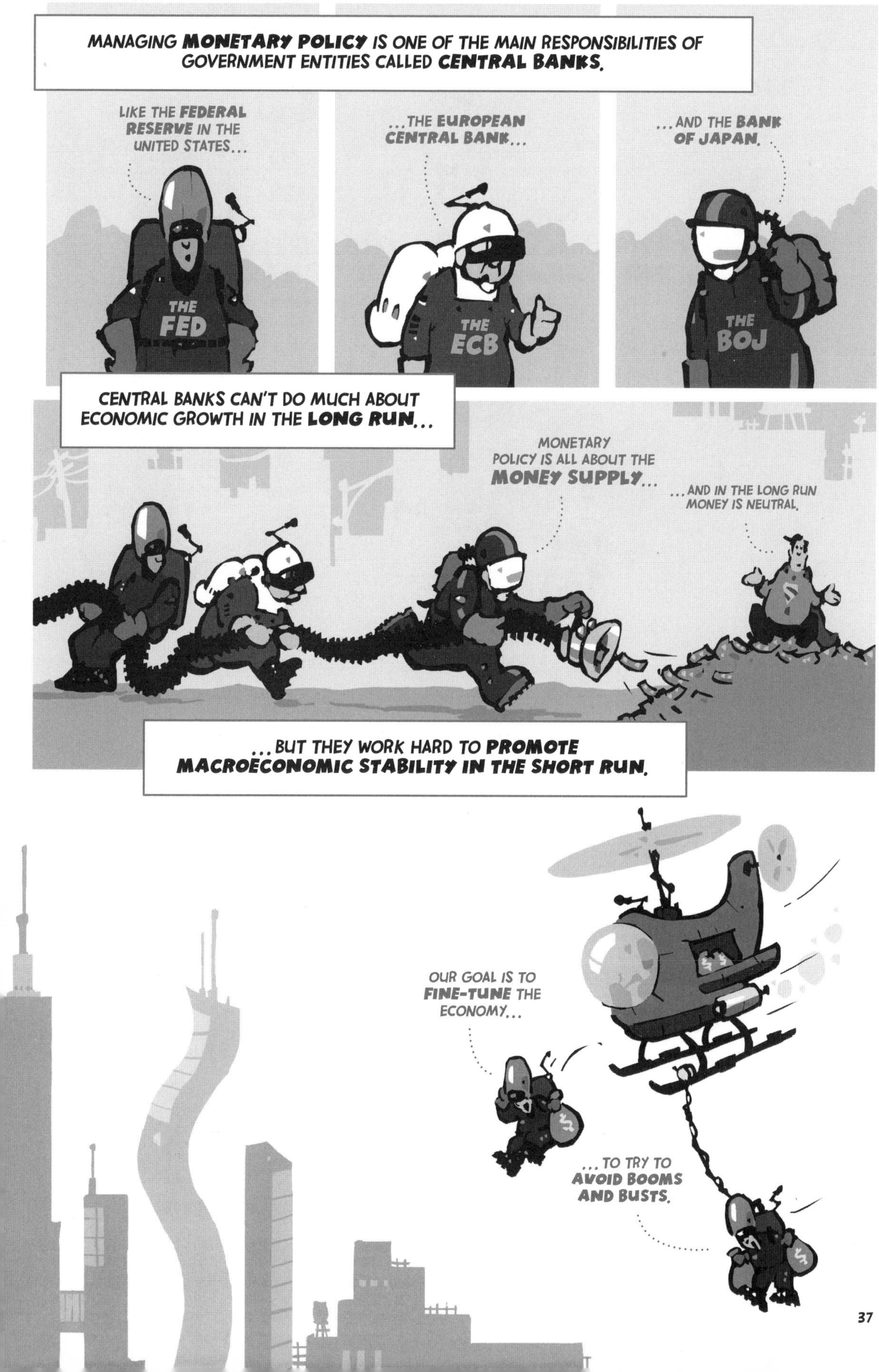

MANAGING **MONETARY POLICY** IS ONE OF THE MAIN RESPONSIBILITIES OF GOVERNMENT ENTITIES CALLED **CENTRAL BANKS**.
LIKE THE **FEDERAL RESERVE** IN THE UNITED STATES...
THE FED
...THE **EUROPEAN CENTRAL BANK**...
THE ECB
...AND THE **BANK OF JAPAN**.
THE BOJ
CENTRAL BANKS CAN'T DO MUCH ABOUT ECONOMIC GROWTH IN THE **LONG RUN**...
MONETARY POLICY IS ALL ABOUT THE **MONEY SUPPLY**...
...AND IN THE LONG RUN MONEY IS NEUTRAL.
...BUT THEY WORK HARD TO **PROMOTE MACROECONOMIC STABILITY IN THE SHORT RUN**.
OUR GOAL IS TO **FINE-TUNE** THE ECONOMY...
...TO TRY TO **AVOID BOOMS AND BUSTS**.

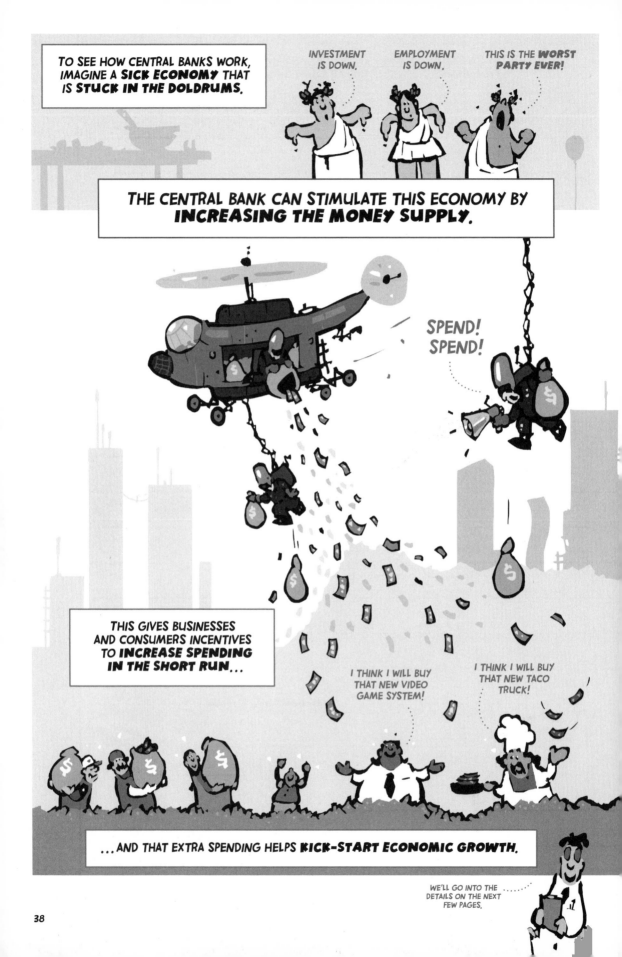

TO SEE HOW CENTRAL BANKS WORK, IMAGINE A **SICK ECONOMY** THAT IS **STUCK IN THE DOLDRUMS.**

INVESTMENT IS DOWN.

EMPLOYMENT IS DOWN.

THIS IS THE **WORST PARTY EVER!**

THE CENTRAL BANK CAN STIMULATE THIS ECONOMY BY **INCREASING THE MONEY SUPPLY.**

SPEND! SPEND!

THIS GIVES BUSINESSES AND CONSUMERS INCENTIVES TO **INCREASE SPENDING IN THE SHORT RUN...**

I THINK I WILL BUY THAT NEW VIDEO GAME SYSTEM!

I THINK I WILL BUY THAT NEW TACO TRUCK!

...AND THAT EXTRA SPENDING HELPS **KICK-START ECONOMIC GROWTH.**

WE'LL GO INTO THE DETAILS ON THE NEXT FEW PAGES.

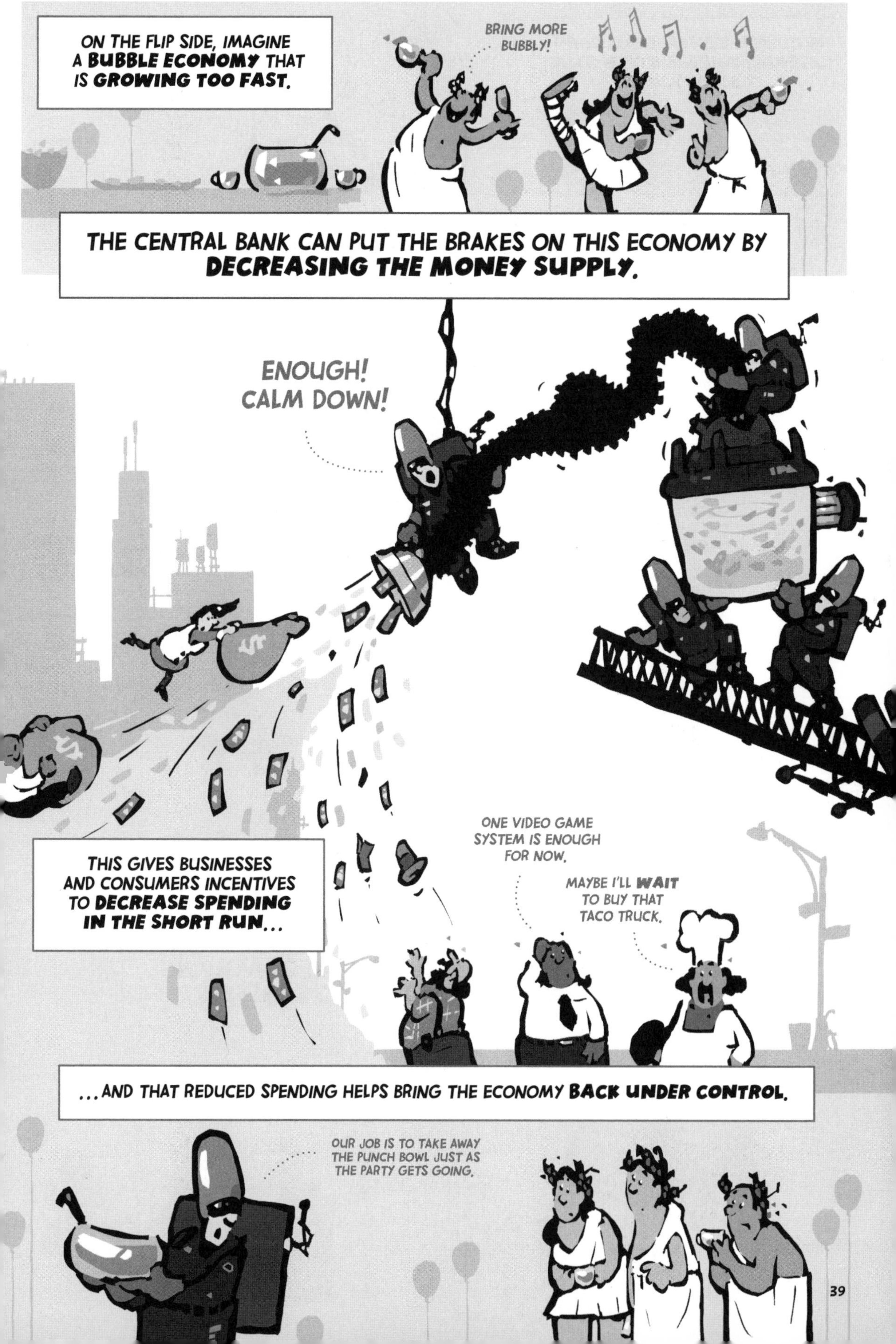

ON THE FLIP SIDE, IMAGINE A **BUBBLE ECONOMY** THAT IS **GROWING TOO FAST.**
BRING MORE BUBBLY!
THE CENTRAL BANK CAN PUT THE BRAKES ON THIS ECONOMY BY **DECREASING THE MONEY SUPPLY.**
ENOUGH! CALM DOWN!
THIS GIVES BUSINESSES AND CONSUMERS INCENTIVES TO **DECREASE SPENDING IN THE SHORT RUN...**
ONE VIDEO GAME SYSTEM IS ENOUGH FOR NOW.
MAYBE I'LL **WAIT** TO BUY THAT TACO TRUCK.
...AND THAT REDUCED SPENDING HELPS BRING THE ECONOMY **BACK UNDER CONTROL.**
OUR JOB IS TO TAKE AWAY THE PUNCH BOWL JUST AS THE PARTY GETS GOING.

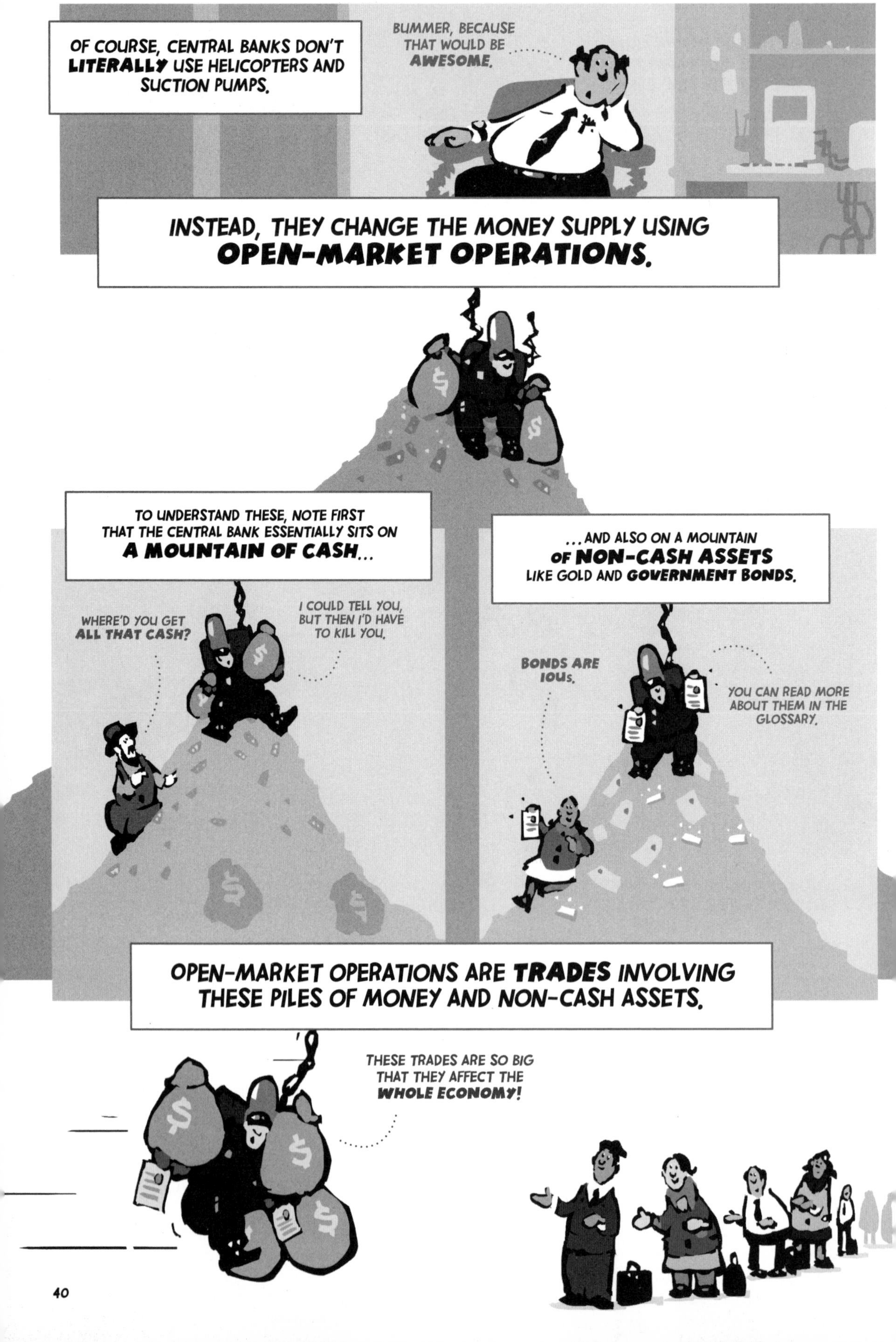

OF COURSE, CENTRAL BANKS DON'T LITERALLY USE HELICOPTERS AND SUCTION PUMPS.
BUMMER, BECAUSE THAT WOULD BE AWESOME.
INSTEAD, THEY CHANGE THE MONEY SUPPLY USING OPEN-MARKET OPERATIONS.
TO UNDERSTAND THESE, NOTE FIRST THAT THE CENTRAL BANK ESSENTIALLY SITS ON A MOUNTAIN OF CASH...
WHERE'D YOU GET ALL THAT CASH?
I COULD TELL YOU, BUT THEN I'D HAVE TO KILL YOU.
...AND ALSO ON A MOUNTAIN OF NON-CASH ASSETS LIKE GOLD AND GOVERNMENT BONDS.
BONDS ARE IOUs.
YOU CAN READ MORE ABOUT THEM IN THE GLOSSARY.
OPEN-MARKET OPERATIONS ARE TRADES INVOLVING THESE PILES OF MONEY AND NON-CASH ASSETS.
THESE TRADES ARE SO BIG THAT THEY AFFECT THE WHOLE ECONOMY!

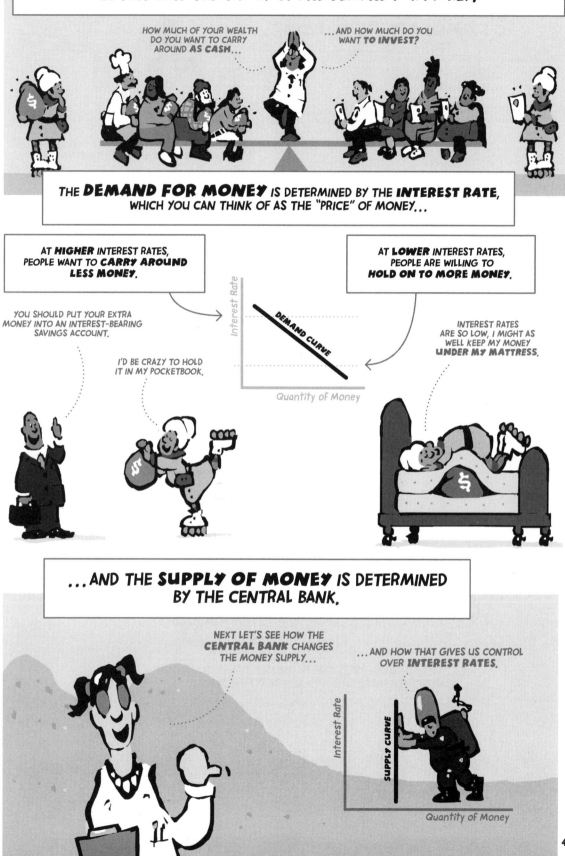

OPEN-MARKET OPERATIONS WORK BECAUSE OF **SUPPLY AND DEMAND**, IN THIS CASE THE SUPPLY OF AND DEMAND FOR MONEY.

HOW MUCH OF YOUR WEALTH DO YOU WANT TO CARRY AROUND **AS CASH**...

...AND HOW MUCH DO YOU WANT **TO INVEST?**

THE **DEMAND FOR MONEY** IS DETERMINED BY THE **INTEREST RATE**, WHICH YOU CAN THINK OF AS THE "PRICE" OF MONEY...

AT **HIGHER** INTEREST RATES, PEOPLE WANT TO **CARRY AROUND LESS MONEY**.

AT **LOWER** INTEREST RATES, PEOPLE ARE WILLING TO **HOLD ON TO MORE MONEY**.

YOU SHOULD PUT YOUR EXTRA MONEY INTO AN INTEREST-BEARING SAVINGS ACCOUNT.

INTEREST RATES ARE SO LOW, I MIGHT AS WELL KEEP MY MONEY **UNDER MY MATTRESS**.

I'D BE CRAZY TO HOLD IT IN MY POCKETBOOK.

Interest Rate

DEMAND CURVE

Quantity of Money

...AND THE **SUPPLY OF MONEY** IS DETERMINED BY THE CENTRAL BANK.

NEXT LET'S SEE HOW THE **CENTRAL BANK** CHANGES THE MONEY SUPPLY...

...AND HOW THAT GIVES US CONTROL OVER **INTEREST RATES**.

Interest Rate

SUPPLY CURVE

Quantity of Money

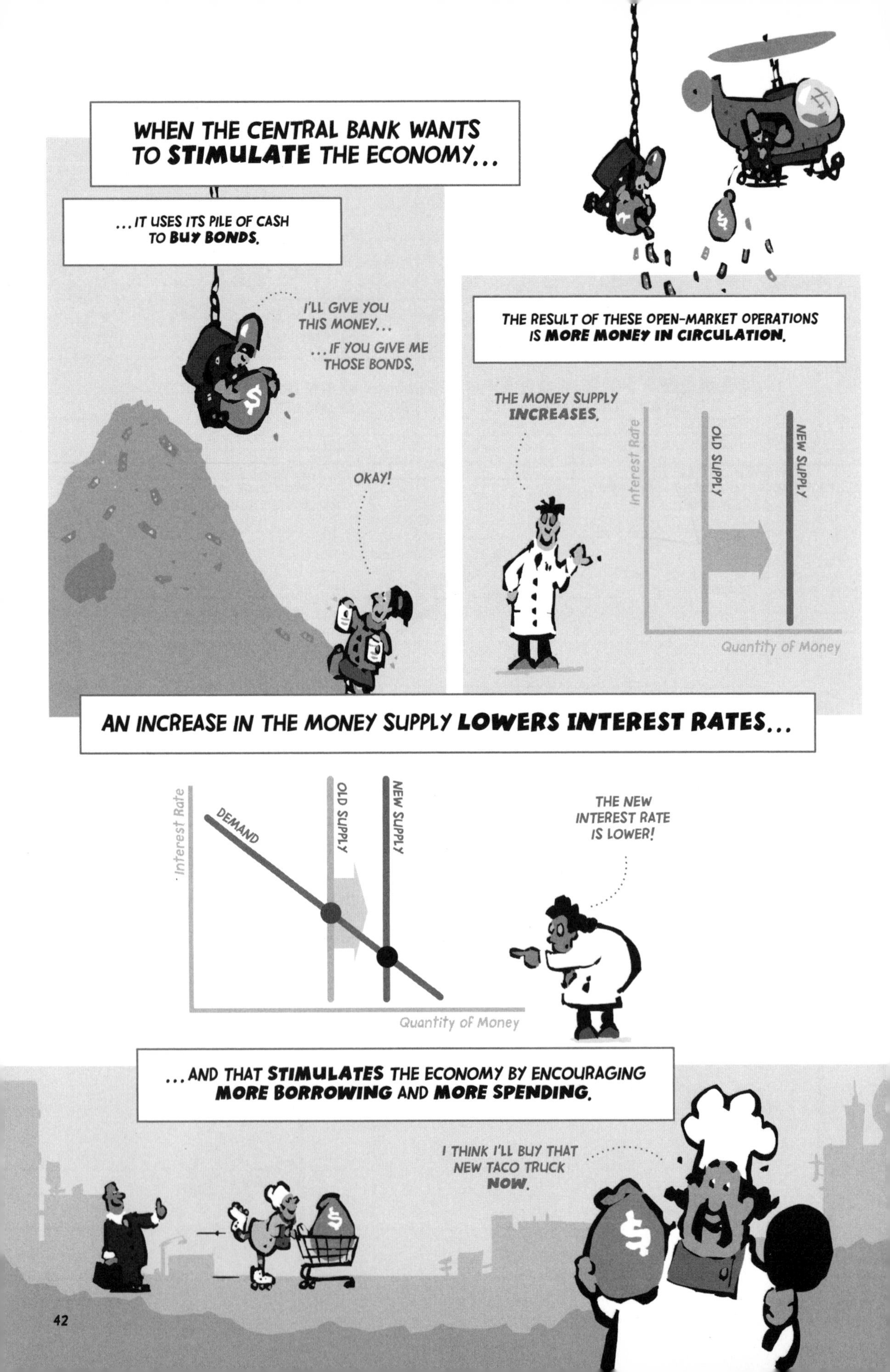

WHEN THE CENTRAL BANK WANTS TO STIMULATE THE ECONOMY...
...IT USES ITS PILE OF CASH TO BUY BONDS.
I'LL GIVE YOU THIS MONEY...
...IF YOU GIVE ME THOSE BONDS.
OKAY!
THE RESULT OF THESE OPEN-MARKET OPERATIONS IS MORE MONEY IN CIRCULATION.
THE MONEY SUPPLY INCREASES.
Interest Rate
OLD SUPPLY
NEW SUPPLY
Quantity of Money
AN INCREASE IN THE MONEY SUPPLY LOWERS INTEREST RATES...
Interest Rate
DEMAND
OLD SUPPLY
NEW SUPPLY
Quantity of Money
THE NEW INTEREST RATE IS LOWER!
...AND THAT STIMULATES THE ECONOMY BY ENCOURAGING MORE BORROWING AND MORE SPENDING.
I THINK I'LL BUY THAT NEW TACO TRUCK NOW.

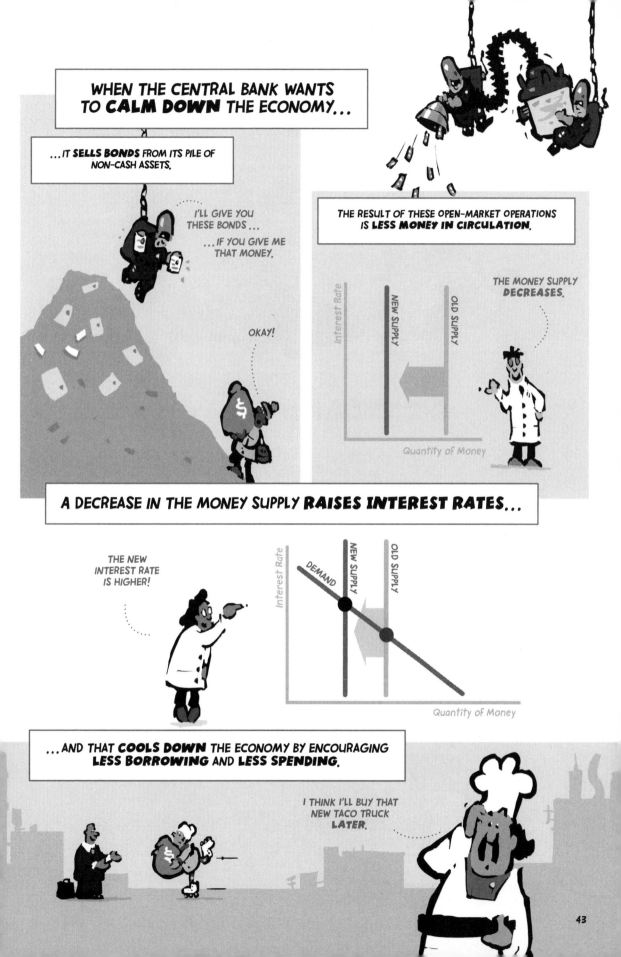

WHEN THE CENTRAL BANK WANTS TO **CALM DOWN** THE ECONOMY...

...IT **SELLS BONDS** FROM ITS PILE OF NON-CASH ASSETS.

I'LL GIVE YOU THESE BONDS ...

...IF YOU GIVE ME THAT MONEY.

OKAY!

THE RESULT OF THESE OPEN-MARKET OPERATIONS IS **LESS MONEY IN CIRCULATION**.

THE MONEY SUPPLY **DECREASES**.

Interest Rate

NEW SUPPLY

OLD SUPPLY

Quantity of Money

A DECREASE IN THE MONEY SUPPLY **RAISES INTEREST RATES**...

THE NEW INTEREST RATE IS HIGHER!

Interest Rate

DEMAND

NEW SUPPLY

OLD SUPPLY

Quantity of Money

...AND THAT **COOLS DOWN** THE ECONOMY BY ENCOURAGING **LESS BORROWING** AND **LESS SPENDING**.

I THINK I'LL BUY THAT NEW TACO TRUCK **LATER**.

BUT REMEMBER, THESE ARE **SHORT-RUN** EFFECTS.

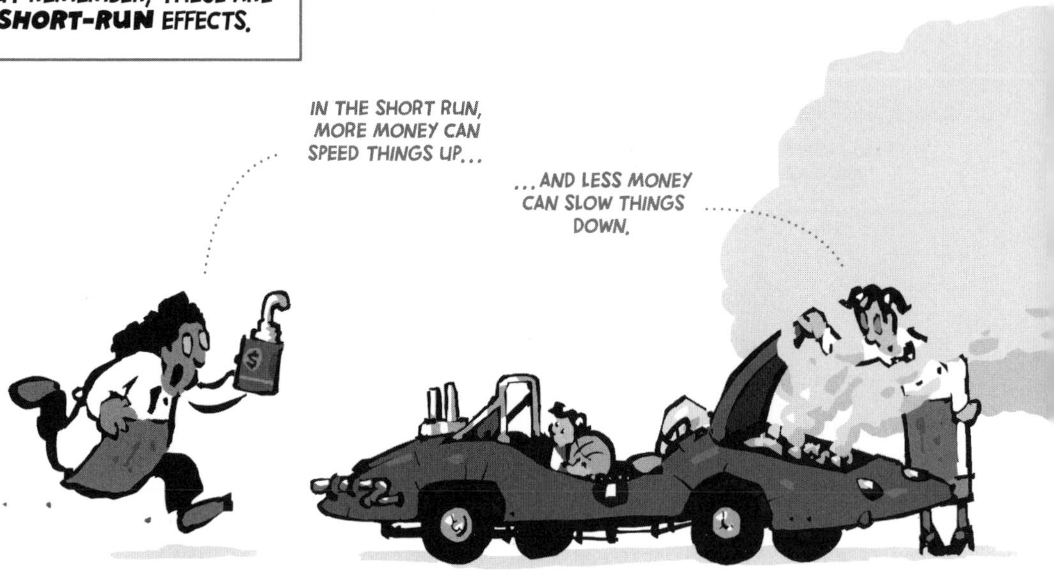
IN THE SHORT RUN, MORE MONEY CAN SPEED THINGS UP...
...AND LESS MONEY CAN SLOW THINGS DOWN.

IN THE LONG RUN, YOU CAN'T GET RICH BY PRINTING MONEY...

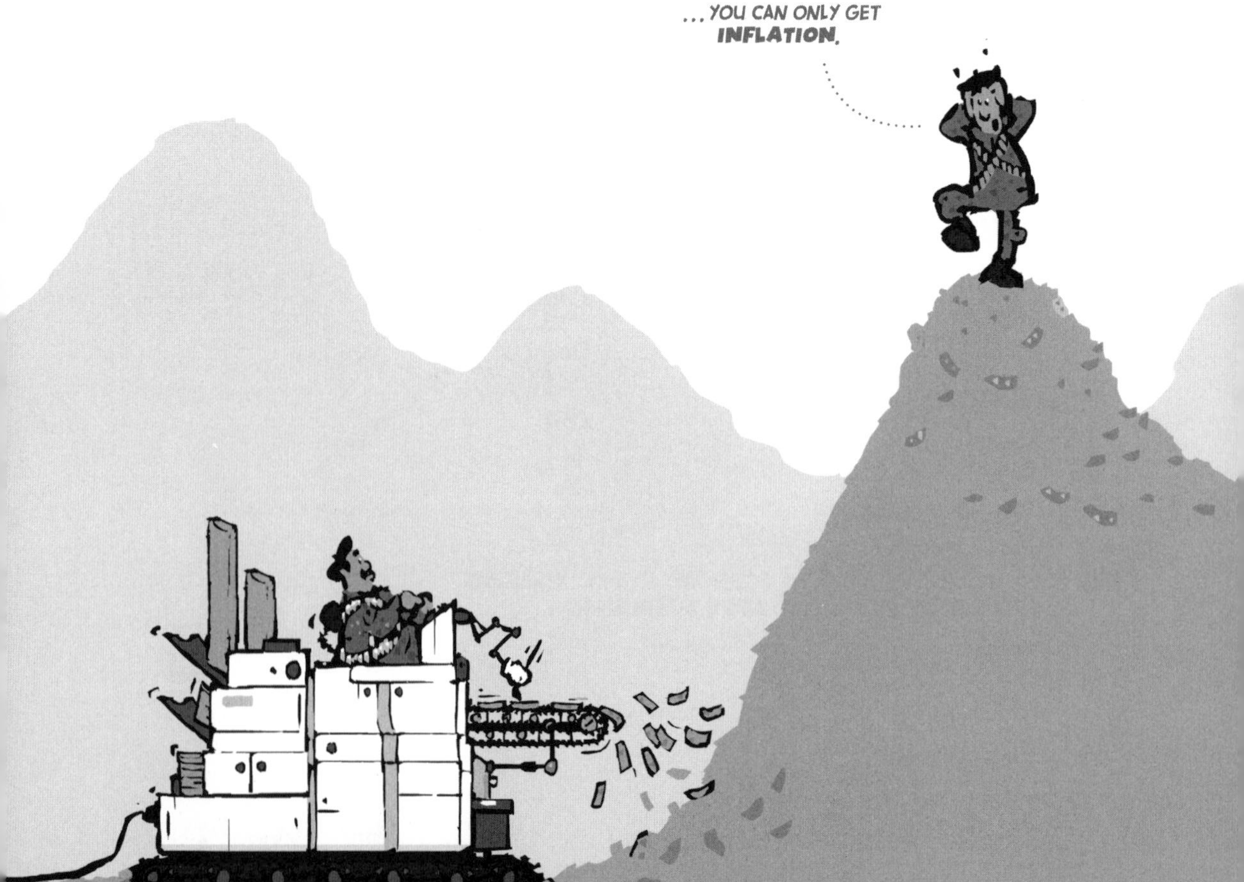
...YOU CAN ONLY GET **INFLATION**.

CHAPTER 4
INFLATION

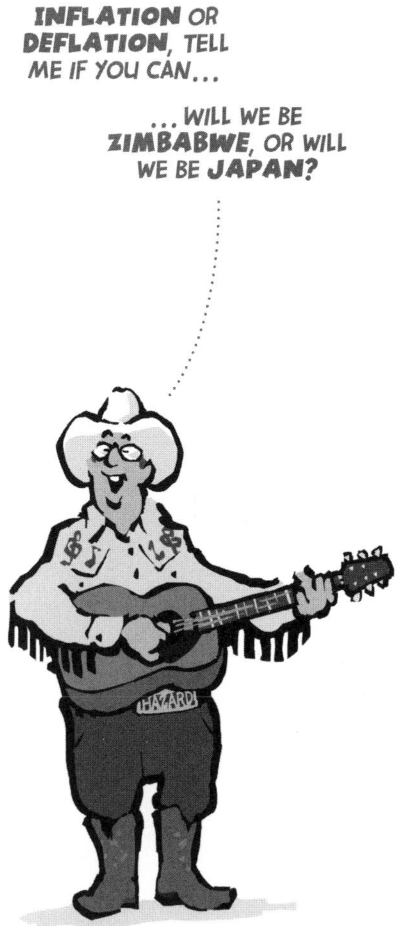
INFLATION OR DEFLATION, TELL ME IF YOU CAN...
...WILL WE BE ZIMBABWE, OR WILL WE BE JAPAN?
HAZARD

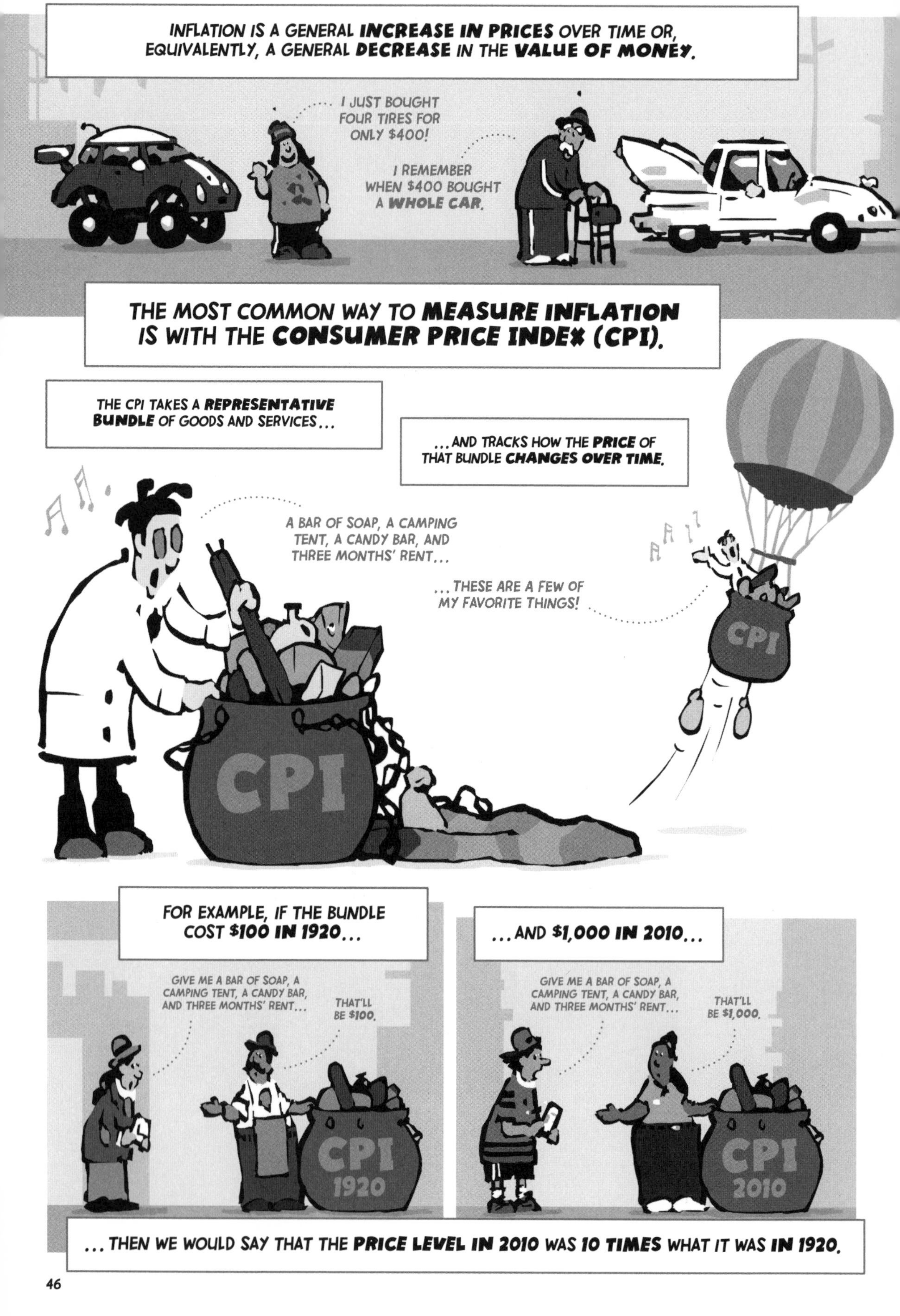
INFLATION IS A GENERAL INCREASE IN PRICES OVER TIME OR, EQUIVALENTLY, A GENERAL DECREASE IN THE VALUE OF MONEY.
I JUST BOUGHT FOUR TIRES FOR ONLY $400!
I REMEMBER WHEN $400 BOUGHT A WHOLE CAR.
THE MOST COMMON WAY TO MEASURE INFLATION IS WITH THE CONSUMER PRICE INDEX (CPI).
THE CPI TAKES A REPRESENTATIVE BUNDLE OF GOODS AND SERVICES...
...AND TRACKS HOW THE PRICE OF THAT BUNDLE CHANGES OVER TIME.
A BAR OF SOAP, A CAMPING TENT, A CANDY BAR, AND THREE MONTHS' RENT...
...THESE ARE A FEW OF MY FAVORITE THINGS!
CPI
CPI
FOR EXAMPLE, IF THE BUNDLE COST $100 IN 1920...
GIVE ME A BAR OF SOAP, A CAMPING TENT, A CANDY BAR, AND THREE MONTHS' RENT...
THAT'LL BE $100.
CPI 1920
...AND $1,000 IN 2010...
GIVE ME A BAR OF SOAP, A CAMPING TENT, A CANDY BAR, AND THREE MONTHS' RENT...
THAT'LL BE $1,000.
CPI 2010
...THEN WE WOULD SAY THAT THE PRICE LEVEL IN 2010 WAS 10 TIMES WHAT IT WAS IN 1920.

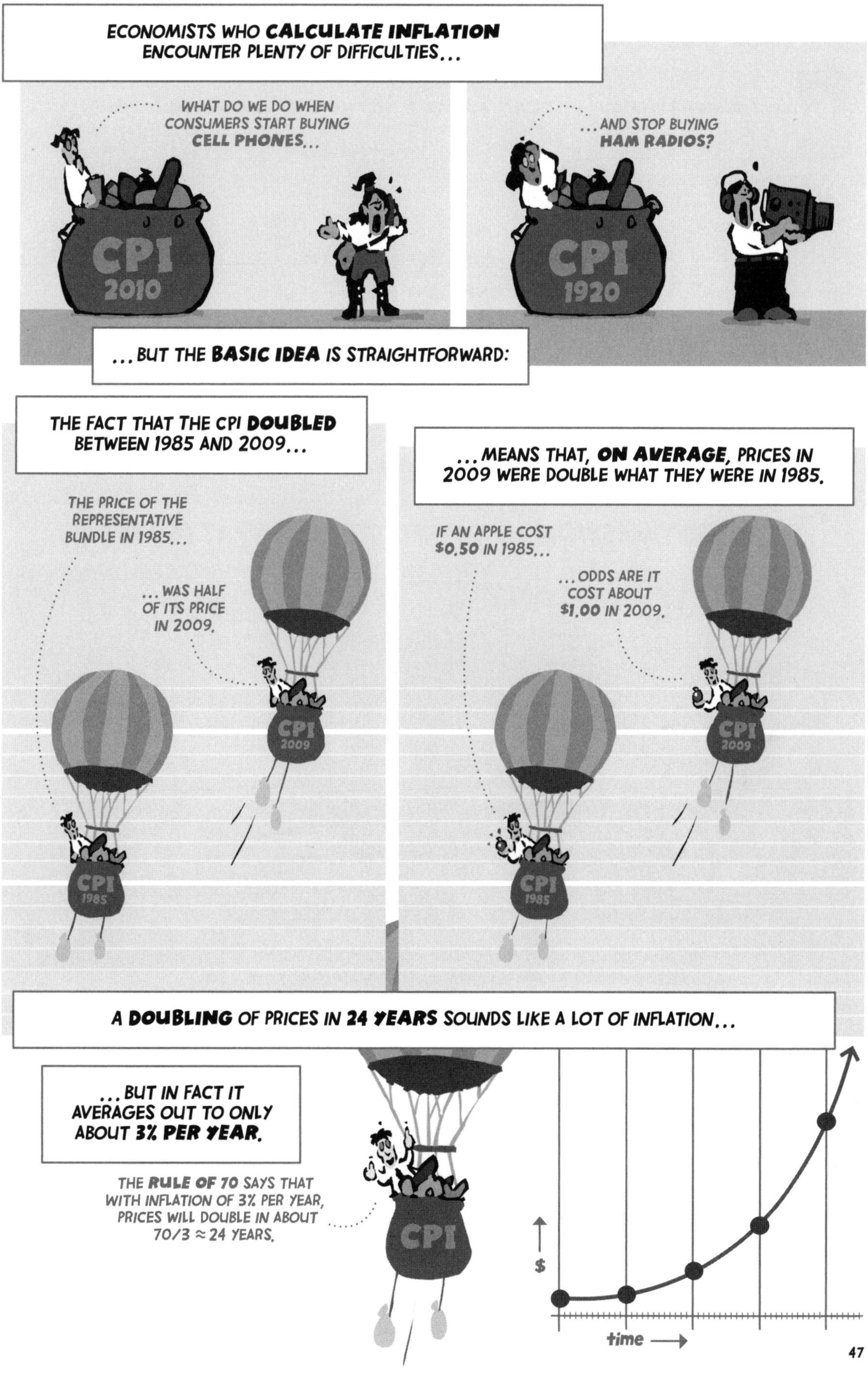
ECONOMISTS WHO CALCULATE INFLATION ENCOUNTER PLENTY OF DIFFICULTIES...
WHAT DO WE DO WHEN CONSUMERS START BUYING CELL PHONES...
CPI 2010
...AND STOP BUYING HAM RADIOS?
CPI 1920
...BUT THE BASIC IDEA IS STRAIGHTFORWARD:
THE FACT THAT THE CPI DOUBLED BETWEEN 1985 AND 2009...
THE PRICE OF THE REPRESENTATIVE BUNDLE IN 1985...
...WAS HALF OF ITS PRICE IN 2009.
CPI 2009
CPI 1985
...MEANS THAT, ON AVERAGE, PRICES IN 2009 WERE DOUBLE WHAT THEY WERE IN 1985.
IF AN APPLE COST $0.50 IN 1985...
...ODDS ARE IT COST ABOUT $1.00 IN 2009.
CPI 2009
CPI 1985
A DOUBLING OF PRICES IN 24 YEARS SOUNDS LIKE A LOT OF INFLATION...
...BUT IN FACT IT AVERAGES OUT TO ONLY ABOUT 3% PER YEAR.
THE RULE OF 70 SAYS THAT WITH INFLATION OF 3% PER YEAR, PRICES WILL DOUBLE IN ABOUT 70/3 ≈ 24 YEARS.
CPI
$
time

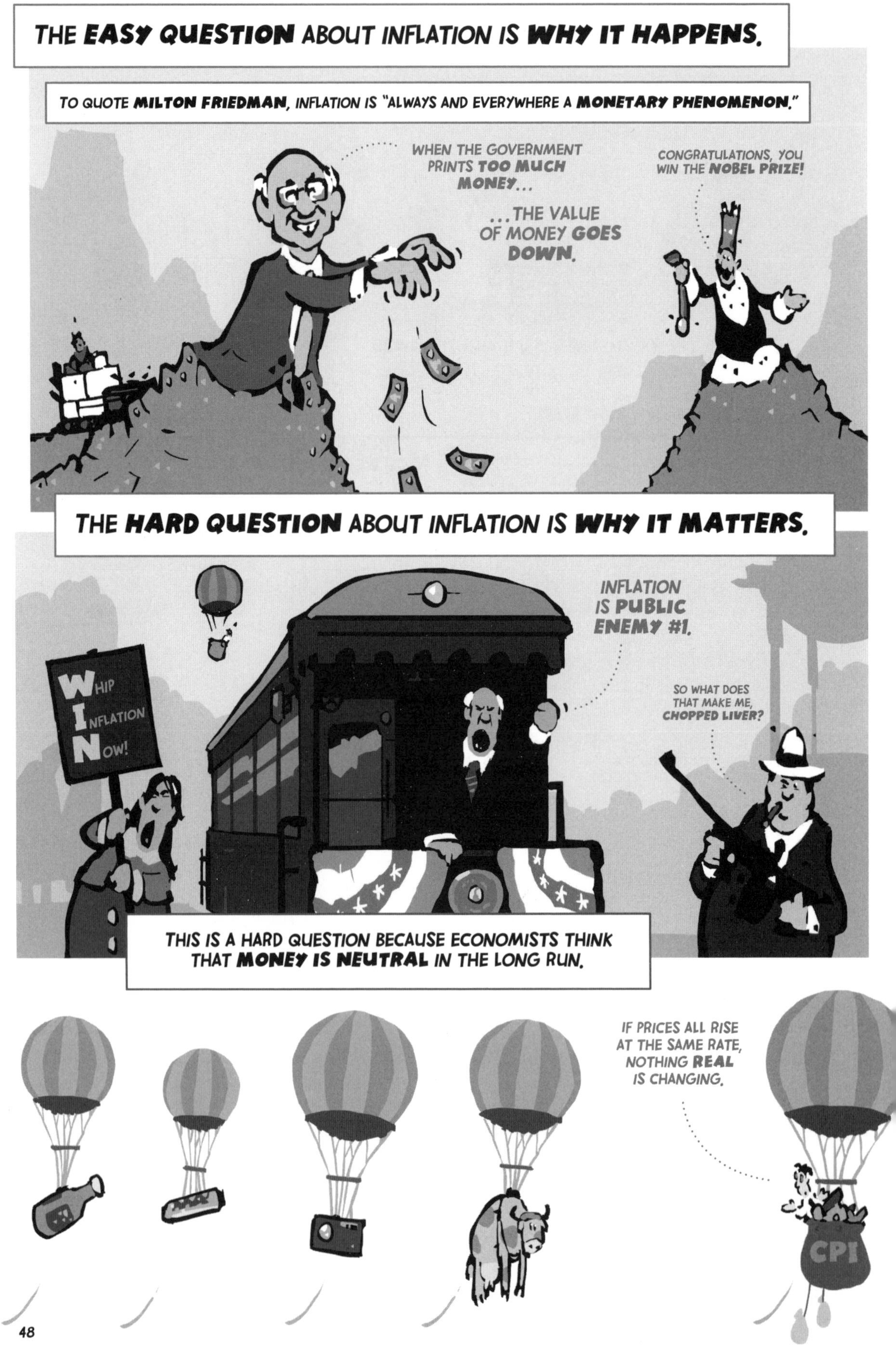
THE EASY QUESTION ABOUT INFLATION IS WHY IT HAPPENS.
TO QUOTE MILTON FRIEDMAN, INFLATION IS "ALWAYS AND EVERYWHERE A MONETARY PHENOMENON."
WHEN THE GOVERNMENT PRINTS TOO MUCH MONEY...
...THE VALUE OF MONEY GOES DOWN.
CONGRATULATIONS, YOU WIN THE NOBEL PRIZE!
THE HARD QUESTION ABOUT INFLATION IS WHY IT MATTERS.
WHIP
INFLATION
NOW!
INFLATION IS PUBLIC ENEMY #1.
SO WHAT DOES THAT MAKE ME, CHOPPED LIVER?
THIS IS A HARD QUESTION BECAUSE ECONOMISTS THINK THAT MONEY IS NEUTRAL IN THE LONG RUN.
IF PRICES ALL RISE AT THE SAME RATE, NOTHING REAL IS CHANGING.
CPI

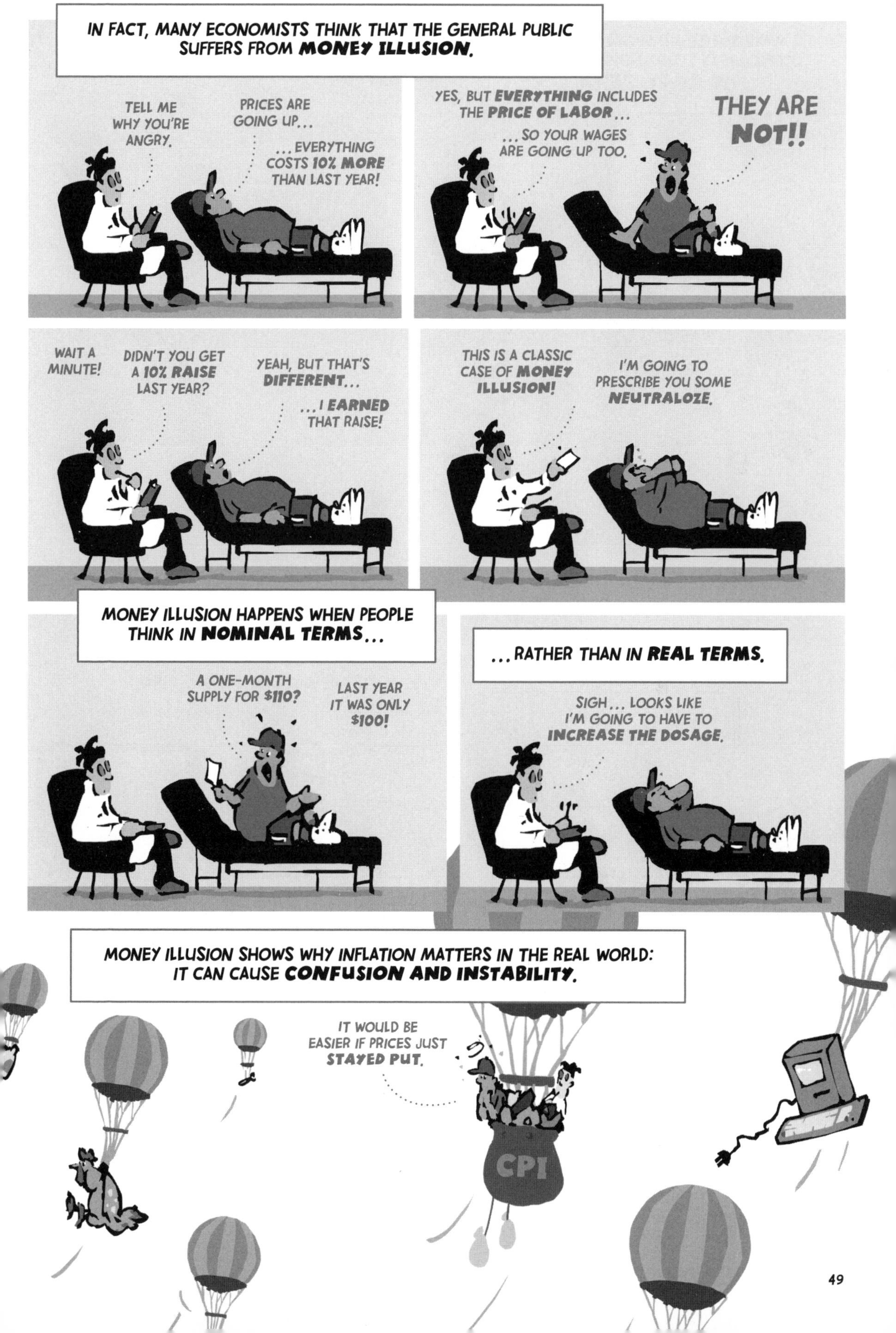
IN FACT, MANY ECONOMISTS THINK THAT THE GENERAL PUBLIC SUFFERS FROM MONEY ILLUSION.
TELL ME WHY YOU'RE ANGRY.
PRICES ARE GOING UP...
...EVERYTHING COSTS 10% MORE THAN LAST YEAR!
YES, BUT EVERYTHING INCLUDES THE PRICE OF LABOR...
...SO YOUR WAGES ARE GOING UP TOO.
THEY ARE NOT!!
WAIT A MINUTE!
DIDN'T YOU GET A 10% RAISE LAST YEAR?
YEAH, BUT THAT'S DIFFERENT...
...I EARNED THAT RAISE!
THIS IS A CLASSIC CASE OF MONEY ILLUSION!
I'M GOING TO PRESCRIBE YOU SOME NEUTRALOZE.
MONEY ILLUSION HAPPENS WHEN PEOPLE THINK IN NOMINAL TERMS...
A ONE-MONTH SUPPLY FOR $110?
LAST YEAR IT WAS ONLY $100!
...RATHER THAN IN REAL TERMS.
SIGH... LOOKS LIKE I'M GOING TO HAVE TO INCREASE THE DOSAGE.
MONEY ILLUSION SHOWS WHY INFLATION MATTERS IN THE REAL WORLD: IT CAN CAUSE CONFUSION AND INSTABILITY.
IT WOULD BE EASIER IF PRICES JUST STAYED PUT.
CPI

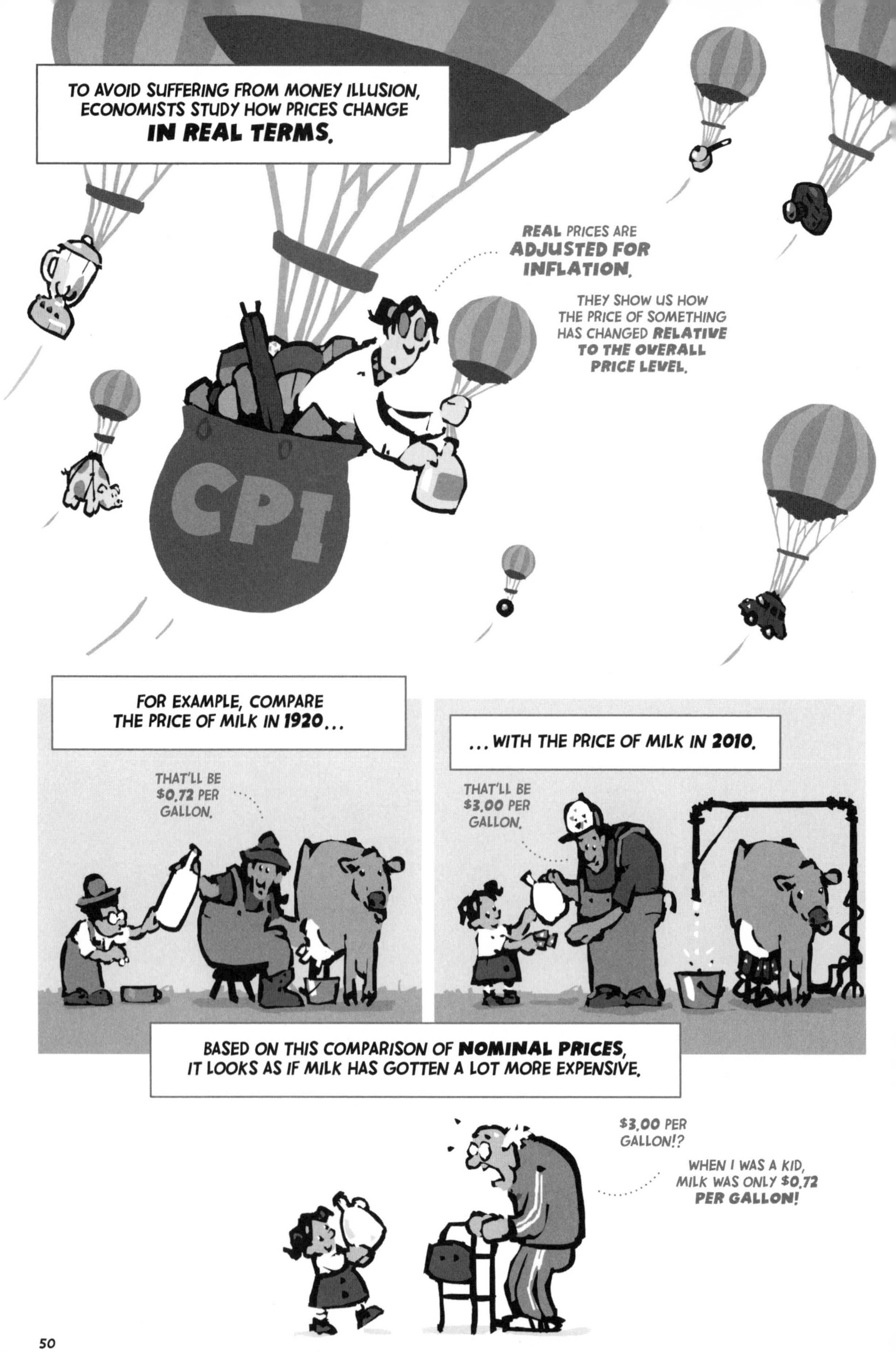
TO AVOID SUFFERING FROM MONEY ILLUSION, ECONOMISTS STUDY HOW PRICES CHANGE **IN REAL TERMS.**
REAL PRICES ARE **ADJUSTED FOR INFLATION.**
THEY SHOW US HOW THE PRICE OF SOMETHING HAS CHANGED **RELATIVE TO THE OVERALL PRICE LEVEL.**
CPI
FOR EXAMPLE, COMPARE THE PRICE OF MILK IN **1920**...
THAT'LL BE **$0.72** PER GALLON.
...WITH THE PRICE OF MILK IN **2010.**
THAT'LL BE **$3.00** PER GALLON.
BASED ON THIS COMPARISON OF **NOMINAL PRICES**, IT LOOKS AS IF MILK HAS GOTTEN A LOT MORE EXPENSIVE.
$3.00 PER GALLON!?
WHEN I WAS A KID, MILK WAS ONLY **$0.72 PER GALLON!**

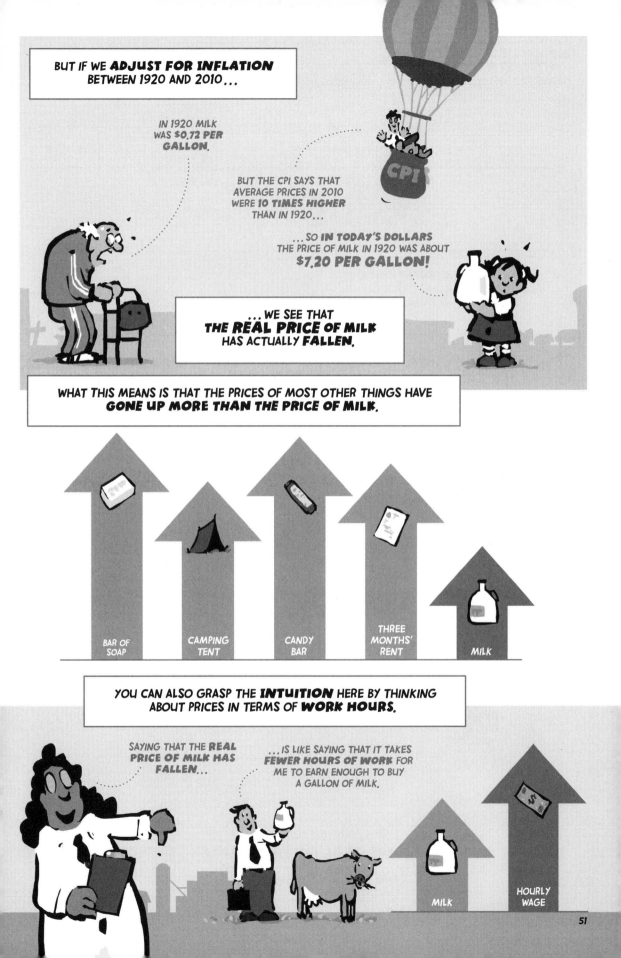

BUT IF WE **ADJUST FOR INFLATION** BETWEEN 1920 AND 2010...

IN 1920 MILK WAS **$0.72 PER GALLON**.

BUT THE CPI SAYS THAT AVERAGE PRICES IN 2010 WERE **10 TIMES HIGHER** THAN IN 1920...

...SO **IN TODAY'S DOLLARS** THE PRICE OF MILK IN 1920 WAS ABOUT **$7.20 PER GALLON!**

... WE SEE THAT **THE REAL PRICE OF MILK** HAS ACTUALLY **FALLEN.**

WHAT THIS MEANS IS THAT THE PRICES OF MOST OTHER THINGS HAVE **GONE UP MORE THAN THE PRICE OF MILK.**

BAR OF SOAP

CAMPING TENT

CANDY BAR

THREE MONTHS' RENT

MILK

YOU CAN ALSO GRASP THE **INTUITION** HERE BY THINKING ABOUT PRICES IN TERMS OF **WORK HOURS.**

SAYING THAT THE **REAL PRICE OF MILK HAS FALLEN**...

...IS LIKE SAYING THAT IT TAKES **FEWER HOURS OF WORK** FOR ME TO EARN ENOUGH TO BUY A GALLON OF MILK.

MILK

HOURLY WAGE

51

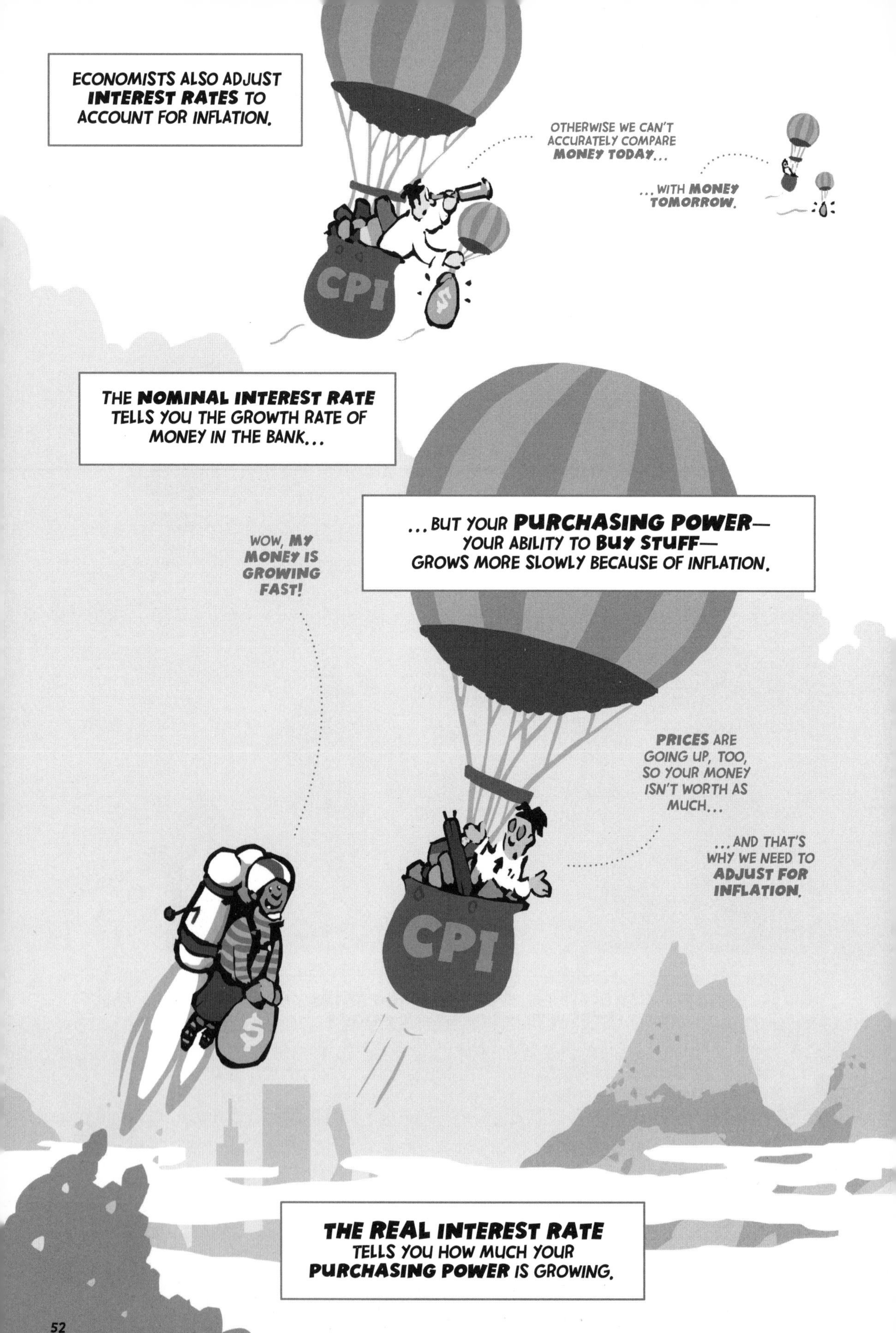

ECONOMISTS ALSO ADJUST **INTEREST RATES** TO ACCOUNT FOR INFLATION.
OTHERWISE WE CAN'T ACCURATELY COMPARE **MONEY TODAY**...
...WITH **MONEY TOMORROW**.
CPI
$
THE **NOMINAL INTEREST RATE** TELLS YOU THE GROWTH RATE OF MONEY IN THE BANK...
...BUT YOUR **PURCHASING POWER**— YOUR ABILITY TO **BUY STUFF**— GROWS MORE SLOWLY BECAUSE OF INFLATION.
WOW, **MY MONEY IS GROWING FAST!**
PRICES ARE GOING UP, TOO, SO YOUR MONEY ISN'T WORTH AS MUCH...
...AND THAT'S WHY WE NEED TO **ADJUST FOR INFLATION**.
CPI
$
THE REAL INTEREST RATE TELLS YOU HOW MUCH YOUR **PURCHASING POWER** IS GROWING.

THERE'S A HANDY **RULE OF THUMB** THAT RELATES **NOMINAL** AND **REAL** INTEREST RATES.

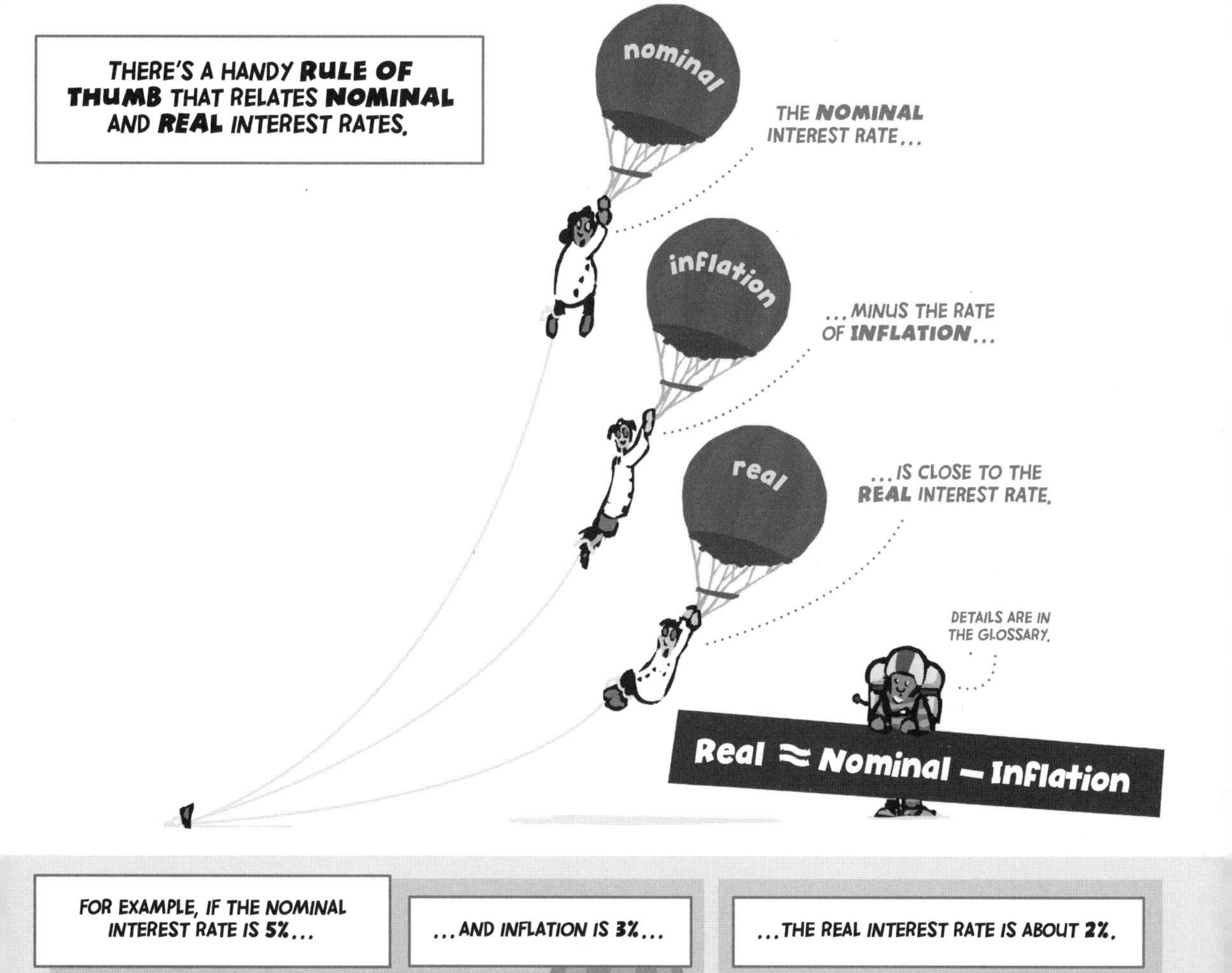

nominal
THE **NOMINAL** INTEREST RATE...
inflation
...MINUS THE RATE OF **INFLATION**...
real
...IS CLOSE TO THE **REAL** INTEREST RATE.
DETAILS ARE IN THE GLOSSARY.
Real ≈ Nominal – Inflation

FOR EXAMPLE, IF THE NOMINAL INTEREST RATE IS **5%**...

...AND INFLATION IS **3%**...

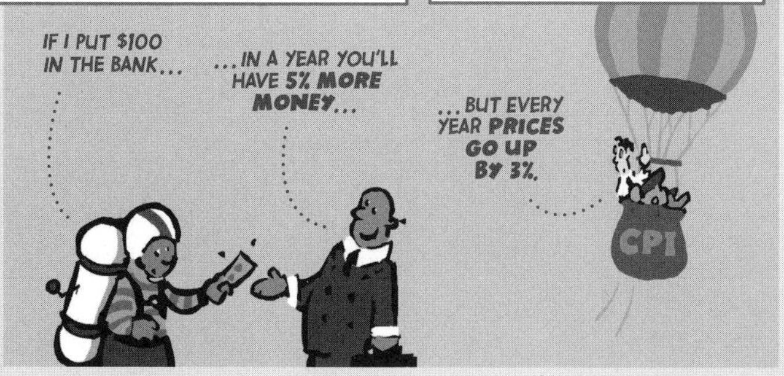

IF I PUT $100 IN THE BANK...
...IN A YEAR YOU'LL HAVE **5% MORE MONEY**...
...BUT EVERY YEAR **PRICES GO UP BY 3%**.
CPI

...THE REAL INTEREST RATE IS ABOUT **2%**.

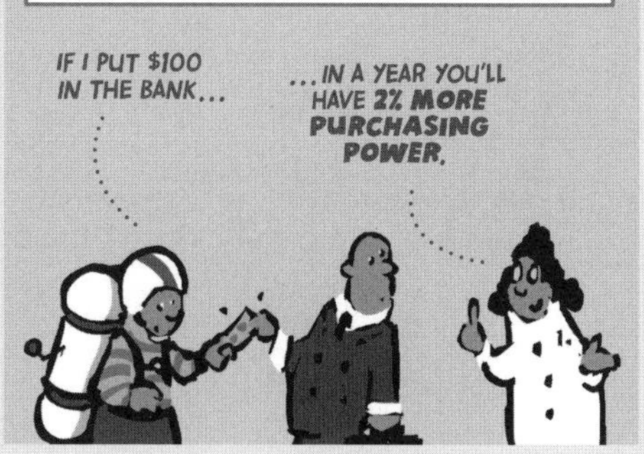

IF I PUT $100 IN THE BANK...
...IN A YEAR YOU'LL HAVE **2% MORE PURCHASING POWER**.

AS WITH PRICES, INTEREST RATES ARE USUALLY GIVEN IN **NOMINAL** TERMS...

...BUT IT'S THE **REAL** INTEREST RATE THAT **DRIVES ECONOMIC DECISIONS**.

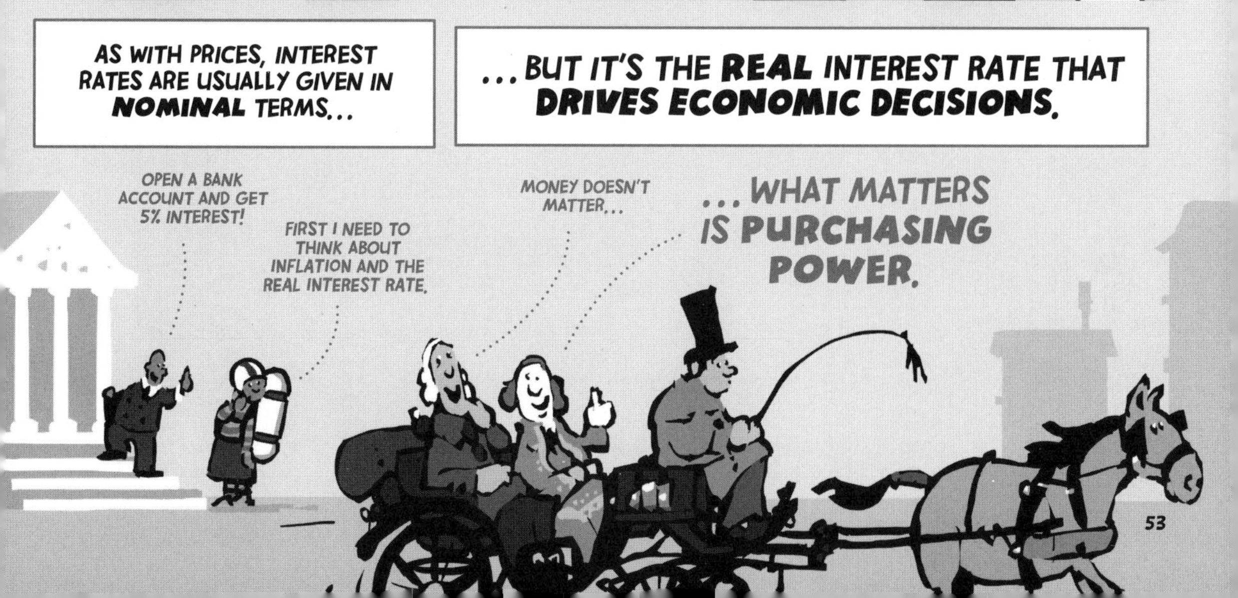

OPEN A BANK ACCOUNT AND GET 5% INTEREST!
FIRST I NEED TO THINK ABOUT INFLATION AND THE REAL INTEREST RATE.
MONEY DOESN'T MATTER...
...WHAT MATTERS IS **PURCHASING POWER**.

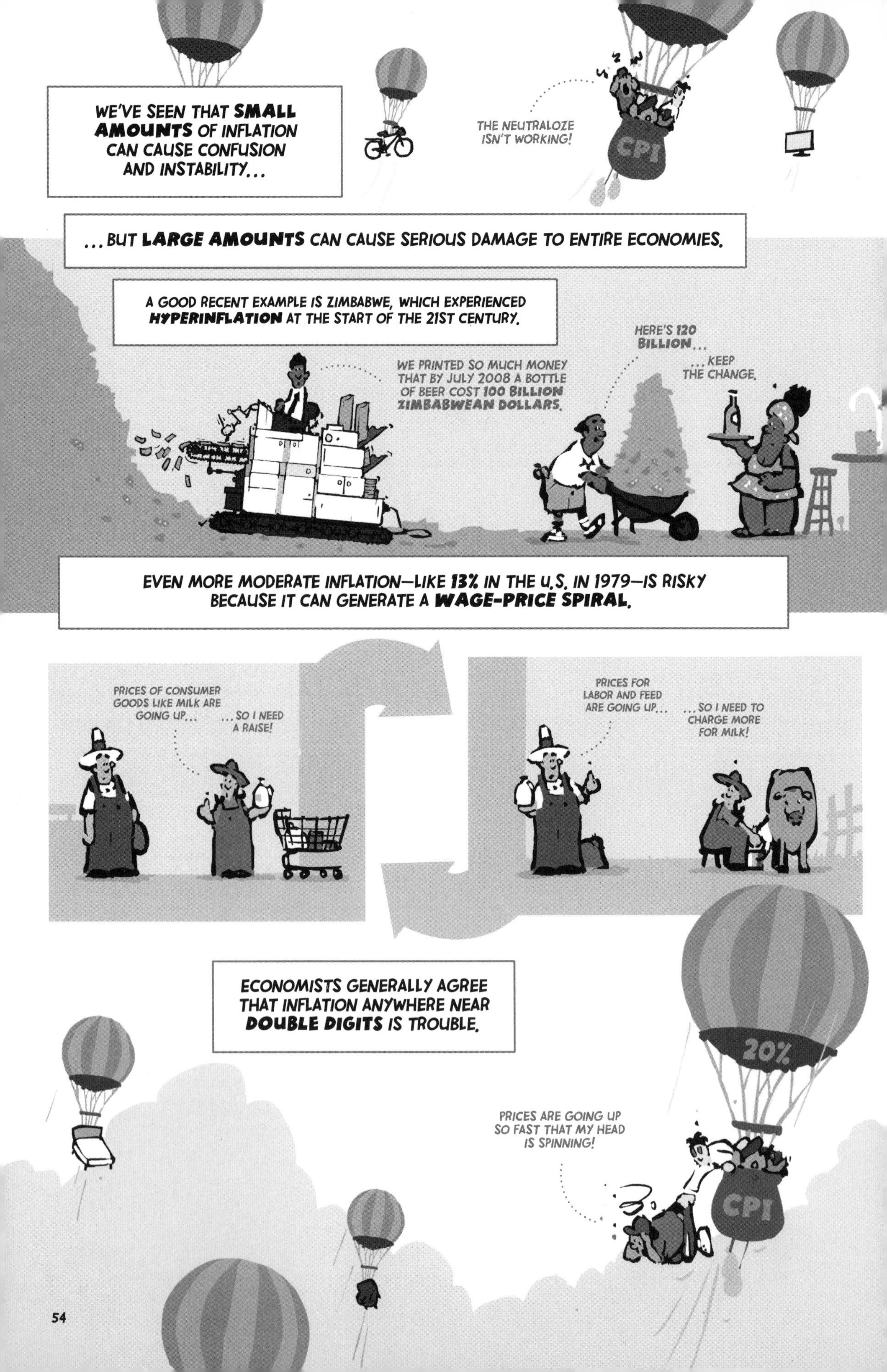
WE'VE SEEN THAT **SMALL AMOUNTS** OF INFLATION CAN CAUSE CONFUSION AND INSTABILITY...
THE NEUTRALOZE ISN'T WORKING!
CPI
...BUT **LARGE AMOUNTS** CAN CAUSE SERIOUS DAMAGE TO ENTIRE ECONOMIES.
A GOOD RECENT EXAMPLE IS ZIMBABWE, WHICH EXPERIENCED **HYPERINFLATION** AT THE START OF THE 21ST CENTURY.
WE PRINTED SO MUCH MONEY THAT BY JULY 2008 A BOTTLE OF BEER COST **100 BILLION ZIMBABWEAN DOLLARS.**
HERE'S **120 BILLION**...
...KEEP THE CHANGE.
EVEN MORE MODERATE INFLATION—LIKE **13%** IN THE U.S. IN 1979—IS RISKY BECAUSE IT CAN GENERATE A **WAGE-PRICE SPIRAL.**
PRICES OF CONSUMER GOODS LIKE MILK ARE GOING UP...
...SO I NEED A RAISE!
PRICES FOR LABOR AND FEED ARE GOING UP...
...SO I NEED TO CHARGE MORE FOR MILK!
ECONOMISTS GENERALLY AGREE THAT INFLATION ANYWHERE NEAR **DOUBLE DIGITS** IS TROUBLE.
20%
PRICES ARE GOING UP SO FAST THAT MY HEAD IS SPINNING!
CPI

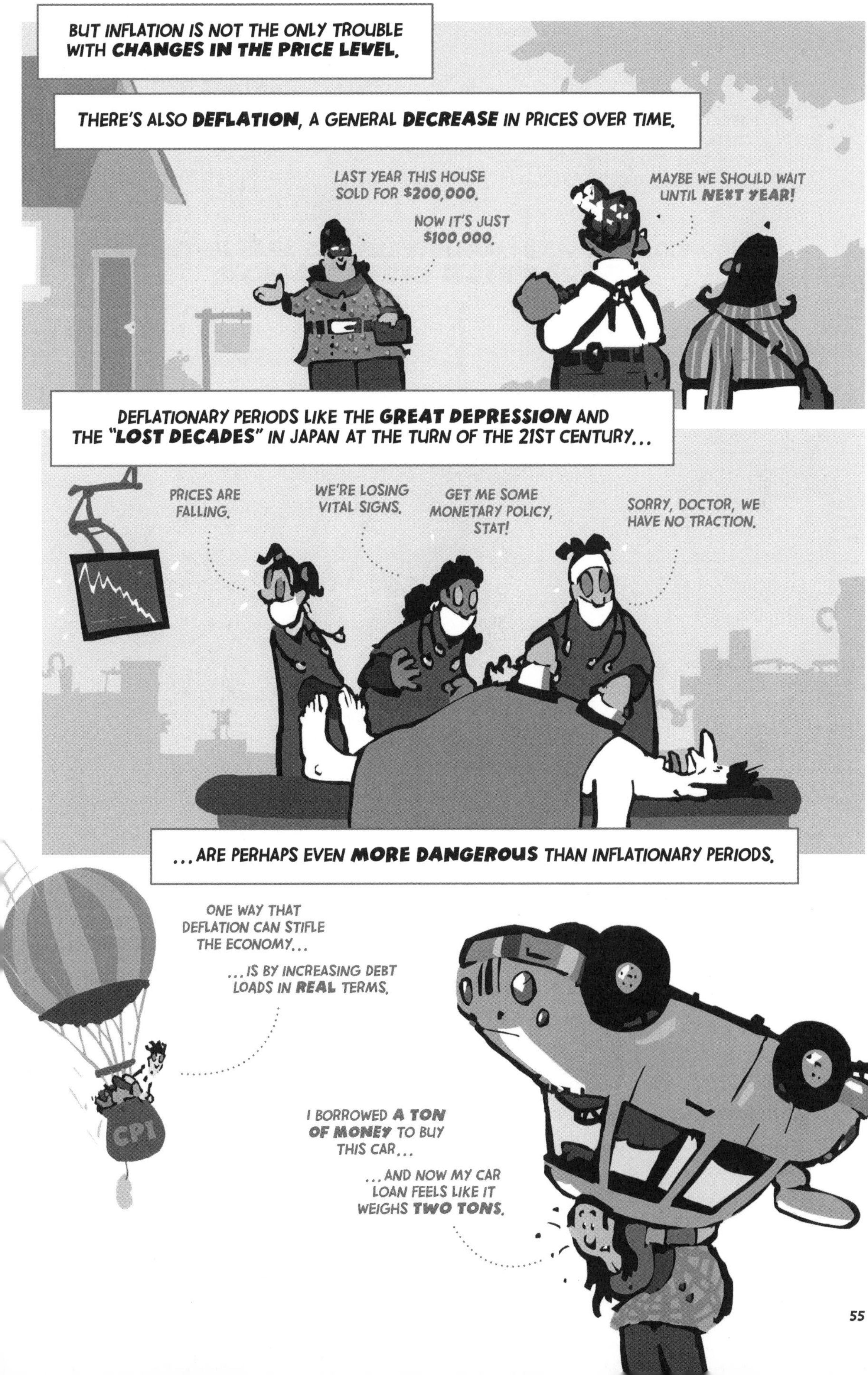
BUT INFLATION IS NOT THE ONLY TROUBLE WITH **CHANGES IN THE PRICE LEVEL.**
THERE'S ALSO **DEFLATION**, A GENERAL **DECREASE** IN PRICES OVER TIME.
LAST YEAR THIS HOUSE SOLD FOR $200,000.
NOW IT'S JUST $100,000.
MAYBE WE SHOULD WAIT UNTIL **NEXT YEAR!**
DEFLATIONARY PERIODS LIKE THE **GREAT DEPRESSION** AND THE **"LOST DECADES"** IN JAPAN AT THE TURN OF THE 21ST CENTURY...
PRICES ARE FALLING.
WE'RE LOSING VITAL SIGNS.
GET ME SOME MONETARY POLICY, STAT!
SORRY, DOCTOR, WE HAVE NO TRACTION.
...ARE PERHAPS EVEN **MORE DANGEROUS** THAN INFLATIONARY PERIODS.
ONE WAY THAT DEFLATION CAN STIFLE THE ECONOMY...
...IS BY INCREASING DEBT LOADS IN **REAL** TERMS.
CPI
I BORROWED **A TON OF MONEY** TO BUY THIS CAR...
...AND NOW MY CAR LOAN FEELS LIKE IT WEIGHS **TWO TONS.**

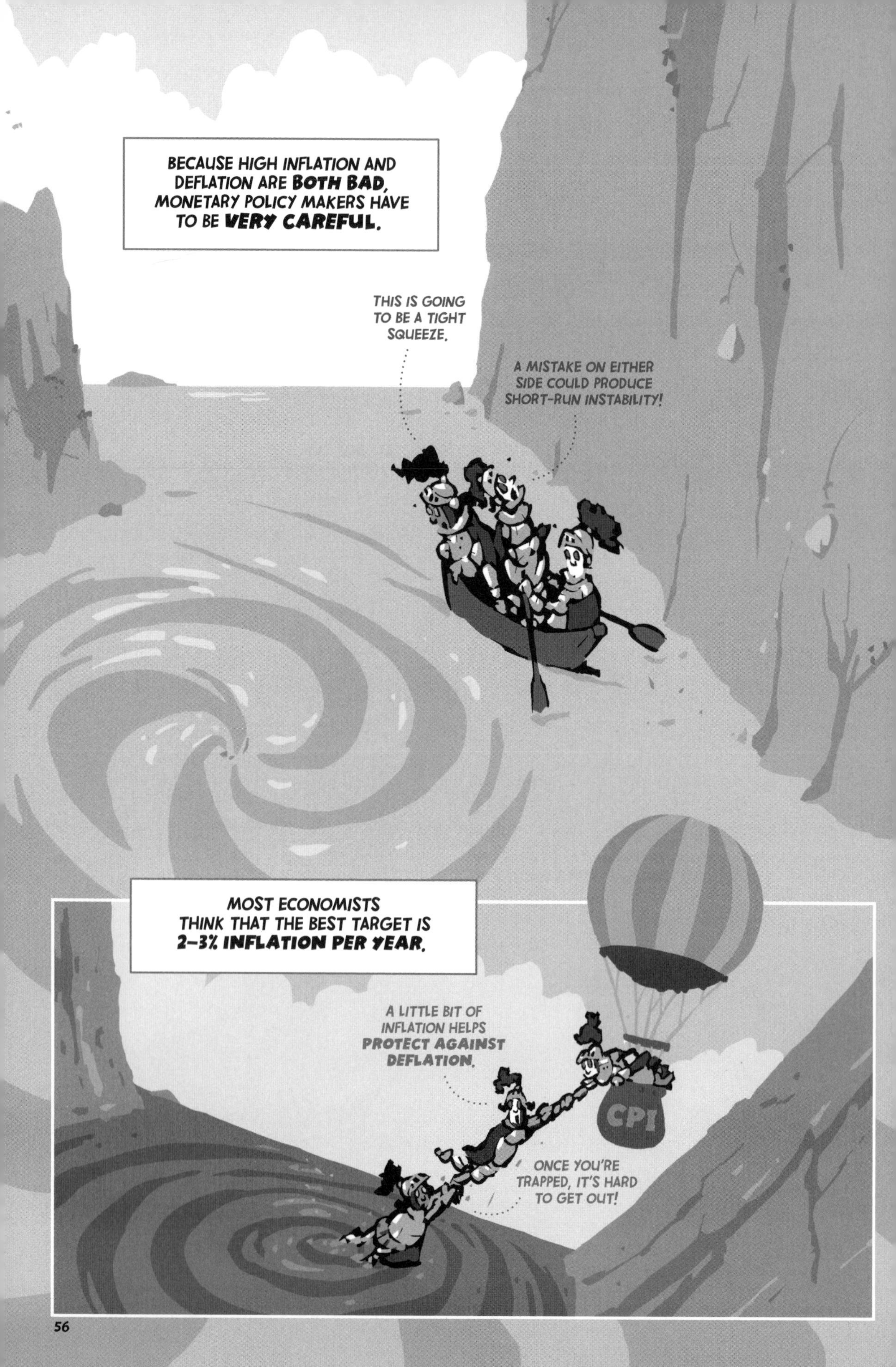

BECAUSE HIGH INFLATION AND DEFLATION ARE **BOTH BAD**, MONETARY POLICY MAKERS HAVE TO BE **VERY CAREFUL.**
THIS IS GOING TO BE A TIGHT SQUEEZE.
A MISTAKE ON EITHER SIDE COULD PRODUCE SHORT-RUN INSTABILITY!
MOST ECONOMISTS THINK THAT THE BEST TARGET IS **2–3% INFLATION PER YEAR.**
A LITTLE BIT OF INFLATION HELPS **PROTECT AGAINST DEFLATION.**
CPI
ONCE YOU'RE TRAPPED, IT'S HARD TO GET OUT!

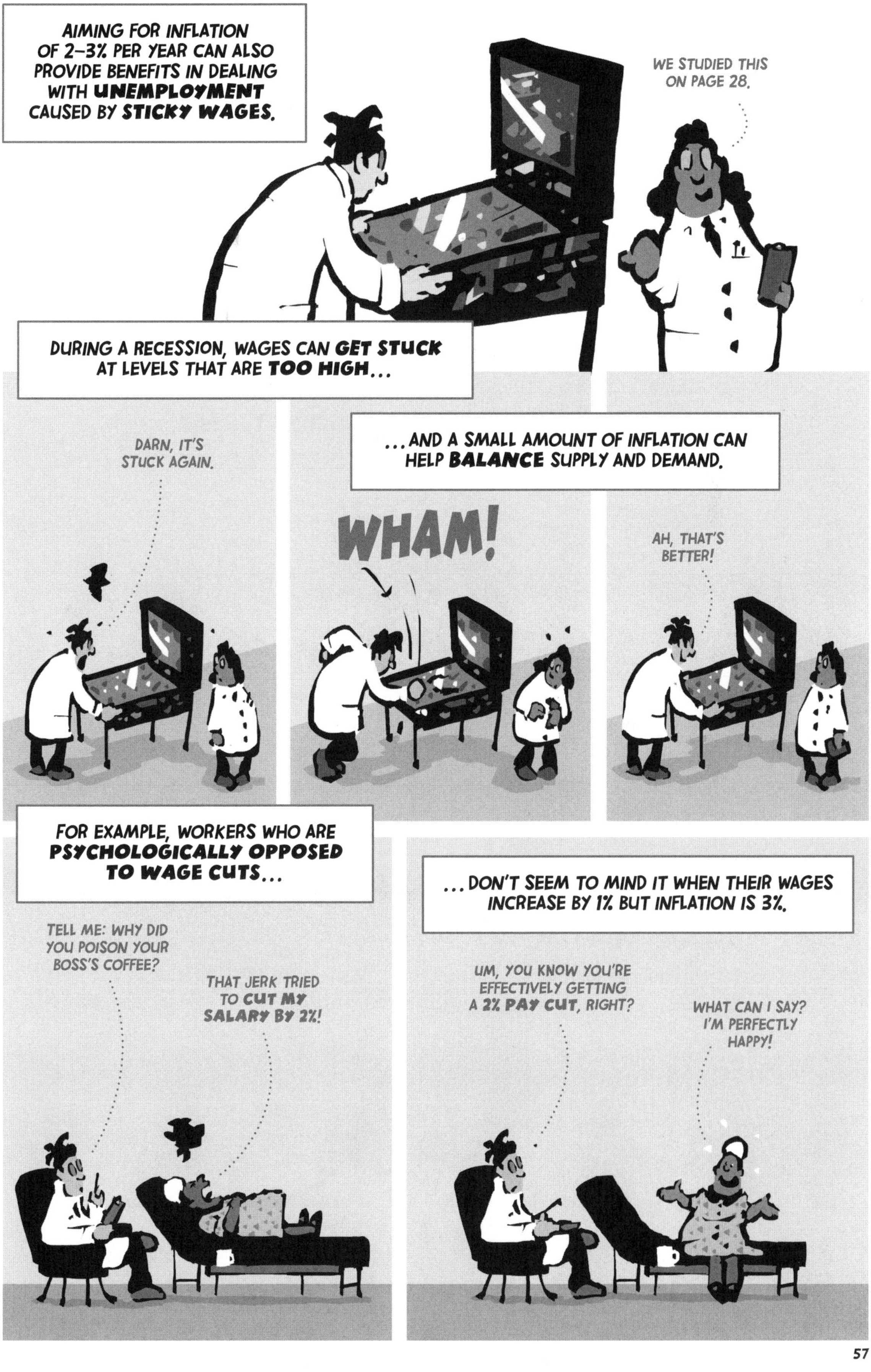
AIMING FOR INFLATION OF 2–3% PER YEAR CAN ALSO PROVIDE BENEFITS IN DEALING WITH **UNEMPLOYMENT** CAUSED BY **STICKY WAGES.**
WE STUDIED THIS ON PAGE 28.
DURING A RECESSION, WAGES CAN **GET STUCK** AT LEVELS THAT ARE **TOO HIGH**...
DARN, IT'S STUCK AGAIN.
...AND A SMALL AMOUNT OF INFLATION CAN HELP **BALANCE** SUPPLY AND DEMAND.
WHAM!
AH, THAT'S BETTER!
FOR EXAMPLE, WORKERS WHO ARE **PSYCHOLOGICALLY OPPOSED TO WAGE CUTS**...
TELL ME: WHY DID YOU POISON YOUR BOSS'S COFFEE?
THAT JERK TRIED TO **CUT MY SALARY BY 2%!**
...DON'T SEEM TO MIND IT WHEN THEIR WAGES INCREASE BY 1% BUT INFLATION IS 3%.
UM, YOU KNOW YOU'RE EFFECTIVELY GETTING A **2% PAY CUT**, RIGHT?
WHAT CAN I SAY? I'M PERFECTLY HAPPY!

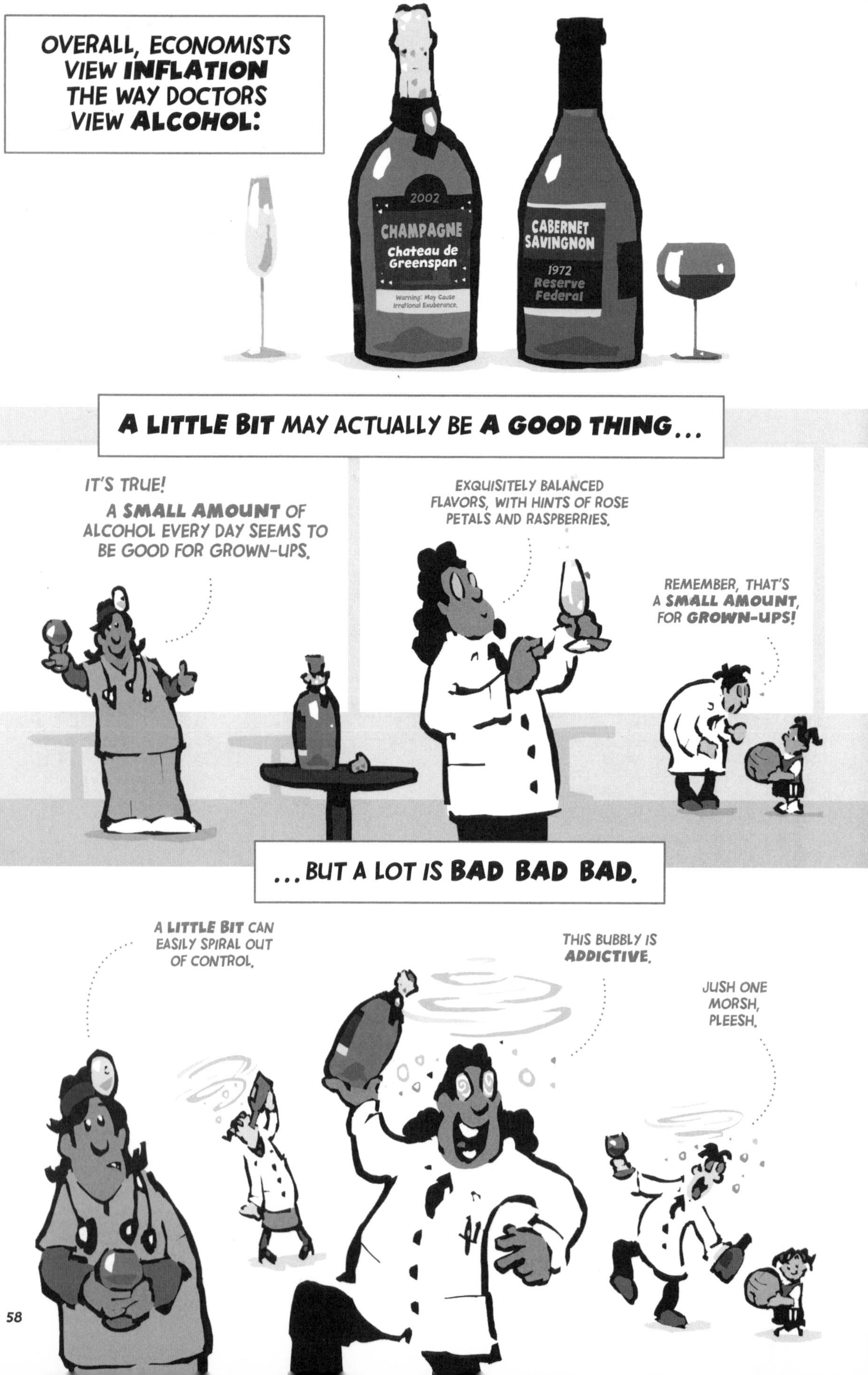
OVERALL, ECONOMISTS VIEW **INFLATION** THE WAY DOCTORS VIEW **ALCOHOL:**
2002
CHAMPAGNE
Chateau de Greenspan
Warning: May Cause Irrational Exuberance.
CABERNET SAVINGNON
1972
Reserve Federal
A LITTLE BIT MAY ACTUALLY BE **A GOOD THING...**
IT'S TRUE! A **SMALL AMOUNT** OF ALCOHOL EVERY DAY SEEMS TO BE GOOD FOR GROWN-UPS.
EXQUISITELY BALANCED FLAVORS, WITH HINTS OF ROSE PETALS AND RASPBERRIES.
REMEMBER, THAT'S A **SMALL AMOUNT**, FOR **GROWN-UPS!**
...BUT A LOT IS **BAD BAD BAD.**
A **LITTLE BIT** CAN EASILY SPIRAL OUT OF CONTROL.
THIS BUBBLY IS **ADDICTIVE.**
JUSH ONE MORSH, PLEESH.

CHAPTER 5
GROSS DOMESTIC PRODUCT (GDP)

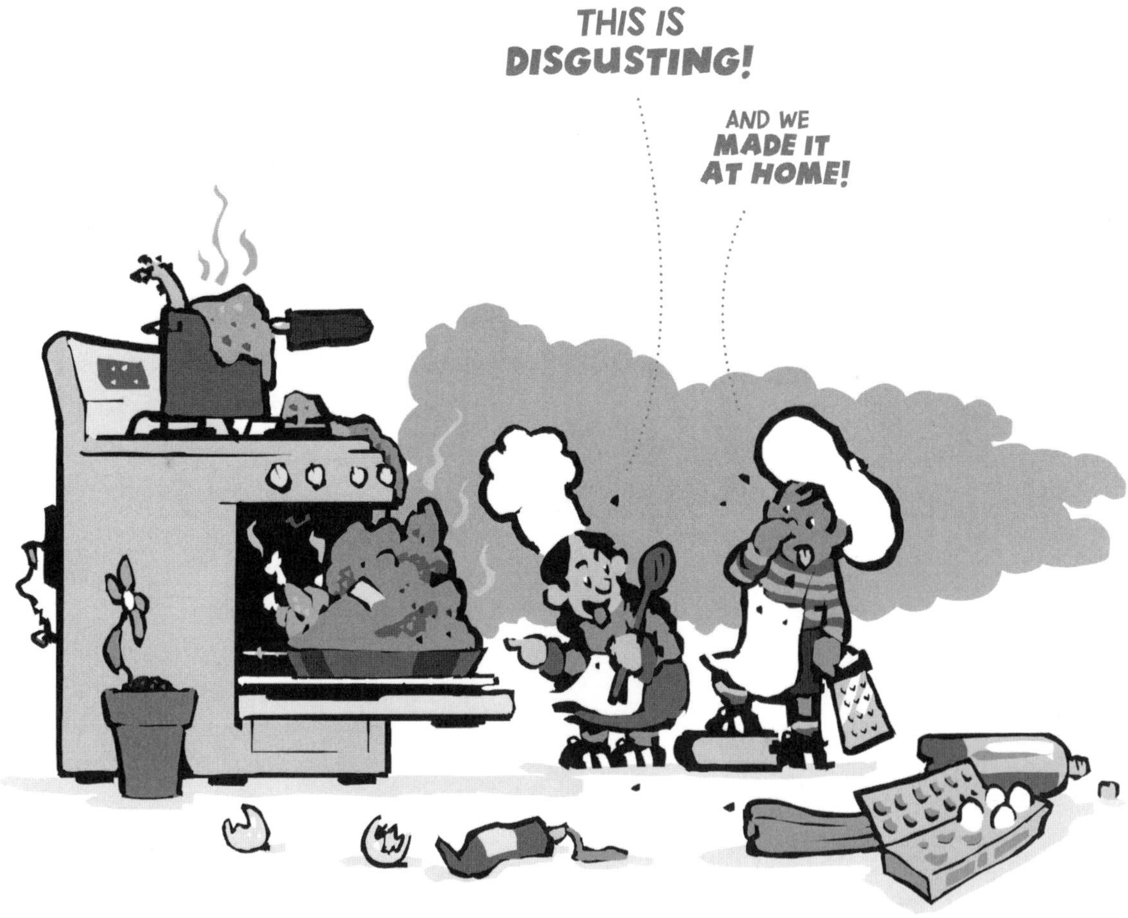
THIS IS **DISGUSTING!**
AND WE **MADE IT AT HOME!**

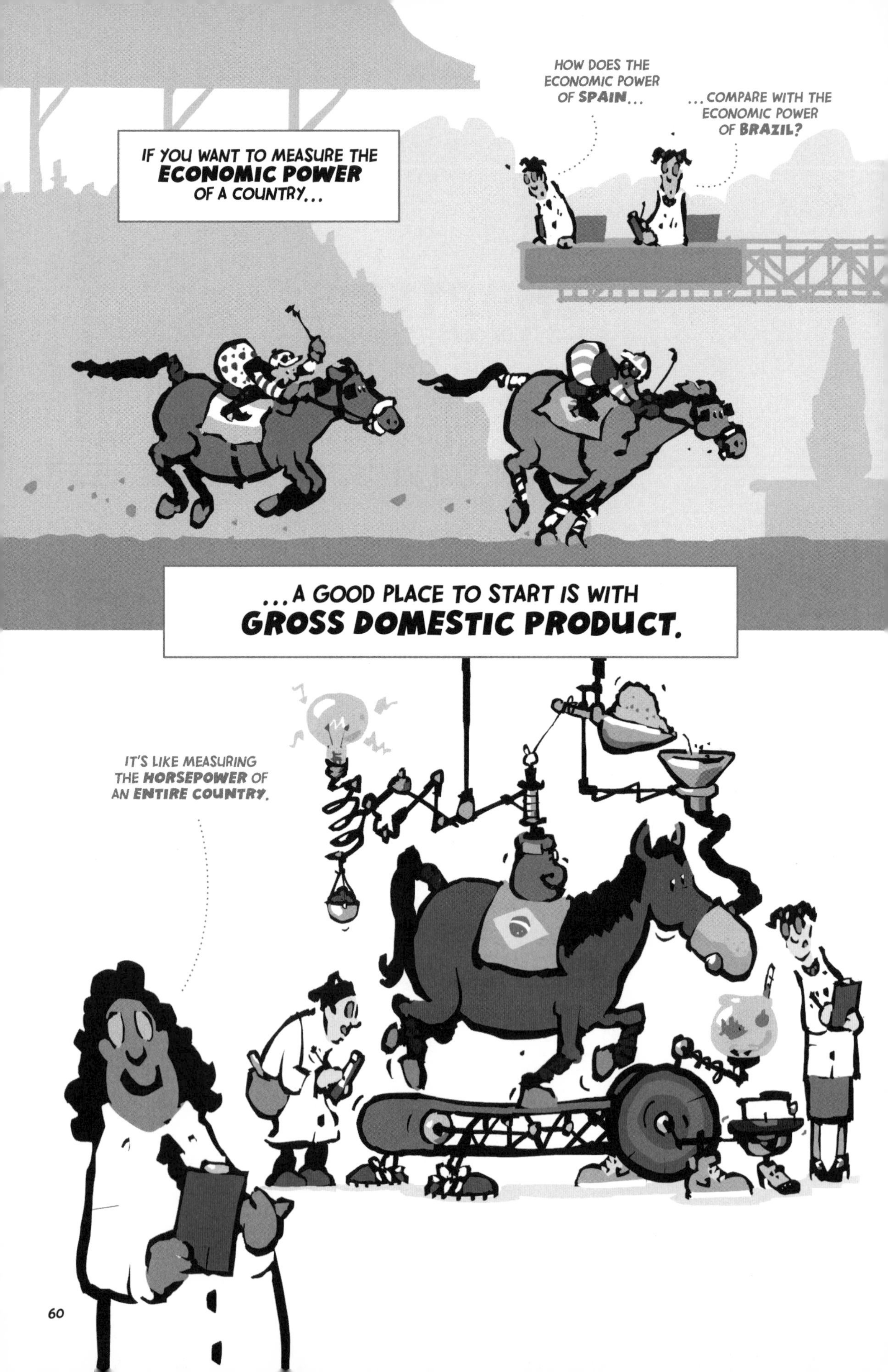
IF YOU WANT TO MEASURE THE ECONOMIC POWER OF A COUNTRY...
HOW DOES THE ECONOMIC POWER OF SPAIN...
...COMPARE WITH THE ECONOMIC POWER OF BRAZIL?
...A GOOD PLACE TO START IS WITH GROSS DOMESTIC PRODUCT.
IT'S LIKE MEASURING THE HORSEPOWER OF AN ENTIRE COUNTRY.

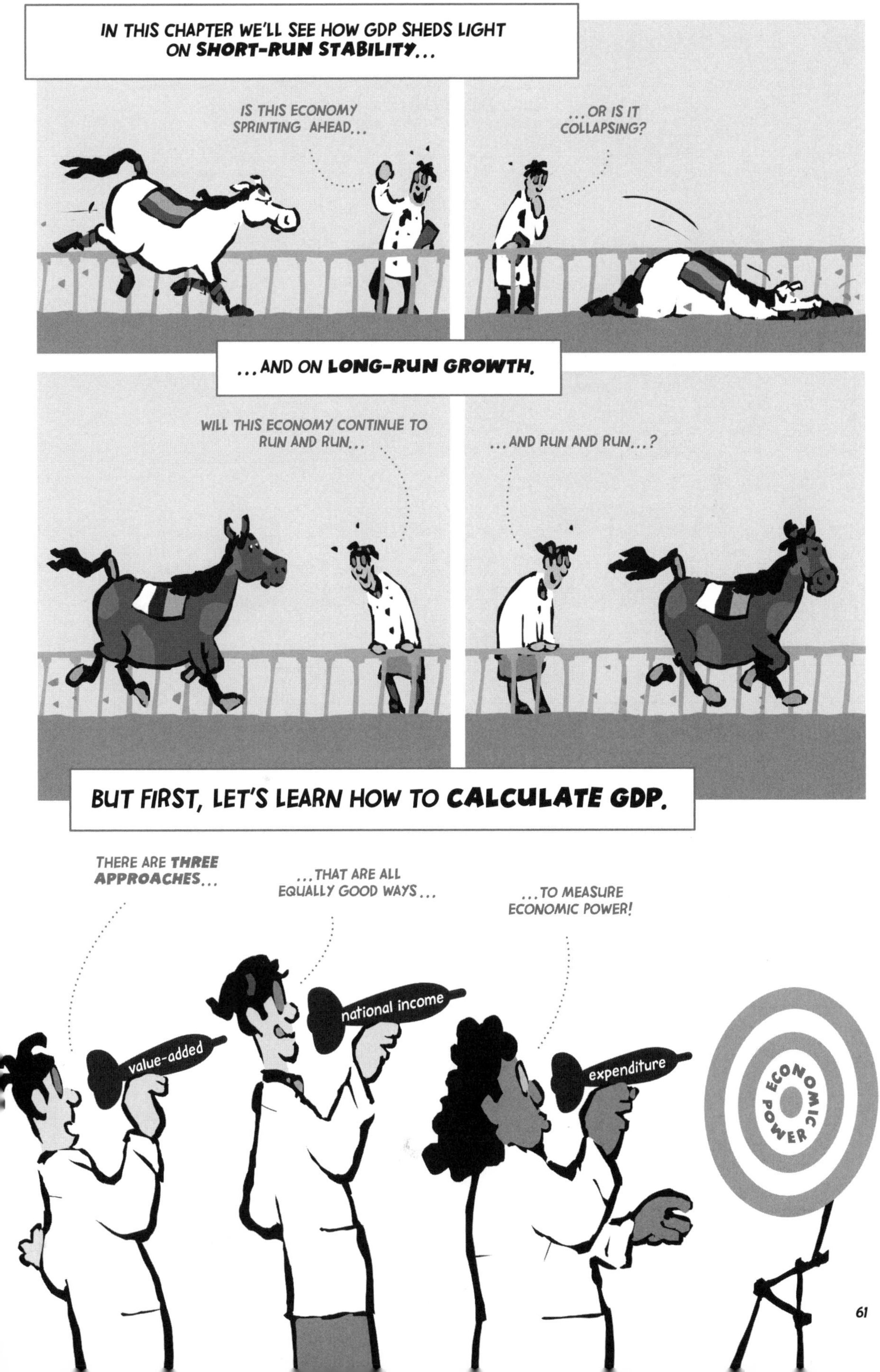
IN THIS CHAPTER WE'LL SEE HOW GDP SHEDS LIGHT ON SHORT-RUN STABILITY...
IS THIS ECONOMY SPRINTING AHEAD...
...OR IS IT COLLAPSING?
...AND ON LONG-RUN GROWTH.
WILL THIS ECONOMY CONTINUE TO RUN AND RUN...
...AND RUN AND RUN...?
BUT FIRST, LET'S LEARN HOW TO CALCULATE GDP.
THERE ARE THREE APPROACHES...
...THAT ARE ALL EQUALLY GOOD WAYS...
...TO MEASURE ECONOMIC POWER!
value-added
national income
expenditure
ECONOMIC POWER

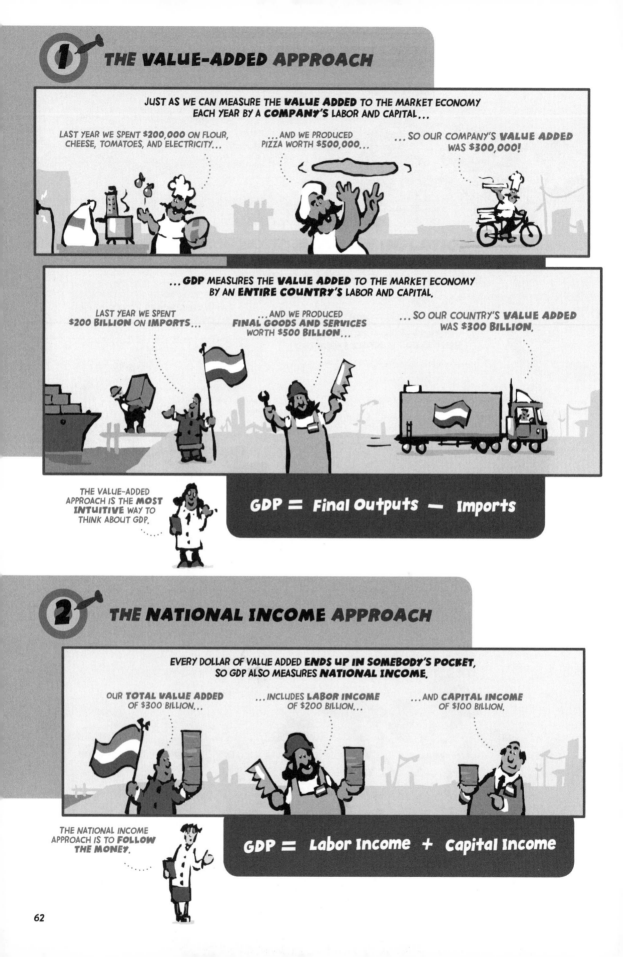

1 THE VALUE-ADDED APPROACH

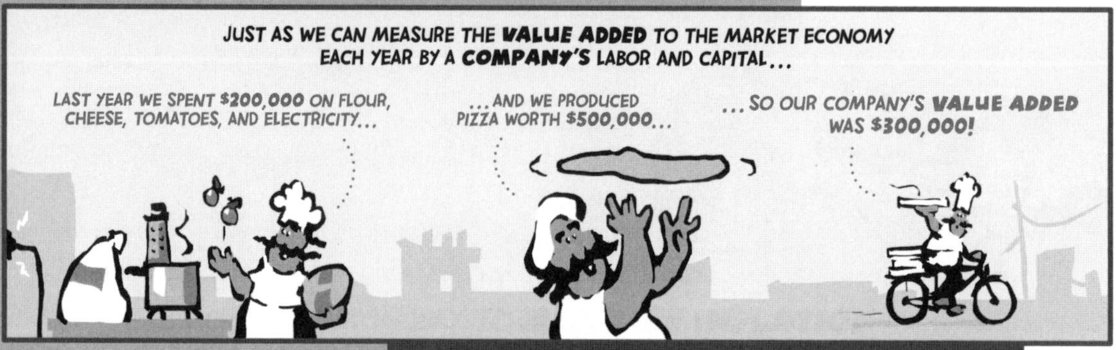
JUST AS WE CAN MEASURE THE VALUE ADDED TO THE MARKET ECONOMY EACH YEAR BY A COMPANY'S LABOR AND CAPITAL...
LAST YEAR WE SPENT $200,000 ON FLOUR, CHEESE, TOMATOES, AND ELECTRICITY...
...AND WE PRODUCED PIZZA WORTH $500,000...
...SO OUR COMPANY'S VALUE ADDED WAS $300,000!

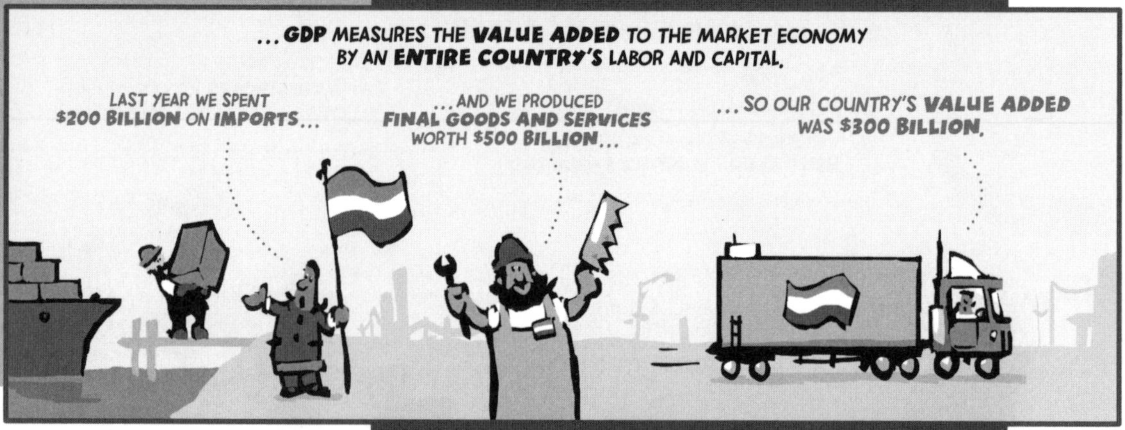
...GDP MEASURES THE VALUE ADDED TO THE MARKET ECONOMY BY AN ENTIRE COUNTRY'S LABOR AND CAPITAL.
LAST YEAR WE SPENT $200 BILLION ON IMPORTS...
...AND WE PRODUCED FINAL GOODS AND SERVICES WORTH $500 BILLION...
...SO OUR COUNTRY'S VALUE ADDED WAS $300 BILLION.

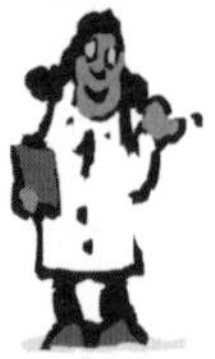
THE VALUE-ADDED APPROACH IS THE MOST INTUITIVE WAY TO THINK ABOUT GDP.

GDP = Final Outputs − Imports

2 THE NATIONAL INCOME APPROACH

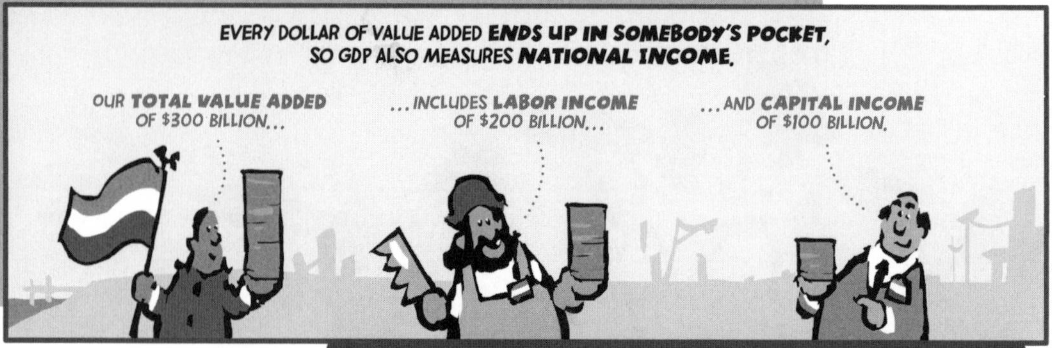
EVERY DOLLAR OF VALUE ADDED ENDS UP IN SOMEBODY'S POCKET, SO GDP ALSO MEASURES NATIONAL INCOME.
OUR TOTAL VALUE ADDED OF $300 BILLION...
...INCLUDES LABOR INCOME OF $200 BILLION...
...AND CAPITAL INCOME OF $100 BILLION.

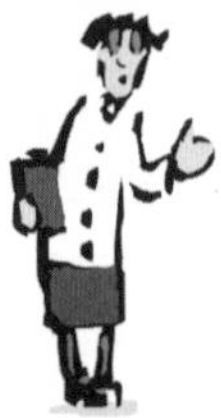
THE NATIONAL INCOME APPROACH IS TO FOLLOW THE MONEY.

GDP = Labor Income + Capital Income

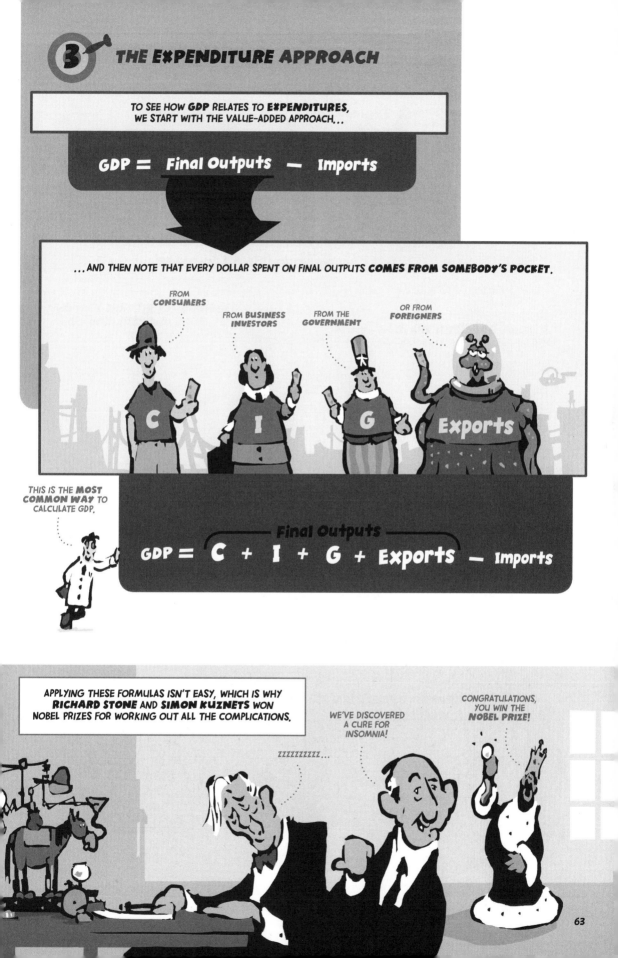

3 THE EXPENDITURE APPROACH

TO SEE HOW **GDP** RELATES TO **EXPENDITURES**, WE START WITH THE VALUE-ADDED APPROACH...

$$GDP = \text{Final Outputs} - \text{Imports}$$

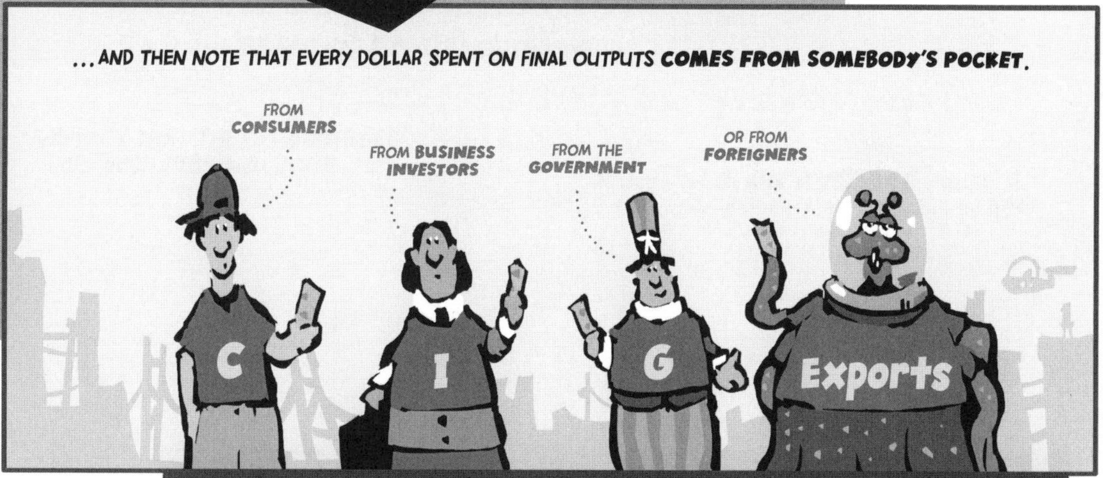
...AND THEN NOTE THAT EVERY DOLLAR SPENT ON FINAL OUTPUTS COMES FROM SOMEBODY'S POCKET.
FROM CONSUMERS
FROM BUSINESS INVESTORS
FROM THE GOVERNMENT
OR FROM FOREIGNERS
C
I
G
Exports

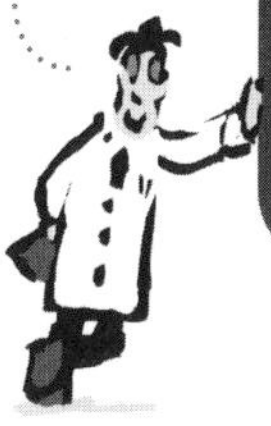
THIS IS THE MOST COMMON WAY TO CALCULATE GDP.

$$GDP = \overbrace{C + I + G + \text{Exports}}^{\text{Final Outputs}} - \text{Imports}$$

APPLYING THESE FORMULAS ISN'T EASY, WHICH IS WHY **RICHARD STONE** AND **SIMON KUZNETS** WON NOBEL PRIZES FOR WORKING OUT ALL THE COMPLICATIONS.

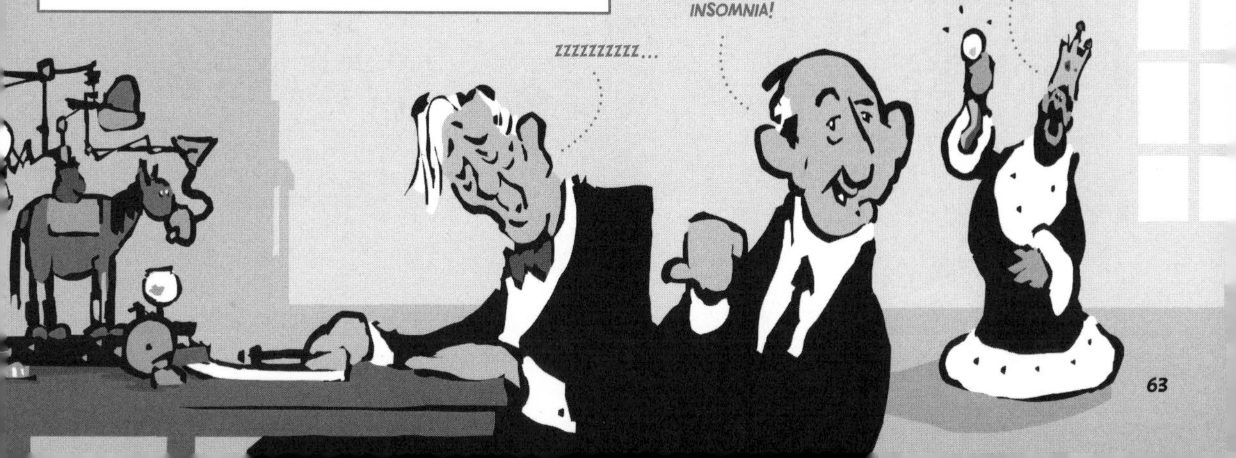
ZZZZZZZZZZ...
WE'VE DISCOVERED A CURE FOR INSOMNIA!
CONGRATULATIONS, YOU WIN THE NOBEL PRIZE!

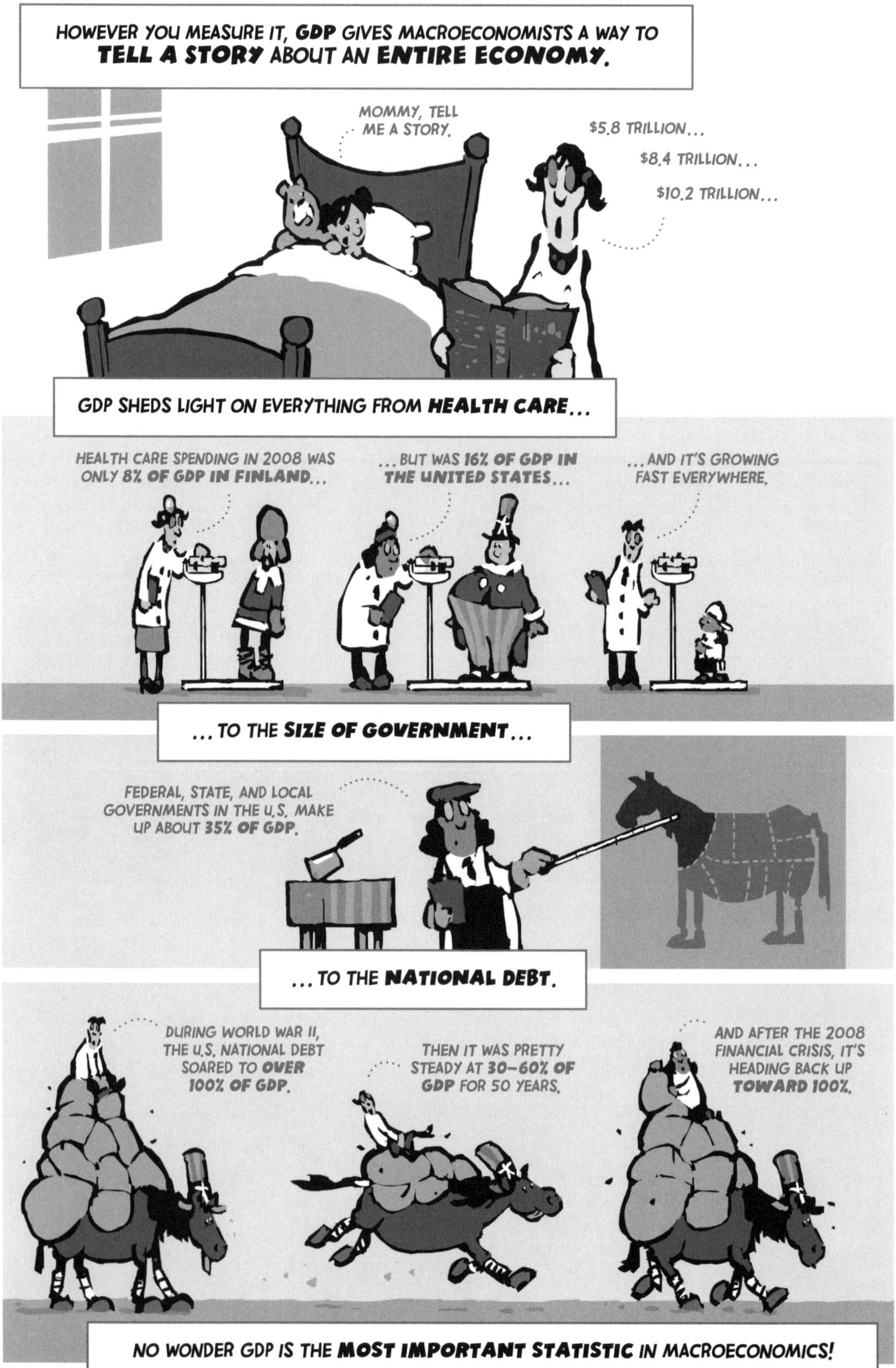
HOWEVER YOU MEASURE IT, GDP GIVES MACROECONOMISTS A WAY TO TELL A STORY ABOUT AN ENTIRE ECONOMY.
MOMMY, TELL ME A STORY.
$5.8 TRILLION...
$8.4 TRILLION...
$10.2 TRILLION...
NIPA
GDP SHEDS LIGHT ON EVERYTHING FROM HEALTH CARE...
HEALTH CARE SPENDING IN 2008 WAS ONLY 8% OF GDP IN FINLAND...
...BUT WAS 16% OF GDP IN THE UNITED STATES...
...AND IT'S GROWING FAST EVERYWHERE.
...TO THE SIZE OF GOVERNMENT...
FEDERAL, STATE, AND LOCAL GOVERNMENTS IN THE U.S. MAKE UP ABOUT 35% OF GDP.
...TO THE NATIONAL DEBT.
DURING WORLD WAR II, THE U.S. NATIONAL DEBT SOARED TO OVER 100% OF GDP.
THEN IT WAS PRETTY STEADY AT 30–60% OF GDP FOR 50 YEARS.
AND AFTER THE 2008 FINANCIAL CRISIS, IT'S HEADING BACK UP TOWARD 100%.
NO WONDER GDP IS THE MOST IMPORTANT STATISTIC IN MACROECONOMICS!

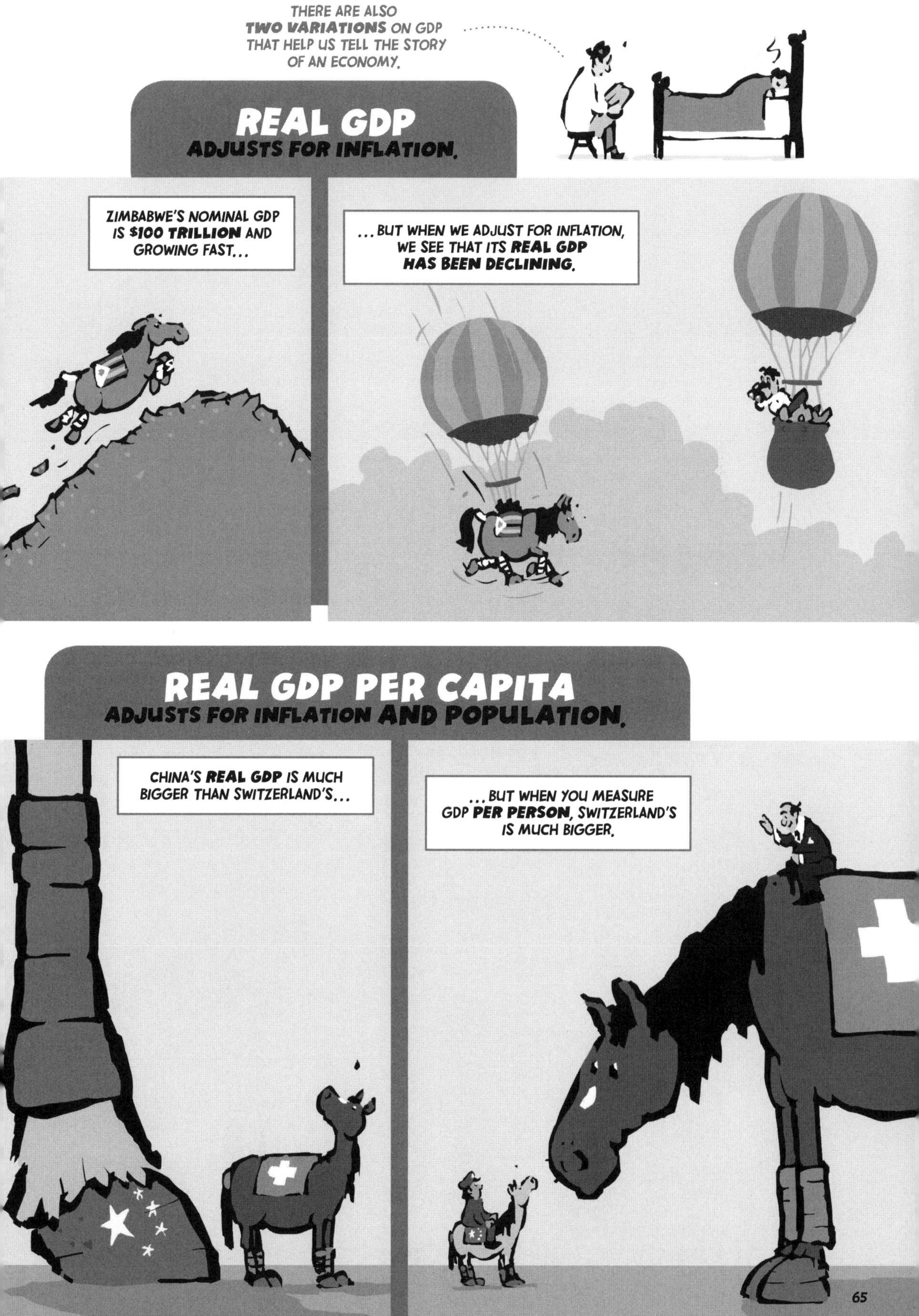
THERE ARE ALSO **TWO VARIATIONS** ON GDP THAT HELP US TELL THE STORY OF AN ECONOMY.
REAL GDP
ADJUSTS FOR INFLATION.
ZIMBABWE'S NOMINAL GDP IS **$100 TRILLION** AND GROWING FAST...
...BUT WHEN WE ADJUST FOR INFLATION, WE SEE THAT ITS **REAL GDP HAS BEEN DECLINING.**
REAL GDP PER CAPITA
ADJUSTS FOR INFLATION AND POPULATION.
CHINA'S **REAL GDP** IS MUCH BIGGER THAN SWITZERLAND'S...
...BUT WHEN YOU MEASURE GDP **PER PERSON**, SWITZERLAND'S IS MUCH BIGGER.

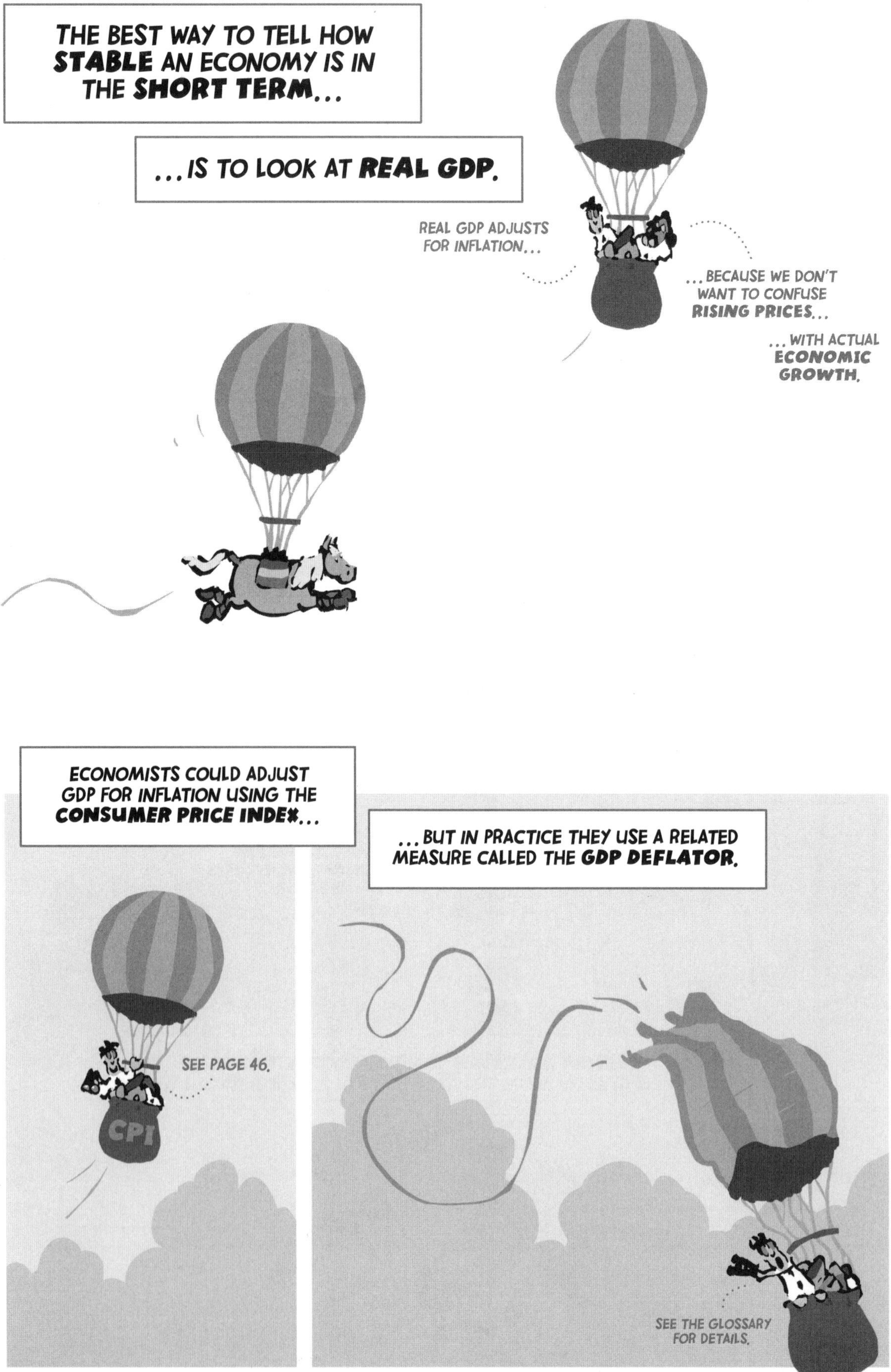
THE BEST WAY TO TELL HOW **STABLE** AN ECONOMY IS IN THE **SHORT TERM**...
...IS TO LOOK AT **REAL GDP**.
REAL GDP ADJUSTS FOR INFLATION...
...BECAUSE WE DON'T WANT TO CONFUSE **RISING PRICES**...
...WITH ACTUAL **ECONOMIC GROWTH**.
ECONOMISTS COULD ADJUST GDP FOR INFLATION USING THE **CONSUMER PRICE INDEX**...
SEE PAGE 46.
CPI
...BUT IN PRACTICE THEY USE A RELATED MEASURE CALLED THE **GDP DEFLATOR**.
SEE THE GLOSSARY FOR DETAILS.

ONCE WE ADJUST FOR INFLATION, **RECESSIONS** SHOW UP AS **DECLINES IN REAL GDP...**

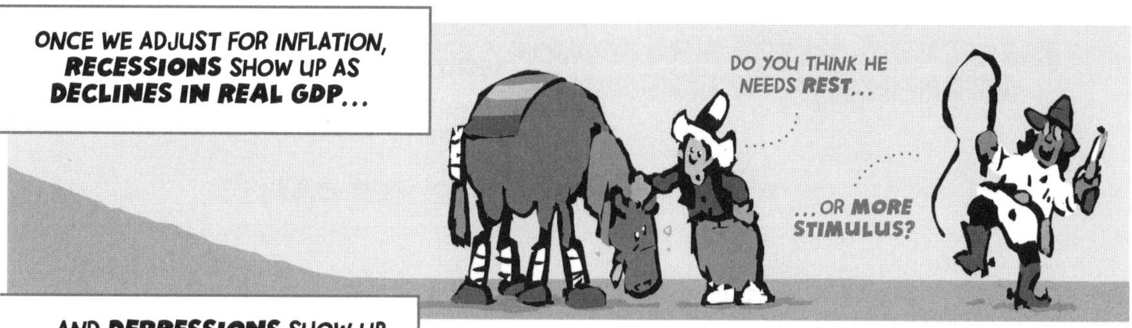
DO YOU THINK HE NEEDS **REST...**
...OR **MORE STIMULUS?**

...AND **DEPRESSIONS** SHOW UP AS **STEEP AND PROLONGED DECLINES IN REAL GDP.**

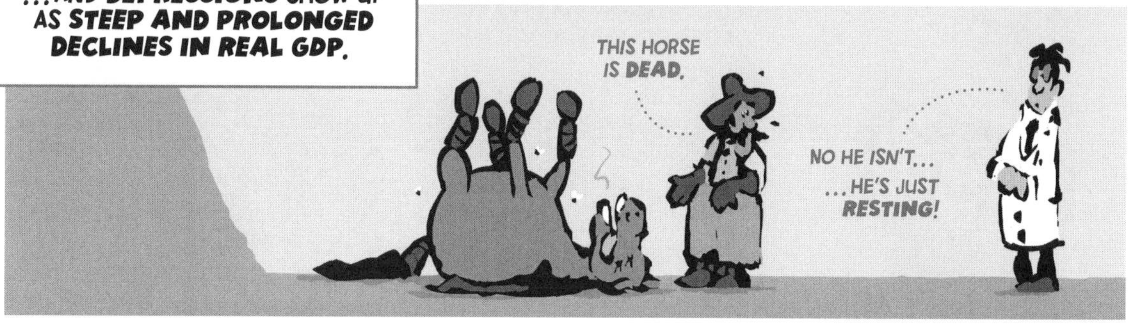
THIS HORSE IS **DEAD.**
NO HE ISN'T...
...HE'S JUST **RESTING!**

SINCE THE GREAT DEPRESSION, THE U.S. ECONOMY HAS GONE THROUGH THE UPS AND DOWNS OF THE **BUSINESS CYCLE** ABOUT A DOZEN TIMES.

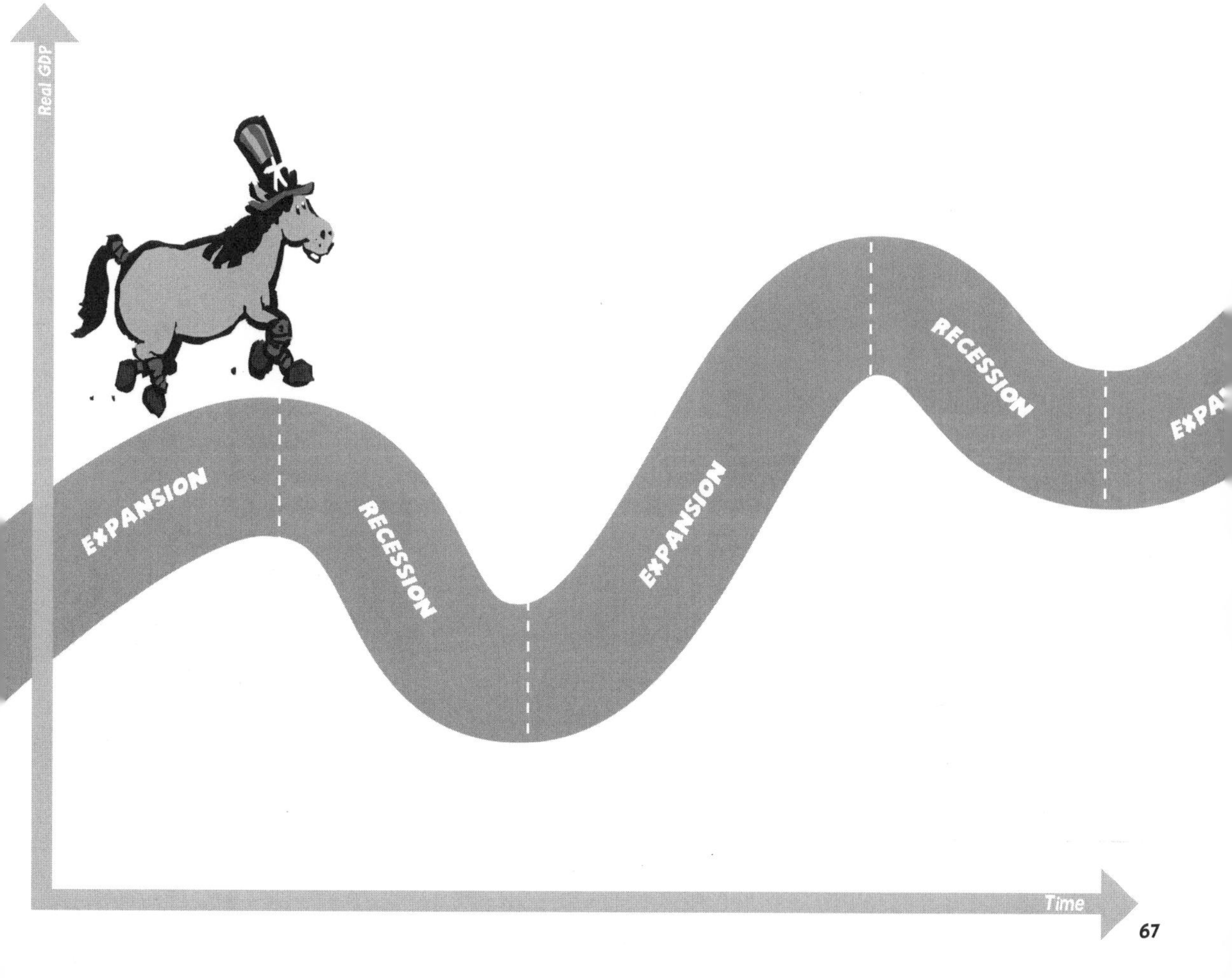
Real GDP
EXPANSION
RECESSION
EXPANSION
RECESSION
Time

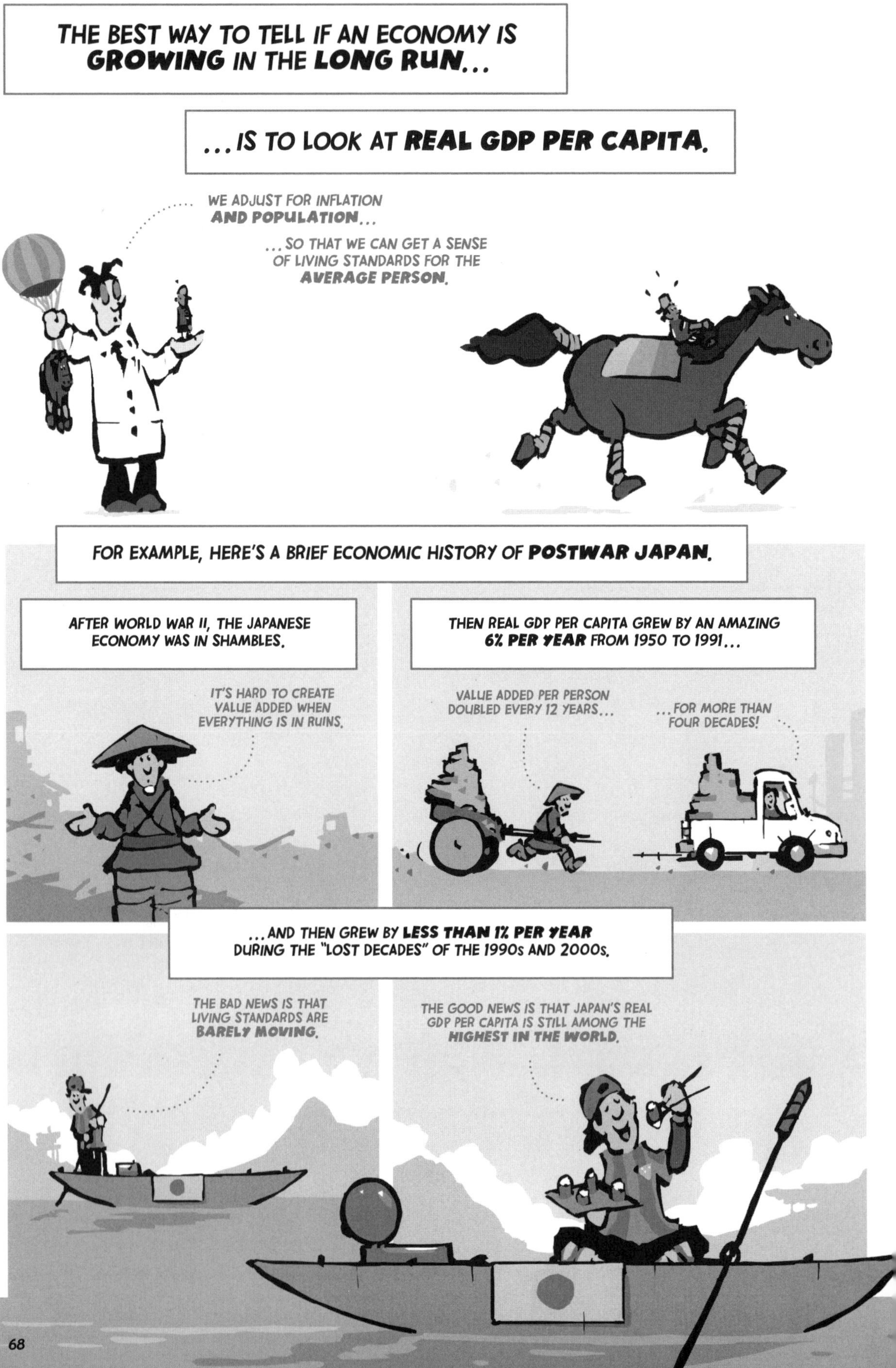
THE BEST WAY TO TELL IF AN ECONOMY IS **GROWING** IN THE **LONG RUN**...
...IS TO LOOK AT **REAL GDP PER CAPITA.**
WE ADJUST FOR INFLATION **AND POPULATION**...
...SO THAT WE CAN GET A SENSE OF LIVING STANDARDS FOR THE **AVERAGE PERSON.**
FOR EXAMPLE, HERE'S A BRIEF ECONOMIC HISTORY OF **POSTWAR JAPAN.**
AFTER WORLD WAR II, THE JAPANESE ECONOMY WAS IN SHAMBLES.
IT'S HARD TO CREATE VALUE ADDED WHEN EVERYTHING IS IN RUINS.
THEN REAL GDP PER CAPITA GREW BY AN AMAZING **6% PER YEAR** FROM 1950 TO 1991...
VALUE ADDED PER PERSON DOUBLED EVERY 12 YEARS...
...FOR MORE THAN FOUR DECADES!
...AND THEN GREW BY **LESS THAN 1% PER YEAR** DURING THE "LOST DECADES" OF THE 1990s AND 2000s.
THE BAD NEWS IS THAT LIVING STANDARDS ARE **BARELY MOVING.**
THE GOOD NEWS IS THAT JAPAN'S REAL GDP PER CAPITA IS STILL AMONG THE **HIGHEST IN THE WORLD.**

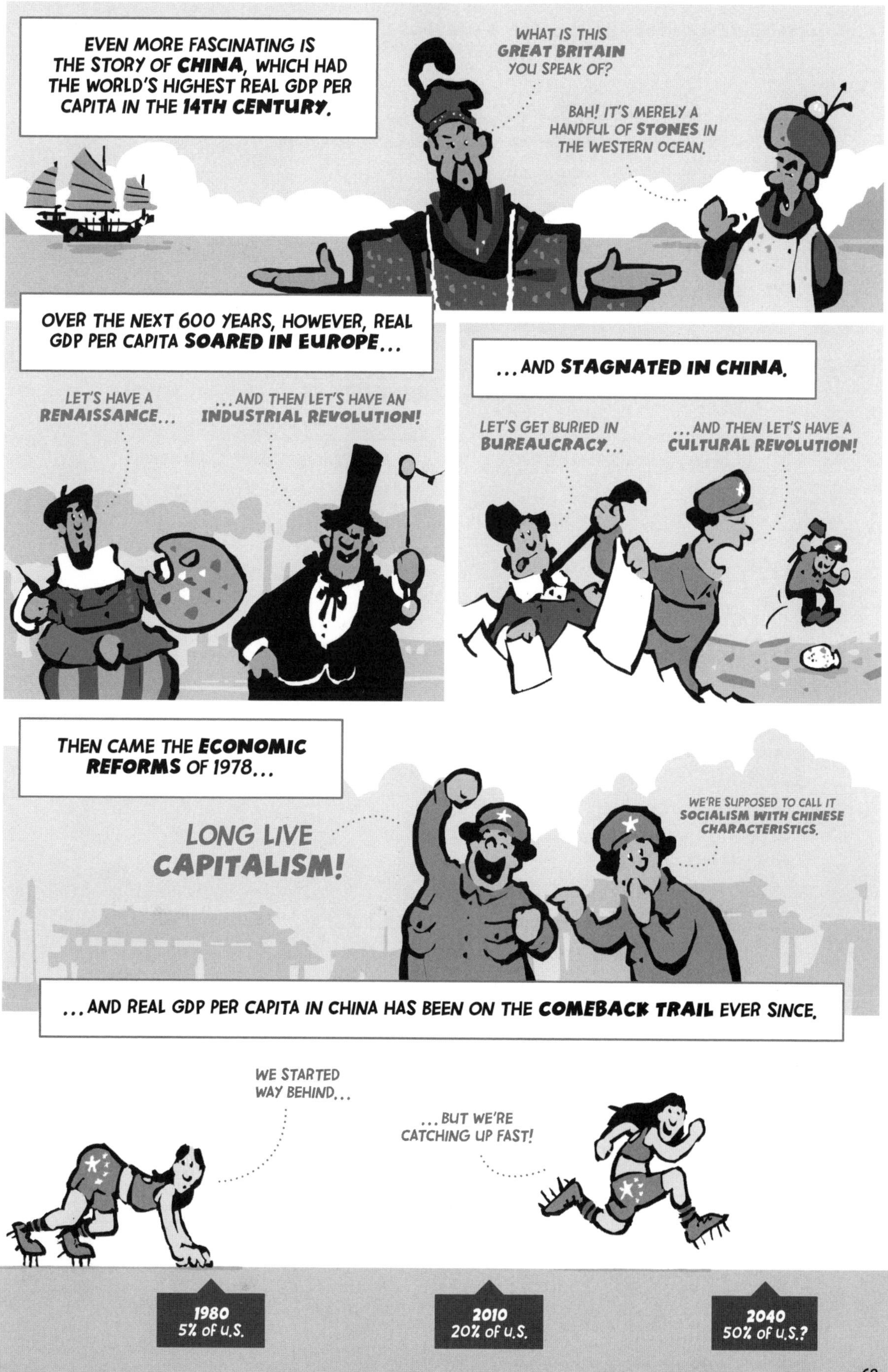
EVEN MORE FASCINATING IS THE STORY OF **CHINA**, WHICH HAD THE WORLD'S HIGHEST REAL GDP PER CAPITA IN THE **14TH CENTURY**.
WHAT IS THIS **GREAT BRITAIN** YOU SPEAK OF?
BAH! IT'S MERELY A HANDFUL OF **STONES** IN THE WESTERN OCEAN.
OVER THE NEXT 600 YEARS, HOWEVER, REAL GDP PER CAPITA **SOARED IN EUROPE**...
LET'S HAVE A **RENAISSANCE**...
...AND THEN LET'S HAVE AN **INDUSTRIAL REVOLUTION!**
...AND **STAGNATED IN CHINA**.
LET'S GET BURIED IN **BUREAUCRACY**...
...AND THEN LET'S HAVE A **CULTURAL REVOLUTION!**
THEN CAME THE **ECONOMIC REFORMS** OF 1978...
LONG LIVE **CAPITALISM!**
WE'RE SUPPOSED TO CALL IT **SOCIALISM WITH CHINESE CHARACTERISTICS**.
...AND REAL GDP PER CAPITA IN CHINA HAS BEEN ON THE **COMEBACK TRAIL** EVER SINCE.
WE STARTED WAY BEHIND...
...BUT WE'RE CATCHING UP FAST!
1980 5% of U.S.
2010 20% of U.S.
2040 50% of U.S.?

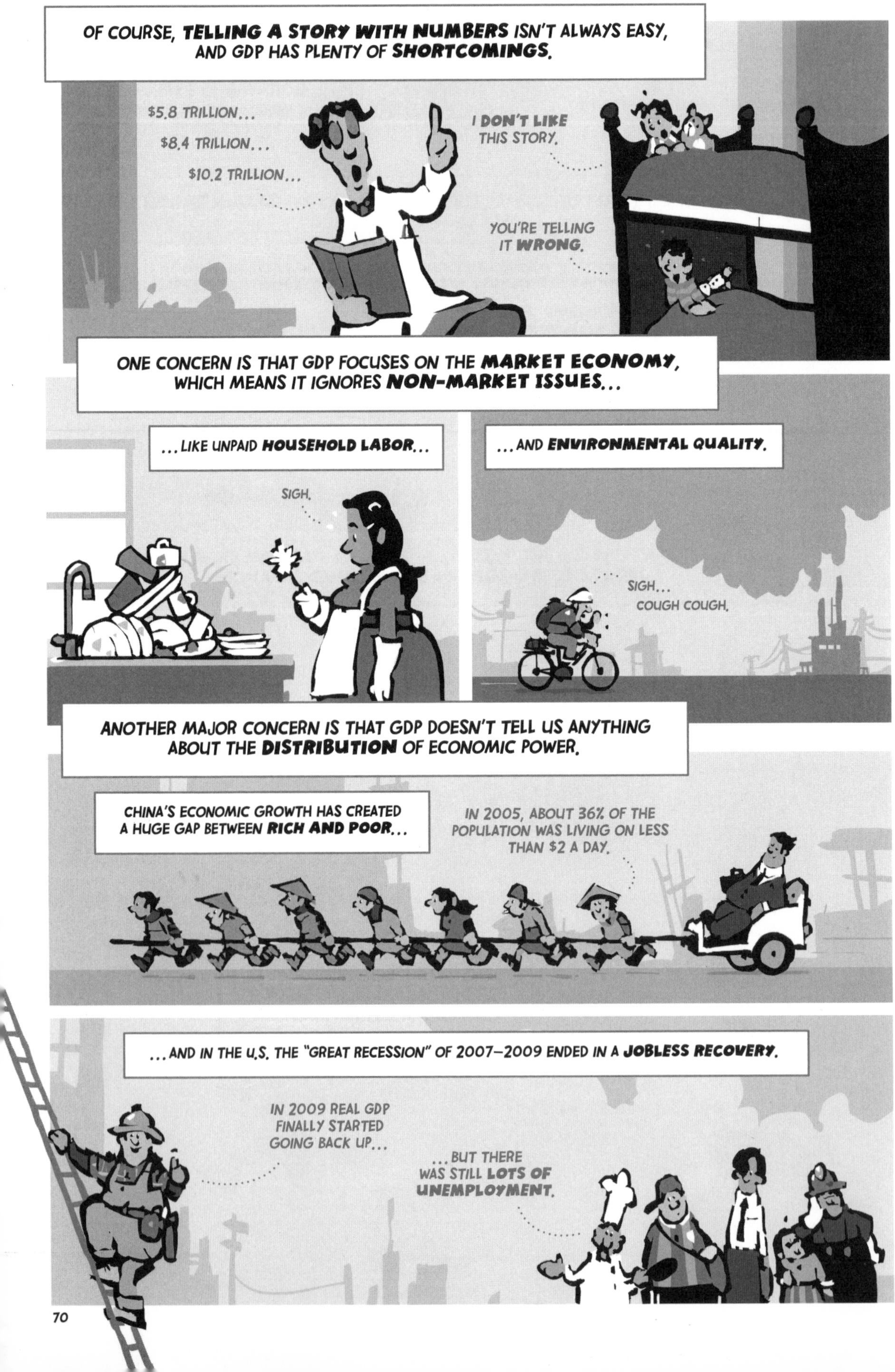
OF COURSE, TELLING A STORY WITH NUMBERS ISN'T ALWAYS EASY, AND GDP HAS PLENTY OF SHORTCOMINGS.
$5.8 TRILLION...
$8.4 TRILLION...
$10.2 TRILLION...
I DON'T LIKE THIS STORY.
YOU'RE TELLING IT WRONG.
ONE CONCERN IS THAT GDP FOCUSES ON THE MARKET ECONOMY, WHICH MEANS IT IGNORES NON-MARKET ISSUES...
...LIKE UNPAID HOUSEHOLD LABOR...
SIGH.
...AND ENVIRONMENTAL QUALITY.
SIGH... COUGH COUGH.
ANOTHER MAJOR CONCERN IS THAT GDP DOESN'T TELL US ANYTHING ABOUT THE DISTRIBUTION OF ECONOMIC POWER.
CHINA'S ECONOMIC GROWTH HAS CREATED A HUGE GAP BETWEEN RICH AND POOR...
IN 2005, ABOUT 36% OF THE POPULATION WAS LIVING ON LESS THAN $2 A DAY.
...AND IN THE U.S. THE "GREAT RECESSION" OF 2007–2009 ENDED IN A JOBLESS RECOVERY.
IN 2009 REAL GDP FINALLY STARTED GOING BACK UP...
...BUT THERE WAS STILL LOTS OF UNEMPLOYMENT.

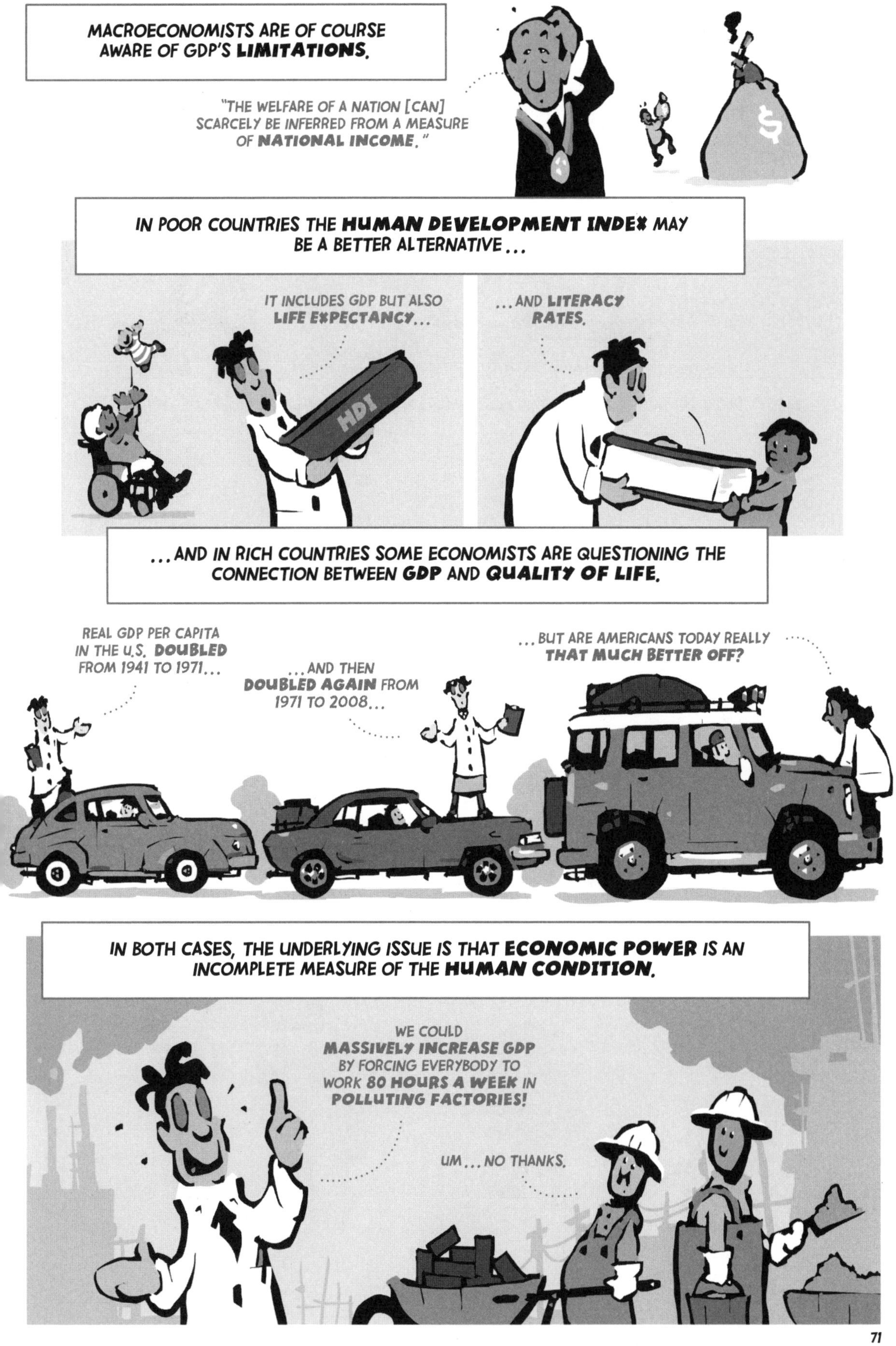
MACROECONOMISTS ARE OF COURSE AWARE OF GDP'S LIMITATIONS.
"THE WELFARE OF A NATION [CAN] SCARCELY BE INFERRED FROM A MEASURE OF NATIONAL INCOME."
IN POOR COUNTRIES THE HUMAN DEVELOPMENT INDEX MAY BE A BETTER ALTERNATIVE...
IT INCLUDES GDP BUT ALSO LIFE EXPECTANCY...
HDI
...AND LITERACY RATES.
...AND IN RICH COUNTRIES SOME ECONOMISTS ARE QUESTIONING THE CONNECTION BETWEEN GDP AND QUALITY OF LIFE.
REAL GDP PER CAPITA IN THE U.S. DOUBLED FROM 1941 TO 1971...
...AND THEN DOUBLED AGAIN FROM 1971 TO 2008...
...BUT ARE AMERICANS TODAY REALLY THAT MUCH BETTER OFF?
IN BOTH CASES, THE UNDERLYING ISSUE IS THAT ECONOMIC POWER IS AN INCOMPLETE MEASURE OF THE HUMAN CONDITION.
WE COULD MASSIVELY INCREASE GDP BY FORCING EVERYBODY TO WORK 80 HOURS A WEEK IN POLLUTING FACTORIES!
UM...NO THANKS.

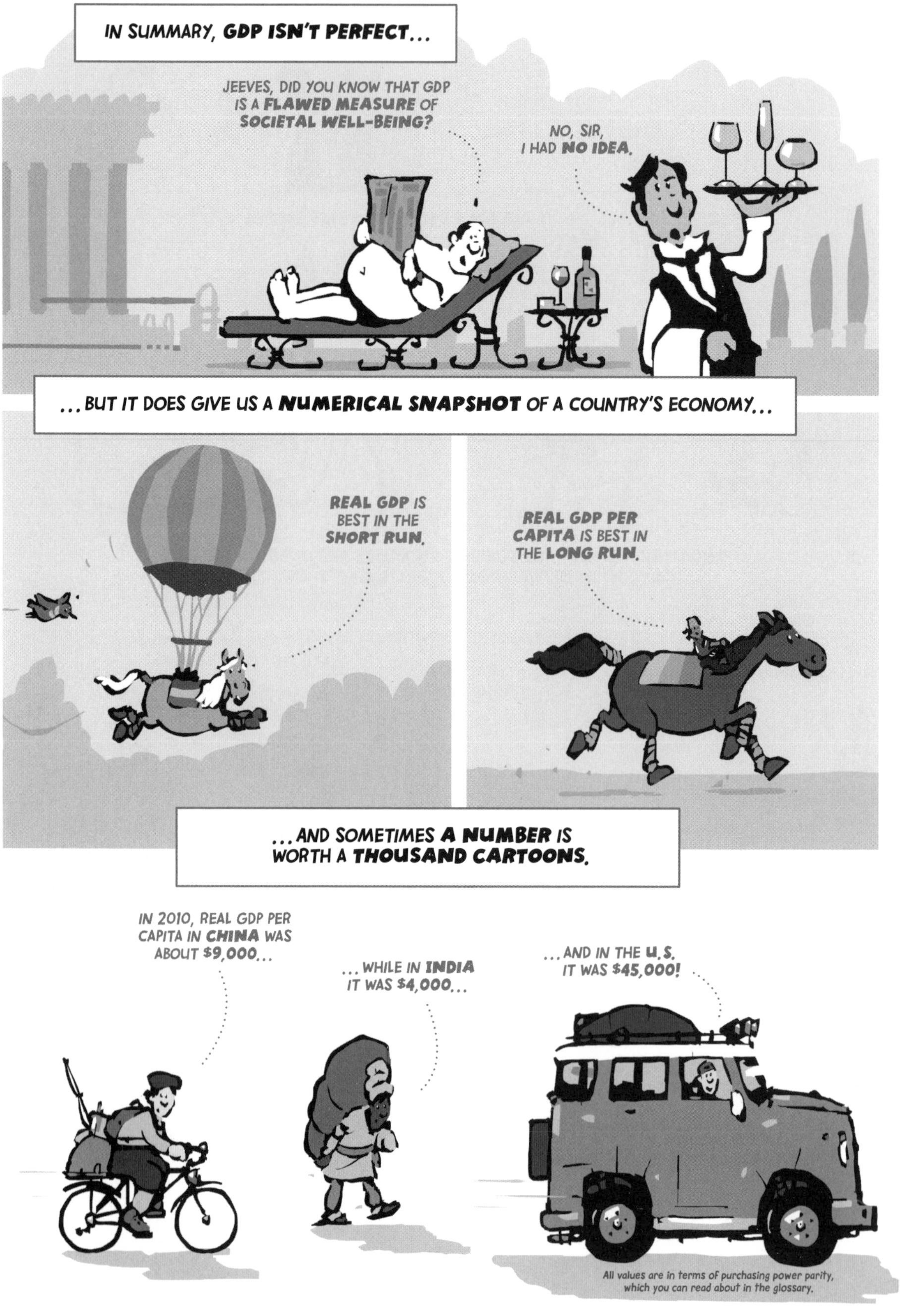
IN SUMMARY, GDP ISN'T PERFECT...
JEEVES, DID YOU KNOW THAT GDP IS A FLAWED MEASURE OF SOCIETAL WELL-BEING?
NO, SIR, I HAD NO IDEA.
...BUT IT DOES GIVE US A NUMERICAL SNAPSHOT OF A COUNTRY'S ECONOMY...
REAL GDP IS BEST IN THE SHORT RUN.
REAL GDP PER CAPITA IS BEST IN THE LONG RUN.
...AND SOMETIMES A NUMBER IS WORTH A THOUSAND CARTOONS.
IN 2010, REAL GDP PER CAPITA IN CHINA WAS ABOUT $9,000...
...WHILE IN INDIA IT WAS $4,000...
...AND IN THE U.S. IT WAS $45,000!
All values are in terms of purchasing power parity, which you can read about in the glossary.

CHAPTER 6
THE ROLE OF GOVERNMENT

HOLD ON...
...WE NEED TO WAIT FOR UNCLE SAM!

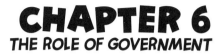

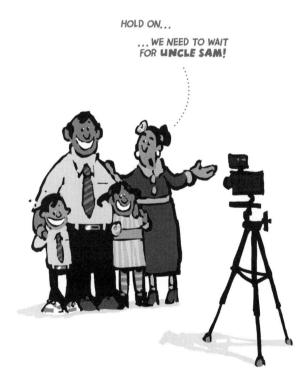

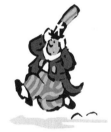

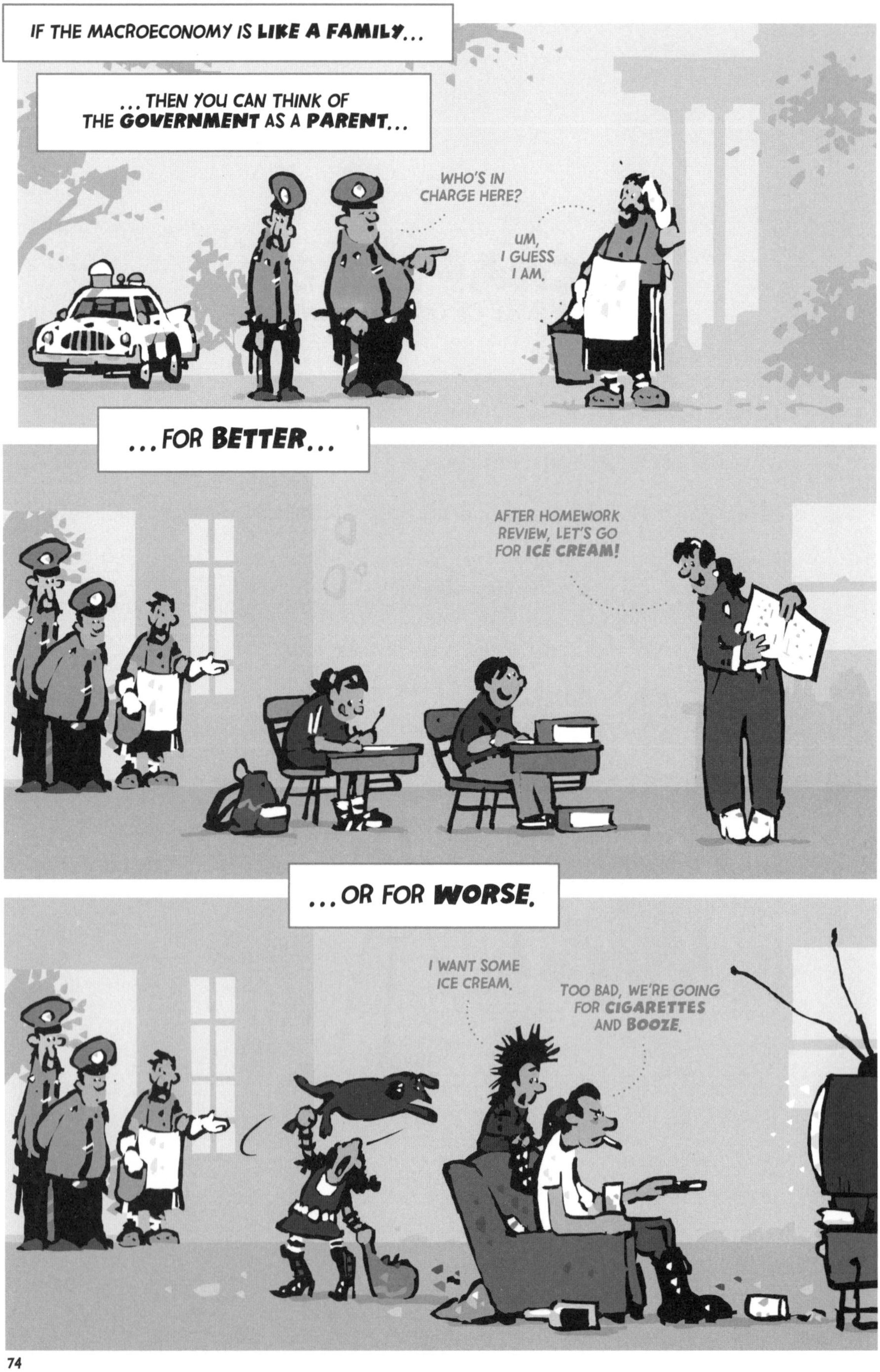
IF THE MACROECONOMY IS **LIKE A FAMILY**...
...THEN YOU CAN THINK OF THE **GOVERNMENT** AS A **PARENT**...
WHO'S IN CHARGE HERE?
UM, I GUESS I AM.
...FOR **BETTER**...
AFTER HOMEWORK REVIEW, LET'S GO FOR **ICE CREAM!**
...OR FOR **WORSE.**
I WANT SOME ICE CREAM.
TOO BAD, WE'RE GOING FOR **CIGARETTES** AND **BOOZE.**

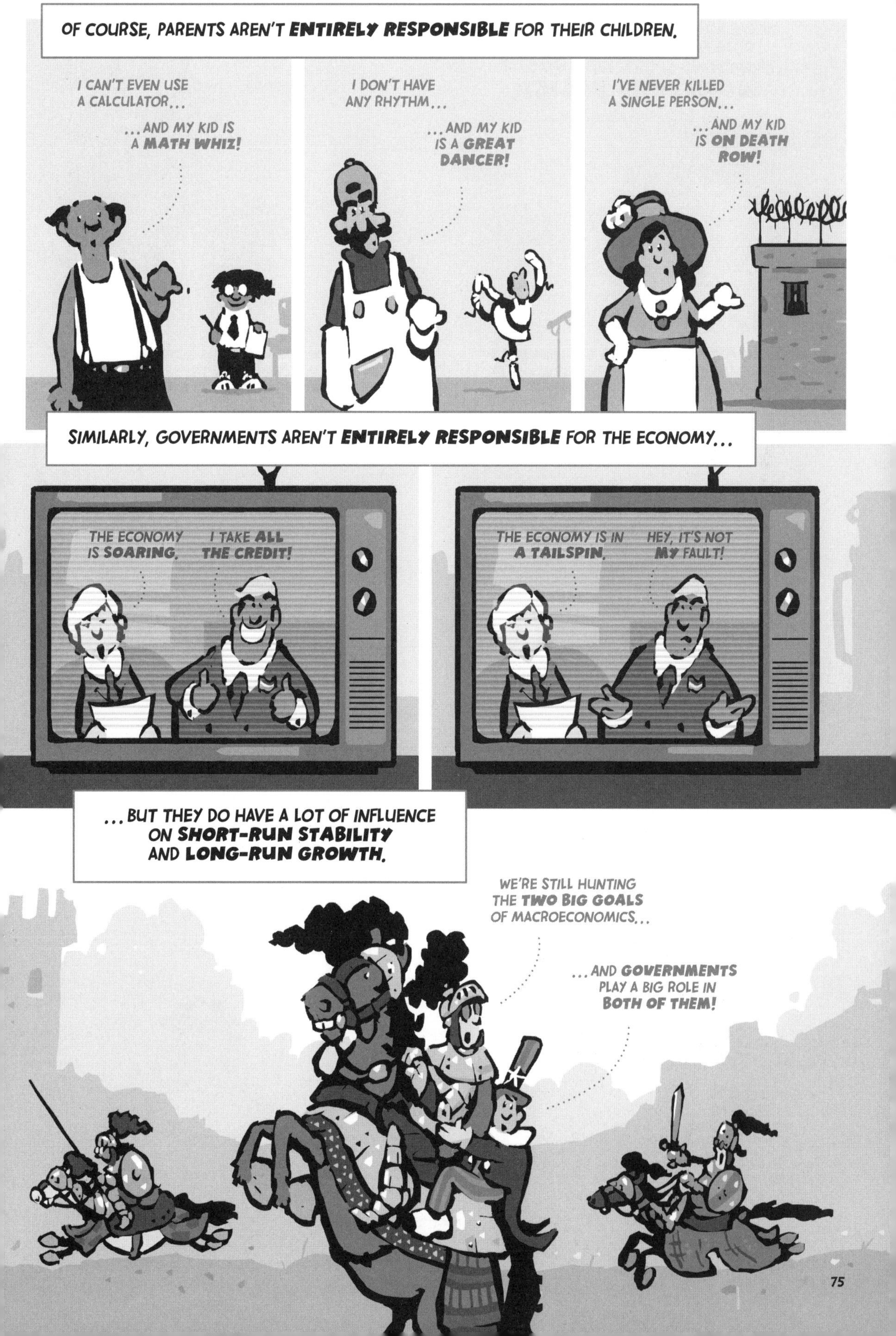
OF COURSE, PARENTS AREN'T ENTIRELY RESPONSIBLE FOR THEIR CHILDREN.
I CAN'T EVEN USE A CALCULATOR...
...AND MY KID IS A MATH WHIZ!
I DON'T HAVE ANY RHYTHM...
...AND MY KID IS A GREAT DANCER!
I'VE NEVER KILLED A SINGLE PERSON...
...AND MY KID IS ON DEATH ROW!
SIMILARLY, GOVERNMENTS AREN'T ENTIRELY RESPONSIBLE FOR THE ECONOMY...
THE ECONOMY IS SOARING.
I TAKE ALL THE CREDIT!
THE ECONOMY IS IN A TAILSPIN.
HEY, IT'S NOT MY FAULT!
...BUT THEY DO HAVE A LOT OF INFLUENCE ON SHORT-RUN STABILITY AND LONG-RUN GROWTH.
WE'RE STILL HUNTING THE TWO BIG GOALS OF MACROECONOMICS...
...AND GOVERNMENTS PLAY A BIG ROLE IN BOTH OF THEM!

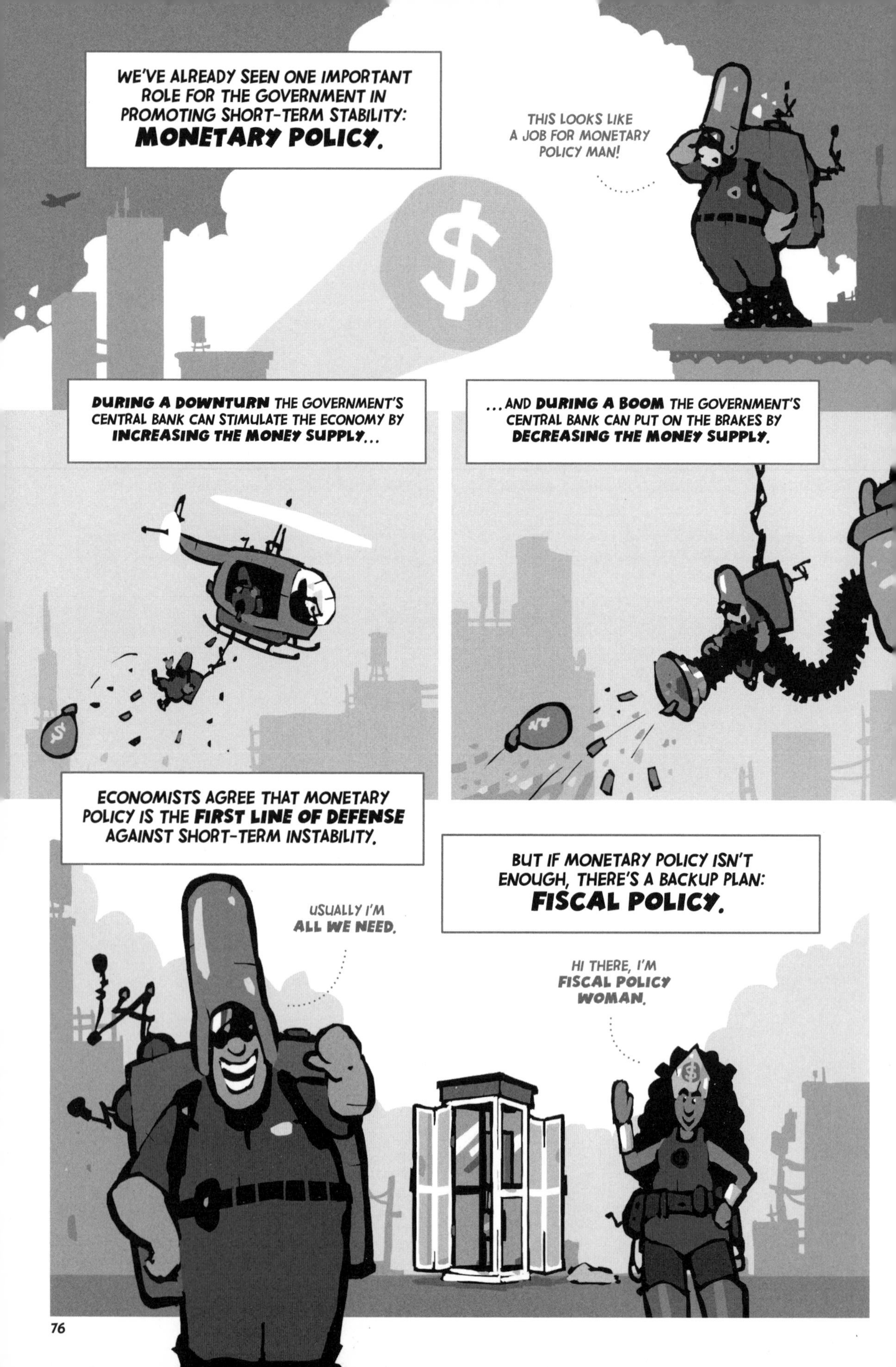
WE'VE ALREADY SEEN ONE IMPORTANT ROLE FOR THE GOVERNMENT IN PROMOTING SHORT-TERM STABILITY: MONETARY POLICY.
THIS LOOKS LIKE A JOB FOR MONETARY POLICY MAN!
DURING A DOWNTURN THE GOVERNMENT'S CENTRAL BANK CAN STIMULATE THE ECONOMY BY INCREASING THE MONEY SUPPLY...
...AND DURING A BOOM THE GOVERNMENT'S CENTRAL BANK CAN PUT ON THE BRAKES BY DECREASING THE MONEY SUPPLY.
ECONOMISTS AGREE THAT MONETARY POLICY IS THE FIRST LINE OF DEFENSE AGAINST SHORT-TERM INSTABILITY.
USUALLY I'M ALL WE NEED.
BUT IF MONETARY POLICY ISN'T ENOUGH, THERE'S A BACKUP PLAN: FISCAL POLICY.
HI THERE, I'M FISCAL POLICY WOMAN.

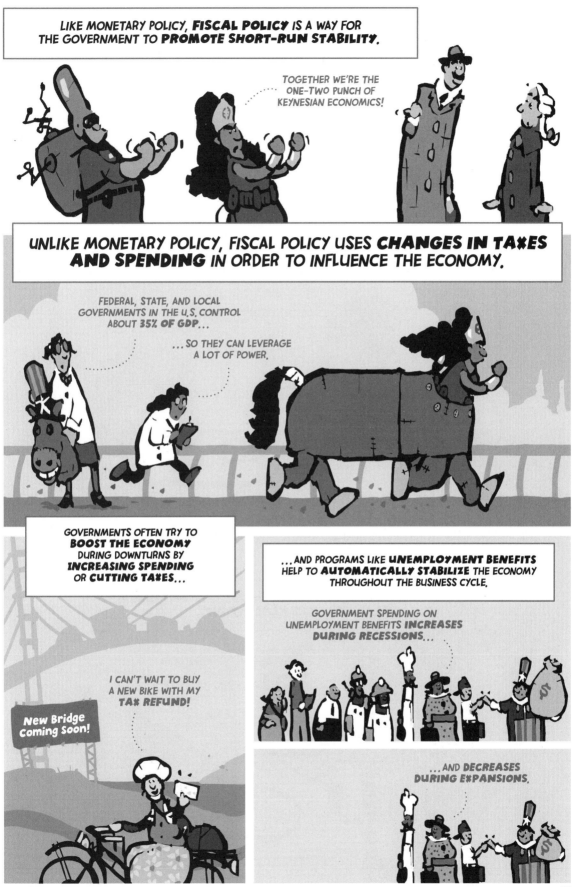

LIKE MONETARY POLICY, **FISCAL POLICY** IS A WAY FOR THE GOVERNMENT TO **PROMOTE SHORT-RUN STABILITY.**

TOGETHER WE'RE THE ONE-TWO PUNCH OF KEYNESIAN ECONOMICS!

UNLIKE MONETARY POLICY, FISCAL POLICY USES **CHANGES IN TAXES AND SPENDING** IN ORDER TO INFLUENCE THE ECONOMY.

FEDERAL, STATE, AND LOCAL GOVERNMENTS IN THE U.S. CONTROL ABOUT **35% OF GDP**...

...SO THEY CAN LEVERAGE A LOT OF POWER.

GOVERNMENTS OFTEN TRY TO **BOOST THE ECONOMY** DURING DOWNTURNS BY **INCREASING SPENDING** OR **CUTTING TAXES**...

...AND PROGRAMS LIKE **UNEMPLOYMENT BENEFITS** HELP TO **AUTOMATICALLY STABILIZE** THE ECONOMY THROUGHOUT THE BUSINESS CYCLE.

GOVERNMENT SPENDING ON UNEMPLOYMENT BENEFITS **INCREASES DURING RECESSIONS**...

I CAN'T WAIT TO BUY A NEW BIKE WITH MY **TAX REFUND!**

New Bridge Coming Soon!

...AND **DECREASES DURING EXPANSIONS.**

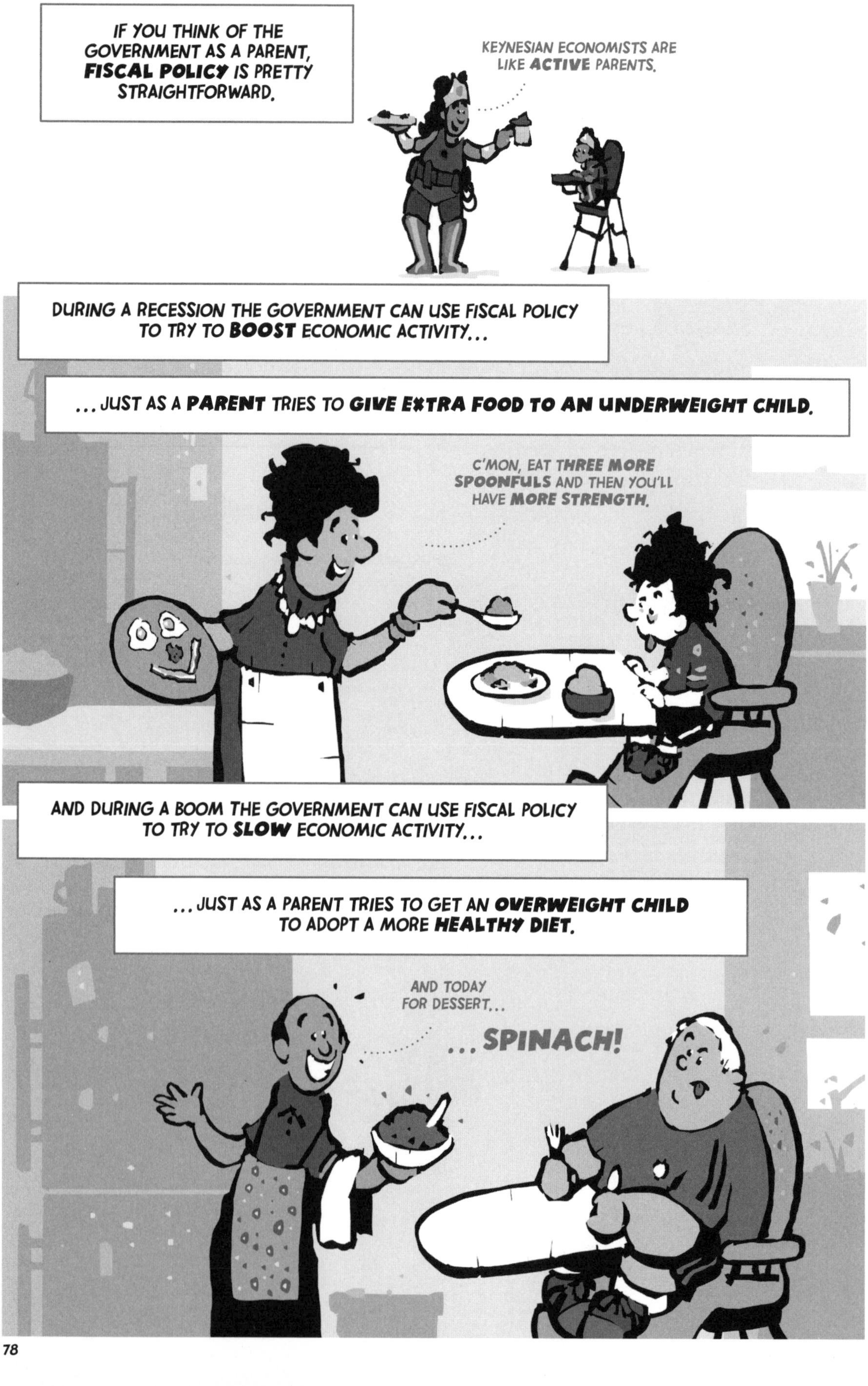
IF YOU THINK OF THE GOVERNMENT AS A PARENT, **FISCAL POLICY** IS PRETTY STRAIGHTFORWARD.
KEYNESIAN ECONOMISTS ARE LIKE **ACTIVE** PARENTS.
DURING A RECESSION THE GOVERNMENT CAN USE FISCAL POLICY TO TRY TO **BOOST** ECONOMIC ACTIVITY...
...JUST AS A **PARENT** TRIES TO **GIVE EXTRA FOOD TO AN UNDERWEIGHT CHILD.**
C'MON, EAT T**HREE MORE SPOONFULS** AND THEN YOU'LL HAVE **MORE STRENGTH.**
AND DURING A BOOM THE GOVERNMENT CAN USE FISCAL POLICY TO TRY TO **SLOW** ECONOMIC ACTIVITY...
...JUST AS A PARENT TRIES TO GET AN **OVERWEIGHT CHILD** TO ADOPT A MORE **HEALTHY DIET.**
AND TODAY FOR DESSERT...
...**SPINACH!**

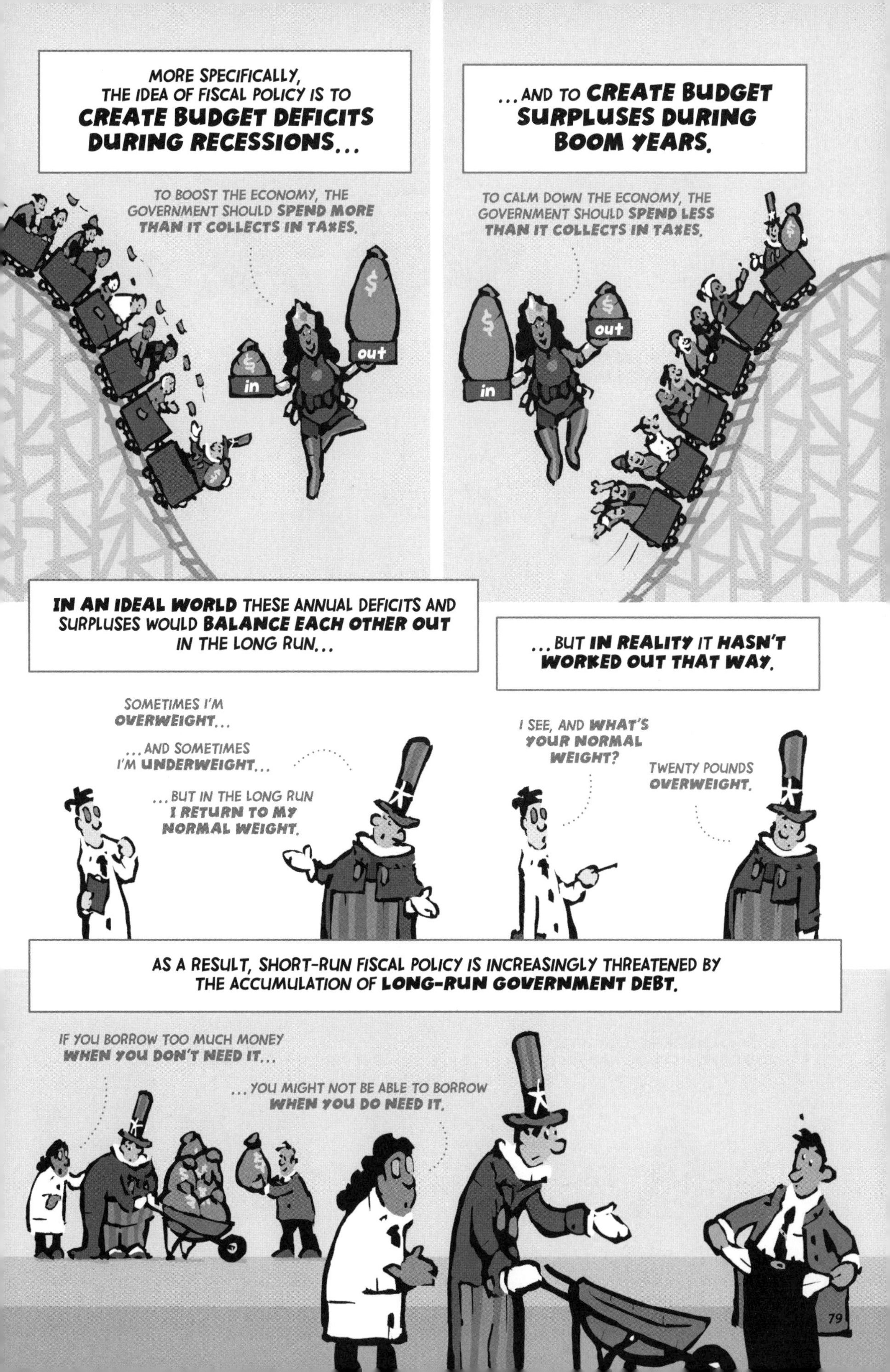
MORE SPECIFICALLY, THE IDEA OF FISCAL POLICY IS TO CREATE BUDGET DEFICITS DURING RECESSIONS...
TO BOOST THE ECONOMY, THE GOVERNMENT SHOULD SPEND MORE THAN IT COLLECTS IN TAXES.
in
out
...AND TO CREATE BUDGET SURPLUSES DURING BOOM YEARS.
TO CALM DOWN THE ECONOMY, THE GOVERNMENT SHOULD SPEND LESS THAN IT COLLECTS IN TAXES.
in
out
IN AN IDEAL WORLD THESE ANNUAL DEFICITS AND SURPLUSES WOULD BALANCE EACH OTHER OUT IN THE LONG RUN...
SOMETIMES I'M OVERWEIGHT...
...AND SOMETIMES I'M UNDERWEIGHT...
...BUT IN THE LONG RUN I RETURN TO MY NORMAL WEIGHT.
...BUT IN REALITY IT HASN'T WORKED OUT THAT WAY.
I SEE, AND WHAT'S YOUR NORMAL WEIGHT?
TWENTY POUNDS OVERWEIGHT.
AS A RESULT, SHORT-RUN FISCAL POLICY IS INCREASINGLY THREATENED BY THE ACCUMULATION OF LONG-RUN GOVERNMENT DEBT.
IF YOU BORROW TOO MUCH MONEY WHEN YOU DON'T NEED IT...
...YOU MIGHT NOT BE ABLE TO BORROW WHEN YOU DO NEED IT.

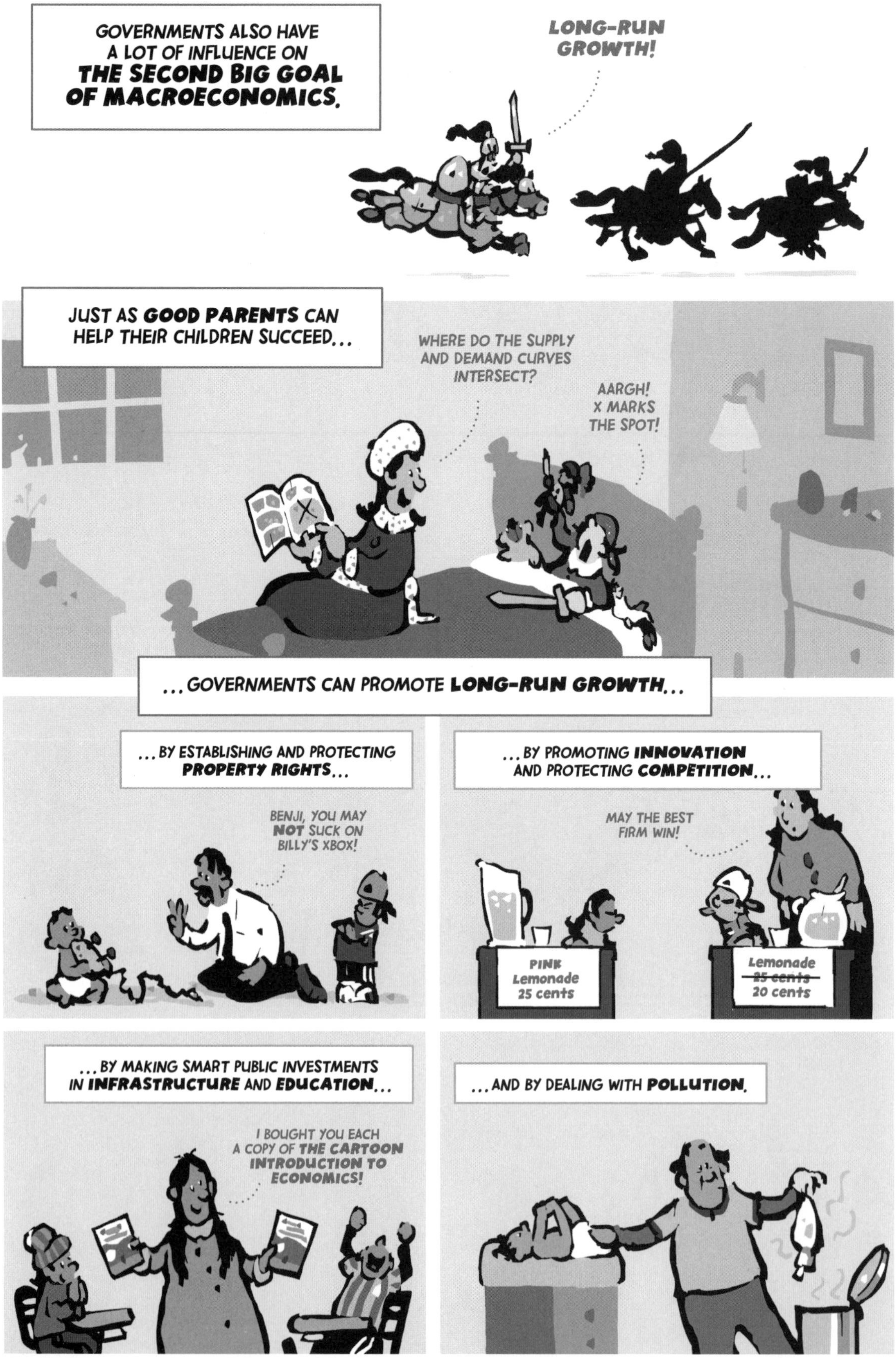
GOVERNMENTS ALSO HAVE A LOT OF INFLUENCE ON **THE SECOND BIG GOAL OF MACROECONOMICS.**
LONG-RUN GROWTH!
JUST AS **GOOD PARENTS** CAN HELP THEIR CHILDREN SUCCEED...
WHERE DO THE SUPPLY AND DEMAND CURVES INTERSECT?
AARGH! X MARKS THE SPOT!
...GOVERNMENTS CAN PROMOTE **LONG-RUN GROWTH**...
...BY ESTABLISHING AND PROTECTING **PROPERTY RIGHTS**...
BENJI, YOU MAY **NOT** SUCK ON BILLY'S XBOX!
...BY PROMOTING **INNOVATION** AND PROTECTING **COMPETITION**...
MAY THE BEST FIRM WIN!
PINK Lemonade 25 cents
Lemonade ~~25 cents~~ 20 cents
...BY MAKING SMART PUBLIC INVESTMENTS IN **INFRASTRUCTURE** AND **EDUCATION**...
I BOUGHT YOU EACH A COPY OF **THE CARTOON INTRODUCTION TO ECONOMICS!**
...AND BY DEALING WITH **POLLUTION.**

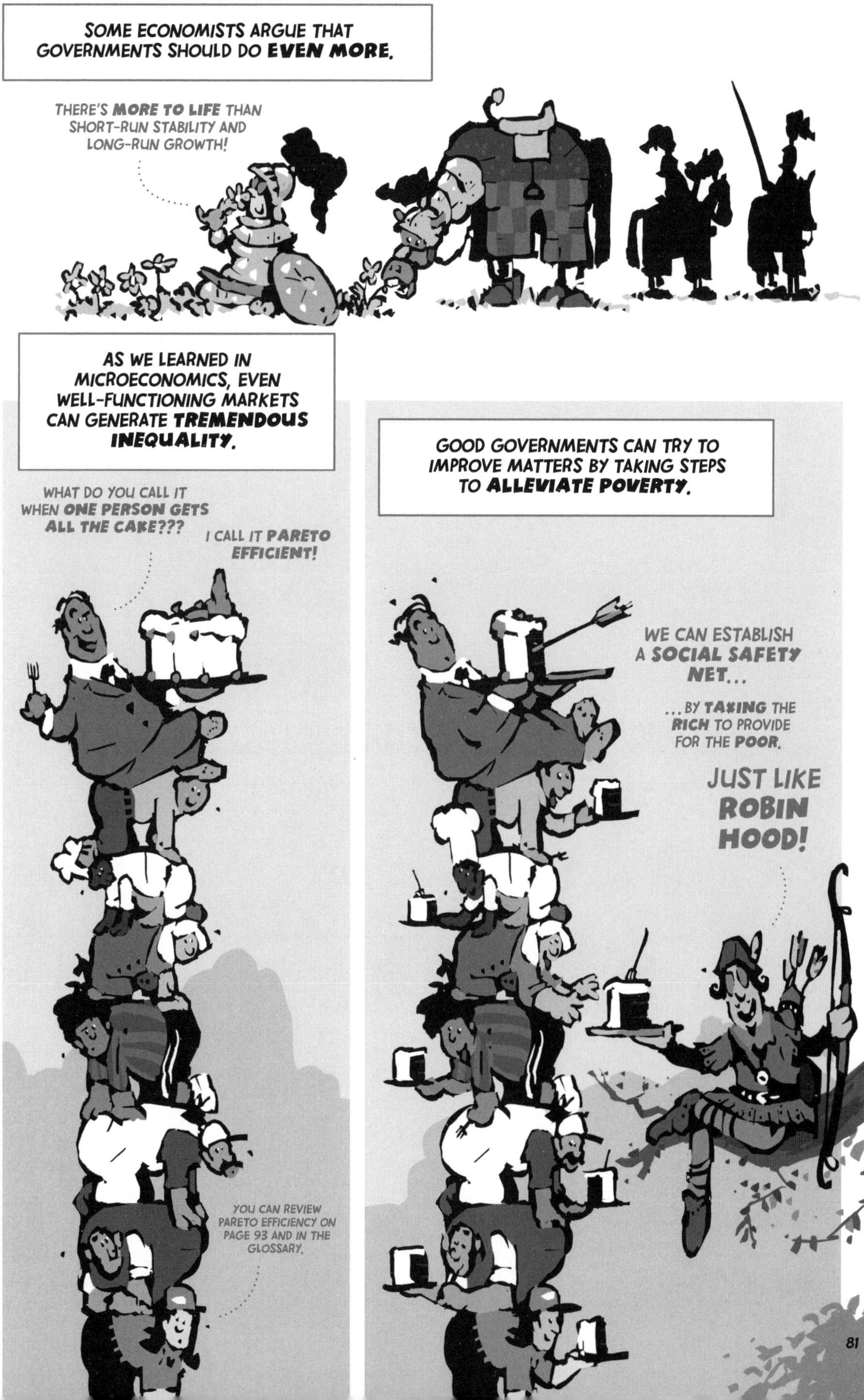
SOME ECONOMISTS ARGUE THAT GOVERNMENTS SHOULD DO **EVEN MORE.**
THERE'S **MORE TO LIFE** THAN SHORT-RUN STABILITY AND LONG-RUN GROWTH!
AS WE LEARNED IN MICROECONOMICS, EVEN WELL-FUNCTIONING MARKETS CAN GENERATE **TREMENDOUS INEQUALITY.**
WHAT DO YOU CALL IT WHEN **ONE PERSON GETS ALL THE CAKE???**
I CALL IT **PARETO EFFICIENT!**
YOU CAN REVIEW PARETO EFFICIENCY ON PAGE 93 AND IN THE GLOSSARY.
GOOD GOVERNMENTS CAN TRY TO IMPROVE MATTERS BY TAKING STEPS TO **ALLEVIATE POVERTY.**
WE CAN ESTABLISH A **SOCIAL SAFETY NET...**
...BY **TAXING** THE **RICH** TO PROVIDE FOR THE **POOR.**
JUST LIKE **ROBIN HOOD!**

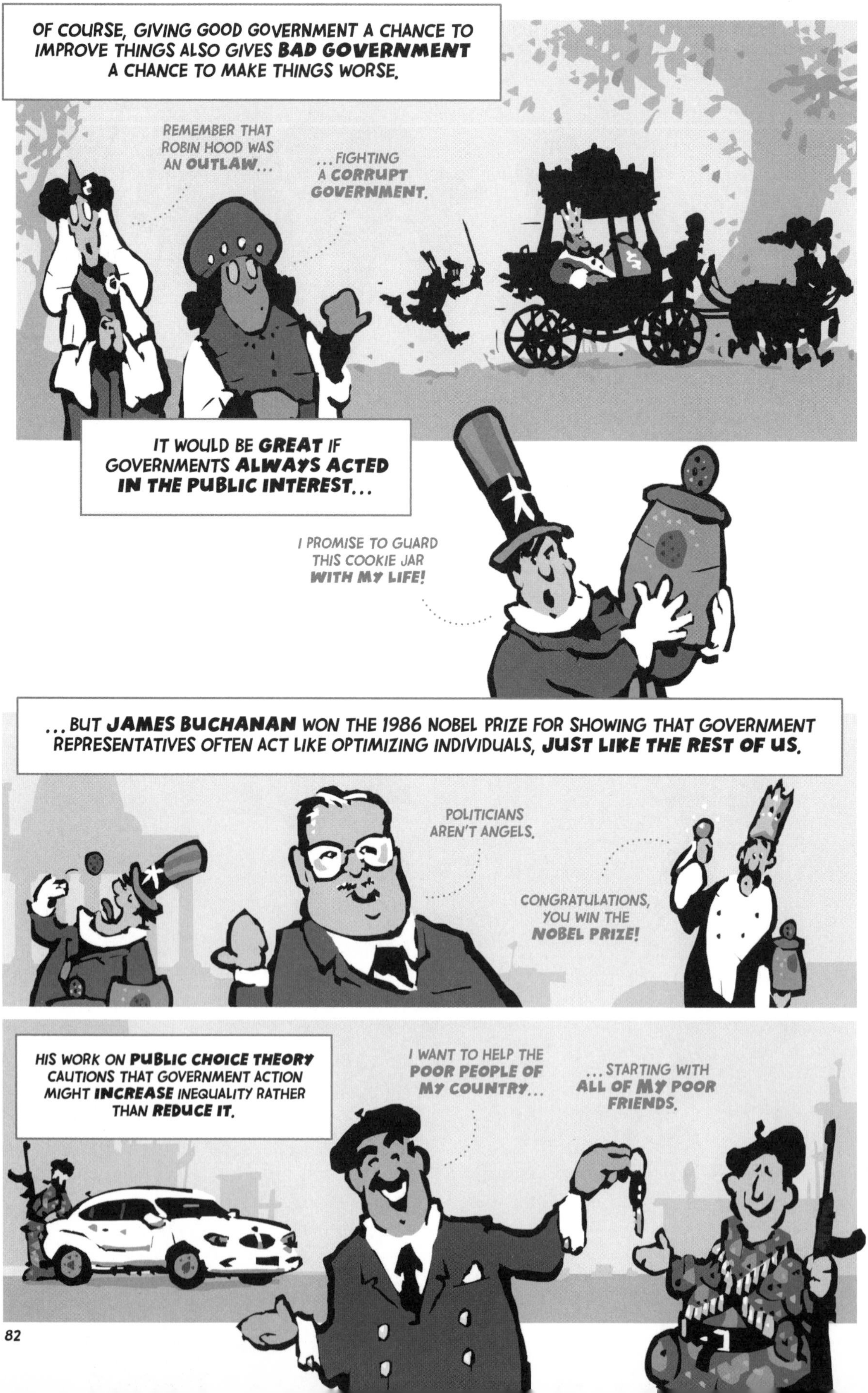
OF COURSE, GIVING GOOD GOVERNMENT A CHANCE TO IMPROVE THINGS ALSO GIVES BAD GOVERNMENT A CHANCE TO MAKE THINGS WORSE.
REMEMBER THAT ROBIN HOOD WAS AN OUTLAW...
...FIGHTING A CORRUPT GOVERNMENT.
IT WOULD BE GREAT IF GOVERNMENTS ALWAYS ACTED IN THE PUBLIC INTEREST...
I PROMISE TO GUARD THIS COOKIE JAR WITH MY LIFE!
...BUT JAMES BUCHANAN WON THE 1986 NOBEL PRIZE FOR SHOWING THAT GOVERNMENT REPRESENTATIVES OFTEN ACT LIKE OPTIMIZING INDIVIDUALS, JUST LIKE THE REST OF US.
POLITICIANS AREN'T ANGELS.
CONGRATULATIONS, YOU WIN THE NOBEL PRIZE!
HIS WORK ON PUBLIC CHOICE THEORY CAUTIONS THAT GOVERNMENT ACTION MIGHT INCREASE INEQUALITY RATHER THAN REDUCE IT.
I WANT TO HELP THE POOR PEOPLE OF MY COUNTRY...
...STARTING WITH ALL OF MY POOR FRIENDS.

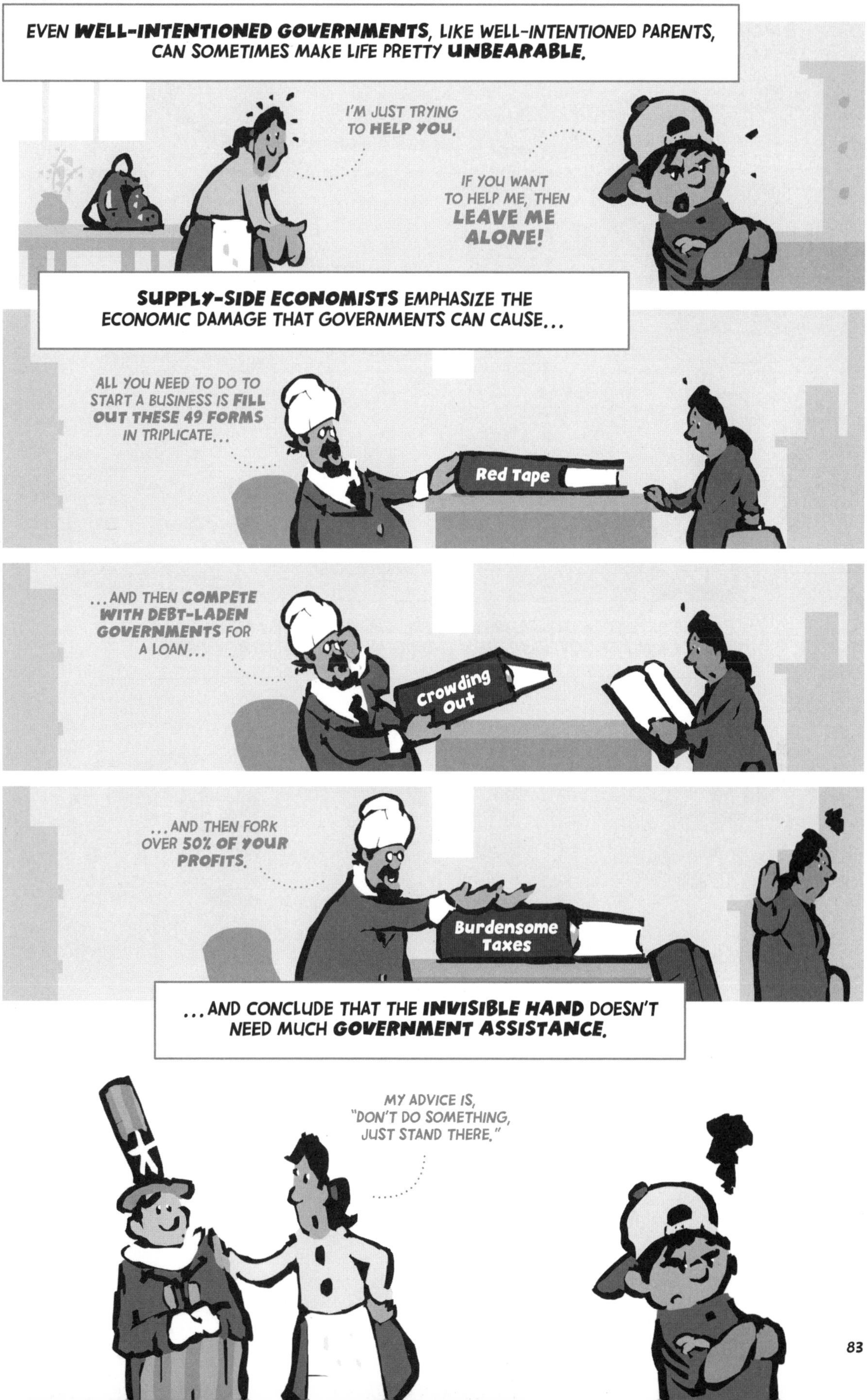
EVEN **WELL-INTENTIONED GOVERNMENTS**, LIKE WELL-INTENTIONED PARENTS, CAN SOMETIMES MAKE LIFE PRETTY **UNBEARABLE.**
I'M JUST TRYING TO **HELP YOU.**
IF YOU WANT TO HELP ME, THEN **LEAVE ME ALONE!**
SUPPLY-SIDE ECONOMISTS EMPHASIZE THE ECONOMIC DAMAGE THAT GOVERNMENTS CAN CAUSE...
ALL YOU NEED TO DO TO START A BUSINESS IS **FILL OUT THESE 49 FORMS** IN TRIPLICATE...
Red Tape
...AND THEN **COMPETE WITH DEBT-LADEN GOVERNMENTS** FOR A LOAN...
Crowding Out
...AND THEN FORK OVER **50% OF YOUR PROFITS.**
Burdensome Taxes
...AND CONCLUDE THAT THE **INVISIBLE HAND** DOESN'T NEED MUCH **GOVERNMENT ASSISTANCE.**
MY ADVICE IS, "DON'T DO SOMETHING, JUST STAND THERE."

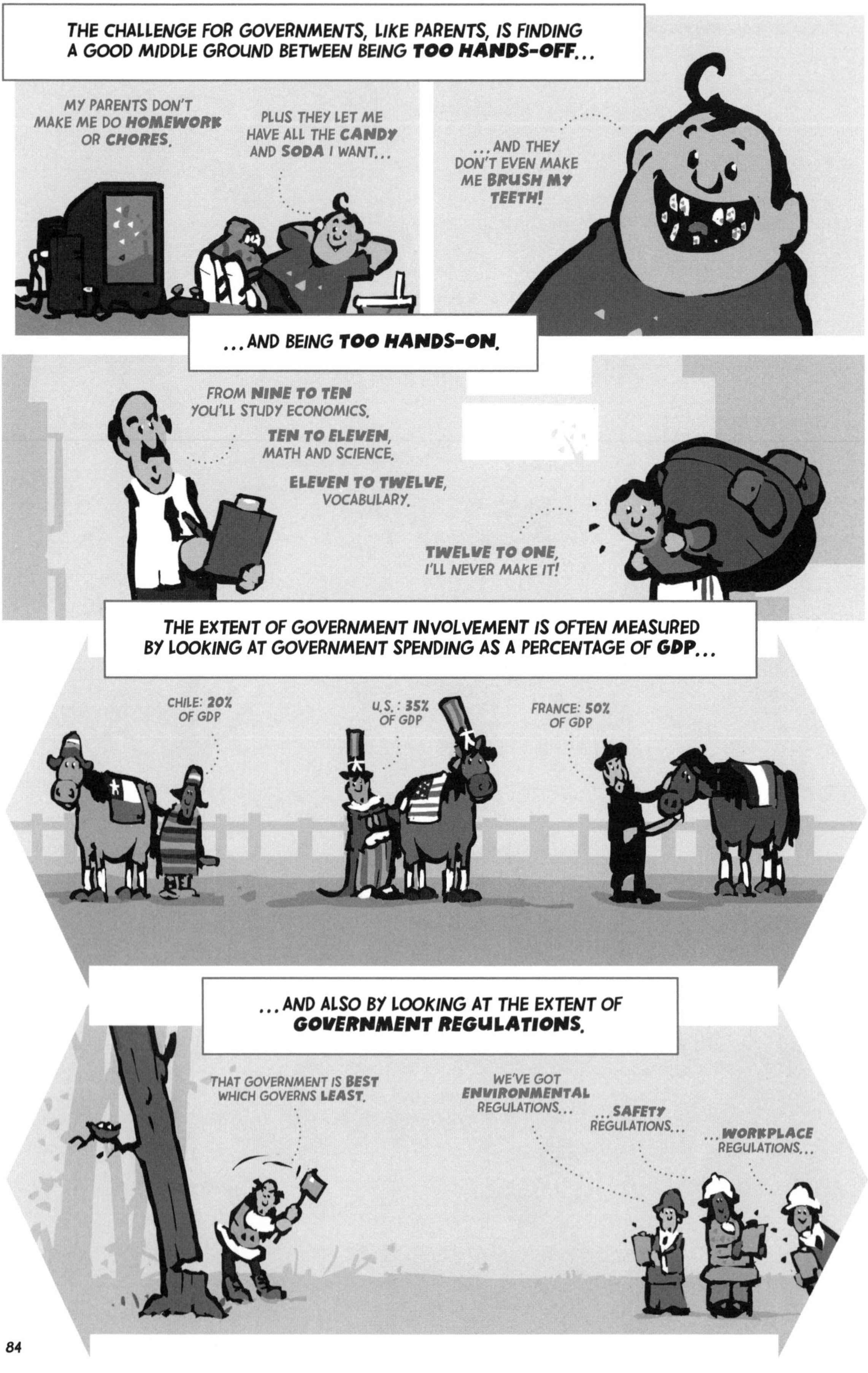
THE CHALLENGE FOR GOVERNMENTS, LIKE PARENTS, IS FINDING A GOOD MIDDLE GROUND BETWEEN BEING **TOO HANDS-OFF**...
MY PARENTS DON'T MAKE ME DO **HOMEWORK** OR **CHORES**.
PLUS THEY LET ME HAVE ALL THE **CANDY** AND **SODA** I WANT...
...AND THEY DON'T EVEN MAKE ME **BRUSH MY TEETH!**
...AND BEING **TOO HANDS-ON**.
FROM **NINE TO TEN** YOU'LL STUDY ECONOMICS.
TEN TO ELEVEN, MATH AND SCIENCE.
ELEVEN TO TWELVE, VOCABULARY.
TWELVE TO ONE, I'LL NEVER MAKE IT!
THE EXTENT OF GOVERNMENT INVOLVEMENT IS OFTEN MEASURED BY LOOKING AT GOVERNMENT SPENDING AS A PERCENTAGE OF **GDP**...
CHILE: **20%** OF GDP
U.S.: **35%** OF GDP
FRANCE: **50%** OF GDP
...AND ALSO BY LOOKING AT THE EXTENT OF **GOVERNMENT REGULATIONS**.
THAT GOVERNMENT IS **BEST** WHICH GOVERNS **LEAST**.
WE'VE GOT **ENVIRONMENTAL** REGULATIONS...
...**SAFETY** REGULATIONS...
...**WORKPLACE** REGULATIONS...

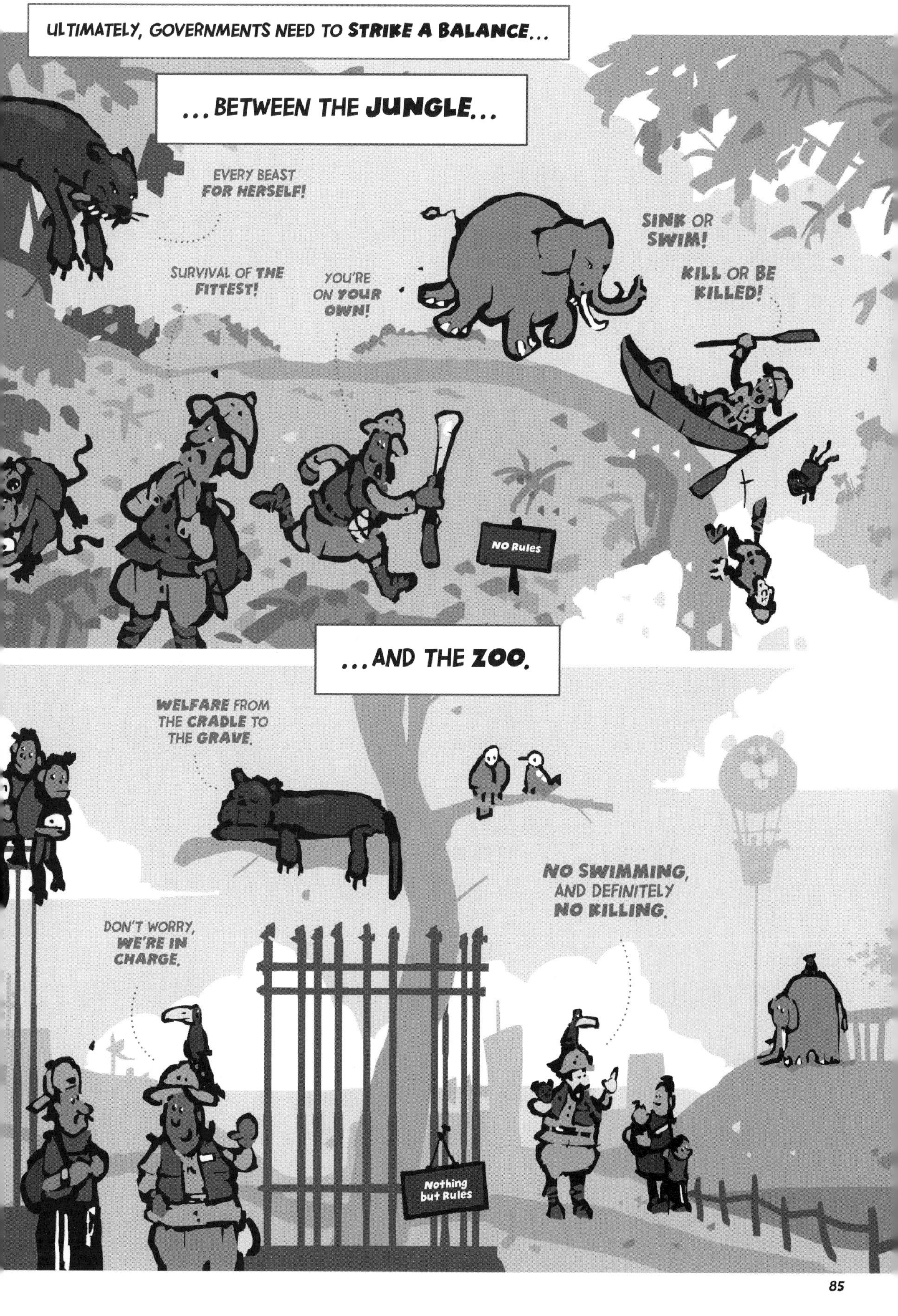
ULTIMATELY, GOVERNMENTS NEED TO STRIKE A BALANCE...
...BETWEEN THE JUNGLE...
EVERY BEAST FOR HERSELF!
SURVIVAL OF THE FITTEST!
YOU'RE ON YOUR OWN!
SINK OR SWIM!
KILL OR BE KILLED!
NO Rules
...AND THE ZOO.
WELFARE FROM THE CRADLE TO THE GRAVE.
DON'T WORRY, WE'RE IN CHARGE.
NO SWIMMING, AND DEFINITELY NO KILLING.
Nothing but Rules

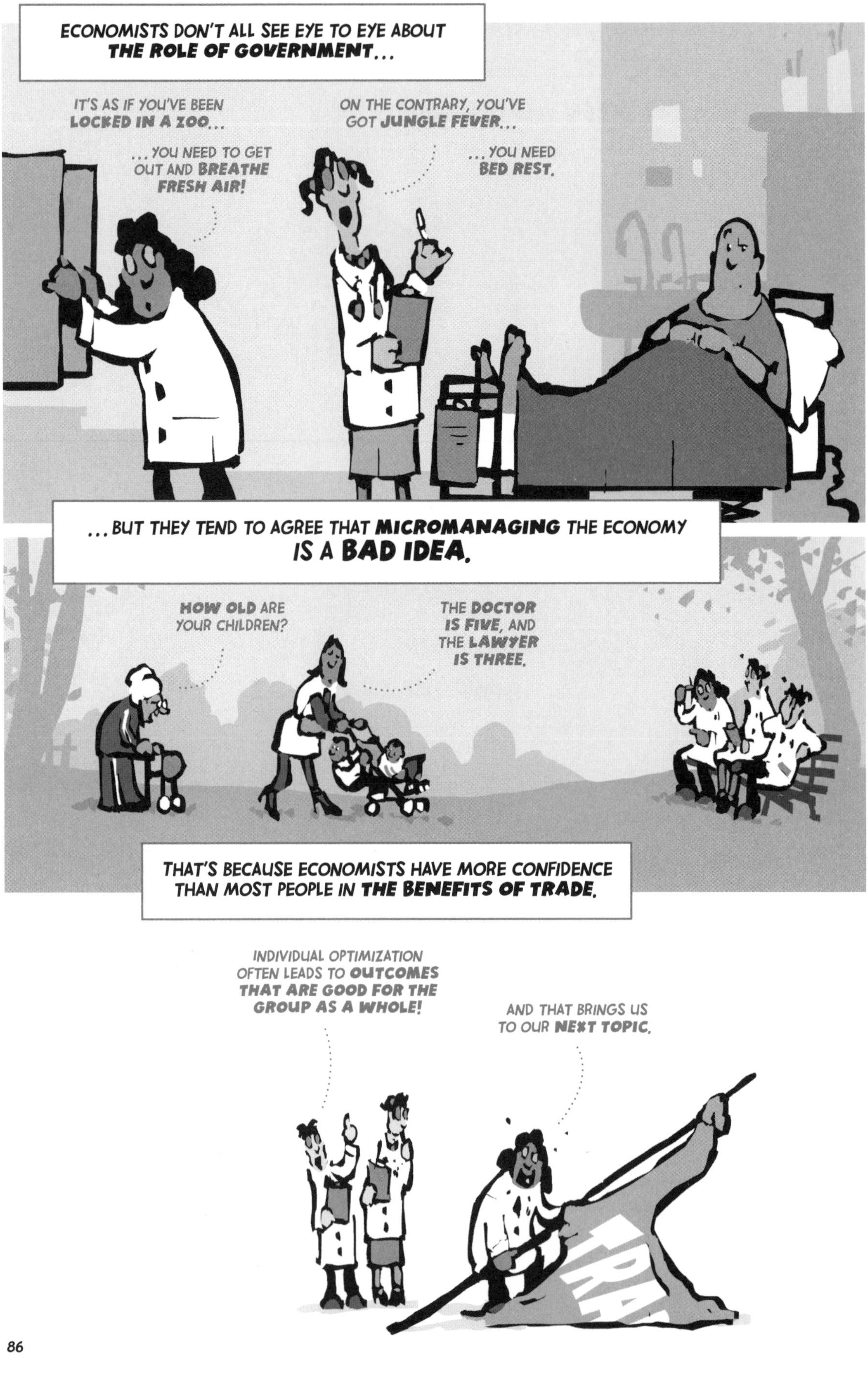
ECONOMISTS DON'T ALL SEE EYE TO EYE ABOUT THE ROLE OF GOVERNMENT...
IT'S AS IF YOU'VE BEEN LOCKED IN A ZOO...
...YOU NEED TO GET OUT AND BREATHE FRESH AIR!
ON THE CONTRARY, YOU'VE GOT JUNGLE FEVER...
...YOU NEED BED REST.
...BUT THEY TEND TO AGREE THAT MICROMANAGING THE ECONOMY IS A BAD IDEA.
HOW OLD ARE YOUR CHILDREN?
THE DOCTOR IS FIVE, AND THE LAWYER IS THREE.
THAT'S BECAUSE ECONOMISTS HAVE MORE CONFIDENCE THAN MOST PEOPLE IN THE BENEFITS OF TRADE.
INDIVIDUAL OPTIMIZATION OFTEN LEADS TO OUTCOMES THAT ARE GOOD FOR THE GROUP AS A WHOLE!
AND THAT BRINGS US TO OUR NEXT TOPIC.

PART TWO
INTERNATIONAL TRADE

CHAPTER 7
TRADE AND TECHNOLOGY

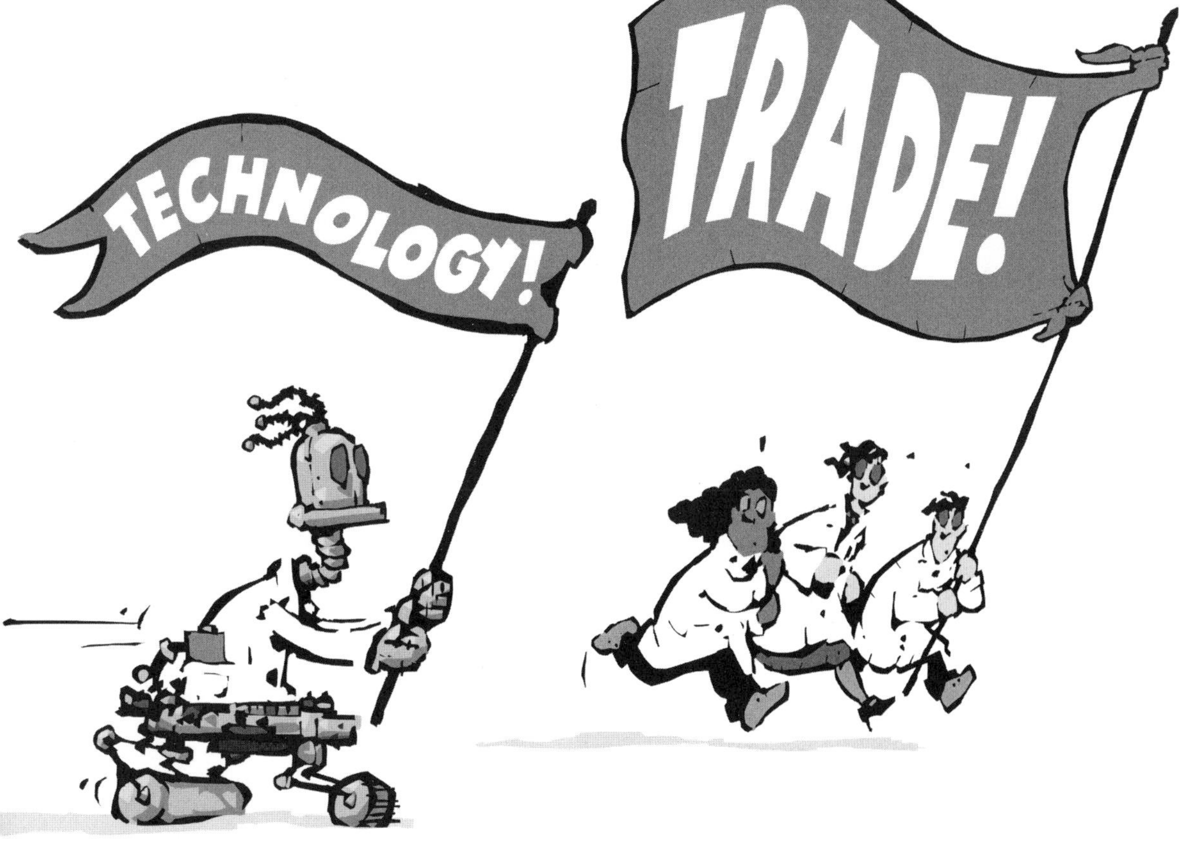
TECHNOLOGY!
TRADE!

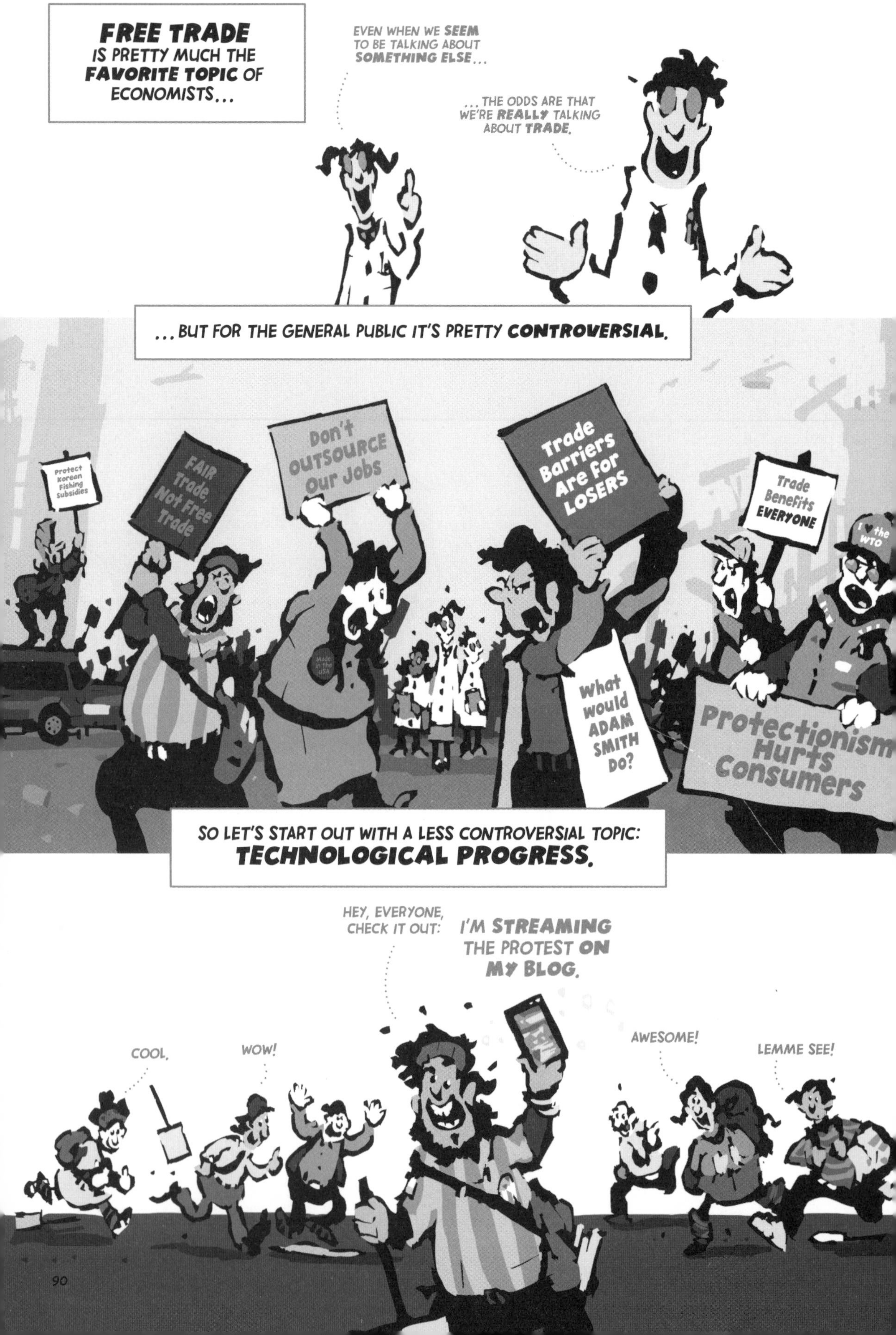

FREE TRADE IS PRETTY MUCH THE FAVORITE TOPIC OF ECONOMISTS...
EVEN WHEN WE SEEM TO BE TALKING ABOUT SOMETHING ELSE...
...THE ODDS ARE THAT WE'RE REALLY TALKING ABOUT TRADE.
...BUT FOR THE GENERAL PUBLIC IT'S PRETTY CONTROVERSIAL.
Protect Korean Fishing Subsidies
FAIR Trade, Not Free Trade
Don't OUTSOURCE Our Jobs
Made in the USA
Trade Barriers Are for LOSERS
What would ADAM SMITH Do?
Trade Benefits EVERYONE
I ♥ the WTO
Protectionism Hurts Consumers
SO LET'S START OUT WITH A LESS CONTROVERSIAL TOPIC: TECHNOLOGICAL PROGRESS.
HEY, EVERYONE, CHECK IT OUT:
I'M STREAMING THE PROTEST ON MY BLOG.
COOL.
WOW!
AWESOME!
LEMME SEE!

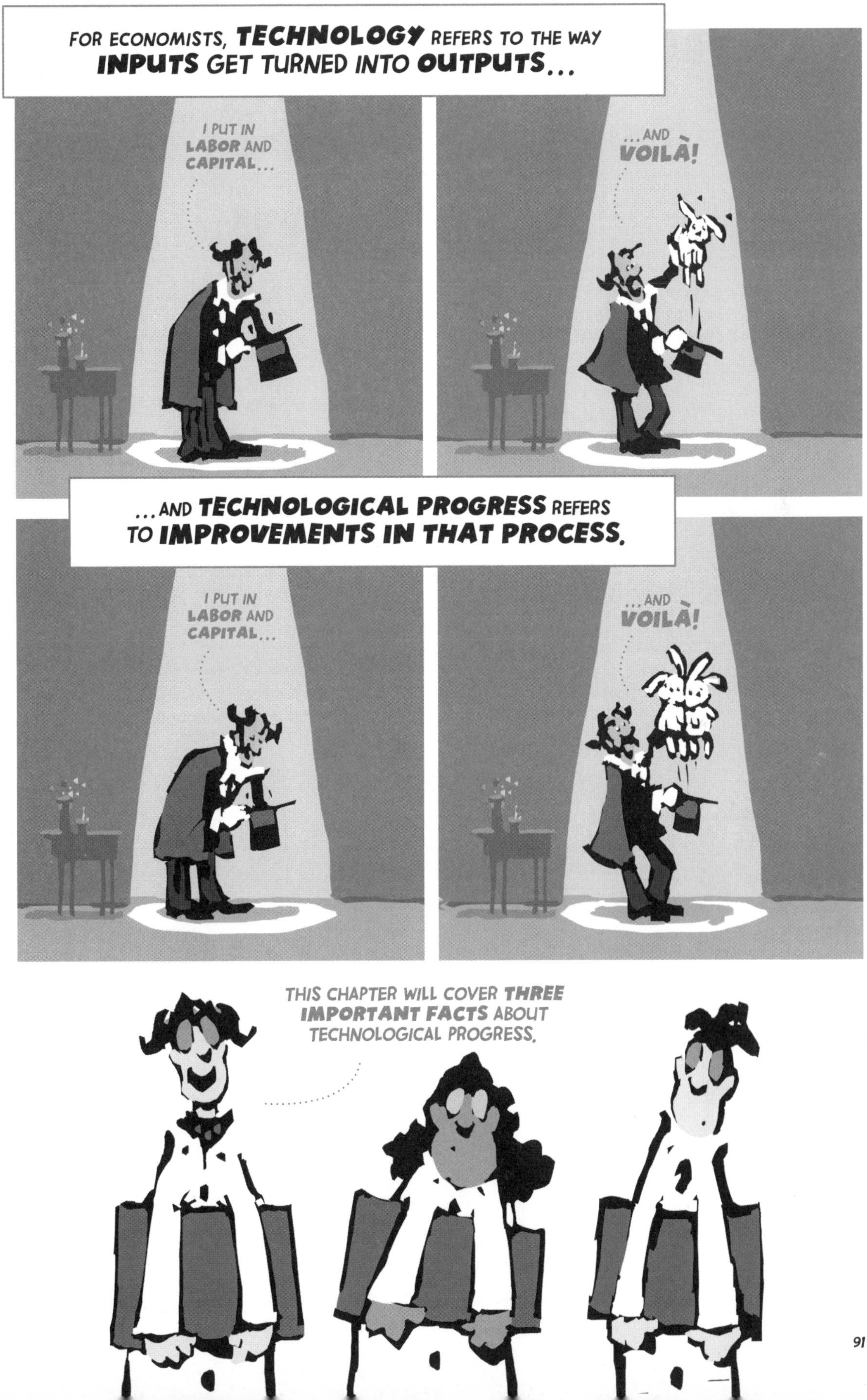
FOR ECONOMISTS, TECHNOLOGY REFERS TO THE WAY INPUTS GET TURNED INTO OUTPUTS...
I PUT IN LABOR AND CAPITAL...
...AND VOILÀ!
...AND TECHNOLOGICAL PROGRESS REFERS TO IMPROVEMENTS IN THAT PROCESS.
I PUT IN LABOR AND CAPITAL...
...AND VOILÀ!
THIS CHAPTER WILL COVER THREE IMPORTANT FACTS ABOUT TECHNOLOGICAL PROGRESS.

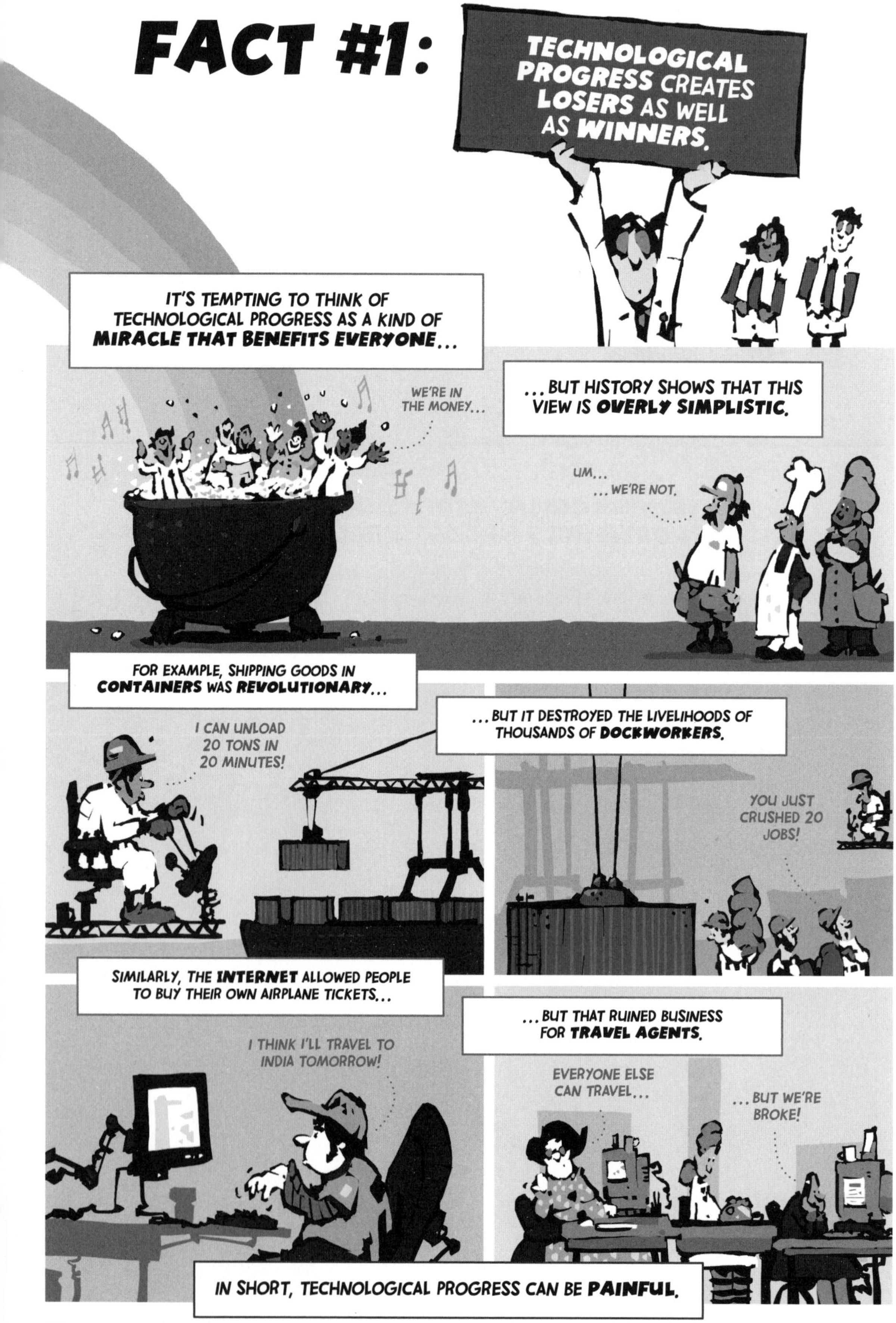
FACT #1:
TECHNOLOGICAL PROGRESS CREATES LOSERS AS WELL AS WINNERS.
IT'S TEMPTING TO THINK OF TECHNOLOGICAL PROGRESS AS A KIND OF MIRACLE THAT BENEFITS EVERYONE...
WE'RE IN THE MONEY...
...BUT HISTORY SHOWS THAT THIS VIEW IS OVERLY SIMPLISTIC.
UM... ...WE'RE NOT.
FOR EXAMPLE, SHIPPING GOODS IN CONTAINERS WAS REVOLUTIONARY...
I CAN UNLOAD 20 TONS IN 20 MINUTES!
...BUT IT DESTROYED THE LIVELIHOODS OF THOUSANDS OF DOCKWORKERS.
YOU JUST CRUSHED 20 JOBS!
SIMILARLY, THE INTERNET ALLOWED PEOPLE TO BUY THEIR OWN AIRPLANE TICKETS...
I THINK I'LL TRAVEL TO INDIA TOMORROW!
...BUT THAT RUINED BUSINESS FOR TRAVEL AGENTS.
EVERYONE ELSE CAN TRAVEL...
...BUT WE'RE BROKE!
IN SHORT, TECHNOLOGICAL PROGRESS CAN BE PAINFUL.

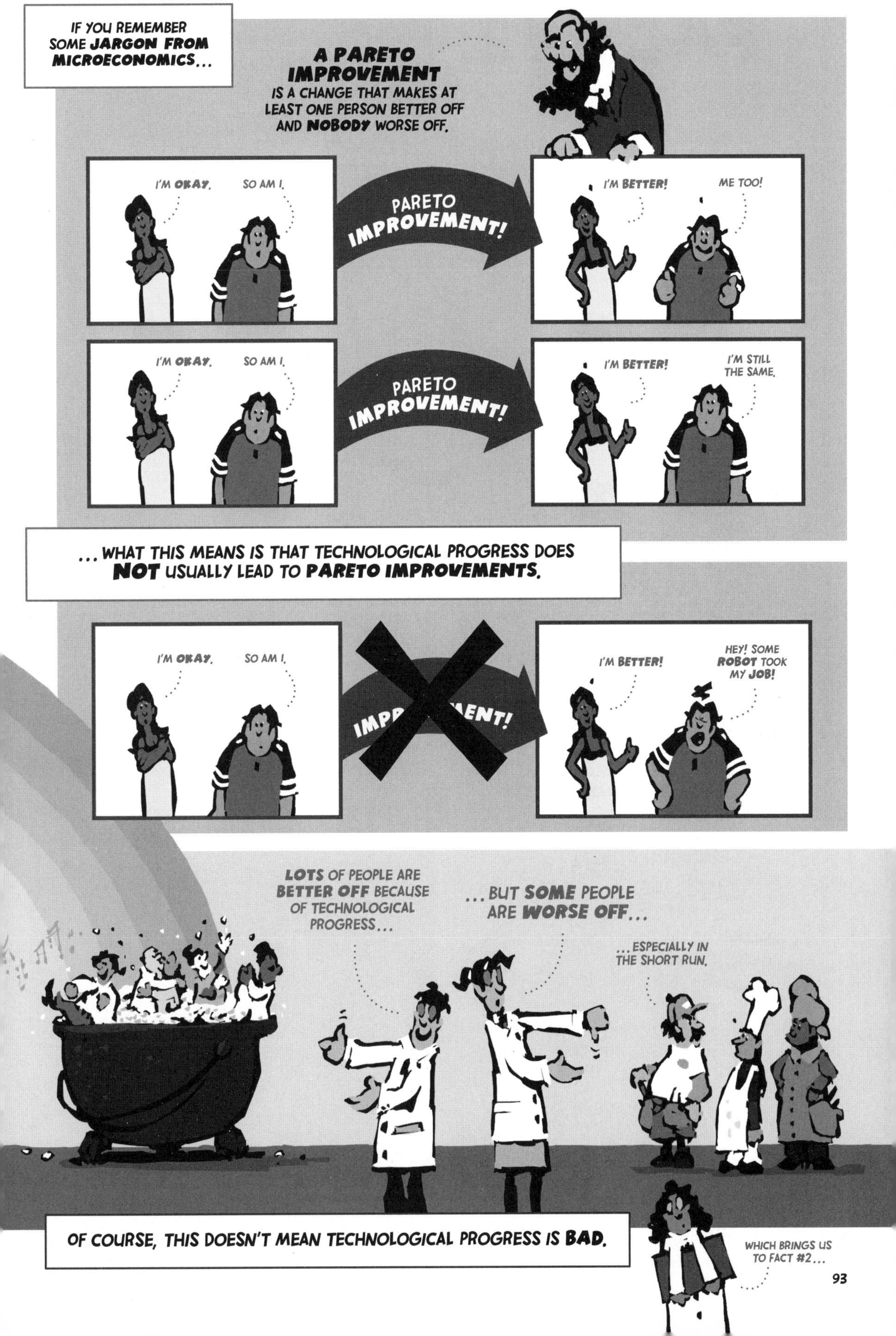
IF YOU REMEMBER SOME JARGON FROM MICROECONOMICS...
A PARETO IMPROVEMENT IS A CHANGE THAT MAKES AT LEAST ONE PERSON BETTER OFF AND NOBODY WORSE OFF.
I'M OKAY.
SO AM I.
PARETO IMPROVEMENT!
I'M BETTER!
ME TOO!
I'M OKAY.
SO AM I.
PARETO IMPROVEMENT!
I'M BETTER!
I'M STILL THE SAME.
...WHAT THIS MEANS IS THAT TECHNOLOGICAL PROGRESS DOES NOT USUALLY LEAD TO PARETO IMPROVEMENTS.
I'M OKAY.
SO AM I.
I'M BETTER!
HEY! SOME ROBOT TOOK MY JOB!
LOTS OF PEOPLE ARE BETTER OFF BECAUSE OF TECHNOLOGICAL PROGRESS...
...BUT SOME PEOPLE ARE WORSE OFF...
...ESPECIALLY IN THE SHORT RUN.
OF COURSE, THIS DOESN'T MEAN TECHNOLOGICAL PROGRESS IS BAD.
WHICH BRINGS US TO FACT #2...

FACT #2:

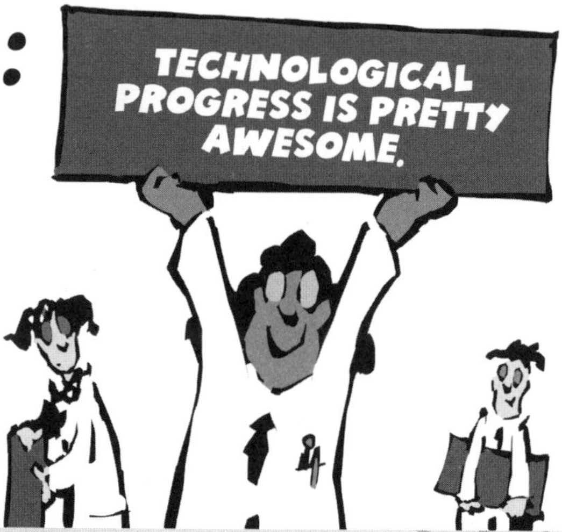

TECHNOLOGICAL PROGRESS IS PRETTY AWESOME.

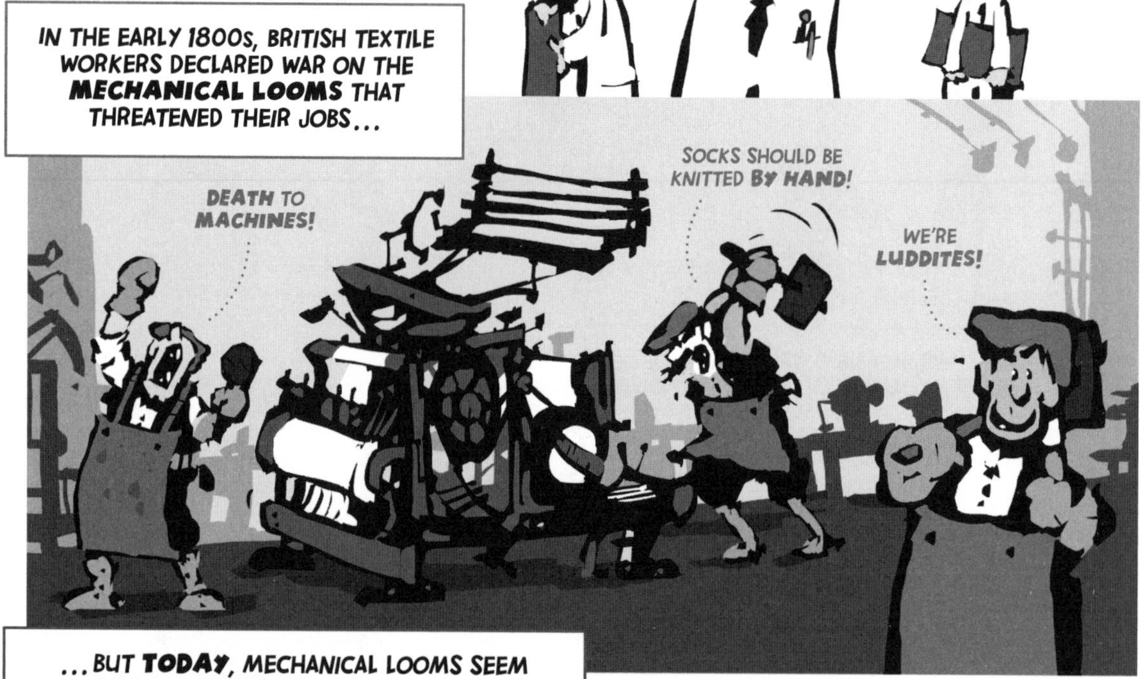

IN THE EARLY 1800s, BRITISH TEXTILE WORKERS DECLARED WAR ON THE **MECHANICAL LOOMS** THAT THREATENED THEIR JOBS...
DEATH TO **MACHINES!**
SOCKS SHOULD BE KNITTED **BY HAND!**
WE'RE **LUDDITES!**

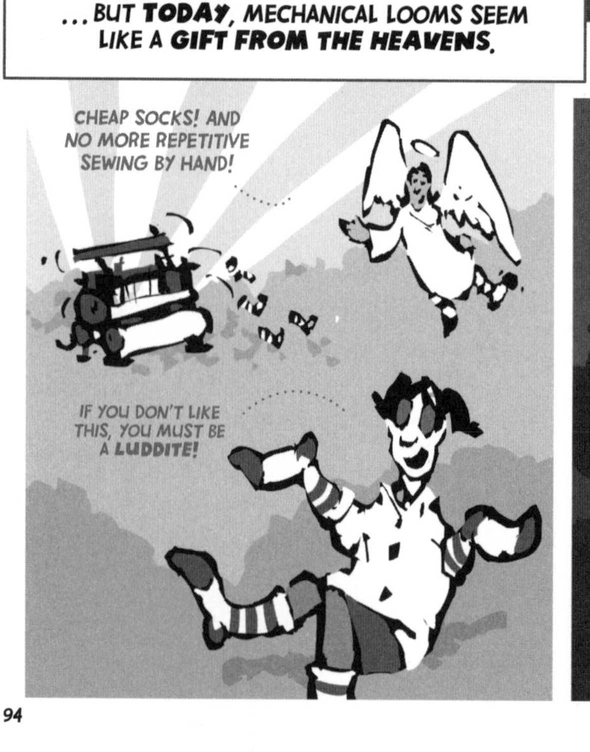

...BUT **TODAY**, MECHANICAL LOOMS SEEM LIKE A **GIFT FROM THE HEAVENS.**
CHEAP SOCKS! AND NO MORE REPETITIVE SEWING BY HAND!
IF YOU DON'T LIKE THIS, YOU MUST BE A **LUDDITE!**

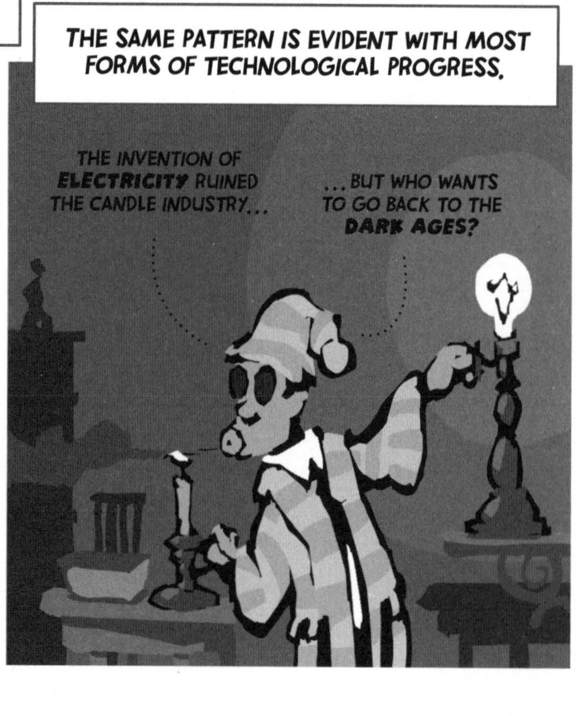

THE SAME PATTERN IS EVIDENT WITH MOST FORMS OF TECHNOLOGICAL PROGRESS.
THE INVENTION OF **ELECTRICITY** RUINED THE CANDLE INDUSTRY...
...BUT WHO WANTS TO GO BACK TO THE **DARK AGES?**

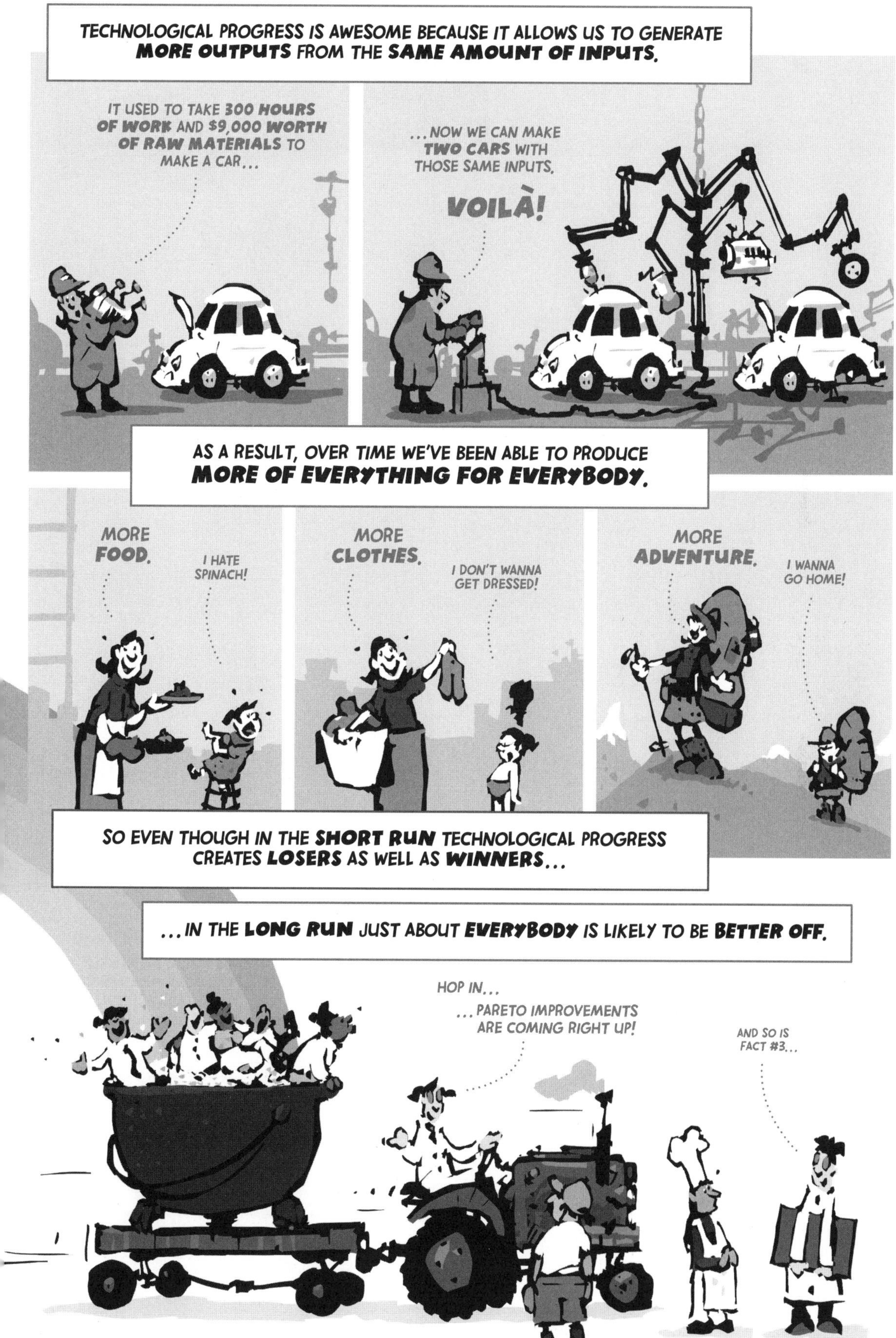

TECHNOLOGICAL PROGRESS IS AWESOME BECAUSE IT ALLOWS US TO GENERATE **MORE OUTPUTS** FROM THE **SAME AMOUNT OF INPUTS.**
IT USED TO TAKE **300 HOURS OF WORK** AND $9,000 **WORTH OF RAW MATERIALS** TO MAKE A CAR...
...NOW WE CAN MAKE **TWO CARS** WITH THOSE SAME INPUTS.
VOILÀ!
AS A RESULT, OVER TIME WE'VE BEEN ABLE TO PRODUCE **MORE OF EVERYTHING FOR EVERYBODY.**
MORE **FOOD.**
I HATE SPINACH!
MORE **CLOTHES.**
I DON'T WANNA GET DRESSED!
MORE **ADVENTURE.**
I WANNA GO HOME!
SO EVEN THOUGH IN THE **SHORT RUN** TECHNOLOGICAL PROGRESS CREATES **LOSERS** AS WELL AS **WINNERS...**
...IN THE **LONG RUN** JUST ABOUT **EVERYBODY** IS LIKELY TO BE **BETTER OFF.**
HOP IN...
...PARETO IMPROVEMENTS ARE COMING RIGHT UP!
AND SO IS FACT #3...

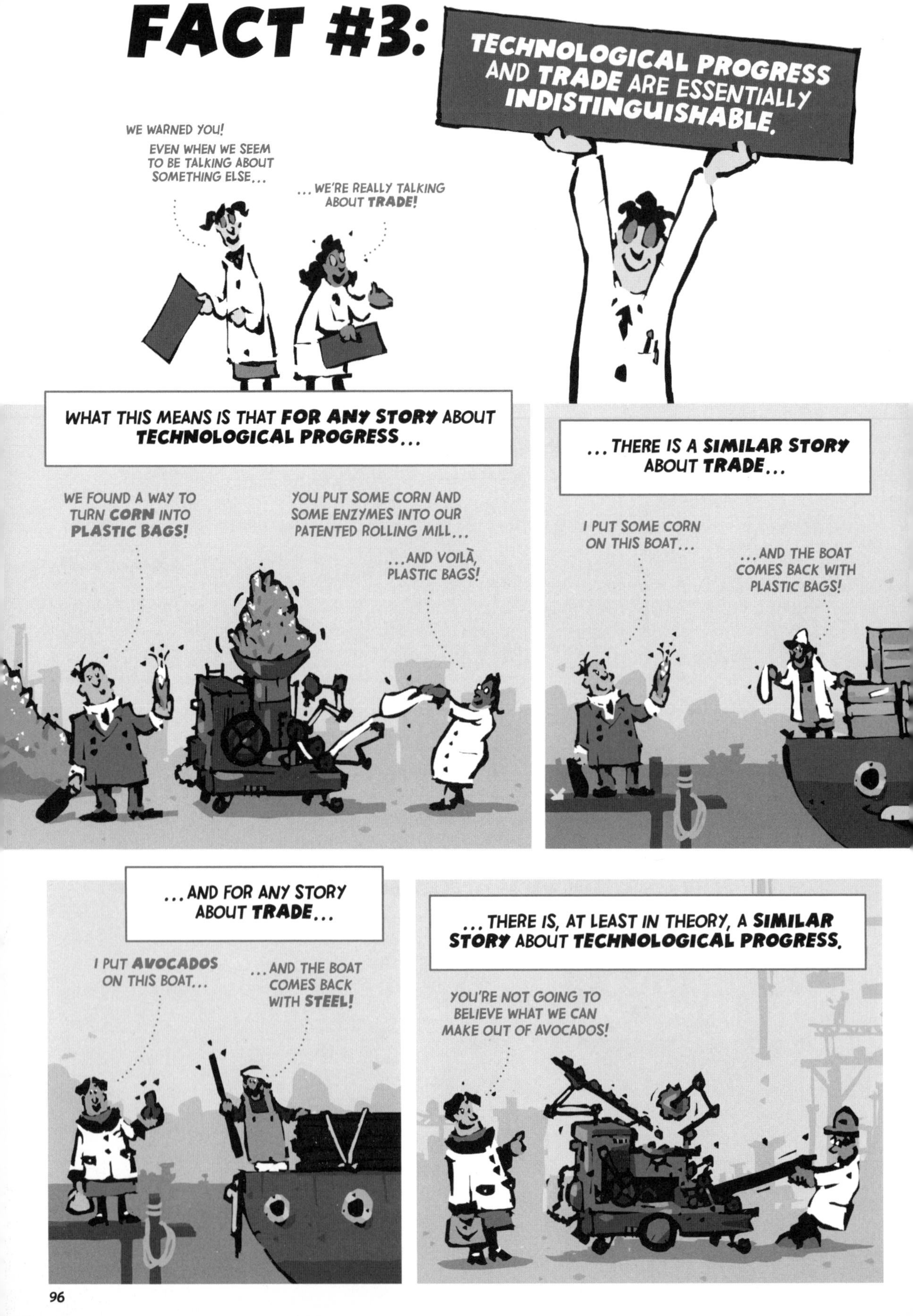
FACT #3:
TECHNOLOGICAL PROGRESS AND TRADE ARE ESSENTIALLY INDISTINGUISHABLE.
WE WARNED YOU!
EVEN WHEN WE SEEM TO BE TALKING ABOUT SOMETHING ELSE...
...WE'RE REALLY TALKING ABOUT TRADE!
WHAT THIS MEANS IS THAT FOR ANY STORY ABOUT TECHNOLOGICAL PROGRESS...
WE FOUND A WAY TO TURN CORN INTO PLASTIC BAGS!
YOU PUT SOME CORN AND SOME ENZYMES INTO OUR PATENTED ROLLING MILL...
...AND VOILÀ, PLASTIC BAGS!
...THERE IS A SIMILAR STORY ABOUT TRADE...
I PUT SOME CORN ON THIS BOAT...
...AND THE BOAT COMES BACK WITH PLASTIC BAGS!
...AND FOR ANY STORY ABOUT TRADE...
I PUT AVOCADOS ON THIS BOAT...
...AND THE BOAT COMES BACK WITH STEEL!
...THERE IS, AT LEAST IN THEORY, A SIMILAR STORY ABOUT TECHNOLOGICAL PROGRESS.
YOU'RE NOT GOING TO BELIEVE WHAT WE CAN MAKE OUT OF AVOCADOS!

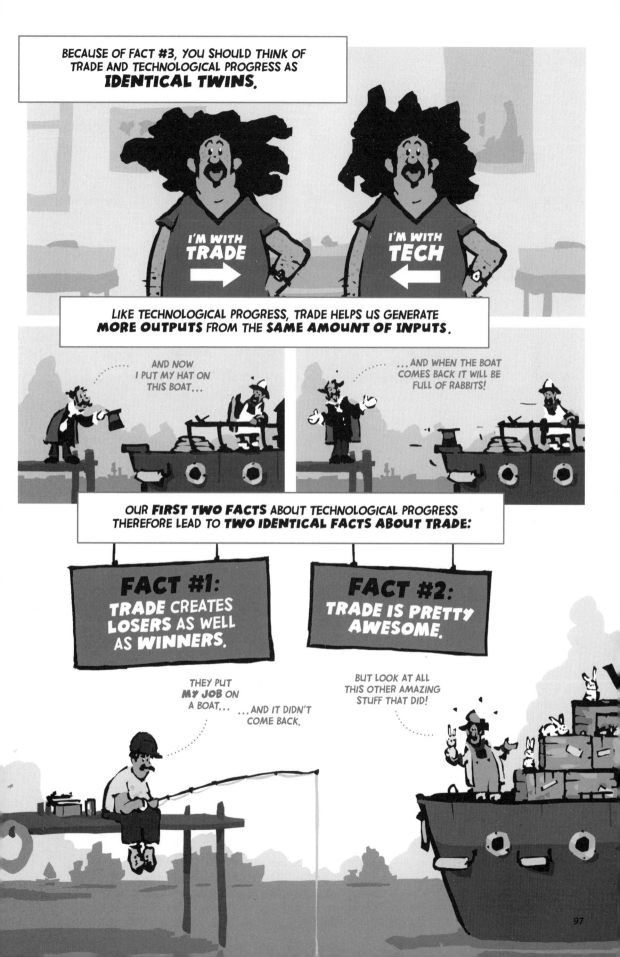

BECAUSE OF FACT #3, YOU SHOULD THINK OF TRADE AND TECHNOLOGICAL PROGRESS AS **IDENTICAL TWINS.**

I'M WITH **TRADE**

I'M WITH **TECH**

LIKE TECHNOLOGICAL PROGRESS, TRADE HELPS US GENERATE **MORE OUTPUTS** FROM THE **SAME AMOUNT OF INPUTS.**

AND NOW I PUT MY HAT ON THIS BOAT...

...AND WHEN THE BOAT COMES BACK IT WILL BE FULL OF RABBITS!

OUR **FIRST TWO FACTS** ABOUT TECHNOLOGICAL PROGRESS THEREFORE LEAD TO **TWO IDENTICAL FACTS ABOUT TRADE:**

FACT #1: **TRADE** CREATES **LOSERS** AS WELL AS **WINNERS.**

FACT #2: **TRADE IS PRETTY AWESOME.**

THEY PUT **MY JOB** ON A BOAT... ...AND IT DIDN'T COME BACK.

BUT LOOK AT ALL THIS OTHER AMAZING STUFF THAT DID!

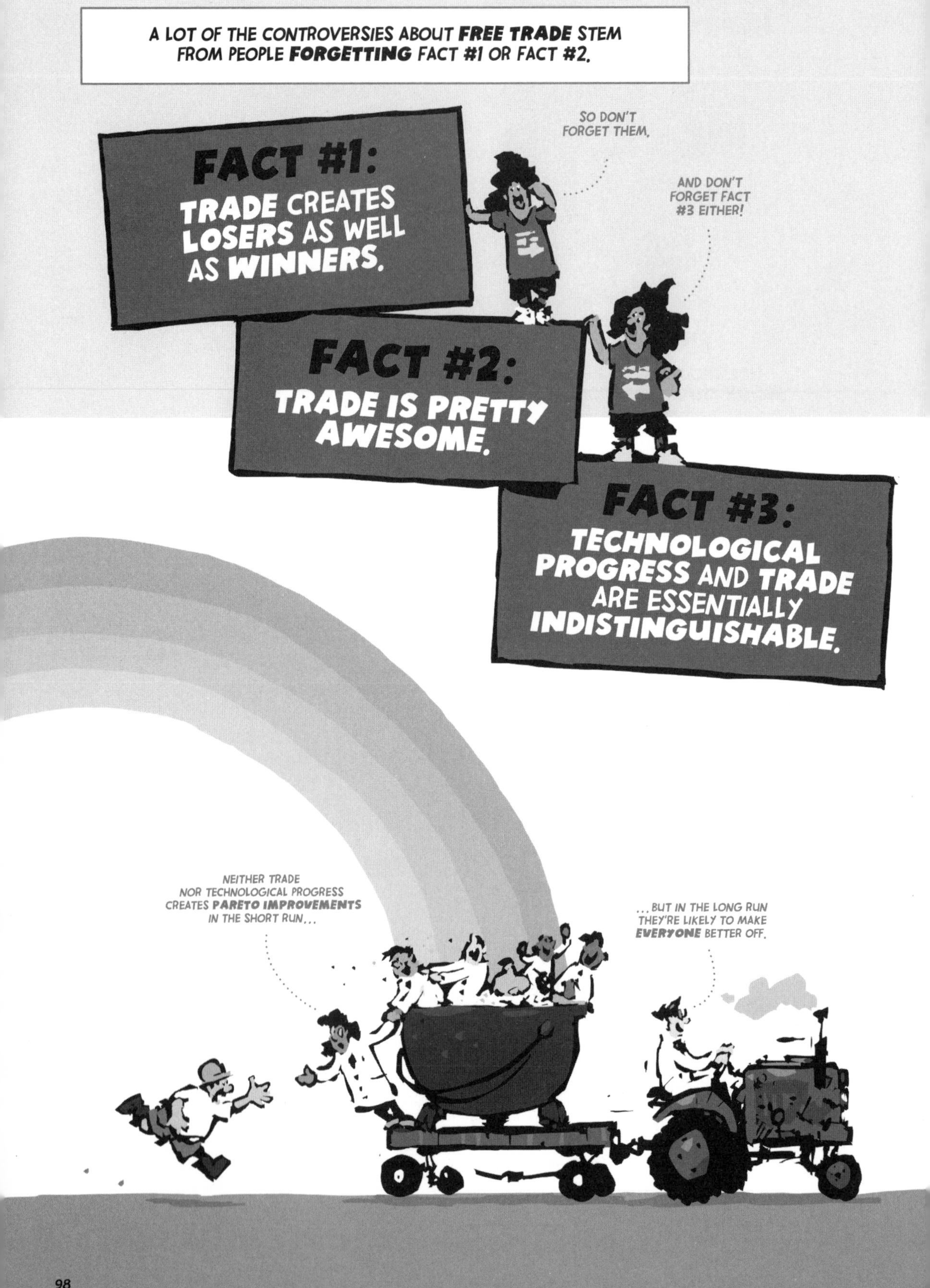
A LOT OF THE CONTROVERSIES ABOUT **FREE TRADE** STEM FROM PEOPLE **FORGETTING** FACT #1 OR FACT #2.
FACT #1: TRADE CREATES LOSERS AS WELL AS WINNERS.
SO DON'T FORGET THEM.
AND DON'T FORGET FACT #3 EITHER!
FACT #2: TRADE IS PRETTY AWESOME.
FACT #3: TECHNOLOGICAL PROGRESS AND TRADE ARE ESSENTIALLY INDISTINGUISHABLE.
NEITHER TRADE NOR TECHNOLOGICAL PROGRESS CREATES **PARETO IMPROVEMENTS** IN THE SHORT RUN...
...BUT IN THE LONG RUN THEY'RE LIKELY TO MAKE **EVERYONE** BETTER OFF.

CHAPTER 8
THE CLASSICAL VIEW OF TRADE

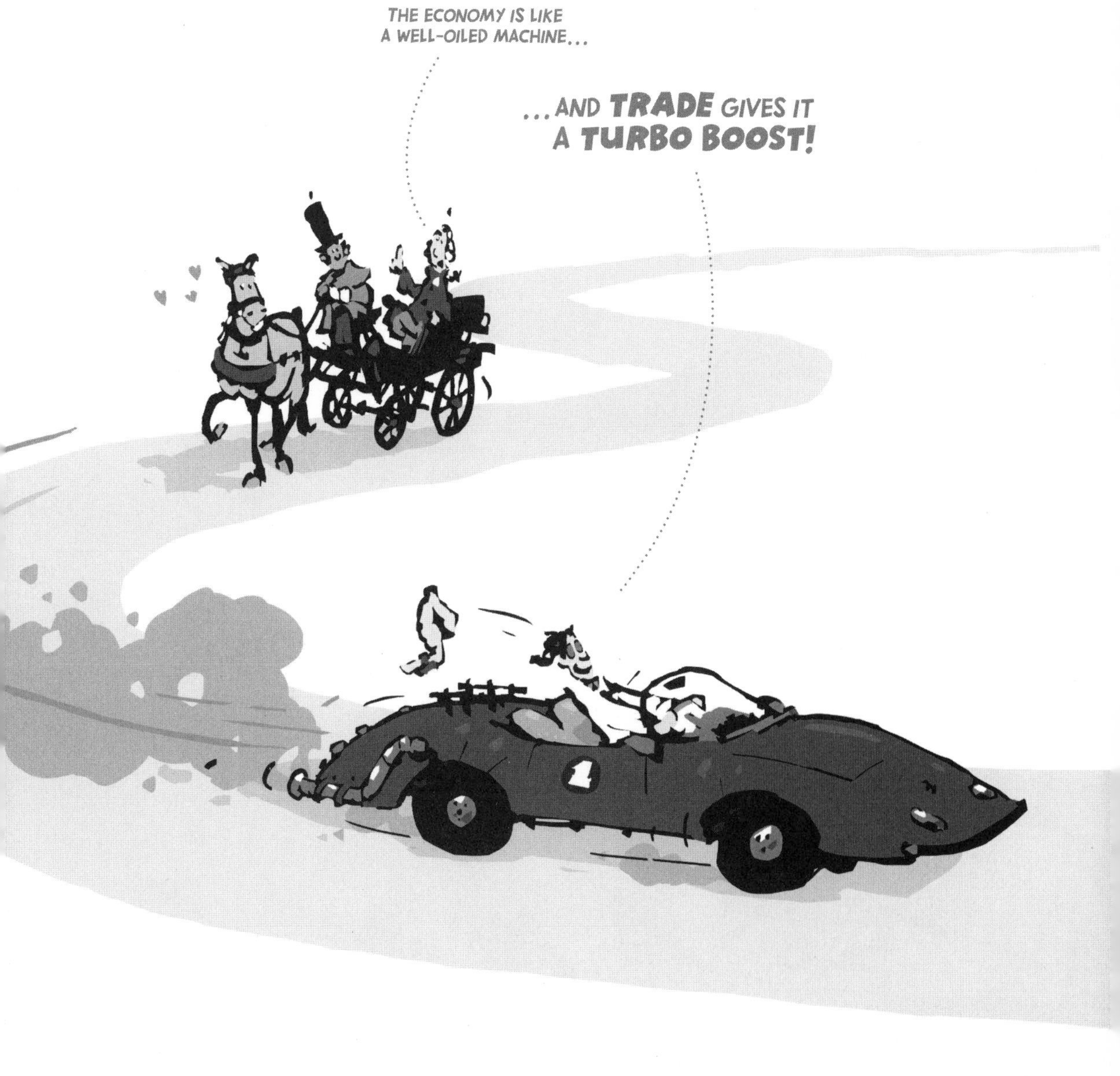
THE ECONOMY IS LIKE A WELL-OILED MACHINE...
...AND TRADE GIVES IT A TURBO BOOST!

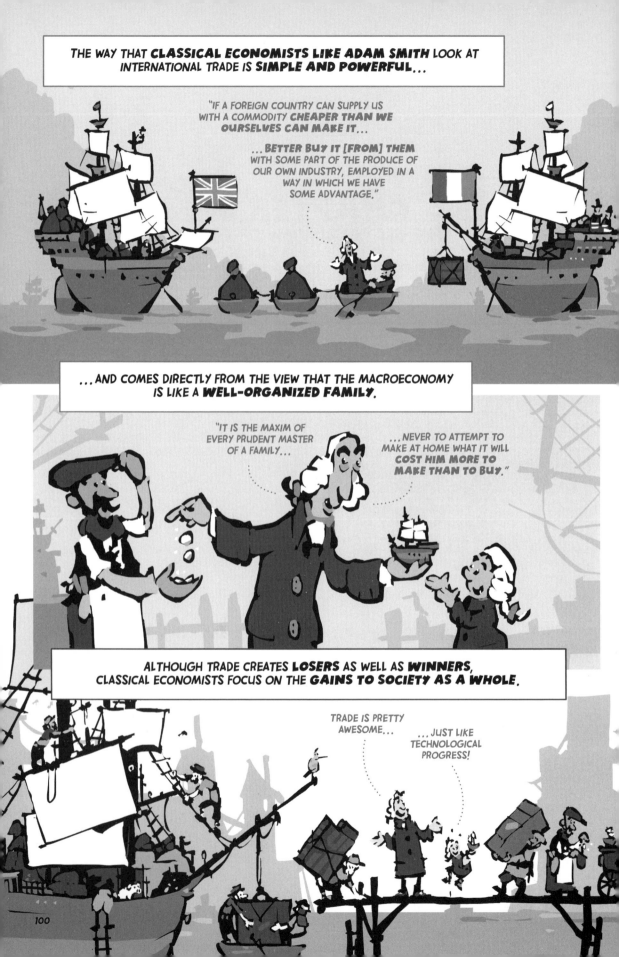

THE WAY THAT **CLASSICAL ECONOMISTS LIKE ADAM SMITH** LOOK AT INTERNATIONAL TRADE IS **SIMPLE AND POWERFUL**...

"IF A FOREIGN COUNTRY CAN SUPPLY US WITH A COMMODITY **CHEAPER THAN WE OURSELVES CAN MAKE IT**...

...**BETTER BUY IT [FROM] THEM** WITH SOME PART OF THE PRODUCE OF OUR OWN INDUSTRY, EMPLOYED IN A WAY IN WHICH WE HAVE SOME ADVANTAGE."

...AND COMES DIRECTLY FROM THE VIEW THAT THE MACROECONOMY IS LIKE A **WELL-ORGANIZED FAMILY**.

"IT IS THE MAXIM OF EVERY PRUDENT MASTER OF A FAMILY...

...NEVER TO ATTEMPT TO MAKE AT HOME WHAT IT WILL **COST HIM MORE TO MAKE THAN TO BUY**."

ALTHOUGH TRADE CREATES **LOSERS** AS WELL AS **WINNERS**, CLASSICAL ECONOMISTS FOCUS ON THE **GAINS TO SOCIETY AS A WHOLE**.

TRADE IS PRETTY AWESOME...

...JUST LIKE TECHNOLOGICAL PROGRESS!

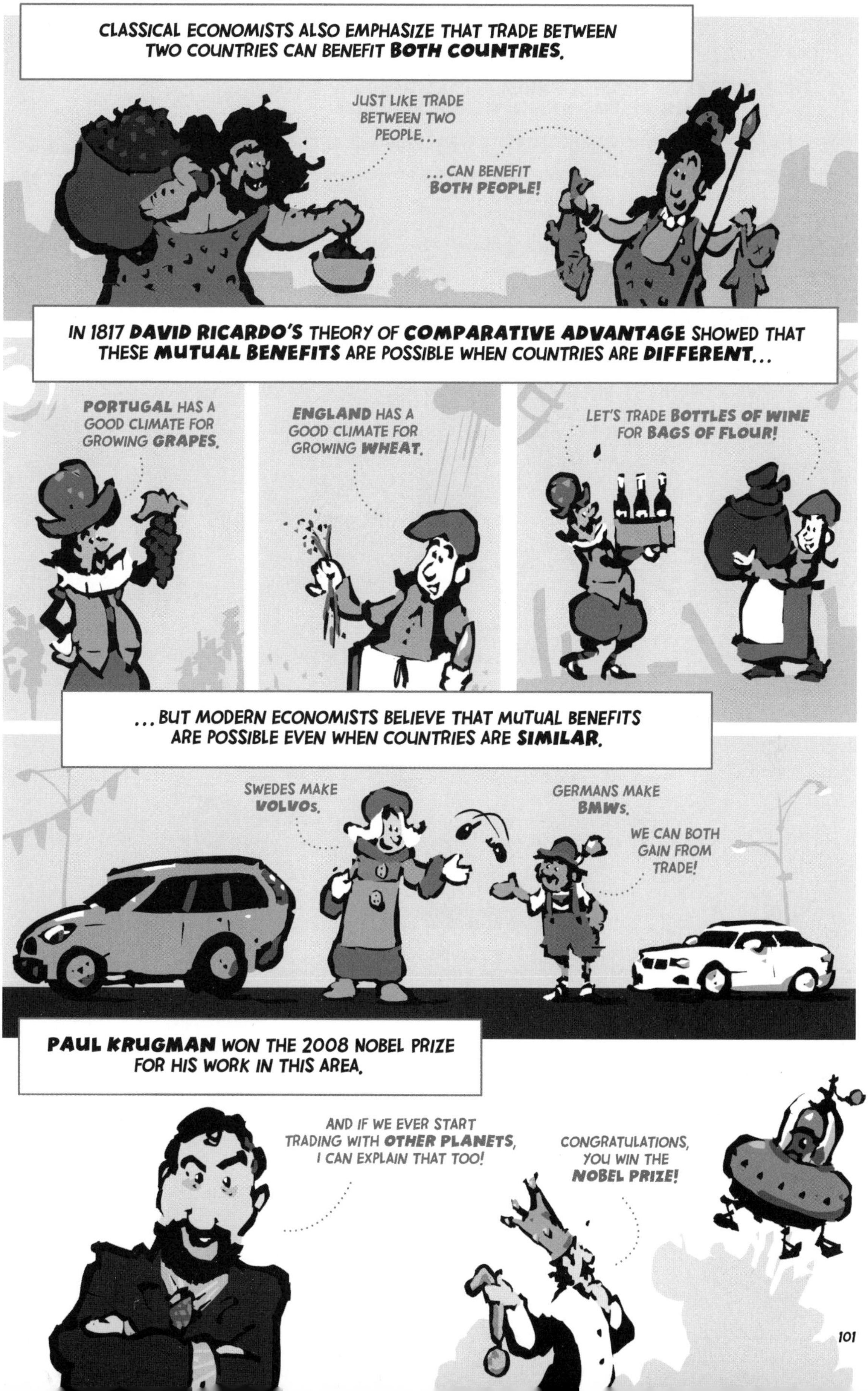
CLASSICAL ECONOMISTS ALSO EMPHASIZE THAT TRADE BETWEEN TWO COUNTRIES CAN BENEFIT **BOTH COUNTRIES.**
JUST LIKE TRADE BETWEEN TWO PEOPLE...
...CAN BENEFIT **BOTH PEOPLE!**
IN 1817 **DAVID RICARDO'S** THEORY OF **COMPARATIVE ADVANTAGE** SHOWED THAT THESE **MUTUAL BENEFITS** ARE POSSIBLE WHEN COUNTRIES ARE **DIFFERENT...**
PORTUGAL HAS A GOOD CLIMATE FOR GROWING **GRAPES.**
ENGLAND HAS A GOOD CLIMATE FOR GROWING **WHEAT.**
LET'S TRADE **BOTTLES OF WINE** FOR **BAGS OF FLOUR!**
...BUT MODERN ECONOMISTS BELIEVE THAT MUTUAL BENEFITS ARE POSSIBLE EVEN WHEN COUNTRIES ARE **SIMILAR.**
SWEDES MAKE **VOLVOS.**
GERMANS MAKE **BMWS.**
WE CAN BOTH GAIN FROM TRADE!
PAUL KRUGMAN WON THE 2008 NOBEL PRIZE FOR HIS WORK IN THIS AREA.
AND IF WE EVER START TRADING WITH **OTHER PLANETS,** I CAN EXPLAIN THAT TOO!
CONGRATULATIONS, YOU WIN THE **NOBEL PRIZE!**

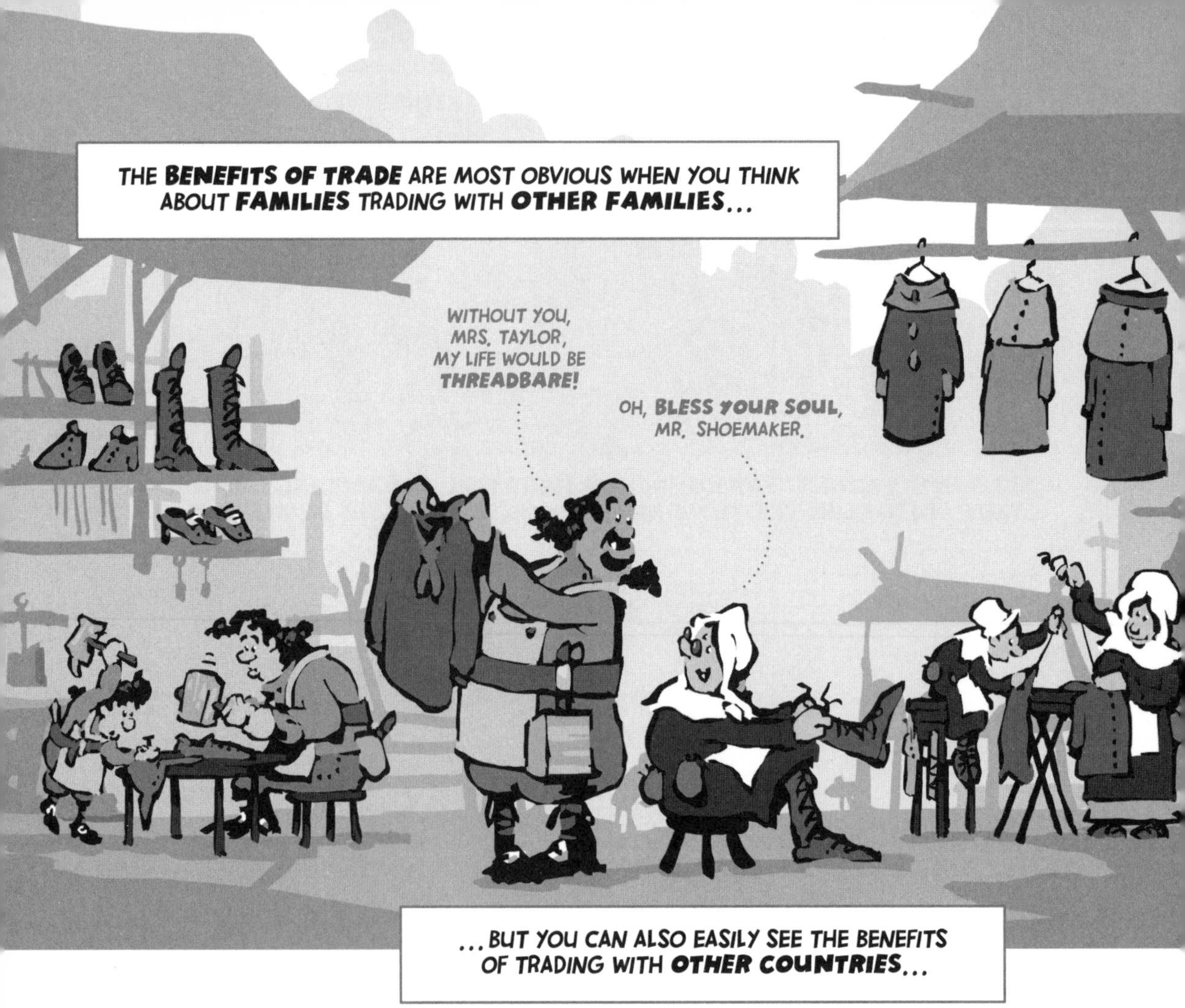
THE **BENEFITS OF TRADE** ARE MOST OBVIOUS WHEN YOU THINK ABOUT **FAMILIES** TRADING WITH **OTHER FAMILIES**...
WITHOUT YOU, MRS. TAYLOR, MY LIFE WOULD BE **THREADBARE!**
OH, **BLESS YOUR SOUL**, MR. SHOEMAKER.
...BUT YOU CAN ALSO EASILY SEE THE BENEFITS OF TRADING WITH **OTHER COUNTRIES**...

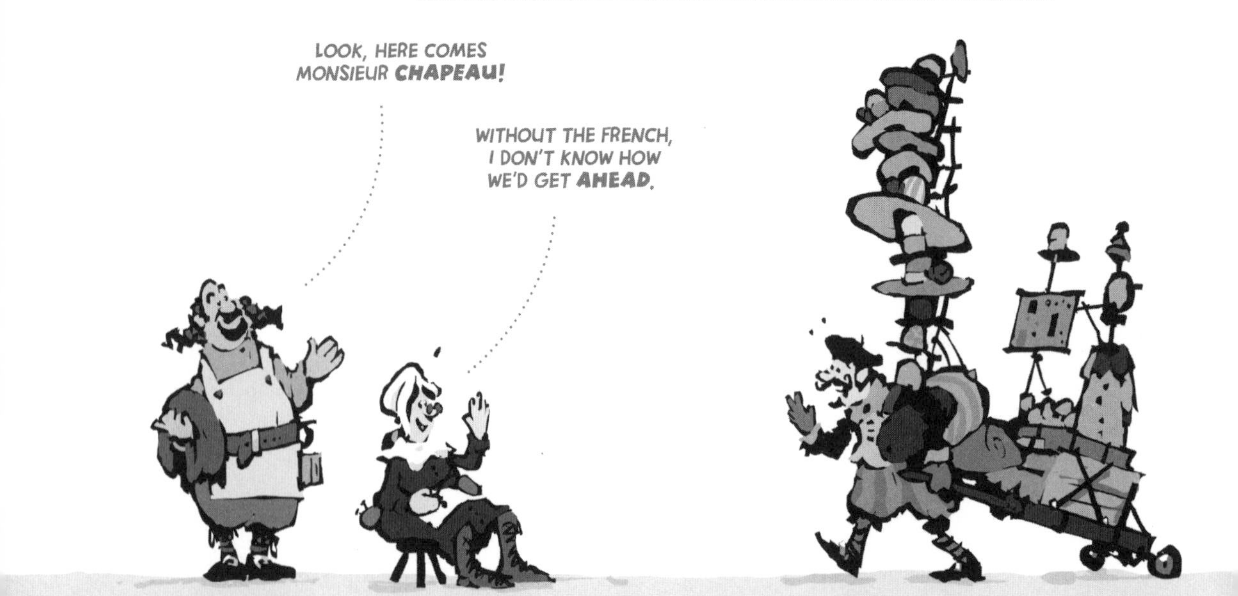
LOOK, HERE COMES MONSIEUR **CHAPEAU!**
WITHOUT THE FRENCH, I DON'T KNOW HOW WE'D GET **AHEAD**.

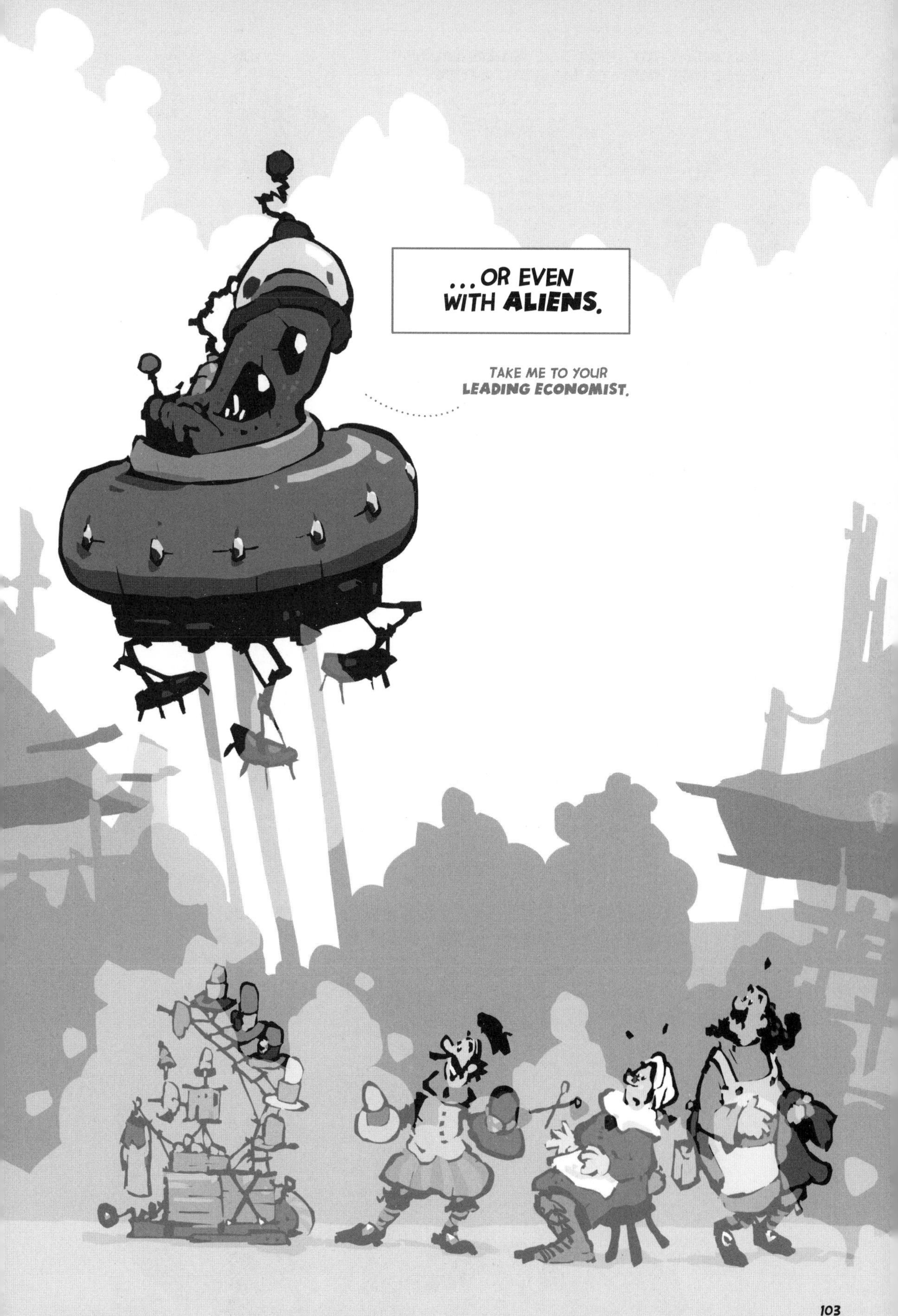
...OR EVEN WITH **ALIENS**.
TAKE ME TO YOUR **LEADING ECONOMIST**.

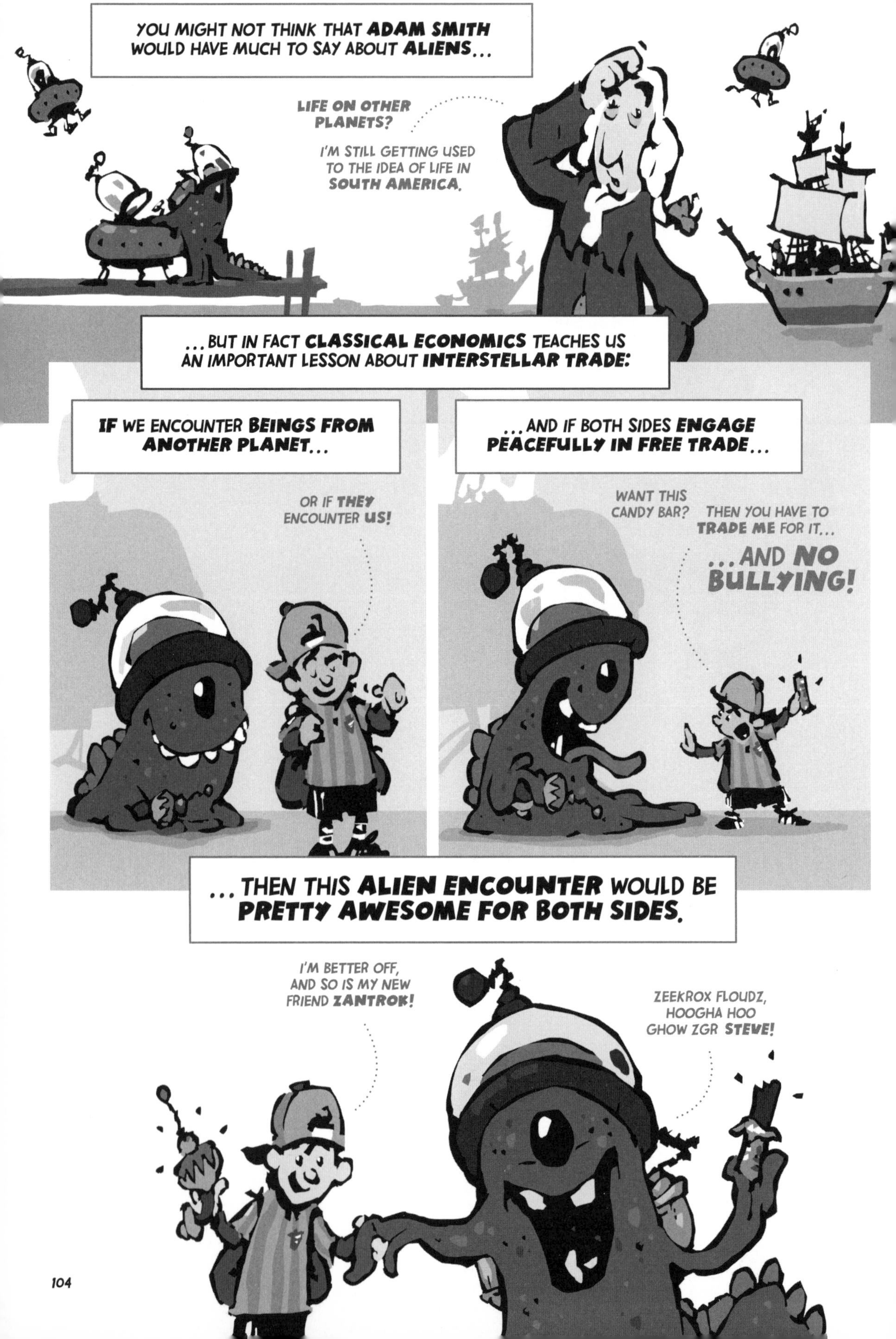
YOU MIGHT NOT THINK THAT ADAM SMITH WOULD HAVE MUCH TO SAY ABOUT ALIENS...
LIFE ON OTHER PLANETS?
I'M STILL GETTING USED TO THE IDEA OF LIFE IN SOUTH AMERICA.
...BUT IN FACT CLASSICAL ECONOMICS TEACHES US AN IMPORTANT LESSON ABOUT INTERSTELLAR TRADE:
IF WE ENCOUNTER BEINGS FROM ANOTHER PLANET...
OR IF THEY ENCOUNTER US!
...AND IF BOTH SIDES ENGAGE PEACEFULLY IN FREE TRADE...
WANT THIS CANDY BAR?
THEN YOU HAVE TO TRADE ME FOR IT...
...AND NO BULLYING!
...THEN THIS ALIEN ENCOUNTER WOULD BE PRETTY AWESOME FOR BOTH SIDES.
I'M BETTER OFF, AND SO IS MY NEW FRIEND ZANTROK!
ZEEKROX FLOUDZ, HOOGHA HOO GHOW ZGR STEVE!

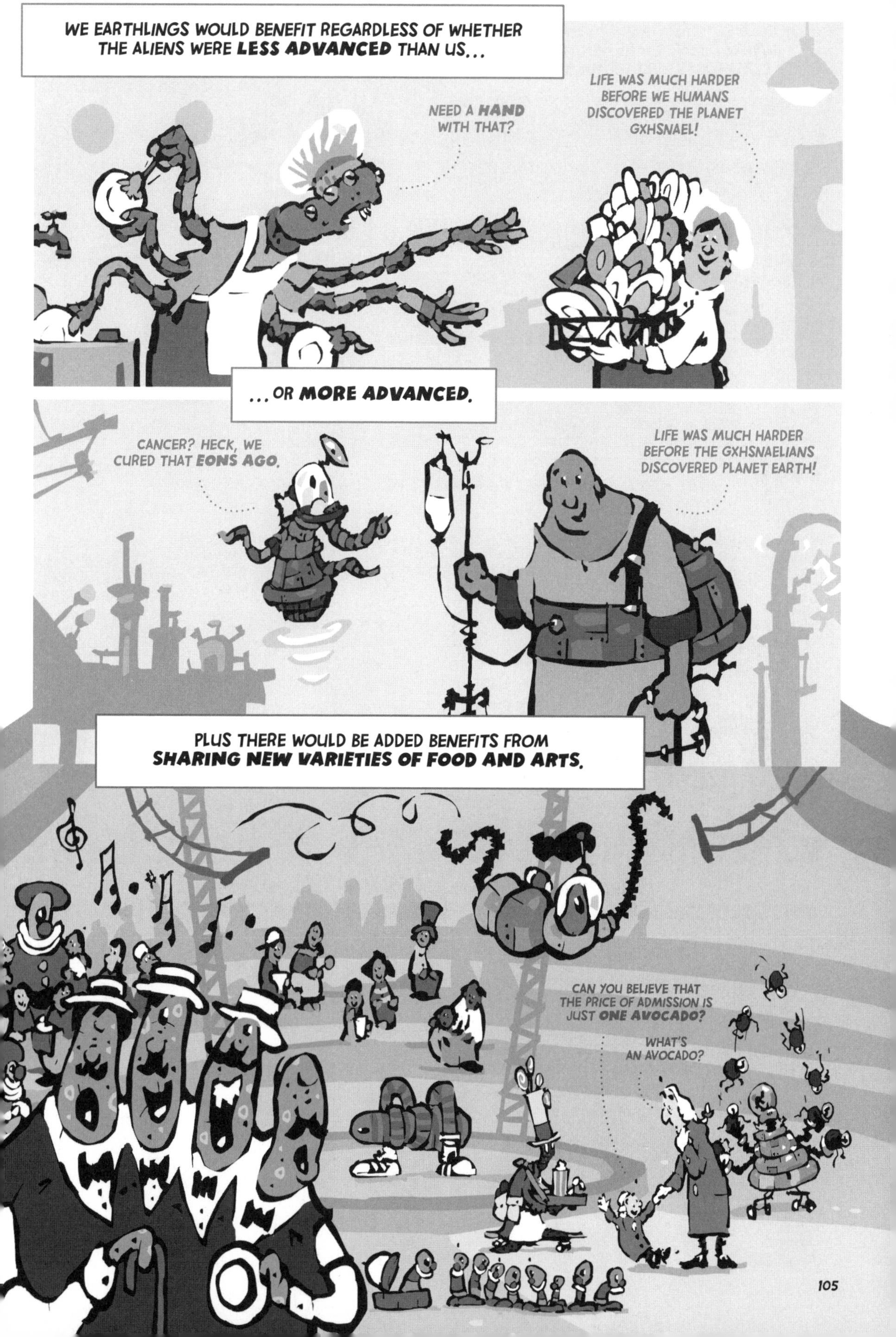

WE EARTHLINGS WOULD BENEFIT REGARDLESS OF WHETHER THE ALIENS WERE **LESS ADVANCED** THAN US...
NEED A **HAND** WITH THAT?
LIFE WAS MUCH HARDER BEFORE WE HUMANS DISCOVERED THE PLANET GXHSNAEL!
...OR **MORE ADVANCED.**
CANCER? HECK, WE CURED THAT **EONS AGO.**
LIFE WAS MUCH HARDER BEFORE THE GXHSNAELIANS DISCOVERED PLANET EARTH!
PLUS THERE WOULD BE ADDED BENEFITS FROM **SHARING NEW VARIETIES OF FOOD AND ARTS.**
CAN YOU BELIEVE THAT THE PRICE OF ADMISSION IS JUST **ONE AVOCADO?**
WHAT'S AN AVOCADO?

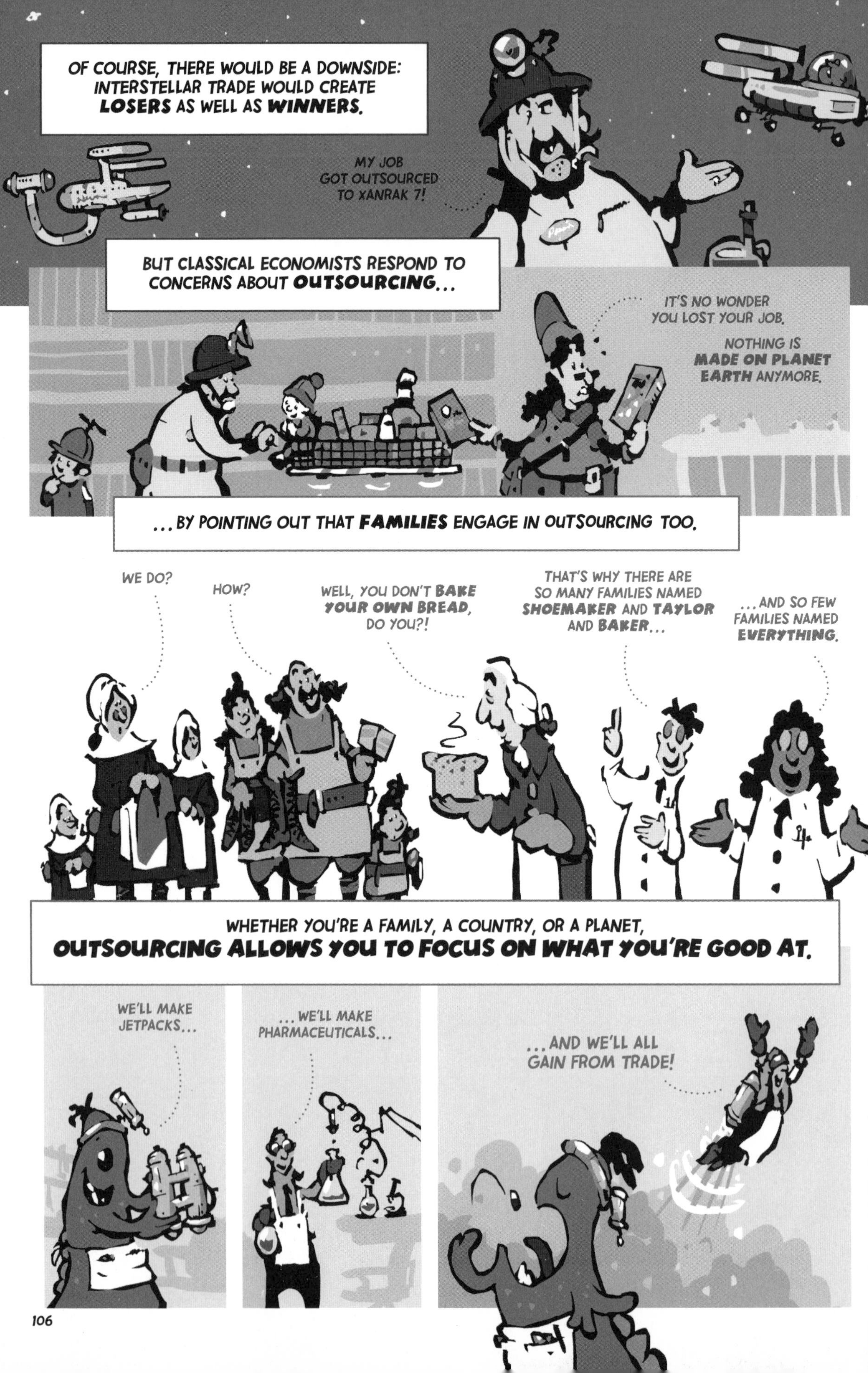
OF COURSE, THERE WOULD BE A DOWNSIDE: INTERSTELLAR TRADE WOULD CREATE **LOSERS** AS WELL AS **WINNERS.**
MY JOB GOT OUTSOURCED TO XANRAK 7!
BUT CLASSICAL ECONOMISTS RESPOND TO CONCERNS ABOUT **OUTSOURCING...**
IT'S NO WONDER YOU LOST YOUR JOB.
NOTHING IS **MADE ON PLANET EARTH** ANYMORE.
...BY POINTING OUT THAT **FAMILIES** ENGAGE IN OUTSOURCING TOO.
WE DO?
HOW?
WELL, YOU DON'T **BAKE YOUR OWN BREAD,** DO YOU?!
THAT'S WHY THERE ARE SO MANY FAMILIES NAMED **SHOEMAKER** AND **TAYLOR** AND **BAKER...**
...AND SO FEW FAMILIES NAMED **EVERYTHING.**
WHETHER YOU'RE A FAMILY, A COUNTRY, OR A PLANET, **OUTSOURCING ALLOWS YOU TO FOCUS ON WHAT YOU'RE GOOD AT.**
WE'LL MAKE JETPACKS...
...WE'LL MAKE PHARMACEUTICALS...
...AND WE'LL ALL GAIN FROM TRADE!

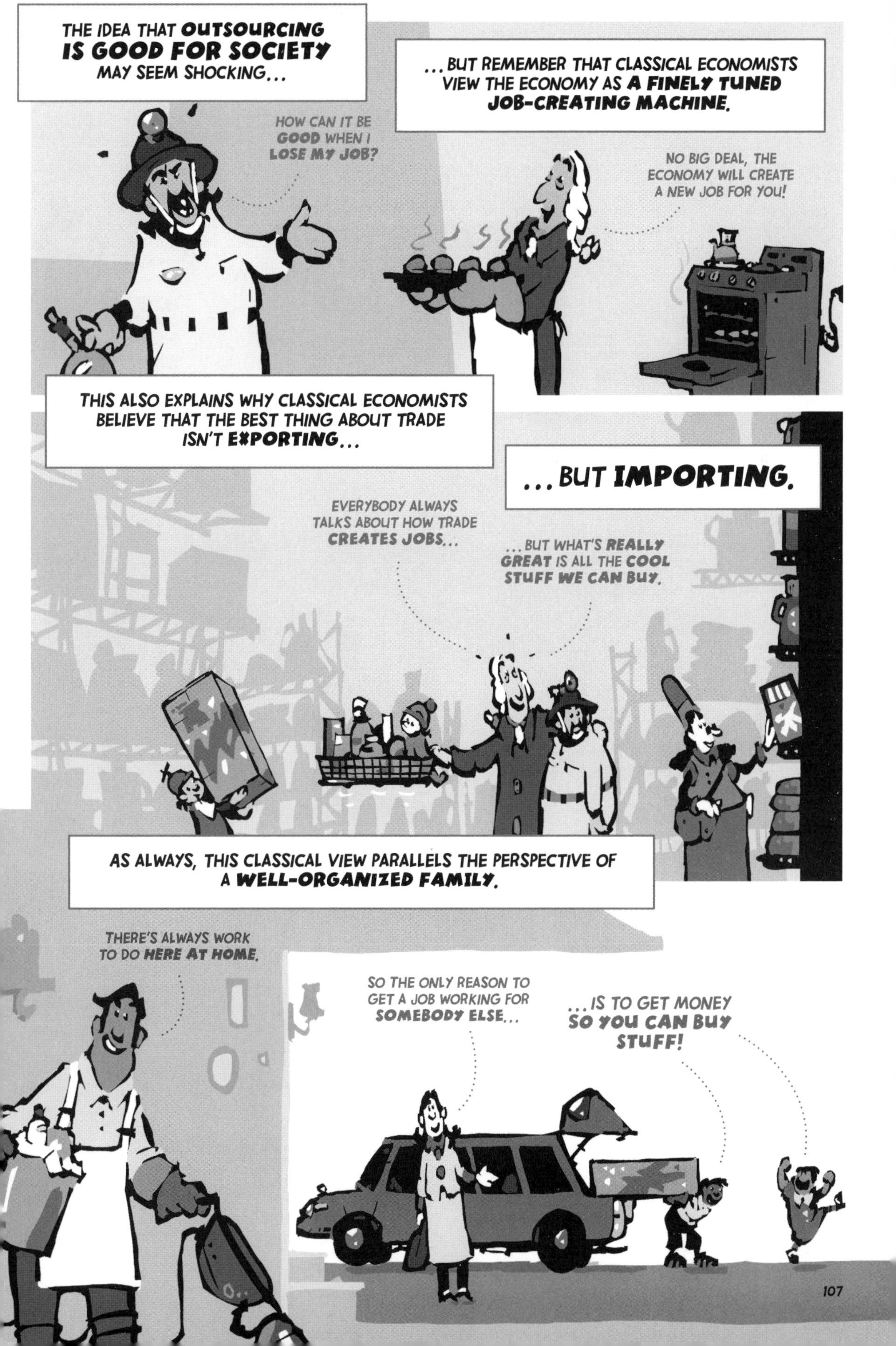

THE IDEA THAT OUTSOURCING IS GOOD FOR SOCIETY MAY SEEM SHOCKING...
HOW CAN IT BE GOOD WHEN I LOSE MY JOB?
...BUT REMEMBER THAT CLASSICAL ECONOMISTS VIEW THE ECONOMY AS A FINELY TUNED JOB-CREATING MACHINE.
NO BIG DEAL, THE ECONOMY WILL CREATE A NEW JOB FOR YOU!
THIS ALSO EXPLAINS WHY CLASSICAL ECONOMISTS BELIEVE THAT THE BEST THING ABOUT TRADE ISN'T EXPORTING...
...BUT IMPORTING.
EVERYBODY ALWAYS TALKS ABOUT HOW TRADE CREATES JOBS...
...BUT WHAT'S REALLY GREAT IS ALL THE COOL STUFF WE CAN BUY.
AS ALWAYS, THIS CLASSICAL VIEW PARALLELS THE PERSPECTIVE OF A WELL-ORGANIZED FAMILY.
THERE'S ALWAYS WORK TO DO HERE AT HOME.
SO THE ONLY REASON TO GET A JOB WORKING FOR SOMEBODY ELSE...
...IS TO GET MONEY SO YOU CAN BUY STUFF!

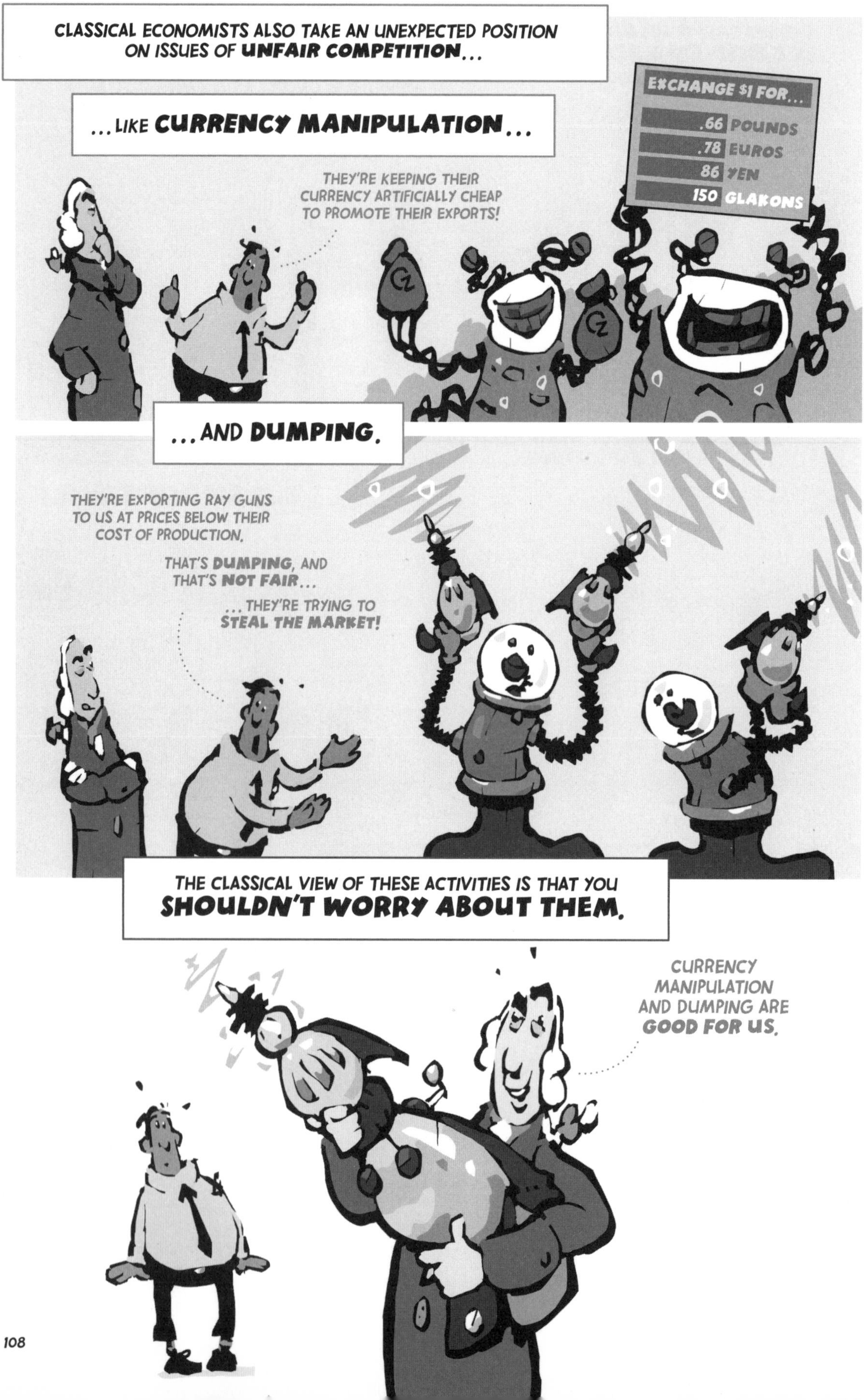

CLASSICAL ECONOMISTS ALSO TAKE AN UNEXPECTED POSITION ON ISSUES OF UNFAIR COMPETITION...
...LIKE CURRENCY MANIPULATION...
EXCHANGE $1 FOR...
.66 POUNDS
.78 EUROS
86 YEN
150 GLAKONS
THEY'RE KEEPING THEIR CURRENCY ARTIFICIALLY CHEAP TO PROMOTE THEIR EXPORTS!
...AND DUMPING.
THEY'RE EXPORTING RAY GUNS TO US AT PRICES BELOW THEIR COST OF PRODUCTION.
THAT'S DUMPING, AND THAT'S NOT FAIR...
...THEY'RE TRYING TO STEAL THE MARKET!
THE CLASSICAL VIEW OF THESE ACTIVITIES IS THAT YOU SHOULDN'T WORRY ABOUT THEM.
CURRENCY MANIPULATION AND DUMPING ARE GOOD FOR US.

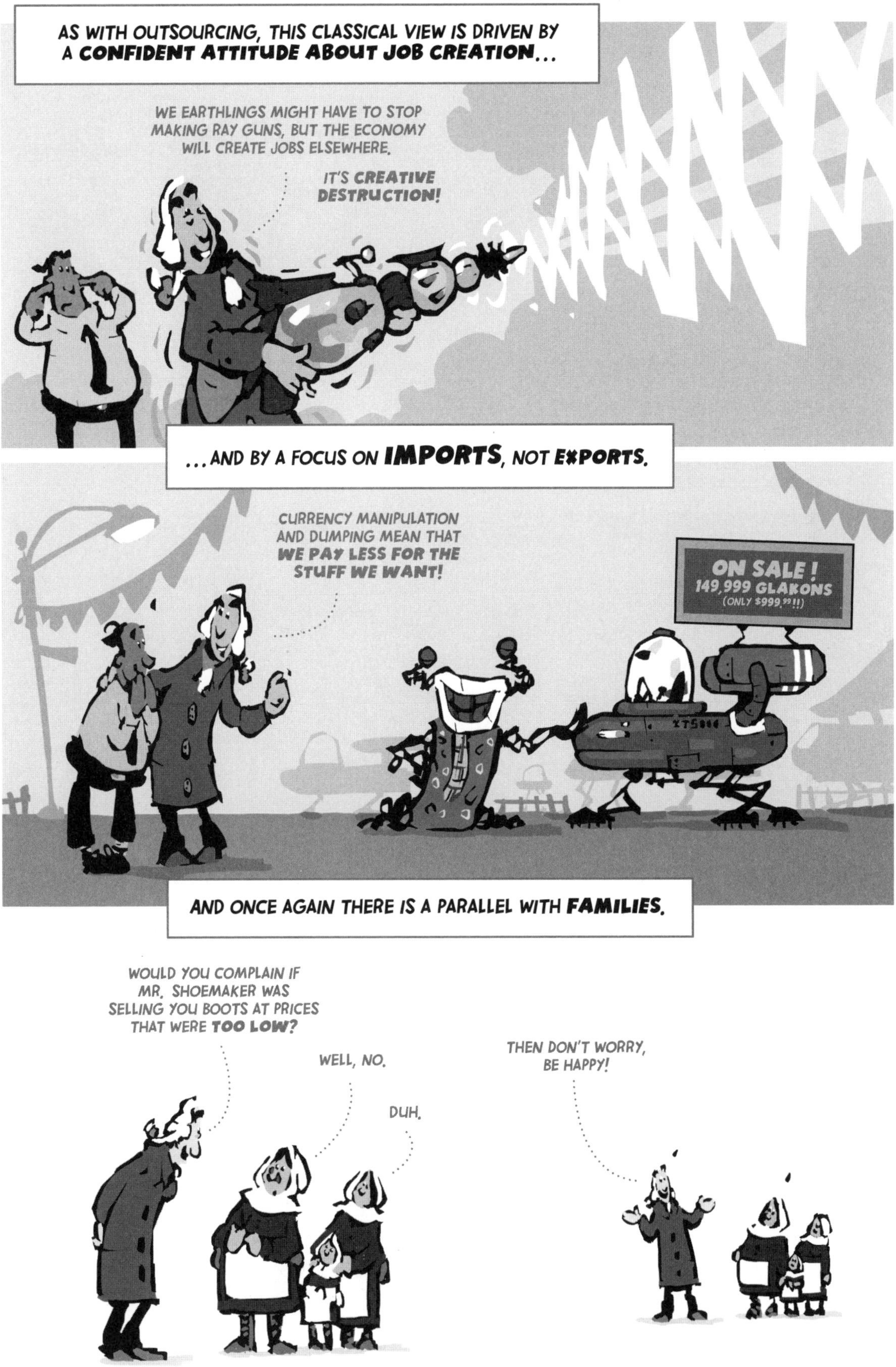
AS WITH OUTSOURCING, THIS CLASSICAL VIEW IS DRIVEN BY A **CONFIDENT ATTITUDE ABOUT JOB CREATION**...
WE EARTHLINGS MIGHT HAVE TO STOP MAKING RAY GUNS, BUT THE ECONOMY WILL CREATE JOBS ELSEWHERE.
IT'S **CREATIVE DESTRUCTION!**
...AND BY A FOCUS ON **IMPORTS**, NOT **EXPORTS**.
CURRENCY MANIPULATION AND DUMPING MEAN THAT **WE PAY LESS FOR THE STUFF WE WANT!**
ON SALE! 149,999 GLAKONS (ONLY $999.99!!)
AND ONCE AGAIN THERE IS A PARALLEL WITH **FAMILIES**.
WOULD YOU COMPLAIN IF MR. SHOEMAKER WAS SELLING YOU BOOTS AT PRICES THAT WERE **TOO LOW?**
WELL, NO.
DUH.
THEN DON'T WORRY, BE HAPPY!

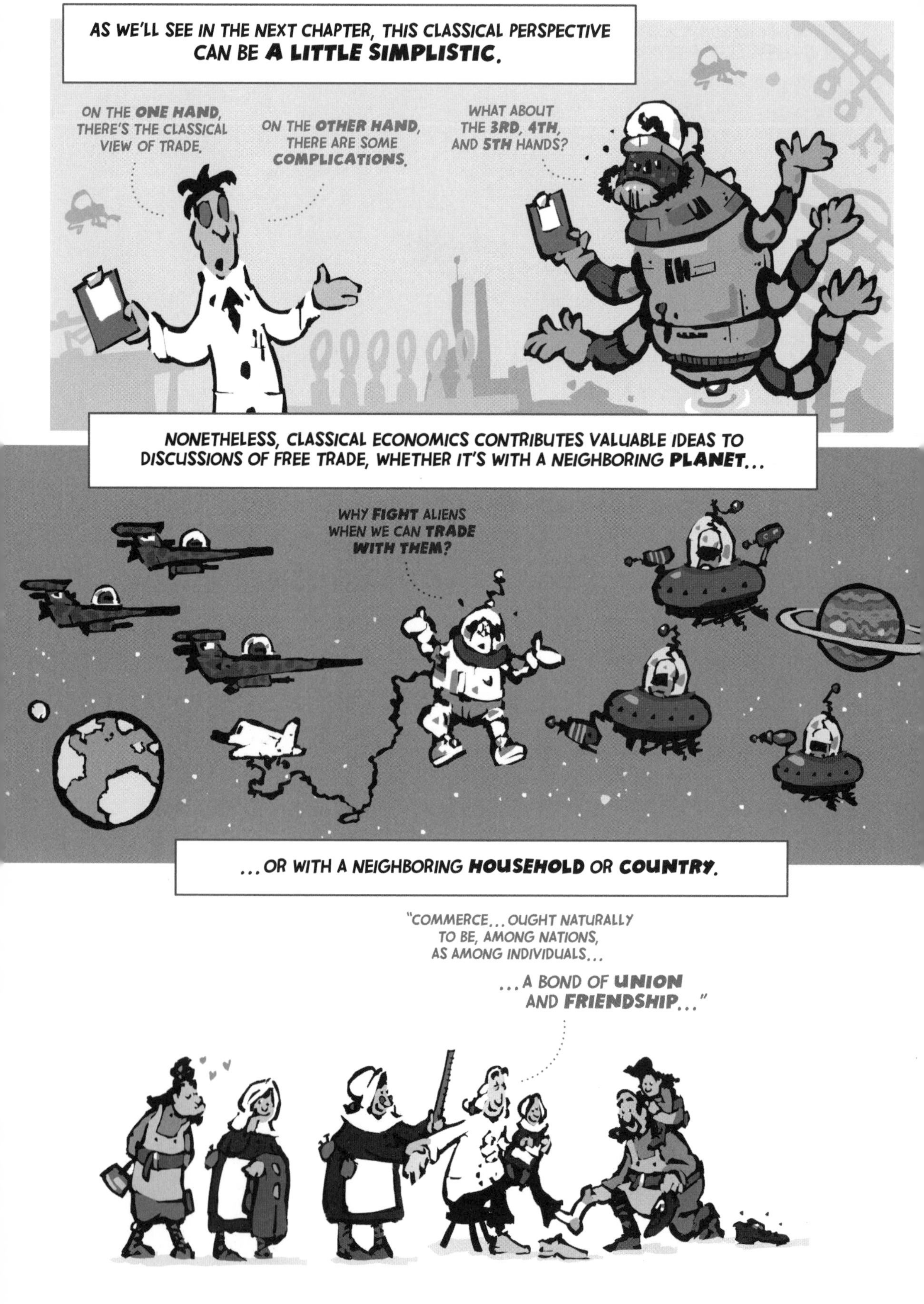
AS WE'LL SEE IN THE NEXT CHAPTER, THIS CLASSICAL PERSPECTIVE CAN BE **A LITTLE SIMPLISTIC.**
ON THE **ONE HAND**, THERE'S THE CLASSICAL VIEW OF TRADE.
ON THE **OTHER HAND**, THERE ARE SOME **COMPLICATIONS**.
WHAT ABOUT THE **3RD, 4TH**, AND **5TH** HANDS?
NONETHELESS, CLASSICAL ECONOMICS CONTRIBUTES VALUABLE IDEAS TO DISCUSSIONS OF FREE TRADE, WHETHER IT'S WITH A NEIGHBORING **PLANET**...
WHY **FIGHT** ALIENS WHEN WE CAN **TRADE WITH THEM?**
...OR WITH A NEIGHBORING **HOUSEHOLD** OR **COUNTRY**.
"COMMERCE... OUGHT NATURALLY TO BE, AMONG NATIONS, AS AMONG INDIVIDUALS...
...A BOND OF **UNION** AND **FRIENDSHIP**..."

CHAPTER 9
COMPLICATIONS

"COMMERCE, WHICH OUGHT NATURALLY TO BE, AMONG NATIONS, AS AMONG INDIVIDUALS, A BOND OF **UNION** AND **FRIENDSHIP**...

...HAS BECOME THE MOST FERTILE SOURCE OF **DISCORD** AND **ANIMOSITY!**"

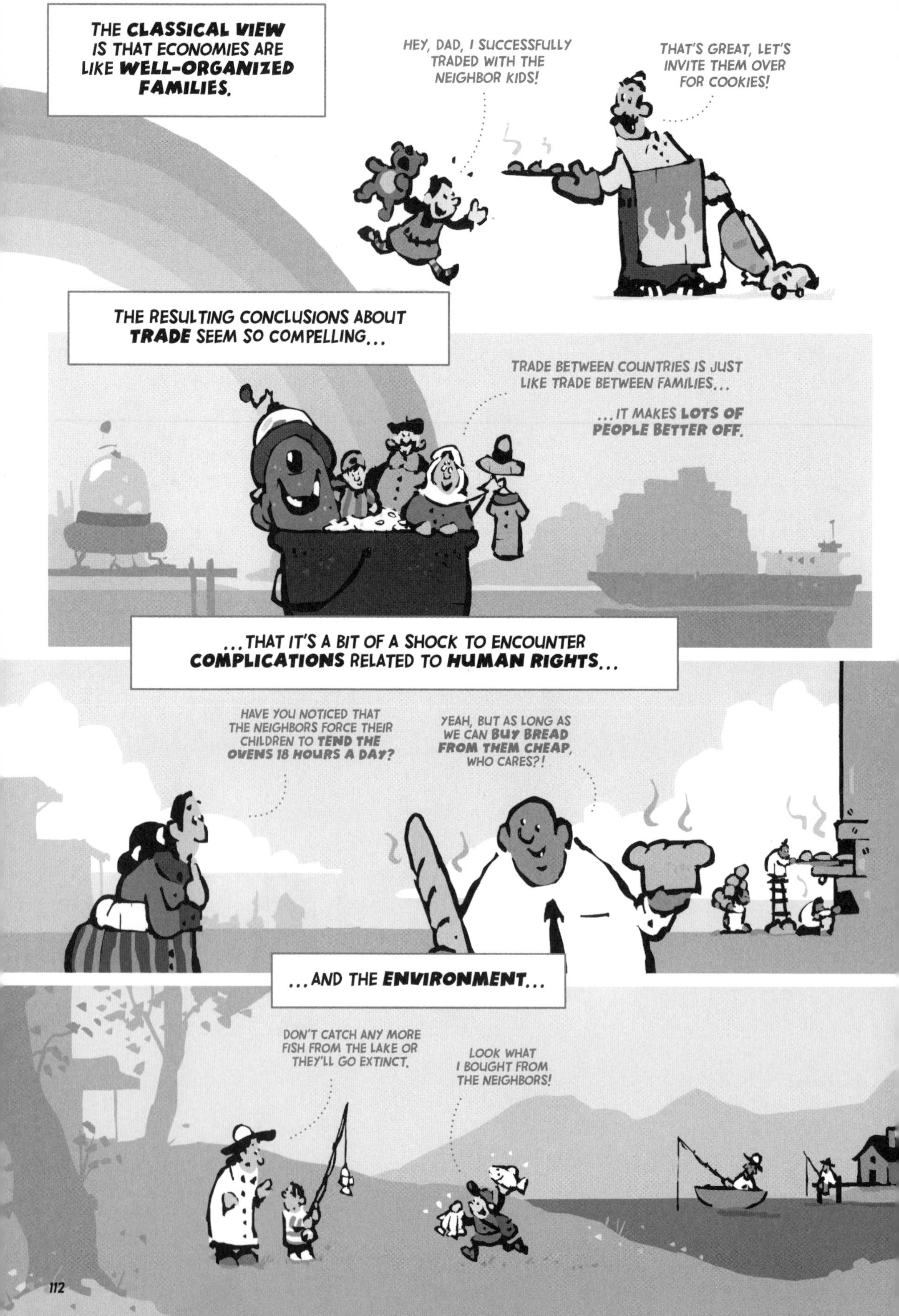
THE CLASSICAL VIEW IS THAT ECONOMIES ARE LIKE WELL-ORGANIZED FAMILIES.
HEY, DAD, I SUCCESSFULLY TRADED WITH THE NEIGHBOR KIDS!
THAT'S GREAT, LET'S INVITE THEM OVER FOR COOKIES!
THE RESULTING CONCLUSIONS ABOUT TRADE SEEM SO COMPELLING...
TRADE BETWEEN COUNTRIES IS JUST LIKE TRADE BETWEEN FAMILIES...
...IT MAKES LOTS OF PEOPLE BETTER OFF.
...THAT IT'S A BIT OF A SHOCK TO ENCOUNTER COMPLICATIONS RELATED TO HUMAN RIGHTS...
HAVE YOU NOTICED THAT THE NEIGHBORS FORCE THEIR CHILDREN TO TEND THE OVENS 18 HOURS A DAY?
YEAH, BUT AS LONG AS WE CAN BUY BREAD FROM THEM CHEAP, WHO CARES?!
...AND THE ENVIRONMENT...
DON'T CATCH ANY MORE FISH FROM THE LAKE OR THEY'LL GO EXTINCT.
LOOK WHAT I BOUGHT FROM THE NEIGHBORS!

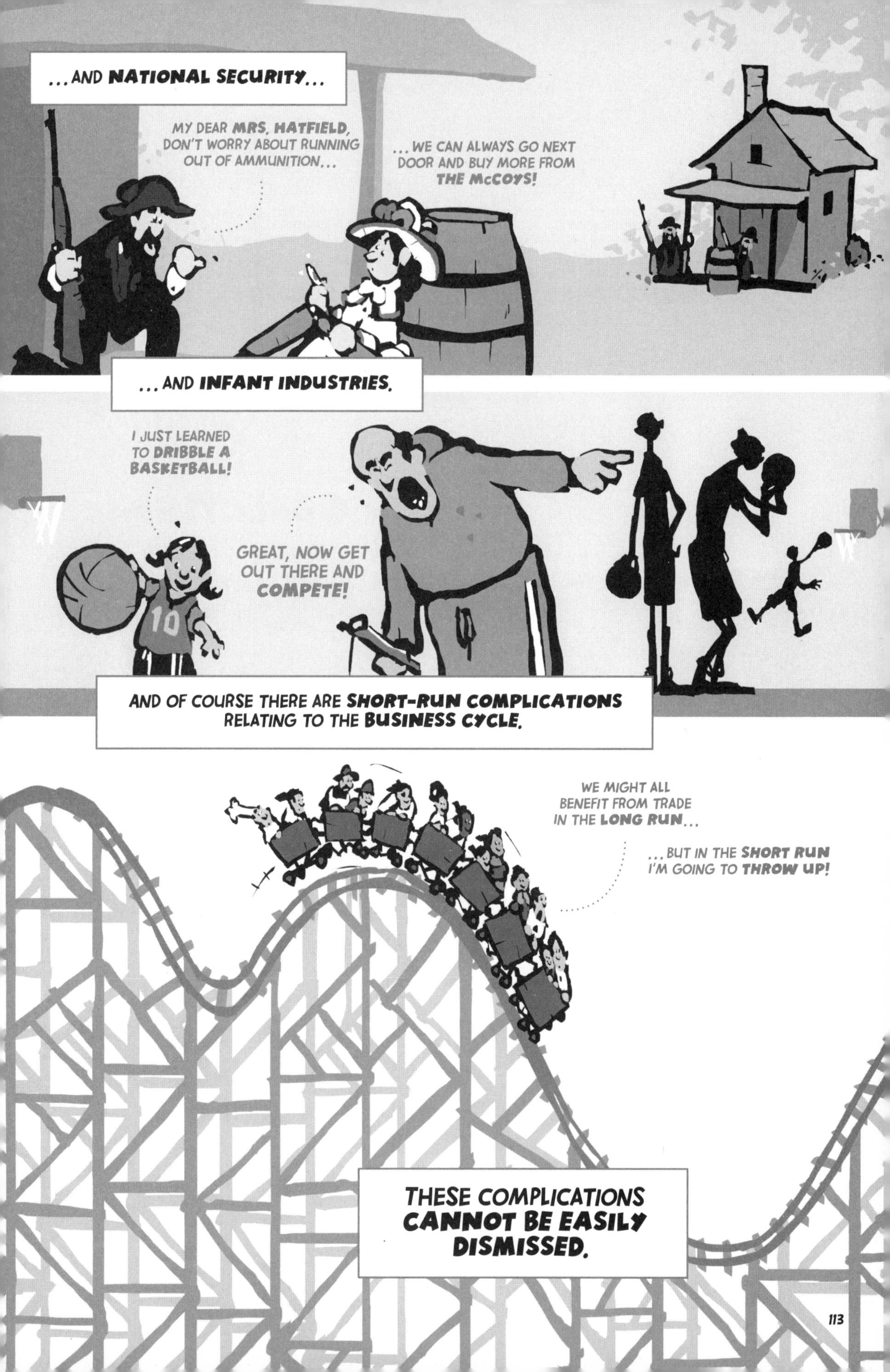
. . . AND **NATIONAL SECURITY . . .**
MY DEAR **MRS. HATFIELD,** DON'T WORRY ABOUT RUNNING OUT OF AMMUNITION . . .
. . . WE CAN ALWAYS GO NEXT DOOR AND BUY MORE FROM **THE McCOYS!**
. . . AND **INFANT INDUSTRIES.**
I JUST LEARNED TO **DRIBBLE A BASKETBALL!**
GREAT, NOW GET OUT THERE AND **COMPETE!**
10
AND OF COURSE THERE ARE **SHORT-RUN COMPLICATIONS** RELATING TO THE **BUSINESS CYCLE.**
WE MIGHT ALL BENEFIT FROM TRADE IN THE **LONG RUN . . .**
. . . BUT IN THE **SHORT RUN** I'M GOING TO **THROW UP!**
THESE COMPLICATIONS **CANNOT BE EASILY DISMISSED.**

THE CLASSICAL PERSPECTIVE PROMISES THAT TRADE BETWEEN COUNTRIES BENEFITS **BOTH** COUNTRIES...

...AND SO, IN THE LONG RUN, TRADE IS LIKELY TO LEAD TO **PARETO IMPROVEMENTS.**

I REST MY CASE!

OBJECTION!

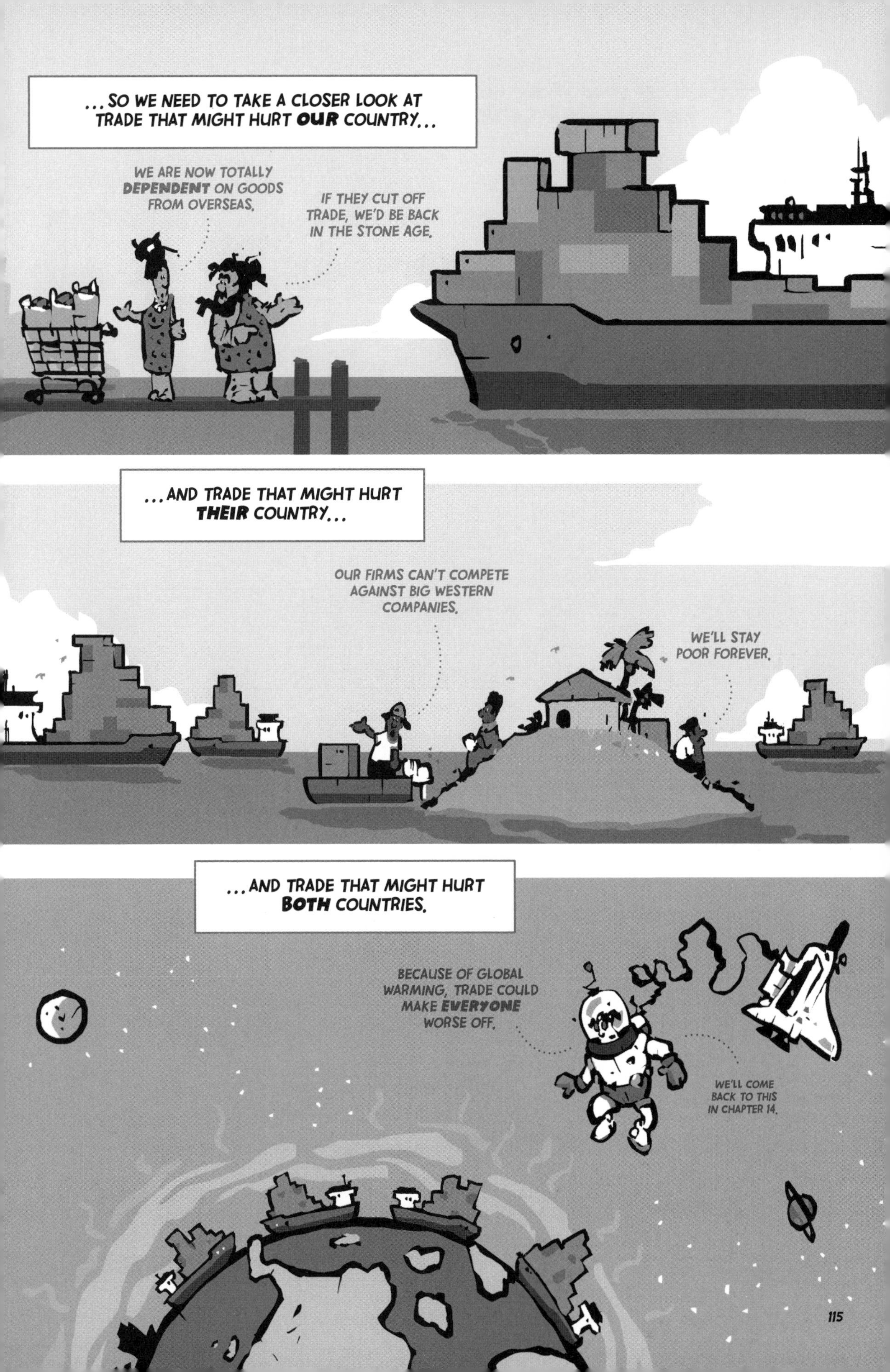
...SO WE NEED TO TAKE A CLOSER LOOK AT TRADE THAT MIGHT HURT OUR COUNTRY...
WE ARE NOW TOTALLY DEPENDENT ON GOODS FROM OVERSEAS.
IF THEY CUT OFF TRADE, WE'D BE BACK IN THE STONE AGE.
...AND TRADE THAT MIGHT HURT THEIR COUNTRY...
OUR FIRMS CAN'T COMPETE AGAINST BIG WESTERN COMPANIES.
WE'LL STAY POOR FOREVER.
...AND TRADE THAT MIGHT HURT BOTH COUNTRIES.
BECAUSE OF GLOBAL WARMING, TRADE COULD MAKE EVERYONE WORSE OFF.
WE'LL COME BACK TO THIS IN CHAPTER 14.

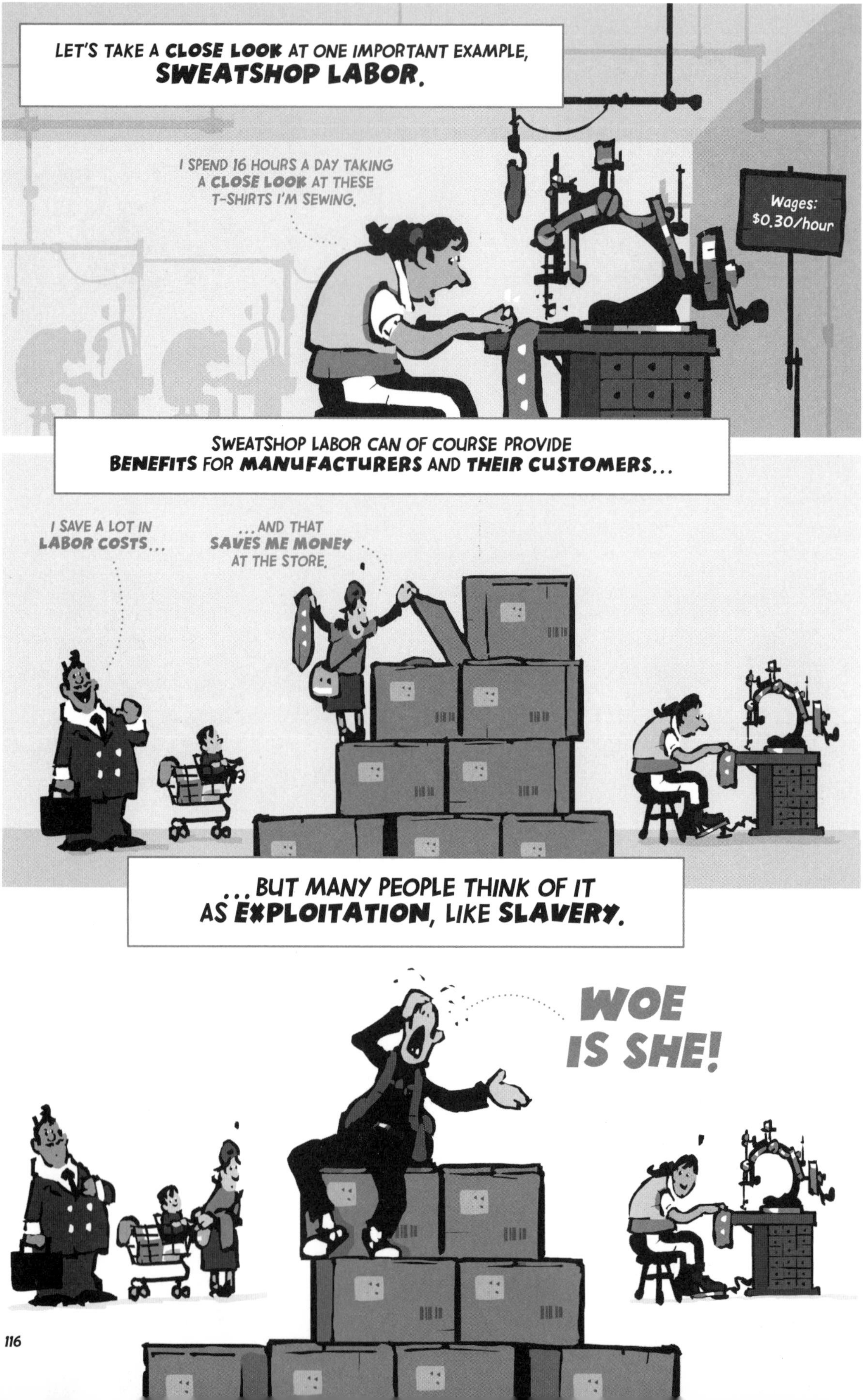
LET'S TAKE A **CLOSE LOOK** AT ONE IMPORTANT EXAMPLE, **SWEATSHOP LABOR.**
I SPEND 16 HOURS A DAY TAKING A **CLOSE LOOK** AT THESE T-SHIRTS I'M SEWING.
Wages: $0.30/hour
SWEATSHOP LABOR CAN OF COURSE PROVIDE **BENEFITS** FOR **MANUFACTURERS** AND **THEIR CUSTOMERS**...
I SAVE A LOT IN **LABOR COSTS**...
...AND THAT **SAVES ME MONEY** AT THE STORE.
...BUT MANY PEOPLE THINK OF IT AS **EXPLOITATION**, LIKE **SLAVERY**.
WOE IS SHE!

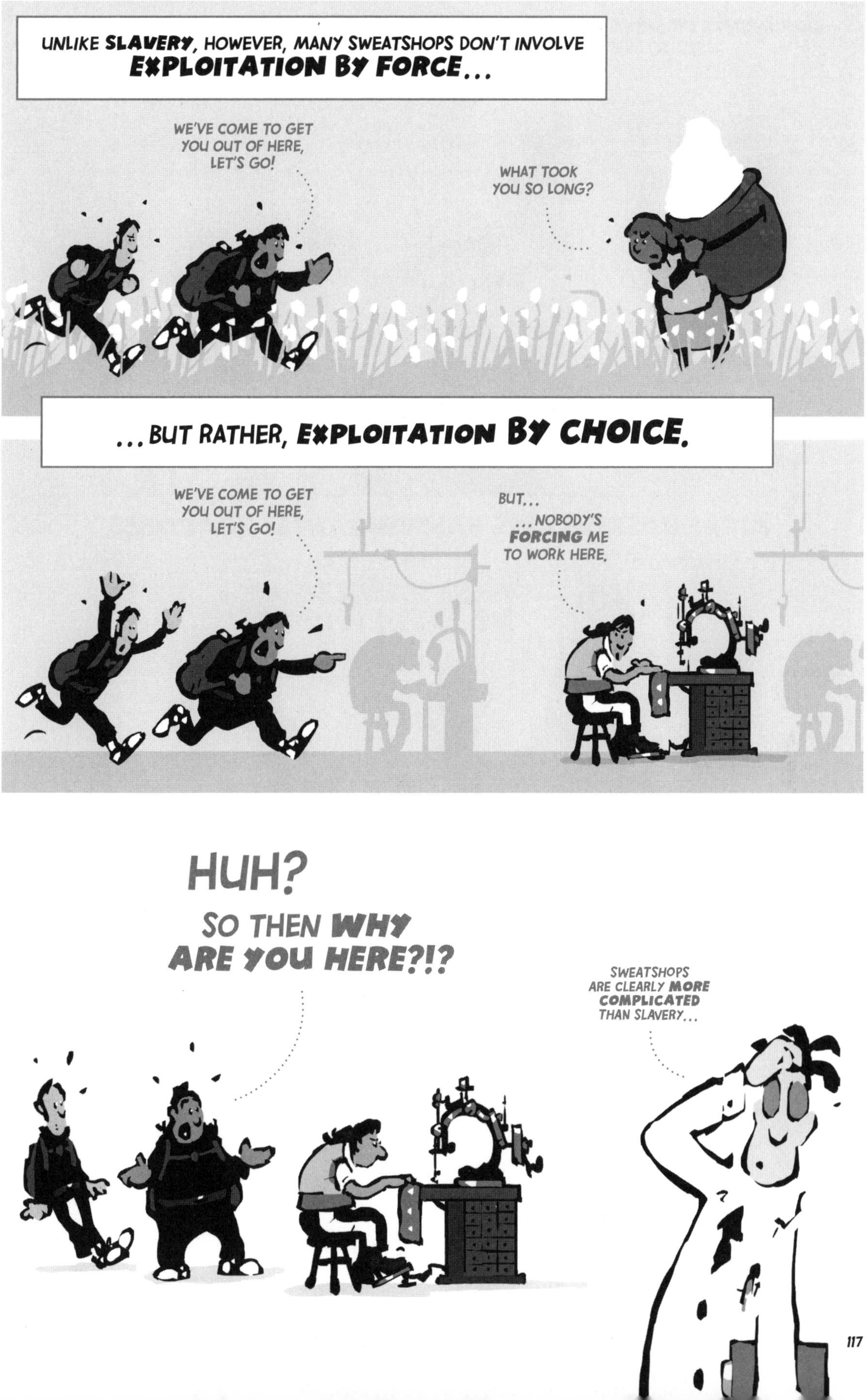
UNLIKE SLAVERY, HOWEVER, MANY SWEATSHOPS DON'T INVOLVE EXPLOITATION BY FORCE...
WE'VE COME TO GET YOU OUT OF HERE, LET'S GO!
WHAT TOOK YOU SO LONG?
...BUT RATHER, EXPLOITATION BY CHOICE.
WE'VE COME TO GET YOU OUT OF HERE, LET'S GO!
BUT...
...NOBODY'S FORCING ME TO WORK HERE.
HUH?
SO THEN WHY ARE YOU HERE?!?
SWEATSHOPS ARE CLEARLY MORE COMPLICATED THAN SLAVERY...

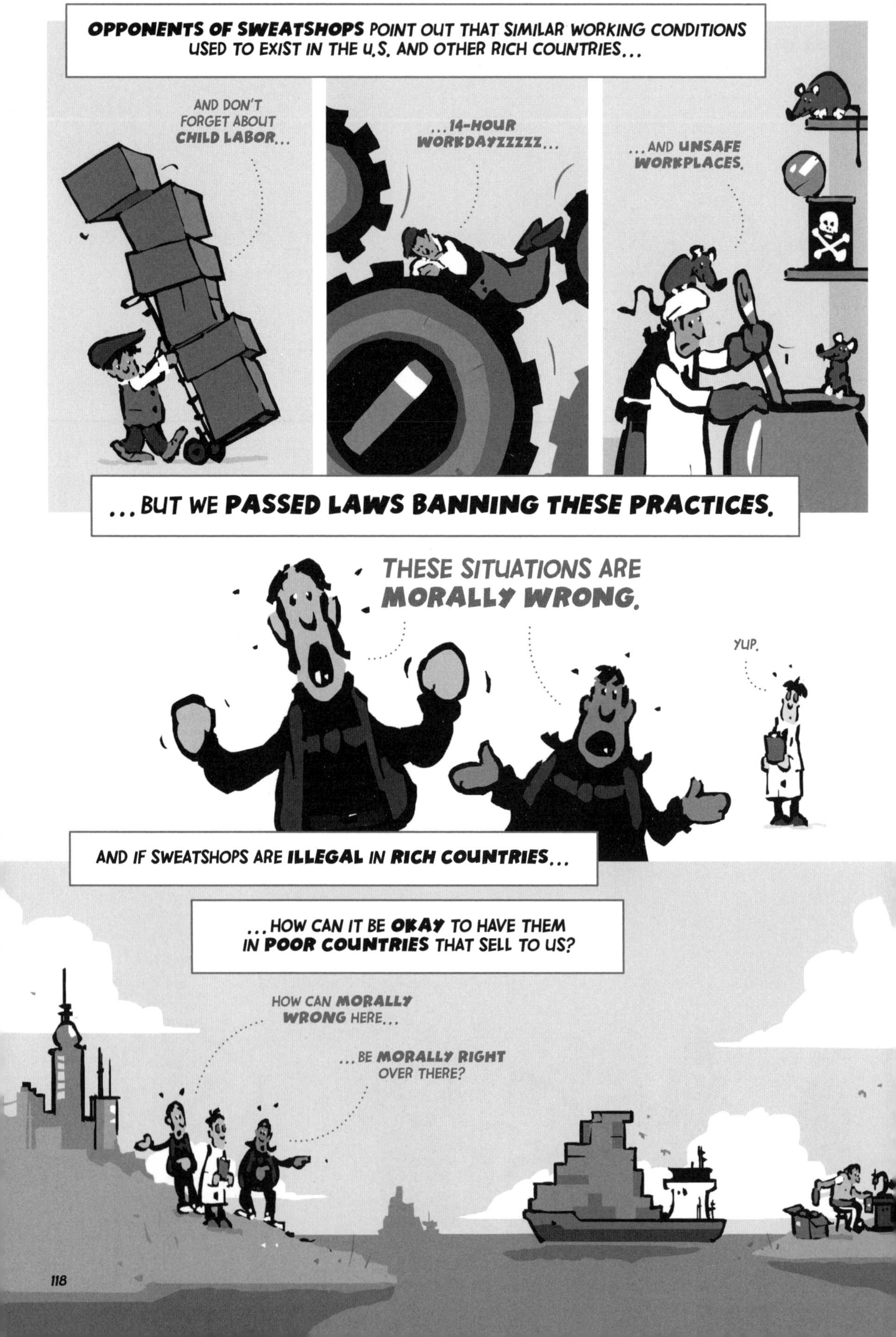
OPPONENTS OF SWEATSHOPS POINT OUT THAT SIMILAR WORKING CONDITIONS USED TO EXIST IN THE U.S. AND OTHER RICH COUNTRIES...
AND DON'T FORGET ABOUT **CHILD LABOR**...
...**14-HOUR WORKDAYZZZZZ**...
...AND **UNSAFE WORKPLACES**.
...BUT WE **PASSED LAWS BANNING THESE PRACTICES.**
THESE SITUATIONS ARE **MORALLY WRONG.**
YUP.
AND IF SWEATSHOPS ARE **ILLEGAL** IN **RICH COUNTRIES**...
...HOW CAN IT BE **OKAY** TO HAVE THEM IN **POOR COUNTRIES** THAT SELL TO US?
HOW CAN **MORALLY WRONG** HERE...
...BE **MORALLY RIGHT** OVER THERE?

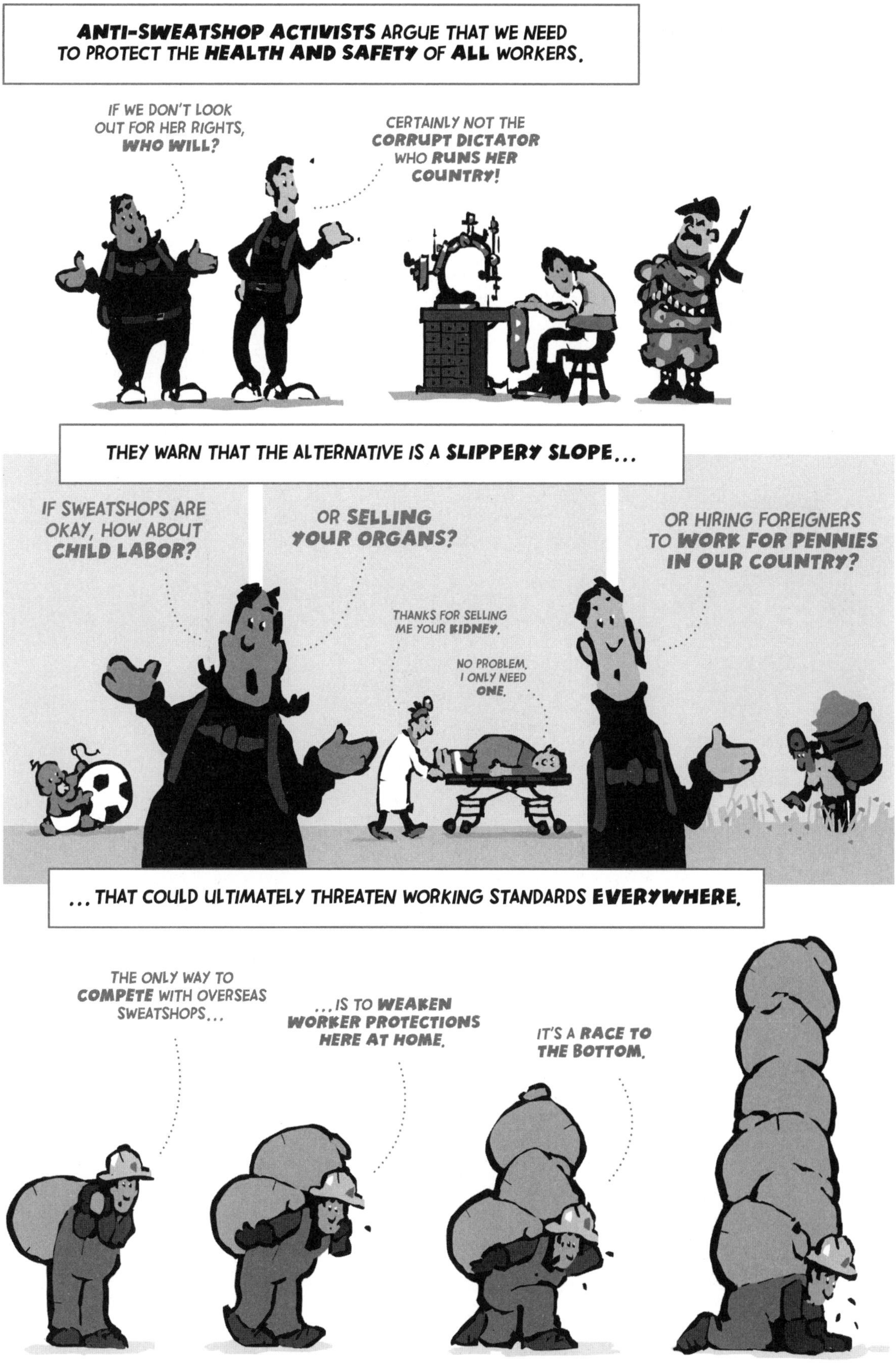
ANTI-SWEATSHOP ACTIVISTS ARGUE THAT WE NEED TO PROTECT THE HEALTH AND SAFETY OF ALL WORKERS.
IF WE DON'T LOOK OUT FOR HER RIGHTS, WHO WILL?
CERTAINLY NOT THE CORRUPT DICTATOR WHO RUNS HER COUNTRY!
THEY WARN THAT THE ALTERNATIVE IS A SLIPPERY SLOPE...
IF SWEATSHOPS ARE OKAY, HOW ABOUT CHILD LABOR?
OR SELLING YOUR ORGANS?
THANKS FOR SELLING ME YOUR KIDNEY.
NO PROBLEM. I ONLY NEED ONE.
OR HIRING FOREIGNERS TO WORK FOR PENNIES IN OUR COUNTRY?
...THAT COULD ULTIMATELY THREATEN WORKING STANDARDS EVERYWHERE.
THE ONLY WAY TO COMPETE WITH OVERSEAS SWEATSHOPS...
...IS TO WEAKEN WORKER PROTECTIONS HERE AT HOME.
IT'S A RACE TO THE BOTTOM.

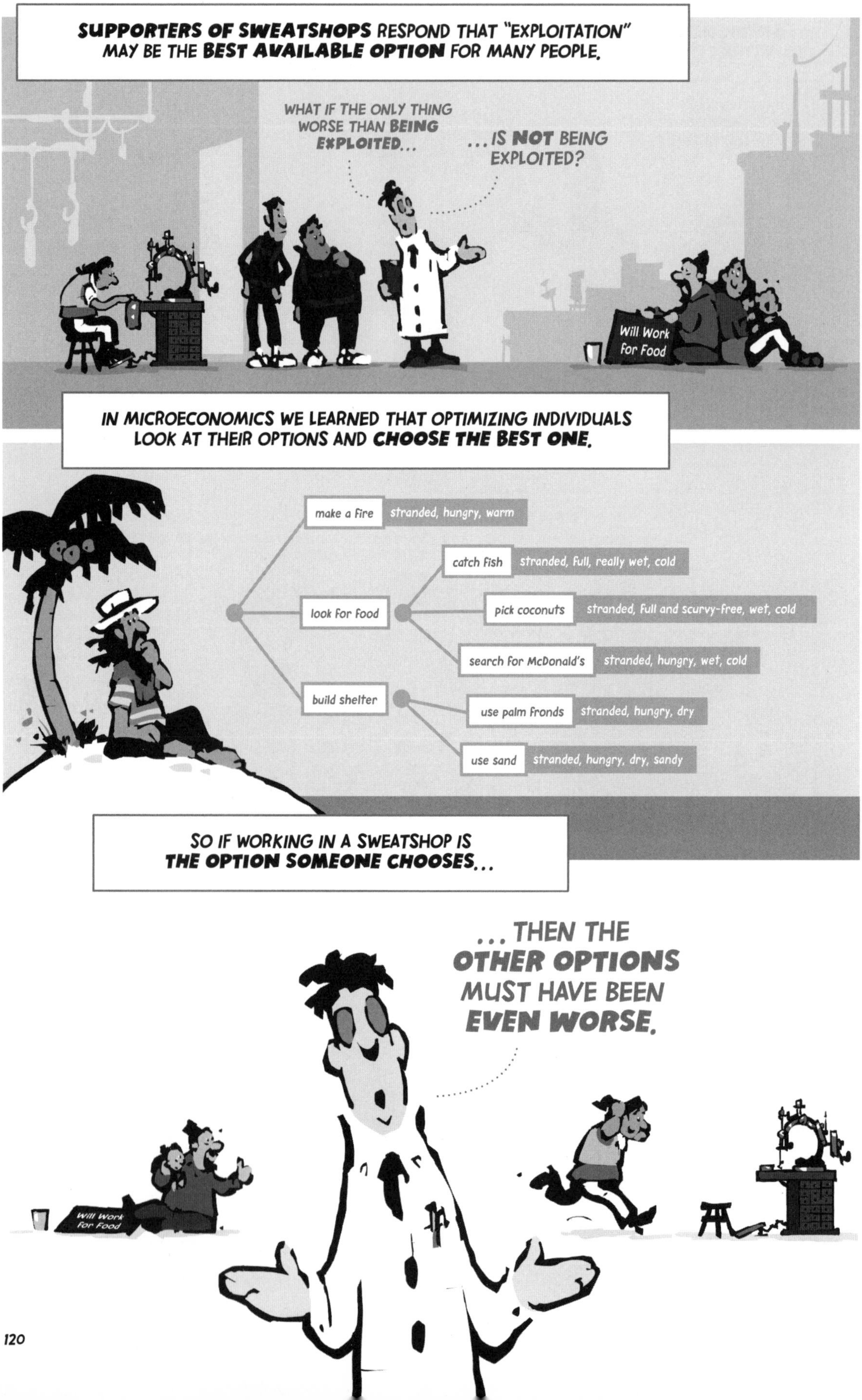
SUPPORTERS OF SWEATSHOPS RESPOND THAT "EXPLOITATION" MAY BE THE BEST AVAILABLE OPTION FOR MANY PEOPLE.
WHAT IF THE ONLY THING WORSE THAN BEING EXPLOITED...
...IS NOT BEING EXPLOITED?
Will Work For Food
IN MICROECONOMICS WE LEARNED THAT OPTIMIZING INDIVIDUALS LOOK AT THEIR OPTIONS AND CHOOSE THE BEST ONE.
make a fire
stranded, hungry, warm
look for food
catch fish
stranded, full, really wet, cold
pick coconuts
stranded, full and scurvy-free, wet, cold
search for McDonald's
stranded, hungry, wet, cold
build shelter
use palm fronds
stranded, hungry, dry
use sand
stranded, hungry, dry, sandy
SO IF WORKING IN A SWEATSHOP IS THE OPTION SOMEONE CHOOSES...
...THEN THE OTHER OPTIONS MUST HAVE BEEN EVEN WORSE.
Will Work For Food

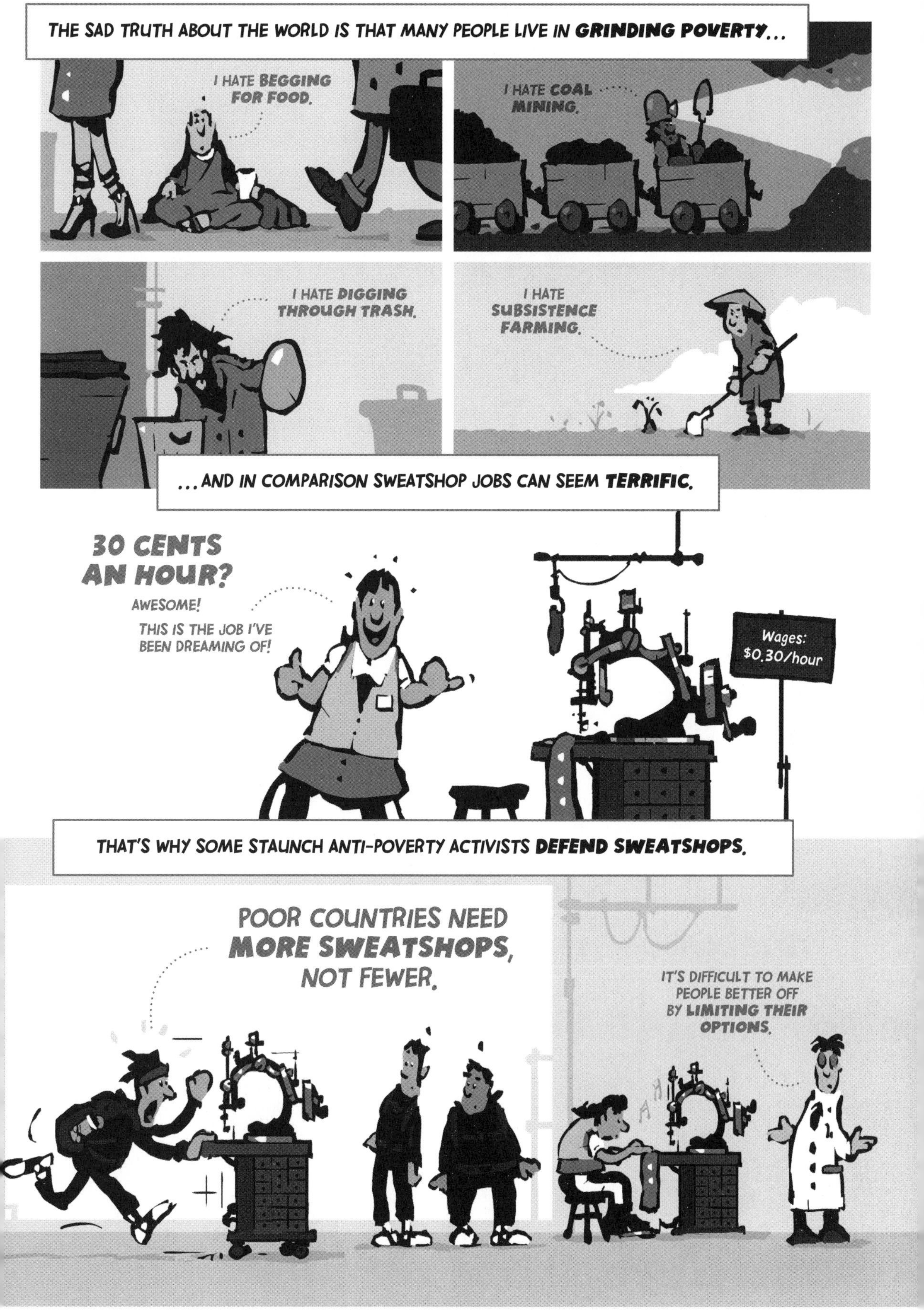
THE SAD TRUTH ABOUT THE WORLD IS THAT MANY PEOPLE LIVE IN GRINDING POVERTY...
I HATE BEGGING FOR FOOD.
I HATE COAL MINING.
I HATE DIGGING THROUGH TRASH.
I HATE SUBSISTENCE FARMING.
...AND IN COMPARISON SWEATSHOP JOBS CAN SEEM TERRIFIC.
30 CENTS AN HOUR?
AWESOME!
THIS IS THE JOB I'VE BEEN DREAMING OF!
Wages: $0.30/hour
THAT'S WHY SOME STAUNCH ANTI-POVERTY ACTIVISTS DEFEND SWEATSHOPS.
POOR COUNTRIES NEED MORE SWEATSHOPS, NOT FEWER.
IT'S DIFFICULT TO MAKE PEOPLE BETTER OFF BY LIMITING THEIR OPTIONS.

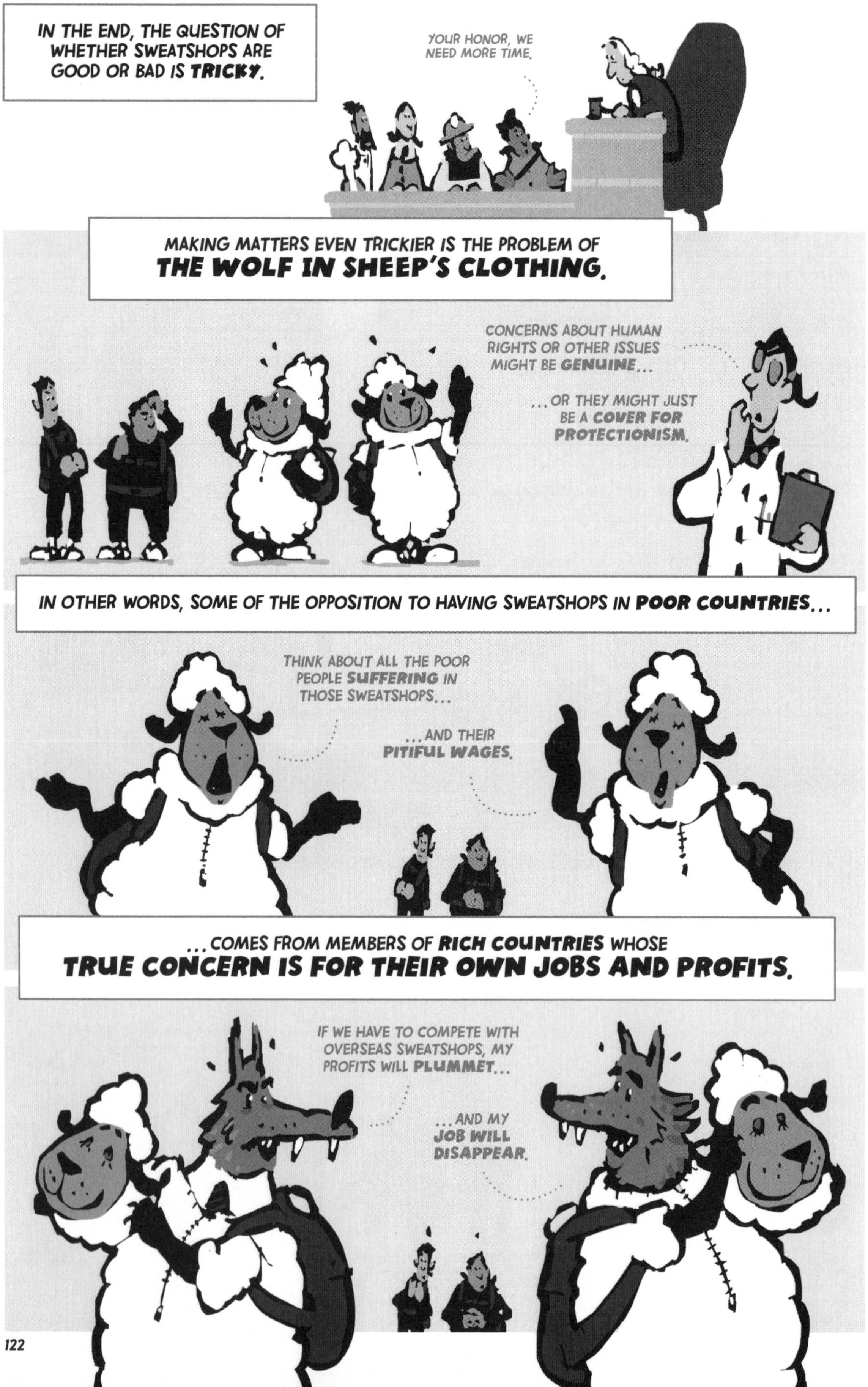

IN THE END, THE QUESTION OF WHETHER SWEATSHOPS ARE GOOD OR BAD IS TRICKY.
YOUR HONOR, WE NEED MORE TIME.
MAKING MATTERS EVEN TRICKIER IS THE PROBLEM OF THE WOLF IN SHEEP'S CLOTHING.
CONCERNS ABOUT HUMAN RIGHTS OR OTHER ISSUES MIGHT BE GENUINE...
...OR THEY MIGHT JUST BE A COVER FOR PROTECTIONISM.
IN OTHER WORDS, SOME OF THE OPPOSITION TO HAVING SWEATSHOPS IN POOR COUNTRIES...
THINK ABOUT ALL THE POOR PEOPLE SUFFERING IN THOSE SWEATSHOPS...
...AND THEIR PITIFUL WAGES.
...COMES FROM MEMBERS OF RICH COUNTRIES WHOSE TRUE CONCERN IS FOR THEIR OWN JOBS AND PROFITS.
IF WE HAVE TO COMPETE WITH OVERSEAS SWEATSHOPS, MY PROFITS WILL PLUMMET...
...AND MY JOB WILL DISAPPEAR.

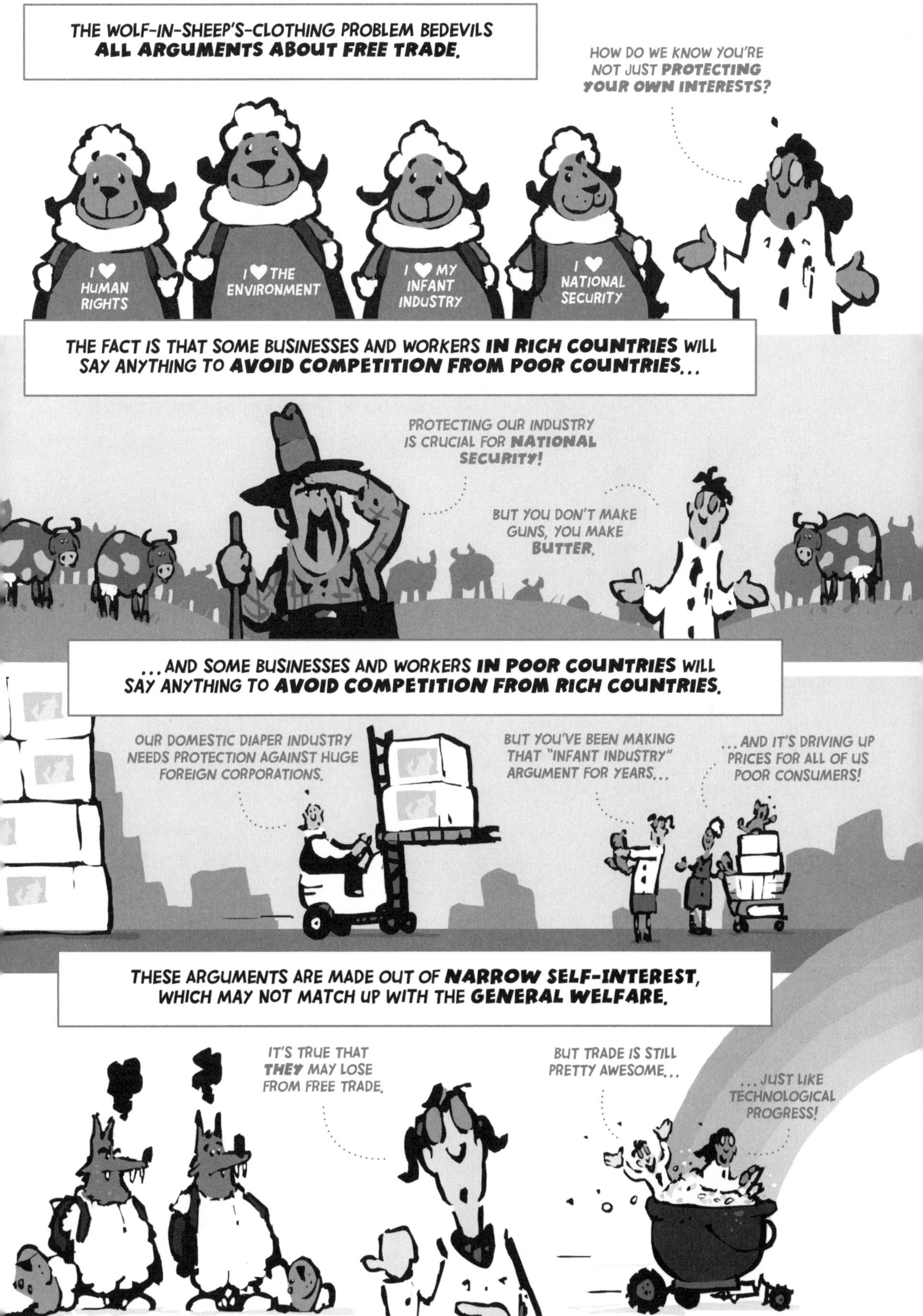
THE WOLF-IN-SHEEP'S-CLOTHING PROBLEM BEDEVILS **ALL ARGUMENTS ABOUT FREE TRADE.**
HOW DO WE KNOW YOU'RE NOT JUST **PROTECTING YOUR OWN INTERESTS?**
I ♥ HUMAN RIGHTS
I ♥ THE ENVIRONMENT
I ♥ MY INFANT INDUSTRY
I ♥ NATIONAL SECURITY
THE FACT IS THAT SOME BUSINESSES AND WORKERS **IN RICH COUNTRIES** WILL SAY ANYTHING TO **AVOID COMPETITION FROM POOR COUNTRIES...**
PROTECTING OUR INDUSTRY IS CRUCIAL FOR **NATIONAL SECURITY!**
BUT YOU DON'T MAKE GUNS, YOU MAKE **BUTTER.**
...AND SOME BUSINESSES AND WORKERS **IN POOR COUNTRIES** WILL SAY ANYTHING TO **AVOID COMPETITION FROM RICH COUNTRIES.**
OUR DOMESTIC DIAPER INDUSTRY NEEDS PROTECTION AGAINST HUGE FOREIGN CORPORATIONS.
BUT YOU'VE BEEN MAKING THAT "INFANT INDUSTRY" ARGUMENT FOR YEARS...
...AND IT'S DRIVING UP PRICES FOR ALL OF US POOR CONSUMERS!
THESE ARGUMENTS ARE MADE OUT OF **NARROW SELF-INTEREST,** WHICH MAY NOT MATCH UP WITH THE **GENERAL WELFARE.**
IT'S TRUE THAT **THEY** MAY LOSE FROM FREE TRADE.
BUT TRADE IS STILL PRETTY AWESOME...
...JUST LIKE TECHNOLOGICAL PROGRESS!

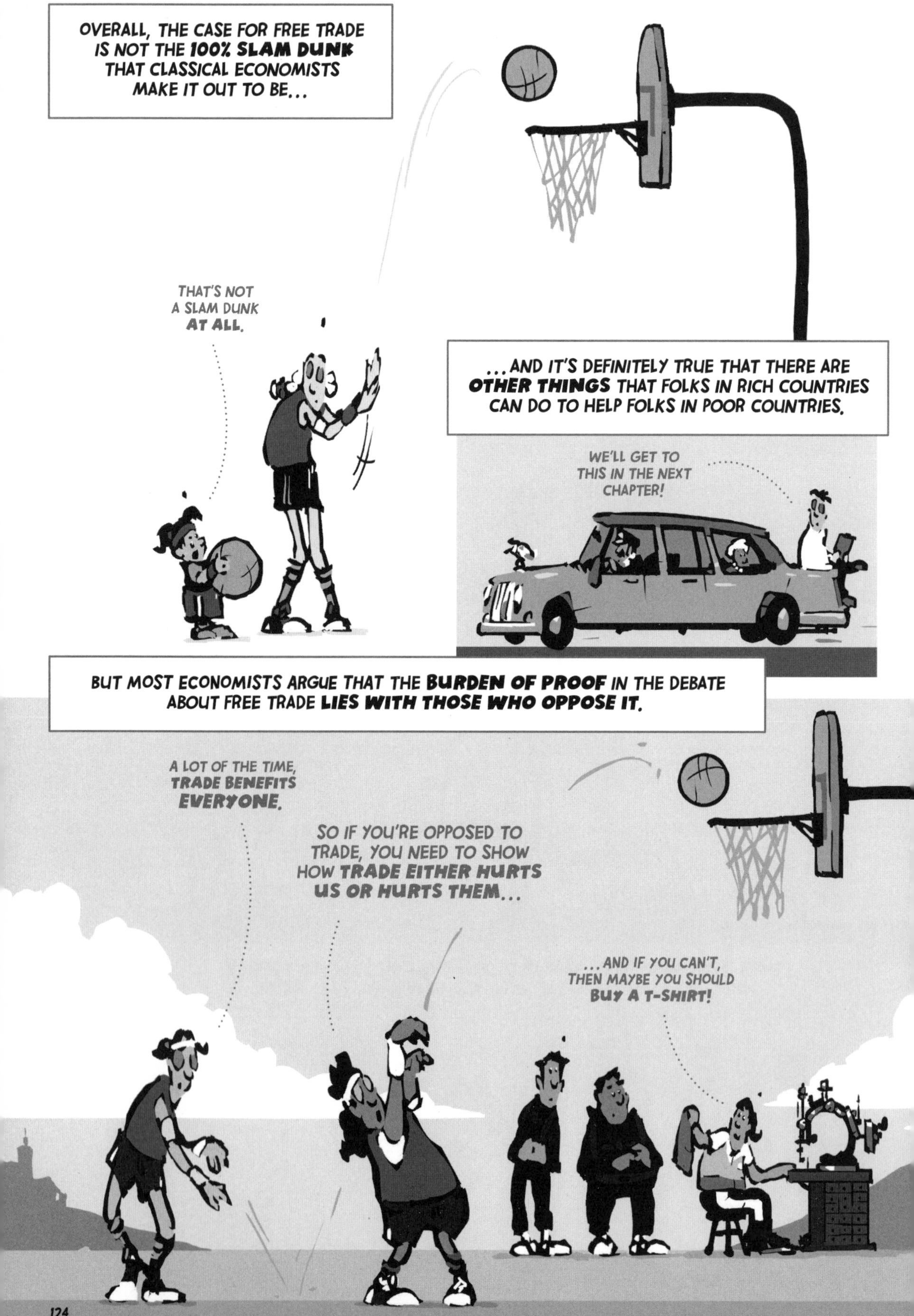

OVERALL, THE CASE FOR FREE TRADE IS NOT THE 100% SLAM DUNK THAT CLASSICAL ECONOMISTS MAKE IT OUT TO BE...
THAT'S NOT A SLAM DUNK AT ALL.
...AND IT'S DEFINITELY TRUE THAT THERE ARE OTHER THINGS THAT FOLKS IN RICH COUNTRIES CAN DO TO HELP FOLKS IN POOR COUNTRIES.
WE'LL GET TO THIS IN THE NEXT CHAPTER!
BUT MOST ECONOMISTS ARGUE THAT THE BURDEN OF PROOF IN THE DEBATE ABOUT FREE TRADE LIES WITH THOSE WHO OPPOSE IT.
A LOT OF THE TIME, TRADE BENEFITS EVERYONE.
SO IF YOU'RE OPPOSED TO TRADE, YOU NEED TO SHOW HOW TRADE EITHER HURTS US OR HURTS THEM...
...AND IF YOU CAN'T, THEN MAYBE YOU SHOULD BUY A T-SHIRT!

CHAPTER 10

FOREIGN AID

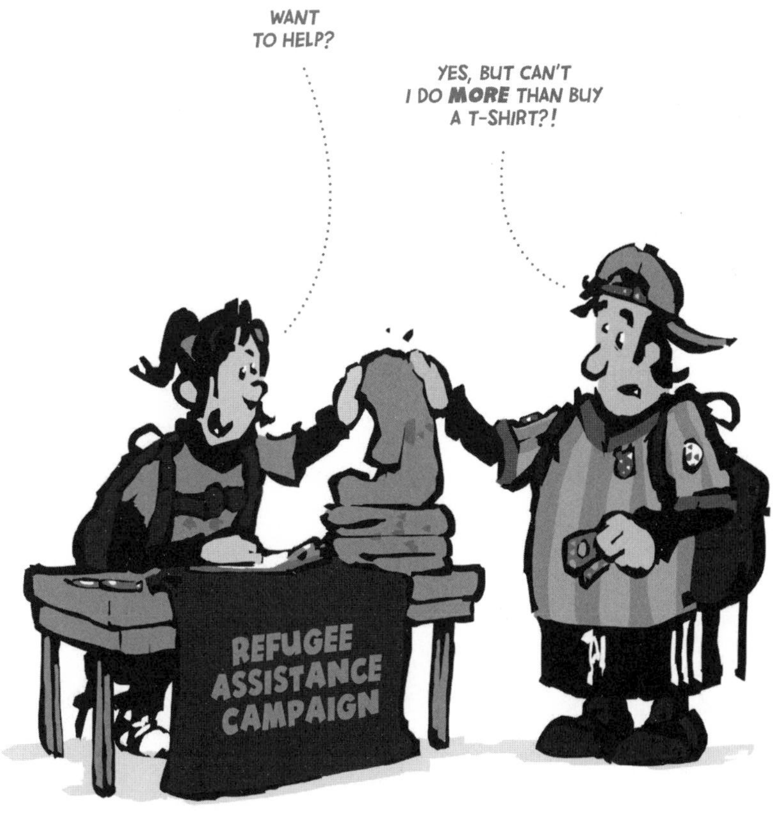
WANT TO HELP?
YES, BUT CAN'T I DO **MORE** THAN BUY A T-SHIRT?!
REFUGEE ASSISTANCE CAMPAIGN

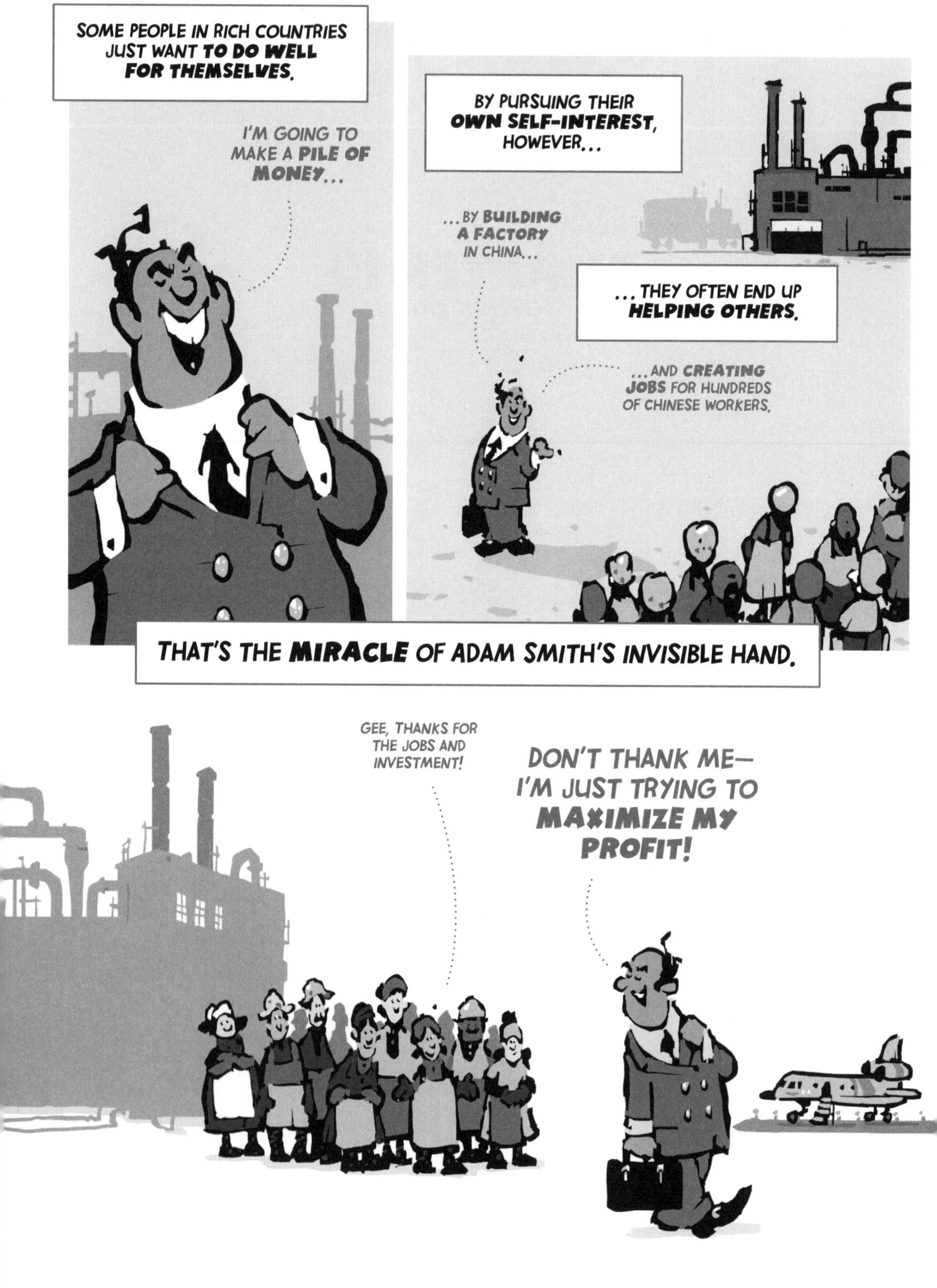

SOME PEOPLE IN RICH COUNTRIES JUST WANT **TO DO WELL FOR THEMSELVES.**
I'M GOING TO MAKE A **PILE OF MONEY**...
BY PURSUING THEIR **OWN SELF-INTEREST**, HOWEVER...
...BY **BUILDING A FACTORY** IN CHINA...
...THEY OFTEN END UP **HELPING OTHERS.**
...AND **CREATING JOBS** FOR HUNDREDS OF CHINESE WORKERS.
THAT'S THE **MIRACLE** OF ADAM SMITH'S INVISIBLE HAND.
GEE, THANKS FOR THE JOBS AND INVESTMENT!
DON'T THANK ME— I'M JUST TRYING TO **MAXIMIZE MY PROFIT!**

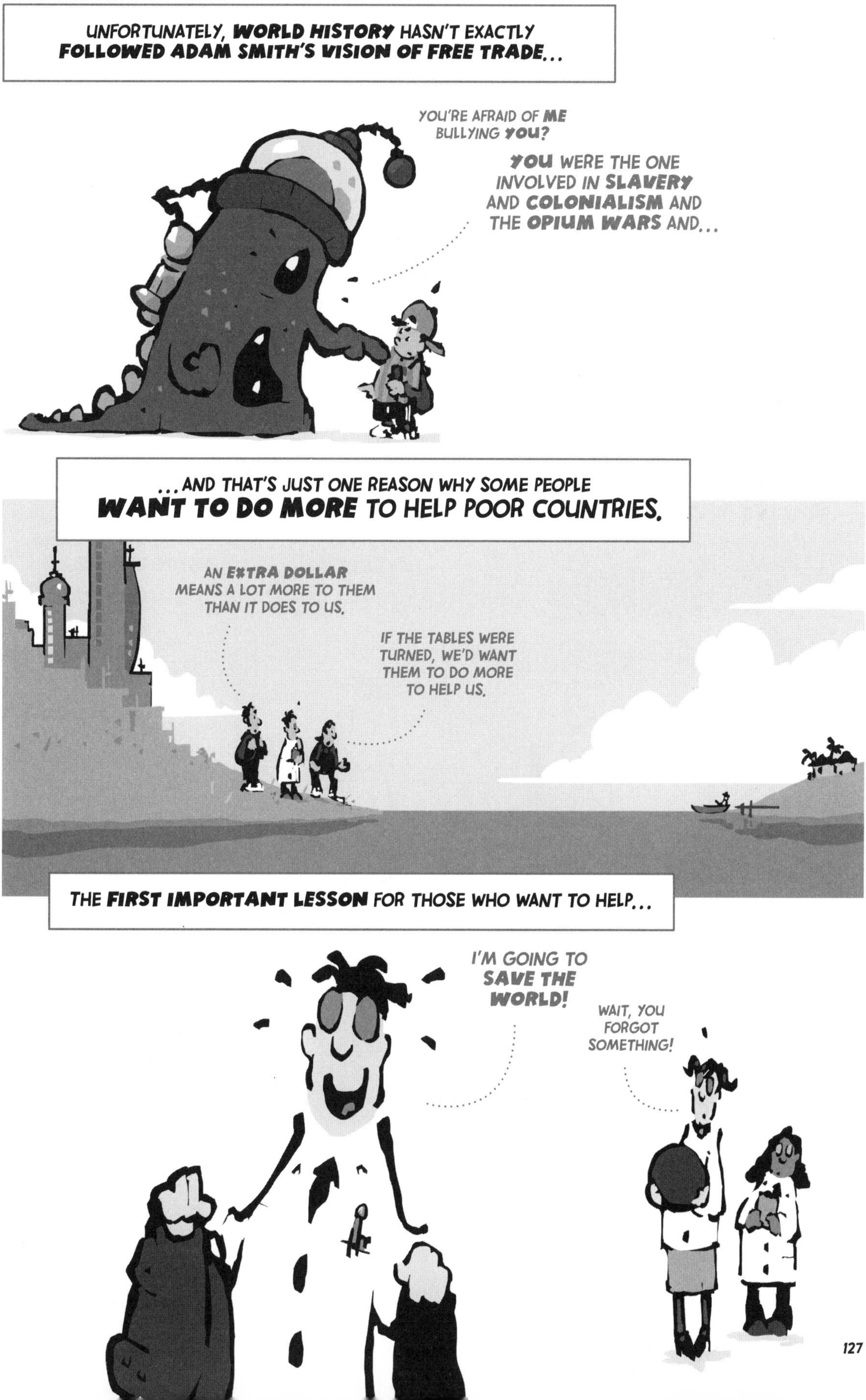
UNFORTUNATELY, WORLD HISTORY HASN'T EXACTLY FOLLOWED ADAM SMITH'S VISION OF FREE TRADE...
YOU'RE AFRAID OF ME BULLYING YOU?
YOU WERE THE ONE INVOLVED IN SLAVERY AND COLONIALISM AND THE OPIUM WARS AND...
...AND THAT'S JUST ONE REASON WHY SOME PEOPLE WANT TO DO MORE TO HELP POOR COUNTRIES.
AN EXTRA DOLLAR MEANS A LOT MORE TO THEM THAN IT DOES TO US.
IF THE TABLES WERE TURNED, WE'D WANT THEM TO DO MORE TO HELP US.
THE FIRST IMPORTANT LESSON FOR THOSE WHO WANT TO HELP...
I'M GOING TO SAVE THE WORLD!
WAIT, YOU FORGOT SOMETHING!

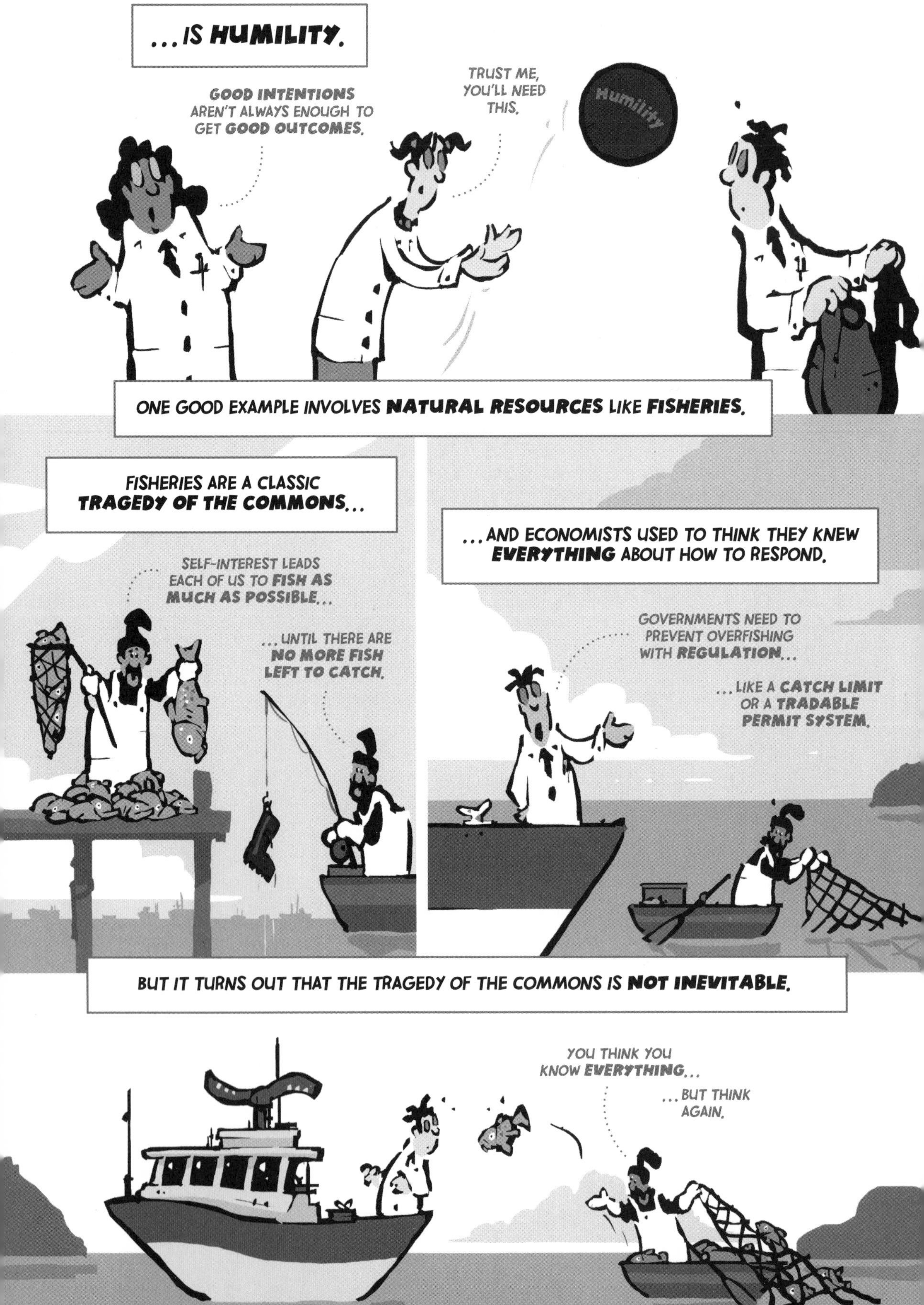

...IS HUMILITY.
GOOD INTENTIONS AREN'T ALWAYS ENOUGH TO GET GOOD OUTCOMES.
TRUST ME, YOU'LL NEED THIS.
Humility
ONE GOOD EXAMPLE INVOLVES NATURAL RESOURCES LIKE FISHERIES.
FISHERIES ARE A CLASSIC TRAGEDY OF THE COMMONS...
SELF-INTEREST LEADS EACH OF US TO FISH AS MUCH AS POSSIBLE...
...UNTIL THERE ARE NO MORE FISH LEFT TO CATCH.
...AND ECONOMISTS USED TO THINK THEY KNEW EVERYTHING ABOUT HOW TO RESPOND.
GOVERNMENTS NEED TO PREVENT OVERFISHING WITH REGULATION...
...LIKE A CATCH LIMIT OR A TRADABLE PERMIT SYSTEM.
BUT IT TURNS OUT THAT THE TRAGEDY OF THE COMMONS IS NOT INEVITABLE.
YOU THINK YOU KNOW EVERYTHING...
...BUT THINK AGAIN.

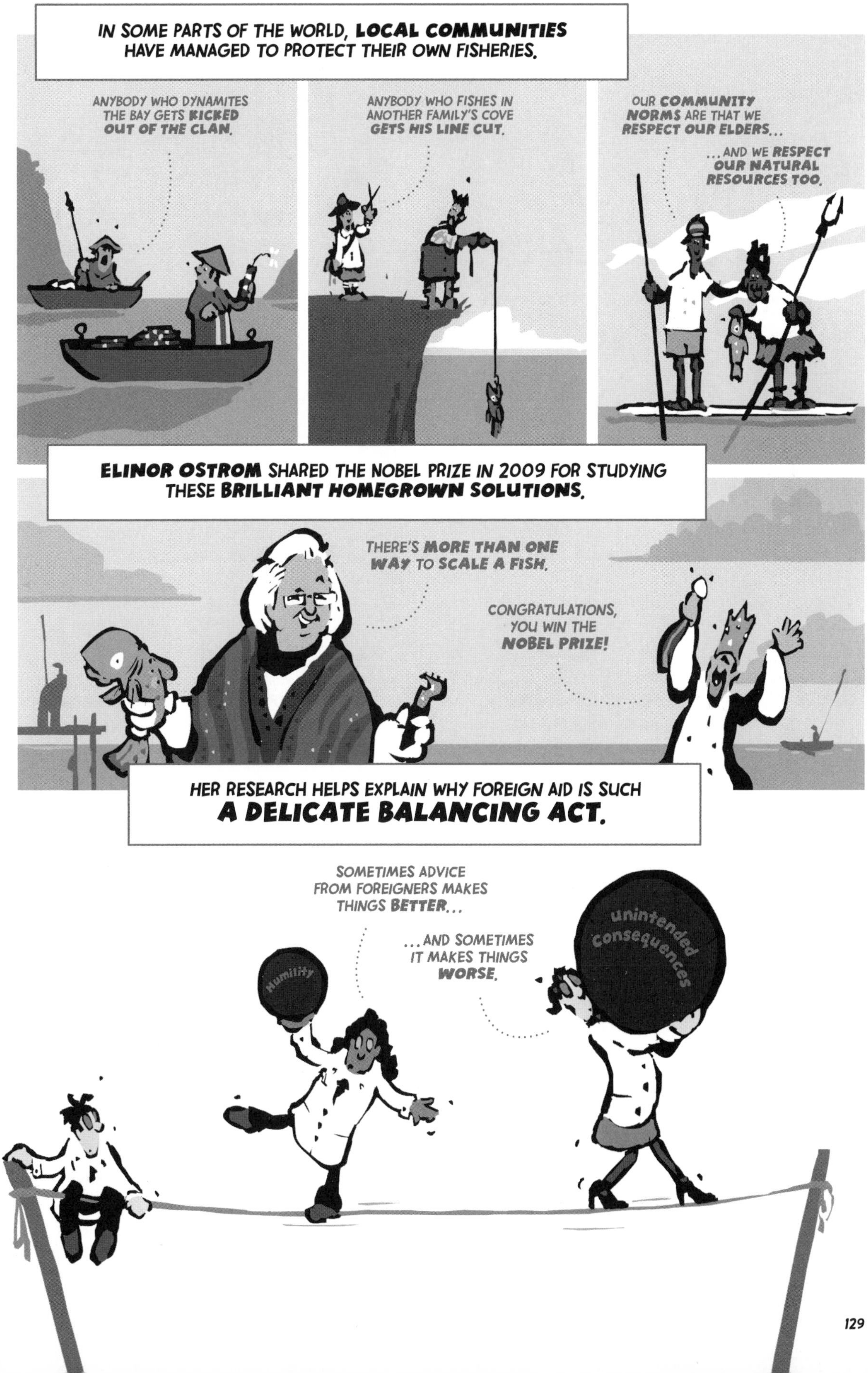
IN SOME PARTS OF THE WORLD, LOCAL COMMUNITIES HAVE MANAGED TO PROTECT THEIR OWN FISHERIES.
ANYBODY WHO DYNAMITES THE BAY GETS KICKED OUT OF THE CLAN.
ANYBODY WHO FISHES IN ANOTHER FAMILY'S COVE GETS HIS LINE CUT.
OUR COMMUNITY NORMS ARE THAT WE RESPECT OUR ELDERS...
...AND WE RESPECT OUR NATURAL RESOURCES TOO.
ELINOR OSTROM SHARED THE NOBEL PRIZE IN 2009 FOR STUDYING THESE BRILLIANT HOMEGROWN SOLUTIONS.
THERE'S MORE THAN ONE WAY TO SCALE A FISH.
CONGRATULATIONS, YOU WIN THE NOBEL PRIZE!
HER RESEARCH HELPS EXPLAIN WHY FOREIGN AID IS SUCH A DELICATE BALANCING ACT.
SOMETIMES ADVICE FROM FOREIGNERS MAKES THINGS BETTER...
...AND SOMETIMES IT MAKES THINGS WORSE.
Humility
unintended consequences

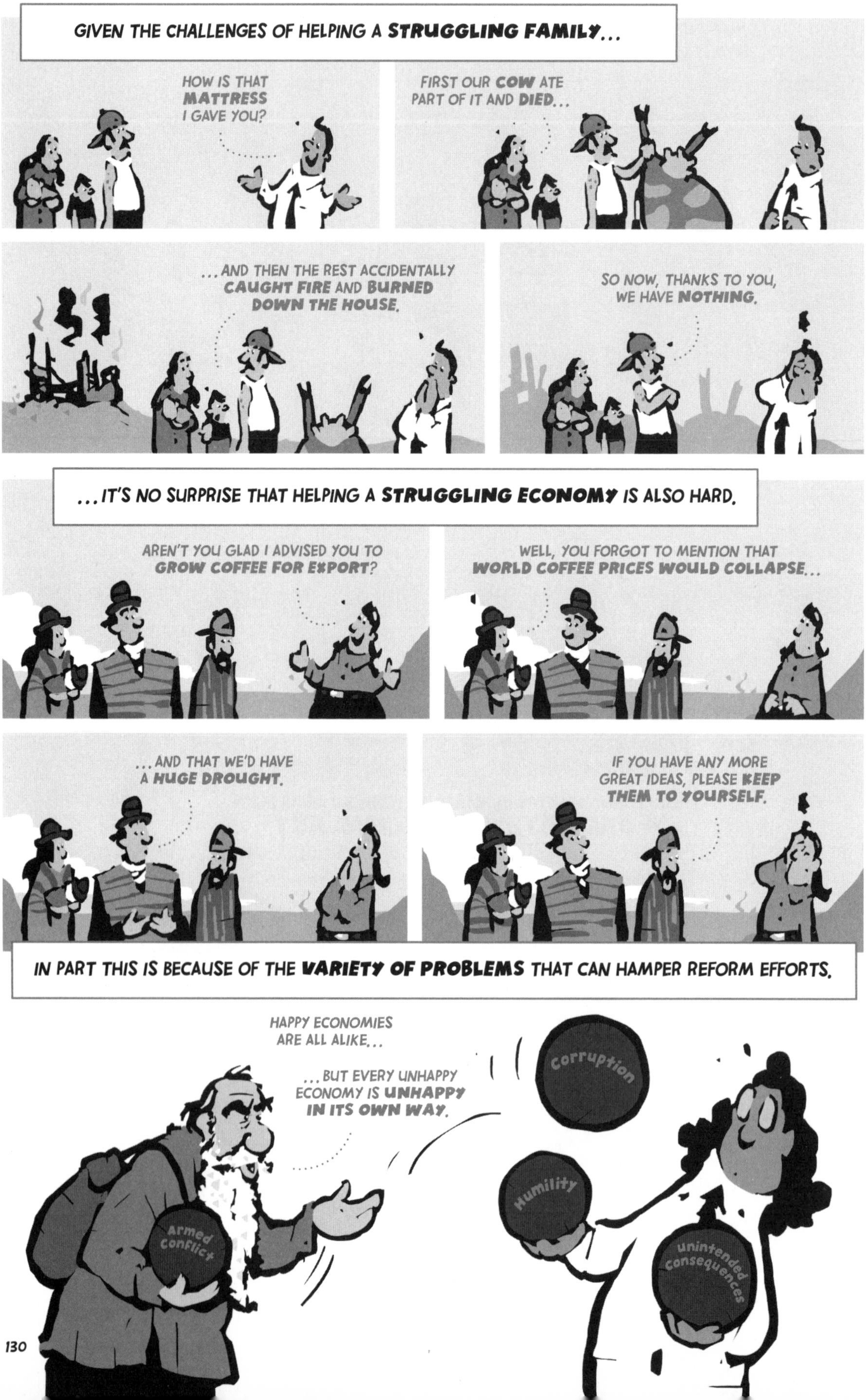

GIVEN THE CHALLENGES OF HELPING A STRUGGLING FAMILY...
HOW IS THAT MATTRESS I GAVE YOU?
FIRST OUR COW ATE PART OF IT AND DIED...
...AND THEN THE REST ACCIDENTALLY CAUGHT FIRE AND BURNED DOWN THE HOUSE.
SO NOW, THANKS TO YOU, WE HAVE NOTHING.
...IT'S NO SURPRISE THAT HELPING A STRUGGLING ECONOMY IS ALSO HARD.
AREN'T YOU GLAD I ADVISED YOU TO GROW COFFEE FOR EXPORT?
WELL, YOU FORGOT TO MENTION THAT WORLD COFFEE PRICES WOULD COLLAPSE...
...AND THAT WE'D HAVE A HUGE DROUGHT.
IF YOU HAVE ANY MORE GREAT IDEAS, PLEASE KEEP THEM TO YOURSELF.
IN PART THIS IS BECAUSE OF THE VARIETY OF PROBLEMS THAT CAN HAMPER REFORM EFFORTS.
HAPPY ECONOMIES ARE ALL ALIKE...
...BUT EVERY UNHAPPY ECONOMY IS UNHAPPY IN ITS OWN WAY.
Corruption
Humility
Armed Conflict
Unintended Consequences

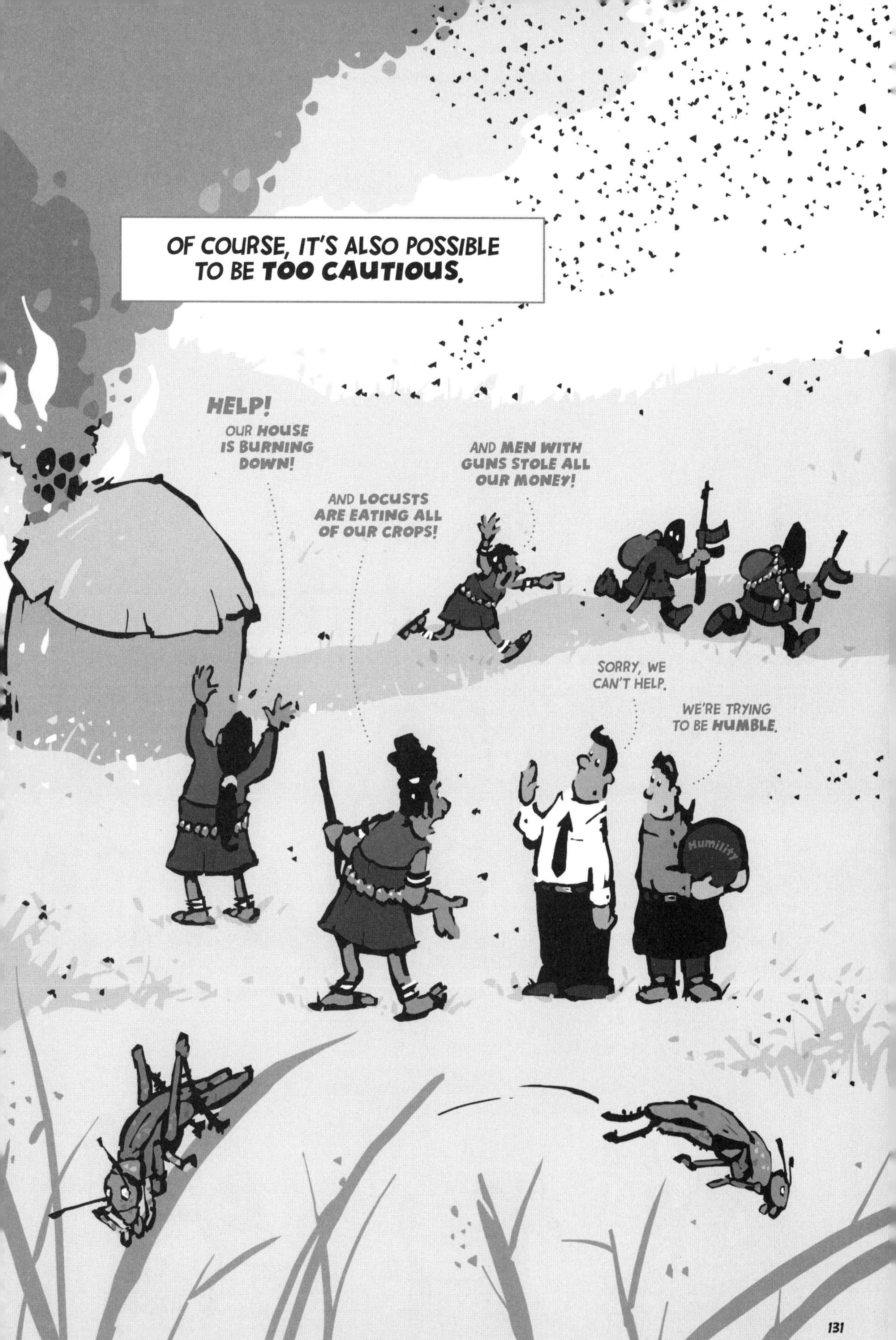
OF COURSE, IT'S ALSO POSSIBLE TO BE **TOO CAUTIOUS.**
HELP!
OUR **HOUSE IS BURNING DOWN!**
AND **LOCUSTS ARE EATING ALL OF OUR CROPS!**
AND **MEN WITH GUNS STOLE ALL OUR MONEY!**
SORRY, WE CAN'T HELP.
WE'RE TRYING TO BE **HUMBLE.**
Humility

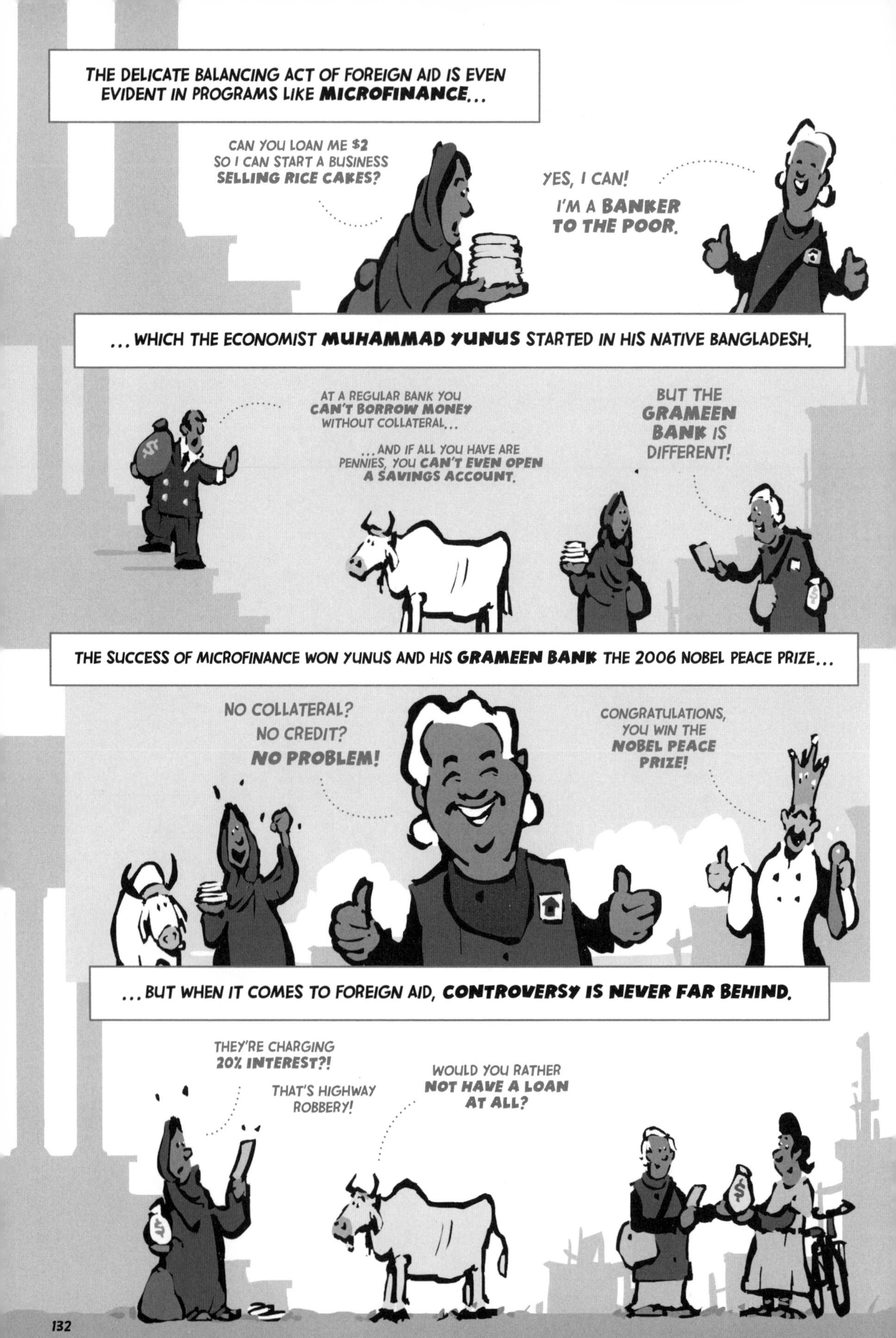
THE DELICATE BALANCING ACT OF FOREIGN AID IS EVEN EVIDENT IN PROGRAMS LIKE MICROFINANCE...
CAN YOU LOAN ME $2 SO I CAN START A BUSINESS SELLING RICE CAKES?
YES, I CAN!
I'M A BANKER TO THE POOR.
...WHICH THE ECONOMIST MUHAMMAD YUNUS STARTED IN HIS NATIVE BANGLADESH.
AT A REGULAR BANK YOU CAN'T BORROW MONEY WITHOUT COLLATERAL...
...AND IF ALL YOU HAVE ARE PENNIES, YOU CAN'T EVEN OPEN A SAVINGS ACCOUNT.
BUT THE GRAMEEN BANK IS DIFFERENT!
THE SUCCESS OF MICROFINANCE WON YUNUS AND HIS GRAMEEN BANK THE 2006 NOBEL PEACE PRIZE...
NO COLLATERAL?
NO CREDIT?
NO PROBLEM!
CONGRATULATIONS, YOU WIN THE NOBEL PEACE PRIZE!
...BUT WHEN IT COMES TO FOREIGN AID, CONTROVERSY IS NEVER FAR BEHIND.
THEY'RE CHARGING 20% INTEREST?!
THAT'S HIGHWAY ROBBERY!
WOULD YOU RATHER NOT HAVE A LOAN AT ALL?

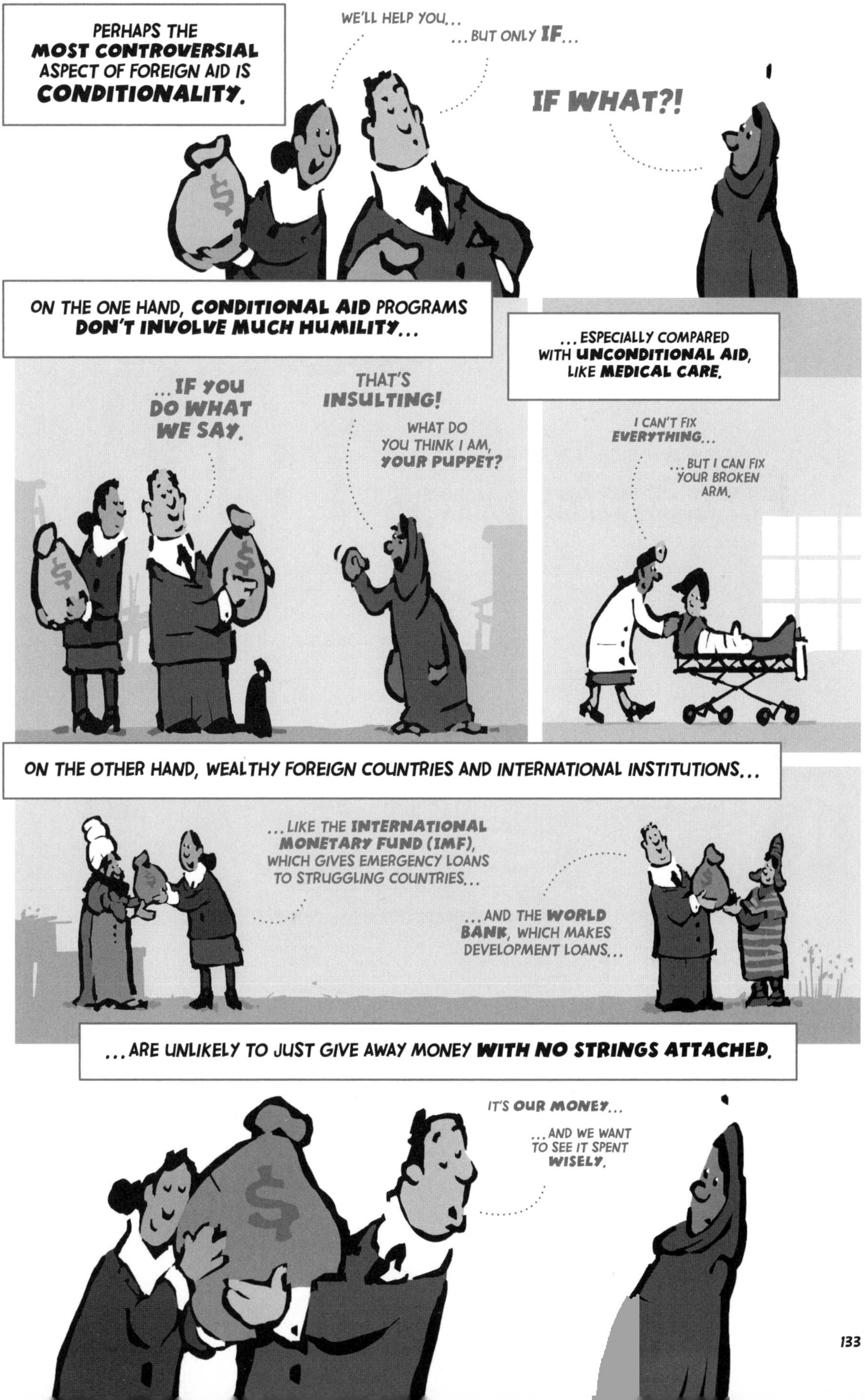
PERHAPS THE **MOST CONTROVERSIAL** ASPECT OF FOREIGN AID IS **CONDITIONALITY.**
WE'LL HELP YOU...
...BUT ONLY **IF**...
IF WHAT?!
ON THE ONE HAND, **CONDITIONAL AID** PROGRAMS **DON'T INVOLVE MUCH HUMILITY**...
...**IF YOU DO WHAT WE SAY.**
THAT'S **INSULTING!**
WHAT DO YOU THINK I AM, **YOUR PUPPET?**
...ESPECIALLY COMPARED WITH **UNCONDITIONAL AID**, LIKE **MEDICAL CARE.**
I CAN'T FIX **EVERYTHING**...
...BUT I CAN FIX YOUR BROKEN ARM.
ON THE OTHER HAND, WEALTHY FOREIGN COUNTRIES AND INTERNATIONAL INSTITUTIONS...
...LIKE THE **INTERNATIONAL MONETARY FUND (IMF)**, WHICH GIVES EMERGENCY LOANS TO STRUGGLING COUNTRIES...
...AND THE **WORLD BANK**, WHICH MAKES DEVELOPMENT LOANS...
...ARE UNLIKELY TO JUST GIVE AWAY MONEY **WITH NO STRINGS ATTACHED.**
IT'S **OUR MONEY**...
...AND WE WANT TO SEE IT SPENT **WISELY.**

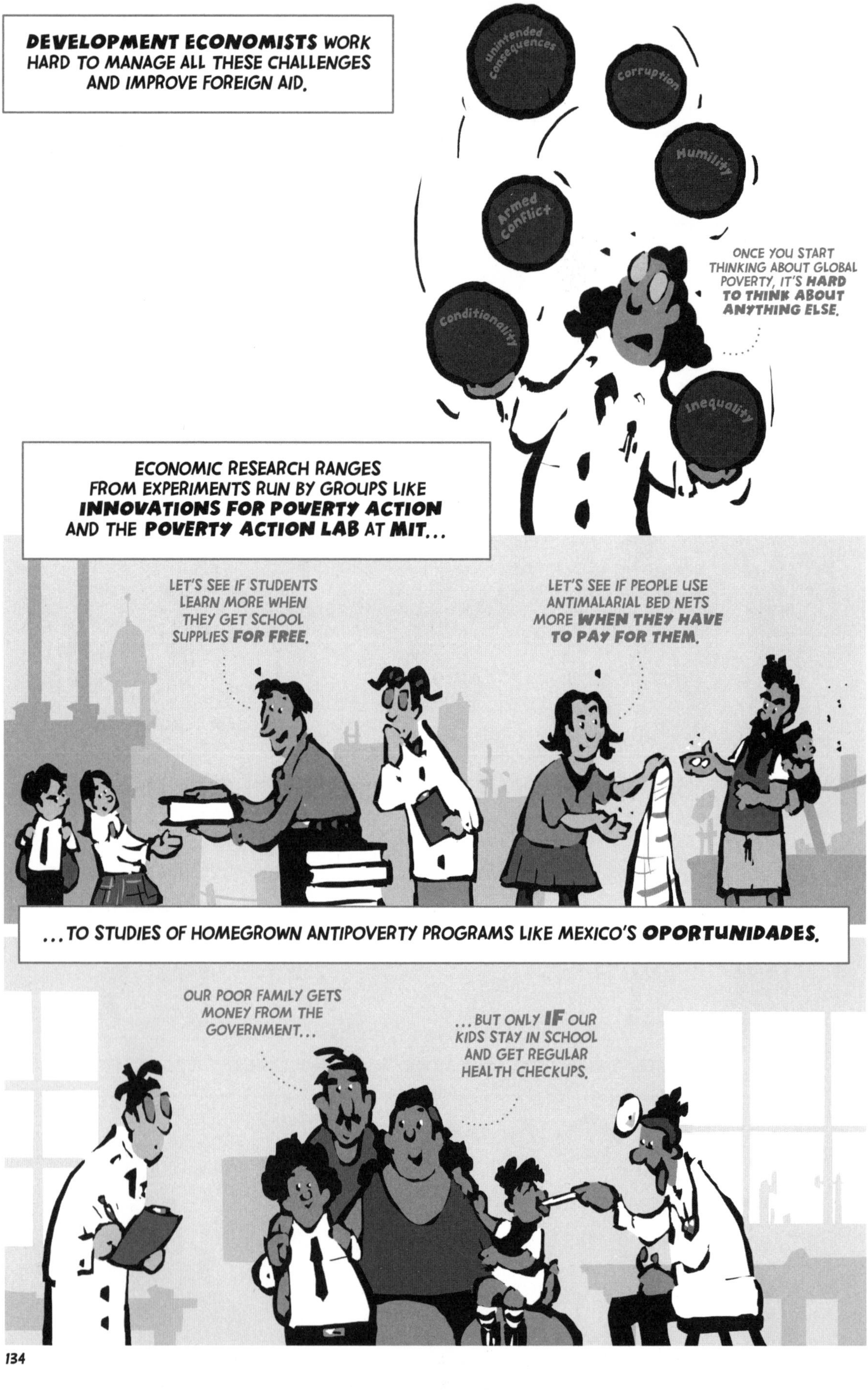
DEVELOPMENT ECONOMISTS WORK HARD TO MANAGE ALL THESE CHALLENGES AND IMPROVE FOREIGN AID.
unintended consequences
Corruption
Humility
Armed conflict
Conditionality
Inequality
ONCE YOU START THINKING ABOUT GLOBAL POVERTY, IT'S HARD TO THINK ABOUT ANYTHING ELSE.
ECONOMIC RESEARCH RANGES FROM EXPERIMENTS RUN BY GROUPS LIKE INNOVATIONS FOR POVERTY ACTION AND THE POVERTY ACTION LAB AT MIT...
LET'S SEE IF STUDENTS LEARN MORE WHEN THEY GET SCHOOL SUPPLIES FOR FREE.
LET'S SEE IF PEOPLE USE ANTIMALARIAL BED NETS MORE WHEN THEY HAVE TO PAY FOR THEM.
...TO STUDIES OF HOMEGROWN ANTIPOVERTY PROGRAMS LIKE MEXICO'S OPORTUNIDADES.
OUR POOR FAMILY GETS MONEY FROM THE GOVERNMENT...
...BUT ONLY IF OUR KIDS STAY IN SCHOOL AND GET REGULAR HEALTH CHECKUPS.

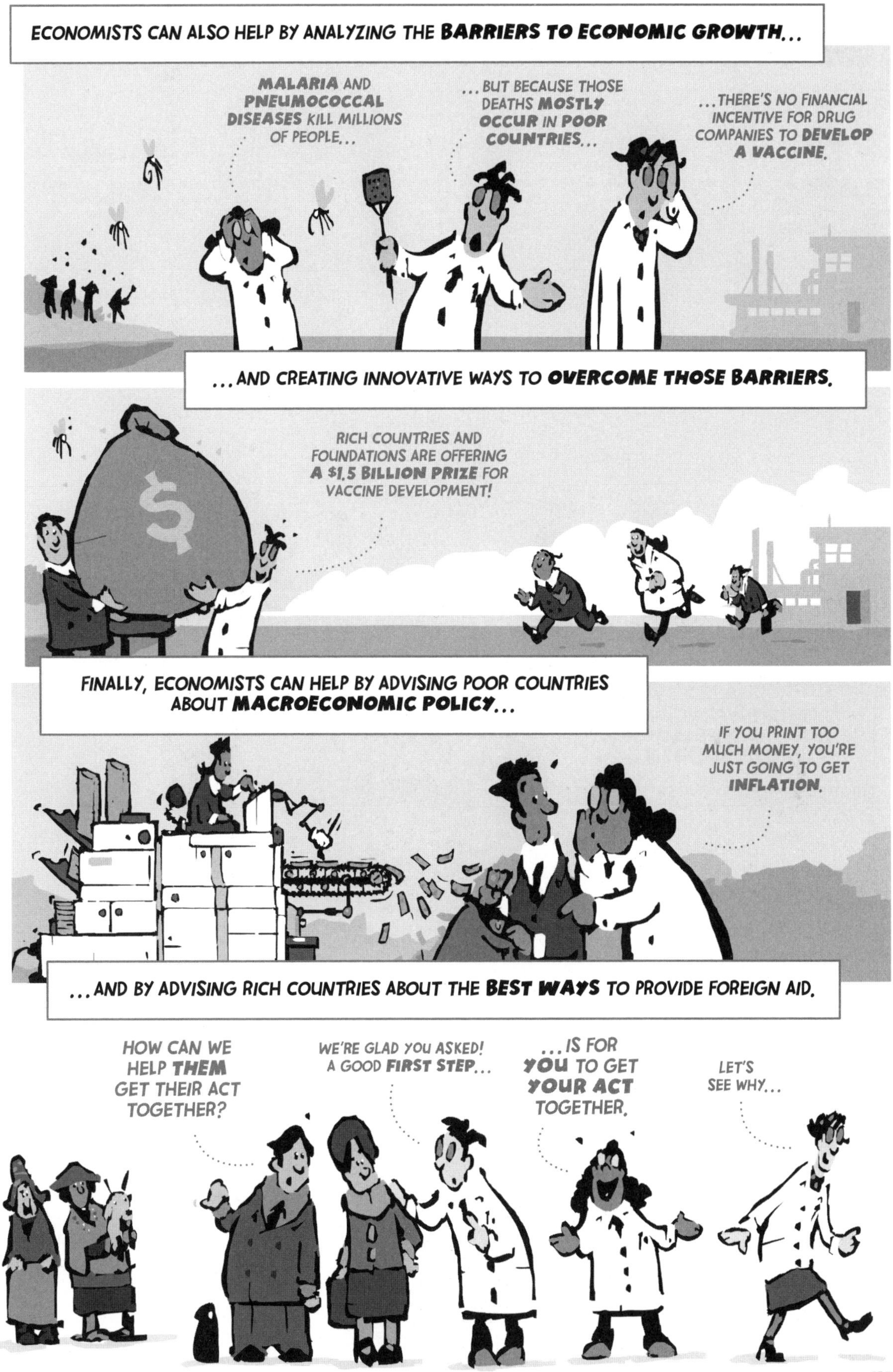
ECONOMISTS CAN ALSO HELP BY ANALYZING THE BARRIERS TO ECONOMIC GROWTH...
MALARIA AND PNEUMOCOCCAL DISEASES KILL MILLIONS OF PEOPLE...
...BUT BECAUSE THOSE DEATHS MOSTLY OCCUR IN POOR COUNTRIES...
...THERE'S NO FINANCIAL INCENTIVE FOR DRUG COMPANIES TO DEVELOP A VACCINE.
...AND CREATING INNOVATIVE WAYS TO OVERCOME THOSE BARRIERS.
RICH COUNTRIES AND FOUNDATIONS ARE OFFERING A $1.5 BILLION PRIZE FOR VACCINE DEVELOPMENT!
$
FINALLY, ECONOMISTS CAN HELP BY ADVISING POOR COUNTRIES ABOUT MACROECONOMIC POLICY...
IF YOU PRINT TOO MUCH MONEY, YOU'RE JUST GOING TO GET INFLATION.
...AND BY ADVISING RICH COUNTRIES ABOUT THE BEST WAYS TO PROVIDE FOREIGN AID.
HOW CAN WE HELP THEM GET THEIR ACT TOGETHER?
WE'RE GLAD YOU ASKED! A GOOD FIRST STEP...
...IS FOR YOU TO GET YOUR ACT TOGETHER.
LET'S SEE WHY...

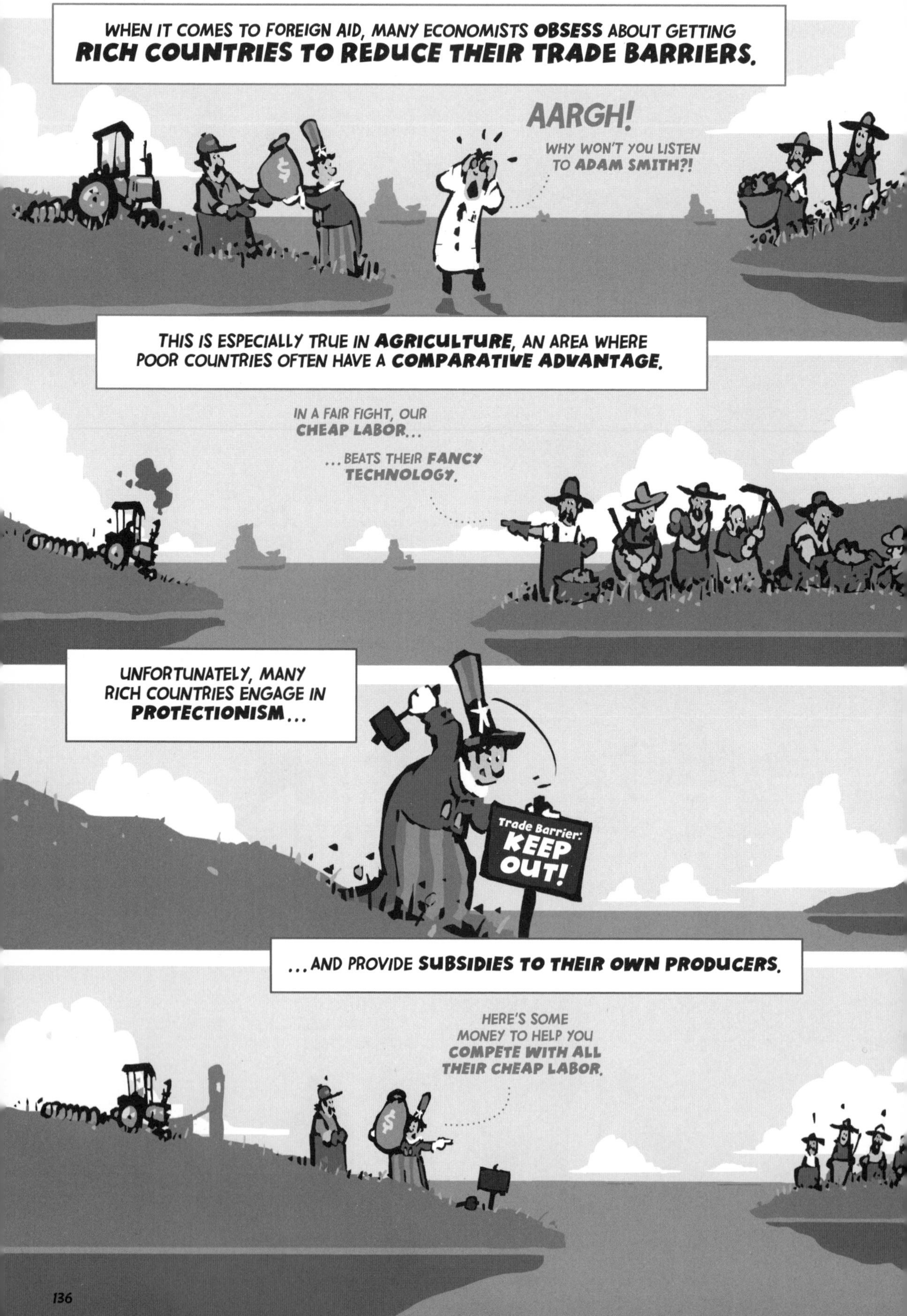
WHEN IT COMES TO FOREIGN AID, MANY ECONOMISTS OBSESS ABOUT GETTING RICH COUNTRIES TO REDUCE THEIR TRADE BARRIERS.
AARGH!
WHY WON'T YOU LISTEN TO ADAM SMITH?!
THIS IS ESPECIALLY TRUE IN AGRICULTURE, AN AREA WHERE POOR COUNTRIES OFTEN HAVE A COMPARATIVE ADVANTAGE.
IN A FAIR FIGHT, OUR CHEAP LABOR...
...BEATS THEIR FANCY TECHNOLOGY.
UNFORTUNATELY, MANY RICH COUNTRIES ENGAGE IN PROTECTIONISM...
Trade Barrier: KEEP OUT!
...AND PROVIDE SUBSIDIES TO THEIR OWN PRODUCERS.
HERE'S SOME MONEY TO HELP YOU COMPETE WITH ALL THEIR CHEAP LABOR.

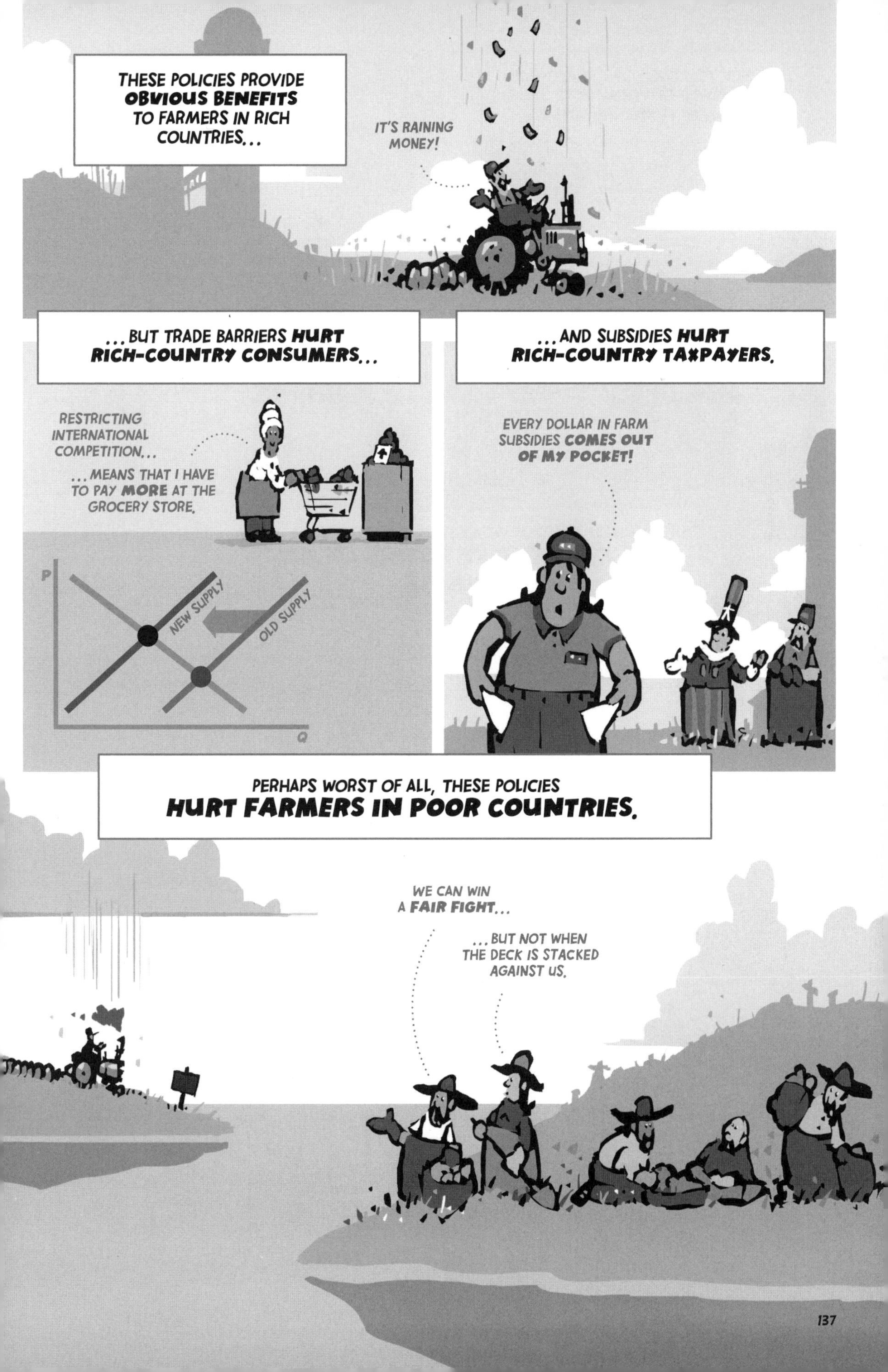
THESE POLICIES PROVIDE **OBVIOUS BENEFITS** TO FARMERS IN RICH COUNTRIES...
IT'S RAINING MONEY!
...BUT TRADE BARRIERS **HURT RICH-COUNTRY CONSUMERS**...
...AND SUBSIDIES **HURT RICH-COUNTRY TAXPAYERS.**
RESTRICTING INTERNATIONAL COMPETITION...
...MEANS THAT I HAVE TO PAY **MORE** AT THE GROCERY STORE.
P
NEW SUPPLY
OLD SUPPLY
Q
EVERY DOLLAR IN FARM SUBSIDIES **COMES OUT OF MY POCKET!**
PERHAPS WORST OF ALL, THESE POLICIES **HURT FARMERS IN POOR COUNTRIES.**
WE CAN WIN A **FAIR FIGHT**...
...BUT NOT WHEN THE DECK IS STACKED AGAINST US.

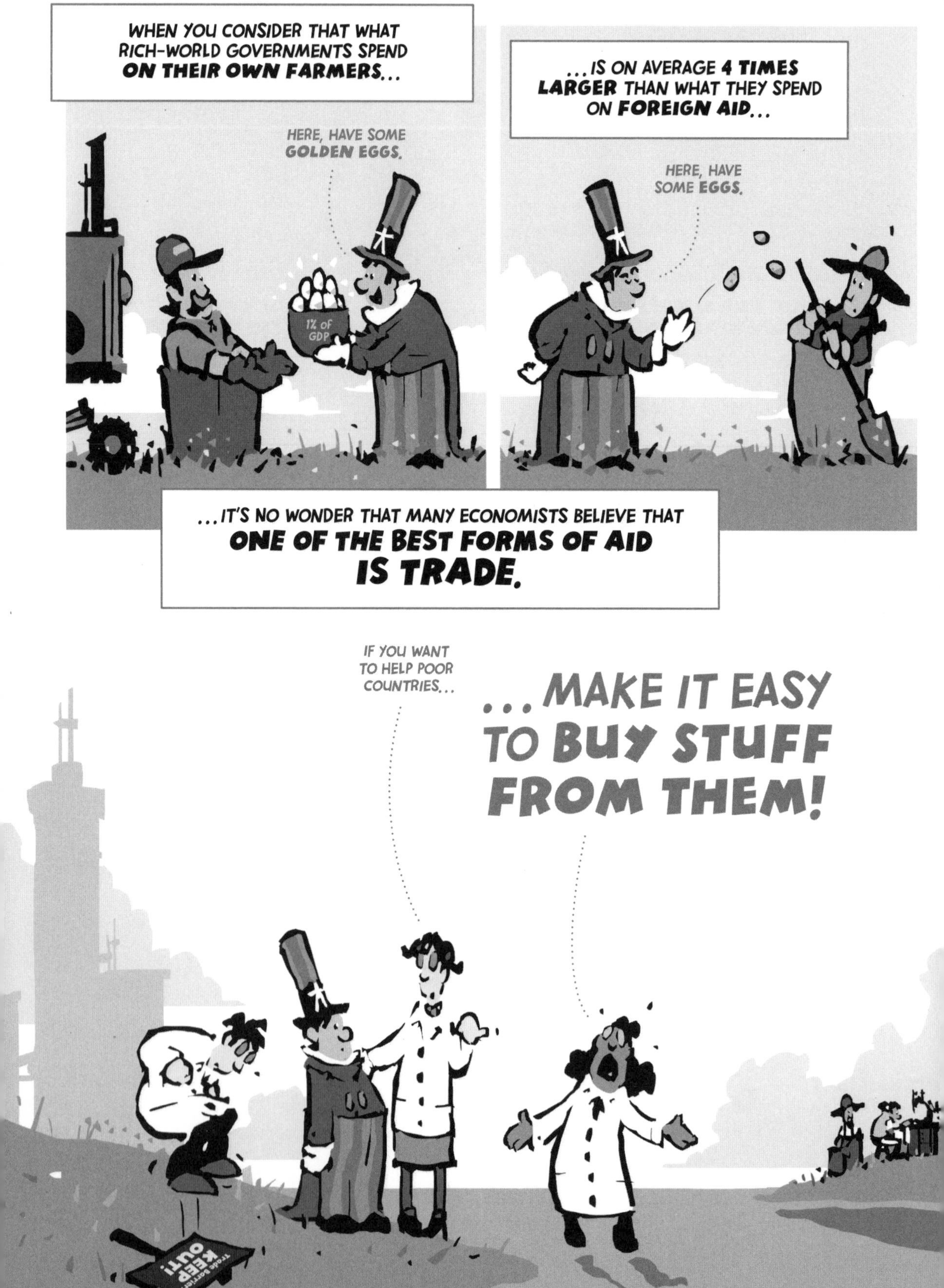
WHEN YOU CONSIDER THAT WHAT RICH-WORLD GOVERNMENTS SPEND **ON THEIR OWN FARMERS...**
HERE, HAVE SOME **GOLDEN EGGS.**
1% of GDP
...IS ON AVERAGE 4 TIMES LARGER THAN WHAT THEY SPEND ON **FOREIGN AID...**
HERE, HAVE SOME **EGGS.**
...IT'S NO WONDER THAT MANY ECONOMISTS BELIEVE THAT **ONE OF THE BEST FORMS OF AID IS TRADE.**
IF YOU WANT TO HELP POOR COUNTRIES...
...MAKE IT EASY TO **BUY STUFF FROM THEM!**
Trade Barrier: KEEP OUT!

CHAPTER 11
FOREIGN CURRENCIES

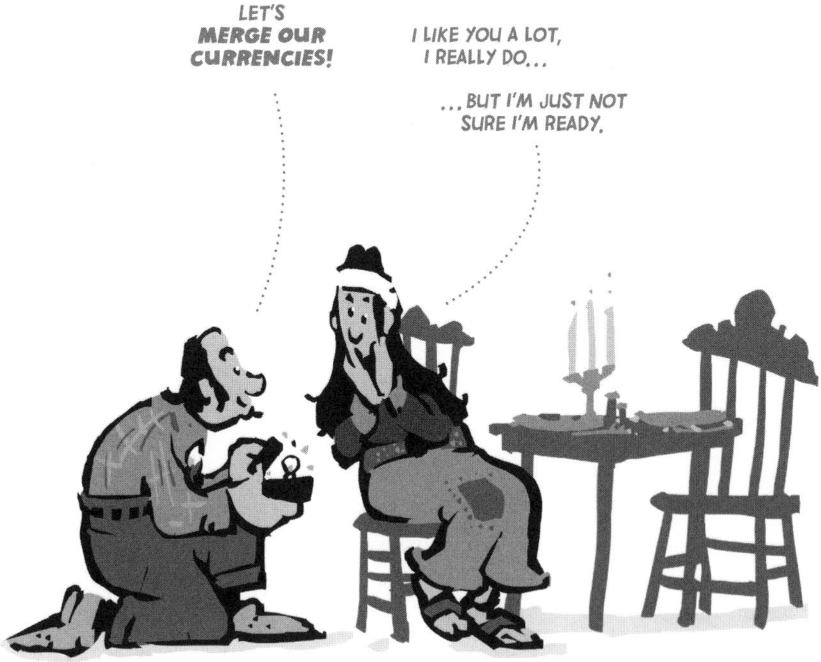
LET'S **MERGE OUR CURRENCIES!**
I LIKE YOU A LOT, I REALLY DO...
...BUT I'M JUST NOT SURE I'M READY.

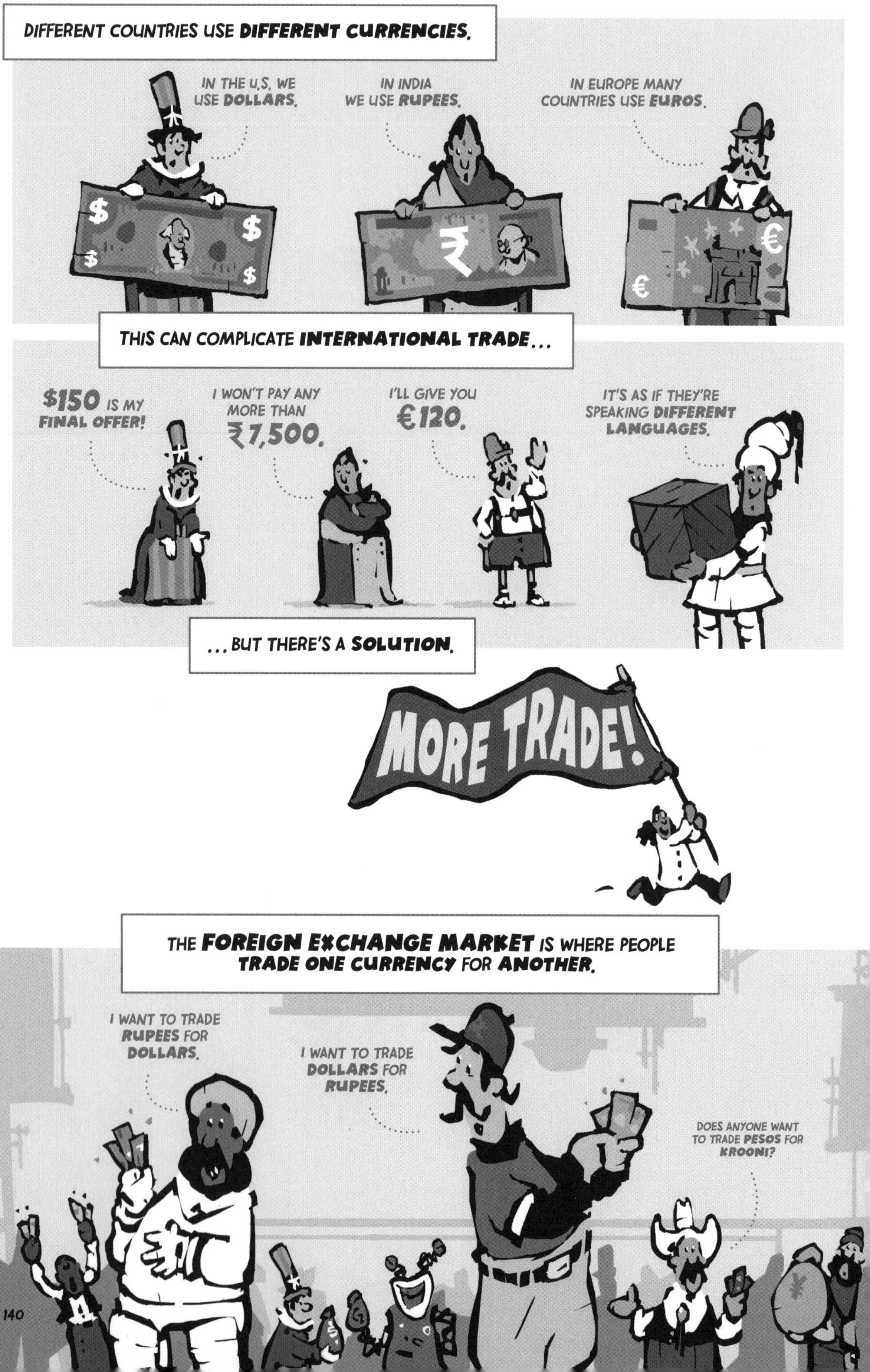
DIFFERENT COUNTRIES USE DIFFERENT CURRENCIES.
IN THE U.S. WE USE DOLLARS.
IN INDIA WE USE RUPEES.
IN EUROPE MANY COUNTRIES USE EUROS.
THIS CAN COMPLICATE INTERNATIONAL TRADE...
$150 IS MY FINAL OFFER!
I WON'T PAY ANY MORE THAN ₹7,500.
I'LL GIVE YOU €120.
IT'S AS IF THEY'RE SPEAKING DIFFERENT LANGUAGES.
...BUT THERE'S A SOLUTION.
MORE TRADE!
THE FOREIGN EXCHANGE MARKET IS WHERE PEOPLE TRADE ONE CURRENCY FOR ANOTHER.
I WANT TO TRADE RUPEES FOR DOLLARS.
I WANT TO TRADE DOLLARS FOR RUPEES.
DOES ANYONE WANT TO TRADE PESOS FOR KROONI?

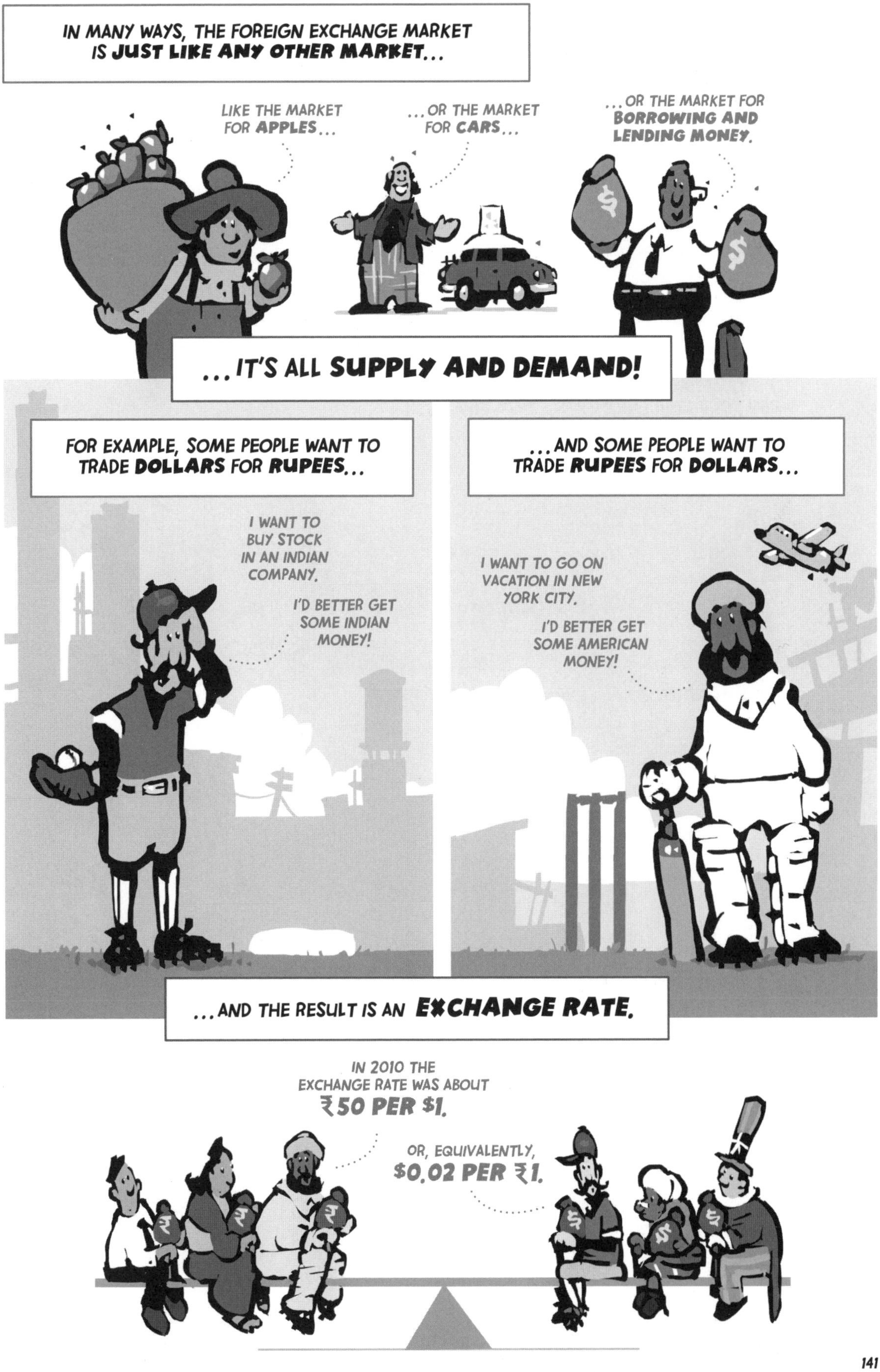
IN MANY WAYS, THE FOREIGN EXCHANGE MARKET IS JUST LIKE ANY OTHER MARKET...
LIKE THE MARKET FOR APPLES...
...OR THE MARKET FOR CARS...
...OR THE MARKET FOR BORROWING AND LENDING MONEY.
...IT'S ALL SUPPLY AND DEMAND!
FOR EXAMPLE, SOME PEOPLE WANT TO TRADE DOLLARS FOR RUPEES...
I WANT TO BUY STOCK IN AN INDIAN COMPANY.
I'D BETTER GET SOME INDIAN MONEY!
...AND SOME PEOPLE WANT TO TRADE RUPEES FOR DOLLARS...
I WANT TO GO ON VACATION IN NEW YORK CITY.
I'D BETTER GET SOME AMERICAN MONEY!
...AND THE RESULT IS AN EXCHANGE RATE.
IN 2010 THE EXCHANGE RATE WAS ABOUT ₹50 PER $1.
OR, EQUIVALENTLY, $0.02 PER ₹1.

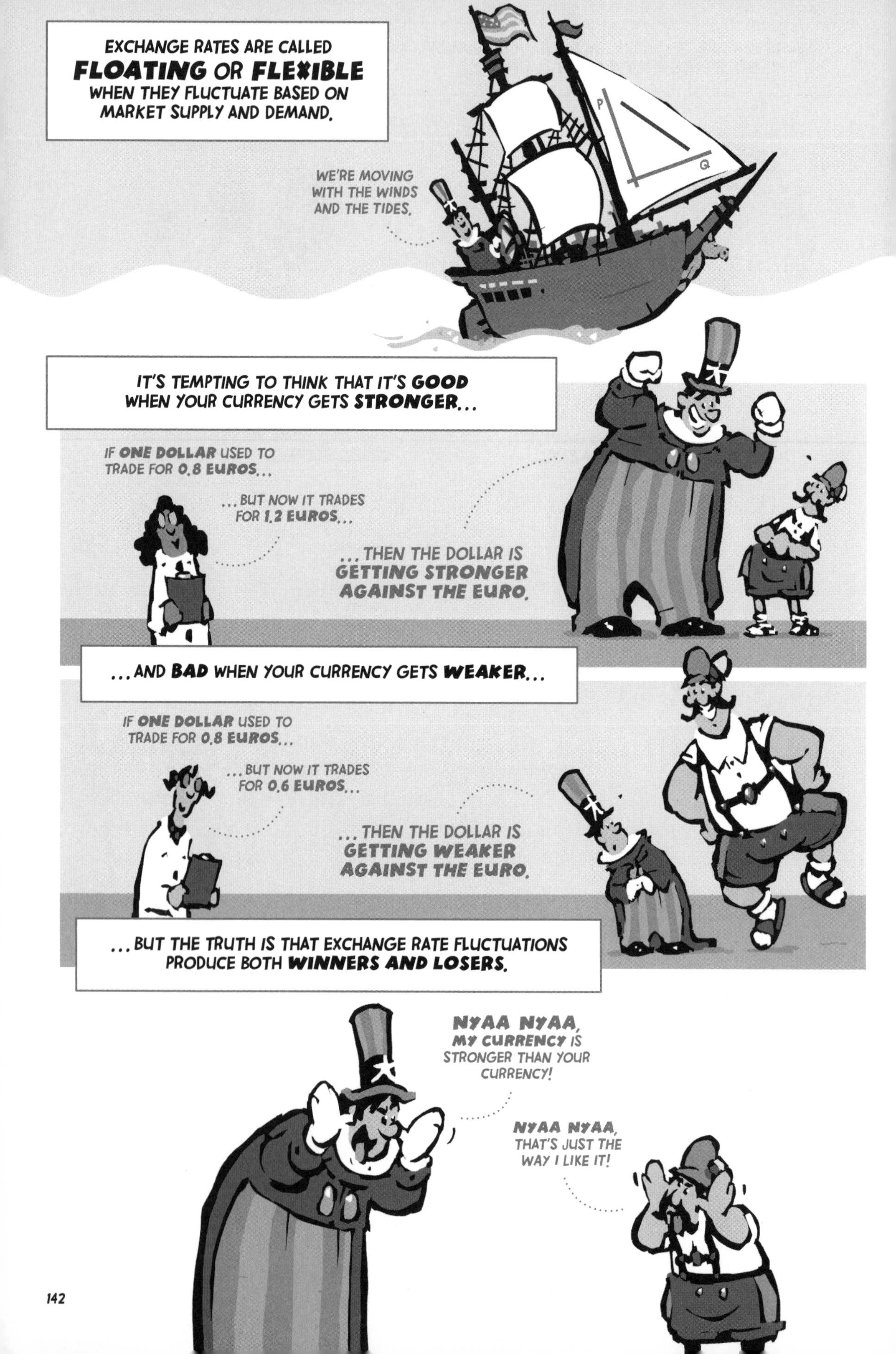
EXCHANGE RATES ARE CALLED **FLOATING** OR **FLEXIBLE** WHEN THEY FLUCTUATE BASED ON MARKET SUPPLY AND DEMAND.
P
Q
WE'RE MOVING WITH THE WINDS AND THE TIDES.
IT'S TEMPTING TO THINK THAT IT'S **GOOD** WHEN YOUR CURRENCY GETS **STRONGER**...
IF **ONE DOLLAR** USED TO TRADE FOR **0.8 EUROS**...
...BUT NOW IT TRADES FOR **1.2 EUROS**...
...THEN THE DOLLAR IS **GETTING STRONGER AGAINST THE EURO.**
...AND **BAD** WHEN YOUR CURRENCY GETS **WEAKER**...
IF **ONE DOLLAR** USED TO TRADE FOR **0.8 EUROS**...
...BUT NOW IT TRADES FOR **0.6 EUROS**...
...THEN THE DOLLAR IS **GETTING WEAKER AGAINST THE EURO.**
...BUT THE TRUTH IS THAT EXCHANGE RATE FLUCTUATIONS PRODUCE BOTH **WINNERS AND LOSERS.**
NYAA NYAA, MY CURRENCY IS STRONGER THAN YOUR CURRENCY!
NYAA NYAA, THAT'S JUST THE WAY I LIKE IT!

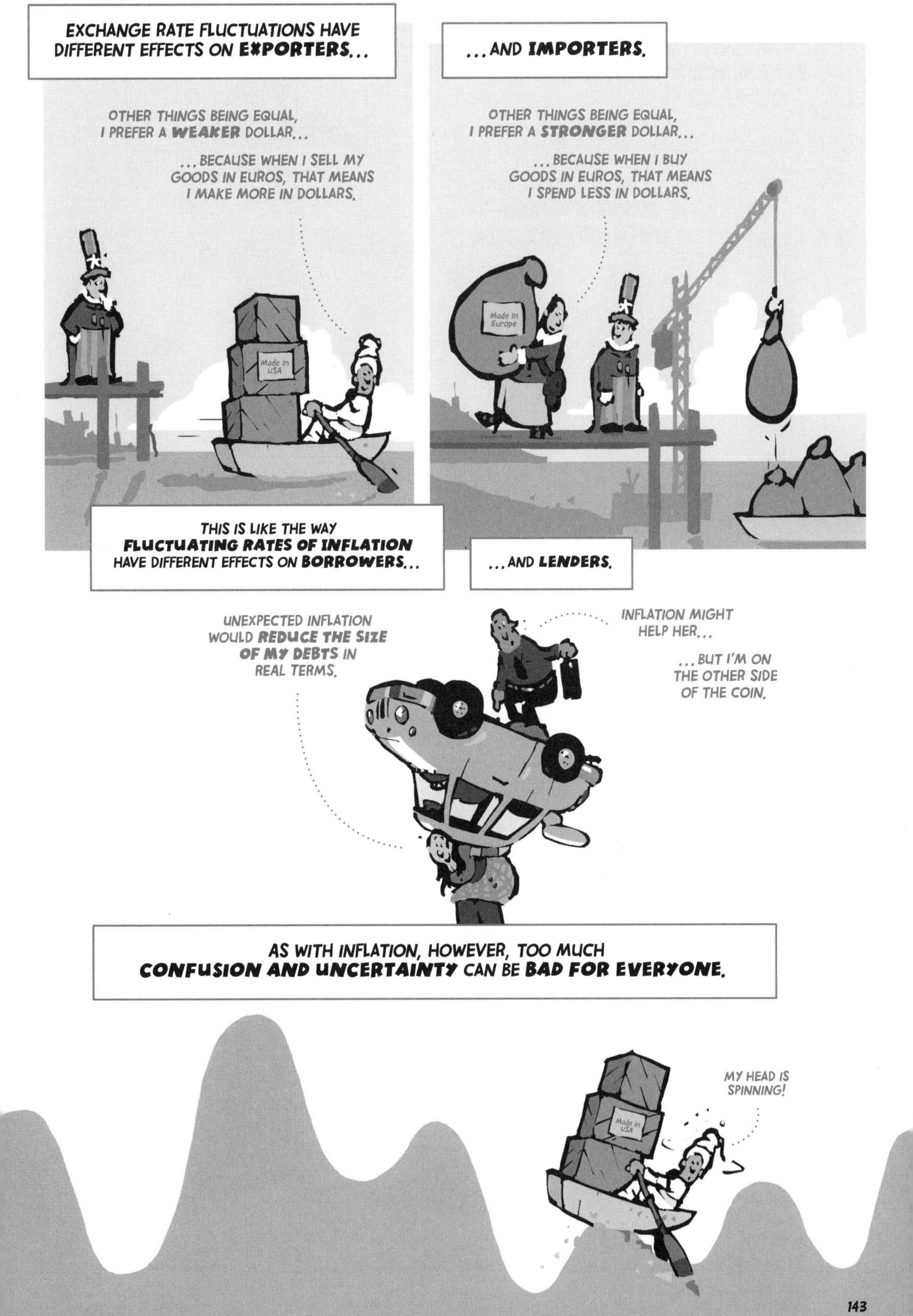
EXCHANGE RATE FLUCTUATIONS HAVE DIFFERENT EFFECTS ON EXPORTERS...
OTHER THINGS BEING EQUAL, I PREFER A WEAKER DOLLAR...
...BECAUSE WHEN I SELL MY GOODS IN EUROS, THAT MEANS I MAKE MORE IN DOLLARS.
Made In USA
...AND IMPORTERS.
OTHER THINGS BEING EQUAL, I PREFER A STRONGER DOLLAR...
...BECAUSE WHEN I BUY GOODS IN EUROS, THAT MEANS I SPEND LESS IN DOLLARS.
Made In Europe
THIS IS LIKE THE WAY FLUCTUATING RATES OF INFLATION HAVE DIFFERENT EFFECTS ON BORROWERS...
...AND LENDERS.
UNEXPECTED INFLATION WOULD REDUCE THE SIZE OF MY DEBTS IN REAL TERMS.
INFLATION MIGHT HELP HER...
...BUT I'M ON THE OTHER SIDE OF THE COIN.
AS WITH INFLATION, HOWEVER, TOO MUCH CONFUSION AND UNCERTAINTY CAN BE BAD FOR EVERYONE.
Made In USA
MY HEAD IS SPINNING!

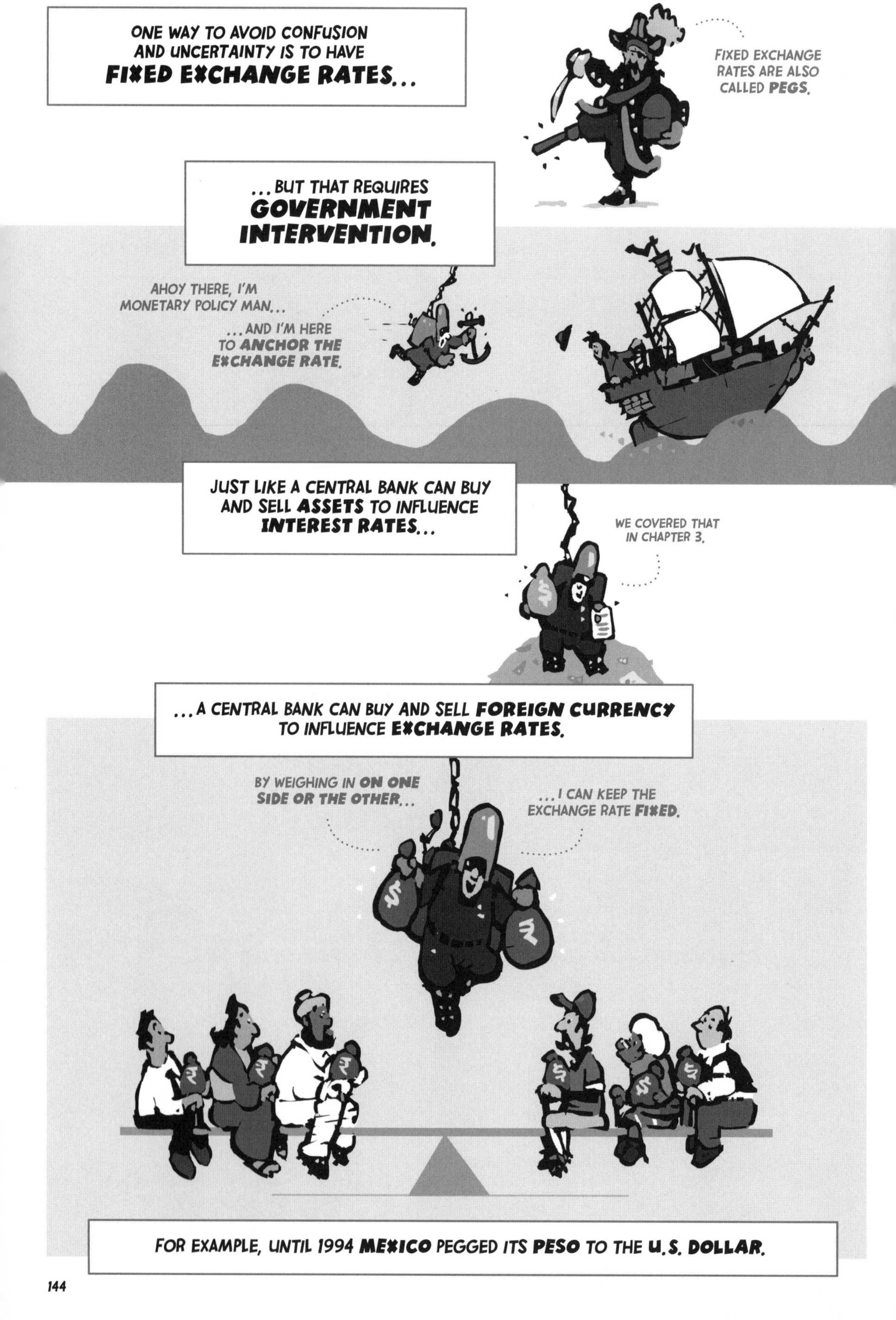
ONE WAY TO AVOID CONFUSION AND UNCERTAINTY IS TO HAVE **FIXED EXCHANGE RATES...**
FIXED EXCHANGE RATES ARE ALSO CALLED **PEGS.**
...BUT THAT REQUIRES **GOVERNMENT INTERVENTION.**
AHOY THERE, I'M MONETARY POLICY MAN...
...AND I'M HERE TO **ANCHOR THE EXCHANGE RATE.**
JUST LIKE A CENTRAL BANK CAN BUY AND SELL **ASSETS** TO INFLUENCE **INTEREST RATES...**
WE COVERED THAT IN CHAPTER 3.
...A CENTRAL BANK CAN BUY AND SELL **FOREIGN CURRENCY** TO INFLUENCE **EXCHANGE RATES.**
BY WEIGHING IN **ON ONE SIDE OR THE OTHER...**
...I CAN KEEP THE EXCHANGE RATE **FIXED.**
FOR EXAMPLE, UNTIL 1994 **MEXICO** PEGGED ITS **PESO** TO THE **U.S. DOLLAR.**

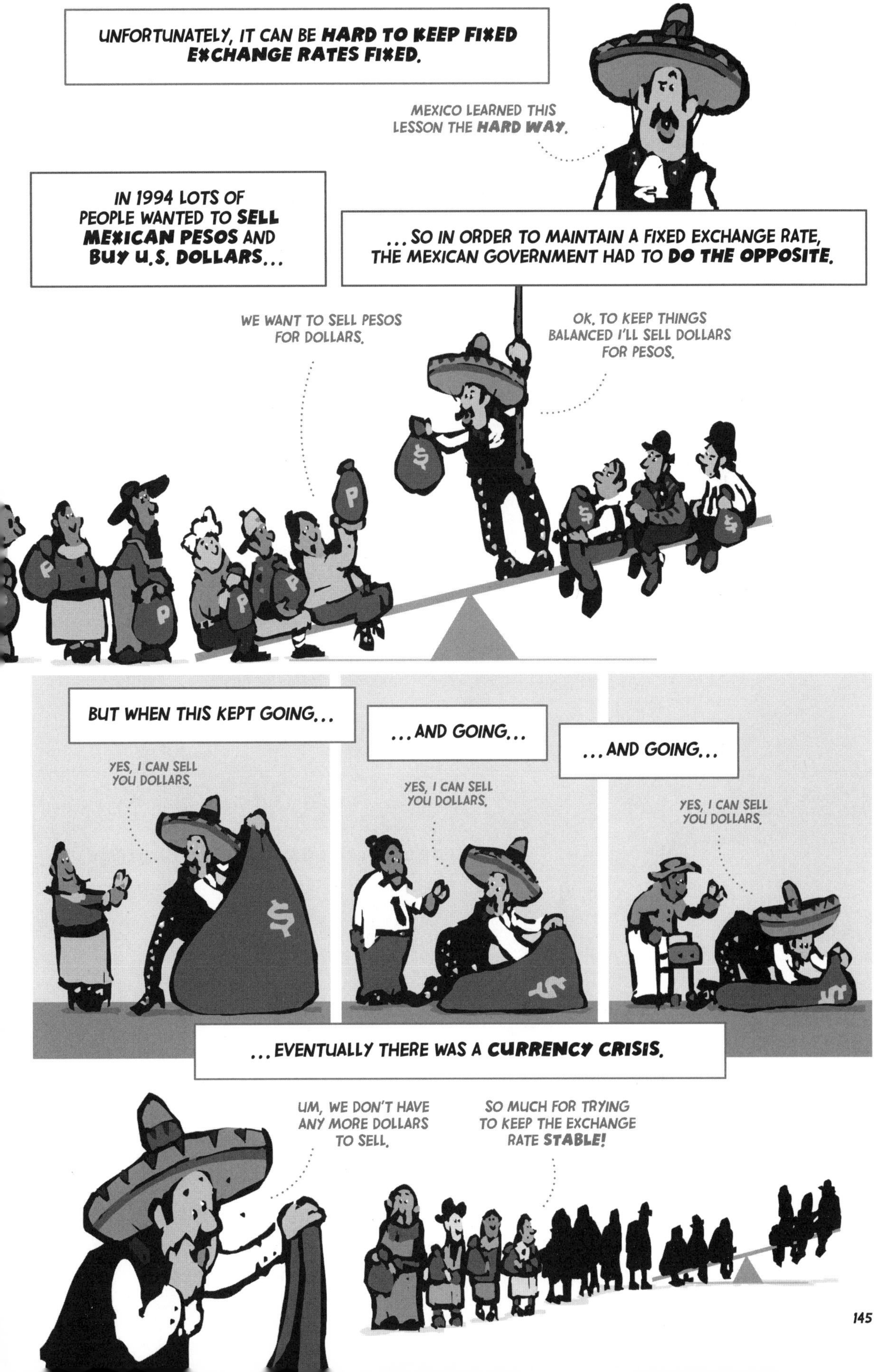
UNFORTUNATELY, IT CAN BE HARD TO KEEP FIXED EXCHANGE RATES FIXED.
MEXICO LEARNED THIS LESSON THE HARD WAY.
IN 1994 LOTS OF PEOPLE WANTED TO SELL MEXICAN PESOS AND BUY U.S. DOLLARS...
...SO IN ORDER TO MAINTAIN A FIXED EXCHANGE RATE, THE MEXICAN GOVERNMENT HAD TO DO THE OPPOSITE.
WE WANT TO SELL PESOS FOR DOLLARS.
OK. TO KEEP THINGS BALANCED I'LL SELL DOLLARS FOR PESOS.
BUT WHEN THIS KEPT GOING...
YES, I CAN SELL YOU DOLLARS.
...AND GOING...
YES, I CAN SELL YOU DOLLARS.
...AND GOING...
YES, I CAN SELL YOU DOLLARS.
...EVENTUALLY THERE WAS A CURRENCY CRISIS.
UM, WE DON'T HAVE ANY MORE DOLLARS TO SELL.
SO MUCH FOR TRYING TO KEEP THE EXCHANGE RATE STABLE!

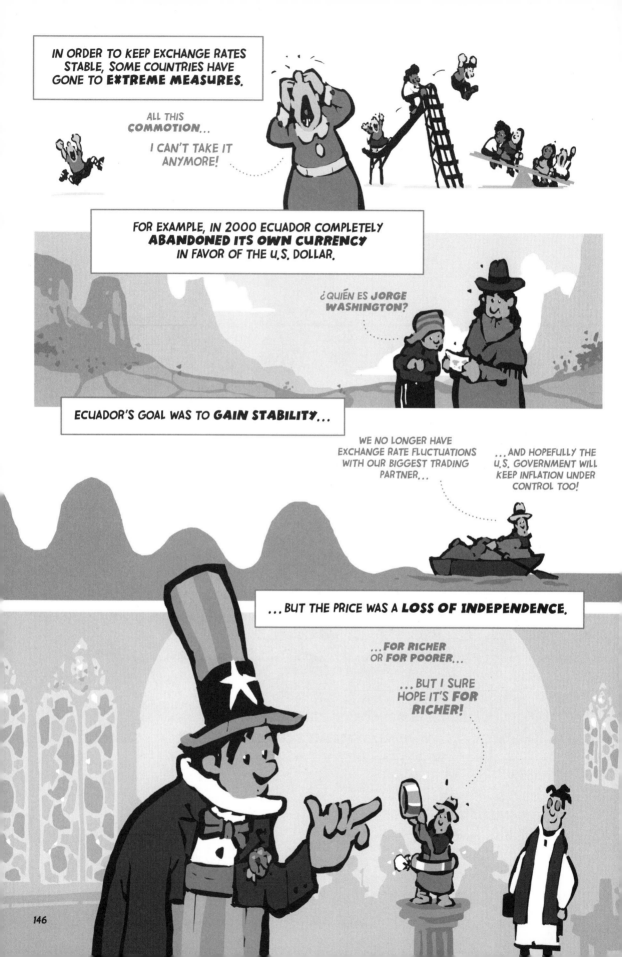

IN ORDER TO KEEP EXCHANGE RATES STABLE, SOME COUNTRIES HAVE GONE TO **EXTREME MEASURES.**

ALL THIS **COMMOTION...**

I CAN'T TAKE IT ANYMORE!

FOR EXAMPLE, IN 2000 ECUADOR COMPLETELY **ABANDONED ITS OWN CURRENCY** IN FAVOR OF THE U.S. DOLLAR.

¿QUIÉN ES **JORGE WASHINGTON?**

ECUADOR'S GOAL WAS TO **GAIN STABILITY...**

WE NO LONGER HAVE EXCHANGE RATE FLUCTUATIONS WITH OUR BIGGEST TRADING PARTNER...

...AND HOPEFULLY THE U.S. GOVERNMENT WILL KEEP INFLATION UNDER CONTROL TOO!

...BUT THE PRICE WAS A **LOSS OF INDEPENDENCE.**

...FOR RICHER OR FOR POORER...

...BUT I SURE HOPE IT'S FOR RICHER!

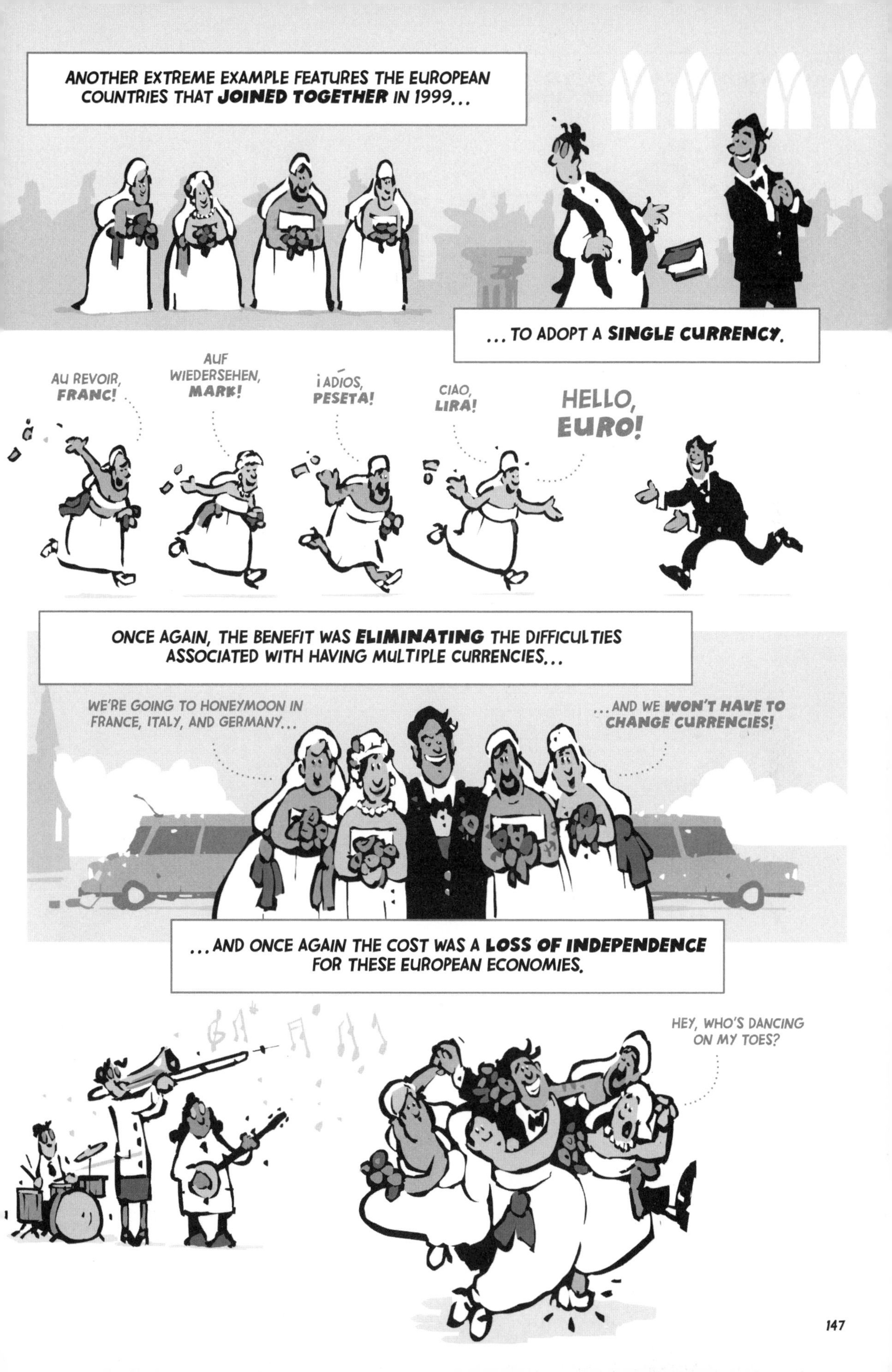

ANOTHER EXTREME EXAMPLE FEATURES THE EUROPEAN COUNTRIES THAT **JOINED TOGETHER** IN 1999...
...TO ADOPT A **SINGLE CURRENCY**.
AU REVOIR, **FRANC!**
AUF WIEDERSEHEN, **MARK!**
¡ADIÓS, **PESETA!**
CIAO, **LIRA!**
HELLO, **EURO!**
ONCE AGAIN, THE BENEFIT WAS **ELIMINATING** THE DIFFICULTIES ASSOCIATED WITH HAVING MULTIPLE CURRENCIES...
WE'RE GOING TO HONEYMOON IN FRANCE, ITALY, AND GERMANY...
...AND WE **WON'T HAVE TO CHANGE CURRENCIES!**
...AND ONCE AGAIN THE COST WAS A **LOSS OF INDEPENDENCE** FOR THESE EUROPEAN ECONOMIES.
HEY, WHO'S DANCING ON MY TOES?

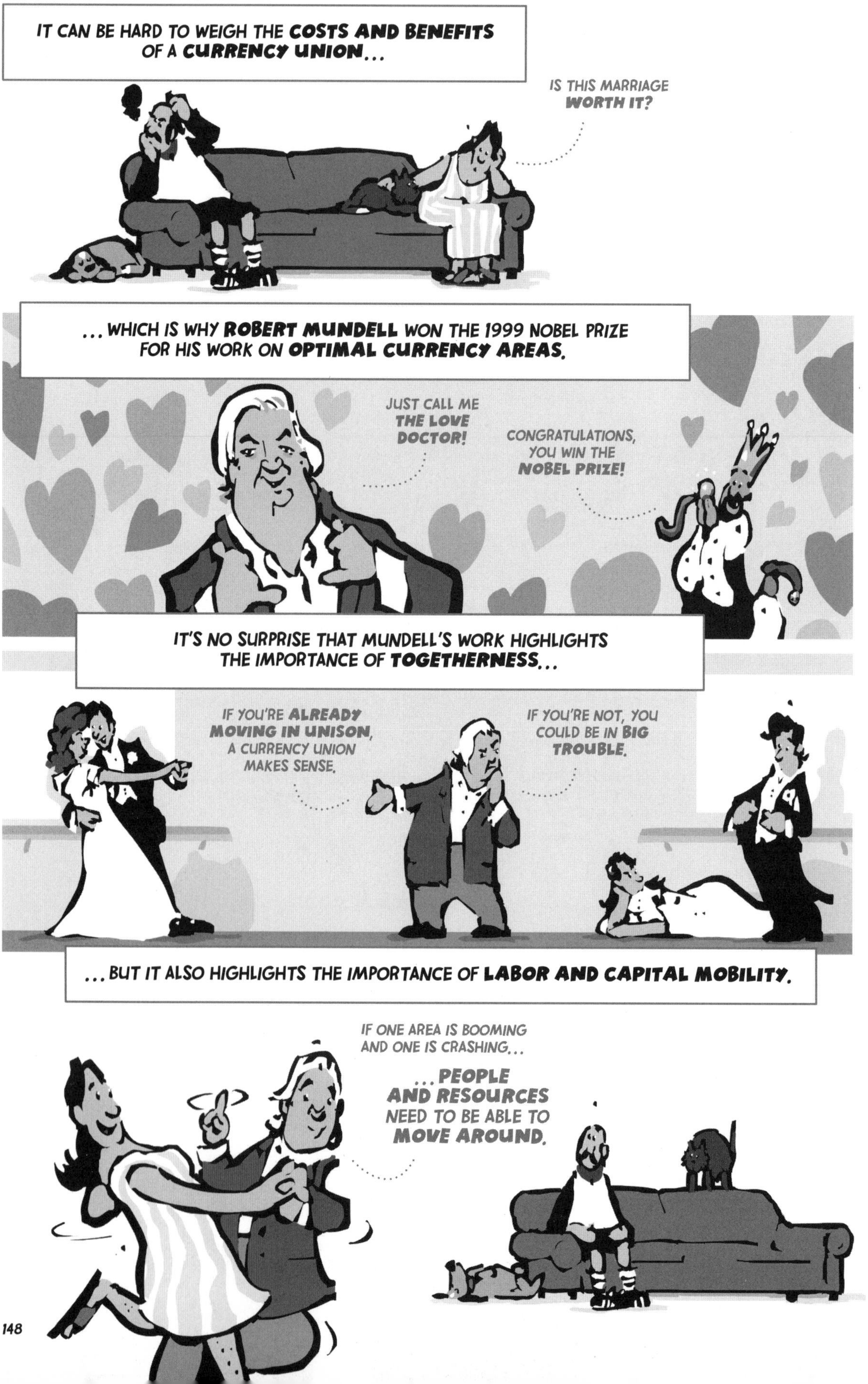

IT CAN BE HARD TO WEIGH THE COSTS AND BENEFITS OF A CURRENCY UNION...
IS THIS MARRIAGE WORTH IT?
...WHICH IS WHY ROBERT MUNDELL WON THE 1999 NOBEL PRIZE FOR HIS WORK ON OPTIMAL CURRENCY AREAS.
JUST CALL ME THE LOVE DOCTOR!
CONGRATULATIONS, YOU WIN THE NOBEL PRIZE!
IT'S NO SURPRISE THAT MUNDELL'S WORK HIGHLIGHTS THE IMPORTANCE OF TOGETHERNESS...
IF YOU'RE ALREADY MOVING IN UNISON, A CURRENCY UNION MAKES SENSE.
IF YOU'RE NOT, YOU COULD BE IN BIG TROUBLE.
...BUT IT ALSO HIGHLIGHTS THE IMPORTANCE OF LABOR AND CAPITAL MOBILITY.
IF ONE AREA IS BOOMING AND ONE IS CRASHING...
...PEOPLE AND RESOURCES NEED TO BE ABLE TO MOVE AROUND.

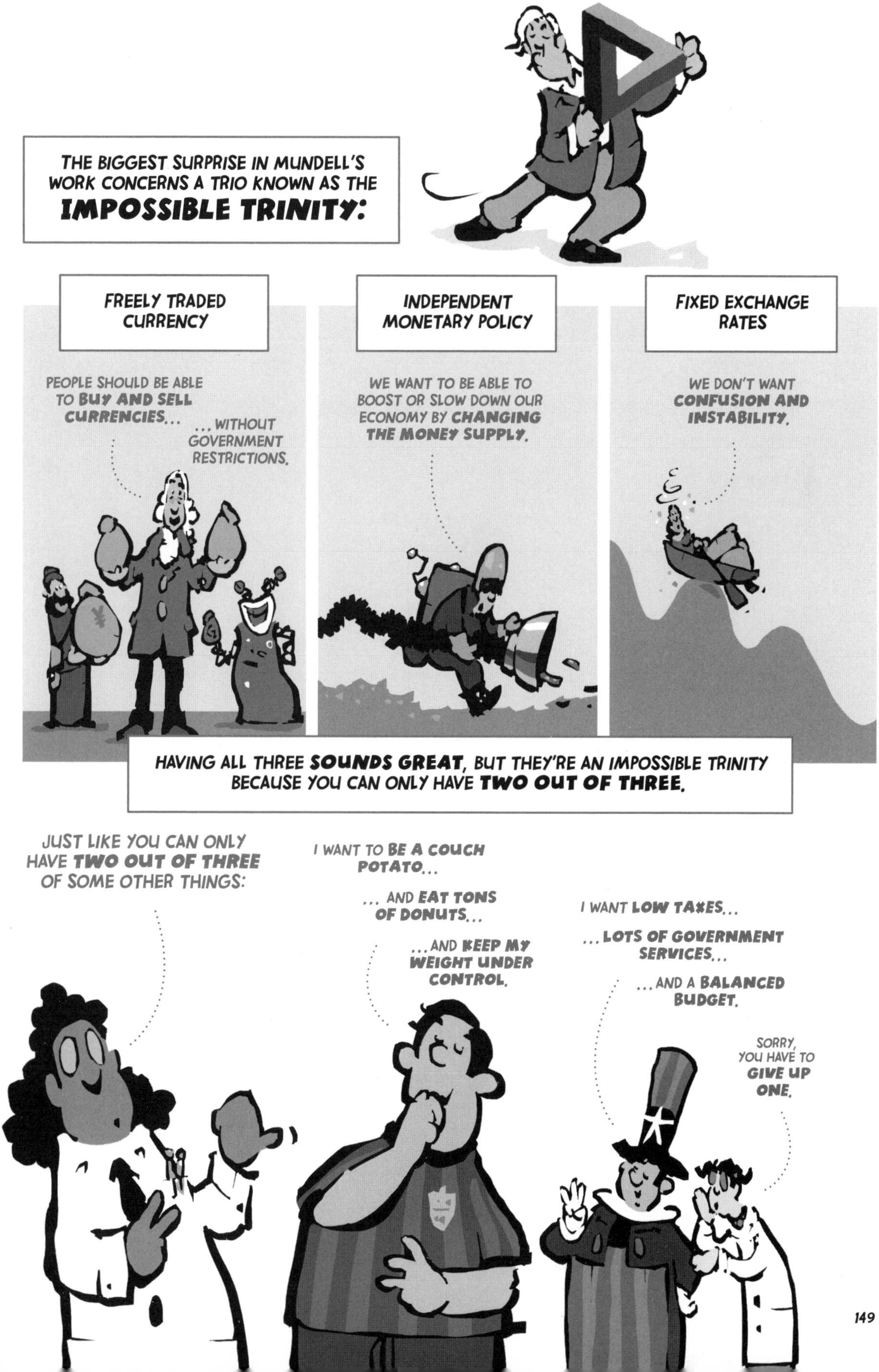
THE BIGGEST SURPRISE IN MUNDELL'S WORK CONCERNS A TRIO KNOWN AS THE **IMPOSSIBLE TRINITY:**
FREELY TRADED CURRENCY
PEOPLE SHOULD BE ABLE TO **BUY AND SELL CURRENCIES**...
...WITHOUT GOVERNMENT RESTRICTIONS.
INDEPENDENT MONETARY POLICY
WE WANT TO BE ABLE TO BOOST OR SLOW DOWN OUR ECONOMY BY **CHANGING THE MONEY SUPPLY.**
FIXED EXCHANGE RATES
WE DON'T WANT **CONFUSION AND INSTABILITY.**
HAVING ALL THREE **SOUNDS GREAT**, BUT THEY'RE AN IMPOSSIBLE TRINITY BECAUSE YOU CAN ONLY HAVE **TWO OUT OF THREE.**
JUST LIKE YOU CAN ONLY HAVE **TWO OUT OF THREE** OF SOME OTHER THINGS:
I WANT TO **BE A COUCH POTATO**...
...AND **EAT TONS OF DONUTS**...
...AND **KEEP MY WEIGHT UNDER CONTROL.**
I WANT **LOW TAXES**...
...**LOTS OF GOVERNMENT SERVICES**...
...AND A **BALANCED BUDGET.**
SORRY, YOU HAVE TO **GIVE UP ONE.**

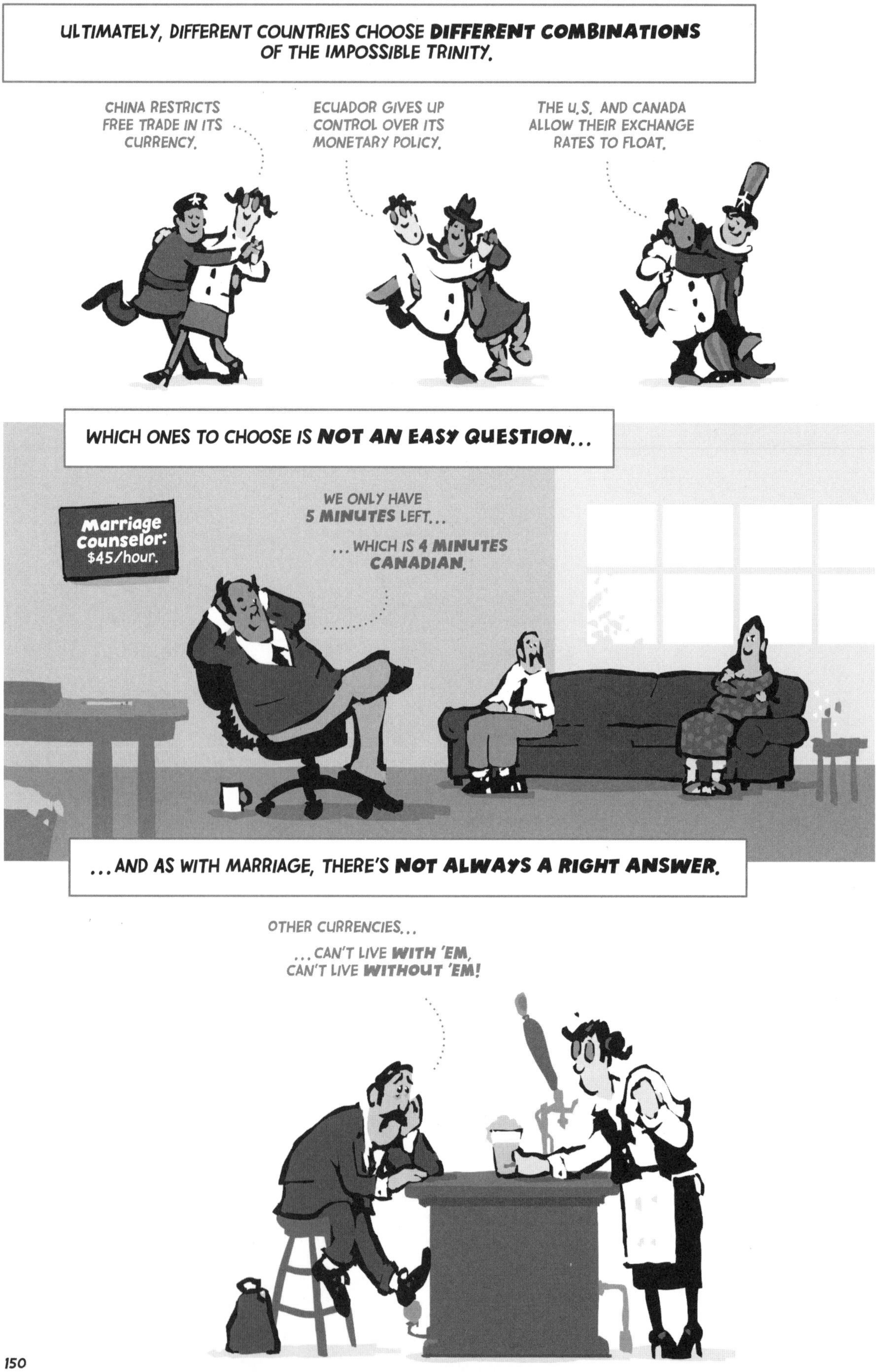
ULTIMATELY, DIFFERENT COUNTRIES CHOOSE **DIFFERENT COMBINATIONS** OF THE IMPOSSIBLE TRINITY.
CHINA RESTRICTS FREE TRADE IN ITS CURRENCY.
ECUADOR GIVES UP CONTROL OVER ITS MONETARY POLICY.
THE U.S. AND CANADA ALLOW THEIR EXCHANGE RATES TO FLOAT.
WHICH ONES TO CHOOSE IS **NOT AN EASY QUESTION**...
Marriage Counselor: $45/hour.
WE ONLY HAVE **5 MINUTES** LEFT...
...WHICH IS **4 MINUTES CANADIAN.**
...AND AS WITH MARRIAGE, THERE'S **NOT ALWAYS A RIGHT ANSWER.**
OTHER CURRENCIES...
...CAN'T LIVE **WITH 'EM**, CAN'T LIVE **WITHOUT 'EM!**

PART THREE
GLOBAL
MACROECONOMICS

CHAPTER 12
THE END OF THE BUSINESS CYCLE?

WILL WE **EVER** SEE THE END OF THE BUSINESS CYCLE?

BE CAREFUL WHAT YOU WISH FOR.

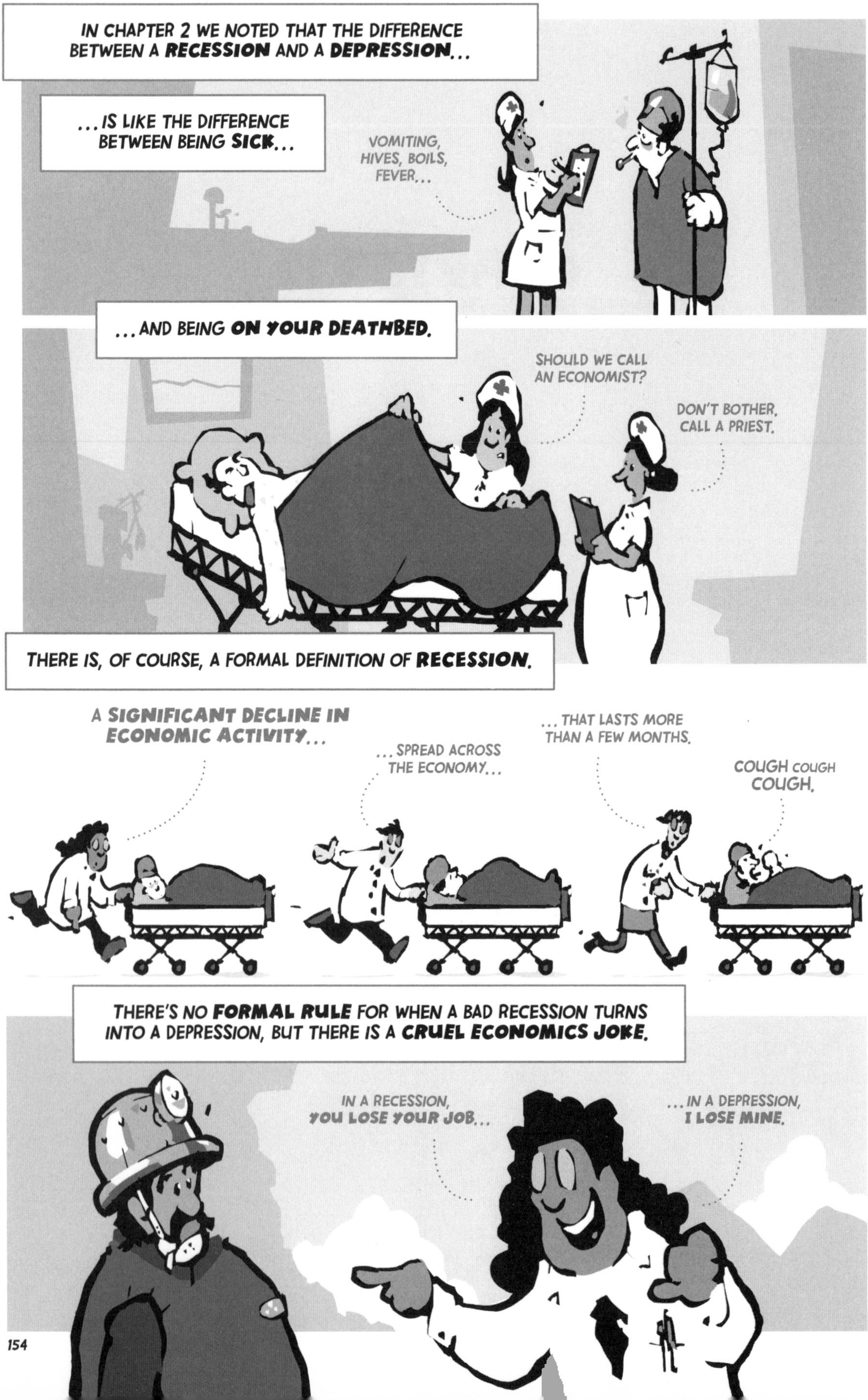
IN CHAPTER 2 WE NOTED THAT THE DIFFERENCE BETWEEN A RECESSION AND A DEPRESSION...
...IS LIKE THE DIFFERENCE BETWEEN BEING SICK...
VOMITING, HIVES, BOILS, FEVER...
...AND BEING ON YOUR DEATHBED.
SHOULD WE CALL AN ECONOMIST?
DON'T BOTHER, CALL A PRIEST.
THERE IS, OF COURSE, A FORMAL DEFINITION OF RECESSION.
A SIGNIFICANT DECLINE IN ECONOMIC ACTIVITY...
...SPREAD ACROSS THE ECONOMY...
...THAT LASTS MORE THAN A FEW MONTHS.
COUGH COUGH COUGH.
THERE'S NO FORMAL RULE FOR WHEN A BAD RECESSION TURNS INTO A DEPRESSION, BUT THERE IS A CRUEL ECONOMICS JOKE.
IN A RECESSION, YOU LOSE YOUR JOB...
...IN A DEPRESSION, I LOSE MINE.

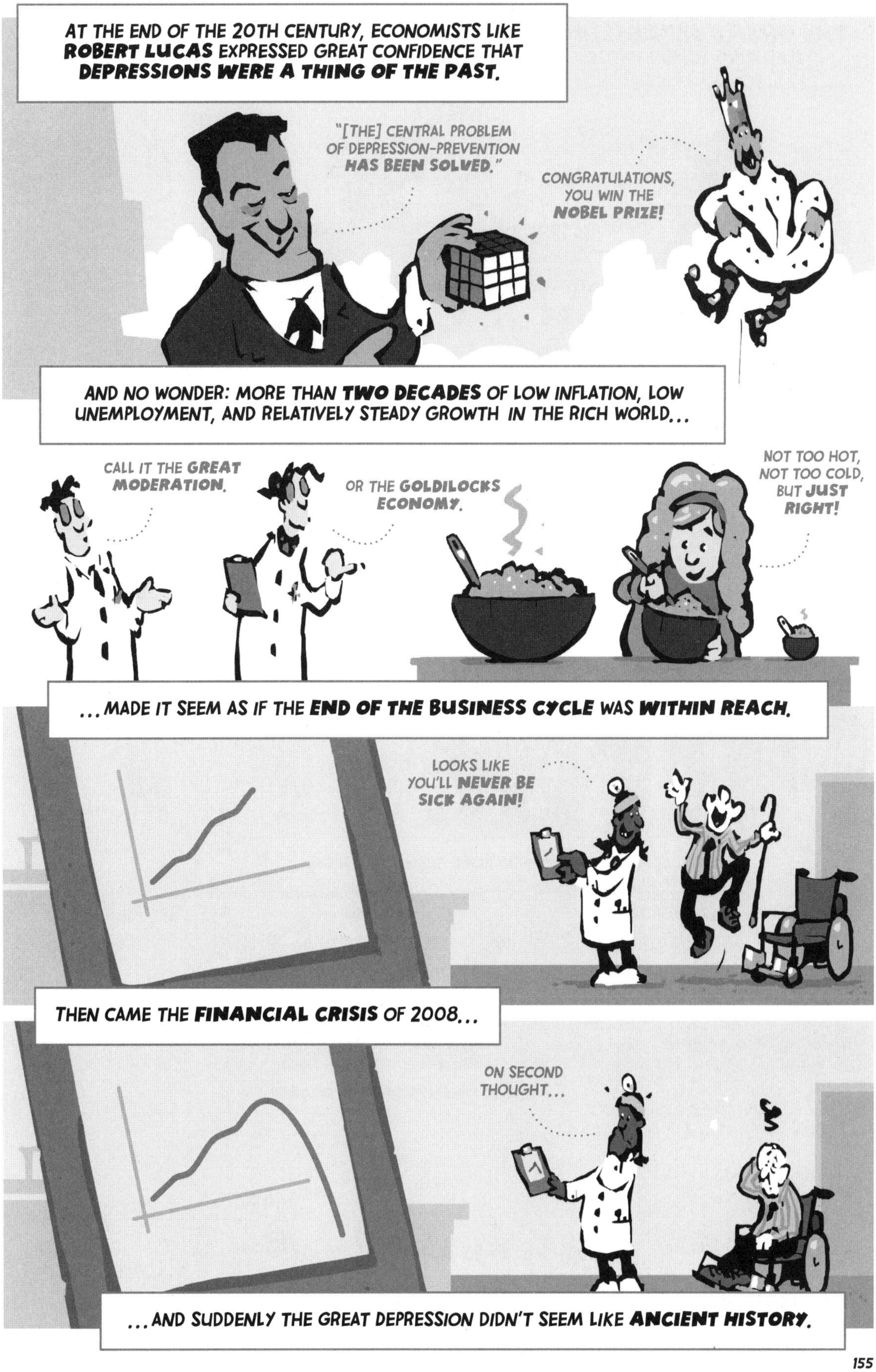
AT THE END OF THE 20TH CENTURY, ECONOMISTS LIKE ROBERT LUCAS EXPRESSED GREAT CONFIDENCE THAT DEPRESSIONS WERE A THING OF THE PAST.
"[THE] CENTRAL PROBLEM OF DEPRESSION-PREVENTION HAS BEEN SOLVED."
CONGRATULATIONS, YOU WIN THE NOBEL PRIZE!
AND NO WONDER: MORE THAN TWO DECADES OF LOW INFLATION, LOW UNEMPLOYMENT, AND RELATIVELY STEADY GROWTH IN THE RICH WORLD...
CALL IT THE GREAT MODERATION.
OR THE GOLDILOCKS ECONOMY.
NOT TOO HOT, NOT TOO COLD, BUT JUST RIGHT!
...MADE IT SEEM AS IF THE END OF THE BUSINESS CYCLE WAS WITHIN REACH.
LOOKS LIKE YOU'LL NEVER BE SICK AGAIN!
THEN CAME THE FINANCIAL CRISIS OF 2008...
ON SECOND THOUGHT...
...AND SUDDENLY THE GREAT DEPRESSION DIDN'T SEEM LIKE ANCIENT HISTORY.

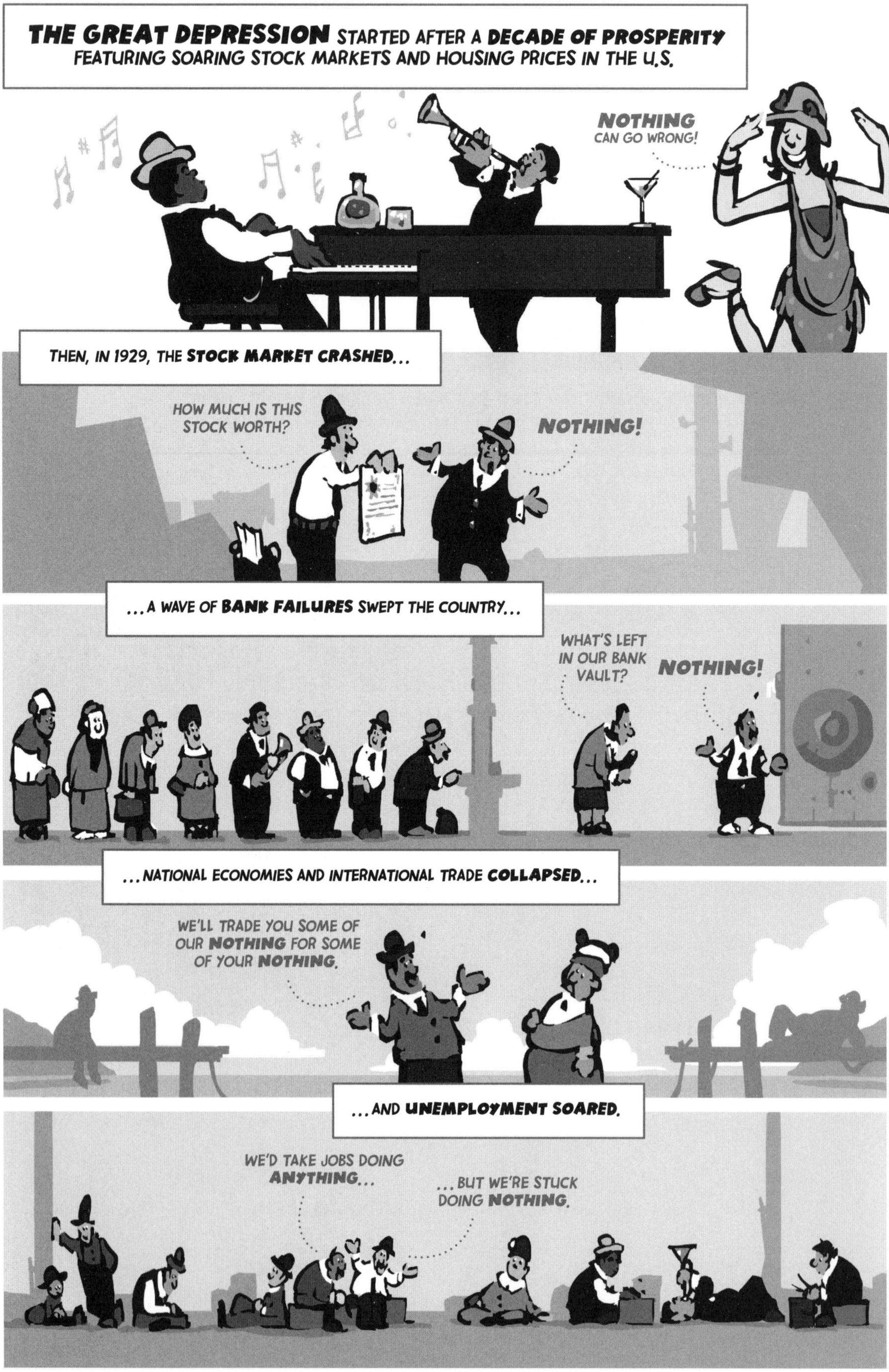

THE GREAT DEPRESSION STARTED AFTER A DECADE OF PROSPERITY FEATURING SOARING STOCK MARKETS AND HOUSING PRICES IN THE U.S.
NOTHING CAN GO WRONG!
THEN, IN 1929, THE STOCK MARKET CRASHED...
HOW MUCH IS THIS STOCK WORTH?
NOTHING!
...A WAVE OF BANK FAILURES SWEPT THE COUNTRY...
WHAT'S LEFT IN OUR BANK VAULT?
NOTHING!
...NATIONAL ECONOMIES AND INTERNATIONAL TRADE COLLAPSED...
WE'LL TRADE YOU SOME OF OUR NOTHING FOR SOME OF YOUR NOTHING.
...AND UNEMPLOYMENT SOARED.
WE'D TAKE JOBS DOING ANYTHING...
...BUT WE'RE STUCK DOING NOTHING.

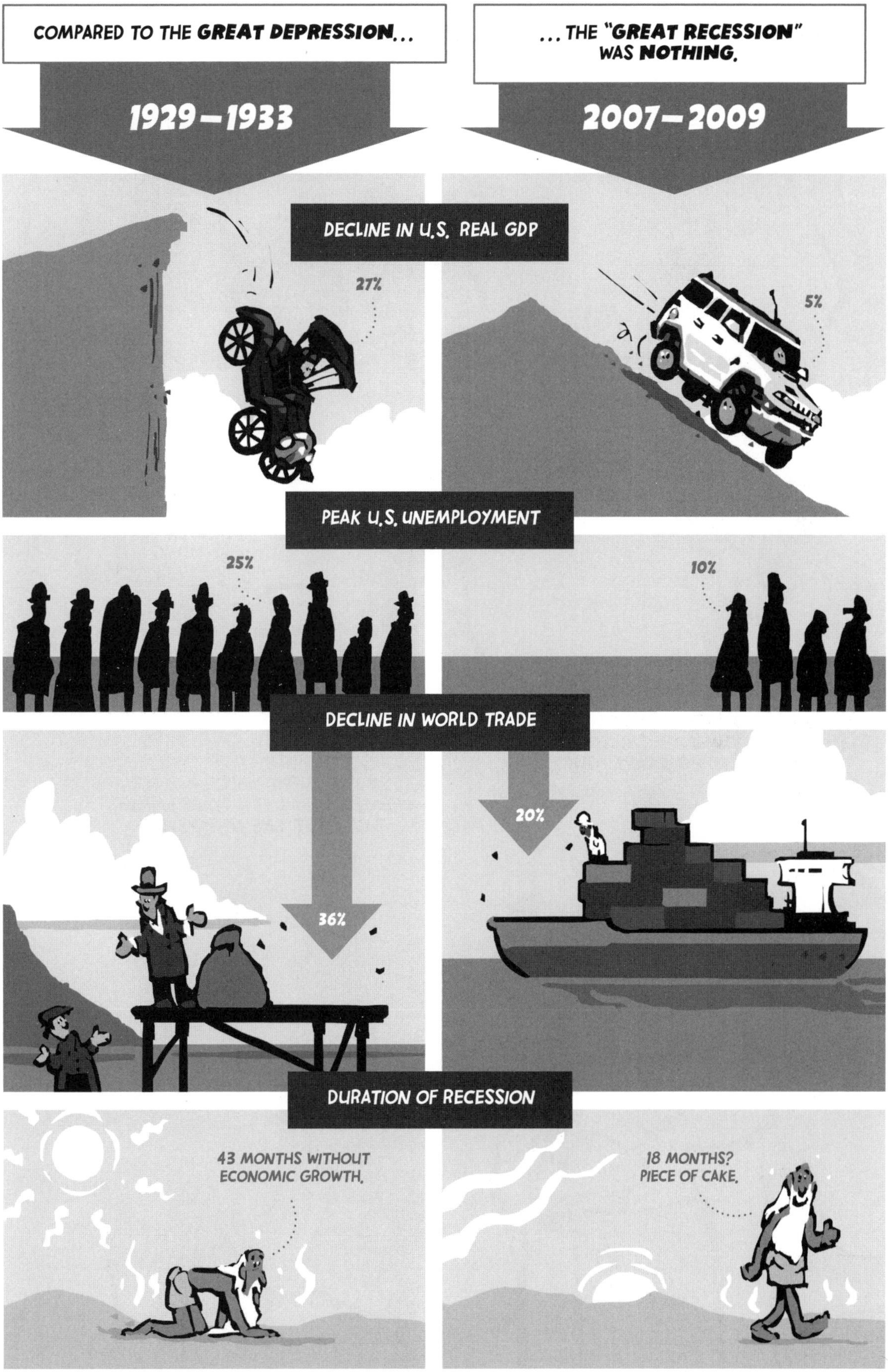
COMPARED TO THE GREAT DEPRESSION...
... THE "GREAT RECESSION" WAS NOTHING.
1929–1933
2007–2009
DECLINE IN U.S. REAL GDP
27%
5%
PEAK U.S. UNEMPLOYMENT
25%
10%
DECLINE IN WORLD TRADE
36%
20%
DURATION OF RECESSION
43 MONTHS WITHOUT ECONOMIC GROWTH.
18 MONTHS? PIECE OF CAKE.

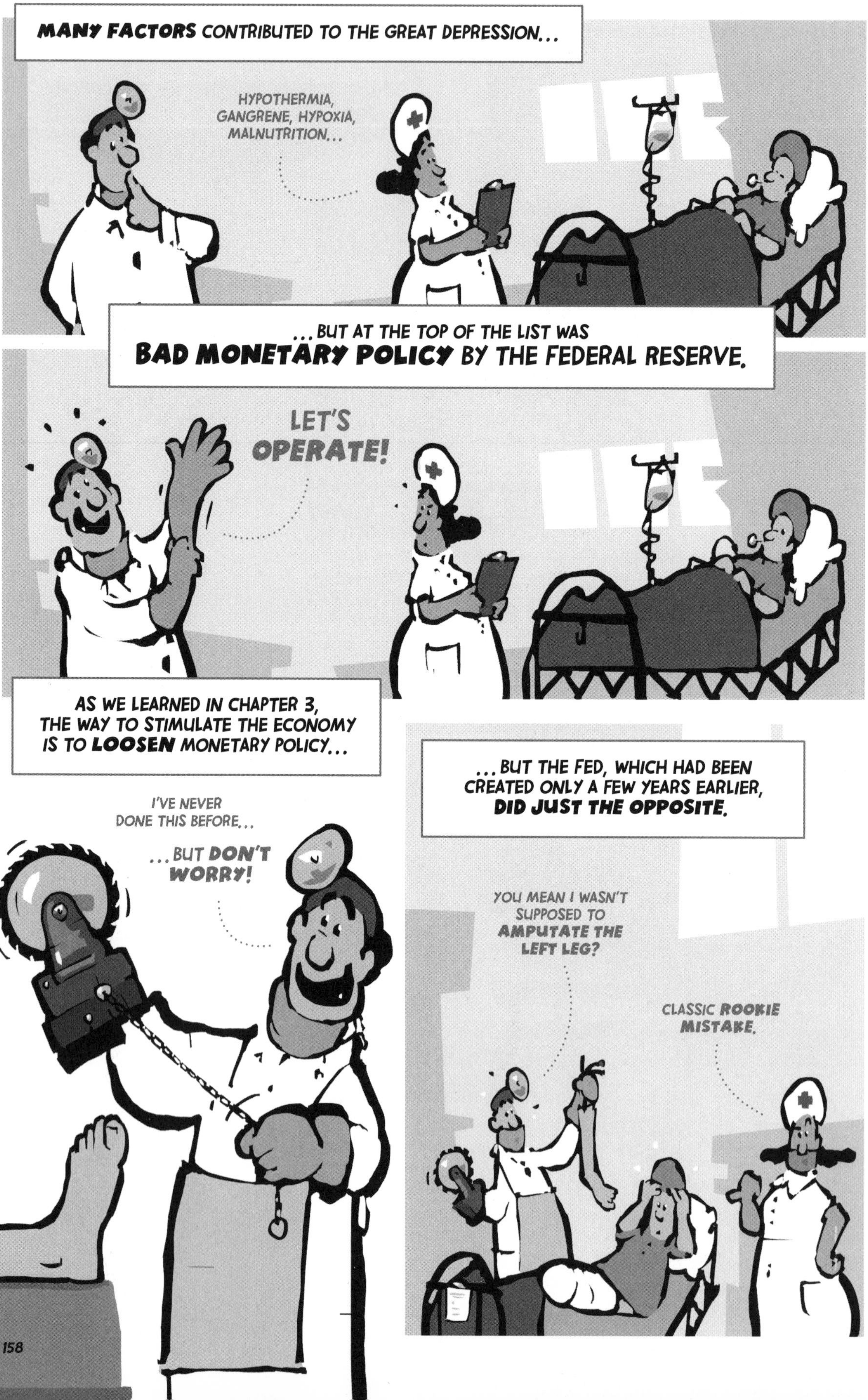
MANY FACTORS CONTRIBUTED TO THE GREAT DEPRESSION...
HYPOTHERMIA, GANGRENE, HYPOXIA, MALNUTRITION...
...BUT AT THE TOP OF THE LIST WAS BAD MONETARY POLICY BY THE FEDERAL RESERVE.
LET'S OPERATE!
AS WE LEARNED IN CHAPTER 3, THE WAY TO STIMULATE THE ECONOMY IS TO LOOSEN MONETARY POLICY...
I'VE NEVER DONE THIS BEFORE...
...BUT DON'T WORRY!
...BUT THE FED, WHICH HAD BEEN CREATED ONLY A FEW YEARS EARLIER, DID JUST THE OPPOSITE.
YOU MEAN I WASN'T SUPPOSED TO AMPUTATE THE LEFT LEG?
CLASSIC ROOKIE MISTAKE.

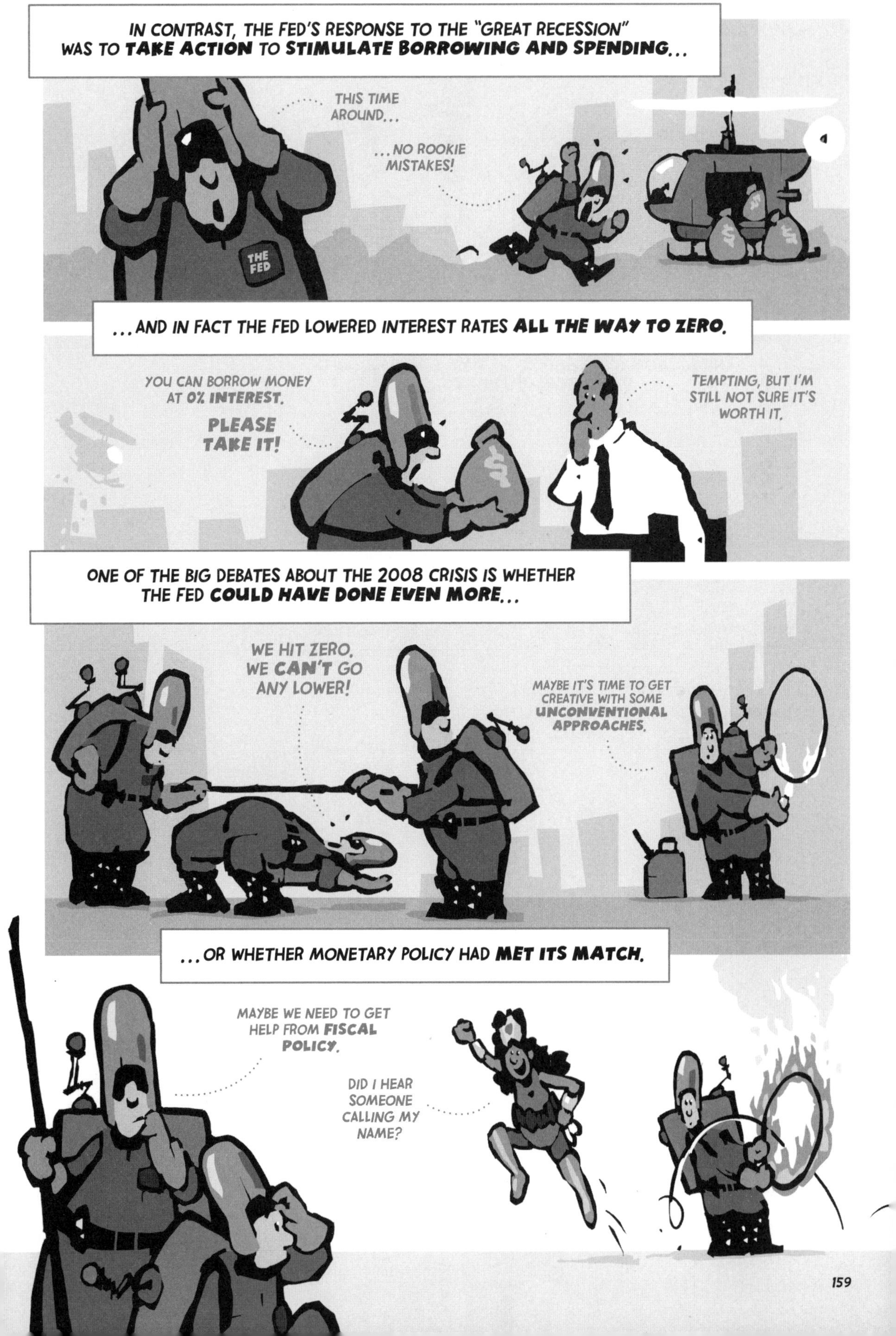
IN CONTRAST, THE FED'S RESPONSE TO THE "GREAT RECESSION" WAS TO TAKE ACTION TO STIMULATE BORROWING AND SPENDING...
THIS TIME AROUND...
...NO ROOKIE MISTAKES!
THE FED
...AND IN FACT THE FED LOWERED INTEREST RATES ALL THE WAY TO ZERO.
YOU CAN BORROW MONEY AT 0% INTEREST.
PLEASE TAKE IT!
TEMPTING, BUT I'M STILL NOT SURE IT'S WORTH IT.
ONE OF THE BIG DEBATES ABOUT THE 2008 CRISIS IS WHETHER THE FED COULD HAVE DONE EVEN MORE...
WE HIT ZERO, WE CAN'T GO ANY LOWER!
MAYBE IT'S TIME TO GET CREATIVE WITH SOME UNCONVENTIONAL APPROACHES.
...OR WHETHER MONETARY POLICY HAD MET ITS MATCH.
MAYBE WE NEED TO GET HELP FROM FISCAL POLICY.
DID I HEAR SOMEONE CALLING MY NAME?

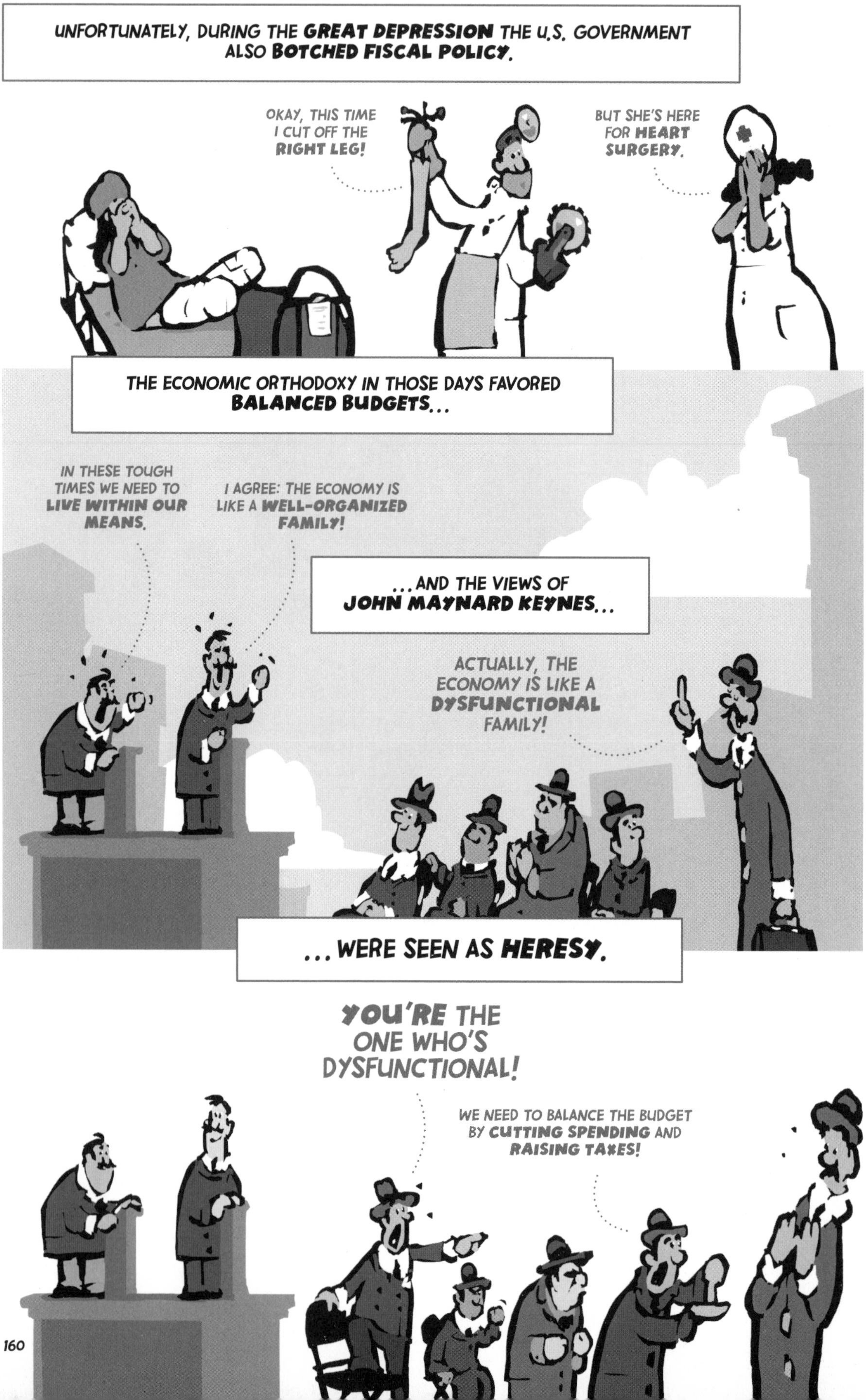
UNFORTUNATELY, DURING THE **GREAT DEPRESSION** THE U.S. GOVERNMENT ALSO **BOTCHED FISCAL POLICY.**
OKAY, THIS TIME I CUT OFF THE **RIGHT LEG!**
BUT SHE'S HERE FOR **HEART SURGERY.**
THE ECONOMIC ORTHODOXY IN THOSE DAYS FAVORED **BALANCED BUDGETS...**
IN THESE TOUGH TIMES WE NEED TO **LIVE WITHIN OUR MEANS.**
I AGREE: THE ECONOMY IS LIKE A **WELL-ORGANIZED FAMILY!**
...AND THE VIEWS OF **JOHN MAYNARD KEYNES...**
ACTUALLY, THE ECONOMY IS LIKE A **DYSFUNCTIONAL** FAMILY!
...WERE SEEN AS **HERESY.**
YOU'RE THE ONE WHO'S DYSFUNCTIONAL!
WE NEED TO BALANCE THE BUDGET BY **CUTTING SPENDING** AND **RAISING TAXES!**

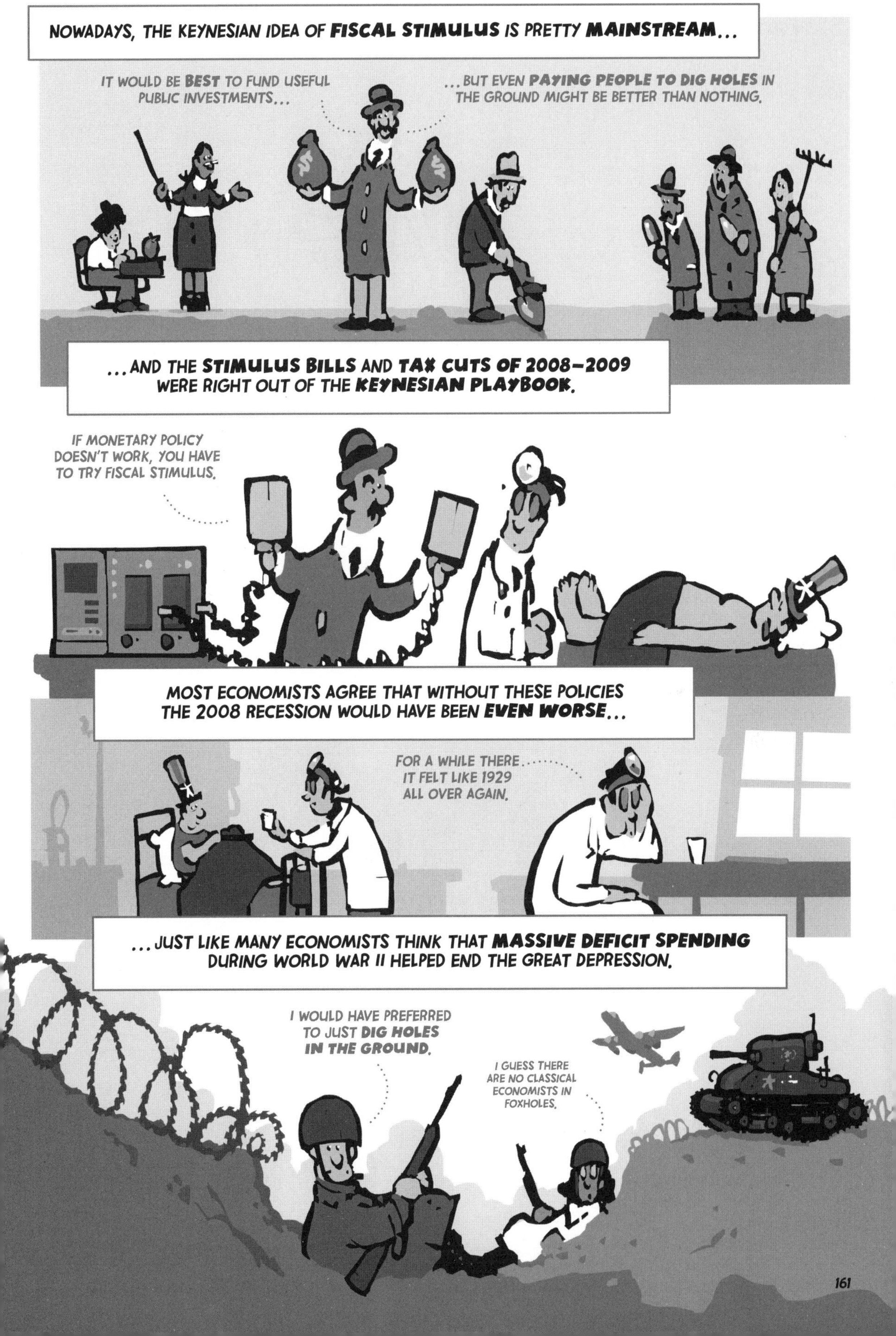
NOWADAYS, THE KEYNESIAN IDEA OF FISCAL STIMULUS IS PRETTY MAINSTREAM...
IT WOULD BE BEST TO FUND USEFUL PUBLIC INVESTMENTS...
...BUT EVEN PAYING PEOPLE TO DIG HOLES IN THE GROUND MIGHT BE BETTER THAN NOTHING.
...AND THE STIMULUS BILLS AND TAX CUTS OF 2008–2009 WERE RIGHT OUT OF THE KEYNESIAN PLAYBOOK.
IF MONETARY POLICY DOESN'T WORK, YOU HAVE TO TRY FISCAL STIMULUS.
MOST ECONOMISTS AGREE THAT WITHOUT THESE POLICIES THE 2008 RECESSION WOULD HAVE BEEN EVEN WORSE...
FOR A WHILE THERE IT FELT LIKE 1929 ALL OVER AGAIN.
...JUST LIKE MANY ECONOMISTS THINK THAT MASSIVE DEFICIT SPENDING DURING WORLD WAR II HELPED END THE GREAT DEPRESSION.
I WOULD HAVE PREFERRED TO JUST DIG HOLES IN THE GROUND.
I GUESS THERE ARE NO CLASSICAL ECONOMISTS IN FOXHOLES.

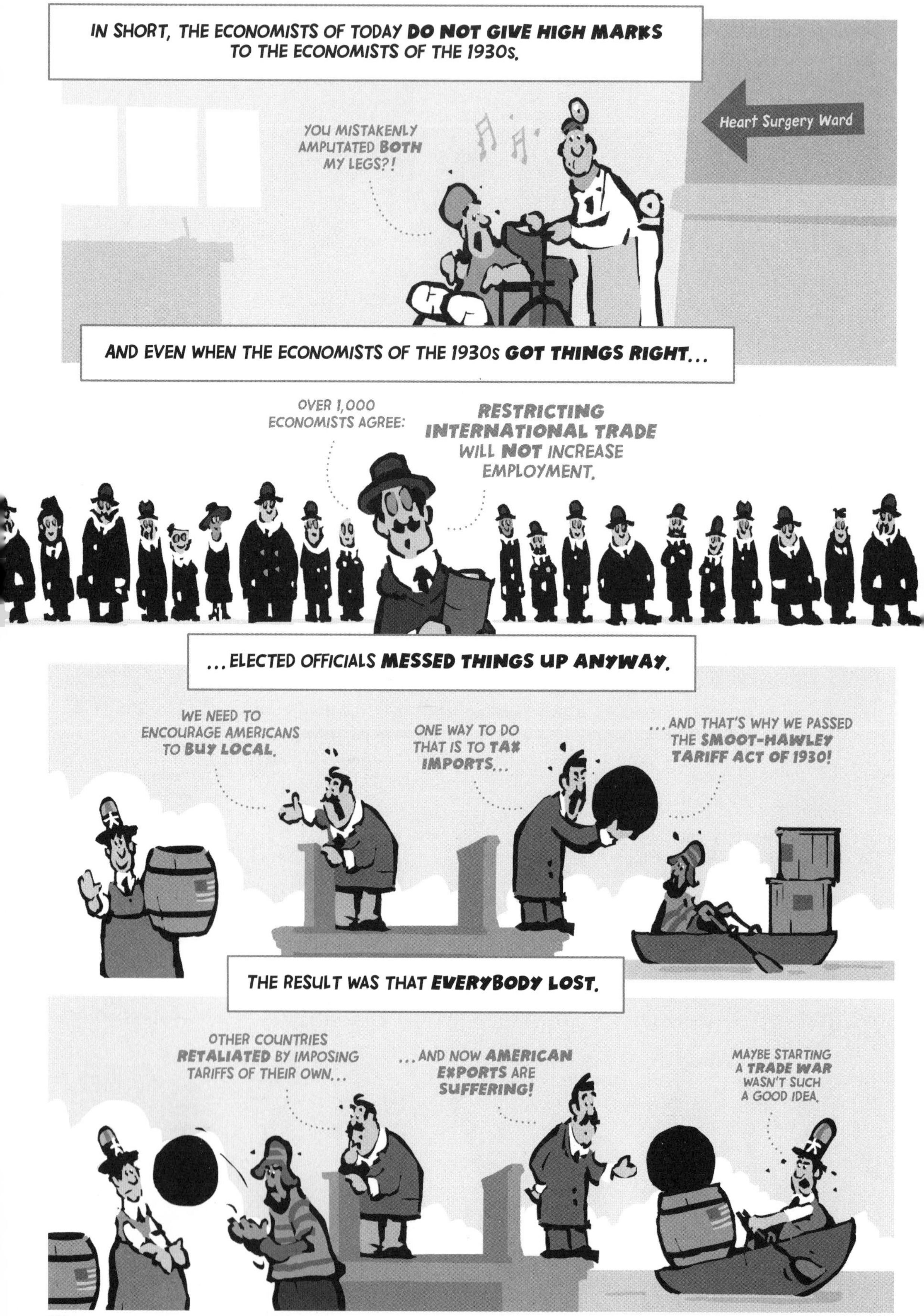
IN SHORT, THE ECONOMISTS OF TODAY DO NOT GIVE HIGH MARKS TO THE ECONOMISTS OF THE 1930s.
YOU MISTAKENLY AMPUTATED BOTH MY LEGS?!
Heart Surgery Ward
AND EVEN WHEN THE ECONOMISTS OF THE 1930s GOT THINGS RIGHT...
OVER 1,000 ECONOMISTS AGREE: RESTRICTING INTERNATIONAL TRADE WILL NOT INCREASE EMPLOYMENT.
...ELECTED OFFICIALS MESSED THINGS UP ANYWAY.
WE NEED TO ENCOURAGE AMERICANS TO BUY LOCAL.
ONE WAY TO DO THAT IS TO TAX IMPORTS...
...AND THAT'S WHY WE PASSED THE SMOOT-HAWLEY TARIFF ACT OF 1930!
THE RESULT WAS THAT EVERYBODY LOST.
OTHER COUNTRIES RETALIATED BY IMPOSING TARIFFS OF THEIR OWN...
...AND NOW AMERICAN EXPORTS ARE SUFFERING!
MAYBE STARTING A TRADE WAR WASN'T SUCH A GOOD IDEA.

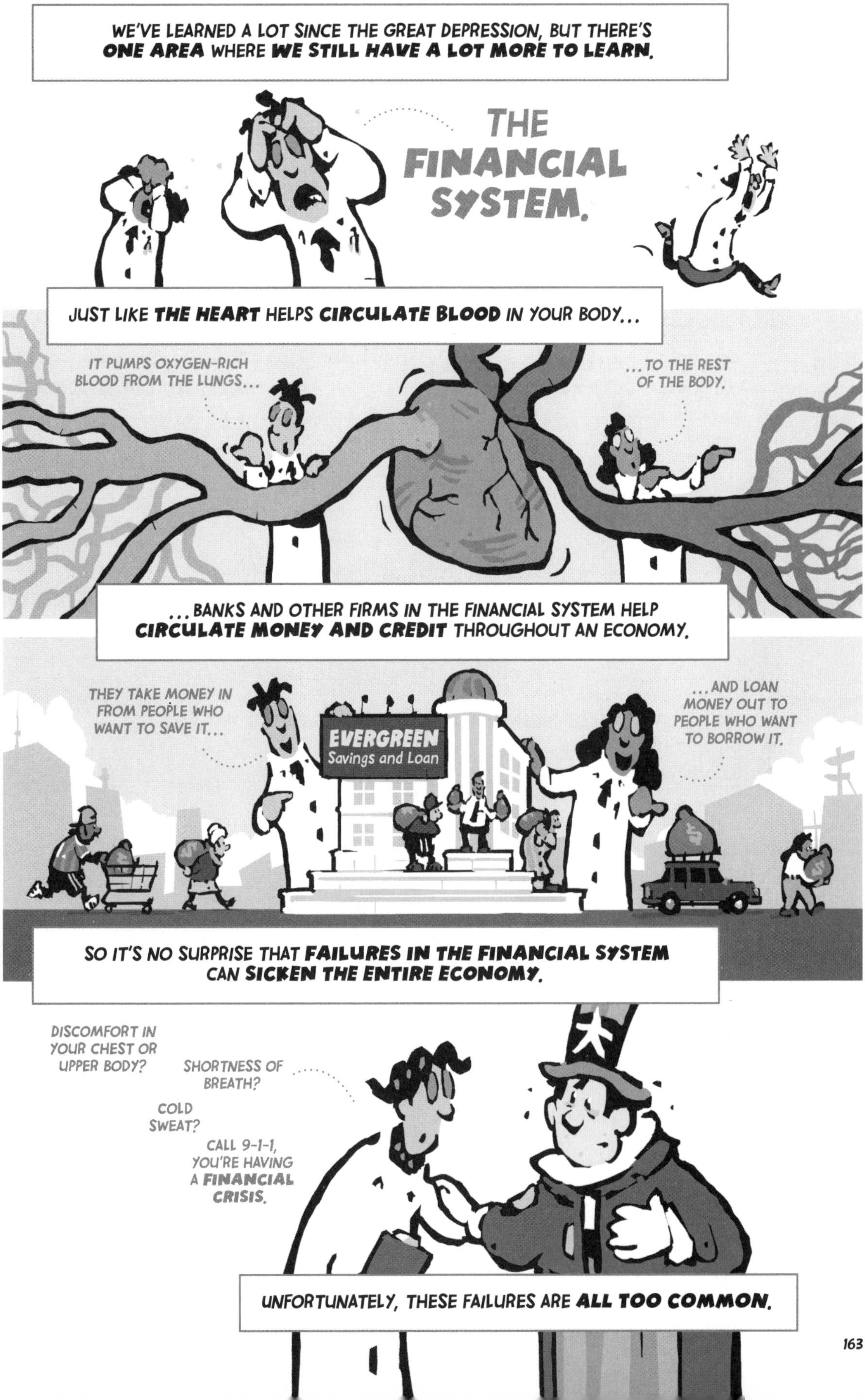
WE'VE LEARNED A LOT SINCE THE GREAT DEPRESSION, BUT THERE'S ONE AREA WHERE WE STILL HAVE A LOT MORE TO LEARN.
THE FINANCIAL SYSTEM.
JUST LIKE THE HEART HELPS CIRCULATE BLOOD IN YOUR BODY...
IT PUMPS OXYGEN-RICH BLOOD FROM THE LUNGS...
...TO THE REST OF THE BODY.
...BANKS AND OTHER FIRMS IN THE FINANCIAL SYSTEM HELP CIRCULATE MONEY AND CREDIT THROUGHOUT AN ECONOMY.
THEY TAKE MONEY IN FROM PEOPLE WHO WANT TO SAVE IT...
EVERGREEN
Savings and Loan
...AND LOAN MONEY OUT TO PEOPLE WHO WANT TO BORROW IT.
SO IT'S NO SURPRISE THAT FAILURES IN THE FINANCIAL SYSTEM CAN SICKEN THE ENTIRE ECONOMY.
DISCOMFORT IN YOUR CHEST OR UPPER BODY?
SHORTNESS OF BREATH?
COLD SWEAT?
CALL 9-1-1, YOU'RE HAVING A FINANCIAL CRISIS.
UNFORTUNATELY, THESE FAILURES ARE ALL TOO COMMON.

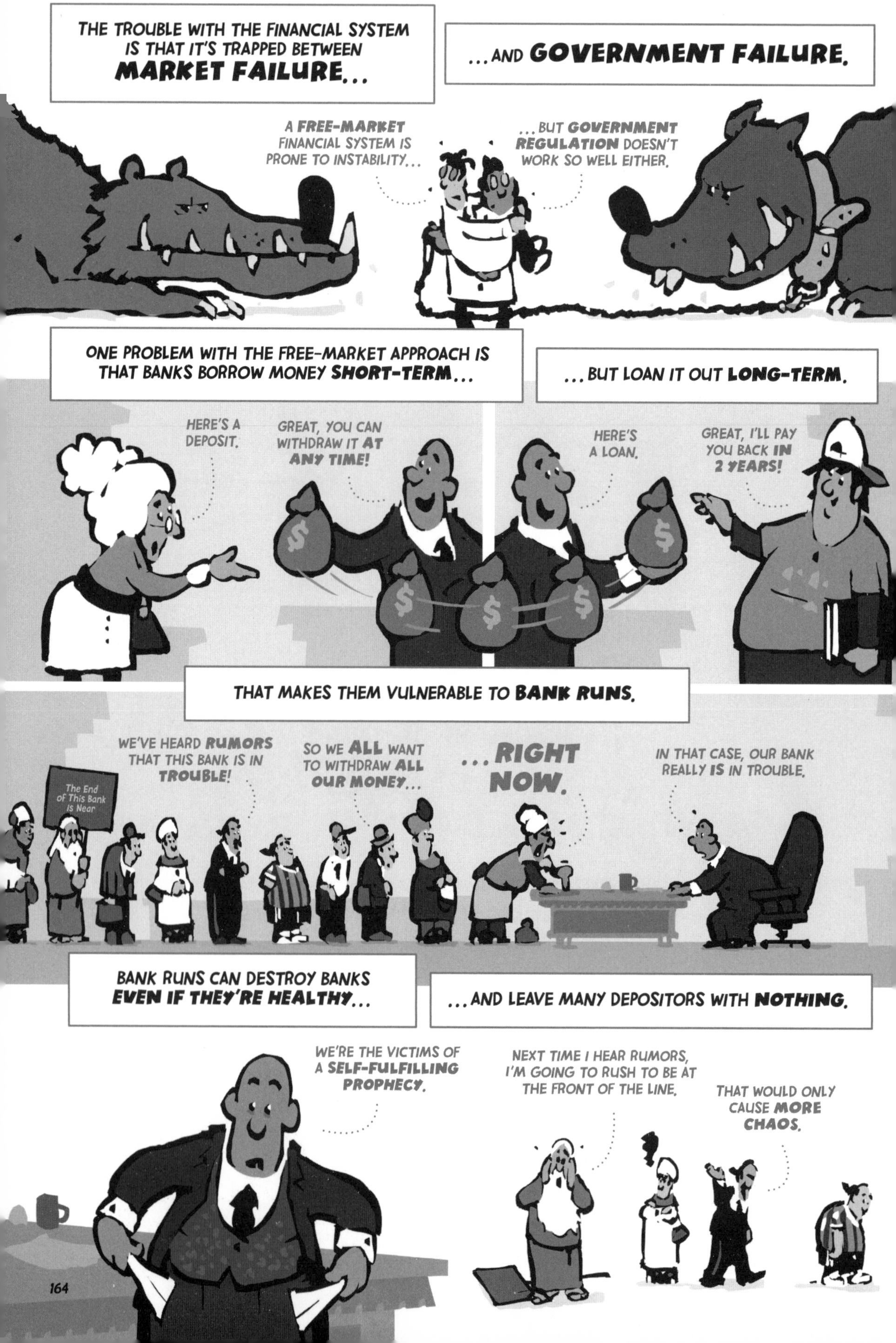
THE TROUBLE WITH THE FINANCIAL SYSTEM IS THAT IT'S TRAPPED BETWEEN **MARKET FAILURE**...
...AND **GOVERNMENT FAILURE.**
A **FREE-MARKET** FINANCIAL SYSTEM IS PRONE TO INSTABILITY...
...BUT **GOVERNMENT REGULATION** DOESN'T WORK SO WELL EITHER.
ONE PROBLEM WITH THE FREE-MARKET APPROACH IS THAT BANKS BORROW MONEY **SHORT-TERM**...
...BUT LOAN IT OUT **LONG-TERM.**
HERE'S A DEPOSIT.
GREAT, YOU CAN WITHDRAW IT **AT ANY TIME!**
HERE'S A LOAN.
GREAT, I'LL PAY YOU BACK **IN 2 YEARS!**
THAT MAKES THEM VULNERABLE TO **BANK RUNS.**
The End of This Bank is Near
WE'VE HEARD **RUMORS** THAT THIS BANK IS IN **TROUBLE!**
SO WE **ALL** WANT TO WITHDRAW **ALL OUR MONEY**...
...**RIGHT NOW.**
IN THAT CASE, OUR BANK REALLY **IS** IN TROUBLE.
BANK RUNS CAN DESTROY BANKS **EVEN IF THEY'RE HEALTHY**...
...AND LEAVE MANY DEPOSITORS WITH **NOTHING.**
WE'RE THE VICTIMS OF A **SELF-FULFILLING PROPHECY.**
NEXT TIME I HEAR RUMORS, I'M GOING TO RUSH TO BE AT THE FRONT OF THE LINE.
THAT WOULD ONLY CAUSE **MORE CHAOS.**

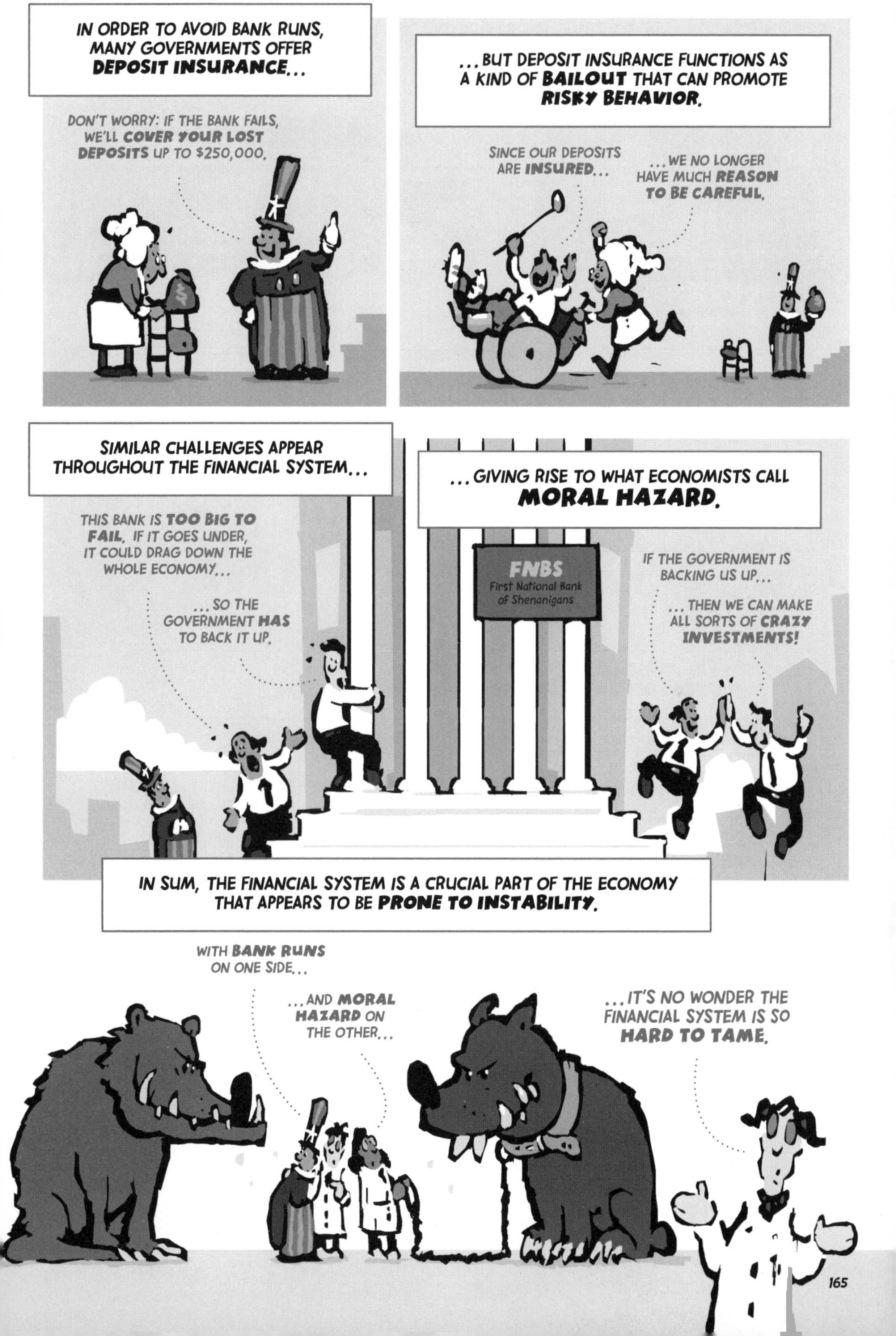
IN ORDER TO AVOID BANK RUNS, MANY GOVERNMENTS OFFER DEPOSIT INSURANCE...
DON'T WORRY: IF THE BANK FAILS, WE'LL COVER YOUR LOST DEPOSITS UP TO $250,000.
...BUT DEPOSIT INSURANCE FUNCTIONS AS A KIND OF BAILOUT THAT CAN PROMOTE RISKY BEHAVIOR.
SINCE OUR DEPOSITS ARE INSURED...
...WE NO LONGER HAVE MUCH REASON TO BE CAREFUL.
SIMILAR CHALLENGES APPEAR THROUGHOUT THE FINANCIAL SYSTEM...
...GIVING RISE TO WHAT ECONOMISTS CALL MORAL HAZARD.
THIS BANK IS TOO BIG TO FAIL. IF IT GOES UNDER, IT COULD DRAG DOWN THE WHOLE ECONOMY...
...SO THE GOVERNMENT HAS TO BACK IT UP.
FNBS
First National Bank of Shenanigans
IF THE GOVERNMENT IS BACKING US UP...
...THEN WE CAN MAKE ALL SORTS OF CRAZY INVESTMENTS!
IN SUM, THE FINANCIAL SYSTEM IS A CRUCIAL PART OF THE ECONOMY THAT APPEARS TO BE PRONE TO INSTABILITY.
WITH BANK RUNS ON ONE SIDE...
...AND MORAL HAZARD ON THE OTHER...
...IT'S NO WONDER THE FINANCIAL SYSTEM IS SO HARD TO TAME.

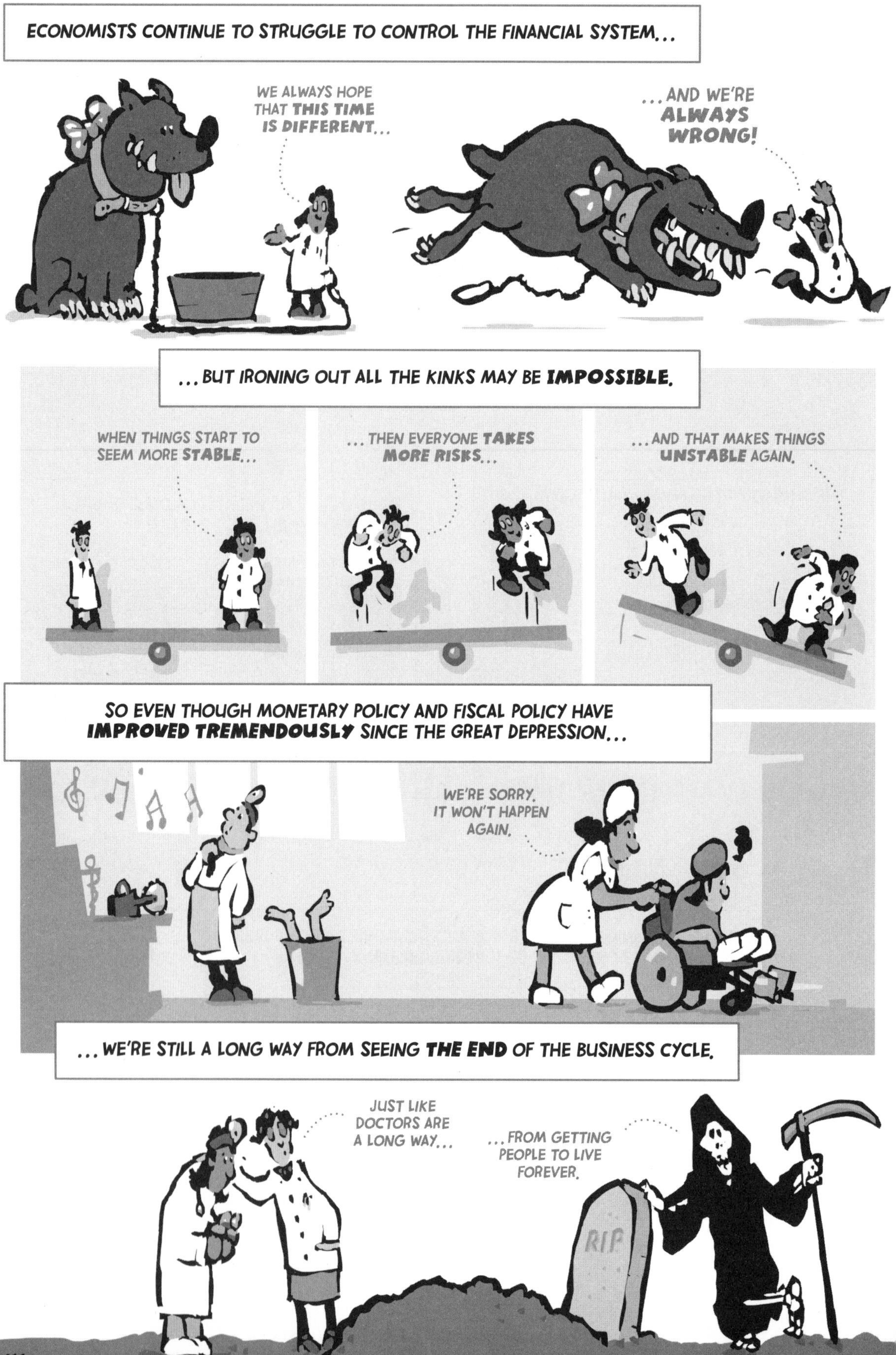
ECONOMISTS CONTINUE TO STRUGGLE TO CONTROL THE FINANCIAL SYSTEM...
WE ALWAYS HOPE THAT THIS TIME IS DIFFERENT...
...AND WE'RE ALWAYS WRONG!
...BUT IRONING OUT ALL THE KINKS MAY BE IMPOSSIBLE.
WHEN THINGS START TO SEEM MORE STABLE...
...THEN EVERYONE TAKES MORE RISKS...
...AND THAT MAKES THINGS UNSTABLE AGAIN.
SO EVEN THOUGH MONETARY POLICY AND FISCAL POLICY HAVE IMPROVED TREMENDOUSLY SINCE THE GREAT DEPRESSION...
WE'RE SORRY. IT WON'T HAPPEN AGAIN.
...WE'RE STILL A LONG WAY FROM SEEING THE END OF THE BUSINESS CYCLE.
JUST LIKE DOCTORS ARE A LONG WAY...
...FROM GETTING PEOPLE TO LIVE FOREVER.
RIP

CHAPTER 13
THE END OF POVERTY?

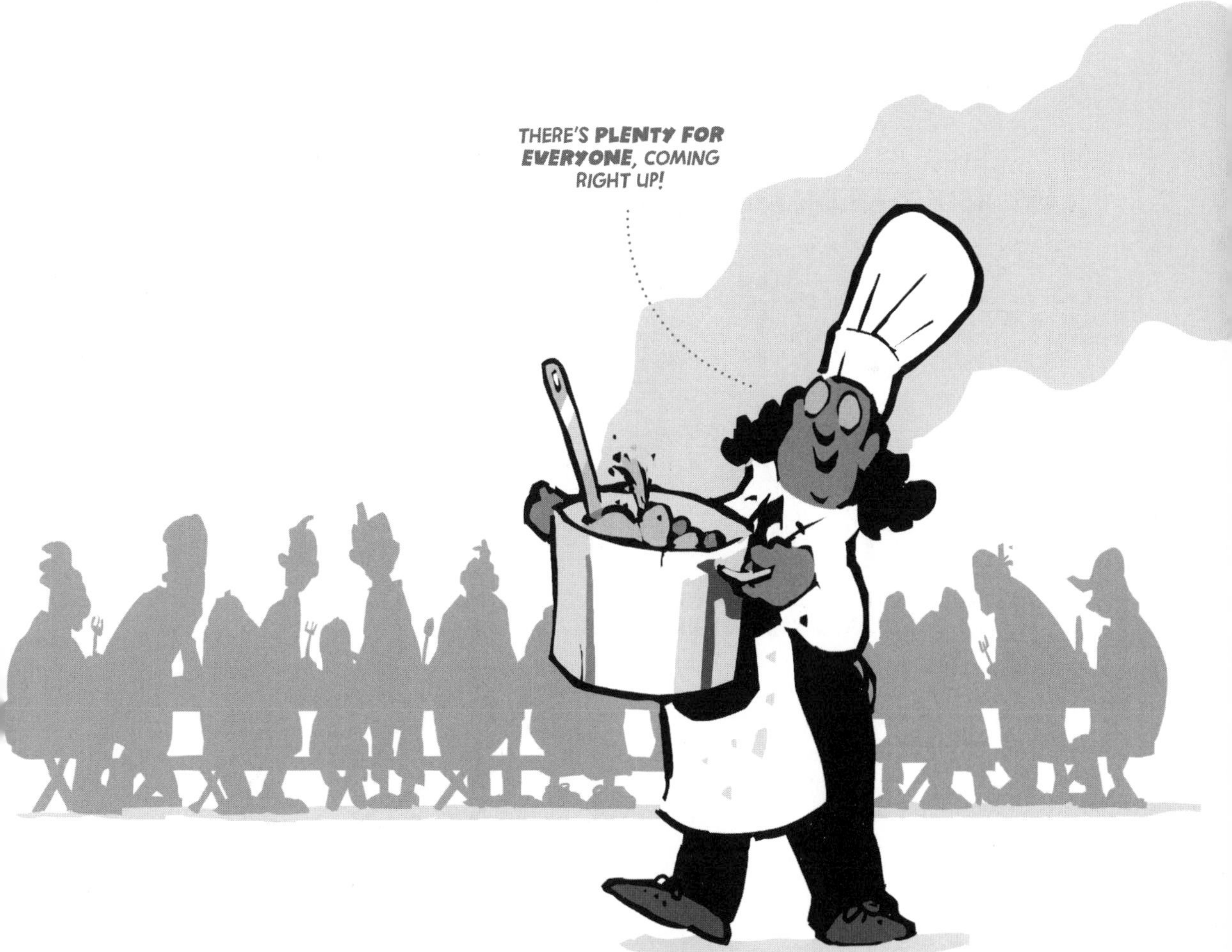
THERE'S PLENTY FOR EVERYONE, COMING RIGHT UP!

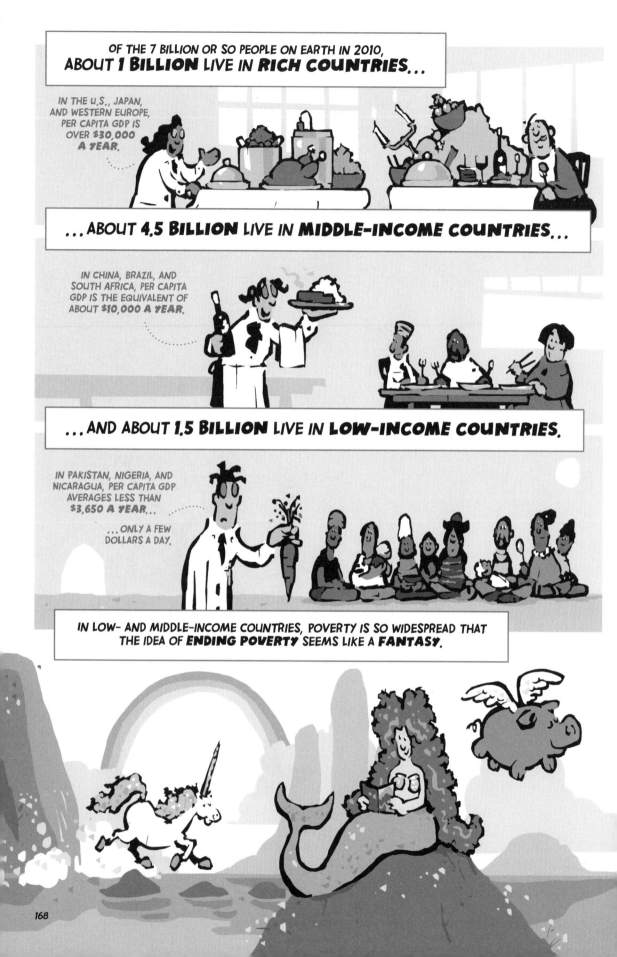

OF THE 7 BILLION OR SO PEOPLE ON EARTH IN 2010, **ABOUT 1 BILLION** LIVE IN **RICH COUNTRIES**...

IN THE U.S., JAPAN, AND WESTERN EUROPE, PER CAPITA GDP IS OVER $30,000 A YEAR.

...**ABOUT 4.5 BILLION** LIVE IN **MIDDLE-INCOME COUNTRIES**...

IN CHINA, BRAZIL, AND SOUTH AFRICA, PER CAPITA GDP IS THE EQUIVALENT OF ABOUT **$10,000 A YEAR.**

...AND ABOUT **1.5 BILLION** LIVE IN **LOW-INCOME COUNTRIES.**

IN PAKISTAN, NIGERIA, AND NICARAGUA, PER CAPITA GDP AVERAGES LESS THAN $3,650 A YEAR...

...ONLY A FEW DOLLARS A DAY.

IN LOW- AND MIDDLE-INCOME COUNTRIES, POVERTY IS SO WIDESPREAD THAT THE IDEA OF **ENDING POVERTY** SEEMS LIKE A **FANTASY.**

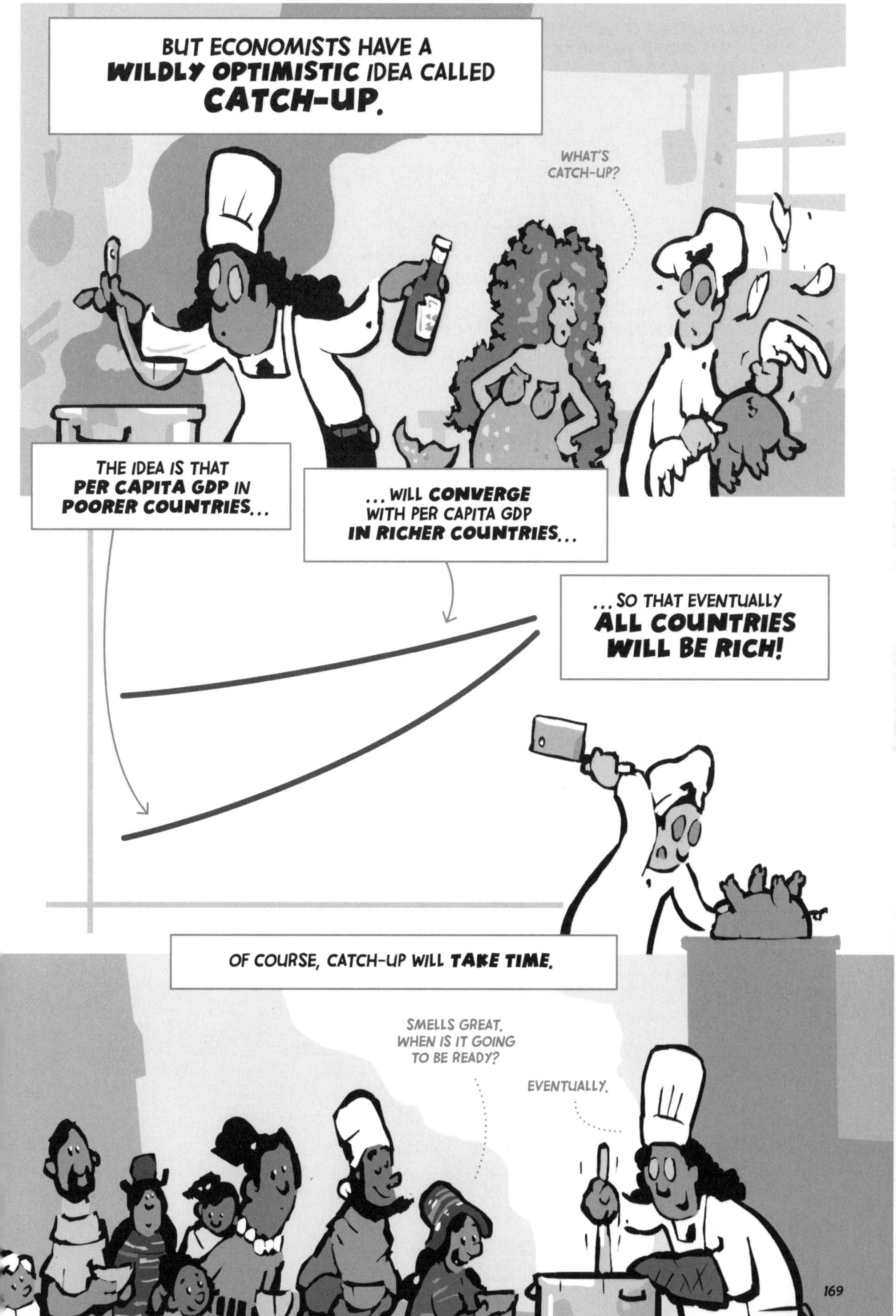

BUT ECONOMISTS HAVE A WILDLY OPTIMISTIC IDEA CALLED CATCH-UP.
WHAT'S CATCH-UP?
THE IDEA IS THAT PER CAPITA GDP IN POORER COUNTRIES...
...WILL CONVERGE WITH PER CAPITA GDP IN RICHER COUNTRIES...
...SO THAT EVENTUALLY ALL COUNTRIES WILL BE RICH!
OF COURSE, CATCH-UP WILL TAKE TIME.
SMELLS GREAT. WHEN IS IT GOING TO BE READY?
EVENTUALLY.

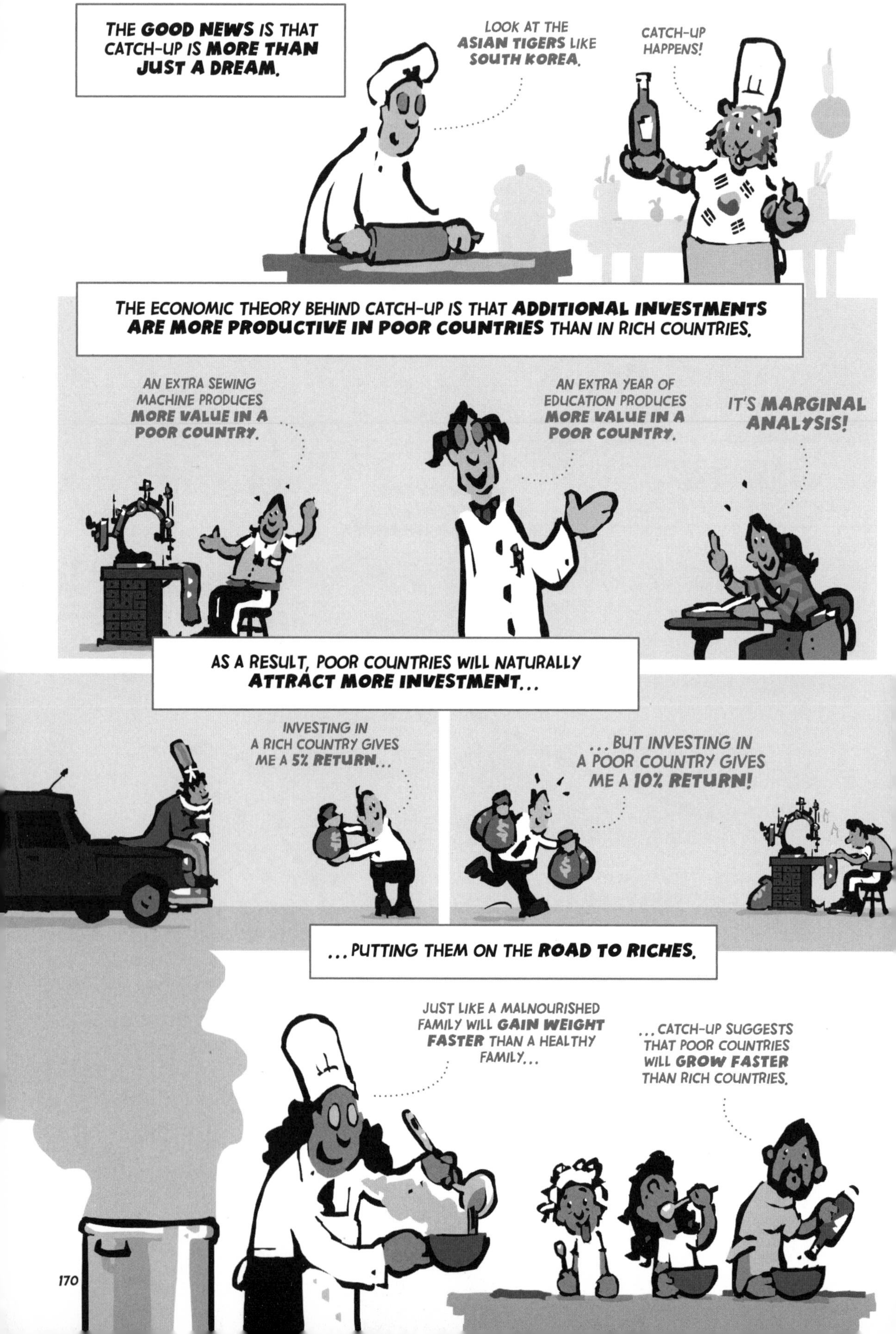
THE GOOD NEWS IS THAT CATCH-UP IS MORE THAN JUST A DREAM.
LOOK AT THE ASIAN TIGERS LIKE SOUTH KOREA.
CATCH-UP HAPPENS!
THE ECONOMIC THEORY BEHIND CATCH-UP IS THAT ADDITIONAL INVESTMENTS ARE MORE PRODUCTIVE IN POOR COUNTRIES THAN IN RICH COUNTRIES.
AN EXTRA SEWING MACHINE PRODUCES MORE VALUE IN A POOR COUNTRY.
AN EXTRA YEAR OF EDUCATION PRODUCES MORE VALUE IN A POOR COUNTRY.
IT'S MARGINAL ANALYSIS!
AS A RESULT, POOR COUNTRIES WILL NATURALLY ATTRACT MORE INVESTMENT...
INVESTING IN A RICH COUNTRY GIVES ME A 5% RETURN...
...BUT INVESTING IN A POOR COUNTRY GIVES ME A 10% RETURN!
...PUTTING THEM ON THE ROAD TO RICHES.
JUST LIKE A MALNOURISHED FAMILY WILL GAIN WEIGHT FASTER THAN A HEALTHY FAMILY...
...CATCH-UP SUGGESTS THAT POOR COUNTRIES WILL GROW FASTER THAN RICH COUNTRIES.

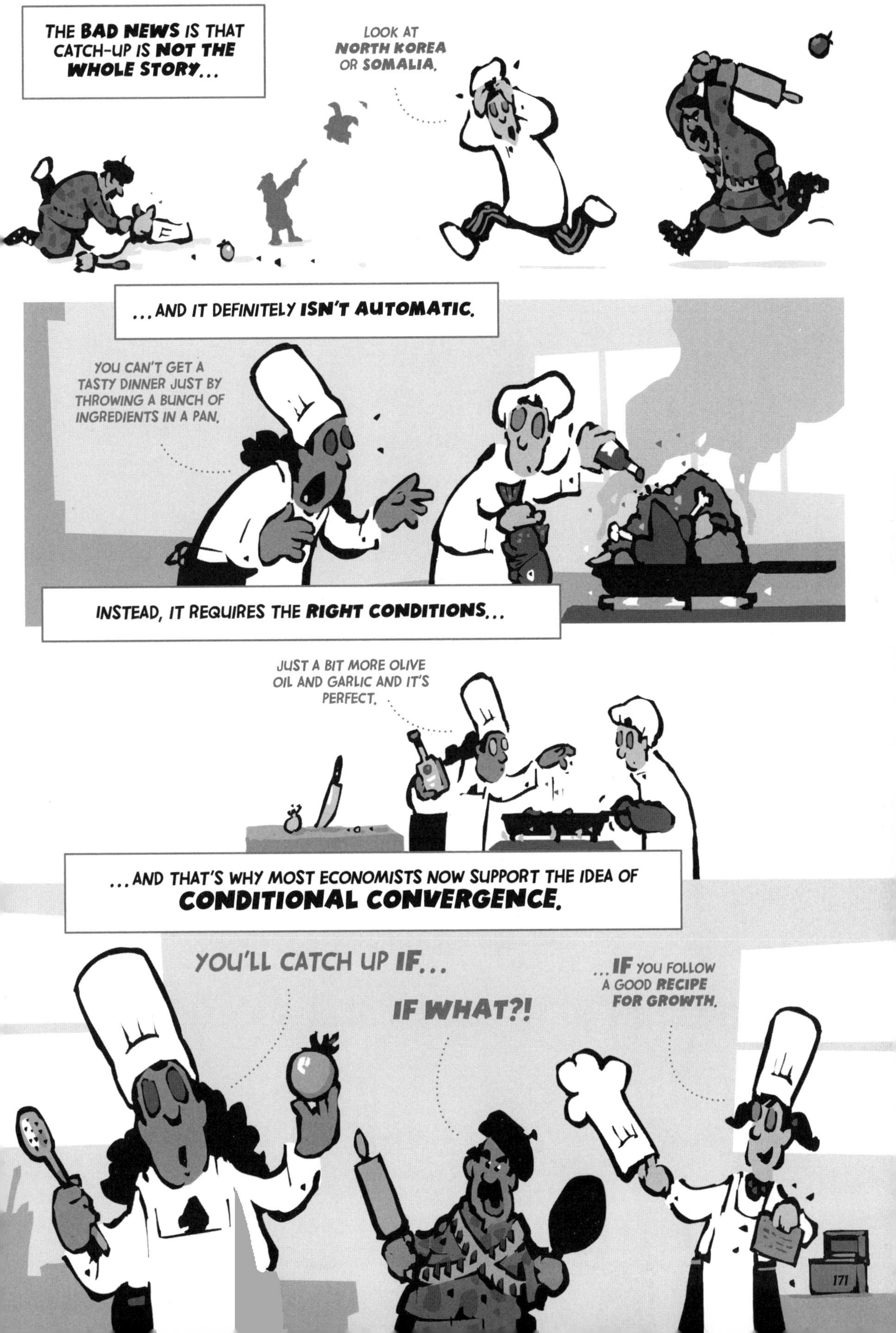

THE BAD NEWS IS THAT CATCH-UP IS NOT THE WHOLE STORY...
LOOK AT NORTH KOREA OR SOMALIA.
...AND IT DEFINITELY ISN'T AUTOMATIC.
YOU CAN'T GET A TASTY DINNER JUST BY THROWING A BUNCH OF INGREDIENTS IN A PAN.
INSTEAD, IT REQUIRES THE RIGHT CONDITIONS...
JUST A BIT MORE OLIVE OIL AND GARLIC AND IT'S PERFECT.
...AND THAT'S WHY MOST ECONOMISTS NOW SUPPORT THE IDEA OF CONDITIONAL CONVERGENCE.
YOU'LL CATCH UP IF...
IF WHAT?!
...IF YOU FOLLOW A GOOD RECIPE FOR GROWTH.

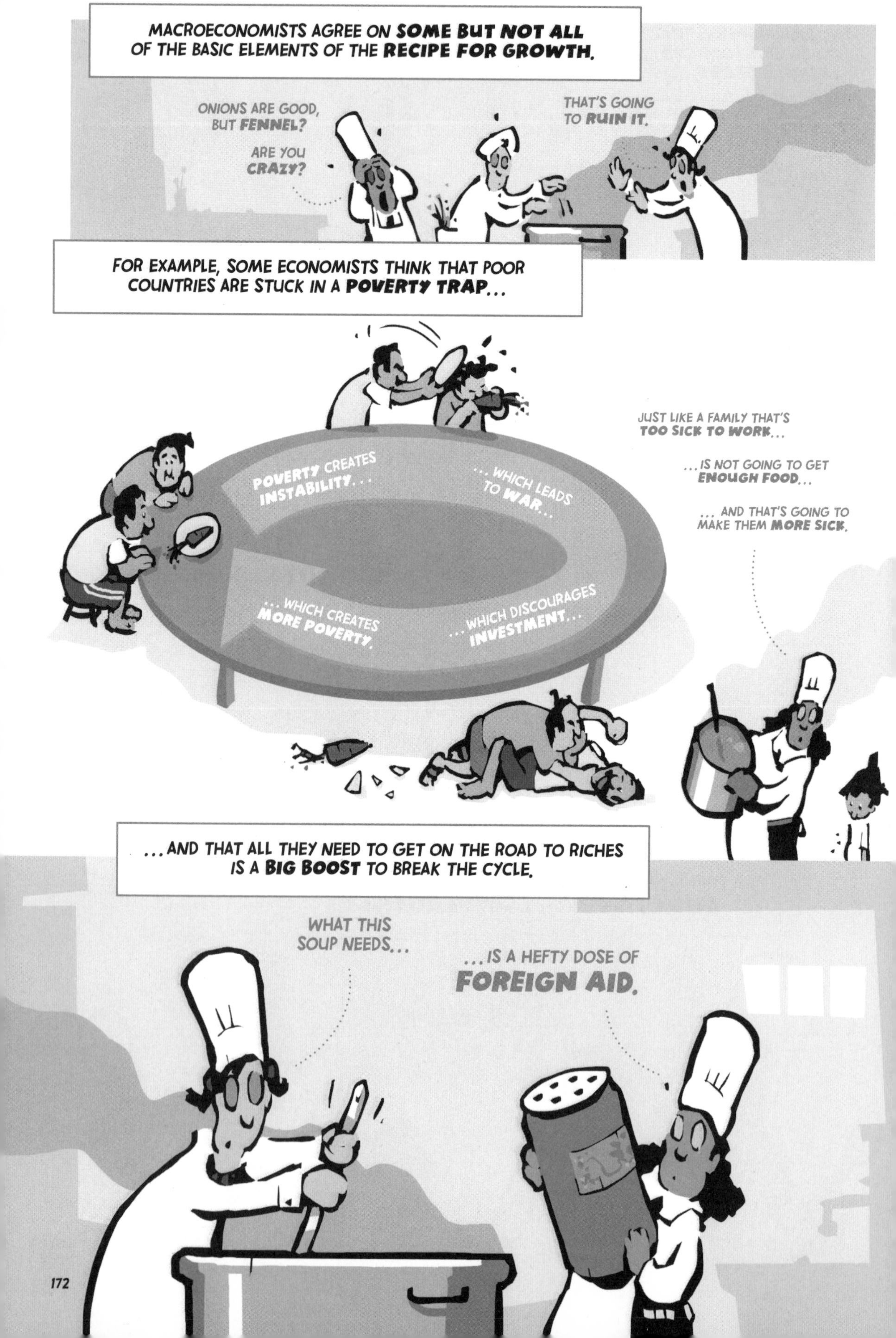
MACROECONOMISTS AGREE ON **SOME BUT NOT ALL** OF THE BASIC ELEMENTS OF THE **RECIPE FOR GROWTH.**
ONIONS ARE GOOD, BUT **FENNEL?**
ARE YOU **CRAZY?**
THAT'S GOING TO **RUIN IT.**
FOR EXAMPLE, SOME ECONOMISTS THINK THAT POOR COUNTRIES ARE STUCK IN A **POVERTY TRAP**...
POVERTY CREATES **INSTABILITY**...
... WHICH LEADS TO **WAR**...
... WHICH DISCOURAGES **INVESTMENT**...
... WHICH CREATES **MORE POVERTY.**
JUST LIKE A FAMILY THAT'S **TOO SICK TO WORK**...
... IS NOT GOING TO GET **ENOUGH FOOD**...
... AND THAT'S GOING TO MAKE THEM **MORE SICK.**
... AND THAT ALL THEY NEED TO GET ON THE ROAD TO RICHES IS A **BIG BOOST** TO BREAK THE CYCLE.
WHAT THIS SOUP NEEDS...
... IS A HEFTY DOSE OF **FOREIGN AID.**

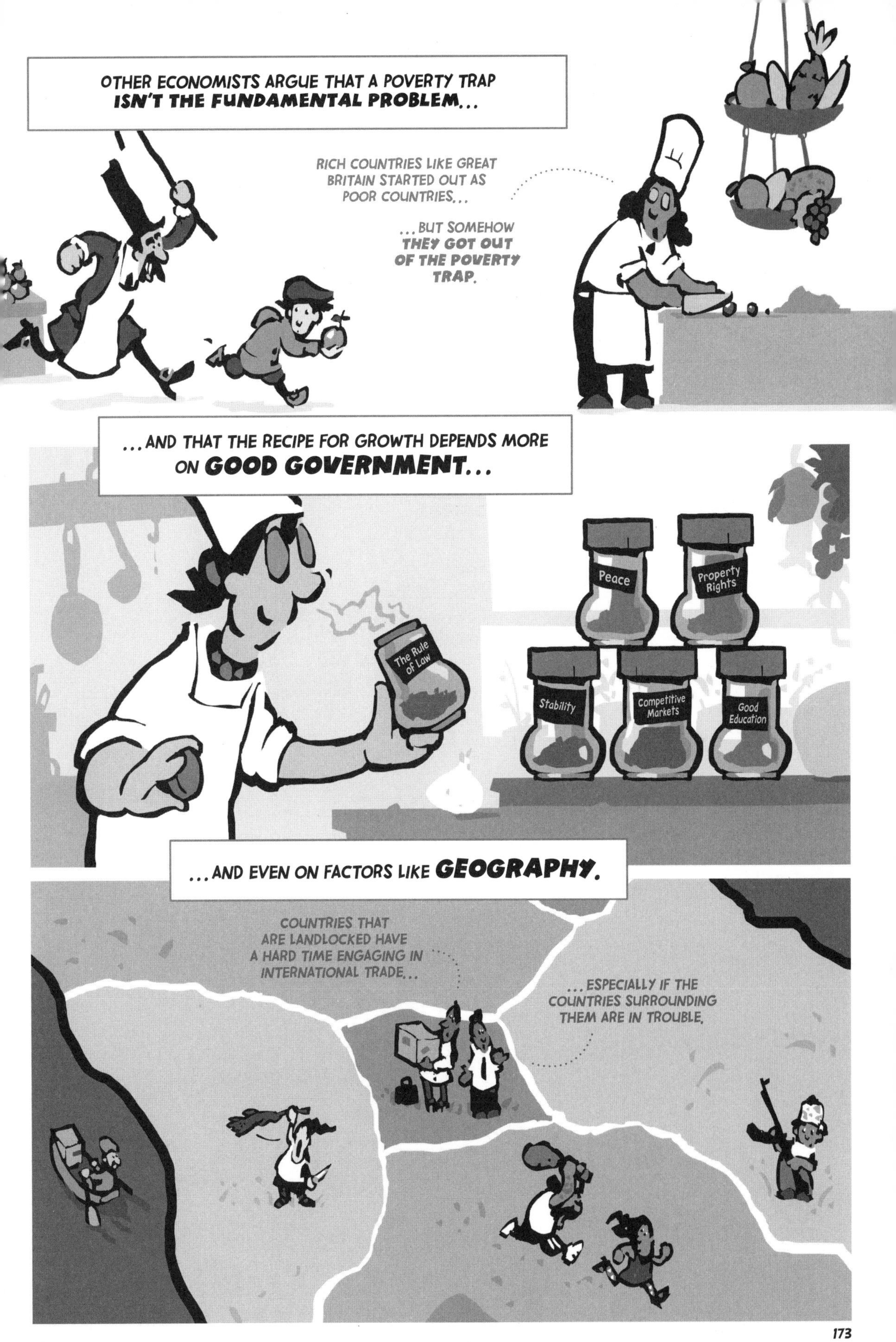
OTHER ECONOMISTS ARGUE THAT A POVERTY TRAP **ISN'T THE FUNDAMENTAL PROBLEM...**
RICH COUNTRIES LIKE GREAT BRITAIN STARTED OUT AS POOR COUNTRIES...
...BUT SOMEHOW **THEY GOT OUT OF THE POVERTY TRAP.**
...AND THAT THE RECIPE FOR GROWTH DEPENDS MORE ON **GOOD GOVERNMENT...**
The Rule of Law
Peace
Property Rights
Stability
Competitive Markets
Good Education
...AND EVEN ON FACTORS LIKE **GEOGRAPHY.**
COUNTRIES THAT ARE LANDLOCKED HAVE A HARD TIME ENGAGING IN INTERNATIONAL TRADE...
...ESPECIALLY IF THE COUNTRIES SURROUNDING THEM ARE IN TROUBLE.

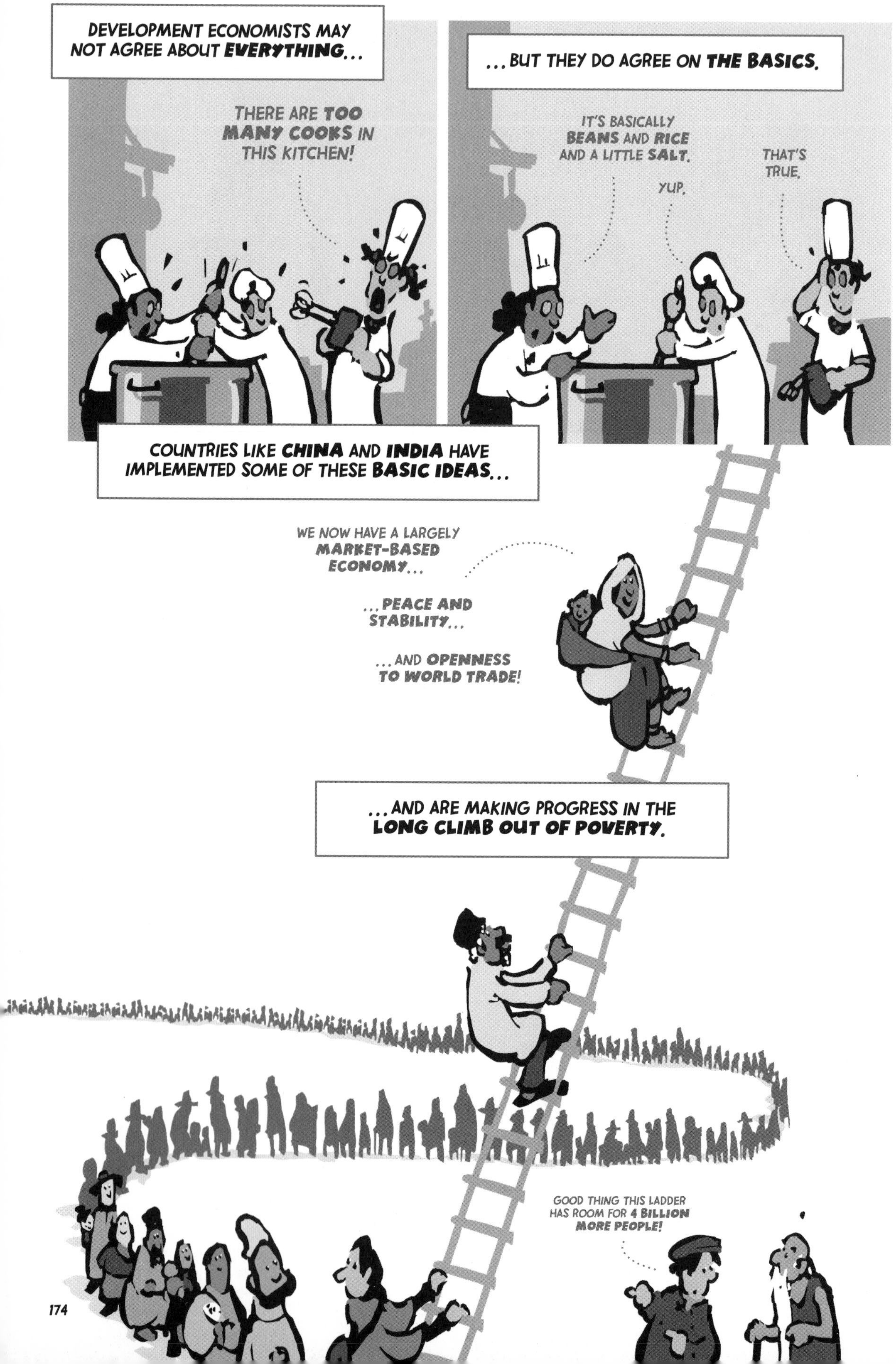

DEVELOPMENT ECONOMISTS MAY NOT AGREE ABOUT EVERYTHING...
THERE ARE TOO MANY COOKS IN THIS KITCHEN!
...BUT THEY DO AGREE ON THE BASICS.
IT'S BASICALLY BEANS AND RICE AND A LITTLE SALT.
YUP.
THAT'S TRUE.
COUNTRIES LIKE CHINA AND INDIA HAVE IMPLEMENTED SOME OF THESE BASIC IDEAS...
WE NOW HAVE A LARGELY MARKET-BASED ECONOMY...
...PEACE AND STABILITY...
...AND OPENNESS TO WORLD TRADE!
...AND ARE MAKING PROGRESS IN THE LONG CLIMB OUT OF POVERTY.
GOOD THING THIS LADDER HAS ROOM FOR 4 BILLION MORE PEOPLE!

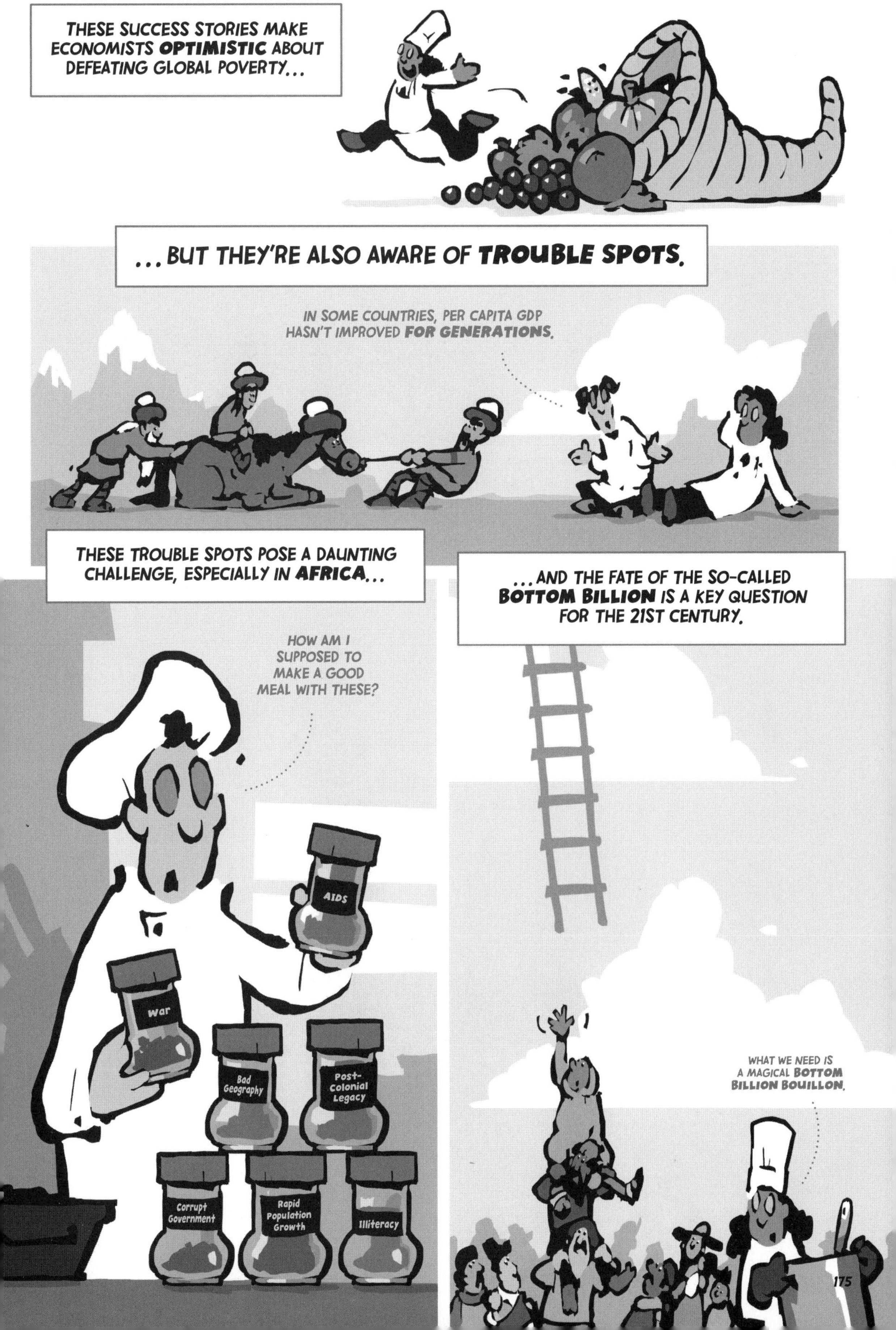
THESE SUCCESS STORIES MAKE ECONOMISTS OPTIMISTIC ABOUT DEFEATING GLOBAL POVERTY...
...BUT THEY'RE ALSO AWARE OF TROUBLE SPOTS.
IN SOME COUNTRIES, PER CAPITA GDP HASN'T IMPROVED FOR GENERATIONS.
THESE TROUBLE SPOTS POSE A DAUNTING CHALLENGE, ESPECIALLY IN AFRICA...
HOW AM I SUPPOSED TO MAKE A GOOD MEAL WITH THESE?
AIDS
War
Bad Geography
Post-Colonial Legacy
Corrupt Government
Rapid Population Growth
Illiteracy
...AND THE FATE OF THE SO-CALLED BOTTOM BILLION IS A KEY QUESTION FOR THE 21ST CENTURY.
WHAT WE NEED IS A MAGICAL BOTTOM BILLION BOUILLON.

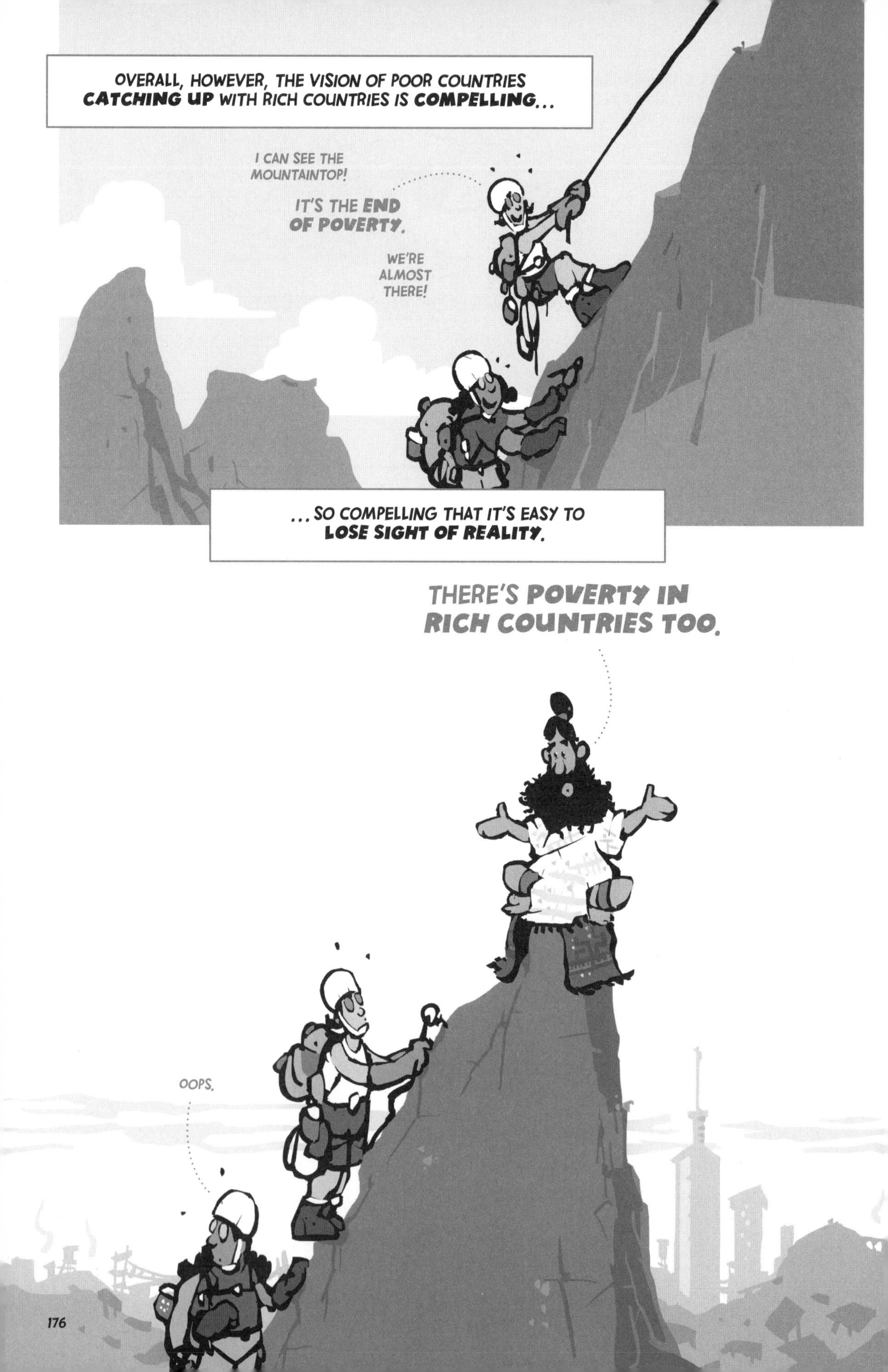
OVERALL, HOWEVER, THE VISION OF POOR COUNTRIES **CATCHING UP** WITH RICH COUNTRIES IS **COMPELLING**...
I CAN SEE THE MOUNTAINTOP!
IT'S THE **END OF POVERTY.**
WE'RE ALMOST THERE!
...SO COMPELLING THAT IT'S EASY TO **LOSE SIGHT OF REALITY.**
THERE'S **POVERTY IN RICH COUNTRIES TOO.**
OOPS.

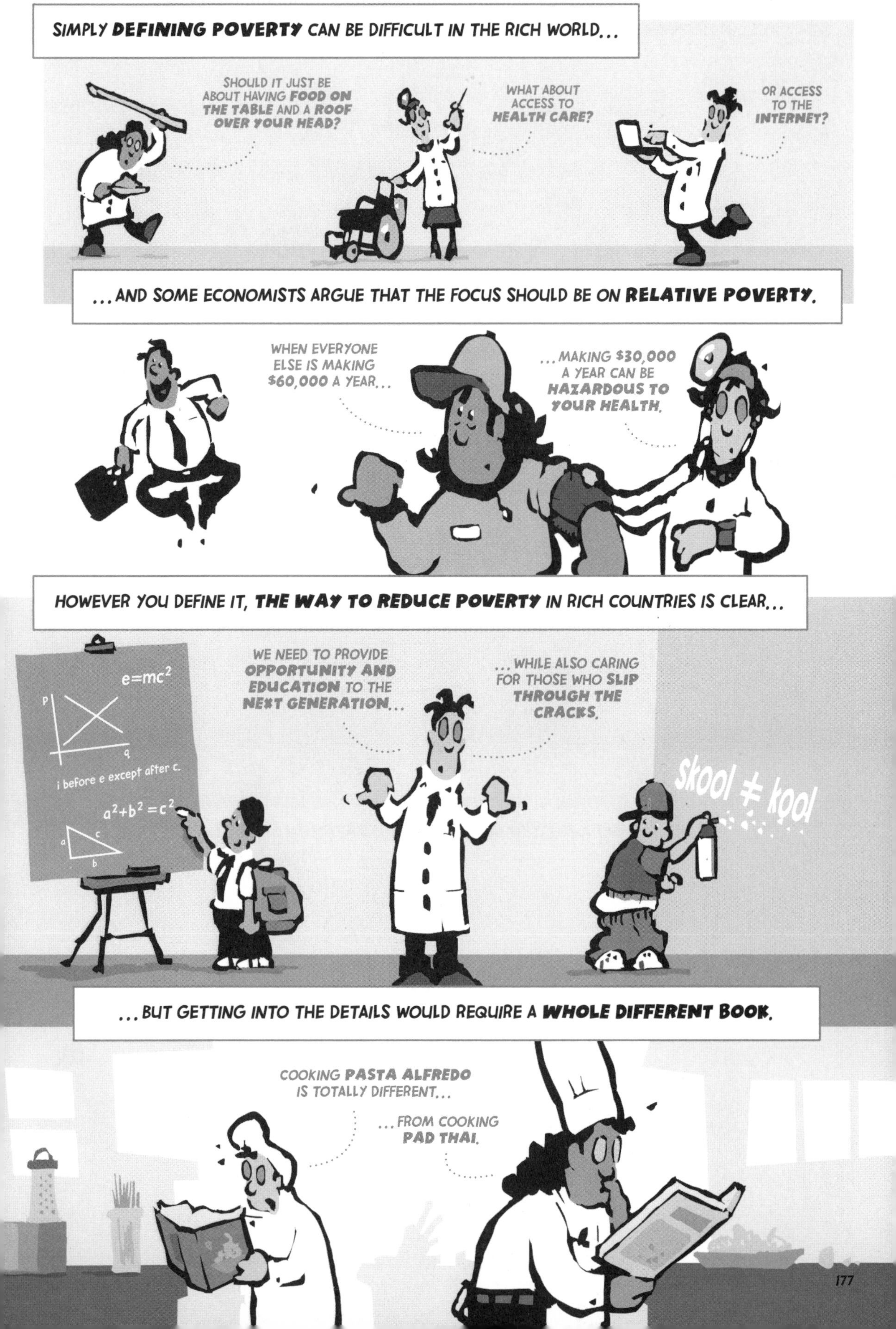
SIMPLY DEFINING POVERTY CAN BE DIFFICULT IN THE RICH WORLD...
SHOULD IT JUST BE ABOUT HAVING FOOD ON THE TABLE AND A ROOF OVER YOUR HEAD?
WHAT ABOUT ACCESS TO HEALTH CARE?
OR ACCESS TO THE INTERNET?
...AND SOME ECONOMISTS ARGUE THAT THE FOCUS SHOULD BE ON RELATIVE POVERTY.
WHEN EVERYONE ELSE IS MAKING $60,000 A YEAR...
...MAKING $30,000 A YEAR CAN BE HAZARDOUS TO YOUR HEALTH.
HOWEVER YOU DEFINE IT, THE WAY TO REDUCE POVERTY IN RICH COUNTRIES IS CLEAR...
e=mc²
P
q
i before e except after c.
a²+b²=c²
a
b
c
WE NEED TO PROVIDE OPPORTUNITY AND EDUCATION TO THE NEXT GENERATION...
...WHILE ALSO CARING FOR THOSE WHO SLIP THROUGH THE CRACKS.
skool ≠ kool
...BUT GETTING INTO THE DETAILS WOULD REQUIRE A WHOLE DIFFERENT BOOK.
COOKING PASTA ALFREDO IS TOTALLY DIFFERENT...
...FROM COOKING PAD THAI.

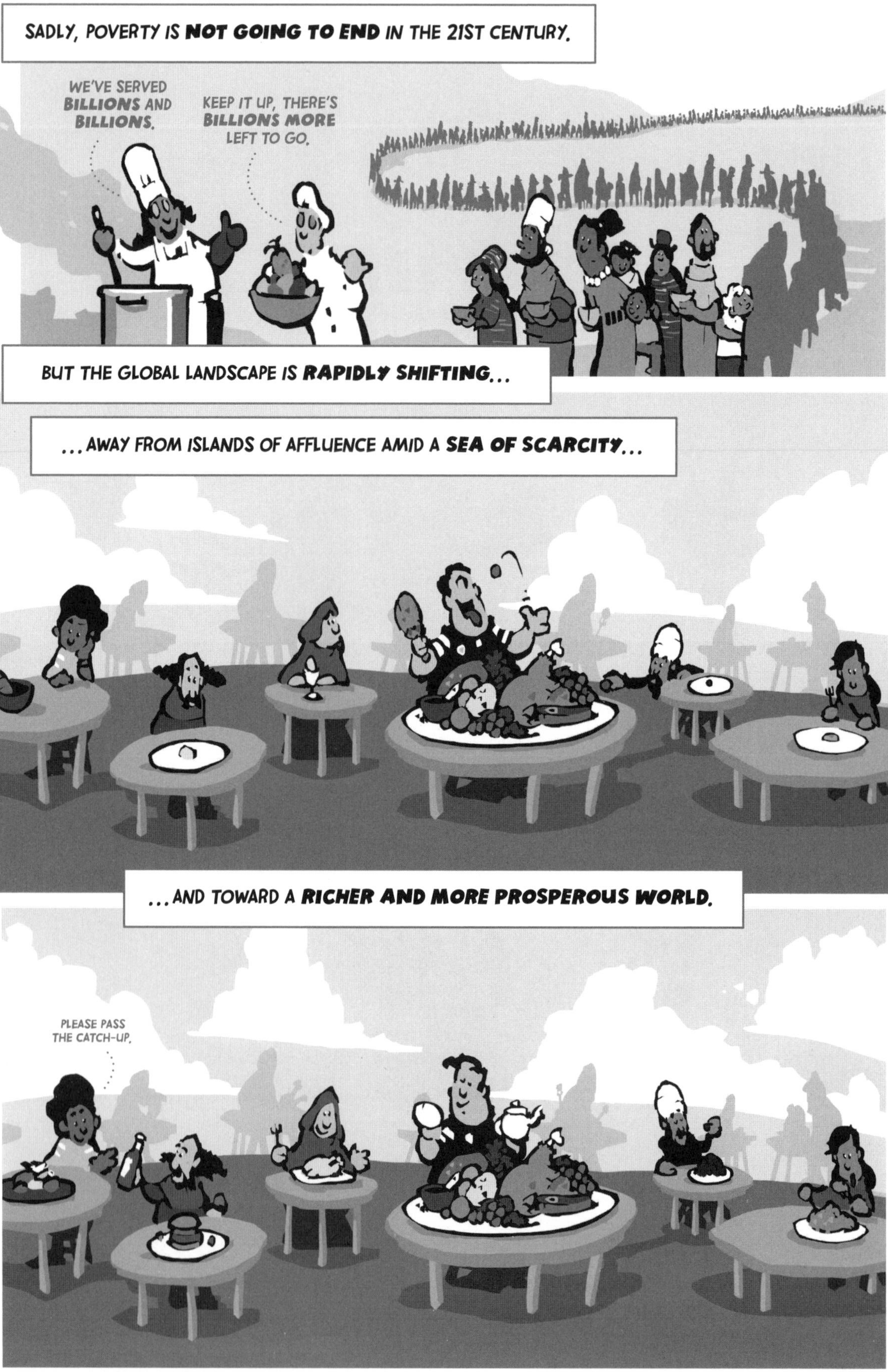
SADLY, POVERTY IS **NOT GOING TO END** IN THE 21ST CENTURY.
WE'VE SERVED **BILLIONS** AND **BILLIONS**.
KEEP IT UP, THERE'S **BILLIONS MORE** LEFT TO GO.
BUT THE GLOBAL LANDSCAPE IS **RAPIDLY SHIFTING**...
...AWAY FROM ISLANDS OF AFFLUENCE AMID A **SEA OF SCARCITY**...
...AND TOWARD A **RICHER AND MORE PROSPEROUS WORLD**.
PLEASE PASS THE CATCH-UP.

CHAPTER 14
THE END OF PLANET EARTH?

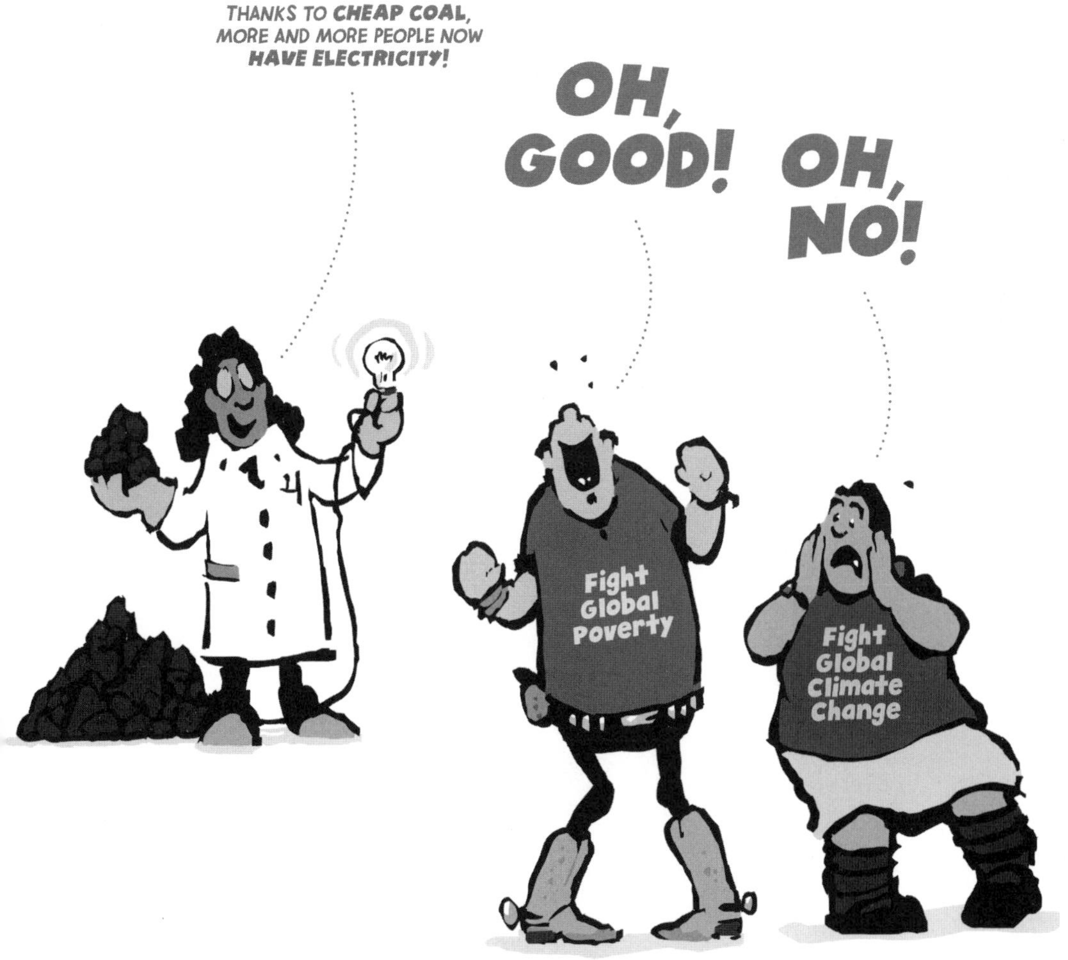
THANKS TO **CHEAP COAL**, MORE AND MORE PEOPLE NOW **HAVE ELECTRICITY**!
OH, GOOD!
OH, NO!
Fight Global Poverty
Fight Global Climate Change

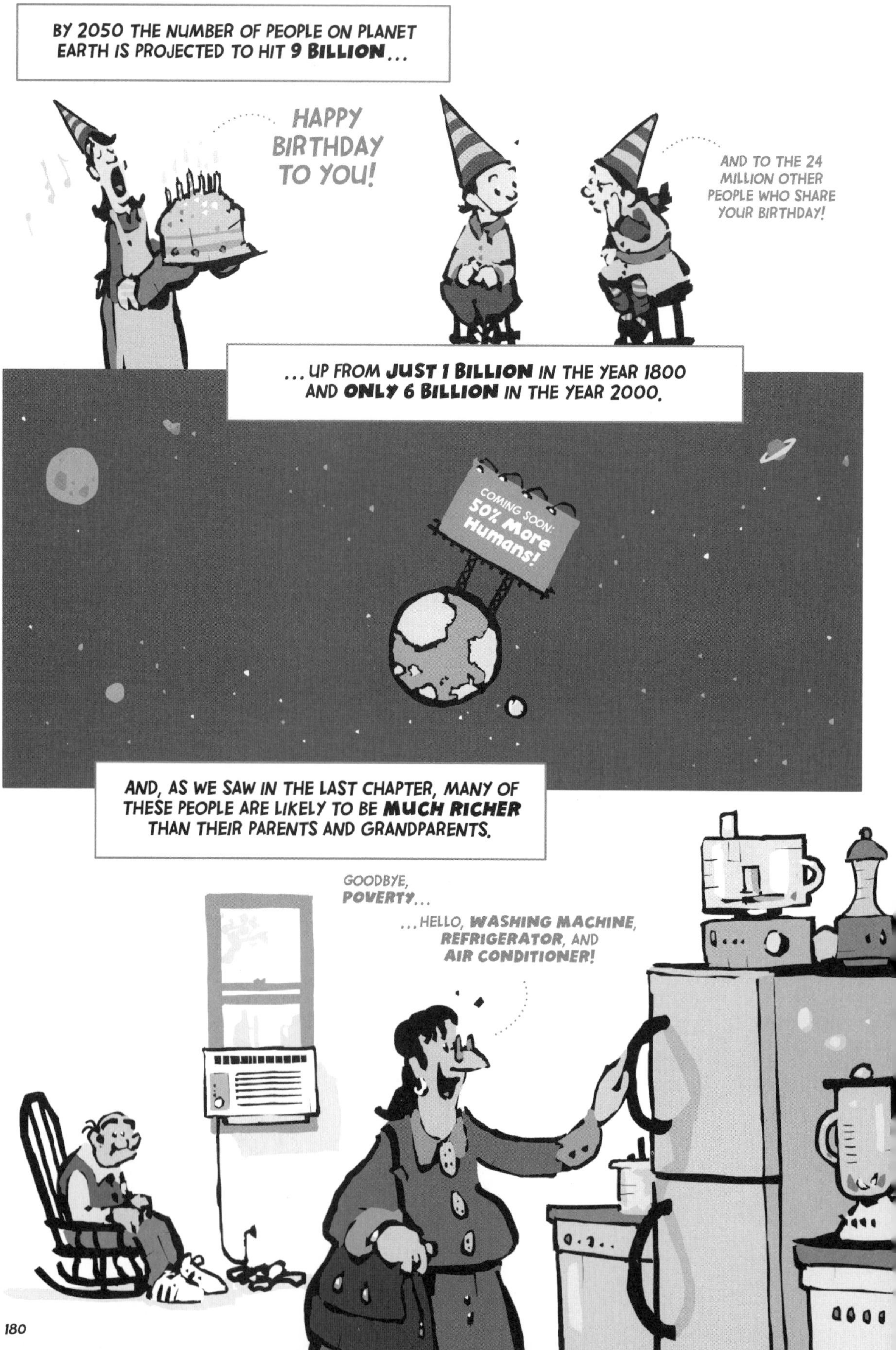
BY 2050 THE NUMBER OF PEOPLE ON PLANET EARTH IS PROJECTED TO HIT 9 BILLION...
HAPPY BIRTHDAY TO YOU!
AND TO THE 24 MILLION OTHER PEOPLE WHO SHARE YOUR BIRTHDAY!
...UP FROM JUST 1 BILLION IN THE YEAR 1800 AND ONLY 6 BILLION IN THE YEAR 2000.
COMING SOON: 50% More Humans!
AND, AS WE SAW IN THE LAST CHAPTER, MANY OF THESE PEOPLE ARE LIKELY TO BE MUCH RICHER THAN THEIR PARENTS AND GRANDPARENTS.
GOODBYE, POVERTY...
...HELLO, WASHING MACHINE, REFRIGERATOR, AND AIR CONDITIONER!

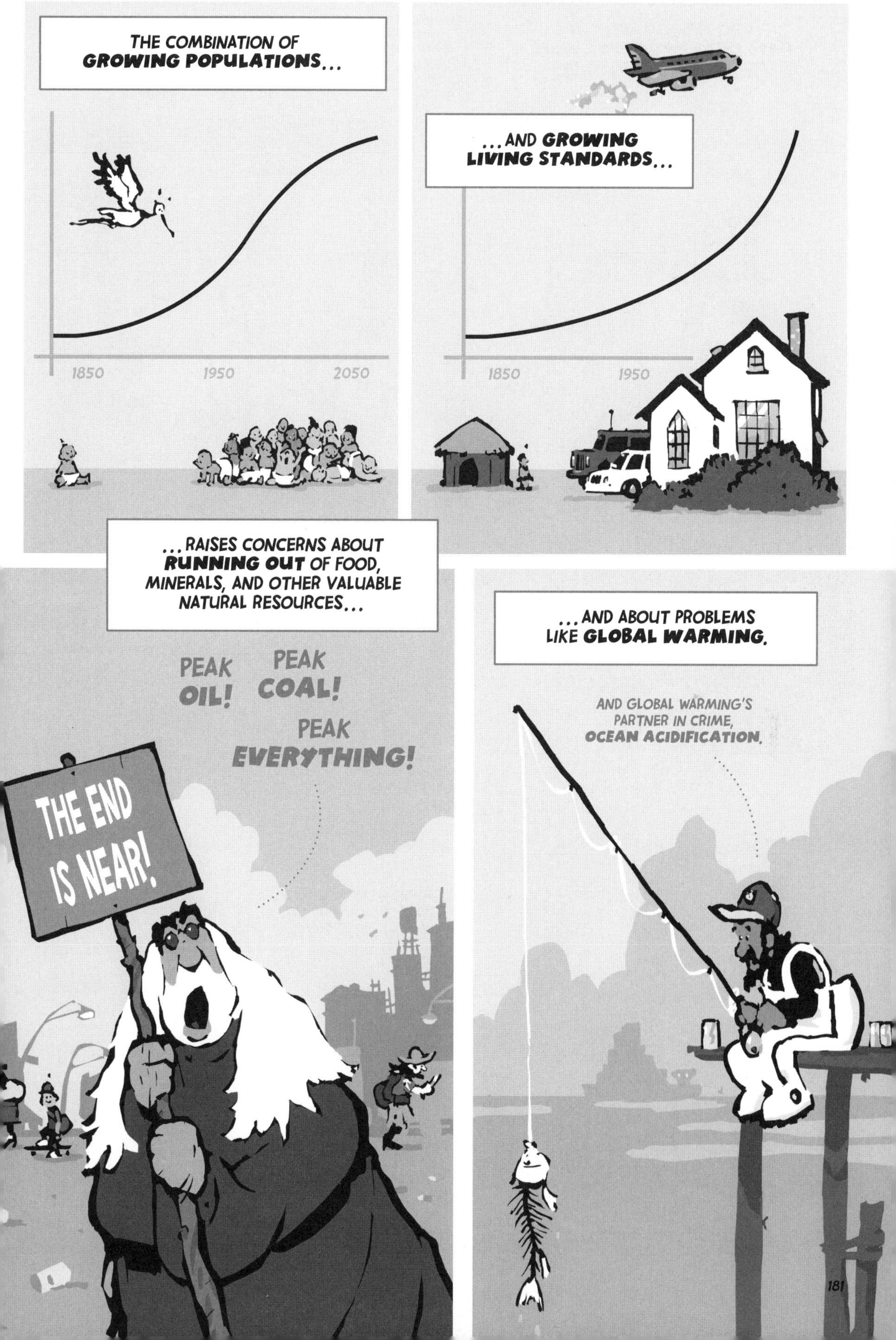
THE COMBINATION OF GROWING POPULATIONS...
1850
1950
2050
...AND GROWING LIVING STANDARDS...
1850
1950
...RAISES CONCERNS ABOUT RUNNING OUT OF FOOD, MINERALS, AND OTHER VALUABLE NATURAL RESOURCES...
PEAK OIL!
PEAK COAL!
PEAK EVERYTHING!
THE END IS NEAR!
...AND ABOUT PROBLEMS LIKE GLOBAL WARMING.
AND GLOBAL WARMING'S PARTNER IN CRIME, OCEAN ACIDIFICATION.

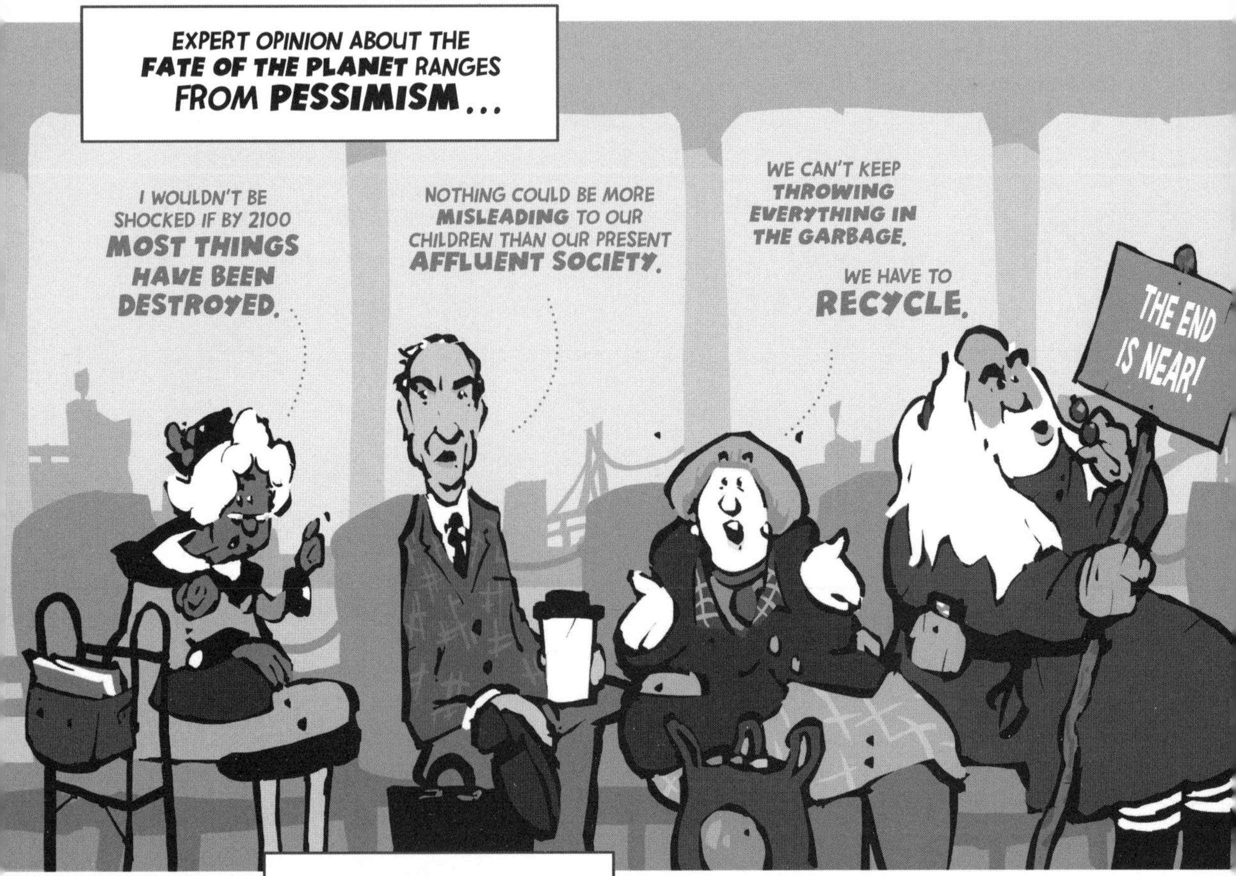
EXPERT OPINION ABOUT THE FATE OF THE PLANET RANGES FROM PESSIMISM...
I WOULDN'T BE SHOCKED IF BY 2100 MOST THINGS HAVE BEEN DESTROYED.
NOTHING COULD BE MORE MISLEADING TO OUR CHILDREN THAN OUR PRESENT AFFLUENT SOCIETY.
WE CAN'T KEEP THROWING EVERYTHING IN THE GARBAGE.
WE HAVE TO RECYCLE.
THE END IS NEAR!

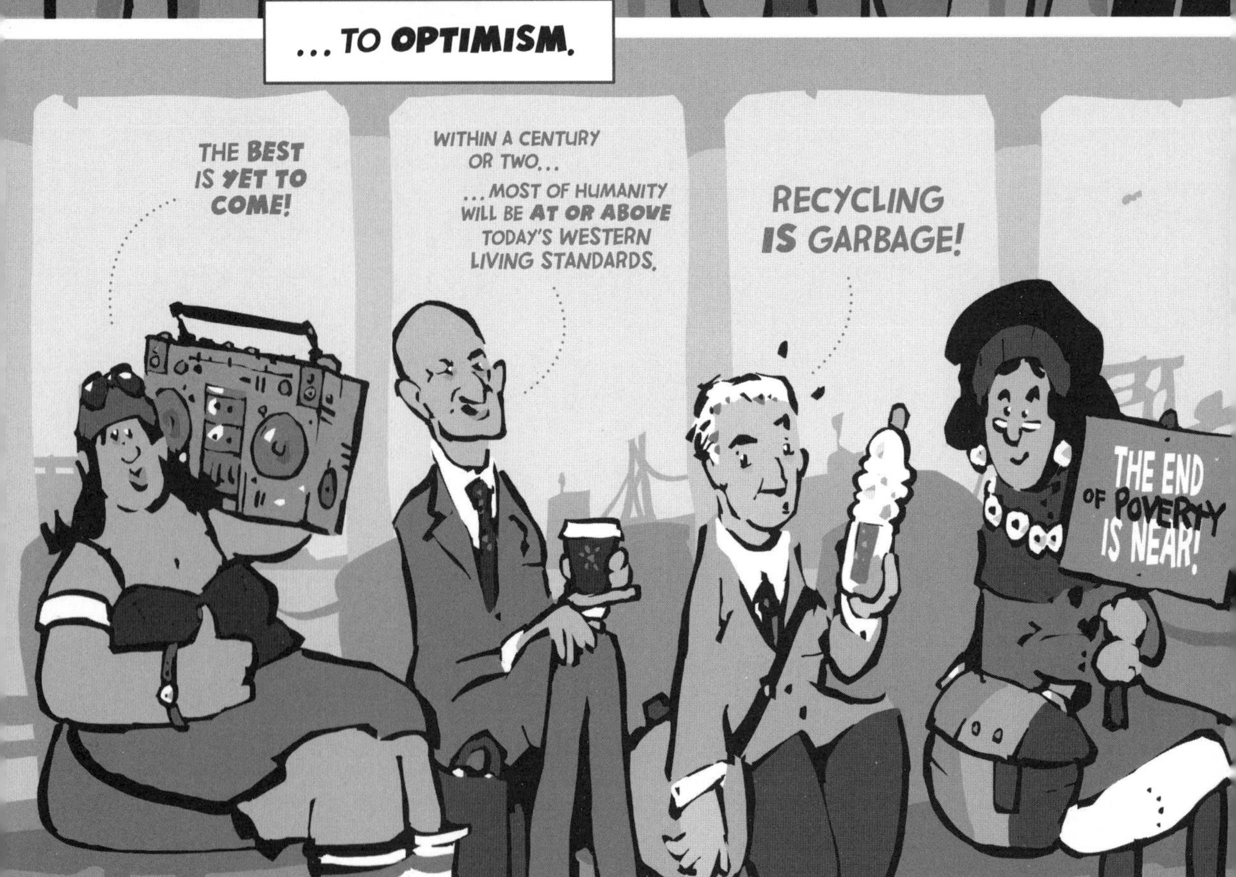
...TO OPTIMISM.
THE BEST IS YET TO COME!
WITHIN A CENTURY OR TWO...
...MOST OF HUMANITY WILL BE AT OR ABOVE TODAY'S WESTERN LIVING STANDARDS.
RECYCLING IS GARBAGE!
THE END OF POVERTY IS NEAR!

THE **PESSIMISTS** ARE WORRIED THAT HUMAN CIVILIZATION IS HEADING **TOWARD THE EDGE OF A CLIFF.**

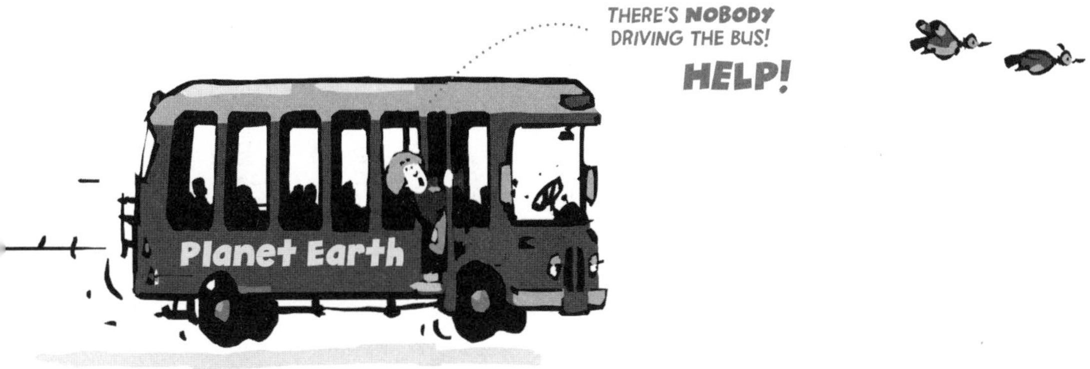
THERE'S NOBODY DRIVING THE BUS!
HELP!
Planet Earth

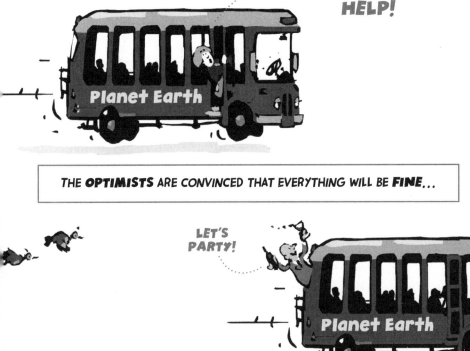

THE **OPTIMISTS** ARE CONVINCED THAT EVERYTHING WILL BE **FINE...**

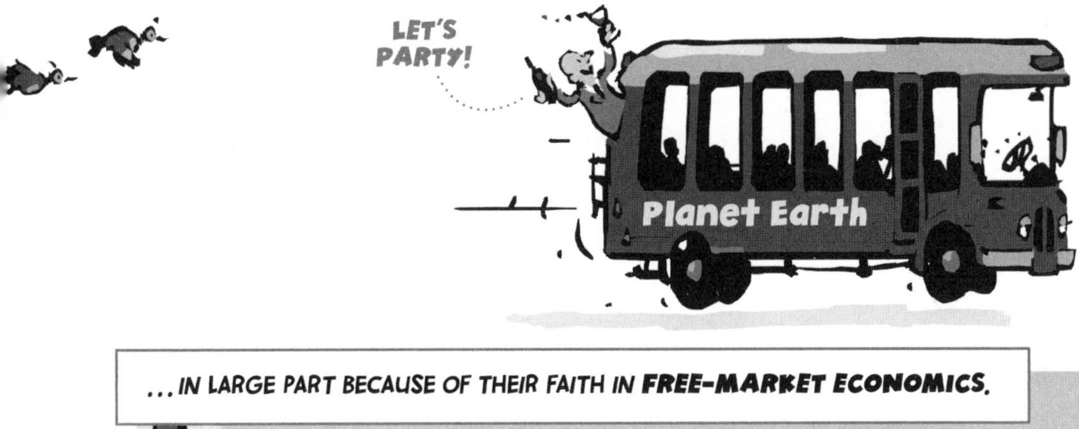
LET'S PARTY!
Planet Earth

...IN LARGE PART BECAUSE OF THEIR FAITH IN **FREE-MARKET ECONOMICS.**

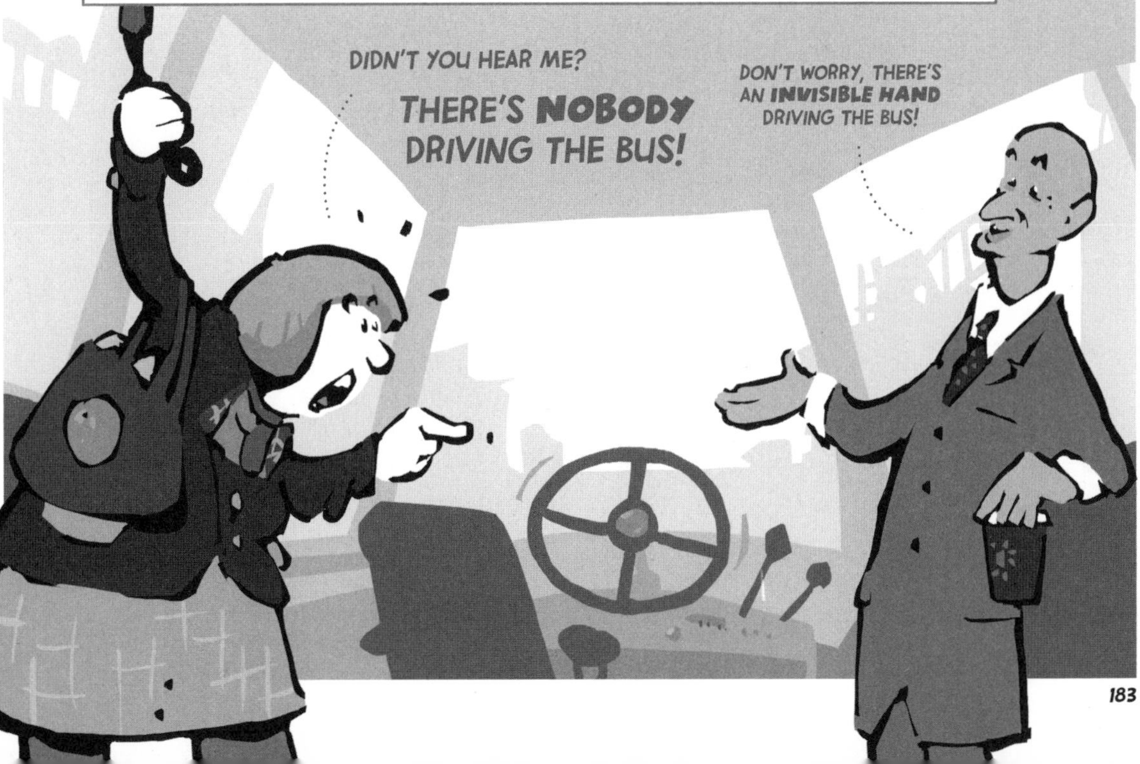
DIDN'T YOU HEAR ME?
THERE'S NOBODY DRIVING THE BUS!
DON'T WORRY, THERE'S AN INVISIBLE HAND DRIVING THE BUS!

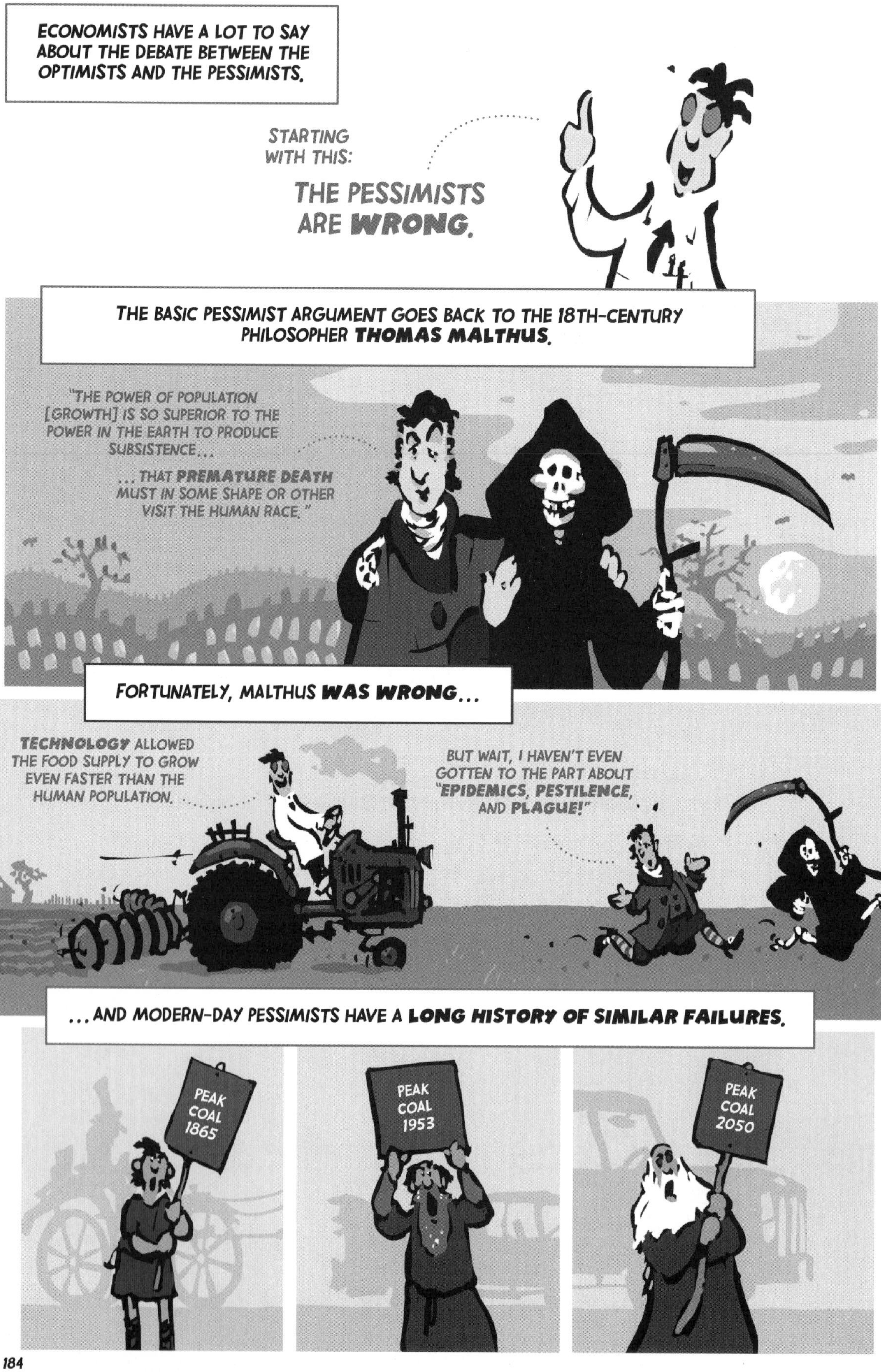
ECONOMISTS HAVE A LOT TO SAY ABOUT THE DEBATE BETWEEN THE OPTIMISTS AND THE PESSIMISTS.
STARTING WITH THIS:
THE PESSIMISTS ARE **WRONG**.
THE BASIC PESSIMIST ARGUMENT GOES BACK TO THE 18TH-CENTURY PHILOSOPHER **THOMAS MALTHUS**.
"THE POWER OF POPULATION [GROWTH] IS SO SUPERIOR TO THE POWER IN THE EARTH TO PRODUCE SUBSISTENCE...
...THAT **PREMATURE DEATH** MUST IN SOME SHAPE OR OTHER VISIT THE HUMAN RACE."
FORTUNATELY, MALTHUS **WAS WRONG**...
TECHNOLOGY ALLOWED THE FOOD SUPPLY TO GROW EVEN FASTER THAN THE HUMAN POPULATION.
BUT WAIT, I HAVEN'T EVEN GOTTEN TO THE PART ABOUT "**EPIDEMICS, PESTILENCE,** AND **PLAGUE!**"
...AND MODERN-DAY PESSIMISTS HAVE A **LONG HISTORY OF SIMILAR FAILURES**.
PEAK COAL 1865
PEAK COAL 1953
PEAK COAL 2050

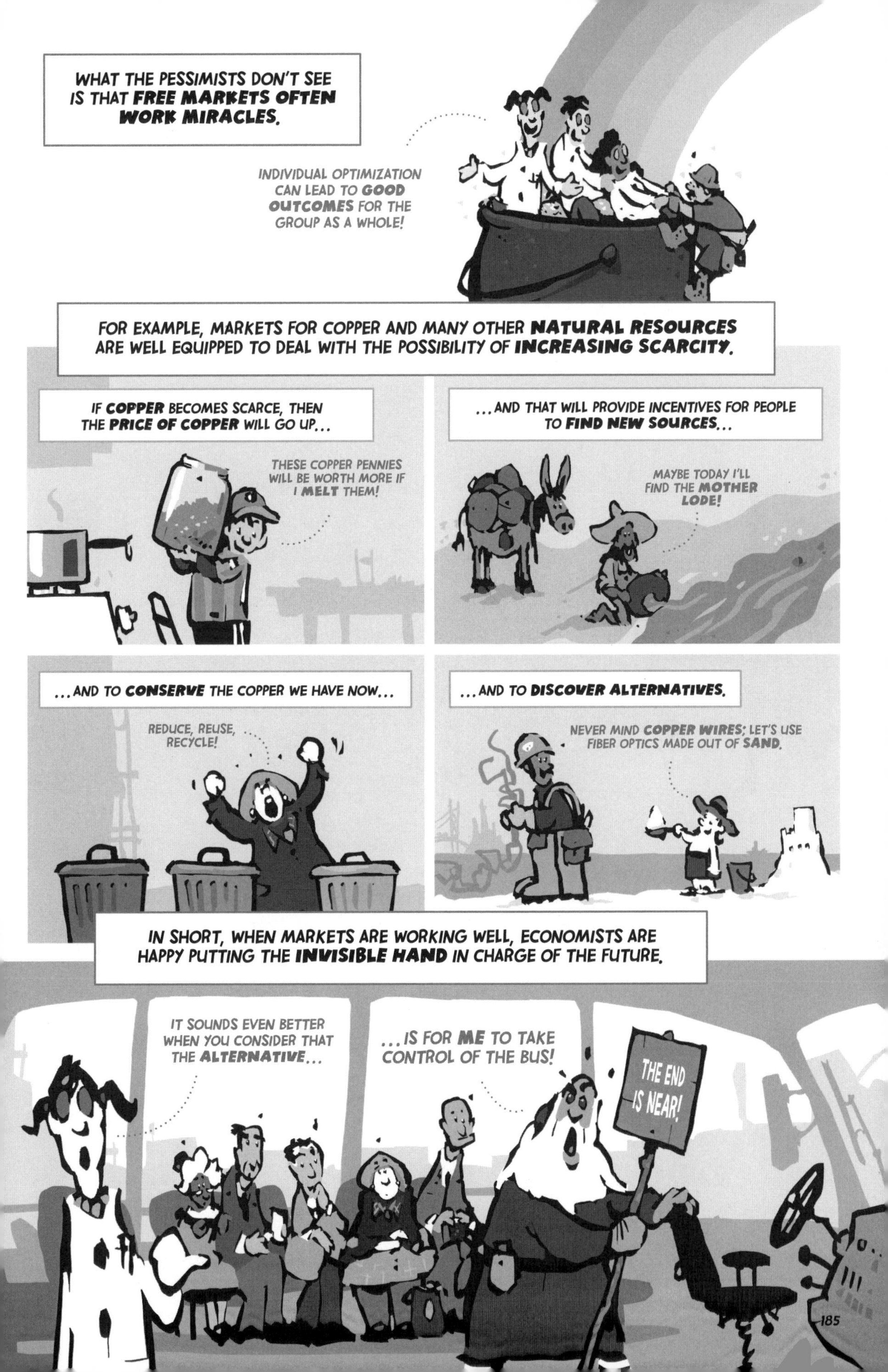
WHAT THE PESSIMISTS DON'T SEE IS THAT FREE MARKETS OFTEN WORK MIRACLES.
INDIVIDUAL OPTIMIZATION CAN LEAD TO GOOD OUTCOMES FOR THE GROUP AS A WHOLE!
FOR EXAMPLE, MARKETS FOR COPPER AND MANY OTHER NATURAL RESOURCES ARE WELL EQUIPPED TO DEAL WITH THE POSSIBILITY OF INCREASING SCARCITY.
IF COPPER BECOMES SCARCE, THEN THE PRICE OF COPPER WILL GO UP...
THESE COPPER PENNIES WILL BE WORTH MORE IF I MELT THEM!
...AND THAT WILL PROVIDE INCENTIVES FOR PEOPLE TO FIND NEW SOURCES...
MAYBE TODAY I'LL FIND THE MOTHER LODE!
...AND TO CONSERVE THE COPPER WE HAVE NOW...
REDUCE, REUSE, RECYCLE!
...AND TO DISCOVER ALTERNATIVES.
NEVER MIND COPPER WIRES; LET'S USE FIBER OPTICS MADE OUT OF SAND.
IN SHORT, WHEN MARKETS ARE WORKING WELL, ECONOMISTS ARE HAPPY PUTTING THE INVISIBLE HAND IN CHARGE OF THE FUTURE.
IT SOUNDS EVEN BETTER WHEN YOU CONSIDER THAT THE ALTERNATIVE...
...IS FOR ME TO TAKE CONTROL OF THE BUS!
THE END IS NEAR!

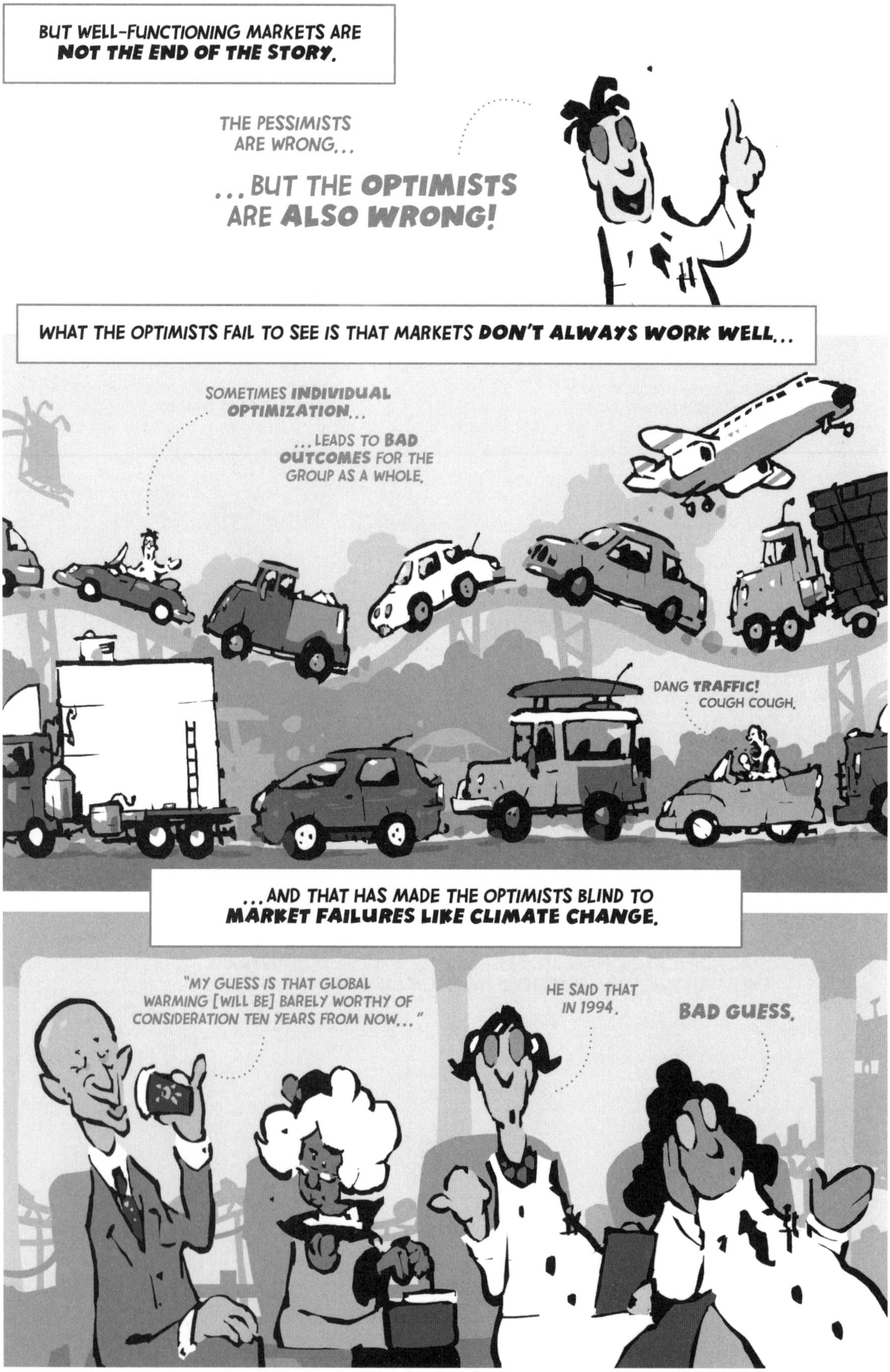
BUT WELL-FUNCTIONING MARKETS ARE NOT THE END OF THE STORY.
THE PESSIMISTS ARE WRONG...
...BUT THE OPTIMISTS ARE ALSO WRONG!
WHAT THE OPTIMISTS FAIL TO SEE IS THAT MARKETS DON'T ALWAYS WORK WELL...
SOMETIMES INDIVIDUAL OPTIMIZATION...
...LEADS TO BAD OUTCOMES FOR THE GROUP AS A WHOLE.
DANG TRAFFIC! COUGH COUGH.
...AND THAT HAS MADE THE OPTIMISTS BLIND TO MARKET FAILURES LIKE CLIMATE CHANGE.
"MY GUESS IS THAT GLOBAL WARMING [WILL BE] BARELY WORTHY OF CONSIDERATION TEN YEARS FROM NOW..."
HE SAID THAT IN 1994.
BAD GUESS.

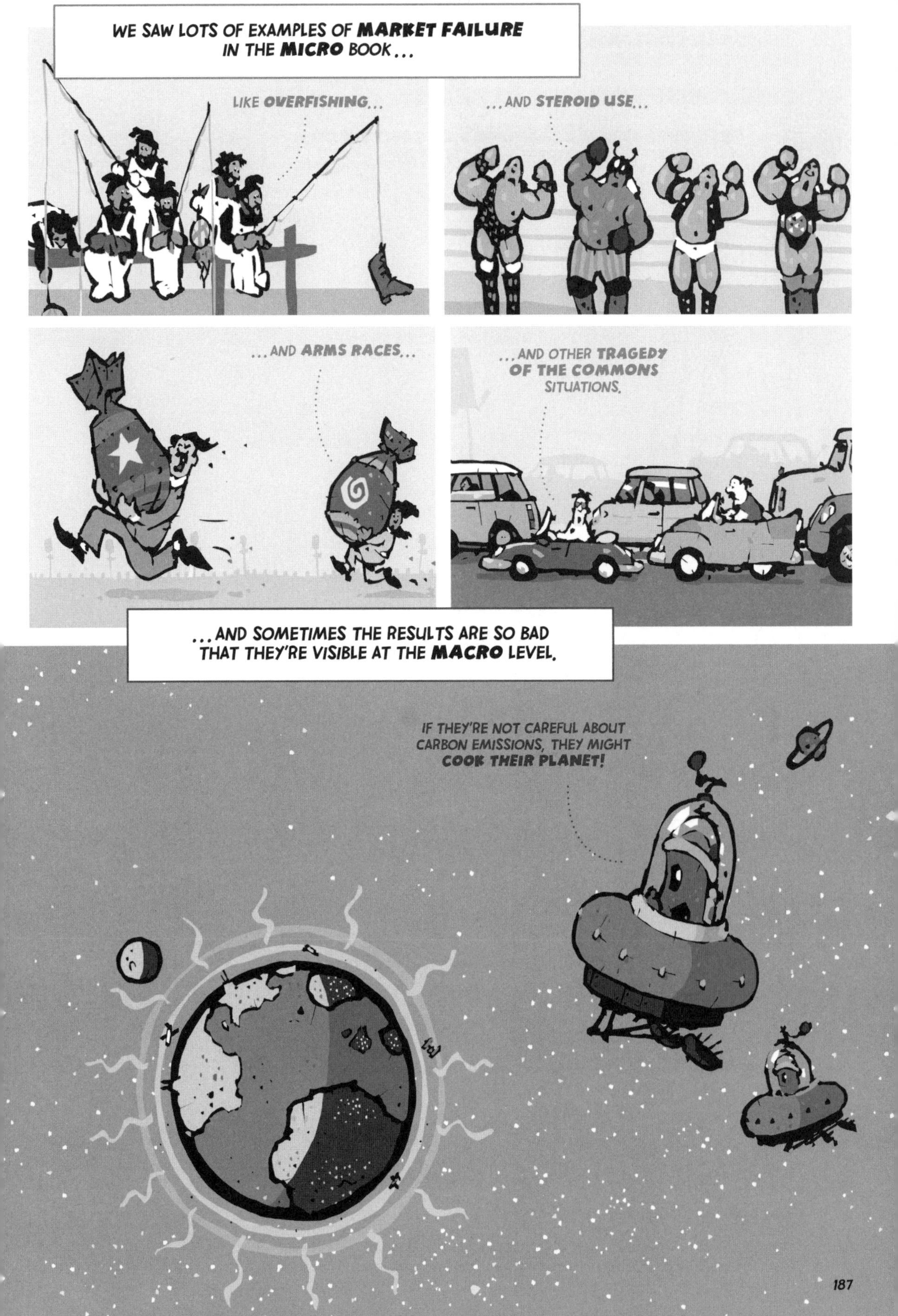

WE SAW LOTS OF EXAMPLES OF **MARKET FAILURE** IN THE **MICRO** BOOK...
LIKE **OVERFISHING**...
...AND **STEROID USE**...
...AND **ARMS RACES**...
...AND OTHER **TRAGEDY OF THE COMMONS** SITUATIONS.
...AND SOMETIMES THE RESULTS ARE SO BAD THAT THEY'RE VISIBLE AT THE **MACRO** LEVEL.
IF THEY'RE NOT CAREFUL ABOUT CARBON EMISSIONS, THEY MIGHT **COOK THEIR PLANET!**

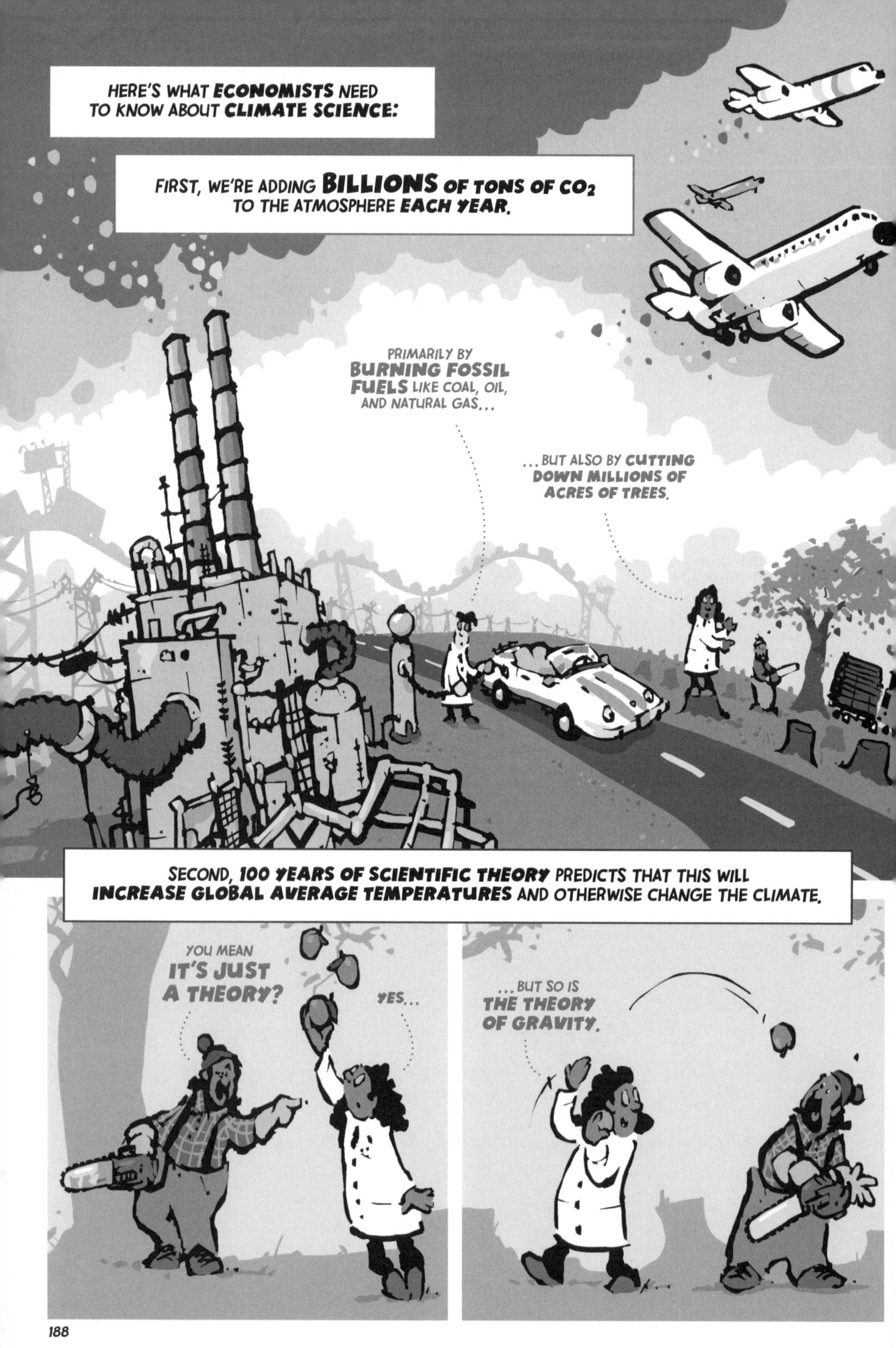

HERE'S WHAT ECONOMISTS NEED TO KNOW ABOUT CLIMATE SCIENCE:
FIRST, WE'RE ADDING BILLIONS OF TONS OF CO_2 TO THE ATMOSPHERE EACH YEAR.
PRIMARILY BY BURNING FOSSIL FUELS LIKE COAL, OIL, AND NATURAL GAS...
...BUT ALSO BY CUTTING DOWN MILLIONS OF ACRES OF TREES.
SECOND, 100 YEARS OF SCIENTIFIC THEORY PREDICTS THAT THIS WILL INCREASE GLOBAL AVERAGE TEMPERATURES AND OTHERWISE CHANGE THE CLIMATE.
YOU MEAN IT'S JUST A THEORY?
YES...
...BUT SO IS THE THEORY OF GRAVITY.

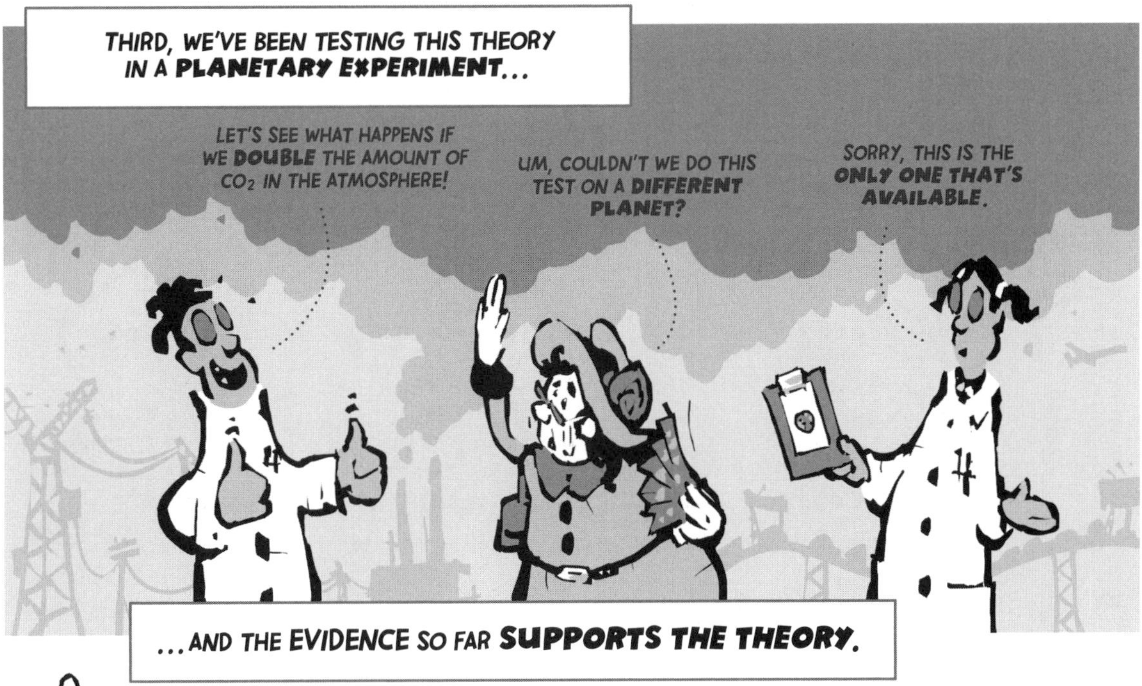
THIRD, WE'VE BEEN TESTING THIS THEORY IN A PLANETARY EXPERIMENT...
LET'S SEE WHAT HAPPENS IF WE DOUBLE THE AMOUNT OF CO_2 IN THE ATMOSPHERE!
UM, COULDN'T WE DO THIS TEST ON A DIFFERENT PLANET?
SORRY, THIS IS THE ONLY ONE THAT'S AVAILABLE.
...AND THE EVIDENCE SO FAR SUPPORTS THE THEORY.

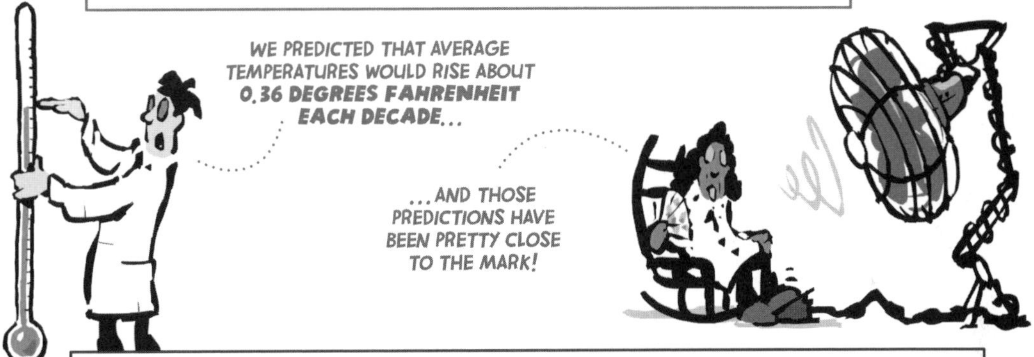
WE PREDICTED THAT AVERAGE TEMPERATURES WOULD RISE ABOUT 0.36 DEGREES FAHRENHEIT EACH DECADE...
...AND THOSE PREDICTIONS HAVE BEEN PRETTY CLOSE TO THE MARK!

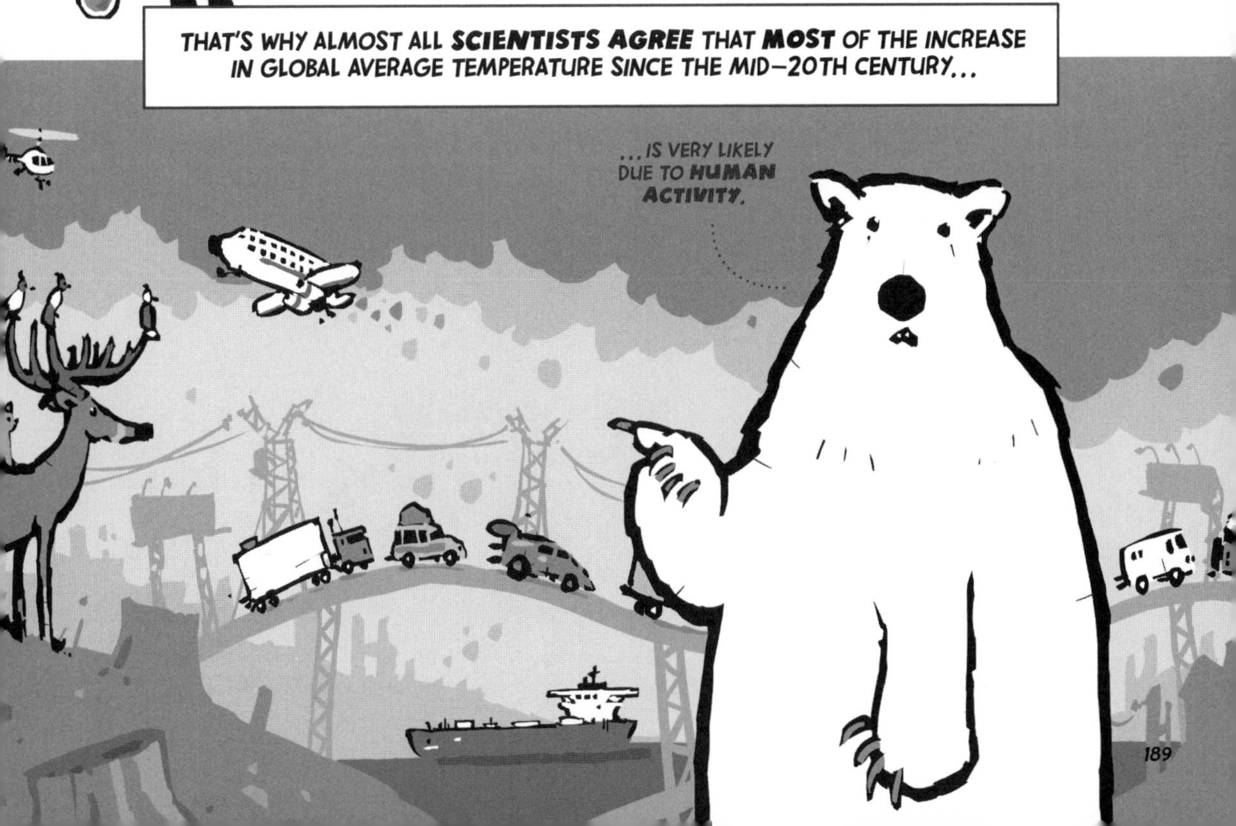
THAT'S WHY ALMOST ALL SCIENTISTS AGREE THAT MOST OF THE INCREASE IN GLOBAL AVERAGE TEMPERATURE SINCE THE MID-20TH CENTURY...
...IS VERY LIKELY DUE TO HUMAN ACTIVITY.

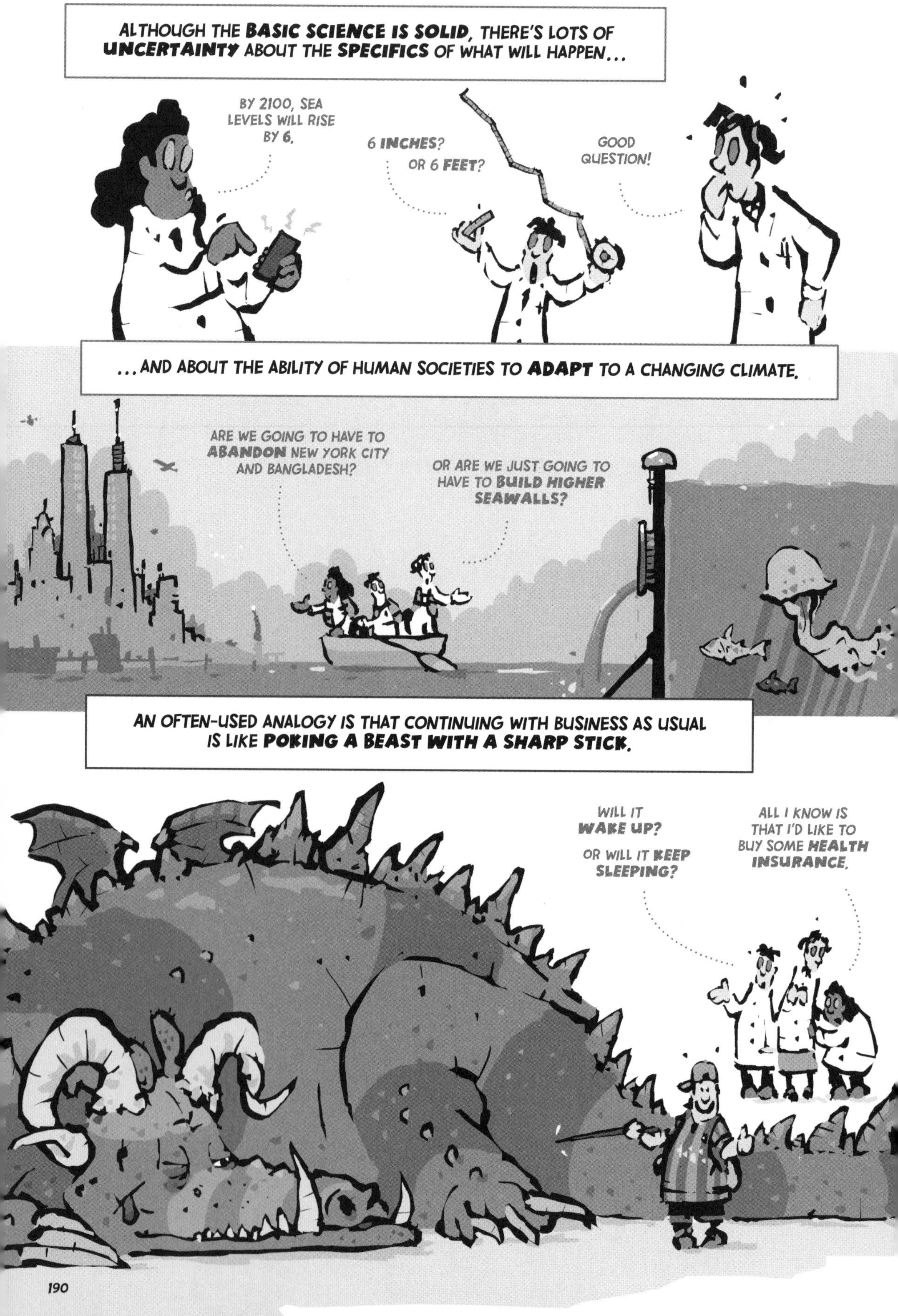
ALTHOUGH THE **BASIC SCIENCE IS SOLID**, THERE'S LOTS OF **UNCERTAINTY** ABOUT THE **SPECIFICS** OF WHAT WILL HAPPEN...
BY 2100, SEA LEVELS WILL RISE BY **6**.
6 **INCHES**? OR 6 **FEET**?
GOOD QUESTION!
...AND ABOUT THE ABILITY OF HUMAN SOCIETIES TO **ADAPT** TO A CHANGING CLIMATE.
ARE WE GOING TO HAVE TO **ABANDON** NEW YORK CITY AND BANGLADESH?
OR ARE WE JUST GOING TO HAVE TO **BUILD HIGHER SEAWALLS?**
AN OFTEN-USED ANALOGY IS THAT CONTINUING WITH BUSINESS AS USUAL IS LIKE **POKING A BEAST WITH A SHARP STICK**.
WILL IT **WAKE UP?**
OR WILL IT **KEEP SLEEPING?**
ALL I KNOW IS THAT I'D LIKE TO BUY SOME **HEALTH INSURANCE**.

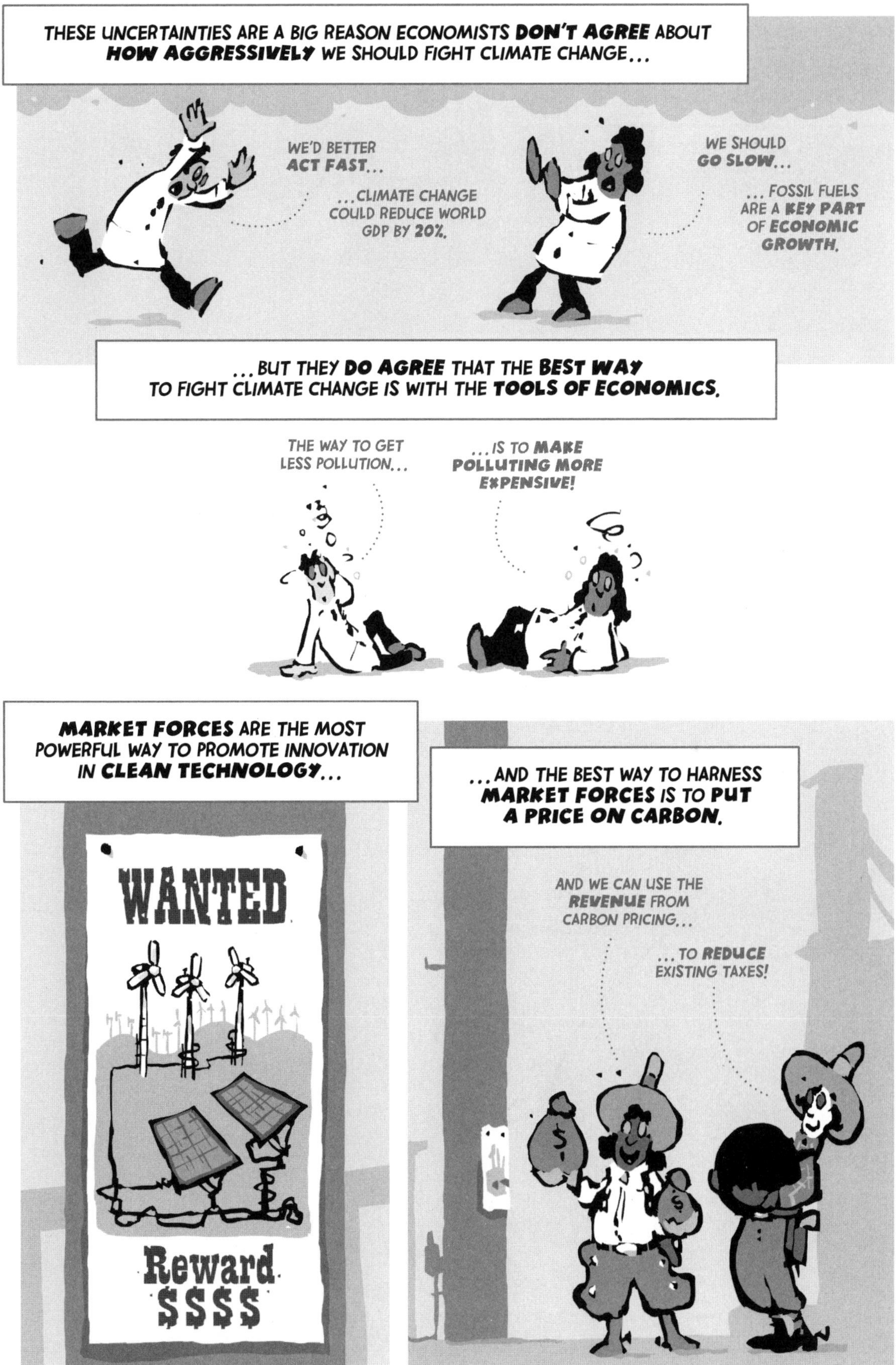
THESE UNCERTAINTIES ARE A BIG REASON ECONOMISTS **DON'T AGREE** ABOUT **HOW AGGRESSIVELY** WE SHOULD FIGHT CLIMATE CHANGE...
WE'D BETTER **ACT FAST...**
...CLIMATE CHANGE COULD REDUCE WORLD GDP BY **20%.**
WE SHOULD **GO SLOW...**
...FOSSIL FUELS ARE A **KEY PART** OF **ECONOMIC GROWTH.**
...BUT THEY **DO AGREE** THAT THE **BEST WAY** TO FIGHT CLIMATE CHANGE IS WITH THE **TOOLS OF ECONOMICS.**
THE WAY TO GET LESS POLLUTION...
...IS TO **MAKE POLLUTING MORE EXPENSIVE!**
MARKET FORCES ARE THE MOST POWERFUL WAY TO PROMOTE INNOVATION IN **CLEAN TECHNOLOGY...**
WANTED
Reward
$$$$
...AND THE BEST WAY TO HARNESS **MARKET FORCES** IS TO **PUT A PRICE ON CARBON.**
AND WE CAN USE THE **REVENUE** FROM CARBON PRICING...
...TO **REDUCE** EXISTING TAXES!

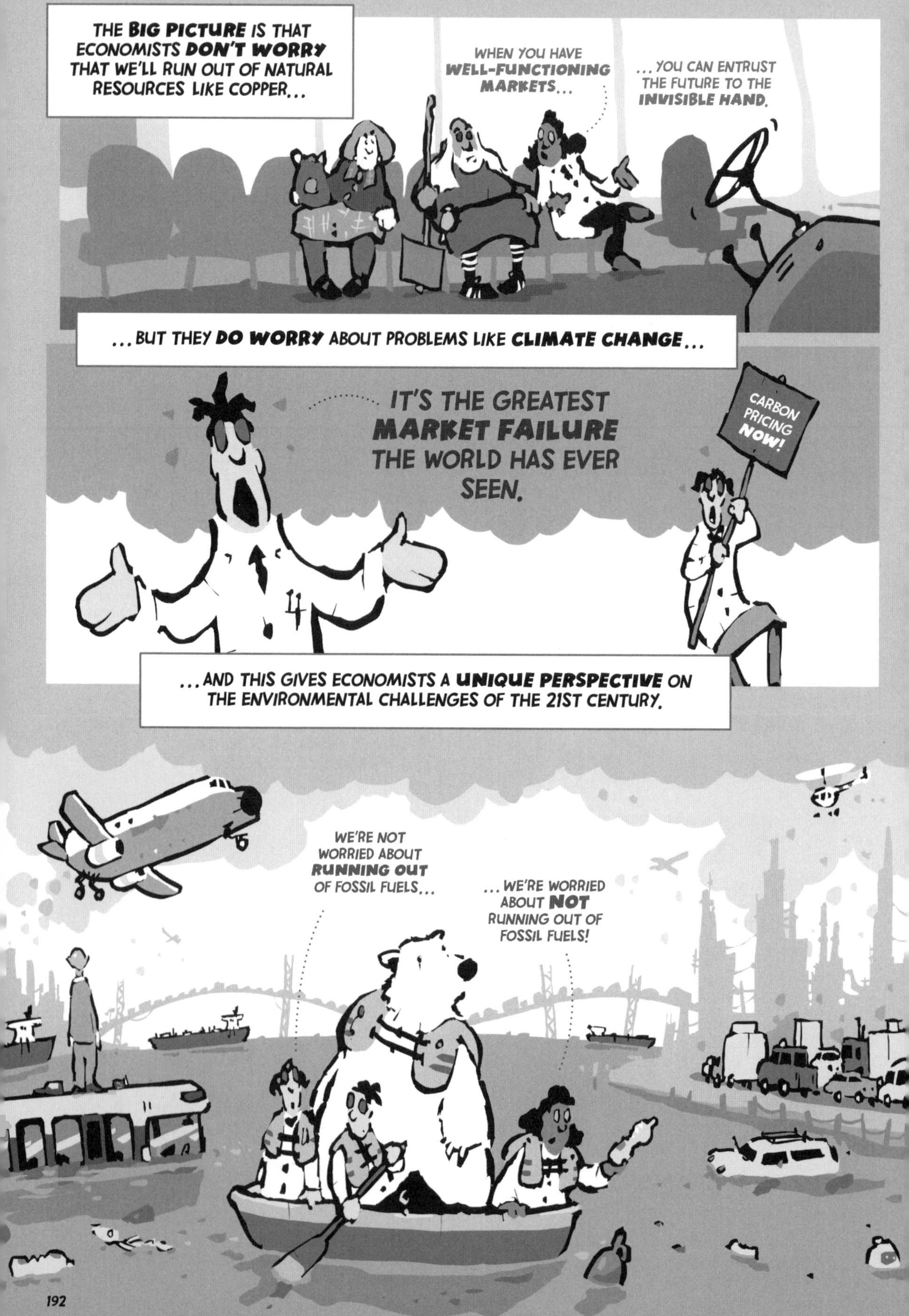
THE BIG PICTURE IS THAT ECONOMISTS DON'T WORRY THAT WE'LL RUN OUT OF NATURAL RESOURCES LIKE COPPER...
WHEN YOU HAVE WELL-FUNCTIONING MARKETS...
...YOU CAN ENTRUST THE FUTURE TO THE INVISIBLE HAND.
...BUT THEY DO WORRY ABOUT PROBLEMS LIKE CLIMATE CHANGE...
IT'S THE GREATEST MARKET FAILURE THE WORLD HAS EVER SEEN.
CARBON PRICING NOW!
...AND THIS GIVES ECONOMISTS A UNIQUE PERSPECTIVE ON THE ENVIRONMENTAL CHALLENGES OF THE 21ST CENTURY.
WE'RE NOT WORRIED ABOUT RUNNING OUT OF FOSSIL FUELS...
...WE'RE WORRIED ABOUT NOT RUNNING OUT OF FOSSIL FUELS!

CHAPTER 15

THE END OF YOUTH?

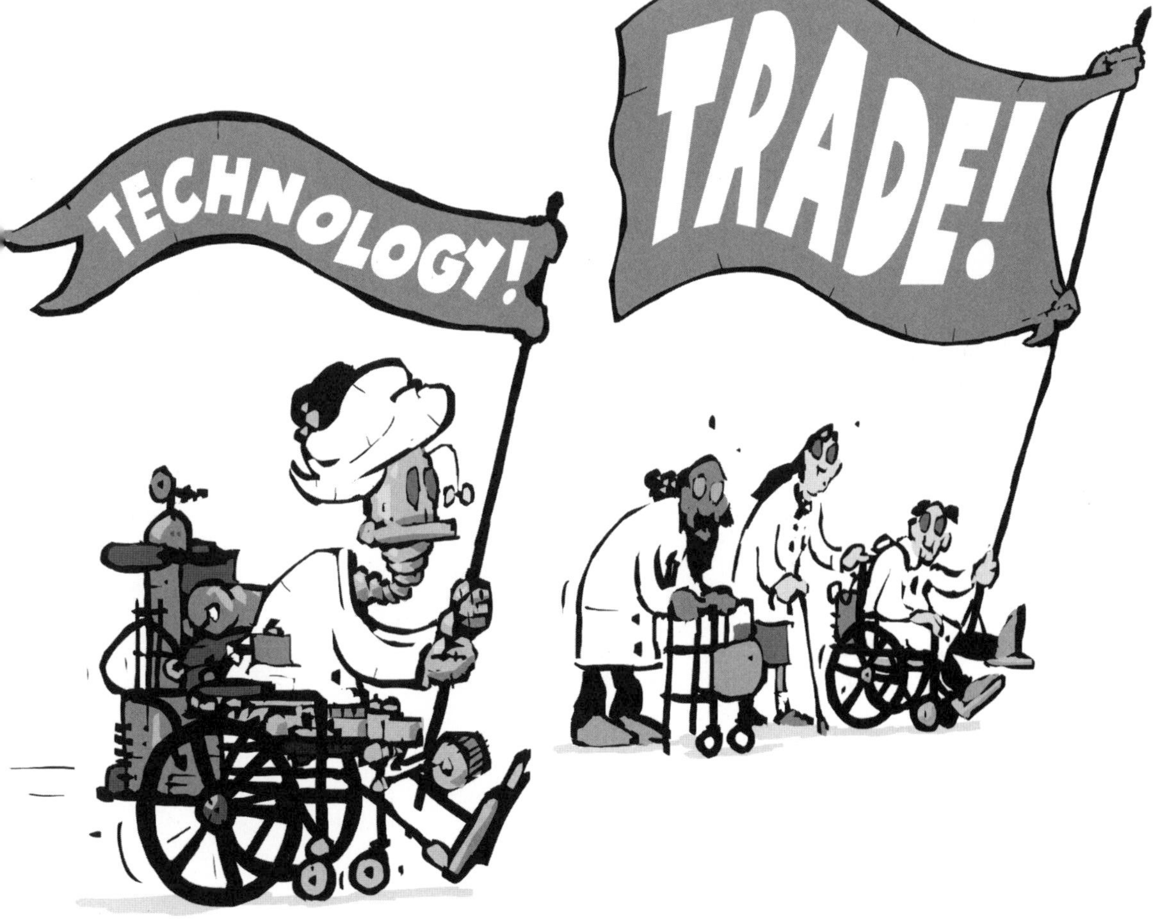
TECHNOLOGY!
TRADE!

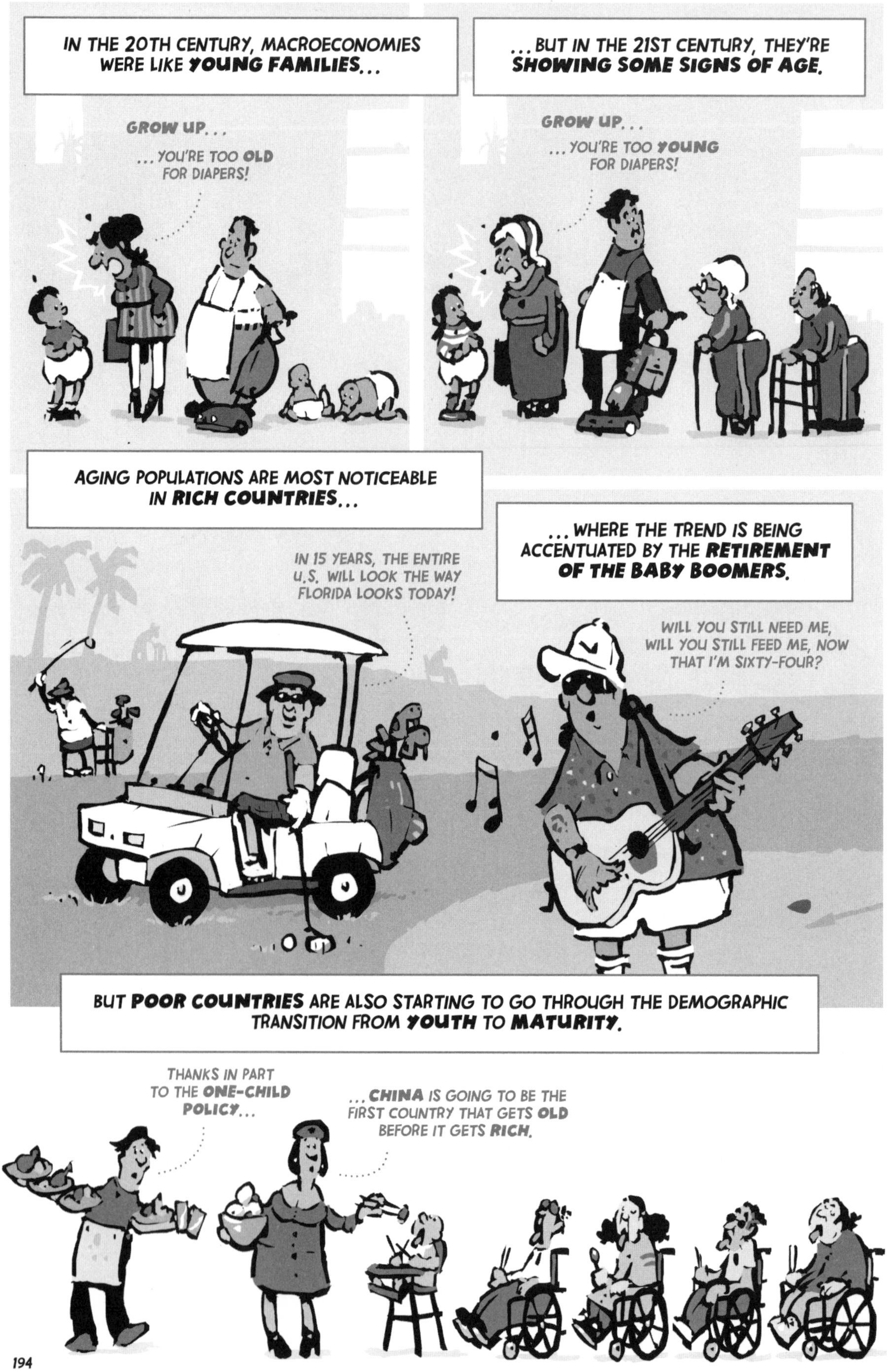

IN THE 20TH CENTURY, MACROECONOMIES WERE LIKE YOUNG FAMILIES...
GROW UP...
...YOU'RE TOO OLD FOR DIAPERS!
...BUT IN THE 21ST CENTURY, THEY'RE SHOWING SOME SIGNS OF AGE.
GROW UP...
...YOU'RE TOO YOUNG FOR DIAPERS!
AGING POPULATIONS ARE MOST NOTICEABLE IN RICH COUNTRIES...
IN 15 YEARS, THE ENTIRE U.S. WILL LOOK THE WAY FLORIDA LOOKS TODAY!
...WHERE THE TREND IS BEING ACCENTUATED BY THE RETIREMENT OF THE BABY BOOMERS.
WILL YOU STILL NEED ME, WILL YOU STILL FEED ME, NOW THAT I'M SIXTY-FOUR?
BUT POOR COUNTRIES ARE ALSO STARTING TO GO THROUGH THE DEMOGRAPHIC TRANSITION FROM YOUTH TO MATURITY.
THANKS IN PART TO THE ONE-CHILD POLICY...
...CHINA IS GOING TO BE THE FIRST COUNTRY THAT GETS OLD BEFORE IT GETS RICH.

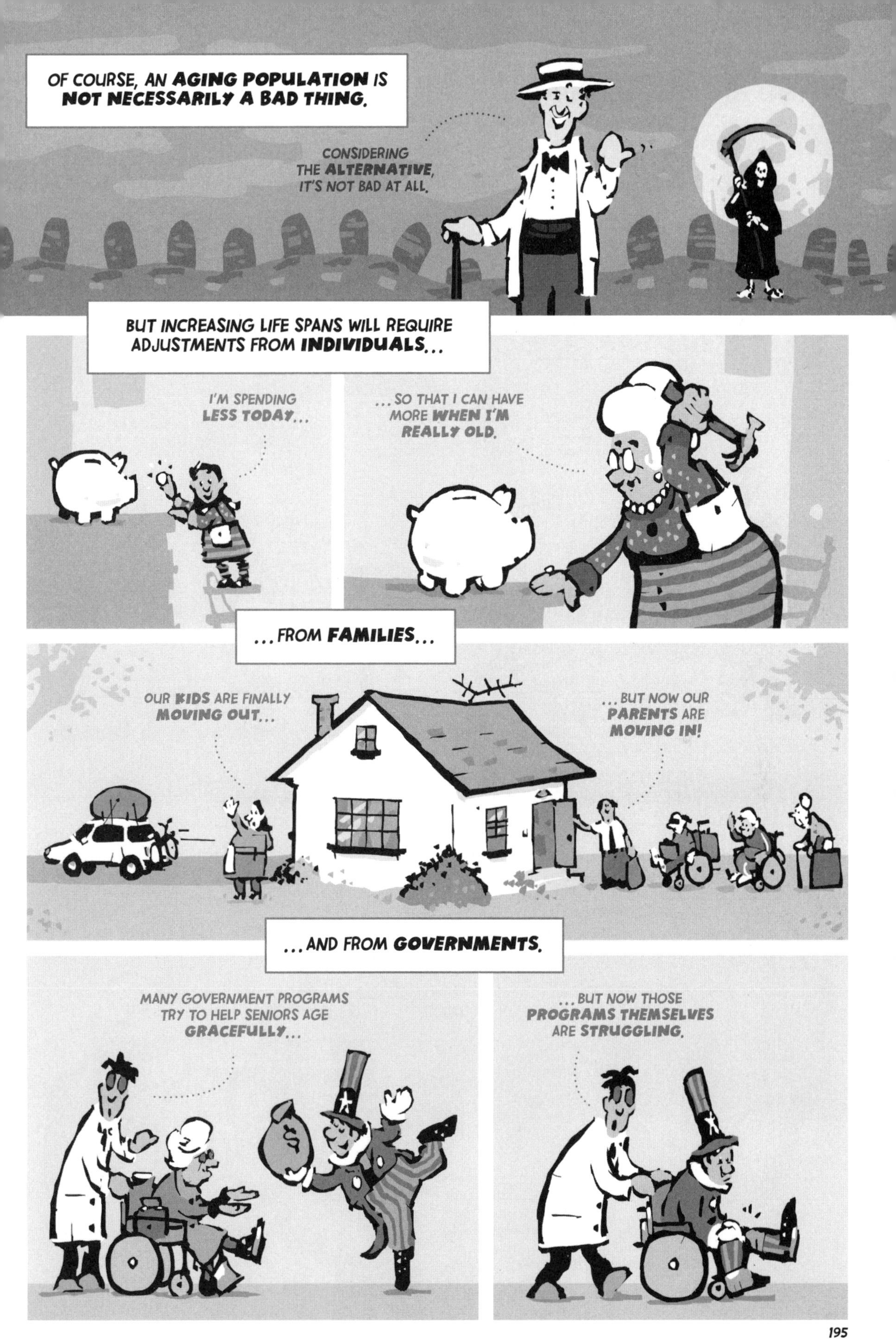
OF COURSE, AN AGING POPULATION IS NOT NECESSARILY A BAD THING.
CONSIDERING THE ALTERNATIVE, IT'S NOT BAD AT ALL.
BUT INCREASING LIFE SPANS WILL REQUIRE ADJUSTMENTS FROM INDIVIDUALS...
I'M SPENDING LESS TODAY...
...SO THAT I CAN HAVE MORE WHEN I'M REALLY OLD.
...FROM FAMILIES...
OUR KIDS ARE FINALLY MOVING OUT...
...BUT NOW OUR PARENTS ARE MOVING IN!
...AND FROM GOVERNMENTS.
MANY GOVERNMENT PROGRAMS TRY TO HELP SENIORS AGE GRACEFULLY...
...BUT NOW THOSE PROGRAMS THEMSELVES ARE STRUGGLING.

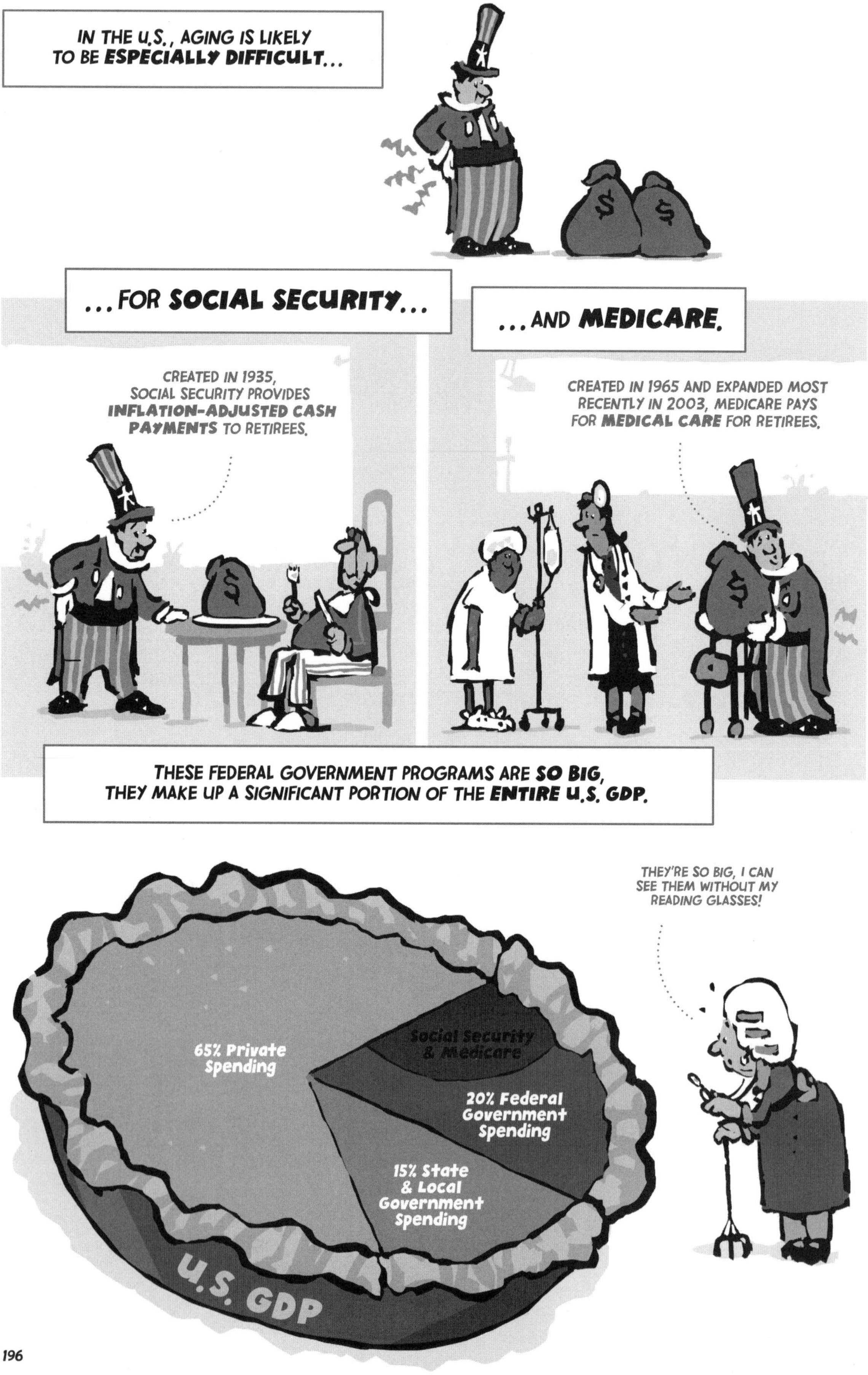
IN THE U.S., AGING IS LIKELY TO BE ESPECIALLY DIFFICULT...
...FOR SOCIAL SECURITY...
CREATED IN 1935, SOCIAL SECURITY PROVIDES INFLATION-ADJUSTED CASH PAYMENTS TO RETIREES.
...AND MEDICARE.
CREATED IN 1965 AND EXPANDED MOST RECENTLY IN 2003, MEDICARE PAYS FOR MEDICAL CARE FOR RETIREES.
THESE FEDERAL GOVERNMENT PROGRAMS ARE SO BIG, THEY MAKE UP A SIGNIFICANT PORTION OF THE ENTIRE U.S. GDP.
65% Private Spending
Social Security & Medicare
20% Federal Government Spending
15% State & Local Government Spending
U.S. GDP
THEY'RE SO BIG, I CAN SEE THEM WITHOUT MY READING GLASSES!

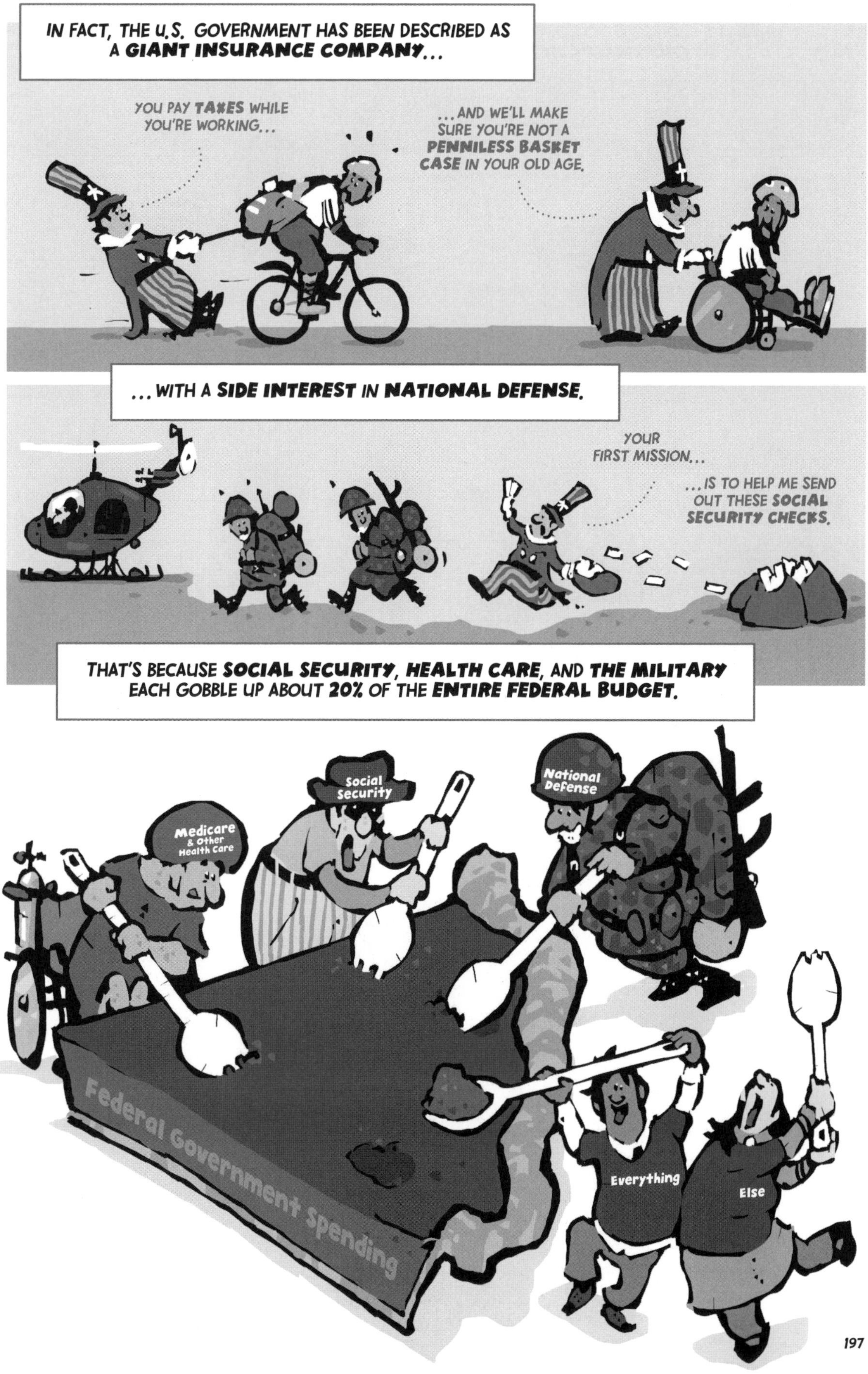
IN FACT, THE U.S. GOVERNMENT HAS BEEN DESCRIBED AS A **GIANT INSURANCE COMPANY**...
YOU PAY **TAXES** WHILE YOU'RE WORKING...
...AND WE'LL MAKE SURE YOU'RE NOT A **PENNILESS BASKET CASE** IN YOUR OLD AGE.
...WITH A **SIDE INTEREST** IN **NATIONAL DEFENSE.**
YOUR FIRST MISSION...
...IS TO HELP ME SEND OUT THESE **SOCIAL SECURITY CHECKS.**
THAT'S BECAUSE **SOCIAL SECURITY, HEALTH CARE,** AND **THE MILITARY** EACH GOBBLE UP ABOUT **20%** OF THE **ENTIRE FEDERAL BUDGET.**
Medicare & Other Health Care
Social Security
National Defense
Everything
Else
Federal Government Spending

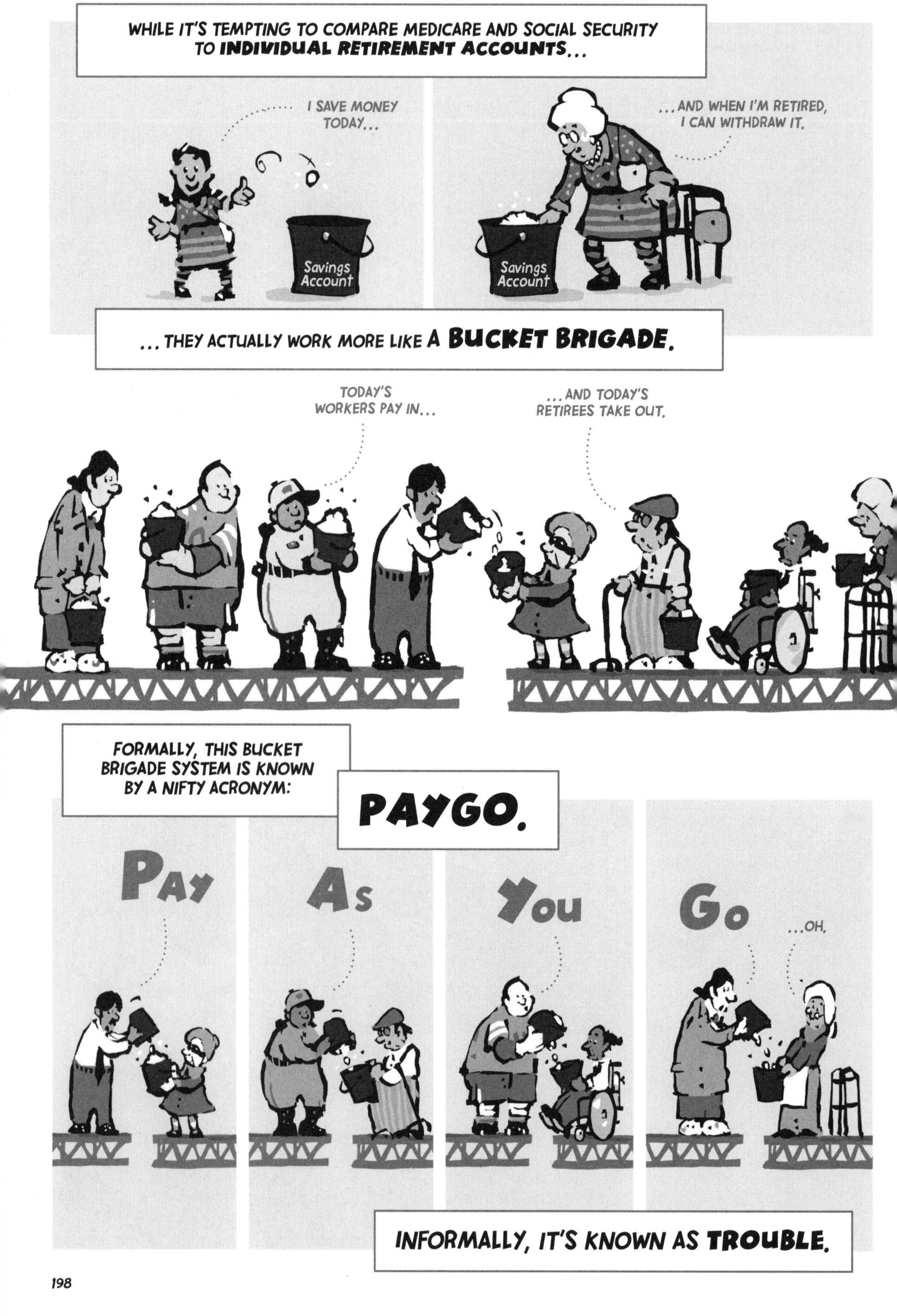

WHILE IT'S TEMPTING TO COMPARE MEDICARE AND SOCIAL SECURITY TO INDIVIDUAL RETIREMENT ACCOUNTS...
I SAVE MONEY TODAY...
Savings Account
...AND WHEN I'M RETIRED, I CAN WITHDRAW IT.
Savings Account
...THEY ACTUALLY WORK MORE LIKE A BUCKET BRIGADE.
TODAY'S WORKERS PAY IN...
...AND TODAY'S RETIREES TAKE OUT.
FORMALLY, THIS BUCKET BRIGADE SYSTEM IS KNOWN BY A NIFTY ACRONYM:
PAYGO.
Pay
As
You
Go
...OH.
INFORMALLY, IT'S KNOWN AS TROUBLE.

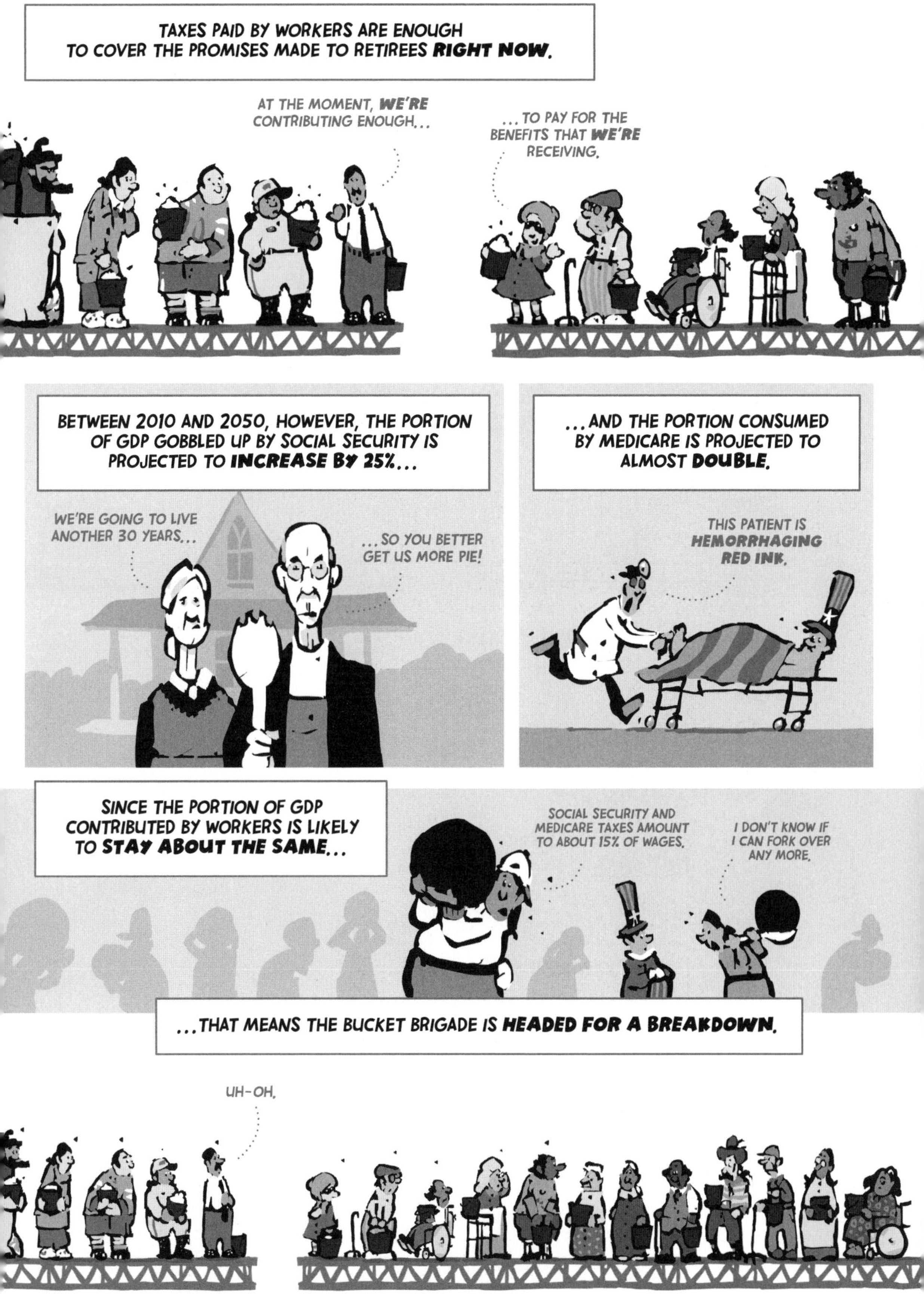
TAXES PAID BY WORKERS ARE ENOUGH TO COVER THE PROMISES MADE TO RETIREES **RIGHT NOW.**
AT THE MOMENT, **WE'RE** CONTRIBUTING ENOUGH...
...TO PAY FOR THE BENEFITS THAT **WE'RE** RECEIVING.
BETWEEN 2010 AND 2050, HOWEVER, THE PORTION OF GDP GOBBLED UP BY SOCIAL SECURITY IS PROJECTED TO **INCREASE BY 25%...**
WE'RE GOING TO LIVE ANOTHER 30 YEARS...
...SO YOU BETTER GET US MORE PIE!
...AND THE PORTION CONSUMED BY MEDICARE IS PROJECTED TO ALMOST **DOUBLE.**
THIS PATIENT IS **HEMORRHAGING RED INK.**
SINCE THE PORTION OF GDP CONTRIBUTED BY WORKERS IS LIKELY TO **STAY ABOUT THE SAME...**
SOCIAL SECURITY AND MEDICARE TAXES AMOUNT TO ABOUT 15% OF WAGES.
I DON'T KNOW IF I CAN FORK OVER ANY MORE.
...THAT MEANS THE BUCKET BRIGADE IS **HEADED FOR A BREAKDOWN.**
UH-OH.

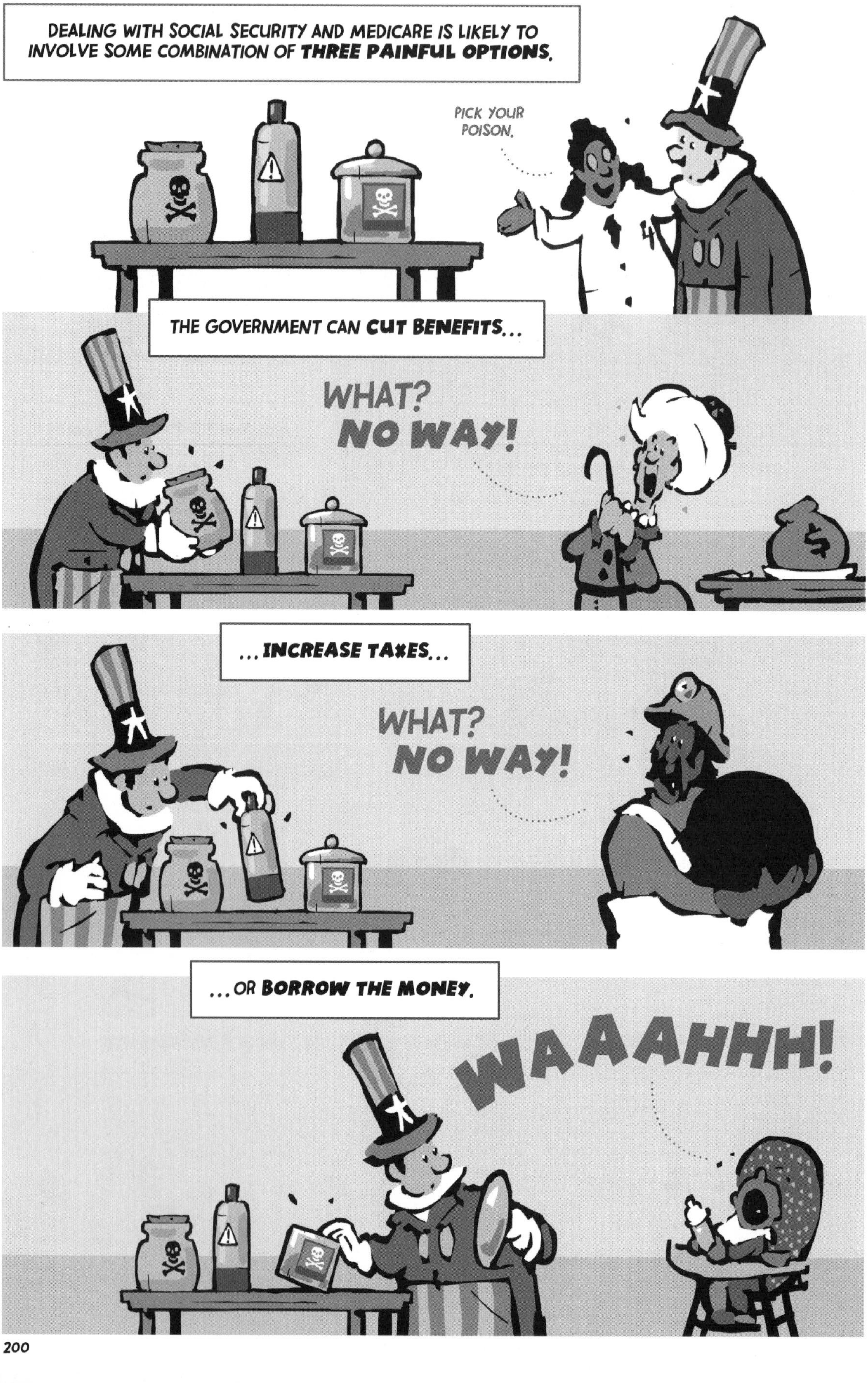
DEALING WITH SOCIAL SECURITY AND MEDICARE IS LIKELY TO INVOLVE SOME COMBINATION OF THREE PAINFUL OPTIONS.
PICK YOUR POISON.
THE GOVERNMENT CAN CUT BENEFITS...
WHAT? NO WAY!
...INCREASE TAXES...
WHAT? NO WAY!
...OR BORROW THE MONEY.
WAAAHHH!

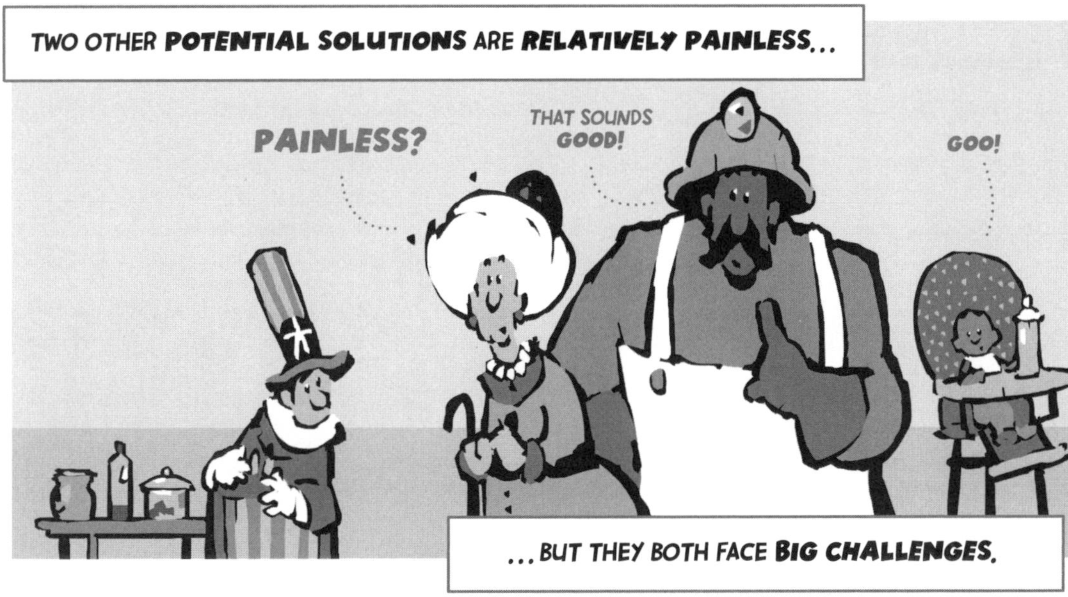
TWO OTHER POTENTIAL SOLUTIONS ARE RELATIVELY PAINLESS...
PAINLESS?
THAT SOUNDS GOOD!
GOO!
...BUT THEY BOTH FACE BIG CHALLENGES.

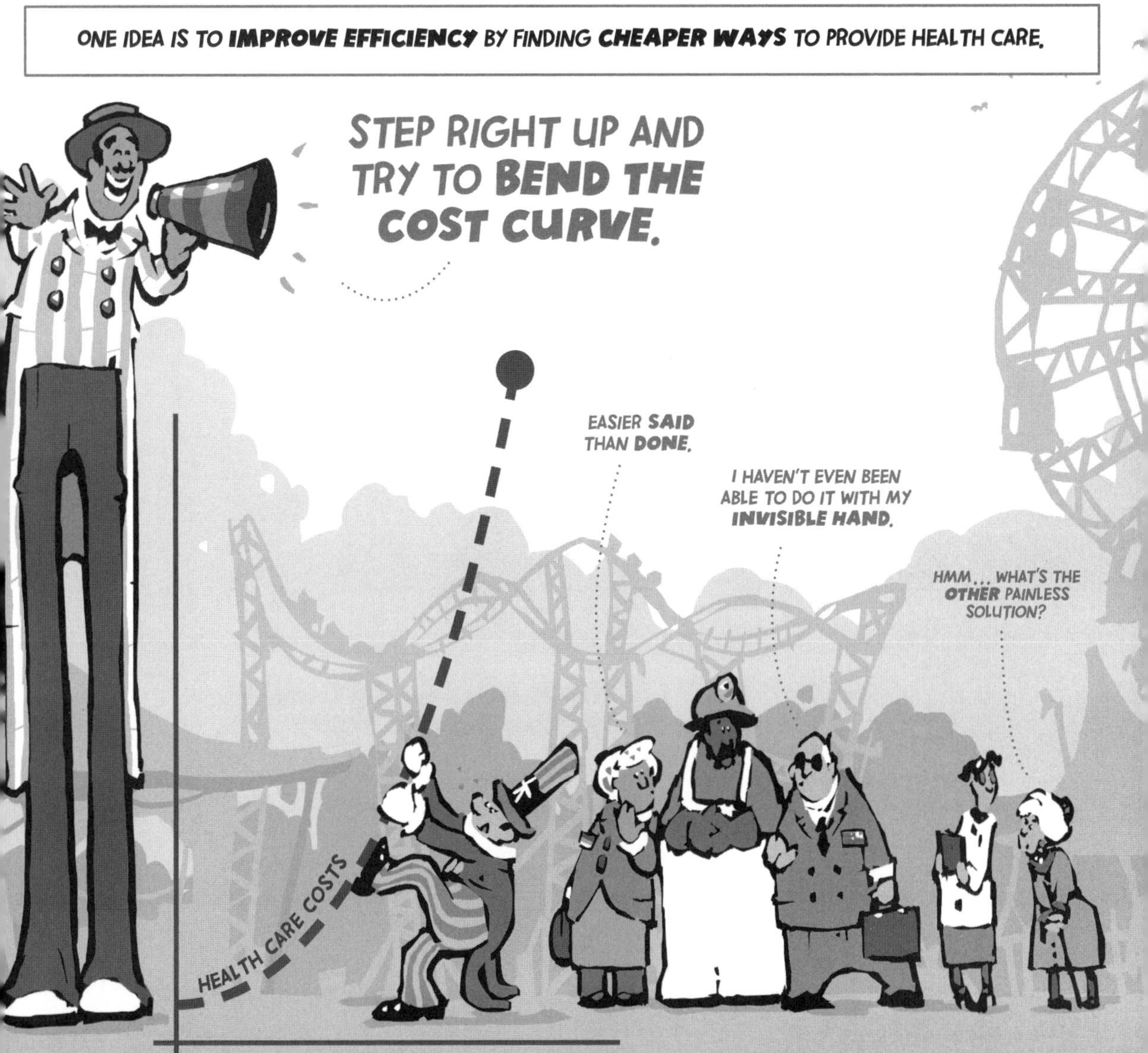
ONE IDEA IS TO IMPROVE EFFICIENCY BY FINDING CHEAPER WAYS TO PROVIDE HEALTH CARE.
STEP RIGHT UP AND TRY TO BEND THE COST CURVE.
EASIER SAID THAN DONE.
I HAVEN'T EVEN BEEN ABLE TO DO IT WITH MY INVISIBLE HAND.
HMM... WHAT'S THE OTHER PAINLESS SOLUTION?
HEALTH CARE COSTS

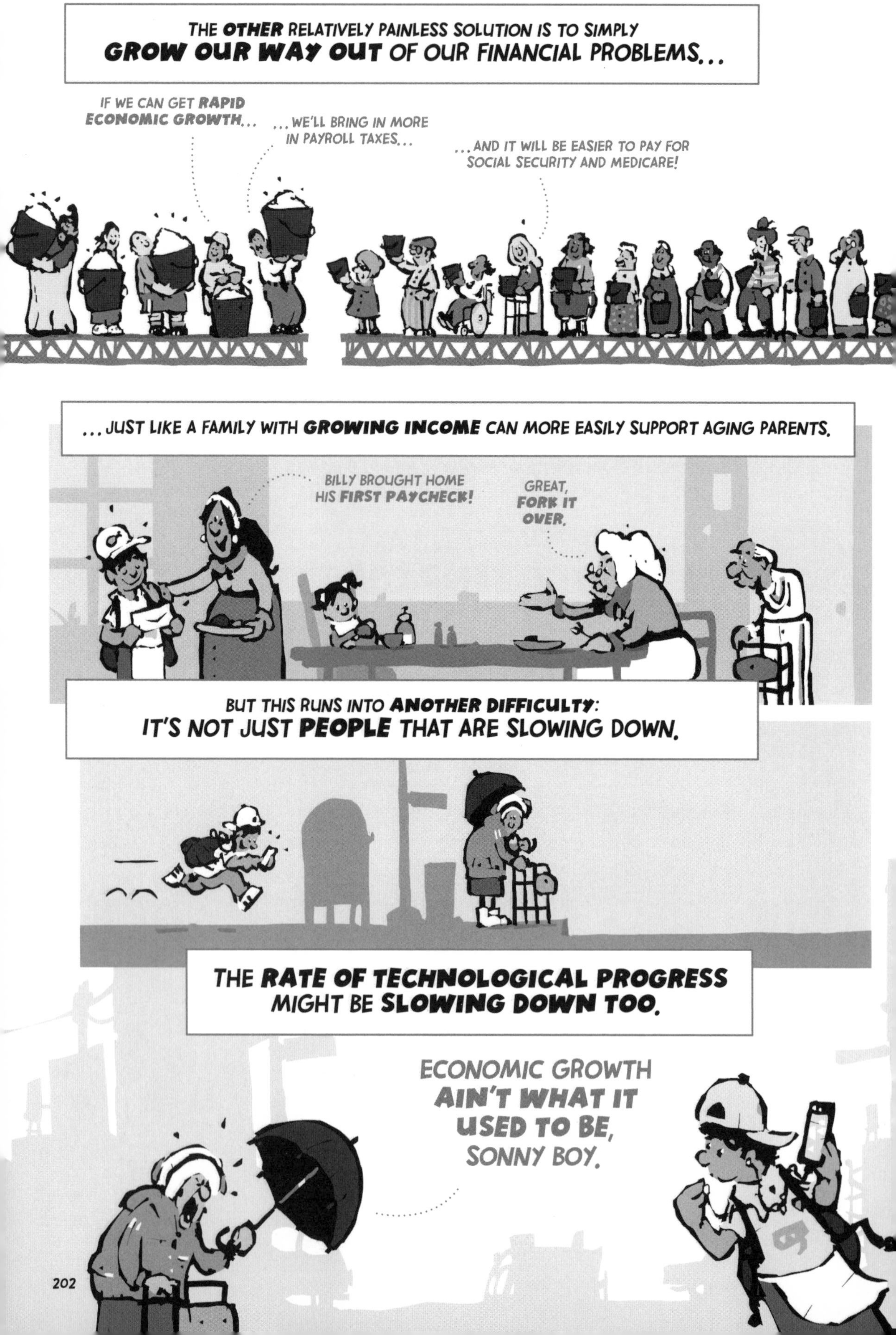
THE OTHER RELATIVELY PAINLESS SOLUTION IS TO SIMPLY GROW OUR WAY OUT OF OUR FINANCIAL PROBLEMS...
IF WE CAN GET RAPID ECONOMIC GROWTH...
...WE'LL BRING IN MORE IN PAYROLL TAXES...
...AND IT WILL BE EASIER TO PAY FOR SOCIAL SECURITY AND MEDICARE!
...JUST LIKE A FAMILY WITH GROWING INCOME CAN MORE EASILY SUPPORT AGING PARENTS.
BILLY BROUGHT HOME HIS FIRST PAYCHECK!
GREAT, FORK IT OVER.
BUT THIS RUNS INTO ANOTHER DIFFICULTY: IT'S NOT JUST PEOPLE THAT ARE SLOWING DOWN.
THE RATE OF TECHNOLOGICAL PROGRESS MIGHT BE SLOWING DOWN TOO.
ECONOMIC GROWTH AIN'T WHAT IT USED TO BE, SONNY BOY.

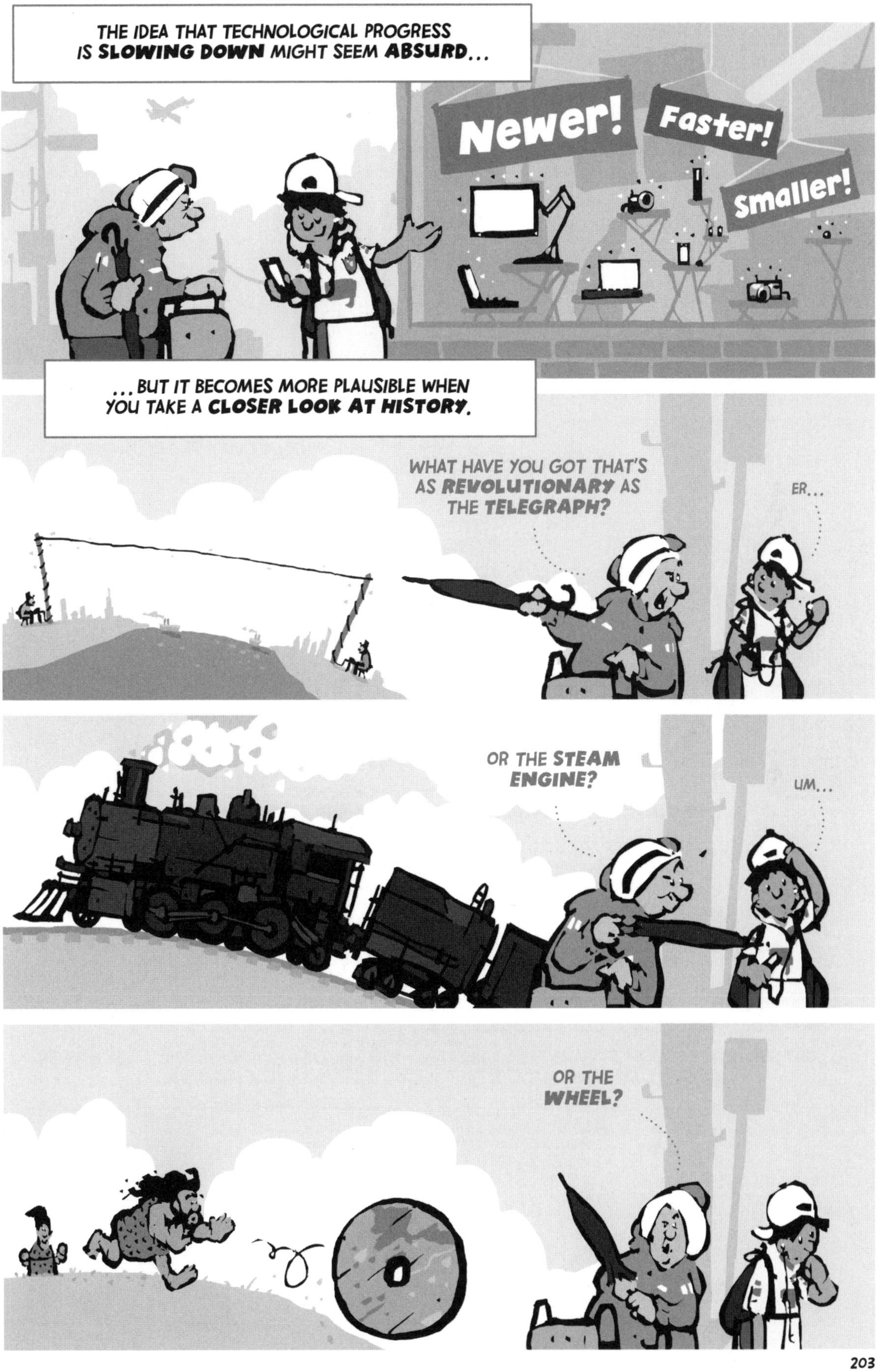
THE IDEA THAT TECHNOLOGICAL PROGRESS IS SLOWING DOWN MIGHT SEEM ABSURD...
Newer!
Faster!
Smaller!
...BUT IT BECOMES MORE PLAUSIBLE WHEN YOU TAKE A CLOSER LOOK AT HISTORY.
WHAT HAVE YOU GOT THAT'S AS REVOLUTIONARY AS THE TELEGRAPH?
ER...
OR THE STEAM ENGINE?
UM...
OR THE WHEEL?

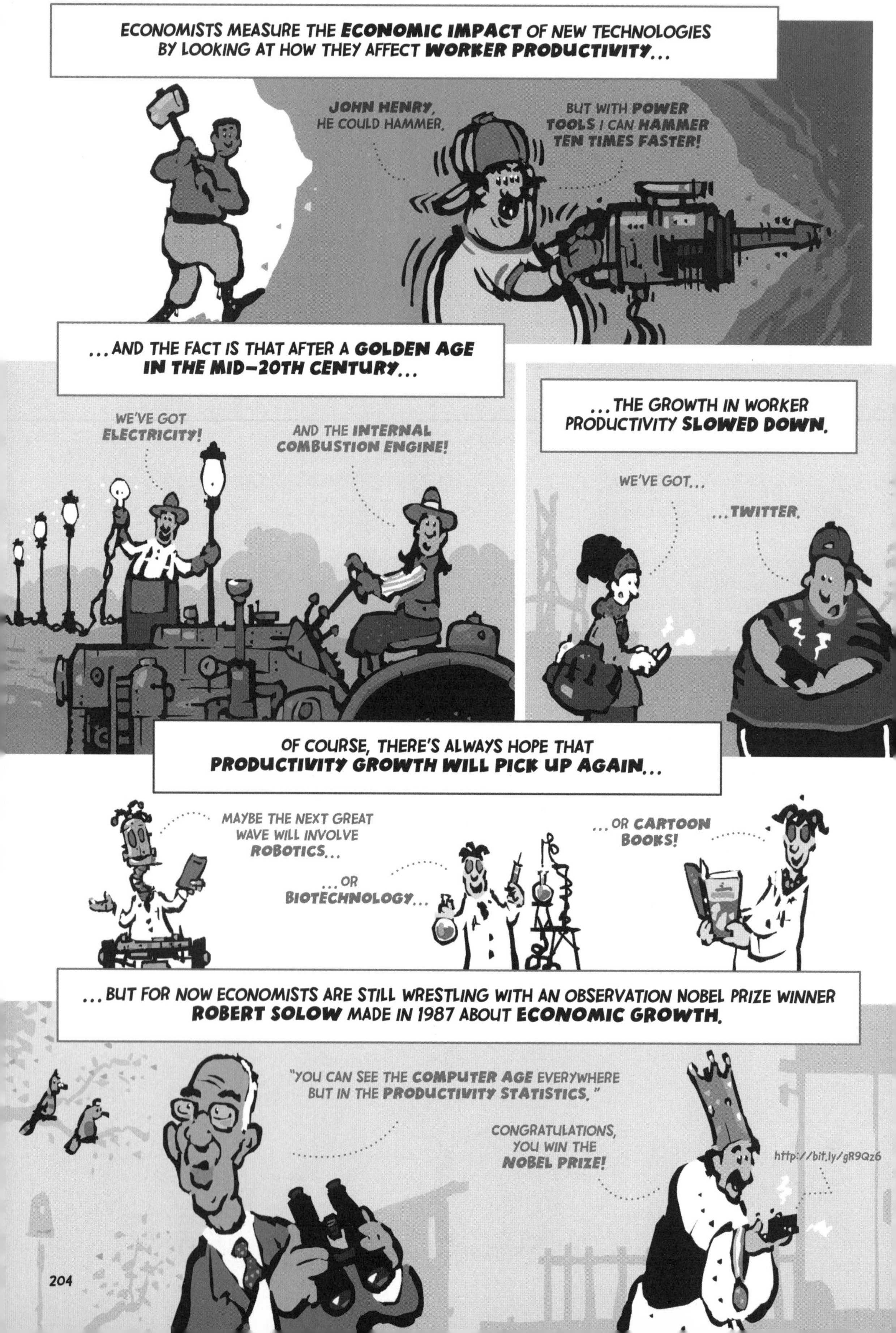

ECONOMISTS MEASURE THE **ECONOMIC IMPACT** OF NEW TECHNOLOGIES BY LOOKING AT HOW THEY AFFECT **WORKER PRODUCTIVITY**...
JOHN HENRY, HE COULD HAMMER.
BUT WITH **POWER TOOLS** I CAN **HAMMER TEN TIMES FASTER!**
...AND THE FACT IS THAT AFTER A **GOLDEN AGE IN THE MID-20TH CENTURY**...
WE'VE GOT **ELECTRICITY!**
AND THE **INTERNAL COMBUSTION ENGINE!**
...THE GROWTH IN WORKER PRODUCTIVITY **SLOWED DOWN.**
WE'VE GOT...
...**TWITTER.**
OF COURSE, THERE'S ALWAYS HOPE THAT **PRODUCTIVITY GROWTH WILL PICK UP AGAIN**...
MAYBE THE NEXT GREAT WAVE WILL INVOLVE **ROBOTICS**...
...OR **BIOTECHNOLOGY**...
...OR **CARTOON BOOKS!**
...BUT FOR NOW ECONOMISTS ARE STILL WRESTLING WITH AN OBSERVATION NOBEL PRIZE WINNER **ROBERT SOLOW** MADE IN 1987 ABOUT **ECONOMIC GROWTH.**
"YOU CAN SEE THE **COMPUTER AGE** EVERYWHERE BUT IN THE **PRODUCTIVITY STATISTICS.**"
CONGRATULATIONS, YOU WIN THE **NOBEL PRIZE!**
http://bit.ly/gR9Qz6

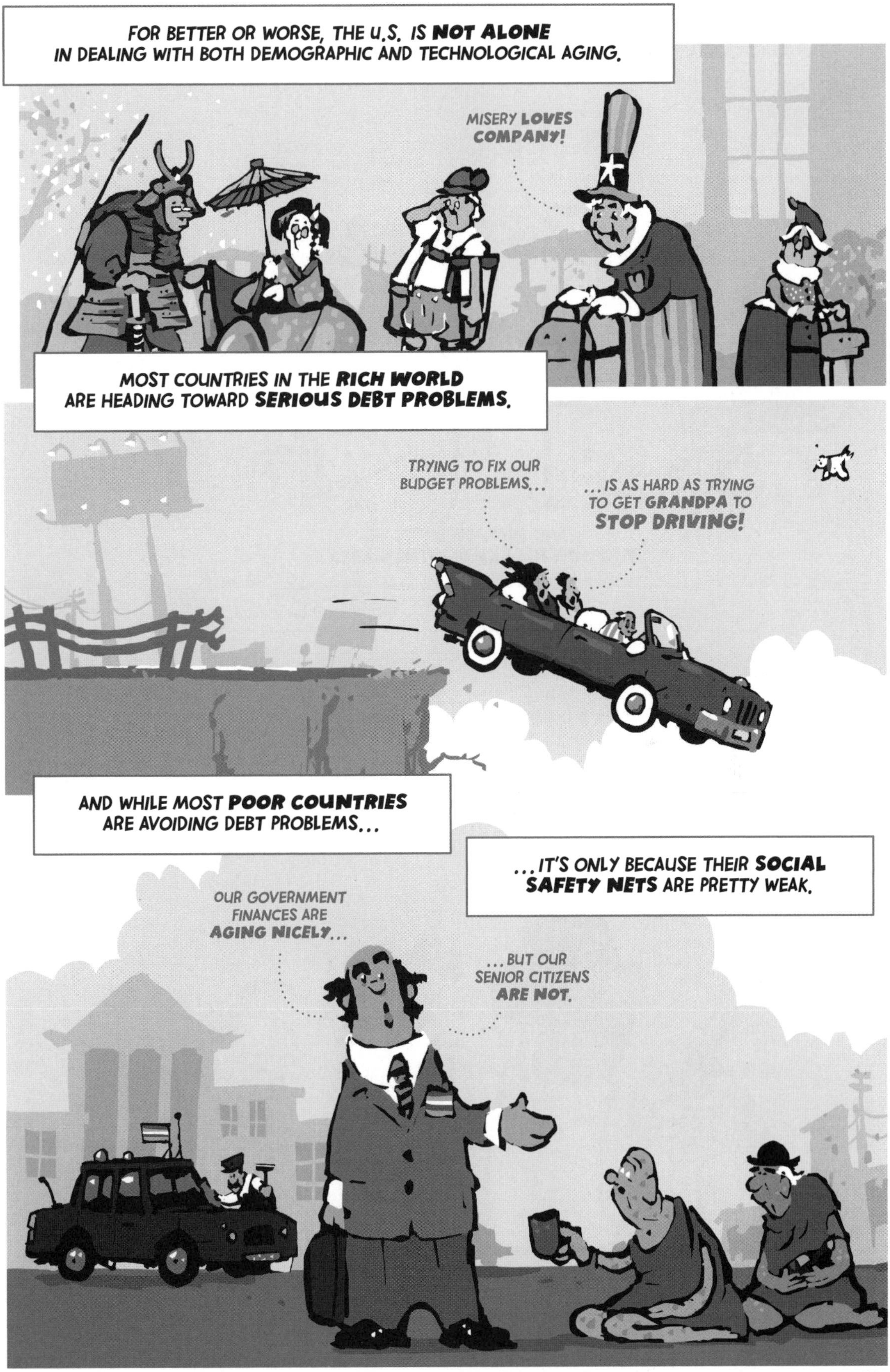
FOR BETTER OR WORSE, THE U.S. IS NOT ALONE IN DEALING WITH BOTH DEMOGRAPHIC AND TECHNOLOGICAL AGING.
MISERY LOVES COMPANY!
MOST COUNTRIES IN THE RICH WORLD ARE HEADING TOWARD SERIOUS DEBT PROBLEMS.
TRYING TO FIX OUR BUDGET PROBLEMS...
...IS AS HARD AS TRYING TO GET GRANDPA TO STOP DRIVING!
AND WHILE MOST POOR COUNTRIES ARE AVOIDING DEBT PROBLEMS...
...IT'S ONLY BECAUSE THEIR SOCIAL SAFETY NETS ARE PRETTY WEAK.
OUR GOVERNMENT FINANCES ARE AGING NICELY...
...BUT OUR SENIOR CITIZENS ARE NOT.

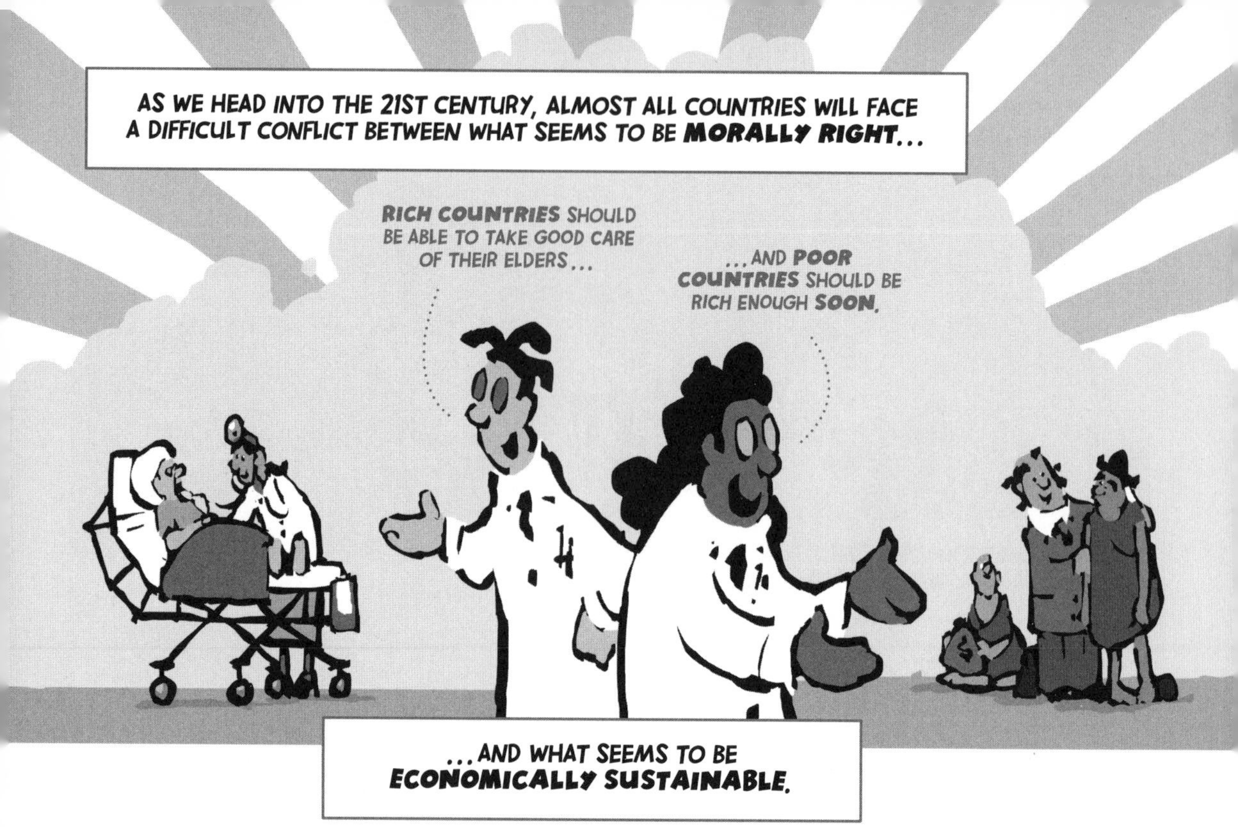
AS WE HEAD INTO THE 21ST CENTURY, ALMOST ALL COUNTRIES WILL FACE A DIFFICULT CONFLICT BETWEEN WHAT SEEMS TO BE **MORALLY RIGHT**...
RICH COUNTRIES SHOULD BE ABLE TO TAKE GOOD CARE OF THEIR ELDERS...
...AND **POOR COUNTRIES** SHOULD BE RICH ENOUGH **SOON**.
...AND WHAT SEEMS TO BE **ECONOMICALLY SUSTAINABLE**.

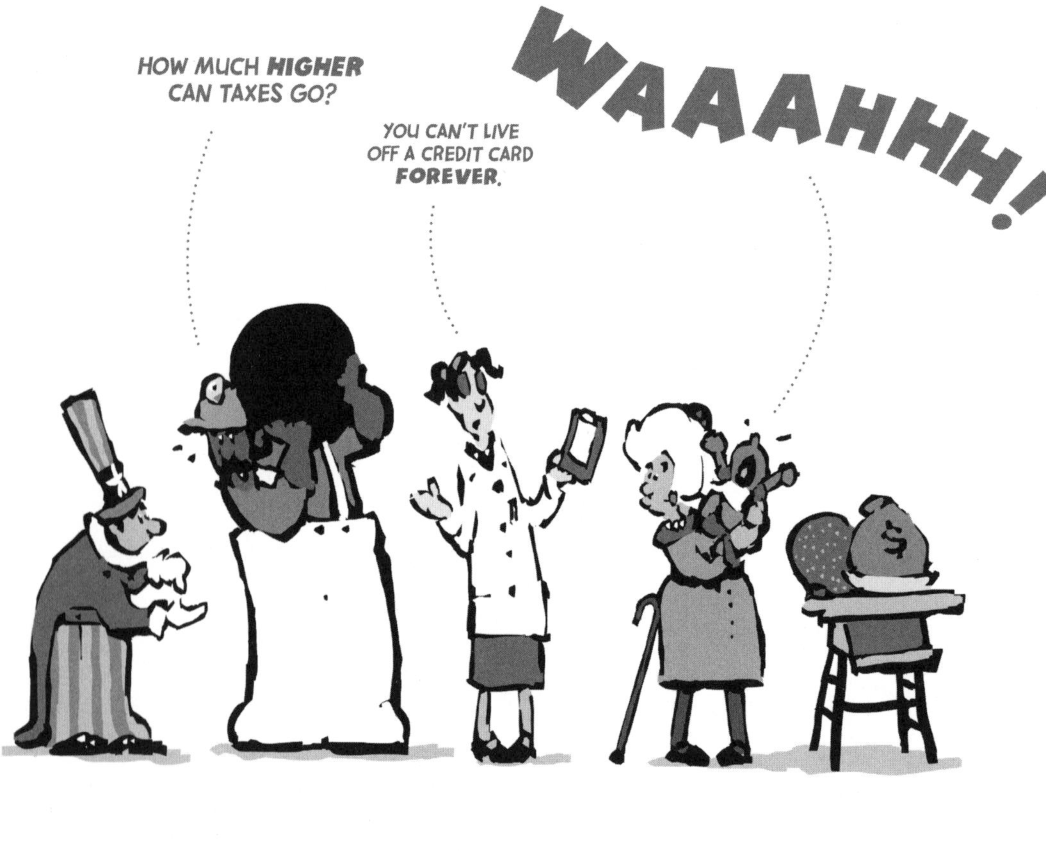
HOW MUCH **HIGHER** CAN TAXES GO?
YOU CAN'T LIVE OFF A CREDIT CARD **FOREVER**.
WAAAHHH!

CHAPTER 16
THE END

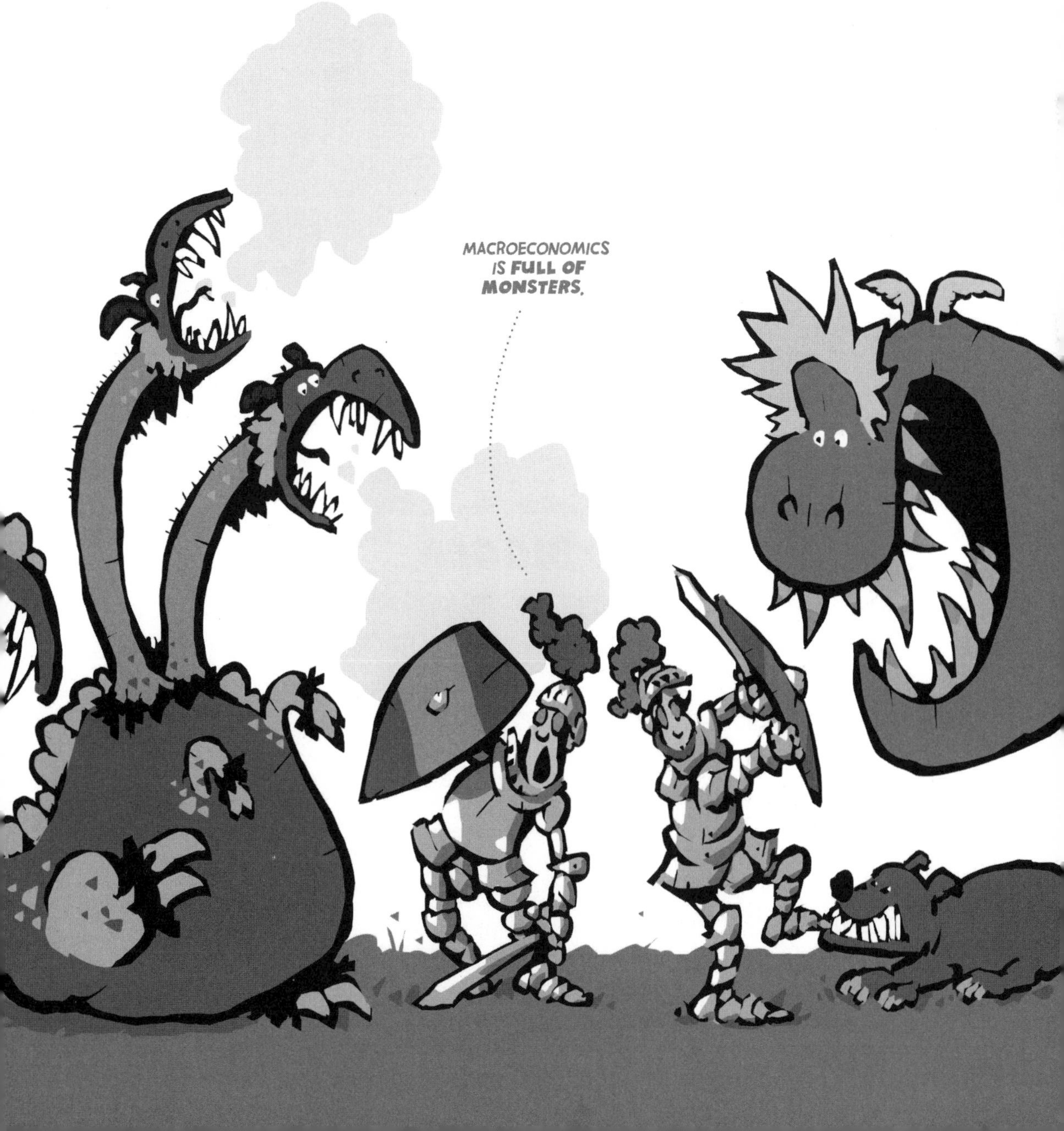
MACROECONOMICS IS FULL OF MONSTERS.

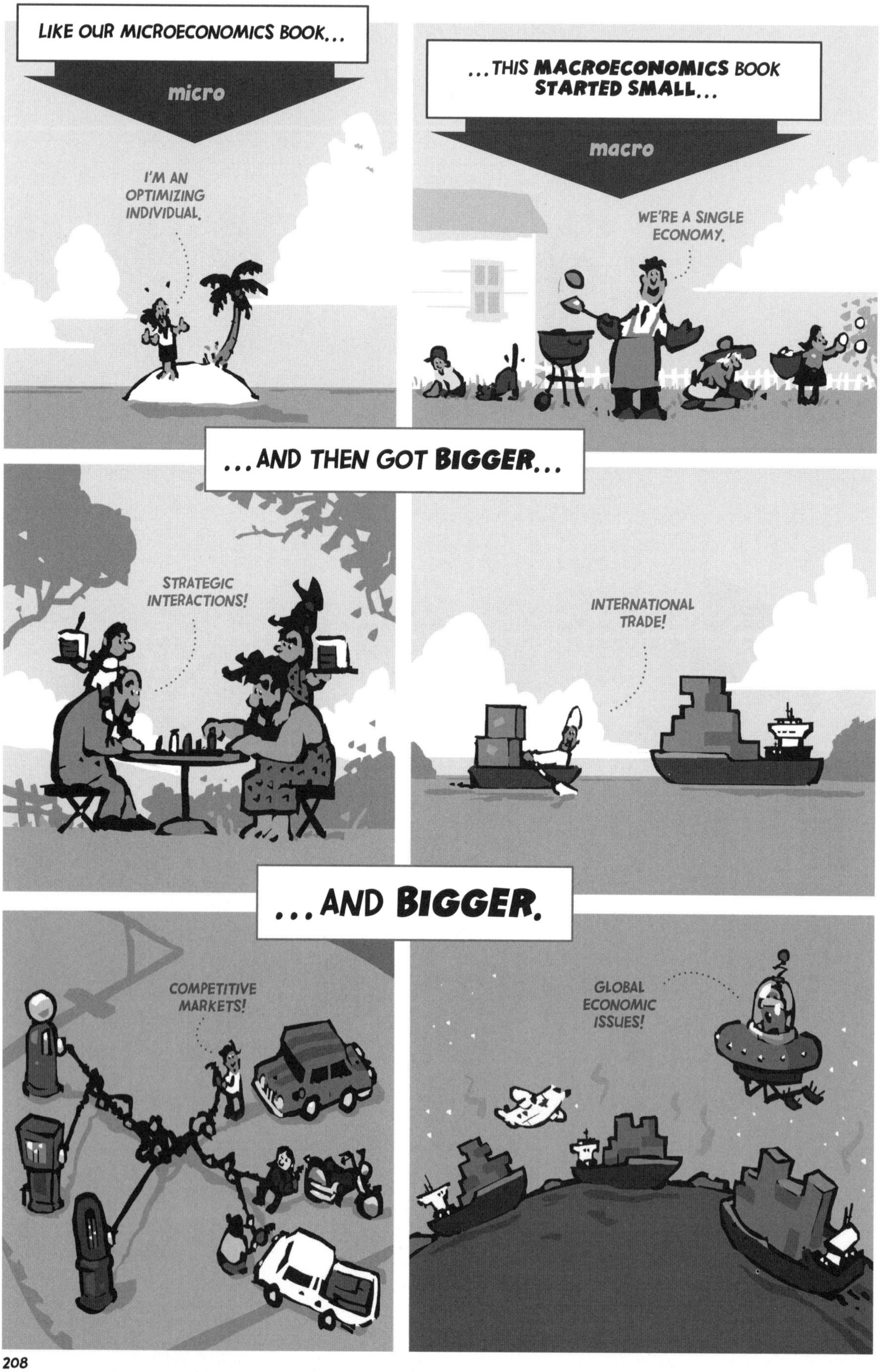
LIKE OUR MICROECONOMICS BOOK...
micro
I'M AN OPTIMIZING INDIVIDUAL.
...THIS MACROECONOMICS BOOK STARTED SMALL...
macro
WE'RE A SINGLE ECONOMY.
...AND THEN GOT BIGGER...
STRATEGIC INTERACTIONS!
INTERNATIONAL TRADE!
...AND BIGGER.
COMPETITIVE MARKETS!
GLOBAL ECONOMIC ISSUES!

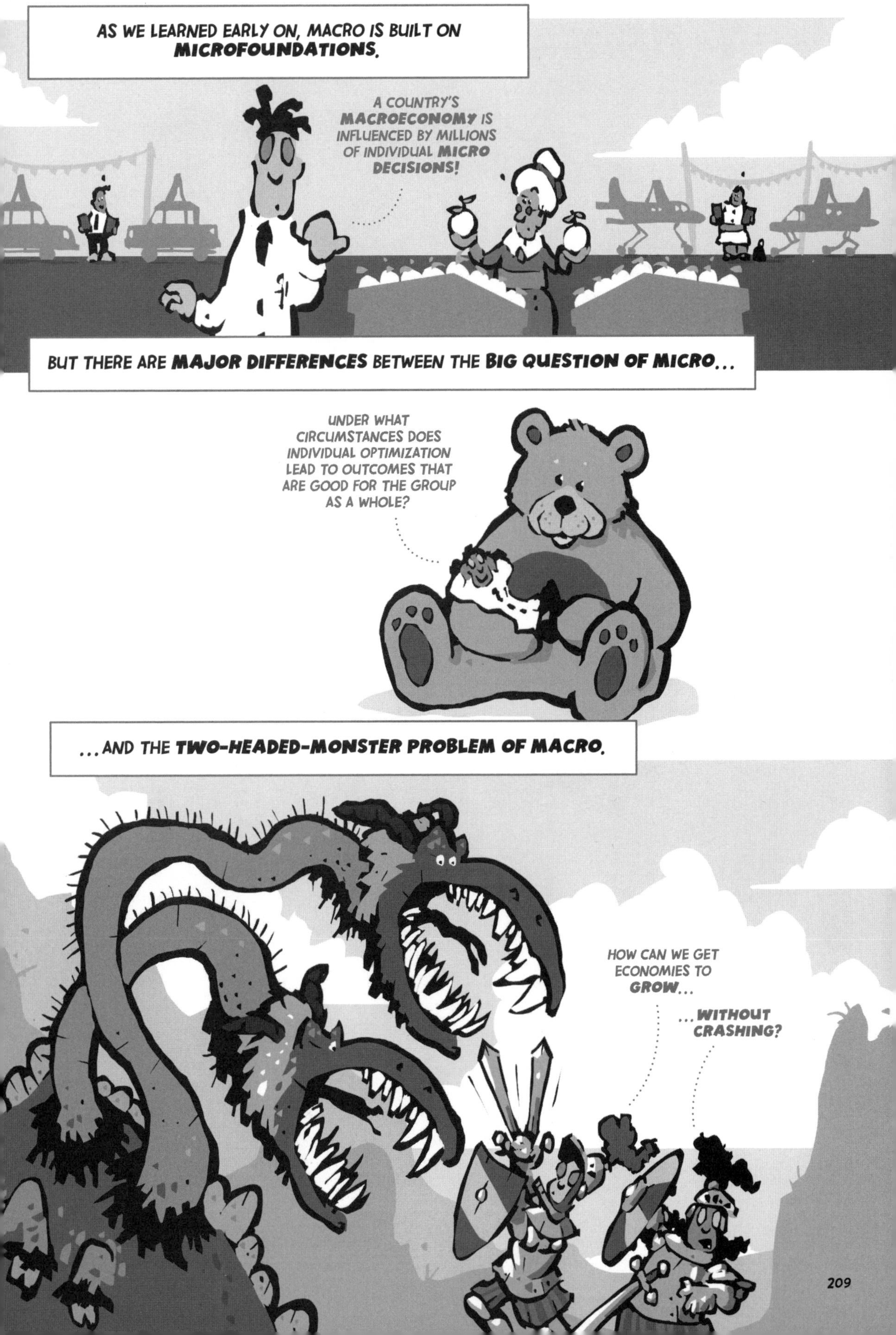
AS WE LEARNED EARLY ON, MACRO IS BUILT ON **MICROFOUNDATIONS.**
A COUNTRY'S **MACROECONOMY** IS INFLUENCED BY MILLIONS OF INDIVIDUAL **MICRO DECISIONS!**
BUT THERE ARE **MAJOR DIFFERENCES** BETWEEN THE **BIG QUESTION OF MICRO...**
UNDER WHAT CIRCUMSTANCES DOES INDIVIDUAL OPTIMIZATION LEAD TO OUTCOMES THAT ARE GOOD FOR THE GROUP AS A WHOLE?
...AND THE **TWO-HEADED-MONSTER PROBLEM OF MACRO.**
HOW CAN WE GET ECONOMIES TO **GROW...**
...**WITHOUT CRASHING?**

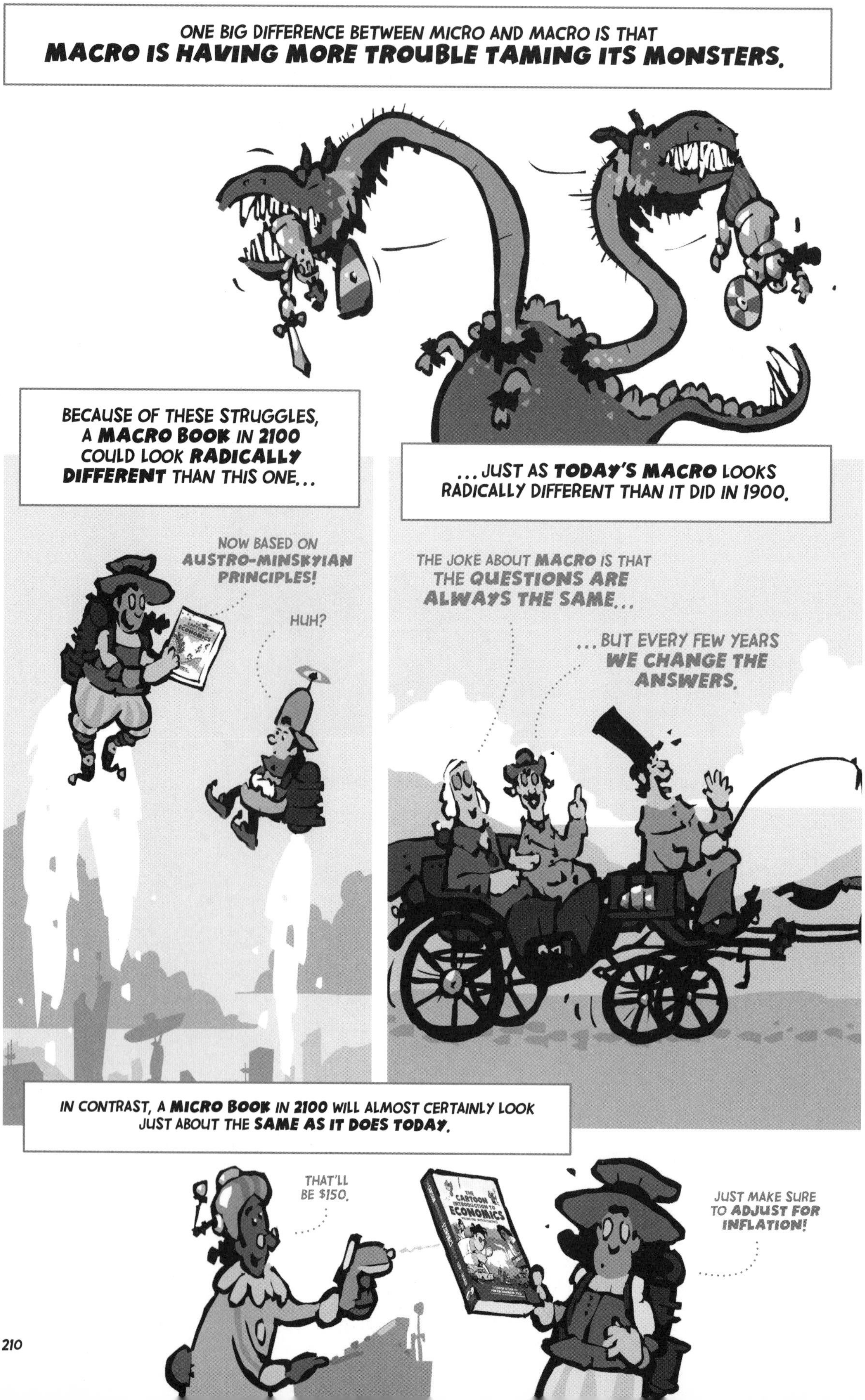
ONE BIG DIFFERENCE BETWEEN MICRO AND MACRO IS THAT
MACRO IS HAVING MORE TROUBLE TAMING ITS MONSTERS.
BECAUSE OF THESE STRUGGLES, A **MACRO BOOK** IN **2100** COULD LOOK **RADICALLY DIFFERENT** THAN THIS ONE...
NOW BASED ON **AUSTRO-MINSKYIAN PRINCIPLES!**
HUH?
...JUST AS **TODAY'S MACRO** LOOKS RADICALLY DIFFERENT THAN IT DID IN 1900.
THE JOKE ABOUT **MACRO** IS THAT THE **QUESTIONS ARE ALWAYS THE SAME...**
...BUT EVERY FEW YEARS **WE CHANGE THE ANSWERS.**
IN CONTRAST, A **MICRO BOOK** IN **2100** WILL ALMOST CERTAINLY LOOK JUST ABOUT THE **SAME AS IT DOES TODAY.**
THAT'LL BE $150.
THE CARTOON INTRODUCTION TO ECONOMICS
JUST MAKE SURE TO **ADJUST FOR INFLATION!**

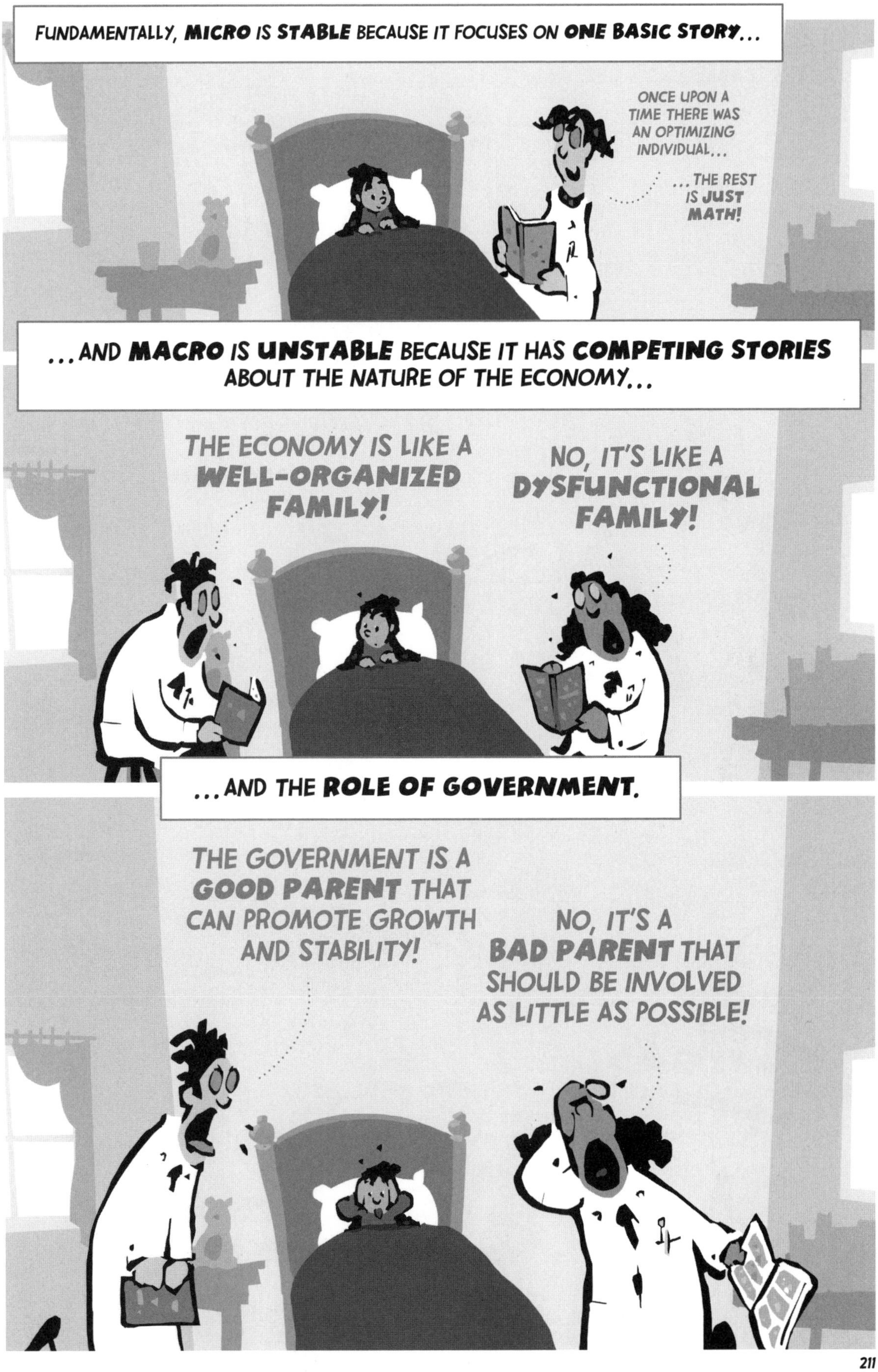
FUNDAMENTALLY, MICRO IS STABLE BECAUSE IT FOCUSES ON ONE BASIC STORY...
ONCE UPON A TIME THERE WAS AN OPTIMIZING INDIVIDUAL...
...THE REST IS JUST MATH!
...AND MACRO IS UNSTABLE BECAUSE IT HAS COMPETING STORIES ABOUT THE NATURE OF THE ECONOMY...
THE ECONOMY IS LIKE A WELL-ORGANIZED FAMILY!
NO, IT'S LIKE A DYSFUNCTIONAL FAMILY!
...AND THE ROLE OF GOVERNMENT.
THE GOVERNMENT IS A GOOD PARENT THAT CAN PROMOTE GROWTH AND STABILITY!
NO, IT'S A BAD PARENT THAT SHOULD BE INVOLVED AS LITTLE AS POSSIBLE!

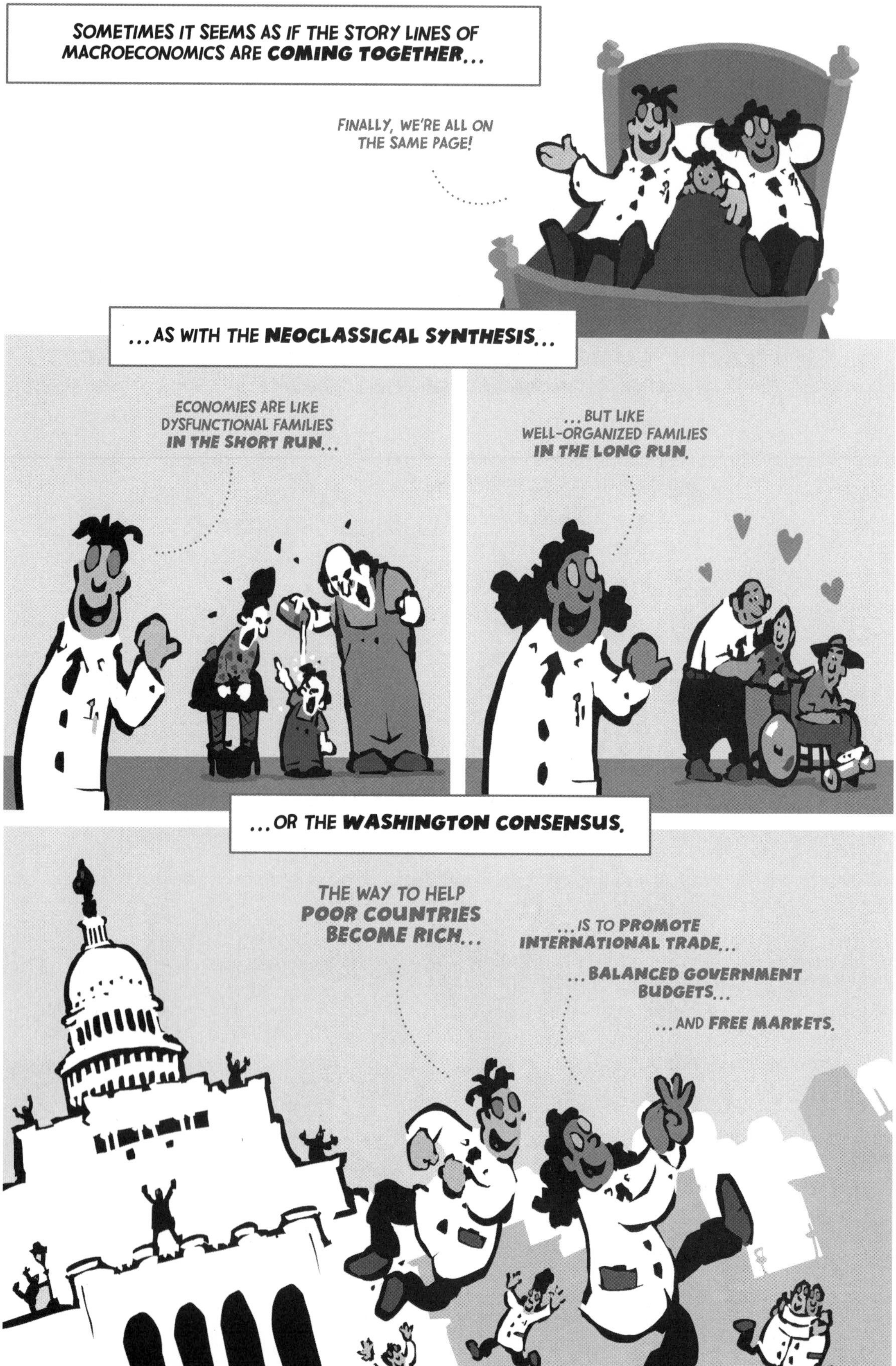
SOMETIMES IT SEEMS AS IF THE STORY LINES OF MACROECONOMICS ARE COMING TOGETHER...
FINALLY, WE'RE ALL ON THE SAME PAGE!
...AS WITH THE NEOCLASSICAL SYNTHESIS...
ECONOMIES ARE LIKE DYSFUNCTIONAL FAMILIES IN THE SHORT RUN...
...BUT LIKE WELL-ORGANIZED FAMILIES IN THE LONG RUN.
...OR THE WASHINGTON CONSENSUS.
THE WAY TO HELP POOR COUNTRIES BECOME RICH...
...IS TO PROMOTE INTERNATIONAL TRADE...
...BALANCED GOVERNMENT BUDGETS...
...AND FREE MARKETS.

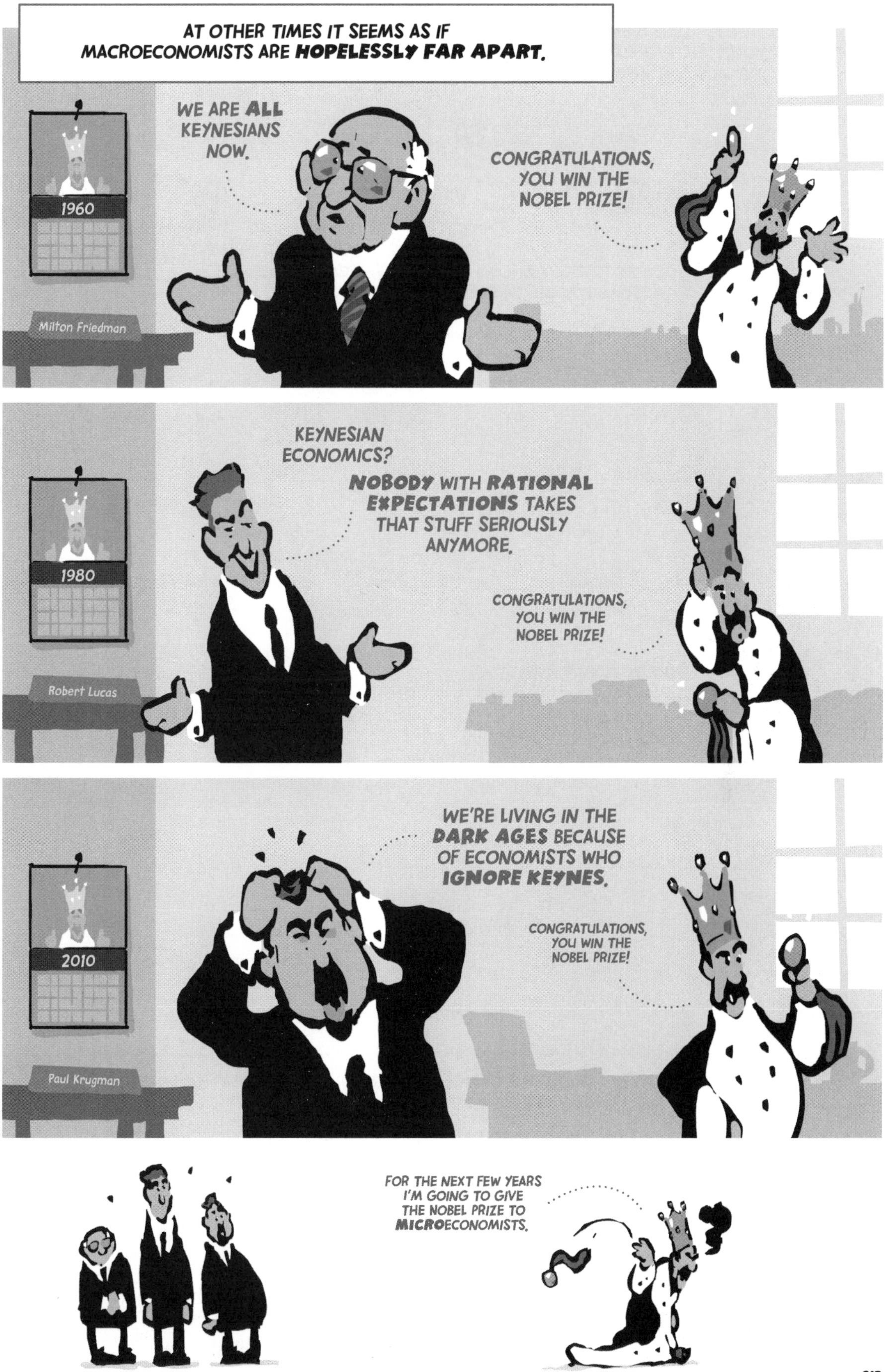
AT OTHER TIMES IT SEEMS AS IF MACROECONOMISTS ARE **HOPELESSLY FAR APART.**
1960
Milton Friedman
WE ARE **ALL** KEYNESIANS NOW.
CONGRATULATIONS, YOU WIN THE NOBEL PRIZE!
1980
Robert Lucas
KEYNESIAN ECONOMICS? **NOBODY** WITH **RATIONAL EXPECTATIONS** TAKES THAT STUFF SERIOUSLY ANYMORE.
CONGRATULATIONS, YOU WIN THE NOBEL PRIZE!
2010
Paul Krugman
WE'RE LIVING IN THE **DARK AGES** BECAUSE OF ECONOMISTS WHO **IGNORE KEYNES.**
CONGRATULATIONS, YOU WIN THE NOBEL PRIZE!
FOR THE NEXT FEW YEARS I'M GOING TO GIVE THE NOBEL PRIZE TO **MICRO**ECONOMISTS.

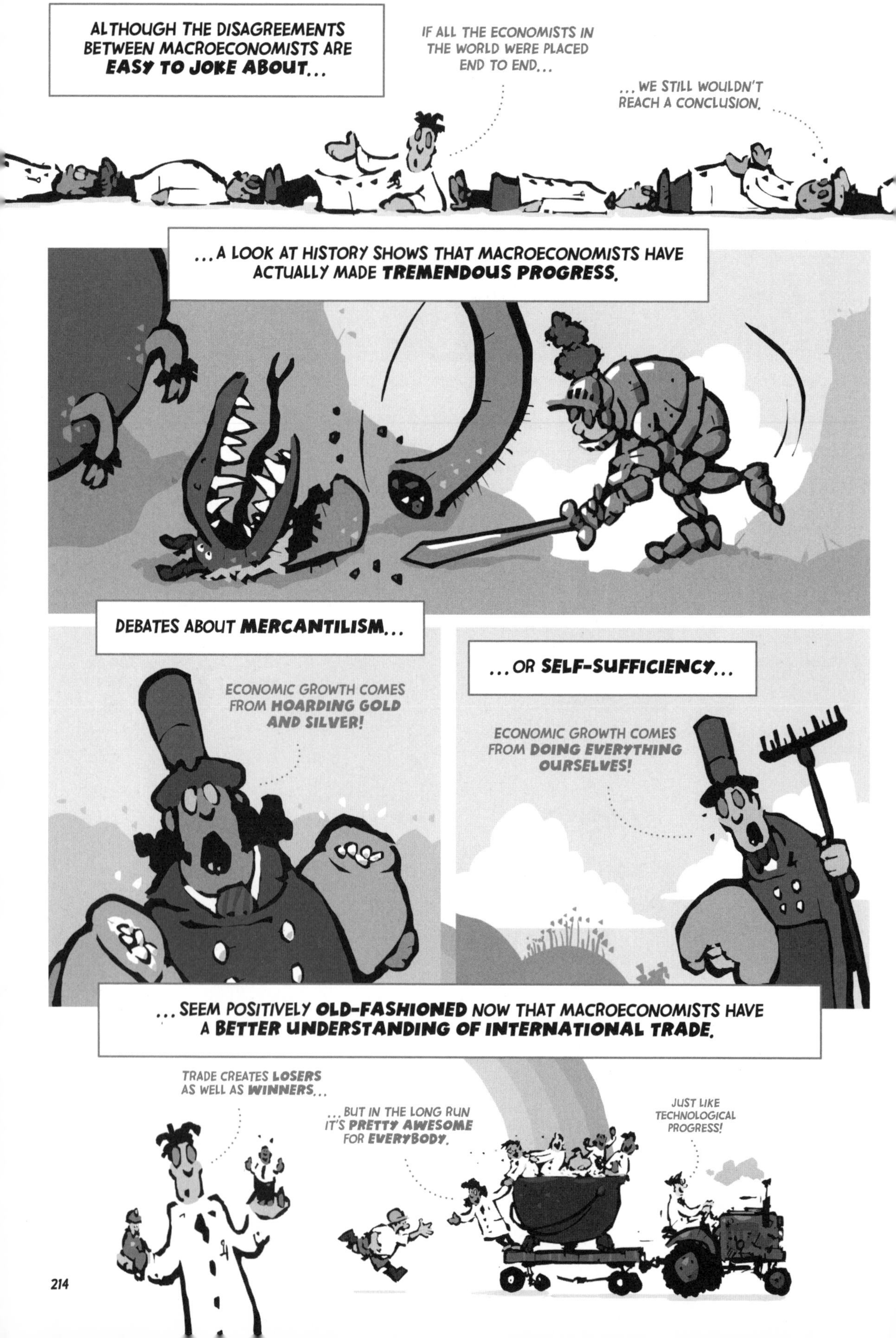
ALTHOUGH THE DISAGREEMENTS BETWEEN MACROECONOMISTS ARE **EASY TO JOKE ABOUT**...
IF ALL THE ECONOMISTS IN THE WORLD WERE PLACED END TO END...
...WE STILL WOULDN'T REACH A CONCLUSION.
...A LOOK AT HISTORY SHOWS THAT MACROECONOMISTS HAVE ACTUALLY MADE **TREMENDOUS PROGRESS.**
DEBATES ABOUT **MERCANTILISM**...
ECONOMIC GROWTH COMES FROM **HOARDING GOLD AND SILVER!**
...OR **SELF-SUFFICIENCY**...
ECONOMIC GROWTH COMES FROM **DOING EVERYTHING OURSELVES!**
...SEEM POSITIVELY **OLD-FASHIONED** NOW THAT MACROECONOMISTS HAVE A **BETTER UNDERSTANDING OF INTERNATIONAL TRADE.**
TRADE CREATES **LOSERS** AS WELL AS **WINNERS**...
...BUT IN THE LONG RUN IT'S **PRETTY AWESOME** FOR **EVERYBODY.**
JUST LIKE TECHNOLOGICAL PROGRESS!

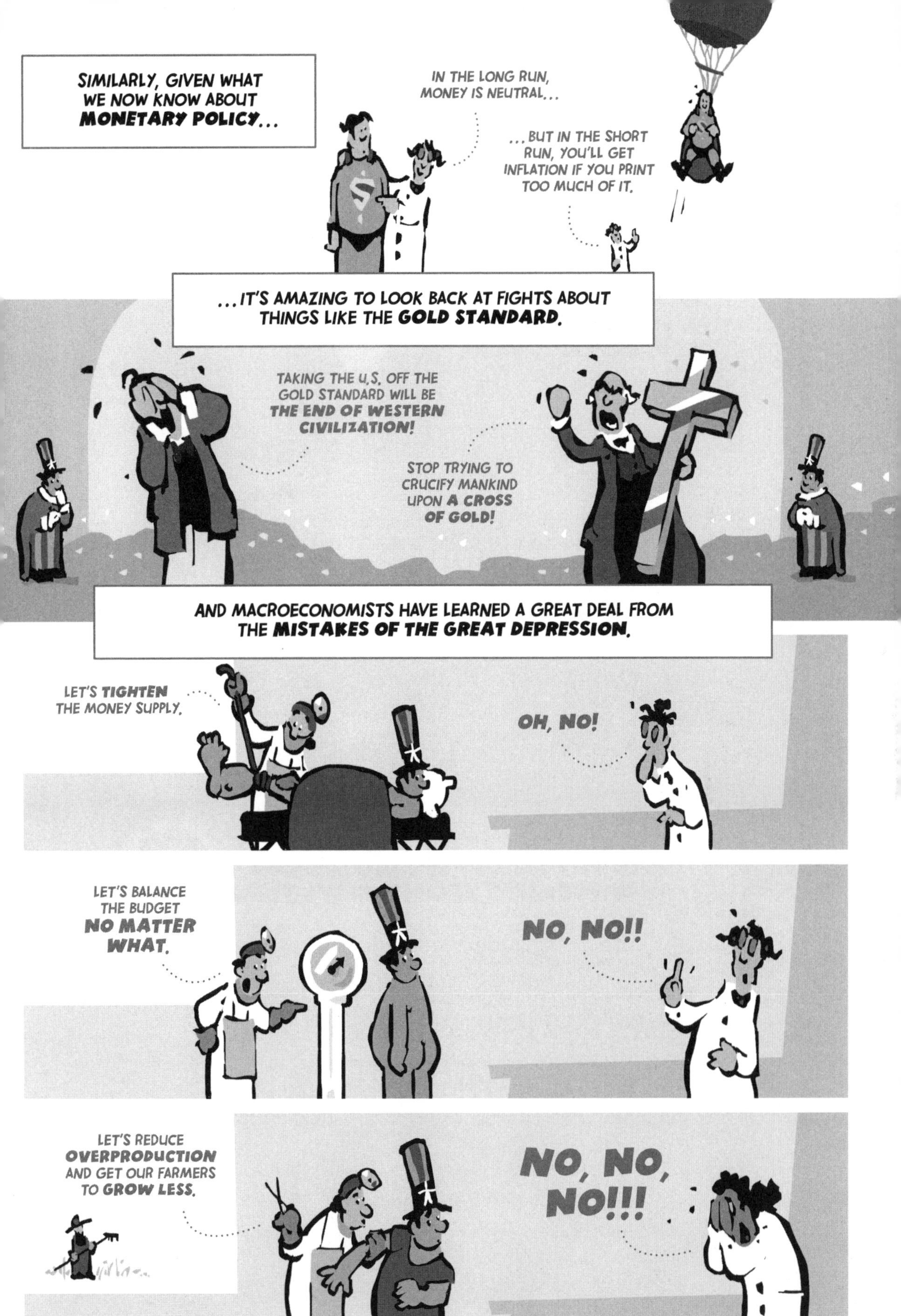
SIMILARLY, GIVEN WHAT WE NOW KNOW ABOUT **MONETARY POLICY...**
IN THE LONG RUN, MONEY IS NEUTRAL...
...BUT IN THE SHORT RUN, YOU'LL GET INFLATION IF YOU PRINT TOO MUCH OF IT.
...IT'S AMAZING TO LOOK BACK AT FIGHTS ABOUT THINGS LIKE THE **GOLD STANDARD.**
TAKING THE U.S. OFF THE GOLD STANDARD WILL BE **THE END OF WESTERN CIVILIZATION!**
STOP TRYING TO CRUCIFY MANKIND UPON **A CROSS OF GOLD!**
AND MACROECONOMISTS HAVE LEARNED A GREAT DEAL FROM THE **MISTAKES OF THE GREAT DEPRESSION.**
LET'S **TIGHTEN** THE MONEY SUPPLY.
OH, NO!
LET'S BALANCE THE BUDGET **NO MATTER WHAT.**
NO, NO!!
LET'S REDUCE **OVERPRODUCTION** AND GET OUR FARMERS TO **GROW LESS.**
NO, NO, NO!!!

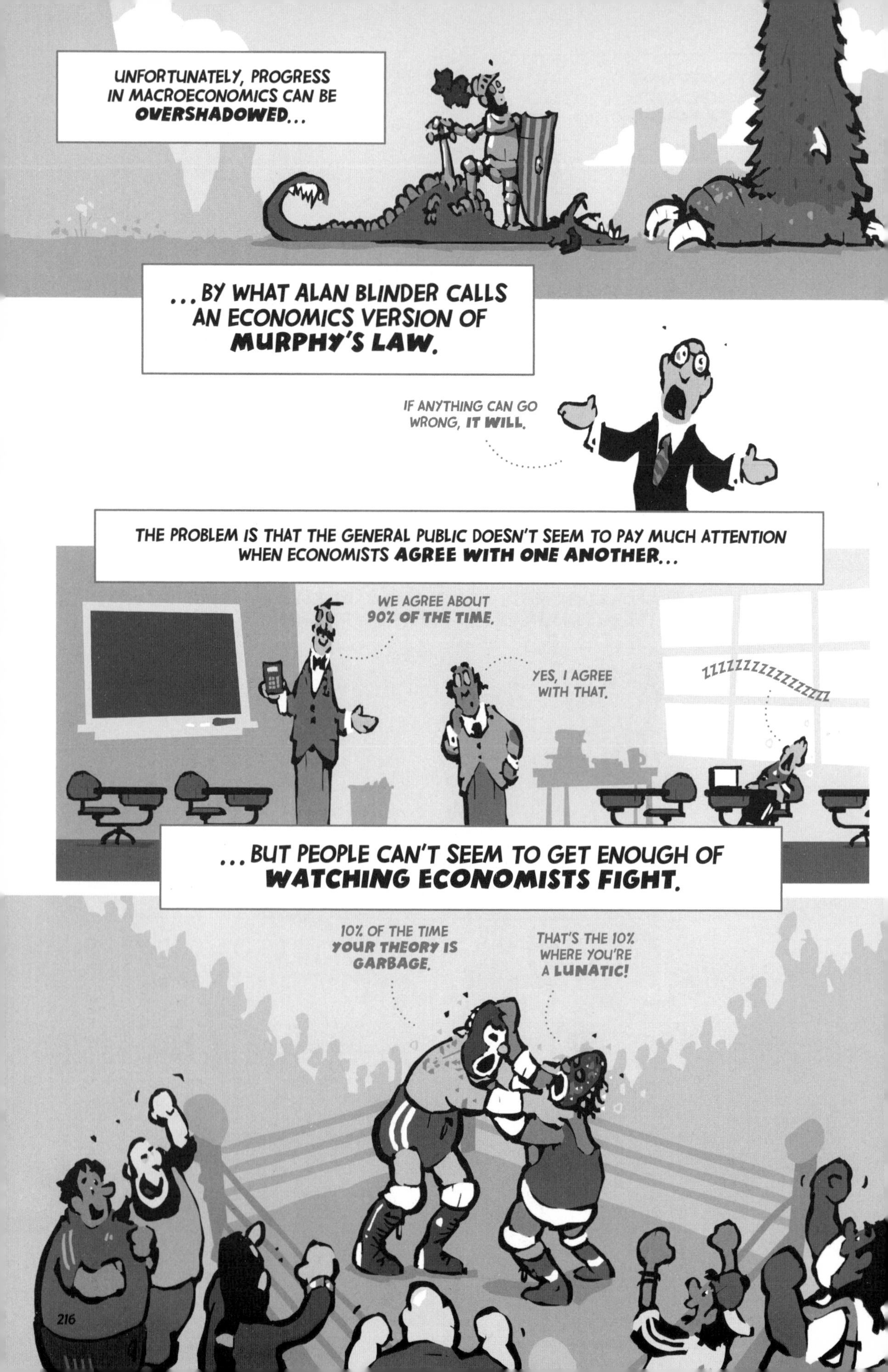
UNFORTUNATELY, PROGRESS IN MACROECONOMICS CAN BE **OVERSHADOWED...**
...BY WHAT ALAN BLINDER CALLS AN ECONOMICS VERSION OF **MURPHY'S LAW.**
IF ANYTHING CAN GO WRONG, **IT WILL.**
THE PROBLEM IS THAT THE GENERAL PUBLIC DOESN'T SEEM TO PAY MUCH ATTENTION WHEN ECONOMISTS **AGREE WITH ONE ANOTHER...**
WE AGREE ABOUT **90% OF THE TIME.**
YES, I AGREE WITH THAT.
ZZZZZZZZZZZZZZZZZZ
...BUT PEOPLE CAN'T SEEM TO GET ENOUGH OF **WATCHING ECONOMISTS FIGHT.**
10% OF THE TIME **YOUR THEORY IS GARBAGE.**
THAT'S THE 10% WHERE YOU'RE A **LUNATIC!**

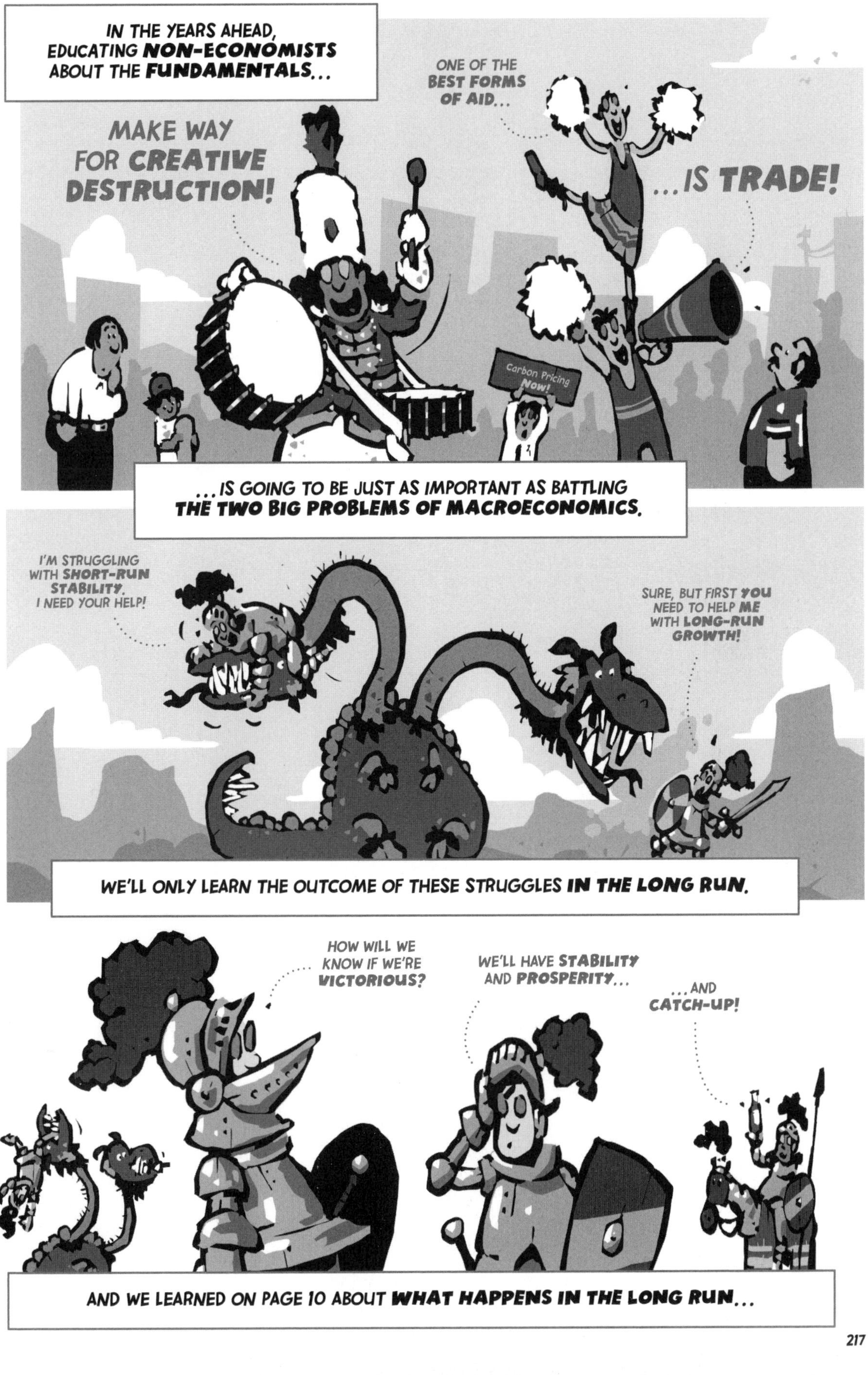
IN THE YEARS AHEAD, EDUCATING NON-ECONOMISTS ABOUT THE FUNDAMENTALS...
MAKE WAY FOR CREATIVE DESTRUCTION!
ONE OF THE BEST FORMS OF AID...
...IS TRADE!
Carbon Pricing Now!
...IS GOING TO BE JUST AS IMPORTANT AS BATTLING THE TWO BIG PROBLEMS OF MACROECONOMICS.
I'M STRUGGLING WITH SHORT-RUN STABILITY. I NEED YOUR HELP!
SURE, BUT FIRST YOU NEED TO HELP ME WITH LONG-RUN GROWTH!
WE'LL ONLY LEARN THE OUTCOME OF THESE STRUGGLES IN THE LONG RUN.
HOW WILL WE KNOW IF WE'RE VICTORIOUS?
WE'LL HAVE STABILITY AND PROSPERITY...
...AND CATCH-UP!
AND WE LEARNED ON PAGE 10 ABOUT WHAT HAPPENS IN THE LONG RUN...

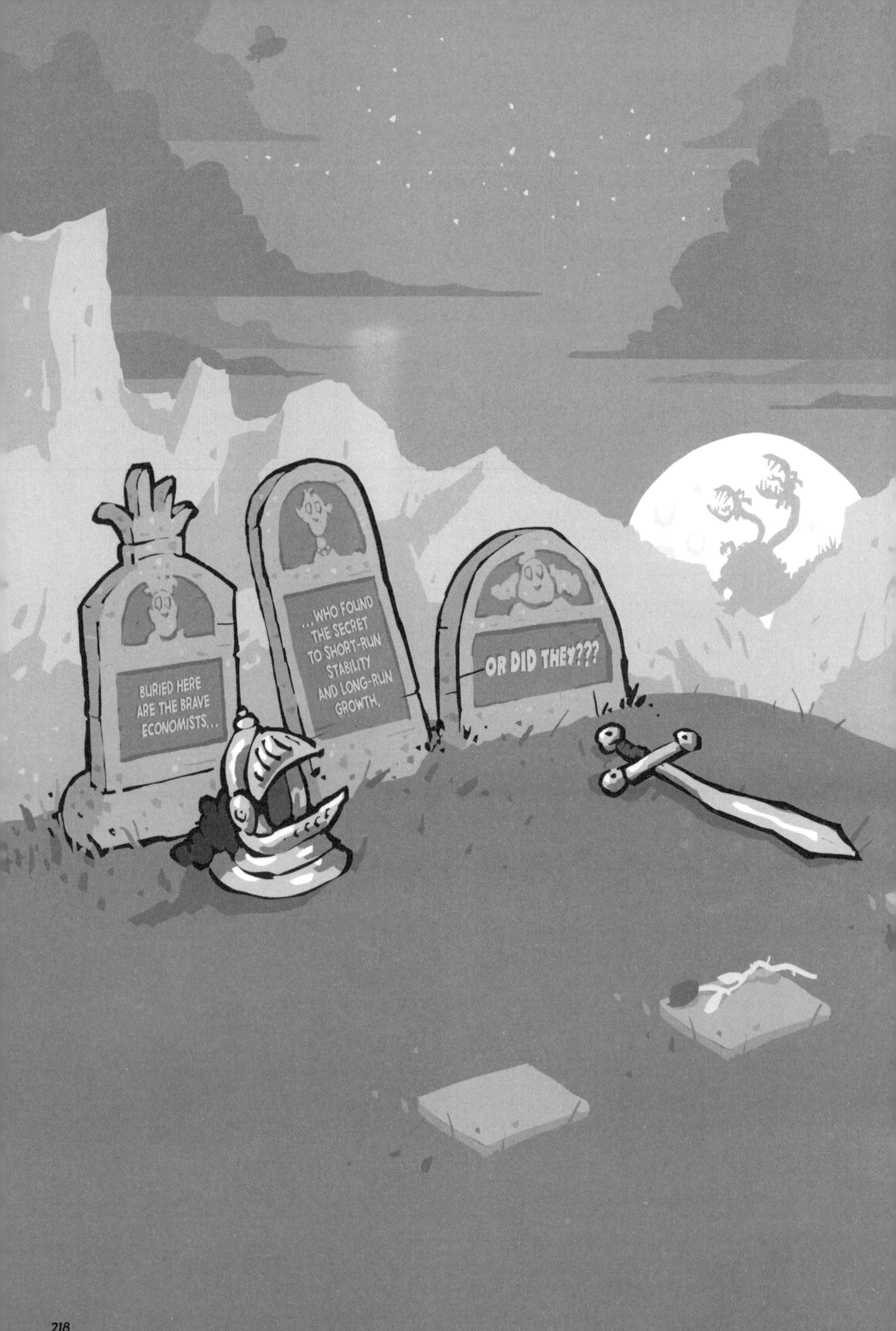
BURIED HERE ARE THE BRAVE ECONOMISTS...
...WHO FOUND THE SECRET TO SHORT-RUN STABILITY AND LONG-RUN GROWTH.
OR DID THEY???

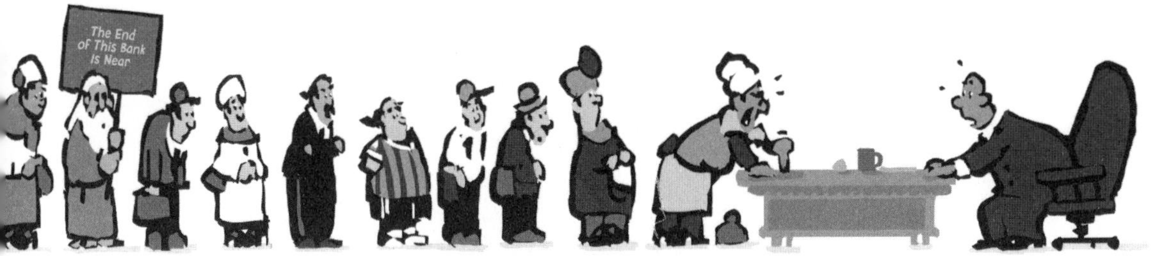
The End
of This Bank
Is Near

GLOSSARY

A

AUTOMATIC STABILIZERS
TAXES OR SPENDING PROGRAMS—SUCH AS UNEMPLOYMENT BENEFITS, WHICH RISE DURING RECESSIONS AND FALL DURING EXPANSIONS—THAT NATURALLY ACT TO COUNTER THE BUSINESS CYCLE: 77

B

BANK RUN
A PANIC IN WHICH DEPOSITORS ALL TRY TO WITHDRAW MONEY FROM A BANK AT THE SAME TIME: 164

BOND
IN RETURN FOR LENDING MONEY TO A COMPANY OR GOVERNMENT, THE LENDER GETS A BOND, WHICH OBLIGATES THE BORROWER TO PAY BACK THE LOAN (PLUS INTEREST) AFTER A SPECIFIED PERIOD OF TIME: 40–43

BUDGET DEFICIT / SURPLUS
A GOVERNMENT RUNS A **BUDGET DEFICIT** IN A GIVEN YEAR IF REVENUES (MONEY IN) ARE LESS THAN EXPENDITURES (MONEY OUT), A **BUDGET SURPLUS** IF REVENUES ARE GREATER THAN EXPENDITURES, AND A **BALANCED BUDGET** IF THE TWO ARE EQUAL; THE ACCUMULATION OF ALL ANNUAL **NATIONAL DEFICITS** IS THE **NATIONAL DEBT**: 79, 149, 160–161

BUSINESS CYCLE
SHORT-TERM ECONOMIC FLUCTUATIONS: 11, 113, 153–166
AND CYCLICAL UNEMPLOYMENT: 26

C

CARBON PRICING
A CARBON TAX OR CAP-AND-TRADE POLICY THAT SEEKS TO REDUCE CARBON EMISSIONS BY MAKING POLLUTING EXPENSIVE: 191–192, 217

COMPARATIVE ADVANTAGE
THE IDEA THAT TWO INDIVIDUALS (OR TWO COUNTRIES) CAN BOTH GAIN FROM TRADE EVEN IF ONE OF THEM IS BETTER THAN THE OTHER AT EVERYTHING: 101, 136

CAPITAL
MACHINERY, HOUSES, OR OTHER ASSETS: 91
CAPITAL INCOME: 62

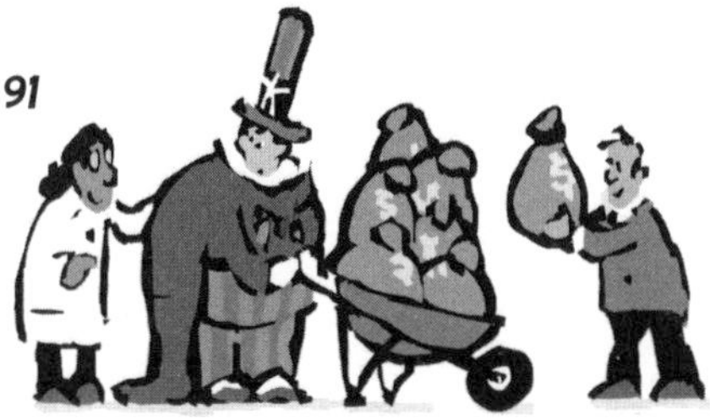

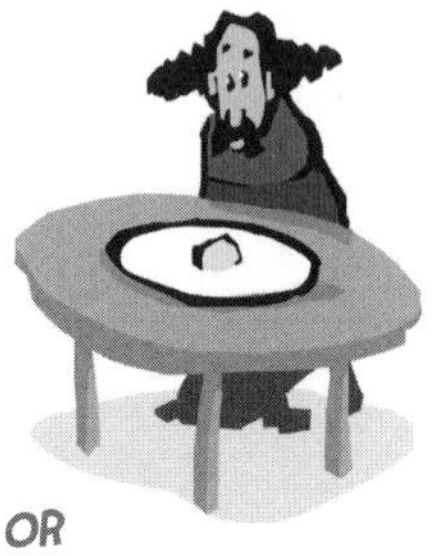

CATCH-UP
THE IDEA—ALSO CALLED **CONVERGENCE**—THAT POOR COUNTRIES WILL GROW FASTER THAN RICH COUNTRIES: 169–171

CENTRAL BANK
A GOVERNMENT AGENCY (SUCH AS THE EUROPEAN CENTRAL BANK OR THE FED) THAT IS IN CHARGE OF THE MONEY SUPPLY: 37

CLASSICAL ECONOMICS
A SCHOOL OF THOUGHT THAT VIEWS THE ECONOMY AS A WELL-ORGANIZED FAMILY AND THEREFORE SEES LITTLE NEED FOR GOVERNMENT INTERVENTION: 9
- CONTRAST WITH KEYNESIAN ECONOMICS: 12–13, 18–19, 22, 27
- AND THE LABOR MARKET: 19–21
- AND MONEY NEUTRALITY: 35
- AND TRADE: 99–110
- AND NEOCLASSICAL SYNTHESIS: 212

CLIMATE CHANGE / GLOBAL WARMING
AN INCREASE IN GLOBAL AVERAGE TEMPERATURE, ESPECIALLY AS A RESULT OF BURNING FOSSIL FUELS AND OTHER HUMAN ACTIVITIES: 115, 181, 186–192

CONDITIONAL AID
FOREIGN AID THAT IS PROVIDED WITH STRINGS ATTACHED: 133

CONSUMER PRICE INDEX (CPI)
A WAY TO MEASURE INFLATION IN CONSUMER PRICES: 46–47, 51
- COMPARED TO GDP DEFLATOR: 222

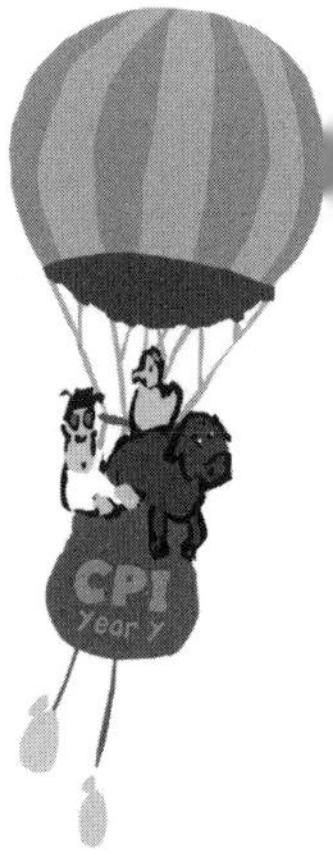
CPI
Year Y

THE CPI COMPARES PRICES IN YEARS X AND Y BY TRACKING THE COST OF A **REPRESENTATIVE BUNDLE** OF CONSUMER GOODS AND SERVICES. HERE'S AN EXAMPLE:

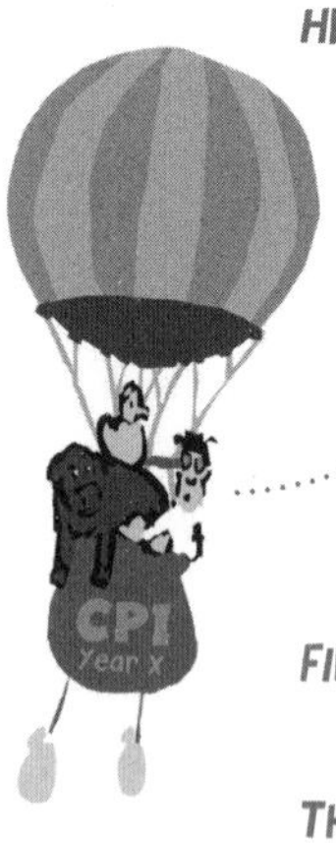
LET'S IMAGINE AN ECONOMY WHERE THERE ARE ONLY TWO CONSUMER GOODS, CHICKEN AND BEEF.
CPI
Year X

	PRICE OF CHICKEN	POUNDS OF CHICKEN IN BUNDLE	PRICE OF BEEF	POUNDS OF BEEF IN BUNDLE
YEAR X	$1/POUND	200	$3/POUND	100
YEAR Y	$2/POUND	200	$4/POUND	100

FIRST WE CALCULATE **THE BUNDLE'S PRICE IN YEAR X:**

$$(\$1 \times 200) + (\$3 \times 100) = \$500.$$

THEN WE CALCULATE **THE BUNDLE'S PRICE IN YEAR Y**:

$$(\$2 \times 200) + (\$4 \times 100) = \$800.$$

FINALLY, WE CONCLUDE THAT INFLATION (AS MEASURED BY THE CPI) WAS **60%** BETWEEN YEAR X AND YEAR Y BY COMPARING THE TWO:

$$\frac{\$800}{\$500} - 1 = 0.60$$

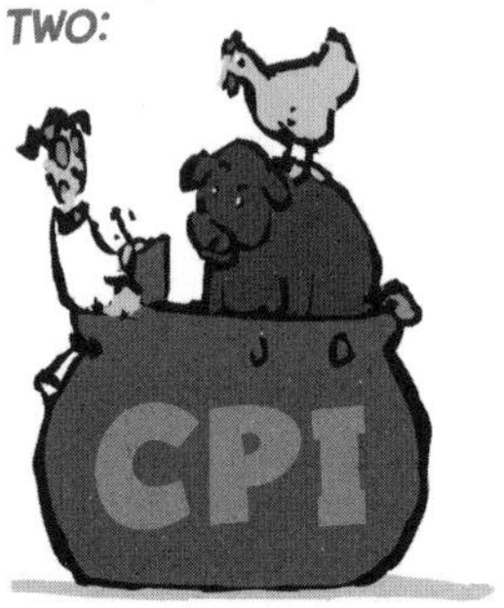
CPI

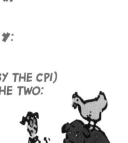

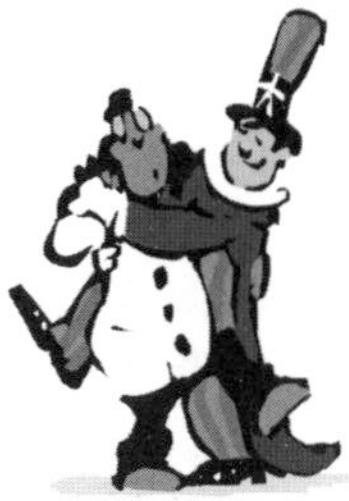

CREATIVE DESTRUCTION
ECONOMIC DEVELOPMENTS THAT BOTH CREATE AND DESTROY JOBS: 20–21, 109, 217

CROWDING OUT
THE IDEA THAT GOVERNMENT ACTIVITY NEGATIVELY AFFECTS BUSINESS: FOR EXAMPLE, THAT BUDGET DEFICITS MAKE IT HARDER FOR BUSINESSES TO BORROW MONEY: 83

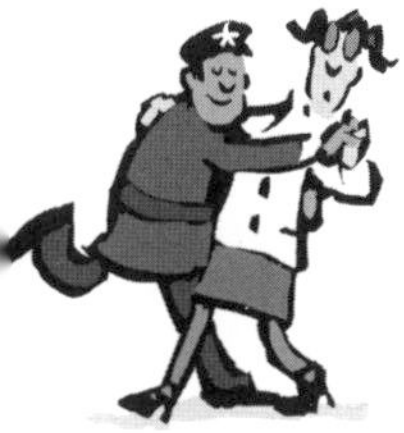

CURRENCY
THE MONEY USED IN A COUNTRY: 139–150
- CURRENCY MANIPULATION: 108–109
- STRONG AND WEAK CURRENCIES: 142–143

CURRENCY UNION
THE USE OF THE SAME CURRENCY IN MULTIPLE COUNTRIES: 146–150

D

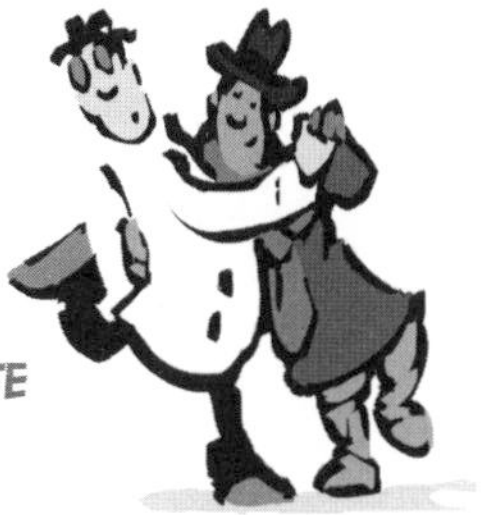

DEFICIT
SEE **BUDGET DEFICIT**

DEFLATION
A GENERAL DECREASE IN PRICES OVER TIME (THE OPPOSITE OF INFLATION): 55–56

DEPRESSION
A VERY BAD RECESSION: 18, 154

E

EFFICIENCY WAGES
THE THEORY THAT EMPLOYERS PAY HIGH WAGES IN ORDER TO AVOID TURNOVER AND MOTIVATE EMPLOYEES: 24

EXCHANGE RATE
A WAY TO COMPARE THE VALUE OF DIFFERENT CURRENCIES: 140–150

MARKET EXCHANGE RATES ARE EITHER **FLOATING** (IF THEY'RE BASED ON SUPPLY AND DEMAND) OR **FIXED** (IF THEY'RE PEGGED AT A SET RATE BY ONE OR MORE GOVERNMENTS). BECAUSE SOME GOODS ARE NOT TRADED INTERNATIONALLY, COMPARISONS OF LIVING STANDARDS IN DIFFERENT COUNTRIES (AS ON PAGE 72) ARE USUALLY MADE USING **PURCHASING POWER PARITY (PPP)** EXCHANGE RATES, WHICH ARE BASED ON THE COST OF LIVING IN DIFFERENT COUNTRIES.

F

FEDERAL RESERVE ("THE FED")
THE CENTRAL BANK OF THE UNITED STATES: 37
- AND GREAT DEPRESSION / GREAT RECESSION: 158–159

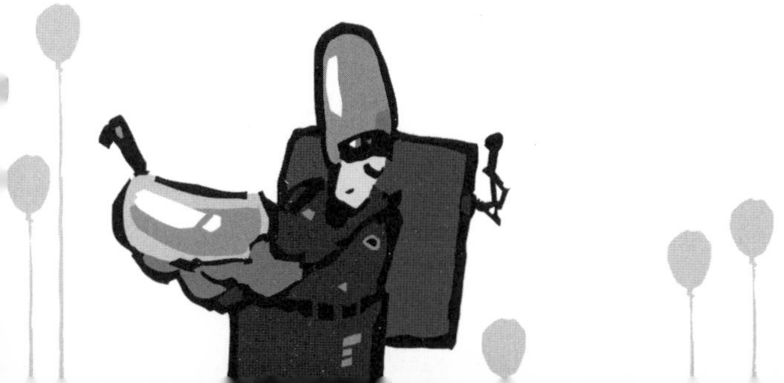

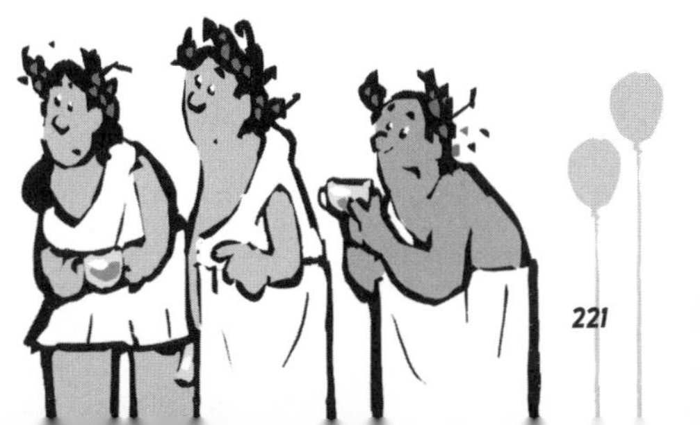

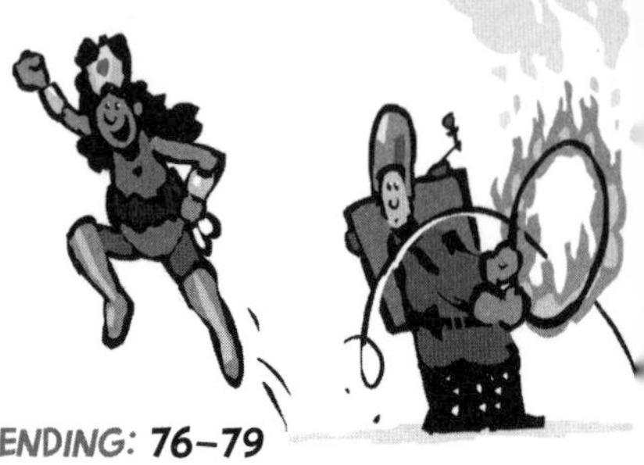

THE GDP DEFLATOR COMPARES PRICES IN YEARS X AND Y BY FIRST CALCULATING **NOMINAL GDP IN YEAR Y** (USING PRICES FROM YEAR Y), THEN CALCULATING **REAL GDP IN YEAR Y** (USING PRICES FROM YEAR X), AND THEN COMPARING THE TWO CALCULATIONS. HERE'S AN EXAMPLE:

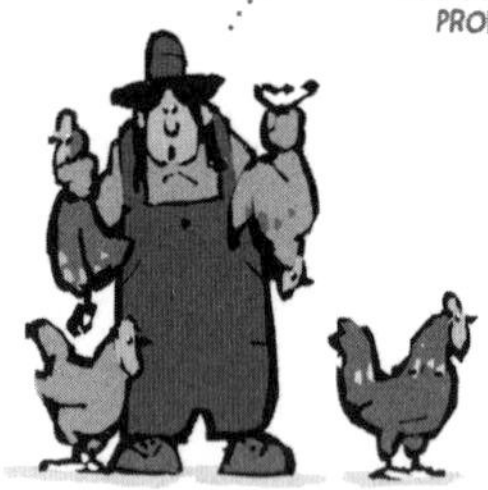

LET'S IMAGINE AN ECONOMY THAT PRODUCES ONLY TWO GOODS, CHICKEN AND BEEF.

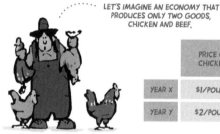

	PRICE OF CHICKEN	POUNDS OF CHICKEN PRODUCED	PRICE OF BEEF	POUNDS OF BEEF PRODUCED
YEAR X	$1/POUND	200	$3/POUND	100
YEAR Y	$2/POUND	250	$4/POUND	150

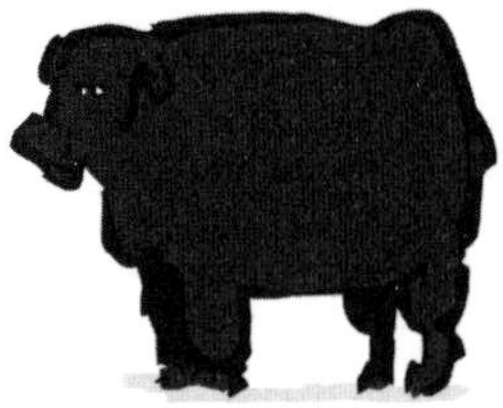

FIRST WE CALCULATE **NOMINAL GDP IN YEAR Y:**

$$(\$2 \times 250) + (\$4 \times 150) = \$1100$$

THEN WE CALCULATE **REAL GDP IN YEAR Y** USING **PRICES FROM YEAR X:**

$$(\$1 \times 250) + (\$3 \times 150) = \$700$$

FINALLY, WE CONCLUDE THAT INFLATION (AS MEASURED BY THE GDP DEFLATOR) WAS **57%** BETWEEN YEAR X AND YEAR Y BY COMPARING THE TWO:

$$\frac{\$1{,}100}{\$700} - 1 = 0.57$$

THE **RULE OF THUMB** RELATING THE NOMINAL INTEREST RATE (r_N), THE REAL INTEREST RATE (r_R), AND THE RATE OF INFLATION (i) IS:

$$r_R \approx r_N - i$$

FOR EXAMPLE, IF THE NOMINAL INTEREST RATE IS 6% ($r_N = 0.06$) AND THE RATE OF INFLATION IS 4% ($i = 0.04$) THE REAL INTEREST RATE IS ABOUT 2% ($r_R \approx 0.06 - 0.04 = 0.02$).

AS LONG AS INFLATION IS NOT TOO HIGH, THIS RULE OF THUMB IS A GOOD APPROXIMATION FOR THE **ACTUAL FORMULA**, WHICH IS:

$$r_R = \frac{1 + r_N}{1 + i} - 1$$

FOR $r_N = 0.06$ AND $i = 0.04$ WE GET $r_R = (1.06)/(1.04) - 1 = 0.019$.

INVISIBLE HAND

ADAM SMITH'S METAPHOR FOR HOW INDIVIDUAL SELF-INTEREST CAN LEAD TO GOOD OUTCOMES FOR THE GROUP AS A WHOLE: 6, 8, 83
    AND UNEMPLOYMENT: 21, 22
    AND FOREIGN AID: 126
    AND ENVIRONMENTAL ISSUES: 183–187, 192

K

KEYNESIAN ECONOMICS

NAMED AFTER 20TH-CENTURY ECONOMIST JOHN MAYNARD KEYNES, THIS SCHOOL OF THOUGHT VIEWS THE ECONOMY AS A DYSFUNCTIONAL FAMILY AND THEREFORE EMPHASIZES THE ROLE THAT GOVERNMENTS CAN PLAY IN TAMING THE BUSINESS CYCLE WITH FISCAL OR MONETARY POLICY: 11
    CONTRAST WITH CLASSICAL ECONOMICS: 12–13, 18–19, 22, 27
    AND THE LABOR MARKET: 18
    AND STICKY WAGES: 28–30
    AND MONEY NEUTRALITY: 36
    AND NEOCLASSICAL SYNTHESIS: 212

L

LABOR FORCE

THE POOL OF POTENTIAL WORKERS, INCLUDING EMPLOYED WORKERS WHO HAVE PAYING JOBS AS WELL AS UNEMPLOYED WORKERS WHO ARE LOOKING FOR PAYING JOBS: 22
    CHANGES IN: 19

LUDDITES

BRITISH TEXTILE WORKERS WHO DESTROYED MECHANICAL LOOMS IN THE 1800s, OR—MORE GENERALLY—PEOPLE WHO OPPOSE TECHNOLOGICAL PROGRESS: 94

M

MICROFINANCE

THE EFFORT TO EXTEND ACCESS TO LOANS, SAVINGS ACCOUNTS, AND OTHER BANKING SERVICES TO THE POOR: 132

MONETARY POLICY

CENTRAL BANK ACTIONS THAT INCREASE OR DECREASE THE MONEY SUPPLY IN ORDER TO PROMOTE SHORT-TERM STABILITY: 37
    CONTRAST WITH FISCAL POLICY: 76
    AND GREAT DEPRESSION: 158

MONEY

ANYTHING THAT FACILITATES TRADE BY SERVING AS A MEDIUM OF EXCHANGE: 32–33

MONEY ILLUSION

THE IDEA THAT PEOPLE RESPOND TO NOMINAL PRICES RATHER THAN REAL (INFLATION-ADJUSTED) PRICES: 49, 57

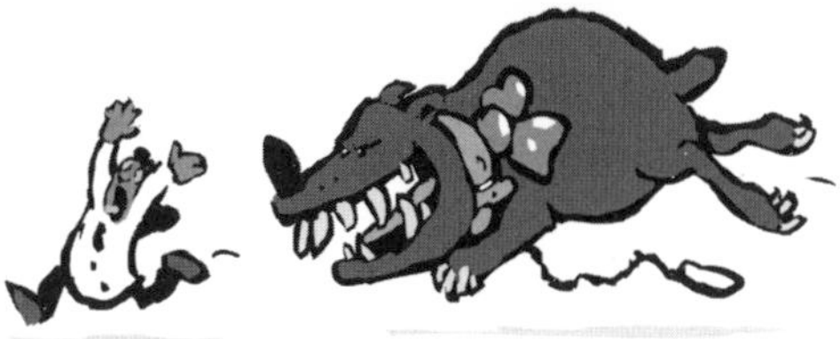

MORAL HAZARD

A SITUATION IN WHICH INSURANCE OR BAILOUTS END UP ENCOURAGING RISKY BEHAVIOR: **165**

N

NEOCLASSICAL SYNTHESIS

THE IDEA THAT MACROECONOMIES ARE KEYNESIAN IN THE SHORT RUN BUT CLASSICAL IN THE LONG RUN: **212**

NEUTRALITY OF MONEY

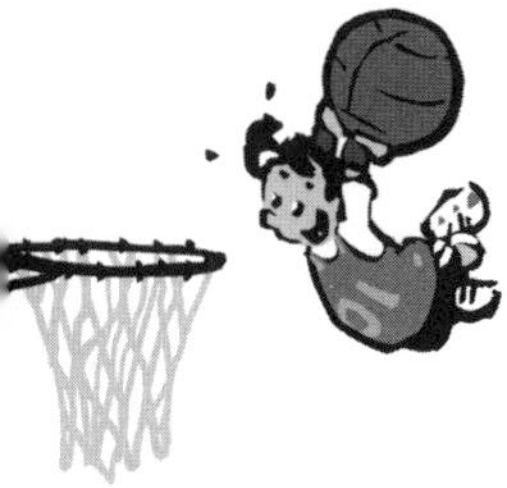

THE IDEA THAT A CHANGE IN THE VALUE OF MONEY—FOR EXAMPLE, A ONE-TIME OCCURRENCE OF 10% INFLATION—WILL NOT AFFECT REAL VARIABLES SUCH AS UNEMPLOYMENT: **34–37**

AND WHY INFLATION MATTERS: **48–49**

BECAUSE IT MAKES FOR FUN DRAWINGS, THIS BOOK ALSO USES (OR, MORE CORRECTLY, MISUSES) THE TERM **SUPER-NEUTRAL**, WHICH IS THE IDEA THAT CHANGES IN THE RATE OF GROWTH OF MONEY—FOR EXAMPLE, MOVING FROM 5% TO 10% INFLATION—WILL NOT AFFECT REAL VARIABLES.

NOMINAL VARIABLES

WAGES, PRICES, INTEREST RATES, OR OTHER VARIABLES THAT—IN CONTRAST TO REAL VARIABLES—CAN BE DISTORTED BY INFLATION, USUALLY BECAUSE THEY ARE EXPRESSED IN DOLLAR TERMS: **49–53**

O

OPEN-MARKET OPERATIONS

PURCHASES OR SALES OF GOVERNMENT BONDS OR OTHER ASSETS BY CENTRAL BANKS IN ORDER TO CHANGE THE MONEY SUPPLY: **40–43**

P

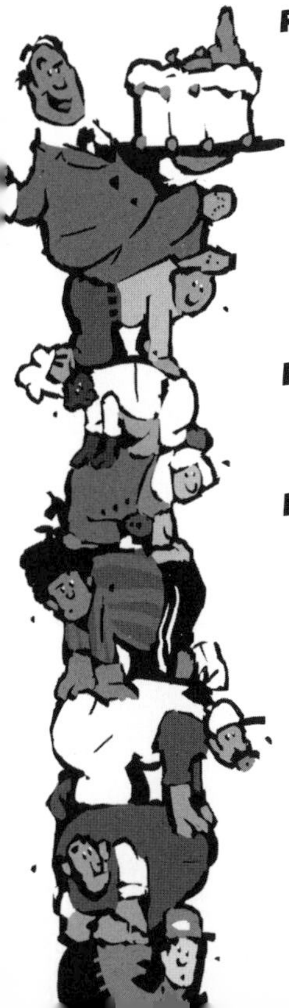

PARETO

THREE TERMS NAMED AFTER ITALIAN ECONOMIST VILFREDO PARETO. ONE OUTCOME IS A **PARETO IMPROVEMENT** OVER ANOTHER IF SWITCHING MAKES AT LEAST ONE PERSON BETTER OFF AND MAKES NOBODY WORSE OFF. ANY PARTICULAR OUTCOME IS EITHER **PARETO INEFFICIENT** OR **PARETO EFFICIENT** DEPENDING ON WHETHER THERE IS OR IS NOT ANY PARETO IMPROVEMENT OVER IT, I.E., ON WHETHER THERE IS OR IS NOT ANOTHER OUTCOME THAT MAKES AT LEAST ONE PERSON BETTER OFF WITHOUT MAKING ANYBODY WORSE OFF: **81, 93, 95, 98, 114**

PEAK COAL, PEAK OIL, ETC.

CONCERNS ABOUT RUNNING OUT OF RESOURCES SUCH AS OIL AND COAL: **181–185**

POVERTY TRAP

A SELF-REINFORCING CYCLE (INSTABILITY, WAR, LOW INVESTMENT, ETC.) THAT KEEPS POOR COUNTRIES TRAPPED IN POVERTY: **172–173**

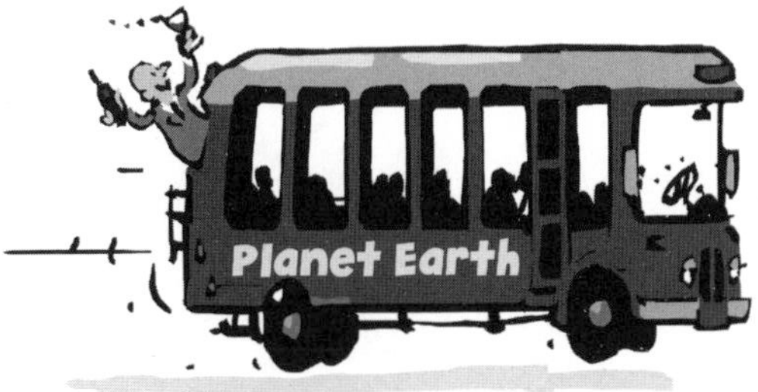
Planet Earth

PROPERTY RIGHTS
LAWS ESTABLISHING OWNERSHIP AND CONTROL OVER
PRIVATE PROPERTY; SECURE PROPERTY RIGHTS ARE CONSIDERED
A KEY INGREDIENT FOR ECONOMIC GROWTH: 80, 173

PROTECTIONISM
EFFORTS TO PROTECT DOMESTIC INDUSTRY FROM FOREIGN
COMPETITION, FOR EXAMPLE, WITH A TARIFF ON IMPORTS OR A SUBSIDY
FOR DOMESTIC INDUSTRY: 122–123
    AND AGRICULTURE: 136

PUBLIC CHOICE THEORY
THE APPLICATION OF ECONOMIC ANALYSIS TO POLITICS: 82

PURCHASING POWER
THE AMOUNT OF GOODS AND SERVICES THAT CAN BE PURCHASED WITH A
CERTAIN AMOUNT OF MONEY: 35, 46, 52, 72

PURCHASING POWER PARITY (PPP)
AN EXCHANGE RATE CALCULATED USING THE PURCHASING POWER OF
DIFFERENT CURRENCIES: 72

R

REAL VARIABLES
VARIABLES THAT—IN CONTRAST TO NOMINAL VARIABLES—ARE
NOT DISTORTED BY INFLATION: 36, 49
    REAL PRICES: 50–51
    REAL INTEREST RATES: 52–53
    REAL GDP: 65–69

RECESSION
DEFINED BY THE NATIONAL BUREAU OF ECONOMIC RESEARCH AS "A
SIGNIFICANT DECLINE IN ECONOMIC ACTIVITY SPREAD ACROSS THE
ECONOMY, LASTING MORE THAN A FEW MONTHS, NORMALLY VISIBLE IN
REAL GDP, REAL INCOME, EMPLOYMENT, INDUSTRIAL PRODUCTION, AND
WHOLESALE-RETAIL SALES": 154
    MEASURED FROM PEAK TO TROUGH: 67

RULE OF 70
A RULE OF THUMB SAYING THAT INFLATION OF 2% PER YEAR WILL DOUBLE
PRICES IN ABOUT 70/2 = 35 YEARS, AND THAT PER CAPITA REAL GDP
GROWTH OF 5% PER YEAR WILL DOUBLE LIVING STANDARDS IN
ABOUT 70/5 = 12 YEARS: 47

S

SMITH, ADAM
AUTHOR OF *THE WEALTH OF NATIONS* (1776), HE COINED
THE "INVISIBLE HAND" METAPHOR: 8–9, 35, 90, 100, 126–127, 136

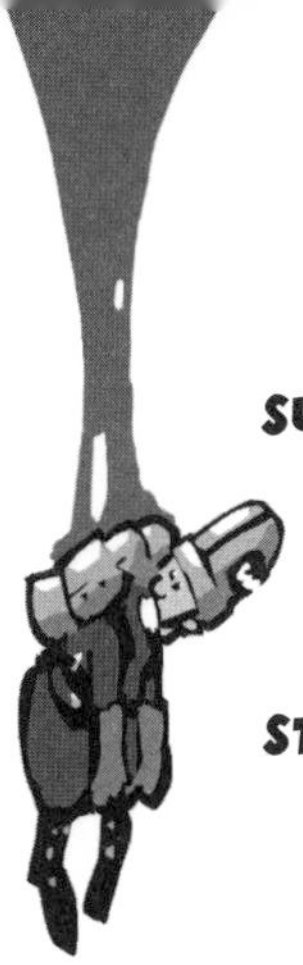

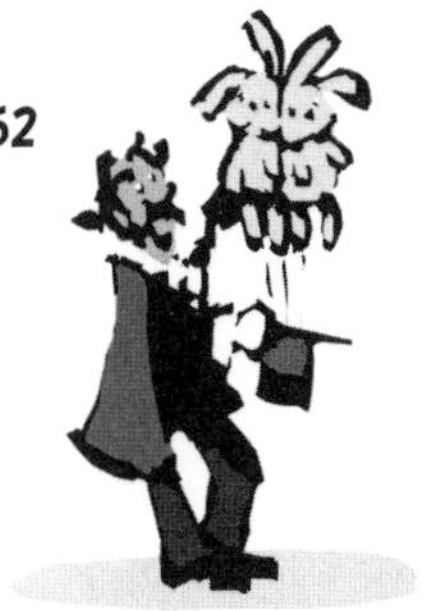

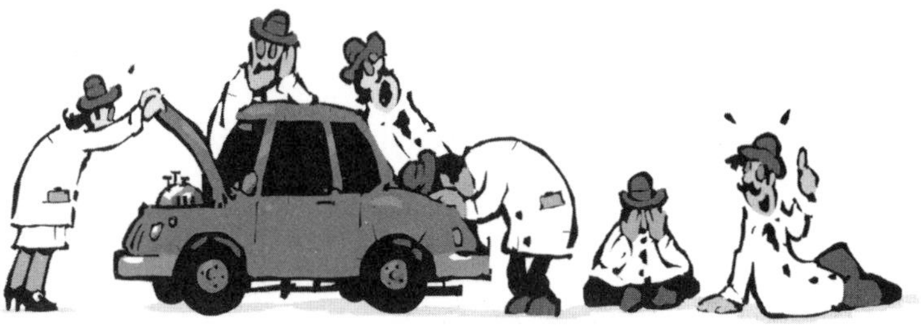